IFIP Advances in Information and Communication Technology

502

Editor-in-Chief

Kai Rannenberg, *Goethe University Frankfurt, Germany*

Editorial Board

IFIP – The International Federation for Information Processing

IFIP was founded in 1960 under the auspices of UNESCO, following the first World Computer Congress held in Paris the previous year. A federation for societies working in information processing, IFIP's aim is two-fold: to support information processing in the countries of its members and to encourage technology transfer to developing nations. As its mission statement clearly states:

IFIP is the global non-profit federation of societies of ICT professionals that aims at achieving a worldwide professional and socially responsible development and application of information and communication technologies.

IFIP is a non-profit-making organization, run almost solely by 2500 volunteers. It operates through a number of technical committees and working groups, which organize events and publications. IFIP's events range from large international open conferences to working conferences and local seminars.

The flagship event is the IFIP World Computer Congress, at which both invited and contributed papers are presented. Contributed papers are rigorously refereed and the rejection rate is high.

As with the Congress, participation in the open conferences is open to all and papers may be invited or submitted. Again, submitted papers are stringently refereed.

The working conferences are structured differently. They are usually run by a working group and attendance is generally smaller and occasionally by invitation only. Their purpose is to create an atmosphere conducive to innovation and development. Refereeing is also rigorous and papers are subjected to extensive group discussion.

Publications arising from IFIP events vary. The papers presented at the IFIP World Computer Congress and at open conferences are published as conference proceedings, while the results of the working conferences are often published as collections of selected and edited papers.

IFIP distinguishes three types of institutional membership: Country Representative Members, Members at Large, and Associate Members. The type of organization that can apply for membership is a wide variety and includes national or international societies of individual computer scientists/ICT professionals, associations or federations of such societies, government institutions/government related organizations, national or international research institutes or consortia, universities, academies of sciences, companies, national or international associations or federations of companies.

More information about this series at http://www.springer.com/series/6102

Sabrina De Capitani di Vimercati
Fabio Martinelli (Eds.)

ICT Systems Security and Privacy Protection

32nd IFIP TC 11 International Conference, SEC 2017
Rome, Italy, May 29–31, 2017
Proceedings

 Springer

Editors
Sabrina De Capitani di Vimercati
Università degli Studi di Milano
Crema
Italy

Fabio Martinelli
National Research Council of Italy
Pisa
Italy

ISSN 1868-4238   ISSN 1868-422X (electronic)
IFIP Advances in Information and Communication Technology
ISBN 978-3-319-86414-3   ISBN 978-3-319-58469-0 (eBook)
DOI 10.1007/978-3-319-58469-0

Printed on acid-free paper

This Springer imprint is published by Springer Nature
The registered company is Springer International Publishing AG
The registered company address is: Gewerbestrasse 11, 6330 Cham, Switzerland

Preface

This volume contains the papers selected for presentation at the 32nd International Conference on ICT Systems Security and Privacy Protection (IFIP SEC 2017), held in Rome, Italy, May 29–31, 2017. IFIP SEC conferences are the flagship events of the International Federation for Information Processing (IFIP) Technical Committee 11 on Information Security and Privacy Protection in Information Processing Systems (TC-11).

In response to the call for papers, 199 papers were submitted to the conference. These papers were evaluated on the basis of their significance, novelty, and technical quality. Each paper was assigned to at least four members of the Program Committee. The Program Committee meeting was held electronically, with intensive discussion over a period of two weeks. Of the papers submitted, 38 were selected for presentation at the conference.

A conference like this does not just happen; it depends on the volunteer efforts of a host of individuals. There is a long list of people who volunteered their time and energy to put together the conference and who deserve acknowledgment. Thanks to all the members of the Program Committee, and the external reviewers, for all their hard work in the paper evaluation. We are very grateful to everyone who gave their assistance and ensured a smooth organization process: Sara Foresti, Luigi V. Mancini (General Chairs); Giovanni Livraga (Publicity Chair); Adriana Lazzaroni (Local Organizing Chair); Patrizia Andronico, Raffaella Casarosa, and Giulia Severino (Local Organizing Secretariat). A special thanks goes to the keynote speakers who accepted our invitation to deliver keynote talks at the conference. We are also sincerely grateful to our sponsor, NECS.

Last but certainly not least, thanks to all the authors who submitted papers and all the conference's attendees. We hope you find the proceedings of IFIP SEC 2017 interesting, stimulating, and inspiring for your future research.

May 2017   Sabrina De Capitani di Vimercati
                                                             Fabio Martinelli

Organization

General Chairs

Sara Foresti	Università degli Studi di Milano, Italy
Luigi V. Mancini	University of Roma La Sapienza, Italy

Program Chairs

Sabrina De Capitani di Vimercati	Università degli Studi di Milano, Italy
Fabio Martinelli	National Research Council of Italy, Italy

Publicity Chair

Giovanni Livraga	Università degli Studi di Milano, Italy

Local Organizing Chair

Adriana Lazzaroni	National Research Council of Italy, Italy

Local Organizing Secretariat

Patrizia Andronico	National Research Council of Italy, Italy
Raffaella Casarosa	National Research Council of Italy, Italy
Giulia Severino	National Research Council of Italy, Italy

Program Committee

Soon Aechun	City University of New York, USA
Vijay Atluri	Rutgers University, USA
Maurizio Aiello	National Research Council of Italy, Italy
Roberto Baldoni	University of Rome La Sapienza, Italy
Matt Bishop	University of California, Davis, USA
Rainer Boehme	University of Innsbruck, Austria
Andrea Bondavalli	Università degli Studi di Firenze, Italy
Joppe Bos	NXP Semiconductors, Belgium
Yazan Boshmaf	Qatar Computing Research Institute, Qatar
Dagmar Brechlerová	Euromise, Czech Republic
William Caelli	IISEC Pty Ltd., Australia
Jan Camenisch	IBM Research Zurich, Switzerland
Iliano Cervesato	Carnegie Mellon University, Qatar
Nathan Clarke	University of Plymouth, UK

Wolter Pieters	TU Delft, The Netherlands
Joachim Posegga	University of Passau, Germany
Alexander Pretschner	Technical University of Munich, Germany
Sihan Qing	Peking University, China
Kai Rannenberg	Goethe University Frankfurt, Germany
Indrajit Ray	Colorado State University, USA
Carlos Rieder	ISec AG, Switzerland
Peter Ryan	University of Luxembourg, Luxembourg
Pierangela Samarati	Università degli Studi di Milano, Italy
Andrea Saracino	National Research Council of Italy, Italy
Damien Sauveron	University of Limoges, France
Nitesh Saxena	University of Alabama at Birmingham, USA
Abbas Shahim	VU University Amsterdam, The Netherlands
Ingrid Schaumüller-Bichl	FH Upper Austria, Austria
Einar Snekkenes	Gjovik University College, Norway
Adesina Sodiya	Federal University of Agric, Nigeria
Scott Stoller	Stony Brook University, USA
Bhavani Thuraisingham	The University of Texas at Dallas, USA
Paulo Verissimo	Universidade de Lisboa, Portugal
Rossouw Von Solms	NMMU, South Africa
Cong Wang	City University of Hong Kong, SAR China
Merrill Warkentin	Mississippi State University, USA
Edgar Weippl	SBA Research, Austria
Tatjana Welzer	University of Maribor, Slovenia
Steffen Wendzel	Hochschule Worms, Germany
Shengzhi Zhang	Florida Tech, USA
Jianying Zhou	Institute for Infocomm Research, Singapore
André Zúquete	IEETA, Portugal

Additional Reviewers

Aysajan Abidin	Olivier Blazy
Mohsen Ahmadvand	Jonas Boehler
Muhamad Erza Aminanto	Dusan Bozilov
S. Abhishek Anand	Alexander Branitskiy
Afonso Arriaga	Jan-Willem Bullee
Arash Atashpendar	Enrico Cambiaso
Monir Azraoui	Michelle Cayford
Fabian Böhm	Andrea Ceccarelli
Sebastian Banescu	Andrey Chechulin
Iulia Bastys	Yueqiang Cheng
Gunjan Batra	Sabarathinam Chockalingam
Daniel Bernau	Rakyong Choi
Arne Bilzhause	Sutanay Choudhury
Anis Bkakria	Warren Connell

Anamaria Costache
Gianpiero Costantino
Kasper Damgaar
Vasily Desnitsky
Lena Doynikova
Kaoutar Elkhiyaoui
David Espes
Chris Everett
Andrey Fedorchenko
Gerardo Fernandez
Simon Foley
Simon Friedberger
Alexander Fromm
Benny Fuhry
Clemente Galdi
Mohamad Gharib
Laszlo Gonczy
Lenka Gondova
Sebastian Groll
Akos Grosz
Marko Hölbl
Florian Hahn
Lukas Hartmann
Majid Hatamian
Kirsi Helkala
Maximilian Hils
Erik Hjelmås
Petra Hochmannova
Matthias Hummer
Vincenzo Iovino
Katharina Issel
Leonardo Iwaya
Jaroslav Janáček
Jonas Lindstrøm Jensen
Olaf Markus Köhler
Johannes Köstler
Severin Kacianka
Christos Kalloniatis
Georgios Kambourakis
Maria Karyda
Marek Klein
Imre Kocsis
Mathias Kohler
Spyros Kokolakis
Andrea Kolberger
Marko Kompara

Tamas Kovacshazy
Katharina Krombholz
Michael Kunz
Stefan Laube
Ibrahim Lazrig
Laurens Lemaire
Fudong Li
Paolo Lollini
Sebastian Luhn
Clara Maathuis
Tobias Marktscheffel
Stefan Meier
Weizhi Meng
Francesco Mercaldo
Georg Merzdovnik
Zoltan Micskei
Tarik Moataz
Nurul Momen
Leonardo Montecchi
Subhojeet Mukherjee
Dieudonne Mulamba
Patrick Murmann
Ajaya Neupane
Ana Nieto
Tomasz Nowak
David Nuñez
Saahil Ognawala
Janos Olah
Maciej Olewiński
Melek Önen
Richard Ostertág
Jaemin Park
Juan D. Parra Rodriguez
Vinh Pham
Federico Pastorino
Cecilia Pasquini
Alexander Puchta
Tobias Pulls
Vincent Raes
Noëlle Rakotondravony
Evangelos Rekleitis
Jenni Reuben
Alfredo Rial
Christian Richthammer
Harmut Richthammer
Ruben Rios

Peter Roenne
Christian Roth
Johannes Saenger
Maliheh Shirvanian
Igor Saenko
Aleieldin Salem
Kiavash Satvat
Enrico Schiavone
Christopher Schmitz
Pascal Schoettle
Mariusz Sepczuk
Ankit Shah
Mina Sheikhalishahi
Prakash Shrestha
Dimitris E. Simos
Albert Sitek
Berit Skjernaa
Marjan Skrobot
Benjamin Smith
Martin Stanek
Michael Stausholm
Adam Szekeres
Masoud Tabatabaei
Tanay Talukdar

Benjamin Taubmann
Welderufael Tesfay
Alberto Trombetta
Anselme Tueno
Marcin Alan Tunia
Muhamed Turkanovic
Theodoros Tzouramanis
Ivan Vaccari
Cédric Van Rompay
Dimitrios Vasilopoulos
Sridhar Venkatesan
Fatbardh Veseli
Marcus Voelp
Jan Vossaert
Artemios Voyiatzis
Jun Wang
Michael Weber
Benjamin Weggenmann
Rea Yaich
Ahmed Seid Yesuf
Jonathan Yung
Tao Zhang
Tommaso Zoppi

Sponsor

Contents

Applied Cryptography and Voting Schemes

Software Security and Privacy

Privacy

Digital Signature, Risk Management, and Code Reuse Attacks

Network Security and Cyber Attacks

Turning Active TLS Scanning to Eleven

Wilfried Mayer[(✉)] and Martin Schmiedecker

SBA Research, Vienna, Austria
{wmayer,mschmiedecker}@sba-research.org

Abstract. Transport Layer Security (TLS) is the fundament of today's web security, but the majority of deployments are misconfigured and left vulnerable to a phletora of attacks. This negatively affects the overall healthiness of the TLS ecosystem, and as such all the protocols that build on top of it. Scanning a larger number of hosts or protocols such as the numerous IPv4-wide scans published recently for a list of known attacks in TLS is non-trivial. This is due to the design of the TLS handshake, where the server chooses the specific cipher suite to be used. Current scanning approaches have to establish an unnecessary large number of connections and amount of traffic. In this paper we present and implemented different optimized strategies for TLS cipher suite scanning that, compared to the current best practice, perform up to 3.2 times faster and with 94% less connections used while being able to do exhaustive scanning for many vulnerabilities at once. We thoroughly evaluated the algorithms using practical scans and an additional simulation for evaluating current cipher suite practices at scale. With this work full TLS cipher suite scans are brought to a new level, making them a practical tool for further empiric research.

Keywords: Cipher suite scanning · SSL · TLS · Network security

1 Introduction

Transport Layer Security (TLS) is the fundament of today's web security and provides confidentiality and authentication for application layer protocols like HTTPS, e-mail-related protocols or smartphone applications. Successful attacks against TLS are irritating the security community on a regular basis. Many of these attacks exploit vulnerabilities in the underlying cryptographic primitives, which, when grouped together, form so-called cipher suites. Often the mitigation of these vulnerabilites is achieved by simply discontinuing the use of insecure cipher suites. Although easily done, this is a *manual* configuration step, which results in a slowly adopting TLS ecosystem. This progress is only observable through Internet-wide measurements.

Full cipher suite scans are important in order to understand in-depth the TLS ecosystem and the impact of discovered vulnerabilities, as demonstrated

© IFIP International Federation for Information Processing 2017
Published by Springer International Publishing AG 2017. All Rights Reserved
S. De Capitani di Vimercati and F. Martinelli (Eds.): SEC 2017, IFIP AICT 502, pp. 3–16, 2017.
DOI: 10.1007/978-3-319-58469-0_1

recently [6, 19]. Only with detailed information it is possible to thoroughly assess the state of online security, ranging from the security of a single host up to the security of the whole ecosystem. With the recent advent of fast-paced scanning tools it has become possible to proactively scan the entire range of IPv4 on a regular basis. This data is invaluable when reacting to newly released attacks.

In this work, we developed three new scanning algorithms that efficiently test TLS configurations in detail. These full cipher suite scans can then be used to cluster configurations based on different cipher suites, identifying common misconfigurations and facilitate TLS stack fingerprinting. We evaluated these algorithms and estimated the performance gain for Internet-wide full cipher suites scans. We then used these algorithms to scan parts of the IPv4-wide Internet and analyzed the results. The specific contributions of this paper are:

- We introduce highly optimized scanning methodologies to perform TLS scanning at scale.
- We evaluate our improved methodologies against the top-10k websites, and are on average 3.2 times faster.
- We show that current cipher suite recommendations are hardly used.
- We publicly release the source code and collected data from our experiments under an open source license[1].

The remainder of this paper is organized as follows: In Sect. 2 we present the relevant background as well as the body of related work. Section 3 introduces our optimized scanning methodologies and the data inputs used for our evaluation. Section 4 illustrates the achievable gain in overall performance and provides insights into the current TLS deployment. We discuss the results in Sect. 5 before we conclude in Sect. 6.

2   Background

TLS itself is specified in a variety of RFCs. The most important one is RFC5246 [7]. It defines the most modern version of TLS, version 1.2, introduced in 2008. Version 1.3 contains significant changes, but is still a working draft [24]. One of the goals of TLS is extensibility, i.e., the possibility of exchanging the used cryptographic functions. This is accomplished through the concept of cipher suites. Cipher suites are combinations of cryptographic primitives, defined as a two-byte value [17]. The used cipher suite and the TLS version are negotiated in the first two exchanged TLS messages (`client_hello`, `server_hello`). First, the client sends a `client_hello` message including a list of supported cipher suites. Second, the server replies with a `server_hello` choosing one of these cipher suites. This cryptographic primitives are subsequently used. A large number of cipher suites exists (over 140), and they can be used in different TLS versions

---

[1] The patterns, the mappings and the source code are available online at: https:// github.com/WilfriedMayer/turning-active-tls-scanning-to-eleven.

(SSLv3, TLSv1, TLSv1.1, TLSv1.2). This results in approx. 550 different combinations that can be tested.

Many security problems are caused by the use of old and deprecated features of TLS, e.g., the support of export-grade algorithms, old TLS versions or insecure ciphers. Two examples are POODLE [20] which is caused by the use of deprecated SSLv3 and DROWN [6] which is based on the active support of SSLv2. Some attempts to get rid of old cryptography were made, e.g., the ban of export-grade crypto in modern TLS versions or RFC7465 [22] that forbids the use of the insecure RC4 cipher. A secure deployment is non-trivial, therefore several guidelines give recommendations on how to (i) configure cipher suite settings and (ii) improve the configuration of TLS-enabled server applications [2,25]. However, these methods all rely on the administrator to actively improve the setup by changing the supported cipher suites manually – hence, the ecosystem is adopting slowly.

In the early days, *nmap* was used to perform these types of scan on a larger scale, but it is rather slow and does not scale to a larger number of hosts in reasonable time. A breakthrough was achieved with the development of *zmap* [11] and *masscan* [13]. Both tools use new methods to optimize large-scale scanning and are so far mainly used for port and vulnerability scanning. However, these improved methods are not applicable to fine-grained TLS scanning. With *zgrab* it is possible to establish TLS connections, but it is still not feasible for examining full cipher suite configurations. A more intense scanning behavior is necessary due to the design of TLS. Tools like *SSLyze* implement naive algorithms that conduct a full scan of all cipher suites by using one TLS handshake for each cipher suite. This is slow and produces a lot of traffic, thus a huge potential for optimization exists. With the results of this work, we are able to efficiently measure cipher suite configurations for TLS, also for large-scale studies.

2.1 Related Work

Prior studies that measured the TLS ecosystem focused primarily on the certificate ecosystem, the overall security was rarely evaluated. An early study was conducted by Lee et al. in 2007 [18]. With only 19,000 evaluated servers, this is a long way from an Internet-wide scale. Nevertheless, the size of measurement studies increased constantly, with larger studies conducted by the EFF [12] a few years later. Also, additional passive data was taken into account (Amann et al. [4,5]). With new scanning methods (e.g., *zmap* [11]), studies were suddenly able to cover the IPv4-wide Internet. These methods implemented new ideas, e.g., no per-connection state. This improved the speed and quality of large-scale scans. Studies that used this new scanning behavior are, e.g., the certificate ecosystem study by Durumeric et al. [9], that doesn't cover supported cryptographic primitives, and studies on vulnerabilities like Heartbleed [10] that solely examine one exclusive issue.

Most of these studies focused on specific details in the configuration, e.g., the properties of a certificate. Fewer studies scanned all cryptographic primitives at once, i.e., all supported cipher suites. Huang et al. [15] describes the results of a complete cipher suite scan to measure perfect forward-secrecy support, but scanned only hosts from the Alexa top 1 million list [3]. Mayer et al. [19] performed cipher suite scans for all e-mail-related ports at an IPv4-wide scale. Both studies used naive algorithms to perform the scan. Other projects like the Qualys SSLTest [23] also scan full TLS configurations, but these projects are designed for single host configuration tests and not for Internet-wide studies. Newer studies tried to draw a complete picture of the certificate ecosystem [26] while missing the underlying security primitives, others decided against scanning full TLS cipher suites, because it would require to establish too many connections [14].

3 Methodology

To improve the scan rate for TLS-specific scanning, we defined the following requirements: First, *time* as the overall time consumption of the scanning process; second, the support for *parallelization* – can different scans be executed in parallel or do they rely on partial results and therefore require a sequential execution? These two requirements are especially important for large-scale scans. Third, the number of *connections* necessary for a scan: How many connections are necessary for a full configuration scan? Also, the generated traffic is derived from the number of connections. Lastly, the *completeness* of the scan, or how much information we can gather from the results: Is it possible to draw a complete picture of the TLS configuration or is it just one specific detail?

The anticipated use cases range from an interested system administrator or CISO who wants to scan infrastructure for security vulnerabilities up to Internet-wide scans for either specific questions or complete ecosystem analysis.

We identified three existing approaches to scan and identify TLS configurations: The *naive approach* establishes one connection for each cipher suite, starting at the same time. For each connection the server replies with either this cipher suite or with an alert that the cipher suite is not supported. This method is currently implemented by the command line tool *SSLyze* [1]. It highly parallelizes all requests, which results in a fast execution time, especially for non-delaying networks. The number of connections and produced traffic is rather large. This can lead to errors for some hosts, because the number of parallel connections may exceed their limit. This disadvantage leads to error-prone results and affects the completeness in a negative way. *SSLyze* (version 0.12) produces exactly 543 connection attempts to test all cipher suite/TLS version combinations and approx. 500KB of traffic (inbound and outbound) per tested host. These numbers clearly don't scale for Internet-wide scans, making *SSLyze* impractical for this task.

The second approach is implemented by *zmap*. This command line tool, created by Durumeric et al. [11], is primarily used for Internet-wide port scans. With *zgrab* they also implemented an application layer scanner capable of scanning TLS configurations. To minimize the number of connections to exactly one per server, the cipher suites in the client_hello message are fixed to a specific research question, e.g., in order to test if RC4 is supported, all cipher suites that use RC4 are included. The server then responds with a server_hello message (showing the support of RC4) or an alert (showing that RC4 is not supported). This one-connection-based approach minimizes traffic and performs fast. The downside is that it does not completely evaluate all cipher suites. It is limited in its expressiveness, since only one question per scan can be evaluated.

The third approach is used by the *SSL Server Test* [23]. This web service is designed to test and evaluate one specific web server configuration. Therefore it utilizes the cipher suite settings from different browsers and browser versions as well as settings to test common misconfigurations. It then establishes one TLS connection per setting to completely evaluate one server configuration. It also includes HTTPS-specific settings and security features, e.g., HSTS or HPKP. The information collected is comprehensive, but the service's design is not suitable for large-scale ecosystem studies.

3.1 Introducing New Approaches

We propose the following new approaches for cipher suite scanning:

Connection-Optimal Approach. This approach tests all cipher suites per TLS version in a serialized way. The process is illustrated in Fig. 1. It starts with one TLS `client_hello` message that includes all available cipher suites for this TLS version. The server then responds with one cipher suite that it accepts. The next handshake includes all cipher suites except the one that was accepted earlier. This procedure is repeated until the server does not accept any of the offered cipher suites and responds with an alert. All remaining cipher suites are then evaluated as rejected. This approach uses the optimal, lowest number of connections necessary, but is not parallelizable for one host. Therefore it needs more time, especially for networks with a delayed round trip.

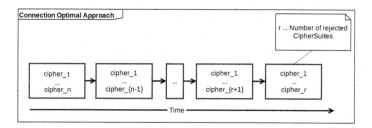

Fig. 1. Connection-optimal approach

Grouped by Cryptographic Primitives. The second approach, presented in Fig. 2, groups cipher suites according to their used cryptographic primitives. It is based on the assumption that server operators disable or enable all cipher suites with a common primitive (e.g., deactivate all RC4-based cipher suites). After the cipher suites are split up in groups, the process follows the methodology of the connection-optimal approach. We currently use groups based on keywords in the cipher suite name, i.e., `SRP`, `PSK`, `EXP`, `NULL`, `(DSA, DSS)`, `(ADH, AECDH)`, `(CAMELLIA, SEED, IDEA, DES-CBC-)`, `RC4`. Primitives that are not supported can be filtered out in the very first round. This approach supports parallel execution of the group tests so that it works with fewer round trips than the connection-optimal approach.

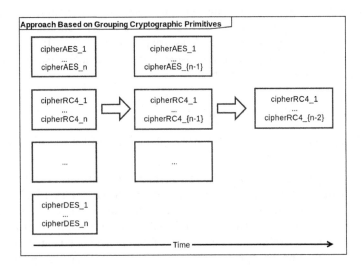

Fig. 2. Approach based on grouping cryptographic primitives

Based on Existing Results. The third approach, as presented in Fig. 3, combines the ideas from the former approach with data from already conducted cipher suite scans. It is based on the fact that many server operators use the same configuration, e.g., a default configuration. The most likely configuration based on former results is calculated before a `client_hello` is sent. After the first round of concurrent handshakes, an intermediary result is evaluated. Based on this result, the next, most probable configuration is computed. The cipher suites used in the next round of parallel sent `client_hello` messages are then adjusted. This goes on until all cipher suites are either rejected or accepted. This approach is based on data described in the next paragraph.

Existing Data. For the last algorithm, we rely on the dataset of an Internet-wide study we conducted from April to August 2015 [19]. We additionally use cipher suite scans of the HTTPS ecosystem, performed in August 2015. These datasets are very extensive w.r.t. the number of scanned cipher suites. Because of the large dataset (approx. 12 million error-free results), we transformed each result for each single host/port combination to a string. This string has a length

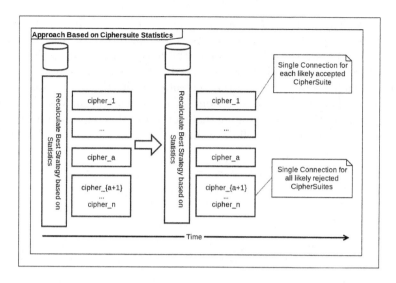

Fig. 3. Approach based on cipher suite statistics

of 551 characters[2]. This represents the total number of TLS version and cipher suite combinations. Each TLS version/cipher suite is either accepted or rejected, which is represented by the characters *a* respectively *r*. We did not take different behaviors of key exchange algorithms or different error messages (for rejected cipher suites) into account. In Table 1, the five most-used combinations for HTTPS are shown (a black bar represents an accepted cipher suite, a white bar a rejected cipher suite). We see that 7.8% of all hosts share one configuration in which all cipher suites for SSLv2 and SSLv3 are rejected and the supported cipher suites for TLSv1 and TLSv1.1 are identical. As an example, the first two bars represent the accepted `AES128-SHA` and `AES256-SHA`, whereas the next cipher suites are rejected (`CAMELLIA128-SHA`, `CAMELLIA256-SHA`).

Table 1. Most-used cipher suite patterns for HTTPS, Internet-wide scan in Aug. 2015

7.8%	
5.5%	
5.3%	
4.3%	
2.7%	

---

[2] 551 cipher suites were tested with *SSLyze* version 0.11. Because the underlying TLS implementation changed, version 0.12 does not test two specific cipher suites for four TLS versions, thus only 543 connections. Existing results for these cipher suites are ignored in the algorithm.

When we take a closer look at the number of existing patterns per TCP port and the percentage of hosts that use these patterns, we see that a small number of patterns are used for most of the hosts. This is especially true for SMTP, where we see that the two most-used patterns cover more than 50% of all SMTP-enabled hosts. In Fig. 4 the percentage of hosts that is covered by an increasing number of patterns for various TCP ports is shown. We assume that it is possible to optimize scanning methods by using this information. Also, the raw data of this patterns is publicly available.[3]

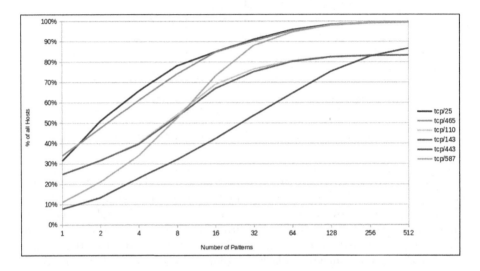

Fig. 4. Host coverarage by number of patterns

3.2   Implemented Approaches

We implemented all approaches by creating an additional mechanism to store partial results. Based on this partial result, the next requests are computed and executed, adding information to the partial result until it is complete. Users are able to choose the algorithm by specifying a command line argument (e.g., `--algorithm=connopt`). The required connections and time are logged for every run. Based on the existing data, we also implemented a simulation that calculates the number of necessary connections and rounds per approach. The complete source code is publicly available.

4   Results

We evaluated the proposed improvements by simulating an Internet-wide scan on IPv4 with existing scan data. We computed two performance values:

---

[3] https://scans.io/study/sba-email.

The number of average established connections necessary to scan one host (C) and the number of average rounds (round trips) to scan one host (R). These two parameters are a good indicator for the defined requirements. Generated traffic and connections are directly mapped to C, the degree of parallelization and therefore the time needed is mapped to R. The results of this simulation are shown in Table 2. We can see that all new approaches use fewer connections than the naive approach. The optimum is achieved with the connection-optimal approach, although this method uses a lot of rounds and is therefore not parallelizable (and probably the slowest of all algorithms), except of the different TLS versions. Thus, the number of connections is five times bigger than the number of rounds. The group-based algorithm lies in between, with further potential to optimize the chosen groups. The algorithm based on existing data shows a low number of connections as well as a low number of rounds. For HTTPS on port 443 it minimizes the number of connections to an average of 37.3 (6.8%) with an average of 1.8 rounds. The simulation is based on the same dataset as the algorithm, so the expressiveness of this method will decrease in the future (as configurations change), but can be easily readopted with newer results.

Table 2. Comparison of simulation results with existing scan data

	Port 25		Port 110		Port 143		Port 443	
	C	R	C	R	C	R	C	R
Naive	551.0	1.0	551.0	1.0	551.0	1.0	551.0	1.0
Connection-optimal	110.0	22.0	42.7	8.5	42.7	8.5	28.2	5.6
Crypto-group-based	252.0	7.3	199.9	3.8	199.8	3.8	187.7	2.4
Existing-data-based	141.0	1.5	52.3	1.5	51.4	1.4	37.3	1.8

4.1   Experimental Results

We tested the performance of our algorithms with scans in the wild. We used *SSLyze* version 0.12 and scanned a predefined set of hosts out of the Alexa Top10k list. We shuffled it and created batches of 100 hosts. With each algorithm we scanned 25 batches and measured the time needed and connections performed. We restrained from changing other aspects of *SSlyze*, like multiprocessing, multithreading or the general process. We also did not optimize kernel settings or other parameters on operating system level in order to compare only the algorithms with the default behavior. We used commodity hardware with an 100MBit/s uplink. The results are presented in Table 3. The naive approach performs worst in terms of speed. Also, connection-wise every new approach performs better than the naive approach. Although it has a more complex implementation, the approach based on existing data performs only slightly better than the algorithm based on crypto groups. Also listed in Table 3 are scans with a slightly larger set of hosts, used in the Sect. 4.2.

Table 3. Experimental results of the different approaches

Approach	# Scans (Hosts)	Valid results	Time (s)				Connections			
			Total	Min	Avg	Max	Total	Min	Avg	Max
Naive	25 (100)	1,866	14,356	0.92	7.69	15.42	1,012,976	542.6	542.9	543.0
Connection-optimal	25 (100)	1,896	4,473	0.92	2.36	4.70	60,723	28.7	32.0	34.7
Crypto-group-based	25 (100)	1,914	5,462	0.64	2.85	4.96	351,534	182.1	183.7	185.8
Existing-data-based	25 (100)	1,870	4,672	0.50	2.50	5.98	268,814	126.1	143.8	156.4
Connection-optimal	5 (2,000)	9,262	5,951	0.56	0.64	0.75	314,398	33.3	33.9	34.4
Connection-optimal	5 (2,000)	7,534	9,493	1.13	1.26	1.38	244,644	31.7	32.5	33.5

Figure 5 visualizes the large performance gain we can achieve with our approaches. It shows the average time for one host and the average number of connections per valid, scanned host of every tested batch.

These results show a large improvement in TLS cipher suite scanning algorithms. The connection-optimal algorithm is 3.2 times faster than the naive implementation (avg. connection-optimal compared with avg. naive) and uses only 6% of the connections (avg. connection-optimal compared with avg. naive) to execute a full TLS cipher suite scan in the wild. The connection-optimal approach and the group-based approach are correctly simulated, but we see that the results of the method based on existing data differ from the simulated results. We argue that this is due to two reasons: First, the algorithm and the simulation are based on the same data. If configurations change, the algorithm gets slower. The second reason is that we practically evaluated top-10k web services and not random hosts, whereas the simulation also considers a large number of small hosts.

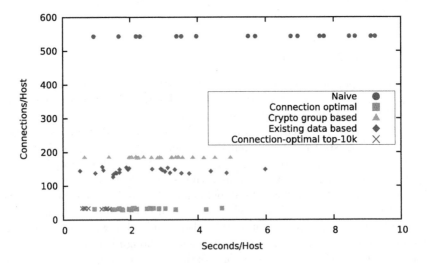

Fig. 5. Experimental results of different approaches

Table 4. Cipher suite patterns

	Umbrella Top10k		Alexa Top10k	
E.g., xx.fbcdn.net	18.53%	1716	8.51%	641
E.g., google.com	13.43%	1244	6.15%	463
E.g., configuration.apple.com	7.63%	707	1.87%	141
Mozilla modern conf.	0.02%	2	0.05%	4
Mozilla intermediate conf.	0.98%	91	3.28%	247
Mozilla old conf.	0.35%	32	0.15%	11

4.2 Cipher Suite Results of Top-10k Domains

We used the connection-optimal algorithm to perform an additional cipher suite scan on the Alexa top-10k domains [3]. Cisco Umbrella recently proposed an alternative to the often-used Alexa Top 1 million list [16], so we decided to scan these top-10k domains as well. We analyzed which patterns occur, if these patterns are secure and if we can find a trend to common and secure TLS configurations. First, we looked at the most-used patterns in the Umbrella top-10k list. Although the three most-used patterns are used by 39.6% of the Umbrella top 10k resp. 26.9% of the Alexa top-10k, 524 and 954 (Umbrella/Alexa) different configurations exist. This indicates a highly diverse ecosystem. Second, we analyzed proposed cipher suite settings. Mozilla introduced a tool, the *Mozilla SSL Configuration Generator* [21], to generate secure configurations for various compatibility requirements, i.e., modern, intermediate and old. We see that the cipher suite pattern for a modern configuration is only used by 2 resp. 4 hosts in the top-10k lists. Their intermediate configuration is used by a recognizable number (91, 247). The exact numbers are also shown in Table 4. Third, we looked at differences between these patterns. All patterns disabled SSLv2 and SSLv3. In contrast to the modern Mozilla configuration (only TLSv1.2), the other configurations support TLSv1 to TLSv1.2. In contrast to the intermediate configuration, TripleDES with DH key exchanges is not supported. The *xx.fbcdn.net* configuration is supporting more cipher suites (CAMELLIA, non-elliptic-curve Diffie-Hellman), whereas configurations like *google.com* support only one cipher suite more than configurations like *configuration.apple.com*, i.e., AES256-SHA. Finally, we tried to compare the results with pattern statistics we used for our simulation. We see that there are differences in the pattern usage, and we argue that the average top-10k host is differently configured than the average host from an Internet-wide scan.

5 Discussion

Internet scanning is not only a technical challenge. It also has to deal with ethical issues. Other studies already pointed out current best practices [11] which include to "scan no larger or more frequent than is necessary". This discouraged studies from performing a full scan, e.g., Holz et al. [14]. They stated that a full TLS cipher suite scan "is a poor trade-off in terms of good Internet citizenship versus lessons that can be learned". With our work, full TLS cipher suite scans can be conducted with less than 6% (approx. 32) of the connections compared to the currently used naive algorithm (543 connections). This minimizes the load each target host has to handle to a manageable minimum and makes the trade-off in terms of good Internet citizenship absolutely arguable. *Good Internet citizenship* is not only about minimizing the impact of one scan. It is also about avoiding unnecessary scans at all. One solution are publicly available results of scans, for which *Censys* [8], a search engine for Internet-wide scans, is a good example. They use the scanning approaches mentioned in Sect. 3, but an integration with the results of full TLS cipher suite scans is possible. We publish all our datasets and the source code.

In this work we optimized the methodology for full TLS cipher suite scans. For the practical evaluation we didn't change important factors of *SSLyze* to speed up the process. Important factors to optimize the bandwidth usage are, e.g., TCP port reuse, optimal settings for the TCP/IP stack or TCP connection reuse. The most influential factor is the parallelization of the scanning infrastructure. *SSLyze* (version 0.12) uses a maximum of 12 processes with 15 threads for all hosts; if the number of hosts is larger than that, the hosts are queued internally. This behavior is not optimal, since the server is idling. The solution is to split up all hosts amongst a large number of concurrent processes to minimize idling. With some optimizations applied, we were able to scan 27 K hosts per hour with the naive approach on commodity hardware (100 MBit/s uplink). We did not bundle these optimizations with our new approaches in order to focus on our comparison.

The approaches are created for TLS versions up to TLS v1.2. With TLSv1.3, which is currently a working draft, many things will change. Many insecure features are dropped, e.g., static RSA or DH key exchanges, insecure ciphers or hash-functions like MD5. Also, the handshake mechanism will be changed, so only one round trip is necessary to establish a full TLS connection. This – and also the question how TLSv1.3. is going to be deployed in the wild – affects the problem of how to efficiently scan full TLSv1.3 configurations.

6 Conclusion

In this paper we presented existing and new approaches for cipher suite scanning which is an important tool to evaluate the current status of the TLS ecosystem. Until now, naive approaches were used which are not optimal in terms of connections, scanning time or traffic transmitted over the wire. We introduced three new approaches that make use of the TLS protocol specification, common configurations and existing results. We evaluated the performance gain of these methods and found that we were able to perform scans 3.2 times faster with only 6% of the connections. We implemented a version of the described methods to work with a commonly used tool, simulated them and then evaluated them in practice by conducting a cipher suite scan for Alexa and the Umbrella top-10k hosts, describing the results and common patterns.

Acknowledgments. The research was funded by COMET K1 and by grant 846028 (TLSiP) from the Austrian Research Promotion Agency (FFG).

References

1. SSLyze - fast and full-featured SSL scanner. https://github.com/nabla-c0d3/sslyze
2. Applied crypto hardening (2015). https://bettercrypto.org
3. Alexa Internet Inc., Top 1,000,000 sites. http://s3.amazonaws.com/alexa-static/top-1m.csv.zip
4. Amann, B., Sommer, R., Vallentin, M., Hall, S.: No attack necessary: the surprising dynamics of SSL trust relationships. In: 29th Annual Computer Security Applications Conference, pp. 179–188. ACM (2013)
5. Amann, B., Vallentin, M., Hall, S., Sommer, R.: Revisiting SSL: a large-scale study of the internet's most trusted protocol. Technical report TR-12-015, ICSI, December 2012
6. Aviram, N., Schinzel, S., Somorovsky, J., Heninger, N., Dankel, M., Steube, J., Valenta, L., Adrian, D., Halderman, J.A., Dukhovni, V., et al.: DROWN: breaking TLS using SSLv2. In: 25th USENIX Security Symposium (2016)
7. Dierks, T., Rescorla, E.: The transport layer security (TLS) protocol version 1.2. RFC 5246 (Proposed Standard), Updated by RFCs 5746, 5878, 6176, August 2008
8. Durumeric, Z., Adrian, D., Mirian, A., Bailey, M., Halderman, J.A.: A search engine backed by internet-wide scanning. In: 22nd Conference on Computer and Communications Security, pp. 542–553. ACM (2015)
9. Durumeric, Z., Kasten, J., Bailey, M., Halderman, J.A.: Analysis of the HTTPS certificate ecosystem. In: 13th ACM Internet Measurement Conference, pp. 291–304, October 2013
10. Durumeric, Z., Li, F., Kasten, J., Amann, J., Beekman, J., Payer, M., Weaver, N., Adrian, D., Paxson, V., Bailey, M., Halderman, J.A.: The matter of heartbleed. In: 14th ACM Internet Measurement Conference, November 2014
11. Durumeric, Z., Wustrow, E., Halderman, J.A.: ZMap: fast internet-wide scanning and its security applications. In: 22nd USENIX Security Symposium, August 2013
12. Eckersley, P., Burns, J.: An observatory for the SSLiverse. DEF CON 18, July 2010. https://www.eff.org/files/defconssliverse.pdf
13. Graham, R.: Masscan: the entire Internet in 3 minutes. https://github.com/robertdavidgraham/masscan/, http://blog.erratasec.com/2013/09/masscan-entire-internet-in-3-minutes.html
14. Holz, R., Amann, J., Mehani, O., Wachs, M., Kaafar, M.A.: TLS in the wild: an internet-wide analysis of TLS-based protocols for electronic communication. In: Network and Distributed System Security Symposium (2016)
15. Huang, L.-S., Adhikarla, S., Boneh, D., Jackson, C.: An experimental study of TLS forward secrecy deployments. IEEE Internet Comput. **18**(6), 43–51 (2014)
16. Hubbard, D.: Cisco umbrella 1 million (2016). https://blog.opendns.com/2016/12/14/cisco-umbrella-1-million/
17. IANA: Transport layer security (TLS) parameters. https://www.iana.org/assignments/tls-parameters/tls-parameters.xhtml#tls-parameters-4

18. Lee, H.K., Malkin, T., Nahum, E.: Cryptographic strength of SSL/TLS servers: current and recent practices. In: 7th ACM Internet Measurement Conference, pp. 83–92, October 2007
19. Mayer, W., Zauner, A., Schmiedecker, M., Huber, M.: No need for black chambers: testing TLS in the e-mail ecosystem at large. In: International Conference on Availability, Reliability and Security (2016)
20. Möller, B., Duong, T., Kotowicz, K.: This POODLE bites: exploiting the SSL 3.0 fallback. Security Advisory (2014)
21. Mozilla: Mozilla SSL configuration generator. https://mozilla.github.io/server-side-tls/ssl-config-generator/
22. Popov, A.: Prohibiting RC4 cipher suites, RFC 7465, February 2015
23. Qualys SSL Labs: SSL server test. https://www.ssllabs.com/ssltest
24. Rescorla, E.: The transport layer security (TLS) protocol version 1.3 draft-ietf-tls-tls13-18 (2016)
25. Sheffer, Y., Holz, R., Saint-Andre, P.: Recommendations for secure use of transport layer security (TLS) and datagram transport layer security (DTLS) (2015)
26. Van der Sloot, B., Amann, J., Bernhard, M., Durumeric, Z., Bailey, M., Halderman, J.A.: Towards a complete view of the certificate ecosystem. In: Internet Measurement Conference, pp. 543–549. ACM (2016)

Slow TCAM Exhaustion DDoS Attack

Túlio A. Pascoal[1]([⊠]), Yuri G. Dantas[2], Iguatemi E. Fonseca[1],
and Vivek Nigam[1,3]

[1] Federal University of Paraíba, João Pessoa, Brazil
tuliopascoal@gmail.com, {iguatemi,vivek}@ci.ufpb.br
[2] TU Darmstadt, Darmstadt, Germany
dantas@mais.informatik.tu-darmstadt.de
[3] fortiss, Munich, Germany

Abstract. Software Defined Networks (SDN) facilitate network management by decoupling the data plane which forwards packets using efficient switches from the control plane by leaving the decisions on how packets should be forwarded to a (centralized) controller. However, due to limitations on the number of forwarding rules a switch can store in its TCAM memory, SDN networks have been subject to saturation and TCAM exhaustion attacks where the attacker is able to deny service by forcing a target switch to install a great number of rules. An underlying assumption is that these attacks are carried out by sending a high rate of unique packets. This paper shows that this assumption is not necessarily true and that SDNs are vulnerable to Slow TCAM exhaustion attacks (Slow-TCAM). We analyse this attack arguing that existing defenses for saturation and TCAM exhaustion attacks are not able to mitigate Slow-TCAM due to its relatively low traffic rate. We then propose a novel defense called SIFT based on selective strategies demonstrating its effectiveness against the Slow-TCAM attack.

Keywords: DDoS attacks · SDN · Low-Rate attacks · Selective defenses

1 Introduction

In Software Defined Networks (SDN), a powerful controller is responsible for taking the decision of where packets should be forward, *i.e.*, defining the network flows (control plane), while the task of forwarding packets is left to powerful switches (data plane). Whenever a packet arrives a switch, it searches whether there is a matching installed rule. This search is efficient because of dedicated

This work has been funded by the DFG as part of the project Secure Refinement of Cryptographic Algorithms (E3) within the CRC 1119 CROSSING, by RNP, by Capes and CNPq.

S. De Capitani di Vimercati and F. Martinelli (Eds.): SEC 2017, IFIP AICT 502, pp. 17–31, 2017.
DOI: 10.1007/978-3-319-58469-0_2

memories called Ternary Content-Addressable Memory (TCAM) where forwarding rules are stored. If no rule is applicable, the switch informs the controller which takes a decision by, for example, installing a new rule.

However, TCAM are expensive and have high power consumption [14]. Therefore, SDN switches have a limited TCAM space [10,14,15] and can store only a limited number of rules (typically 1500 to 3000 rules) [10,13,14,25,27]. This limitation has led to TCAM exhaustion [10,13,17,24,29] and saturation attacks [2,11,12,14,28,29,31]. In a saturation attack, the attacker forces the target switch to install a great number of new rules consuming the switch TCAM capacity and moreover causing the whole network controller to crash because of increased traffic between the switch and the controller.

We describe some approaches for mitigating saturation and TCAM attacks:

1. Setting rule timeouts which remove a rule whenever it is not used for some given duration. This timeout is called *idle timeout* in the OpenFlow protocol used in SDNs as the basic mechanism for removing obsolete rules. There have been proposals [25] for optimizing timeout values according to the network behavior and by flow aggregation.
2. Monitoring the number of unpaired rules, *i.e.*, rules for which there is an incoming flow, but no outgoing flow. The purpose is to detect DDoS attacks in general, as it can be used to detect when a packet has a spoofed IP. Similarly, there have been defenses that evaluate TCP SYN cookies in order to validate TCP Handshake of the packets in order to detect IP spoofing [26].
3. Monitoring the rate that rules are installed. If the rate of rule installation is too high, then it is likely that the network is suffering an attack and defense mechanisms may be triggered [10].
4. CPU and memory of SDN Switches and Controllers also provide indications that a system is suffering a DDoS attack and trigger countermeasures [28].

The main underlying assumption of these measures, however, is that attackers will send unique packets in a very high rate by, for example, spoofing IPs. This causes some of these parameters to change abruptly triggering counter-measures.

1.1 Slow TCAM Exhaustion Attacks

The assumption that attackers only generate high traffic is not necessarily true. Indeed as witnessed by the class of Low-Rate Application Layer DDoS attacks, such as Slowloris, attackers can deny service of a web-server or a VoIP server by sending a very low rate of requests to the target server [8,9,18]. Attackers can also carry out Low-Rate attacks on not powerful devices using SlowDroid [3,6] and exploit new vulnerabilities on application layer protocols in order to evade detection mechanisms, *e.g.*, SlowNext [5].

Inspired by Low-Rate Application DDoS Attacks, our first contribution is the identification of the vulnerability of SDN to Slow TCAM attacks. We propose a novel attack called *Slow TCAM Exhaustion attack* (Slow-TCAM) which is carried out as follows:

1. Recruit a large enough number of bots, typically a number a bit greater than a half the rule capacity of the target switch. A number between 1500–3000 is enough. Notice that the attacker is not spoofing IPs.
2. Each bot sends a unique packet to the target switch. Whenever the switch receives the first packet, a new rule is installed. Moreover, since there is no IP spoofing, two flows, an incoming and outgoing flow, are eventually installed.
3. The unique packet generation rate is controlled so that the rate that new rules are installed is not too high. In our experiments, the attacker generates a traffic of up to 40 packets per second, while typical flooding and saturation attacks generate a traffic greater than 1000 packets per second [10,13,26,28].
4. Finally, each bot keeps sending at a low rate a packet to the switch within its rule idle timeout. The idle timeout can be inferred by the attacker by try and error using SDN SCANNER [25]. Therefore, no rule is uninstalled leaving the TCAM always full and not allowing new rules to be installed.

After the Slow-TCAM attack is carried out, the controller and the switch operate normally, but they are forced to serve only flow rules installed by the attacker thus denying service to legitimate clients.

Our second contribution is the proposal of SIFT, *SelectIve DeFense for TCAM*, a selective defense for Slow-TCAM attack. Our previous work used selective strategies to mitigate Low-Rate Application-Layer DDoS attacks on web and VoIP servers [8,9,18,19]. This paper shows that selective strategies can mitigate Slow-TCAM attack by randomly selecting rules to be dropped whenever the system is overloaded. We built SIFT over the Openflow protocol, *i.e.*, no additional SDN machinery is necessary nor hardware, and it runs in conjunction with the controller. Whenever a switch has its rule capacity full, *i.e.*, the controller receives a TABLE-FULL message, SIFT is activated and decides using a probability distribution whether a new rule is going to be installed or not. We demonstrate that SIFT is a lightweight defense for Slow-TCAM attacks with low impacting on the controller's CPU and memory consumption. Moreover, when under attack, SIFT mitigates the attack leading to high levels of availability.

Similarly to our previous work on selective strategies for Low-Rate Application-Layer DDoS attacks [9], we have also formalized the Slow-TCAM and SIFT in Maude and used Statistical Model Checking techniques to validate our results. The formalization can be found at [1], but due to space limitations is left out of the scope of this paper which focuses on the experimental results obtained.

The rest of the paper is structured as follows: Section 2 details the Slow-TCAM attack arguing why it is a fatal attack on SDN. Section 3 details our experimental results demonstrating the efficiency of the attack. Section 4 discusses means to mitigate Slow-TCAM attack and introduces the defense SIFT based on selective strategies showing that it can mitigate Slow-TCAM attacks. Finally, in Sect. 5, we conclude by discussing related and future work.

2   Slow TCAM Exhaustion Attack (Slow-TCAM)

While we assume that the reader is familiar with the OpenFlow protocol used in SDN, we review some of the messages exchanged between a SDN switch and the controller. Whenever a packet is received by a SDN switch, it checks whether there is a matching forwarding rule. If so, it applies the rule to this packet. However, if no rule is applicable, *i.e.*, it is a *new unique packet*, the switch exchanges the following messages with the controller:

Switch → Controller : PACKET-IN
Controller → Switch : FLOW-MOD

The message PACKET-IN contains the incoming packet information, *e.g.*, header, buffer_id, in_port, payload, etc. It will contain simply the header if the switch's incoming buffer[1] is not full, and it will contain the whole packet if its buffer is full. FLOW-MOD contains the rule that should be installed by the switch. Once the message FLOW-MOD is received by the switch, it checks whether there is enough space in the switch's TCAM memory for installing a new rule. If this is the case, the rule is installed and the packet is forwarded using it. Otherwise, the switch drops the packet and informs the controller that its TCAM memory is full by sending the following message:

Switch → Controller : TABLE-FULL

The controller can specify a rule idle timeout. (OpenFlow comes with a hard timeout which is deprecated.) Given a rule timeout of TO, a rule is uninstalled by the switch if it is not triggered for TO time units. The use of timeouts is a mechanism to remove less used rules freeing TCAM memory for other rules to be installed. Typically, the timeout TO is a value between 9–11 s [31].

Finally, we point out that the communication between a SDN switch and the controller is expensive as it builds a secure channel for their communication. Therefore, a defense should avoid switcher-controller communication overhead.

2.1   Attacking SDN

As TCAM are expensive and consume a great amount of energy, SDN switches have limited TCAM space, consequently are not able to store many rules, typically a number between 1500 and 3000 rules [10,13,14,25,27]. There have been attacks on SDN which attempt to (1) consume the TCAM memory of switches (TCAM exhaustion attack) and (2) overload the controller (saturation attack).

These attacks are carried out by sending a great number of unique packets, normally by spoofing IPs. Once the TCAM is exhausted, the switch starts to drop packets leading to the TCAM exhaustion attack. Moreover, the saturation attack goes even further by sending unique packets at a even greater rate consuming

---

[1] Not to confuse the incoming packet buffer which stores packets with the TCAM which stores rules.

not only the switch's TCAM memory, but also the switch's incoming buffer. The switch, then, starts sending to the controller the whole packet instead of only the packet header. This overloads the controller leading it to crash thus affecting the whole SDN.

Defenses for the TCAM exhaustion attack and the saturation attack assume that the attacker necessarily sends a great number of unique packets, *i.e.*, flood the switch, to deny its service. Existing defenses monitor parameters that could be affected when receiving a large number of unique packets, *e.g.*, rule installation rate, CPU and Memory, number of unpaired rules.

However, this assumption is not necessarily true. We identify that SDNs are vulnerable to Slow TCAM exhaustion attacks, where the attacker exhausts a switch's TCAM memory without sending unique packets at a high rate.

2.2 Slow-TCAM

Inspired by Low-Rate Application DDoS attacks [4,8,9,18], such as Slowloris, we propose a variant of the TCAM exhaustion attack, called Slow TCAM Exhaustion Attack (Slow-TCAM), which does not need to send a great number of unique packets, *i.e.*, flood the system, but rather is able to slowly occupy all a switch's TCAM resources and deny service to legitimate.

In order to carry out a Slow-TCAM attack, we assume that the attacker has a botnet with more than the rule capacity of the target switch, *i.e.*, typically 1500 – 3000 bots.[2] This is feasible as he can recruit a botnet using standard methods, *e.g.*, phishing or purchasing such botnet[3]. We also assume that the attacker knows the rule timeout TO. This can be easily inferred by using existing tools such as an SDN Scanner [25][4] which uses a try and error approach applying statistical testing methods, *e.g.*, t-test analysis.

The Slow-TCAM attack then proceeds as follows:

- **Rule installation:** Coordinates its botnet to send a unique packet to the target switch directed to some service in the SDN, for example a web-server, at a low rate. Once a unique packet is received, the target switch follows the OpenFlow protocol which causes it to install a rule. As the rate of unique packets that are arriving is low, the rate of rule installation is also low.
- **Rule Activation:** Once a bot has send its first unique packet causing the target switch to install a rule, it sends packets in intervals of less than the timeout TO. This causes the corresponding rule to be fired and therefore to not be removed by the rule timeout mechanism.

As we demonstrated by our experiments in Sect. 3, Slow-TCAM can be quite effective:

- **Low Attacker Effort:** The main effort from the attacker is to recruit a large enough botnet. Once he possesses such botnet, the traffic generated by the

---

[2] One can reduce this number by half as a flow has an incoming and outgoing flows.

[3] https://tinyurl.com/zf27emp.

[4] It is possible to carry out a Slow-TCAM attack by IP spoofing. However, this attack could be easily mitigated by checking for unpaired rules.

botnet is very low compared to usual traffic. Bots have to send a single packet in intervals of less than TO, which is typically every 10 s;

– **Disguised Attack:** As the traffic generated is low, it is hard to detect the Slow-TCAM attack. Indeed, differently from the saturation attack which causes the controller to crash, a Slow-TCAM attack does not stress the controller's memory and CPU resources. This renders defense that monitor these parameters ineffectively. Moreover, the rule installation rate is low thus not indicating a malicious over use of the network. In fact, the attack can be in principle made to be as slow as desired as bots can install rules in a slower rate bypassing defenses based on traffic monitoring.

– **Effectiveness:** It effectively denies service to legitimate clients. As the attacker occupies the target switch's TCAM, legitimate clients packets are no longer forwarded being dropped and therefore they cannot access the services provided by the SDN.

Table 1. Slow-TCAM: Time to service and availability. The value on Success Rate corresponds to the number of clients that are able to obtain a response after the attacker has carried out the attack and occupied all the TCAM memory.

Average attack rate	Success Rate	TTS	Time to DoS	CPU	Memory usage
No attack	100%	12,6 ms	–	–	–
3.2 unique packets/s	0.0%	∞	478 s	2.5%	42.3 MB
4.6 unique packets/s	0.0%	∞	324 s	3.83%	43.0 MB
5.8 unique packets/s	0.0%	∞	258 s	4.74%	42.3 MB
9.2 unique packets/s	0.0%	∞	162 s	4.98%	42.5 MB
13.6 unique packets/s	0.0%	∞	110 s	6.39%	42.2 MB
15.6 unique packets/s	0.0%	∞	96 s	7.17%	41.9 MB
23.6 unique packets/s	0.0%	∞	63 s	10.43%	41.8 MB
39.5 unique packets/s	0.0%	∞	38 s	10.97%	42.3 MB

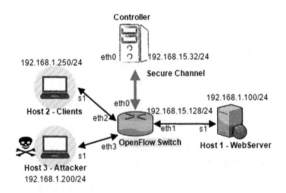

Fig. 1. Experimental set-up.

3 Slow-TCAM Experimental Analysis

We implemented the Slow-TCAM attack and carried out a number of experiments. Figure 1 shows the set-up of our experiments. We used two virtual machines, one executing Mininet [20] along with Open vSwitch 2.5.0 [22], which are a well-known network emulator and open-source virtual switch, respectively. Another virtual machine executed the SDN controller Ryu [23] using Open-Flow 1.3 [21]. The Mininet machine was a Ubuntu 14.04 LTS, Intel i7-5500U CPU@2,40 GHz with 3 GB of RAM memory, while the Ryu machine was a Ubuntu 16.04.1 LTS, Intel i7-5500U CPU@2,40 GHz with 1 GB of RAM memory. The host machine was a Windows 10 64 bit, Intel i7-5500U CPU@2,40 GHz with 8 GB of RAM memory.

We set the SDN switch rule capacity to 1500 rules with rule timeout TO of 10 s as recommended in the literature [31].

Legitimate client traffic (Host 2) consisted of 375 unique connections, which means the installation of 750 rules (incoming and outgoing rules) in a switch, *i.e.*, half the switch rule capacity. We implemented the Slow-TCAM attack where the attacker (Host 2) possesses a botnet with more than 760 bots and no more than 800 bots. Both legitimate and attacker's bots accessed the web-server (Host 1).

Table 1 summarizes our experimental results. It shows that Slow-TCAM attack can be effective in denying service to legitimate clients accessing the network using a SDN switch. We carried out a number of experiments with different attack intensities from 3.2 unique packets per second to 39.5 unique packets per second. In comparison typical flooding attacks has a rule installation rate of 1000 unique packets per second [10, 13, 26, 28]. Once the attacker successfully occupied all the TCAM memory, every one of its bots sends with periodicity of 3 s a packet to keep its corresponding rule active in the SDN switch.

We measured the legitimate client availability after the attacker has occupied all the TCAM memory, time to service (TTS), the time for the attacker to deny service, the controller's average CPU and memory usage. We observed that the attacker can carry out the attack very slowly occupying all the TCAM memory in around 8 min or more quickly in only 38 s. There is little impact on the controller CPU usage and memory.

Figure 2 illustrates the TCAM usage by the Slow-Attack with intensity of 5.8 rules per second. It takes a bit more than 4 min to occupy all the rule capacity by installing 1500 rules. The remaining scenarios with different attack intensities had the same behavior. For our slowest attack with intensity of 3.2 unique packets per second, the attacker can deny service even more silently in around 8 min with practically no impact on the controller's CPU usage. On the other hand, the attacker can also deny service more quickly in 38 s by carrying out a Slow-TCAM attack with intensity of 39.5 unique packets per second with still a very low impact on the controller's CPU usage. Notice that the attacker is able to keep the rules installed in the switch by avoiding their timeout to be fired. This can be observed by the fact that no rules are uninstalled. Once all 1500 rules are installed, there is no more room for new rules thus denying service to legitimate clients.

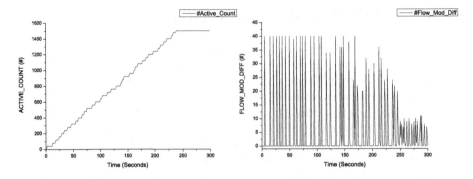

Fig. 2. Number of installed rules in the target SDN switch and the number of FLOW-MOD messages sent by the controller for a Slow-TCAM attack with intensity of 5.8 unique packets per second.

We also measured the number of FLOW-MOD messages sent by the controller (also illustrated in Fig. 2). As the attack is slow, it causes the controller to send a low amount of FLOW-MOD messages (less than 40) and once the TCAM is occupied the number of FLOW-MOD messages reduces even further. Notice as well that this number can also be reduced if the attacker is willing to carry out an attack with an even lower rate.

We measured the CPU and memory effort of the controller during the Slow-TCAM attack depicted in Fig. 3. The Slow-TCAM attack causes a low overhead on the CPU usage of less than 5% and little impact to the switch's memory usage from 34 MB to less than 43 MB which is due to the installation of new rules.

These results demonstrate that the Slow-TCAM attack is indeed an effective and silent attack as it denies service to legitimate clients without changing in abrupt ways the main parameters used by monitoring defenses (see Sect. 5 for

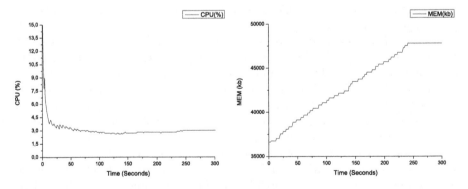

Fig. 3. Slow-TCAM: CPU and memory usage during a Slow-TCAM attack with intensity of 5.8 unique packets per second.

further details). The rule rate installation and of FLOW-MOD messages is kept low and there is little impact to the Switch's CPU and Memory. Moreover, as the attacker is not spoofing IPs, all rules installed in the switch to handle his packets are paired, *i.e.*, have an incoming and outgoing rules.

Algorithm 1. SIFT Execution During a Round

1: **procedure** SIFT-ROUND
2:     **if** *Received FLOW-MOD with ruleIns* **then**
3:         *ruleList.insert(ruleIns)*
4:         *lastFlowMod ← ruleIns*
5:     **if** *Received TABLE-FULL* **then**
6:         pmod ← pmod + inc
7:         *ruleList.remove(lastFlowMod)*
8:         **if** $random() < \frac{k}{k+\text{pmod}}$ **then**
9:             *iRuleInd ← random(k)*
10:             *ruleDr ← ruleList.get(iRuleInd)*
11:             *ruleList.remove(ruleDr)*
12:             send *OFPFC_DELETE with ruleDr*
13:             **if** *hasPairRule(ruleDr,ruleList)* **then**
14:                 *rulePair ← ruleList.getPair(ruleDr)*
15:                 *ruleList.remove(rulePair)*
16:                 send *OFPFC_DELETE with rulePair*
17:     **if** *Received* OFPRR_DELETE or OFPRR_IDLE_TIMEOUT with *ruleDr* **then**
18:         *ruleList.remove(ruleDr)*

---

4   Mitigating Slow-TCAM

Before we introduce our new defense SIFT for mitigating Slow-TCAM attacks, we discuss some alternative defenses mechanisms. A detailed analysis of their applicability is left to future work:

- **Rule aggregation:** It seems possible to mitigate Slow-TCAM attack by aggregating different rules into broader rules. The controller can reduce the impact of Slow-TCAM as the attacker would not be able to consume all the target switch's TCAM. The downside of using rule aggregation is that the controller has a coarser definition of unique packet and therefore, the system becomes more vulnerable to other attacks, such as volumetric attacks.
- **Dynamic Timeouts:** If the controller is able to distinguish a bot from a legitimate client, the controller can set different timeouts allowing rules created for possible clients to have longer timeouts. It is not yet clear how to set these timeouts with the Slow-TCAM attack as bots may behave very close to legitimate clients, *e.g.*, access a web-page with an expected behavior.

– **Improving TCAM usage:** The switch may improve its TCAM usage by storing less data for example. This mechanism may increase a switch's rule capacity and therefore, the attacker would need to hire a larger botnet to carry-out a Slow-TCAM attack.

4.1   SIFT

We propose a new defense called *SelectIve DeFense for TCAM* (SIFT) for defending against the Slow-TCAM attack. It is based on selective strategies [8,9,18] which have already been used to mitigate Low-Rate Application Layer DDoS attacks on web-servers and VoIP servers, such as Slowloris.

SIFT is executed together with the controller at the controller-layer. Assume that the switch rule capacity is k. SIFT maintains three variables:

`ruleList`,   `lastFlowMod`,   and   `pmod`

where `ruleList` is a mirror list of the rules installed in the switch and `pmod` is a counter. Selective strategies including SIFT work in rounds with duration of T_R time units. Our experiments demonstrate that $T_R = 0.1$ s is a suitable value for a round duration being able to mitigate attacks with very little overhead on the controller's CPU and memory usage. At the beginning of a round, SIFT sets a counter `pmod := 0`.

During a round, SIFT follows Algorithm 1. Whenever a new rule `ruleIns` is to be installed, *i.e.*, a FLOW-MOD is generated, then SIFT adds this rule to `ruleList` (lines 2–3). If a TABLE-FULL is received from the switch informing that a rule `ruleTB` was not able to be installed, then SIFT proceeds as follows: first it increments `pmod` by a value `inc` (line 6). Our experiments show that `inc` = 100 is a good value for a switch with rule size 1500.

SIFT then generates a random number between 0 and 1 and checks whether this number is less than (line 8):

$$\frac{k}{k + \text{pmod}}$$

If this is not true, then SIFT simply rejects the rule *ruleTB* and leaves the currently installed rules as they are. Otherwise, SIFT drops a randomly chosen installed rule *ruleDr* so that new rules may be added. As `pmod` increases, the probability of installing new rules decreases with the rate of incoming traffic (for more formal justification for this rule see [16]).

If SIFT decides to install *ruleTB* (lines 9–16), SIFT selects a number *iRuleDr* between 1 and k and removes the rule *ruleDr* at the index *iRuleDr* from `ruleList` (lines 9–11). It then sends the OpenFlow message OFPFC_DELETE to the switch specifying that the rule *ruleDr* should be uninstalled (line 12). As the rule *ruleDr* has been uninstalled, we also search whether it has a pair rule and uninstall it as well (lines 14–16) as it would no longer have an incoming or outgoing flow.

Finally, whenever the switch uninstalls a rule sending an OFPRR_DELETE or an OFPRR_IDLE_TIMEOUT message, the corresponding rule is removed from `ruleList` (lines 17–18).

Notice that SIFT has a concrete effect on the switch only when its rule capacity is reached. If there is still space in the TCAM for new rules, the network behaves as if SIFT is not present.

Rationale of Why SIFT Works: The objective of the attacker is to keep its rules installed for long periods of time. Therefore, whenever a switch's rule capacity is reached, which is likely due to an attack, SIFT has a greater probability of selecting an attacker rule and enabling new rules for serving possibly legitimate clients to be installed.

Variations of SIFT: The results obtained in this paper assumes a uniform probability mechanism for choosing which rule to drop. Our experiments indicate that this strategy is effective for mitigating Slow-TCAM attacks. However, there are other selective strategies [8,18,19] that could be used, *e.g.*, taking into account the time a rule has been installed or the number of packets that fired a rule, etc. We leave this investigation to future work.

4.2   Experimental Results with SIFT

We carried out load tests with scenarios with SIFT and without SIFT when under an Slow-TCAM attack of intensity of 5.8 unique packets per second. These tests provide us with *lower bounds* on the performance of our defense. We varied the intensity of legitimate client traffic from 1 packet in intervals of 1–3 s (chosen randomly), to 15 packets every 1–3 s. We also tested SIFT when there is a burst of legitimate client traffic with 100 packets every 10 s.

Table 2 summarizes the results with different scenarios. It first shows that SIFT does not have an impact when the system is not under attack. Then, it shows that the Slow-TCAM attack is effective in denying service resulting in 0% availability in all cases when not running SIFT. With SIFT, on the other hand, one is able to maintain high levels of availability with levels above 95% for each scenario. SIFT had, however, an impact on the time to service (TTS) specially when there are burst of client demand reaching 2.4 s. We are currently investigating how to improve TTS by using different selective strategies and incorporating other defense technique such as those described at the beginning of Sect. 4. This is left to future work.

Finally, we measured the impact of SIFT on the controller's memory and CPU. It is a lightweight defense not impacting the CPU and Memory consumption of the controller. This can be observed by the graphs depicted in Fig. 4. SIFT did not cause overhead on the CPU and memory usage when compared with the data in Fig. 3.

Table 2. SIFT: Time to service and availability when under an attack of intensity of 5.8 unique packets per second. The value on Success Rate corresponds to the number of clients that are able to obtain a response after the attacker has carried out the attack and occupied all the TCAM memory.

Client traffic	Without SIFT		With SIFT	
	Success Rate	Median TTS	Success Rate	Median TTS
No attack	100%	23.7 ms	100%	20.2 ms
1 packet every 1–3 s	0%	∞	97.3%	97 ms
5 packets every 1–3 s	0%	∞	96.9%	1061 ms
10 packets every 1–3 s	0%	∞	97.9%	1082 ms
15 packets every 1–3 s	0%	∞	98.9%	1149 ms
100 packets every 10 s	0%	∞	95.6%	2454 ms

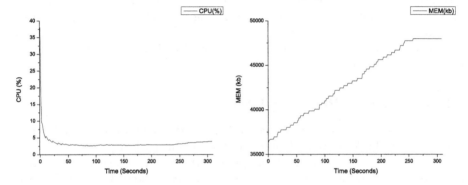

Fig. 4. SIFT: CPU and memory usage during a Slow-TCAM attack of intensity of 5.8 unique packets per second.

5   Related and Future Work

The main objective of TCAM exhaustion attacks is to force the switch to install rules. In the literature, this is accomplished by sending a high rate of unique packets, *e.g.*, using spoofing and sending UDP packets [10,13,17]. Furthermore the saturation attack [2,11,12,14,28,29,31] has as main objective to crash the controller by sending a large amount of traffic to a SDN switch occupying its incoming buffer. This causes the switch send to the controller the whole packet instead of only sending the packet header.

Dhawan *et al.* [10] propose the detection of DoS attacks by monitoring the rate of rule creation by the SDN controller. If this rate passes a threshold, then mitigation actions are taken. Since the Slow-TCAM attack can be configured to set a particular rate of rule creation, this defense is not effective in mitigating the Slow-TCAM attack.

Shin and Gu [25] propose two mechanisms to detect TCAM exhaustion and saturation attacks. The first mechanism is compute an optimal rule timeout according to the complexity of the network. While this mechanism can mitigate flooding attacks which use IP Spoofing of UDP packets, for example, it is not efficient for mitigating Slow-TCAM attacks as the bots are continuously sending valid packets thus resetting timeouts. The second mechanism is the technique of Flow Aggregation which generates more general rules, defining macroflows, instead of using more specific rules, defining microflows. This strategy can mitigate the Slow-TCAM, but at the expense of leaving the network more vulnerable to other attacks, *e.g.*, Get-Flooding, allowing malicious traffic to use the network. Moreover, as pointed out by [28], Flow Aggregation is not capable of mitigating saturation attacks such as the ones proposed by [7].

The strategy AVANT GUARD [26] detects when a TCP-handshake is completed before creating rules in the network. It has been recently shown [2] that this defense is vulnerable to a modification of the saturation attack capable to consume all AVANT GUARD's resources. AVANT GUARD's strategy cannot detect Slow-TCAM attacks as the attacker's bots complete TCP-handshakes.

Wang *et al.* [28] propose to monitor switch buffer, controller's CPU and memory usage to mitigate saturation attacks. As the Slow-TCAM attack has little impact to these parameters, it seems that the defense proposed by Wang *et al.* is not effective in detecting Slow-TCAM attacks.

Shen [24] proposes a peer support strategy where SDN switches share their unused TCAM memory space among them when they are reaching its TCAM limit. This is done by installing flow rules in the attacked switch (they keep a reserved space in TCAM) in order to divert flows to other peer switches according to: not being full, nearest to the attacker switch, less busy, connects to more other switches. However they can only retard the attack and has the problem of when the majority or many switches are full they will divert traffic between them ending up in loop.

Some proposals [15, 30] suggest modifications to the OpenFlow protocol used in SDN and in the structure of TCAM memory in order to improve memory management. Kandoi and Antikainen [13] comment the possibility of using Optimal Timeout technique and Flow Aggregation. However, their goal is to enhance SDN general performance, whereas we expose the TCAM limited space SDN vulnerability as a mean to deny its service.

We are currently investigating the use of alternative selective strategies for mitigating not only Slow-TCAM attack, but also saturation attacks. These selective strategies would use parameters such as CPU, Memory usage, number of times a rules has been fired. The probability of dropping a rule would then depend on such parameters. For example, rules that have not been frequently used should have a higher probability of being dropped. We believe that by using more parameters we can improve SIFT and mitigate other TCAM attacks.

References

1. SIFT (2016). https://github.com/ygdantas/SIFT.git
2. Ambrosin, M., Conti, M., De Gaspari, F., Poovendran, R.: Lineswitch: efficiently managing switch flow in software-defined networking while effectively tackling DoS attacks. In: ASIACCS, pp. 639–644. ACM (2015)
3. Cambiaso, E., Papaleo, G., Aiello, M.: SlowDroid: turning a smartphone into a mobile attack vector. In: FiCloud 2014, pp. 405–410 (2014)
4. Cambiaso, E., Papaleo, G., Chiola, G., Aiello, M.: Slow DoS attacks: definition and categorisation. IJTMCC **1**(3–4), 300–319 (2013)
5. Cambiaso, E., Papaleo, G., Chiola, G., Aiello, M.: Designing and modeling the slow next DoS attack. In: Herrero, Á., Baruque, B., Sedano, J., Quintián, H., Corchado, E. (eds.) International Joint Conference. AISC, vol. 369. Springer, Cham (2015)
6. Cambiaso, E., Papaleo, G., Chiola, G., Aiello, M.: Mobile executions of slow DoS attacks. Log. J. IGPL **24**(1), 54–67 (2016). Oxford University Press (2015)
7. Curtis, A.R., Kim, W., Yalagandula, P.: Mahout: low-overhead datacenter traffic management using end-host-based elephant detection. In: INFOCOM, pp. 1629–1637. IEEE (2011)
8. Dantas, Y.G., Lemos, M.O.O., Fonseca, I.E., Nigam, V.: Formal specification and verification of a selective defense for TDoS attacks. In: Lucanu, D. (ed.) WRLA 2016. LNCS, vol. 9942, pp. 82–97. Springer, Cham (2016). doi:10.1007/978-3-319-44802-2_5
9. Dantas, Y.G., Nigam, V., Fonseca, I.E.: A selective defense for application layer DDoS attacks. In: JISIC 2014, pp. 75–82 (2014)
10. Dhawan, M., Poddar, R., Mahajan, K., Mann, V.: Detecting security attacks in software-defined networks. In: NDSS, SPHINX (2015)
11. Dong, X., Lin, H., Tan, R., Iyer, R.K., Kalbarczyk, Z.: Software-defined networking for smart grid resilience: opportunities and challenges. In: CPSS (2015)
12. Hong, S., Lei, X., Wang, H., Gu, G.: New attacks and countermeasures. In: NDSS, Poisoning Network Visibility in Software-Defined Networks (2015)
13. Kandoi, R., Antikainen, M.: Denial-of-service attacks in OpenFlow SDN networks. In: IM (2015)
14. Kannan, K., Banerjee, S.: Compact TCAM: flow entry compaction in TCAM for power aware SDN. In: Frey, D., Raynal, M., Sarkar, S., Shyamasundar, R.K., Sinha, P. (eds.) ICDCN 2013. LNCS, vol. 7730, pp. 439–444. Springer, Heidelberg (2013). doi:10.1007/978-3-642-35668-1_32
15. Katta, N., Alipourfard, O., Rexford, J., Walker, D.: Infinite cacheflow in software-defined networks. In: HotSDN, pp. 175–180. ACM (2014)
16. Khanna, S., Venkatesh, S.S., Fatemieh, O., Khan, F., Gunter, C.A.: Adaptive selective verification: an efficient adaptive countermeasure to Thwart DoS attacks. IEEE/ACM Trans. Netw. **20**(3), 715–728 (2012)
17. Klöti, R., Kotronis, V., Smith, P.: Openflow: a security analysis. In: ICNP (2013)
18. Lemos, M.O.O, Dantas, Y.G., Fonseca, I., Nigam, V., Sampaio, G.: A selective defense for mitigating coordinated call attacks. In: SBRC (2016)
19. Lemos, M.O.O., Dantas, Y.G., Fonseca, I.E., Nigam, V.: On the accuracy of formal verification of selective defenses for TDoS attacks (under review)
20. Mininet (2016). http://www.mininet.org/. Accessed 02 Nov 2016
21. OpenFlow: Open Networking Foundation. https://www.opennetworking.org/
22. OpenVSwitch (2016). http://openvswitch.org/. Accessed 14 Nov 2016
23. Ryu (2016). https://osrg.github.io/ryu/. Accessed 10 Nov 2016

24. Shen, J.: Defending against flow table overloading attack in software-defined networks. IEEE Trans. Serv. Comput. **PP**(99) (2016). doi:10.1109/TSC.2016.2602861
25. Shin, S., Gu, G.: Attacking software-defined networks: a first feasibility study. In: HotSDN, pp. 165–166. ACM (2013)
26. Shin, S., Yegneswaran, V., Porras, P., Gu, G.: AVANT-GUARD: scalable and vigilant switch flow management in software-defined networks. In: CCS (2013)
27. Vishnoi, A., Poddar, R., Mann, V., Bhattacharya, S.: Effective switch memory management in OpenFlow networks. In: DEBS (2014)
28. Wang, H., Xu, L., Gu, G.: FloodGuard: a DoS attack prevention extension in software-defined networks. In: DSN, pp. 239–250. IEEE (2015)
29. Wang, M., Zhou, H., Chen, J., Tong, B.: An approach for protecting the OpenFlow switch from the saturation attack (2016)
30. Yu, M., Rexford, J., Freedman, M.J., Wang, J.: Scalable flow-based networking with DIFANE. ACM Comput. Commun. Rev. **40**(4), 351–362 (2010)
31. Zarek, A., Ganjali, Y., Lie, D.: OpenFlow timeouts demystified. Master thesis, University of Toronto, Canada (2012)

Evasive Malware Detection Using Groups of Processes

Gheorghe Hăjmăşan[1,2(✉)] (iD), Alexandra Mondoc[1,3] (iD), Radu Portase[1,2] (iD), and Octavian Creţ[2] (iD)

[1] Bitdefender, Cluj-Napoca, Romania
{amondoc,rportase}@bitdefender.com
[2] Technical University of Cluj-Napoca, Cluj-Napoca, Romania
{Gheorghe.Hajmasan,Octavian.Cret}@cs.utcluj.ro
[3] Babeş-Bolyai University, Cluj-Napoca, Romania

Abstract. Fueled by a recent boost in revenue, cybercriminals are developing increasingly sophisticated and advanced malicious applications. This new generation of malware is able to avoid most of the existing detection methods. Even behavioral detection solutions are no longer immune to evasion, mostly because existing solutions focus on the actions or characteristics of a single process. We propose shifting the focus from malware as a single component to a more accurate perspective of malware as multi-component systems. We propose a dynamic behavioral detection solution that identifies groups of related processes, analyzes the actions performed by processes in these groups using behavioral heuristics and evaluates their behavior such that even evasive, multiprocess malware can be detected. Using the information provided by groups of processes, once a malware has been detected, a more comprehensive system cleanup can be performed, to ensure that all traces of an attack have been removed and the system is no longer at risk.

1 Introduction

Malicious software has become the foundation of a highly profitable industry. To maximize profit, malware authors are developing increasingly sophisticated attacks. The new breed of malware is able to avoid static detection through various methods, like obfuscation or encryption. To make detection even more difficult, thousands of new malware or variants of existing malware are being released every day. Consequently, dynamic detection has become more important, representing a last line of defense in security solutions.

Currently, the majority of dynamic malware detection techniques evaluate the behavior of a process and, using a set of rules, decide if that process is malicious or not. The rule set must accurately differentiate between malicious and non-malicious processes. Because a balance between detection rate and number of false positives must be assured, a dynamic detection system can not be too aggressive when evaluating a single process. Advanced malware may take

S. De Capitani di Vimercati and F. Martinelli (Eds.): SEC 2017, IFIP AICT 502, pp. 32–45, 2017.
DOI: 10.1007/978-3-319-58469-0_3

advantage of this lack of aggression. They can evade being detected by separating malicious actions into multiple processes through process creation or code injection. This separation causes current dynamic detection systems to be unable to detect some of the malware components or, even worse, not to detect the malware at all. This is a major issue, because if a malware attack is only partially detected and the malicious components are not entirely removed from a system, they will continue to represent a serious security risk for the user.

We propose a behavioral detection solution that overcomes the issue of detecting evasive malware. We propose renouncing the current view of malware as single component systems and adopting a more accurate and comprehensive, multi-component based, method of evaluation and detection.

The following sections present a method to detect malicious groups of processes instead of single malicious processes. This research will provide a method for constructing such groups, together with a way to evaluate their actions so that malware groups can be detected. We also present a way to clean the infected system based on the actions performed by the processes in the detected group.

This paper is organized as follows: Section 2 presents the current state of research concerning behavioral malware detection and how most common solutions can be evaded. The proposed solution is described in Sect. 3 and the results of the proposed solution are presented in Sect. 4. The conclusions are mentioned in Sect. 5.

2   Related Work

An approach used in behavioral malware detection consists of extracting features based on the API calls performed by an analyzed sample. Devesa et al. [2] propose identifying which actions were performed, based on API calls records. These actions represent features, used to classify a sample as malicious or clean.

Constructing graphs based on the relations between system calls represents another approach in behavioral malware detection. Elhadi et al. [3] propose creating data dependent graphs, with nodes representing system calls and the edges, relations between their parameters or return values. An algorithm based on the Longest Common Subsequence is used to match the obtained graph to those of known malware stored in a database. Behavior graphs are also used in [7]. Compared to other similar solutions, the solution proposed by Kolbitsch et al. has the advantage of matching the behavior graphs in real time, providing protection on the end host. Naval et al. [10] propose representing the behavior of a sample as an ordered system call graph and extracting relevant paths, which are considered features used for classifying the sample as malicious or benign.

Most dynamic malware detection solutions that focus on analyzing the behavior of individual processes are highly vulnerable to a certain type of evasion that is increasingly used by sophisticated malware and advanced threats. The evasion mechanism is quite simple: instead of executing all the malicious actions from a single process - which could be more easily detected by advanced security solutions - the malicious payload is distributed to multiple, distinct processes, and may be executed over a long period of time. Because behavior based detection solutions can not usually detect a process based on a single action, multiple individual processes, each performing a smaller set of actions, may go unnoticed, allowing the malware to achieve its target goal undetected.

Ma et al. [8] developed a prototype tool, working at compiler level, that can generate multiple "shadow" processes from the original malware code. Each "shadow" process executes some of the payload, such that the original behavior of a process remains unchanged. Various methods to deliver malware distributed into multiple files are presented in [11]. Another method of distributing the malicious payload, presented in [4] consists of injecting parts of the payload into clean processes running on a system. This approach makes cleanup more difficult because, if only one injected process is terminated, the malware is capable of reinstantiating itself from another injected process. The distinct malicious processes may communicate using traditional inter process communication, supported by the operating system, or through purposely implemented special mechanisms.

This evasion mechanism is extremely effective especially against detectors based on API or code flow graph. Since the API calls are distributed to multiple distinct processes, this type of detectors may have difficulties in matching the obtained graphs, or may be unable to do so. The effectiveness of distributing malicious behavior to multiple processes is also recognized by [6,12].

A solution designed to combat multi-process malware is proposed in [5]. In the approach presented by Ji et al., the actions performed by each process are represented as feature vectors and then correlated with the actions performed by its child processes. The correlation phase in malware detection may be a complex problem, both in terms of implementation and efficiency. Additionally, this solution does not consider code injection when correlating processes.

Evasion mechanisms such as those previously described represent a strong argument to show that behavioral-based security solutions need to evolve past analyzing a single process, individually and in isolation from other entities. Focus should shift to developing more advanced security solutions, capable of analyzing each process in the broader context of all the processes executed on a computing system and taking into account any relations between them.

3   Proposed Solution

A high level view of the proposed solution, illustrating its major components and the interactions between them is presented in Fig. 1. Our implementation is intended for the Windows Operating System (OS), but the proposed approach may be applied for other operating systems.

The essential requirement for a behavioral detection solution is to monitor the actions performed by processes. This is implemented within the *Event Interceptors*. They use mechanisms specific to the Windows OS and are located both in Kernel Mode and User Mode (UM). In Kernel Mode, the solution uses a

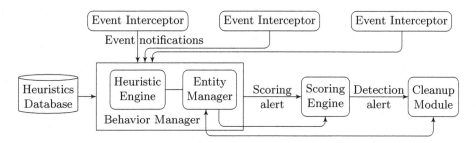

Fig. 1. Behavioral detection solution

minifilter driver [9] that registers callback routines, which are notified whenever changes occur in the file system, registry keys or when processes are created. At User Mode level, the actions are filtered using API interception (hooking) through a DLL injection [1] into the monitored process. The intercepted actions are encapsulated in events and sent to the *Behavior Manager*, consisting of the *Heuristic Engine* and the *Entity Manager*.

The detection is based on behavioral heuristics located in the *Heuristic Engine*. A heuristic is an algorithm that analyzes the actions performed by processes, using the intercepted events. Some heuristics are defined in signature files and are retrieved by the engine from the *Heuristics Database*.

The *Entity Manager* uses information provided by the Event Interceptors, together with information from some heuristics (e.g. for detecting code injection) to manage the processes and groups on a system and their relations.

When a heuristic decides a malicious action has been performed, it sends an alert to the *Scoring Engine*, where it is evaluated. This component computes scores for the entities that caused the alert and decides whether they are potentially malicious. If a process or group of processes is considered malicious a *detection alert* will be sent to the *Cleanup Module*. This module is responsible with taking anti-malware actions against the target entity. The *Cleanup Module* and the *Scoring Engine* use the information provided by the Entity Manager in order to identify all the relations between the malicious entities.

In a broader perspective such a solution should be integrated (as a last line of defense) in a modern security application, together with other components such as URL blocking, firewall, classic AV signatures, etc.

3.1   The Management of Groups

In order to function effectively, the solution must have a complete overview of the running processes. To accomplish that, the *Entity Manager* maintains a collection of processes executing on the client system. The Entity Manager dynamically updates this collection to reflect the addition of new processes in response to process creation, and the removal of other processes in response to process termination. The Entity Manager divides the processes in the collection into one or multiple *groups* and maintains a set of associations indicating the

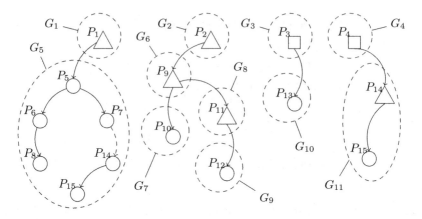

Fig. 2. Groups of processes

groups each of those process belongs to. An example illustrating multiple groups of processes is presented in Fig. 2.

Categories of Processes. Processes are divided into three distinct categories: *group creators* - illustrated using triangles, *group inheritors* - circles and *unmonitored processes* - squares. By assigning a category - or a role - to each process, the groups of processes are much easier to identify and manage. Smaller groups, consisting of processes that are actually related, can be created, avoiding the creation of a single, large group per system. The category which a process belongs to is identified based on certain features of the respective process. Examples of such features are the file path, the digital signature or a hash computed for the executable file corresponding to the process.

Relations of Processes. The solid arrows indicate process creation, while the dashed arrows indicate code injection. The direction of each arrow indicates the direction of the relationship between the respective entities. For example, process P_6 is a child of process P_5 while process P_7 has injected code into process P_{14}. Groups of related processes are represented as dashed lines, encircling those processes, and are denoted as G_i, $i \in \{1, 11\}$. For example, P_1 is the sole member of group G_1, while G_5 contains processes $P_5 \ldots P_8$, P_{14} and P_{15}.

Group creators are processes that are known to create other processes, not necessarily related to them. As their name suggests, whenever a process from this category spawns a process, a new group will be created, initially consisting of the child process. This category includes, among others, *winlogon.exe*, *svchost.exe*, *cmd.exe* and other processes or services of the OS, Windows Explorer, Total Commander and similar file manager applications, Internet Explorer, Firefox, Chrome and other browsers. When a group creator spawns a process a new group is created (e.g. group creator P_1 creates group G_5 when it spawns P_5).

Processes that are *unmonitored* by the security application include the various components of the security solution and certain components of the OS, for example *csrss.exe* and *smss.exe* on the Windows OS. These processes are implicitly treated as group creators.

The *group inheritor* category includes the majority of user processes, as well as processes that are unknown or are not identified as group creators. Whenever a group inheritor spawns a process or injects code into another process, the other process is included in the same group as the group inheritor (e.g. process P_6 is included in the same group with its parent process, P_5; P_{14} is included in the same group as process P_7, as a result of receiving injected code from P_7).

The category of a process is updated in response to certain events or when it becomes part of a group. In Fig. 2, process P_{14} was initially a group creator, as shown in group G_{11}. At a later moment, it received code injected by process P_7, a member of G_5. As a result, process P_{14} was included in the group of the injector process, G_5, and was re-marked as a group inheritor.

A process may also simultaneously belong to multiple groups, due to code injection. However, such situations are not so frequent. In the example illustrated in Fig. 2, process P_{14} has become a group inheritor and is included in both G_5 and G_{11} groups, as described above. When process P_{14} - now a group inheritor - spawns the new process P_{15}, the latter will be included in both the G_5 and G_{11} groups. In other words, changing the category of a process impacts how the processes it spawns or injects code into are handled.

The groups of processes are managed by the Entity Manager, which receives notifications from various Event Interceptors whenever an event related to the life cycle of a process occurs. Process life cycle events consist of process creation, code injection and process termination. If the event indicates the creation of a new process, the Entity Manager determines whether the parent process is a group inheritor or not, in order to assign the newly created process to the appropriate group. If the parent is a group inheritor, the manager will add the child process to the parent's group and will mark it as a group inheritor. Otherwise, the manager determines if the parent process is a group creator. If so, a new group will be created and the child process will be added to that group.

Figure 3 presents a real-world example using a TrojanSpy.MSIL[1] malware. During the two minutes the sample was run, it launched multiple processes, including *cmd.exe* and *reg.exe* (used to modify registry). Under normal circumstances, *cmd.exe* is a group creator, but because the first process in the group is a group inheritor, all its descendant processes become group inheritors.

If the process life cycle event is a code injection, the Entity Manager will determine if it represents a trusted injection. Usually, each code injection event is considered suspicious, possibly indicating a malicious action. However, some processes of the OS may, in some specific situations, legitimately inject code into other processes. These situations should not be considered malicious in order to avoid false positives. The Entity Manager attempts to match the details of the code injection event to a *whitelist*, containing details of legitimate injections.

---

[1] MD5 hash: 0x143FCC07CEB0F779FF1E204CEF4A20D6.

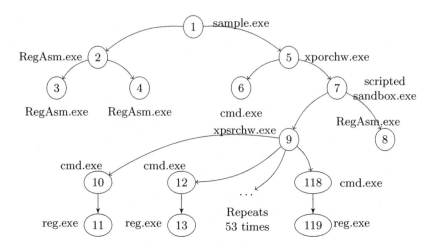

Fig. 3. TrojanSpy:MSIL malware

If the current event is not recognized as a known kind of legitimate injection, the Entity Manager will add the processes receiving the injected code to the group of the process performing the code injection. Then the injected process is marked as a group inheritor, even if initially it was categorized as a group creator.

If the analyzed event indicates the termination of a process, that process is marked as dead. However, it will not be removed from a group until all the other processes in that group have terminated. This strategy will allow a security solution to perform a comprehensive cleanup of the protected system, eliminating even evasive malware that, for instance, only spawn child entities and then exit.

3.2 Heuristics

The proposed security solution relies on *behavioral heuristics* to analyze the actions performed by processes, based on the information provided by Event Interceptors. Whenever a heuristic identifies that a targeted action is being performed, it triggers an alert to the Scoring Engine. Each alert consists of several information about the detected action and the entity that performed it. An alert also has an associated score, that is used to evaluate the potential of a process or group of being malicious.

Some of the actions that can be identified using heuristics are: creating a copy of the original file, hiding a file, injecting code into another process, creating a startup registry key such that the malicious application will be executed after a system restart, deactivating some critical OS functionalities (e.g. Windows Update), terminating critical processes or processes associated with security solutions or modifying an executable file belonging to the OS.

Figure 4A illustrates a heuristic that listens for events to identify six actions in a certain time order. If these actions are identified, the heuristic will trigger

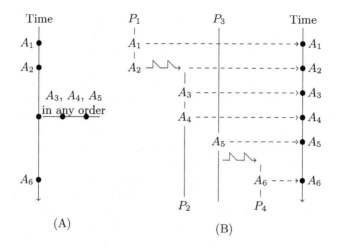

Fig. 4. Heuristic's logic example

an alert. In the proposed solution the logic of the heuristic is implemented in two ways, as function-callbacks or as heuristic signatures, depending on the complexity of the heuristic. In the first case the heuristics are procedures (functions) that are called whenever an event that they registered for occurs. The second one uses signatures to store the logic of simpler heuristics and an engine that tries to match the signatures with the intercepted events.

If a heuristic listens for actions performed only by a process it is called *process heuristic*. If it listens for actions performed by all the processes inside a group it is called *group heuristics*. An example of group heuristic is illustrated in Fig. 4B. Whenever processes $P_1 \dots P_4$ perform actions $A_1 \dots A_6$ in a specific order, such a heuristic will trigger an alert for the group that contains, among others, processes $P_1 \dots P_4$. Process creation is illustrated as a zigzagged arrow. The life history of each process is represented as a solid vertical line. For example, process P_1 terminates after it spawns process P_2. Process P_3 becomes a part of the illustrated group in response to receiving injected code from P_2. Some actions of the respective processes are not part of the heuristic presented in Fig. 4B, for example the spawning of process P_4 by process P_3, mainly because they are not invariants between multiple executions.

The sequence of actions $A_1 \dots A_6$ describes a ransomware attack. Ransomware is a type of malware that encrypts a set of files on the user's computer and demands a ransom payment in order to recover the files. It has become very popular recently among malware authors, because it represents an almost sure source of revenue. In this example, the malicious actions are distributed among a group of processes $P_1 \dots P_4$. Each member of the malicious group performs only a small amount of these actions. The actions performed by the ransomware are: A_1: dropping a copy of itself on disk, A_2: launching a copy of itself, A_3: deleting backup (shadow) files, A_4: injecting code into another process, A_5: enumerating and encrypting files, A_6: displaying a message demanding the ransom.

Individually, each action $A_1 \ldots A_6$ may be performed legitimately by a clean application. For example, dropping a copy of itself on disk or launching it (actions A_1 and A_2) are commonly performed by installers. Additionally, deleting backup files (action A_3) may be performed by certain tools or the Operating System to free disk space. Many clean applications perform code injection (action A_4) for various purposes, such as adding functionalities to an existing, previously released product. Most applications for management of media libraries can legitimately enumerate or modify certain files (action A_5). Finally, displaying a message to the user (action A_6) is specific to almost every GUI application.

An experienced behavior-based detection researcher may observe that a more generic heuristic is possible, that triggers when the group executed the action A_3 or A_4, but the presented heuristic was extended for the sake of the example. Also, one may observe that the flexibility granted by using such heuristics may allow detecting various versions, variants or an entire class of malware. For example, the heuristic presented in Fig. 4 triggers an alert for the CTB Locker[2] sample, whose group is presented in Fig. 5. Regardless of how the actions $A_1 \ldots A_6$ are distributed among processes within the group, if they are executed in the same order as presented in Fig. 4A, the heuristic will trigger an alert on the group.

Heuristic's Evaluation. The Scoring Engine receives *scoring alerts* from the Heuristic Engine whenever a heuristic determines that the occurrence of an event indicates a malicious action. Based on these alerts, the Scoring Engine maintains and updates the *aggregated scores* for the involved entities, process or group. Depending on the heuristic, the alert can influence the aggregated scores of a single process, of a group of processes or of both types of entities.

Using these scores, the Entity Manager determines whether a malware is present on the client system (e.g. a score threshold is reached). When this happens a *detection alert* is sent to the Cleanup Module, that will take the actions necessary to remove the malicious component from the system. Using

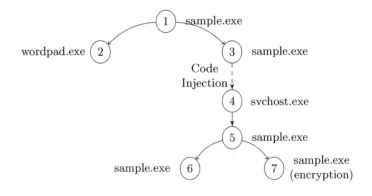

Fig. 5. CTB Locker ransomware

---

[2] MD5 hash: 0x82F941FBD483E0684DAED99F006488F1.

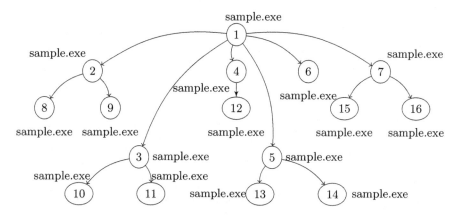

Fig. 6. Trojan-PSW malware

these evaluation methods, even if malicious actions are distributed between several members of a group, and the aggregated scores corresponding to each individual processes are not sufficient to trigger a detection, the group-wide score may exceed the detection threshold. This is very useful for malware such as the Trojan-PSW[3] sample, illustrated in Fig. 6. This malware creates many processes from the same executable file, each having different command line arguments, distributing its payload in this way.

3.3   Remediation

In order to assure the best protection of a system, once a malicious entity is detected, whether it is a process or group of processes, all traces of that entity must be removed from the system and any changes performed by it must be undone. The *Cleanup Module* is responsible for taking such actions, based on information received from the Scoring Engine and the Entity Manager.

When the module receives the detection alert, it will first identify the process that triggered the detection and determine if it belongs to a single group or to multiple groups. If the suspect process belongs to a single group, the module will proceed to clean the entire group of that process, by applying the appropriate cleanup operation on each member of that group. Cleanup operations usually start with suspending or terminating the execution of the targeted entity. Then, the operation may continue with deleting the disk files that contain the code of that entity and undoing or rolling back a set of changes performed by the respective entity, such as changes to a registry of the OS or to the file system. In some situations, malicious activities may be related to a code injection event. In that case, the Cleanup Module terminates the process that received the injection. Special attention should be given to situations where a malware uses a clean process of the OS to carry out part of a malicious attack through code injection.

---

[3] MD5 hash: 0x609614B508622E90EEEDAA875226FEA4.

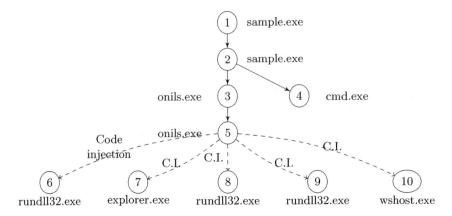

Fig. 7. ZBot malware

In this case, the module may terminate the respective clean process, but it should not delete its executable file so that no damages are made to the OS. An example for this case is the ZBot[4] malware, illustrated in Fig. 7, which injects code into multiple clean processes.

If the suspect process belongs to multiple groups, the Cleanup Module attempts to identify which of those groups is malicious. For example, it could determine how the suspect process became a member of each group: by process creation or code injection. Next, by identifying which heuristic triggered the detection, the Cleanup Module could determine what action the suspect process has performed. For example, we consider a suspect process that is member of a first group via process creation and a member of a second group via code injection. The Cleanup module will attempt to determine the source of the code that was executing when the scoring alert that caused the detection was triggered. If the alert was triggered while the suspected process was executing code from its main executable module, the Cleanup Module will determine that the first group is malicious. Otherwise, if the injected code was being executed, the Cleanup Module will determine that the second group is the malicious one. If the malicious group is successfully identified, the module will proceed with cleaning that group. Otherwise, it will only clean the suspect process, to prevent potential data loss for the user in case of a false positive detection.

4   Technical Results

When evaluating a security solution the detection rate, false positive rate and performance impact are the most important criteria to be considered. A good security solution must have a high detection rate, a low false positive rate and unnoticeable performance impact.

---

[4] MD5 hash: 0x43A6DD7D5BE93F4E5224940C67E40FF8.

4.1   Detection Tests

A comparison between the detection rate of the group based approach and a non group based solution is presented. The detection tests were performed in a virtual environment consisting of machines running Windows 8.1. Each sample was run for two minutes in the virtual machine, then the results were collected and the execution was ended. For false positives tests, each sample was run for ten minutes in the virtual machine before terminating the execution.

For the detection test, two malware collections were used, the first consisting of ransomware that were collected in November 2016, while the other contains malware samples collected from various sources like: honeypots, spam email attachments, infected WEB sites and URLs used to spread malware in November 2016. The clean samples (for the false positive test) are popular applications used in 2016.

Table 1. Malware detection test

Samples	Detected (no groups)	Detected (no groups)	Detected (with groups)	Detected (with groups)
47933	37054	77.3%	42142	87.91%
16490	13084	79.34%	13935	84.5%

Table 1 shows that the detection was improved for both collections with 10.61% and 5.16%. This shows that at least 5% of the malware in both collections are multi-component or multi-process, thus proving the need of changing the detection approach to a group based solution. This amount may not seem much at first glance, but such small differences make the distinction between an average security solutions and a good, competitive one.

Table 2. False positive test

Samples	Detected (no groups)	Detected (no groups)	Detected (with groups)	Detected (with groups)
1128	10	0.88%	10	0.88%

The results of the false positives test, presented in Table 2, show that the number of false positives does not change when augmenting the security solution with group awareness. This is due to the fact that the groups generated for legitimate applications usually contained a small number of processes with few triggered heuristics.

4.2 Limitations of the Solution

The implementation of the solution involves maintaining in memory a set of information associated to each process in a group until the group is terminated. For some samples, such as the TrojanSpy.MSIL sample the memory requirements are high. This can be prevented by detecting the sample before the process group contains too many processes or for clean processes, by simply making that process a group creator.

Clean processes are added to malware groups because malware use such processes to perform different actions (e.g. *reg.exe* to access the registry). This problem indicates that a *whitelist* is needed, that will be consulted when cleaning the infected system to prevent any data loss for the user or producing any damages to the Operating System.

The solution can only detect samples which interact on the current machine. If by some means a process uses an external (i.e. not on the same machine) communication channel to force the creation of another process on the original machine the Entity Manager can not link the parent with the child and it is not able to create the group correctly.

Finally the solution is limited by the platform it runs on. Because Windows does not keep a strict relation between child processes and parent processes, managing groups can prove to be difficult, requiring OS specific knowledge. Furthermore, because Windows allows code to be injected in a trivial way and does not provide a synchronous notification for when injections occur, detecting all code injection methods is also considerably hard. The proposed solution attempts to solve this issue by identifying the most common methods for injecting code through dedicated heuristics.

5 Conclusions

We highlighted the problem of evasive, multi-process malware and proposed shifting the focus from evaluating the behavior of individual processes to evaluating and correlating the actions of related processes. We presented real-world malware samples, in order to better exemplify the behavior of multi-process malware. The proposed solution detected all these samples and constructed their groups correctly.

We described how groups of related processes are constructed, by dividing the processes into *creators* and *inheritors*. We presented the way groups are influenced by process creation and code injection events. We introduced group-based behavioral heuristics, described how the behavior of processes and groups is evaluated and how detected entities can be cleaned.

A major contribution of our solution is that it automatically correlates the behavior of individual processes within a group, thus eliminating the need for a distinct correlation phase, as presented in [5], which is both costly and complex. As a result, the heuristics are easier to develop, the evaluation is more straightforward and cleanup is better performed.

We implemented the presented concepts into a behavior-based solution and compared this approach to a non-group solution. The improvement was quite consistent: the detection rate was increased with over 10% for the ransomware samples test, a type of malware known to be highly evasive (multi-process).

References

1. Blunden, B.: The Rootkit Arsenal: Escape and Evasion in the Dark Corners of the System. Jones and Bartlett Publishers Inc., USA (2009)
2. Devesa, J., Santos, I., Cantero, X., Penya, Y.K., Bringas, P.G.: Automatic behaviour-based analysis and classification system for malware detection. In: ICEIS 2010 - Proceedings of the 12th International Conference on Enterprise Information Systems, AIDSS, Funchal, Madeira, Portugal, 8–12 June 2010, vol. 2, pp. 395–399 (2010)
3. Elhadi, A.A.E., Maarof, M.A., Barry, B.I.: Improving the detection of malware behaviour using simplified data dependent API call graph. Int. J. Secur. Appl. **7**(5), 29–42 (2013)
4. Ispoglou, K.K., Payer, M.: malWASH: washing malware to evade dynamic analysis. In: Proceedings of the 10th USENIX Conference on Offensive Technologies, WOOT 2016, pp. 106–117. USENIX Association, Berkeley (2016)
5. Ji, Y., He, Y., Jiang, X., Cao, J., Li, Q.: Combating the evasion mechanisms of social bots. Comput. Secur. **58**(C), 230–249 (2016)
6. Ji, Y., He, Y., Zhu, D., Li, Q., Guo, D.: A mulitiprocess mechanism of evading behavior-based bot detection approaches. In: Huang, X., Zhou, J. (eds.) ISPEC 2014. LNCS, vol. 8434, pp. 75–89. Springer, Cham (2014). doi:10.1007/978-3-319-06320-1_7
7. Kolbitsch, C., Comparetti, P.M., Kruegel, C., Kirda, E., Zhou, X., Wang, X.: Effective and efficient malware detection at the end host. In: Proceedings of the 18th Conference on USENIX Security Symposium, SSYM 2009, pp. 351–366. USENIX Association, Berkeley (2009)
8. Ma, W., Duan, P., Liu, S., Gu, G., Liu, J.C.: Shadow attacks: automatically evading system-call-behavior based malware detection. J. Comput. Virol. **8**(1–2), 1–13 (2012)
9. MSDN: file system minifilter drivers. http://msdn.microsoft.com/en-us/library/windows/hardware/ff540402%28v=vs.85%29.aspx
10. Naval, S., Laxmi, V., Rajarajan, M., Gaur, M.S., Conti, M.: Employing program semantics for malware detection. IEEE Trans. Inf. Forensics Secur. **10**(12), 2591–2604 (2015)
11. Ramilli, M., Bishop, M.: Multi-stage delivery of malware. In: 5th International Conference on Malicious and Unwanted Software (MALWARE), pp. 91–97, October 2010
12. Ramilli, M., Bishop, M., Sun, S.: Multiprocess malware. In: Proceedings of the 2011 6th International Conference on Malicious and Unwanted Software, MALWARE 2011, pp. 8–13. IEEE Computer Society, Washington, DC (2011)

A Malware-Tolerant, Self-Healing Industrial Control System Framework

Michael Denzel$^{(\boxtimes)}$, Mark Ryan, and Eike Ritter

School of Computer Science, University of Birmingham,
Birmingham B15 2TT, UK
{m.denzel,m.d.ryan,e.ritter}@cs.bham.ac.uk

Abstract. Industrial Control Systems (ICSs) are computers managing many critical infrastructures like power plants, aeroplanes, production lines, etc. While ICS were specialised hardware circuits without internet connection in former times, they are nowadays commodity computers with network connection, TCP/IP stack, and a full operating system, making them vulnerable to common attacks. The defensive mechanisms, however, are still lacking behind due to the strong requirement for availability of ICSs which prohibits to deploy typical countermeasures like e.g. an anti-virus. New techniques are needed to defend these systems under their distinct prerequisites.

We introduce the concept of a malware-tolerant ICS network architecture which can still operate securely even when some components are entirely compromised by an attacker. This was done by replacing all single point-of-failures with multiple components verifying each other. We provide ProVerif proofs to show the correctness of the network protocol one-by-one assuming each device compromised.

Furthermore, we added a self-healing mechanism based on invariants to the architecture on network as well as system level which will reset failed or compromised systems. To demonstrate system level self-healing, we implemented it on top of FreeRTOS and ARM TrustZone. The network level self-healing was incorporated into the ProVerif proofs by formally verifying the absence of type 1 (falsely identified attacks) and type 2 errors (missed attacks).

Keywords: Malware tolerance · Self-healing · Industrial Control System (ICS) · Security

1 Introduction

Industrial Control Systems (ICSs) received a lot of media attention with the Stuxnet attack [18]. But there are also more examples like Duqu, Flame, Red October, MiniDuke [31], Gauss, Energetic Bear, Epic Turla [15], and the attack on a German steel mill [4].

© IFIP International Federation for Information Processing 2017
Published by Springer International Publishing AG 2017. All Rights Reserved
S. De Capitani di Vimercati and F. Martinelli (Eds.): SEC 2017, IFIP AICT 502, pp. 46–60, 2017.
DOI: 10.1007/978-3-319-58469-0_4

ICSs are sensor-actuator networks that control physical systems. The core components are so-called Programmable Logic Controllers (PLCs), which nowadays are essentially commodity computers with specialised software to satisfy the requirement for high availability and real-time operation. Due to these requirements, they cannot run common defensive measures like an anti-virus. Defensive mechanisms have, thus, to be deployed (less effective) elsewhere in the network. Moreover, PLCs have a long lifetime (10–20 years) and are not usually patched to avoid downtime and bricking the devices [26]. A corrupted patch can render a PLC unusable possibly leading to a shutdown of part of the network which is potentially life-threatening. In combination with historic protocols which do not even offer basic authentication (like the Modbus protocol [10]) these systems fall in the hands of attackers as soon as the attacker has network access.

Governmental organisations [13,26] recommend a strategy called "defence in depth" which tries to deploy defences at every layer of the network. We want to go one step further and, instead of only defending problematic devices, we aim to distribute trust over several independent components in a way that an individual component infected with malware cannot break the security policy. We call this approach *malware-tolerance*. Simply put, we want to remove every single point-of-failure at critical intersections throughout the entire ICS architecture. Our secondary goal is to enable the architecture to automatically repair ordinary and malicious faults, so-called self-healing. With this approach, it is also possible to recover from corrupted or incomplete patches.

Contributions:

- We design the architecture of a malware-tolerant ICS that has no single point-of-failure at critical intersection points and can self-heal failed or (maliciously) misbehaving PLCs.
- We also formally prove the network architecture with state-of-the-art protocol verifier ProVerif[1]. The proofs can be found online[2].
- To achieve our architecture, we also develop a self-healing mechanism which detects incorrect behaviour by verifying invariants, and recovers to a good state. We adjusted FreeRTOS[3] to include our mechanism and released our implementation as open-source[4].

2   Overview

2.1   Traditional Industrial Control System Architecture

Traditional ICSs separate the network into zones which are isolated from each other by firewalls resulting in a layered network with Intrusion Detection System (IDS) at intersection points (defence in depth). The innermost part of an ICS is

---

[1] http://prosecco.gforge.inria.fr/personal/bblanche/proverif/.

[2] https://github.com/mdenzel/malware-tolerant_ICS_proofs.

[3] www.freertos.org.

[4] https://github.com/mdenzel/self-healing_FreeRTOS.

called *control loop* and consists of a PLC as well as sensors and actuators. This part of the system is the actual cyber-physical system and has hardly any (often no) defensive measures apart from the firewall in front of it due to availability and real-time constraints. The control loop can be at a different location (*field site*) than the control centre. An example for such a control loop would be a temperature control system with e.g. some water tanks which should neither freeze nor boil. The PLC would read the temperature from a sensor and adjust the heating/cooling of the water to maintain a temperature between 0 to 100 °C.

2.2 Assumptions

1. We assume a Dolev-Yao attacker [8] on the network who interacts with software-side technologies. The attacker has no physical access to the facilities and cannot change cabling or remotely introduce electrical signals directly into wires (apart from assumption 2).
2. Additionally, the attacker can choose one[5] device (except the actuator) of which he gains full control – i.e. also access to corresponding cryptographic keys and "software" access to the physical wires connected to the chosen device. If the attacker chooses e.g. a PLC, he has access to the connected sensors, can read their values, but cannot change wiring or sensors. The attacker can manipulate the hardware of a chosen device once (during production) but has no physical access afterwards any more. If the chosen device has network access, the attacker can update software and firmware.
3. We are initially not aware which device the attacker chose.
4. We assume the 2-out-of-3 circuit is hardware-only and in scope of verification.
5. Attacks on cryptography and phishing attacks are out of scope.
6. PLCs and sensors work synchronously or are buffered.

2.3 Proposed Architecture

Our approach is an extension to already existent firewalls, network zones, IDSs etc. and changes the control loop at the field site. Figure 1 displays our infrastructure with the changes being highlighted in red. Our concept adds hardware in form of reset-circuits; data by images and policies; and software in form of a self-healing Real-Time Operating System (RTOS) and the netboot firmware of the reset-chip. Additionally, we leverage existent redundancy of PLCs and a 2-out-of-3 (2oo3) circuit which are already in place in some ICS facilities.

Basis of the malware-tolerant architecture are three diverse PLCs combined with trusted computing. The 2-out-of-3 hardware circuit combines the results of the PLCs and forward them to the actuator. That means none of the PLCs has to be invulnerable to attacks or failures, it is enough if two of the three work. The PLCs must differ in their soft- as well as hardware which we achieve with a special kind of N-variant system and diverse hardware (details in Sect. 4.2).

---

[5] We only show the basic case of an attacker compromising one system. Tolerating attacks on multiple systems is more challenging but similarly possible.

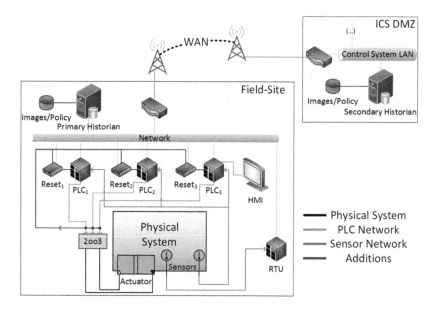

Fig. 1. Proposed Industrial Control System architecture

We also added self-healing functionality that can recover failed and compromised PLCs with (1) a RTOS based on ARM TrustZone that can reset user level tasks and (2) a network protocol and reset-circuits to defend against attacks on Trusted Execution Environment (TEE).

Self-healing RTOS: To demonstrate the RTOS, we created a proof-of-concept implementation based on ARM TrustZone and the FreeRTOS operating system which we ported to ARM TrustZone to protect critical functionality like scheduling and interrupts. ARM TrustZone, is a TEE which consists of two separated environments: the *secure world* and the *normal world*. While the secure world has full access to the system, the normal world is restricted in its capabilities. The switch between the two worlds is handled by the so-called *monitor*. TrustZone chips usually come with the TrustZone Interrupt Controller (TZIC) and functionality to manage memory, i.e. a TrustZone-aware Memory Management Unit, routines to forbid Direct Memory Access, and so on. We refer to the ARM documentation [2] for more details.

Figure 2 shows the control flow of our TrustZone-aware RTOS. Periodically, the TZIC will generate a timer interrupt (1.) which is setup as an Fast Interrupt (FIQ) trapping into monitor mode (2.). The monitor will save the context and jump to the interrupt handler (3.) which will, for timer interrupts, call the FreeR-TOS scheduler (4.). After scheduler (5.) and interrupt handler (6.) return, the next *task* is determined. At this point, the monitor will invoke a detection routine (7.). To reveal faults or malicious behaviour of certain tasks, the detection routine checks various system variables and external values (e.g. sensor values)

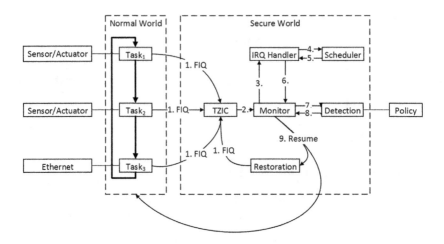

Fig. 2. TrustZone-aware real-time operating system

against invariants which are stored in form of a policy, cryptographically signed, on at least two servers. These invariants are implicitly given by the set-points the operator of the system placed. For our water tank example, the operator could e.g. set the temperature t to 0 to 100 °C, forbid heating for $t > 50$ °C, and forbid cooling for $t < 50$ °C. If the temperature is below or above this range and the task does not enable the actuator, our task is faulty. The result of the detection routine is returned to the monitor (8.) which then (9.) either runs the task or dispatches a restoration routine if the task was misbehaving. The restoration routine only runs during the time-slice of the misbehaving task which ensures availability of the rest of the system including other tasks and operating system functionality. The restoration terminates the task and loads an image of the original task from a protected memory region inside the secure world. Lastly, the task is added to the scheduler again. The critical steps are run inside the TrustZone secure world to protect them from manipulation.

To avoid unnecessary resets due to false positives, we created a specification-based detection technique. These have a lower rate of false alarms than non-specification-based techniques but might miss some attacks [24]. If the presented online self-healing mechanism fails, the network level self-healing approach (see following paragraph) will restore the particular PLC but at the cost of a restart.

Reset-Circuits and Network Protocol: Our reset-circuits consist of a network boot chip (e.g. iPXE[6]) and a logical circuit to control resets (Fig. 3). A low frequency clock signal restricts resets to a certain interval. Optionally, the inputs to the circuit (label 1. in Fig. 3) can be replaced with flipflops to enable synchronising the PLCs. Circuits for PLC_2 and PLC_3 can be similarly derived.

---

[6] www.ipxe.org.

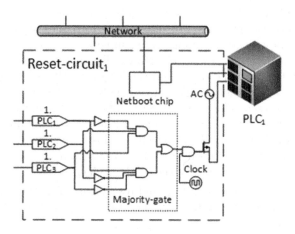

Fig. 3. Reset-circuit for PLC_1

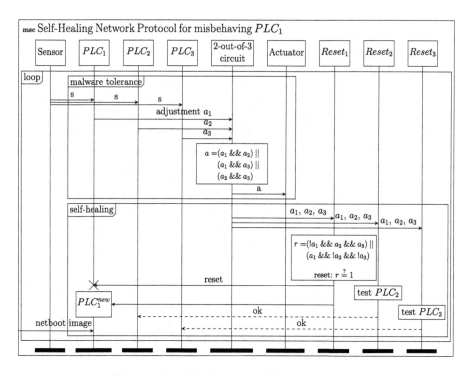

Fig. 4. Malware-tolerant, self-healing protocol

Since network-based detection indicates that system level self-healing (taking place beforehand) failed, we intentionally clear the state to recover from the attack. We re-initialise state either by discovery or by requesting it from the other PLCs. In our temperature maintenance example, discovering the temperature and adjusting the actuator is straight forward. For more complex scenarios, the reset PLC would request the state from the other two PLCs and compare it.

The full message sequence chart of our malware-tolerant, self-healing network protocol is presented in Fig. 4: Every PLC reads the current sensor value s (for simplicity we drew only one sensor but multiple sensors are possible) and computes the adjustment a_i of the actuator. This is sent to the 2-out-of-3 circuit which forwards the end result a to the actuator. Parallel, each reset-circuit receives the three response values of the PLCs, each checks if a reset for its corresponding PLC should happen ($r \stackrel{?}{=} 1$), and resets it if this is the case. Rebooting PLCs load the netboot image from the network. The figure displays a reset of PLC_1 as an example.

3   Security Analysis and Results

3.1   ProVerif Proofs

To give evidence of the security features of our architecture, we utilised ProVerif – a state-of-the-art protocol verifier – to test our network protocol. We modelled the protocol as shown in Fig. 4 for various configurations (see Table 1) where we grant the attacker control over different sets of devices.

In order to reason about malware-tolerant systems, we analysed the system based on multiple Trusted Computing Bases (TCBs). A TCB is the minimum set of honest components needed to secure the system; multiple such sets can exist. A system is malware-tolerant if there are at least two disjoint TCBs that provide the same property. Each independent component of the system – i.e. mostly entire devices as e.g. the CPU depends on the computer and is not an independent component – can be part of multiple TCBs.

With this notation, we can reason about a system based on TCBs. The system is secure if any TCB_i is secure. E.g. if device d_1 and d_2 are part of TCB_1 and device d_2 and d_3 are part of TCB_2, then the system is secure if $(d_1 \wedge d_2) \vee (d_2 \wedge d_3)$ is secure. As we can see here, d_2 is part of all TCBs and is, thus, the single point-of-failure. The system is not malware-tolerant because there are no disjoint TCBs (TCB_1 and TCB_2 overlap).

The TCB model of our proposed ICS is shown in expression 1. R_i stands for the reset-circuit of PLC number i. Since R_i controls PLC_i, we have to consider (R_i, PLC_i) pairs as they are the smallest subset of *independent* components. Our system is malware tolerant, because no (R_i, PLC_i) pair is part of all TCBs.

$$TCB_1 = \{(R_1, PLC_1), (R_2, PLC_2)\}.$$
$$TCB_2 = \{(R_1, PLC_1), (R_3, PLC_3)\}. \tag{1}$$
$$TCB_3 = \{(R_2, PLC_2), (R_3, PLC_3)\}.$$

We formally verified our architecture by testing five properties of our protocol (Fig. 4) with ProVerif (results shown in Table 1):

1./2. $1^{st}/2^{nd}$ iteration: As ProVerif cannot verify loops, we modelled two iterations of the protocol. These two iterations are sufficient, since computations are independent from each other and resets only affect the next loop iteration. For each iteration, we tested if the actuator received the correct value.

3./4. Self-healing: The self-healing column in Table 1 consists of two proofs; the absence of type I errors and the absence of type II errors.

- Type I error (false positive): Regarding our protocol, a false positive is the case where we reset an honest PLC. In ProVerif this has to be expressed as: For all *reset* events of PLC_i, PLC_i misbehaved.
  At first, this seems to not prove that *if PLC_i misbehaved, a reset happens* but in combination with the type II error and knowing that reset is a binary event (it can either happen or not happen), we prove the property.
- Type II error (false negative): False negative refers to the case where a misbehaving PLC is not reset (missed attack). In ProVerif: For all *not_reset* events of PLC_i, PLC_i behaved correctly.
  Again, it seems that *if PLC_i is honest, no reset happens* is not proven. This is applicable, similar to before, by the absence of type I errors.

Table 1. ProVerif results

№	Compromised Devices	1st Iteration (1.)	2nd Iteration (2.)	Self-Healing (3.) (4.)	End reached (5.)
1	None	✓	✓	✓ ✓	✓
2	PLC_1	✓	✓	✓ ✓	✓
3	PLC_2	✓	✓	✓ ✓	✓
4	PLC_3	✓	✓	✓ ✓	✓
5	2oo3				✓
6	R_1	✓	✓		✓
7	R_2	✓	✓		✓
8	R_3	✓	✓		✓
9	PLC_1, R_1	✓	✓		✓
10	PLC_2, R_2	✓	✓		✓
11	PLC_3, R_3	✓	✓		✓
12	PLC_1, R_2	✓			✓
13	PLC_1, PLC_2				✓
14	PLC_1, 2oo3				✓
15	2oo3, R_1				✓
16	R_1, R_2	✓			✓
17	PLC_{1-3}				✓
18	PLC_{1-2}, 2oo3				✓
19	PLC_1, 2oo3, R_1				✓
20	2oo3, R_{1-2}				✓
21	PLC_1, R_{1-2}	✓			✓
22	PLC_1, R_{2-3}	✓			✓
23	R_{1-3}	✓			✓
24	All				✓

5. End reached: We tested if the protocol runs through. This is done in ProVerif by detecting the deliberate leak of a secret value at the end of the protocol.

The proofs (Table 1) show that the physical system, i.e. the actuator, is supplied with correct values for the cases where the adversary controls one device (cases 2–4 and 6–8) or one $(PLC_i, Reset_i)$-pair (cases 9–11). Self-healing works for one compromised PLC but functional reset-circuits (cases 2–4). Also, everything works if there is no attack (case 1). We tested more hypothetical cases as sanity checks, e.g. the case where the attacker can physically change the 2-out-of-3 circuit (case 5) which is a validation of our assumption. The expected result is that the protocol fails since we hand the asset to the attacker from the very beginning. Case 24 is a special sanity check where we give the adversary control over literally everything. Both cases (case 5 and 24) fail as predicted.

3.2   Evaluation of Self-healing FreeRTOS

Since we are not aware of any Common Vulnerabilities and Exposures (CVE) for FreeRTOS, we could not test any real-world attacks against our extended FreeRTOS operating system (a broader analysis of attacks follows in Sect. 4.1).

To test the system level self-healing capability of our proof-of-concept implementation, we introduced a buffer overflow in our Input/Output (I/O) driver using the vulnerable C-function *strcpy*. We exploited this vulnerability by overflowing the buffer and overwriting the settings in the PLC. We chose this attack as it is the most common vulnerability in C and is similar to a range of attacks, e.g. format string attacks and return-oriented-programming.

Our simplified detection routine checks that the settings are within an accepted range and otherwise triggers restoration. The results show that the task and the temperature driver are reset to their original if the maximum temperature is changed to values outside the range (for more details see code of adjusted FreeRTOS implementation).

3.3   Performance Analysis of TrustZone

We conducted a performance analysis of the TrustZone world switch on a FreeScale i.MX53 Quick Start Board with 1 GB DDR3 SDRAM running a 1 GHz ARM Cortex-A8. For this, we measured the time of 1531 task switches on a system running four tasks and FreeRTOS. The measurements start from the timer interrupt until restoring the context of the next task. This experiment was executed twice, once with and once without TrustZone. To measure the time accurately, we read the CCNT-register which stores the cycle count. The overhead of our timing function calls was $0.9\,\mu s$, allowing us an accuracy of microseconds. The average overhead of a TrustZone task switch was $29\,\mu s$. Figure 5 presents the overhead as box-and-whisker diagram and the values are listed in Table 2.

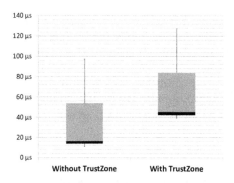

Fig. 5. Box-and-whisker diagram
of time for task switches

Table 2. Data values of the Box-and-whisker diagram in Fig. 5

Value	Without TrustZone	With TrustZone
Maximum	$97 \pm 1\,\mu s$	$126 \pm 1\,\mu s$
75%-Quantile	$54 \pm 1\,\mu s$	$84 \pm 1\,\mu s$
Mean	$16 \pm 1\,\mu s$	$45 \pm 1\,\mu s$
25%-Quantile	$14 \pm 1\,\mu s$	$42 \pm 1\,\mu s$
Minimum	$11 \pm 1\,\mu s$	$39 \pm 1\,\mu s$

A TrustZone task switch in comparison to a non-TrustZone one is equal to 3.6 *malloc* system calls (average time for *malloc* on our system: $8\,\mu s$) overhead; in other words memory management overhead is comparable to TrustZone.

4   Discussion

4.1   Attacks

We examine how our architecture behaves in different attack classes.

– Attacks that change invariants: Let us assume an adversary compromises a PLC but changes some invariants – e.g. he overflows a buffer and inserts a new task but the policy states that there are only N tasks. The system level self-healing will immediately reset the tasks, removing the malicious task. This type of defence was demonstrated in a simple fashion by the buffer overflow above (Sect. 3.2).
– Stealthy attacks (Advanced Persistent Threats (APTs), backdoors, rootkits, trojans etc.): Suppose an attacker manages to deploy a stealthy rootkit on a PLC without being detected. He can now manipulate the PLC as he likes, but the other two PLCs continue to function correctly. If the rogue PLC affects outputs, its reset-circuit will notice this and reinstall the PLC, thus removing the rootkit. If the rootkit resides in the normal world, it will be removed even earlier by the system level self-healing.
– Firmware/hardware attacks: Suppose the attacker deploys a firmware or hardware rootkit in a PLC or in a reset-circuit, then software-based self-healing becomes impossible. However, if the other two PLCs remain operational, then manipulations of outputs are still detected and outvoted by those other two PLCs (through the 2-out-of-3 circuit).
– Attacks on network protocol flaws (e.g. Modbus): Since all PLCs presumably have to support the same protocols, exploits targeting the protocol itself (in contrast to its implementation) are not prevented. To defend against these attacks, one has to modify the protocol standard which is beyond our scope.

- Attacks on the policy/administrator account: We rely on the information in the (cryptographically signed) policy. If the account in charge of it is compromised, the adversary can change the policy freely. To prevent this, trusted input techniques as in [33] should be utilised.
- Denial of Service (DoS): Since we deliberately grant the attacker full control over some devices (see assumption 2 Sect. 2.2), he already has the ability to turn these devices off, but we aim at not enabling further DoS attacks.

4.2   Diversity of PLCs

It is crucial for our architecture that PLCs are diverse in their software as well as hardware. To achieve this, we suggest to use different reset-chips and different CPU architectures, e.g. ARM TrustZone, Intel Software Guard Extensions (SGX), and a PowerPC with a TPM chip. Since the architectures are different, an adversary has to craft different exploits, however, he can still use the same exploit idea to attack the software of all PLCs.

N-version programming was shown to be ineffective against malicious attacks [5,23] as people make correlated mistakes. Hence, we suggest to use a form of artificial N-variant systems where N systems are crafted such that they are distinct by design [32]. Cox et al. [7] used address space partitioning and instruction set tagging to create different programs that cannot be compromised with the same exploit. Salamat et al. [22] proposed to invert the stack and demonstrated this by a special compiler. There is also a compiler which splits stack into data and control structures [17].

By utilising N-variant system techniques, we can artificially create distinct software, that cannot be compromised with the same exploit idea – e.g. a RTOS with the stack growing downwards, one with the stack growing upwards, and one with separate data and control stack cannot all be exploited with the same stack-based attack. If we additionally require each netboot image to be diverse from the last one, similar to [25], an attacker would need to learn the properties of the new image to compromise it. That means, it is considerably harder for an attacker to compromise two PLCs at the same time.

4.3   Implications

The practical implications of our architecture for the real world are that an attacker would have to find twice the amount of vulnerabilities for an ICS since he has to compromise two different devices (e.g. an ARM TrustZone and an Intel SGX PLC). Hence, our system would double the cost for the attacker.

The cost for the defender will not double. Considering that a lot of companies already have redundant PLCs, the hardware cost for the company would roughly stay the same. Diverse software versions can be created similar to the artificial N-variant systems. As the special compilers used to generate these variants [7,22] demonstrate, software can be automatically diversified except for architecture dependent code. In our proof-of-concept implementation based on FreeRTOS 7.8% is platform specific code (780 lines Assembly; 9956 lines C-code)[7].

Another advantage is that network-based self-healing prevents bricking PLCs. If a PLC is partially flashed with an image and crashes, it would automatically reboot triggering the netboot chip to reinstall the image. Thus, patching of the PLCs can now be done conveniently by central image servers with signed images.

5   Related Work and Comparison

Industrial Control Systems: The ICS architecture was already analysed in general: Virvilis et al. [31] studied a variety of APT attacks in depth and their countermeasures. They suggest proper patch management, network segregation, white-listing of outgoing connections, filtering dynamic content execution, and employing trusted computing. Fitzek et al. combined ARM TrustZone with an ICS but relied on a single TCB [9]. Another new TEE is Intel SGX [12] but we are not aware of any studies considering APTs or ICSs.

On the defence side, there is the term *secure control*, i.e. controlling a cyber-physical system while preventing attacks [6]. Also governmental organisations already approached the topic [13,26] focusing on thoroughly enhancing every layer of the architecture, so-called *Defence in Depth*. Coexisting, there is also a *Defence in Breadth* which is not clearly defined but is described as the use of multiple instances of a security technology within a security layer [20]. Commonly, intrusion detection and tolerance systems [16] and firewalls are deployed to prevent or limit damage through attackers. Intrusion tolerance draws its ideas from the field of fault-tolerance [1,30] which focuses on safe operation of a system by using redundancy. Totel et al. [27] proposed to use multiple diverse off-the-shelf devices in combination with an IDS proxy to detect attacks. They demonstrated this on the example of a webserver. However, their proxy is a single point-of-failure.

Self-healing Systems: The field of self-healing is not well established, especially considering security. Ghosh et al. [11] gave a detailed overview of existing techniques. The closest ones to our technique are Finite State Automaton (FSA) approaches [14,28] which model the systems as an FSA and rejuvenate it when invalid states are reached. Our self-healing technique based on invariants is more efficient than FSA as we do not actively keep track of the state. Since invariants can be declared as regular expressions and every FSA can be translated into a regular expression [19], our technique is as representative as FSA.

Bessani et al. [3] use proactive-reactive rejuvenation to restore intrusion-tolerant Crutial Information Switches (a firewall device) throughout the network. It is an example of a hybrid distributed system [29]. While their system targets the firewall in front of critical devices like PLCs, our approach is aimed at PLCs

---

[7] Measured with the CLOC Linux tool.

directly. Platania et al. [21] proposed a rejuvenation architecture similar to ours. Instead of self-healing upon detected misbehaviour, they proactively rejuvenate PLCs periodically; each on its own to ensure availability of the whole system.

Periodic system resets can defend against attacks before visible effects occur – independently of any detection algorithm – however, they impose an overhead on the system even though the system is mostly in a valid state. In contrast to Bessani et al. and Platania et al., we removed single point-of-failures[8] and kept the system running as long as possible through system level reactive measurements making it more applicable to scenarios were availability is a major concern.

6   Conclusion

We presented a malware-tolerant Industrial Control System architecture without single point-of-failures at critical intersection points. We achieve this by relying on diverse, redundant PLCs and a 2-out-of-3 circuit. The infrastructure can push an attacker out of any single PLC using its offline self-healing abilities on the network level. By also employing online self-healing at system level, we maintain high availability during basic failures or simple attacks. To prove our claims, we utilised ProVerif, a state-of-the-art protocol verifier, and implemented proof-of-concept self-healing capabilities on top of FreeRTOS and ARM TrustZone. Proofs as well as RTOS implementation are open-source.

References

1. Amir, Y., Coan, B., Kirsch, J., Lane, J.: Prime: Byzantine replication under attack. IEEE Trans. Dependable Secur. Comput. **8**(4), 564–577 (2011)
2. ARM: Building a secure system using trustzone technology. Technical report, ARM, April 2009. http://infocenter.arm.com/help/topic/com.arm.doc. prd29-genc-009492c/PRD29-GENC-009492C_trustzone_security_whitepaper.pdf
3. Bessani, A.N., Sousa, P., Correia, M., Neves, N.F., Verissimo, P.: The crutial way of critical infrastructure protection. IEEE Secur. Priv. **6**(6), 44–51 (2008)
4. BSI: Die lage der it-sicherheit in deutschland 2014. Technical report, Bundesamt für Sicherheit in der Informationstechnik (2014). https://www.bsi.bund.de/ SharedDocs/Downloads/DE/BSI/Publikationen/Lageberichte/Lagebericht2014. pdf
5. Cai, X., Lyu, M.R., Vouk, M.A.: An experimental evaluation on reliability features of N-version programming. In: Proceedings of the International Symposium on Software Reliability Engineering (ISSRE 2005). IEEE (2005)
6. Cardenas, A.A., Amin, S., Sastry, S.: Secure control: towards survivable cyber-physical systems. In: Proceedings of the International Conference on Distributed Computing Systems. IEEE (2008)

---

[8] The wormhole devices of Bessani et al. storing the cryptographic key and the rejuvenation device of Platania et al. are single point-of-failures.

7. Cox, B., Evans, D., Filipi, A., Rowanhill, J., Hu, W., Davidson, J., Knight, J., Nguyen-Tuong, A., Hiser, J.: N-variant systems: a secretless framework for security through diversity. Usenix Secur. **6**, 105–120 (2006)
8. Dolev, D., Yao, A.C.: On the security of public key protocols. IEEE Trans. Inf. Theor. **29**(2), 198–208 (1983)
9. Fitzek, A., Achleitner, F., Winter, J., Hein, D.: The ANDIX research OS-ARM trustzone meets industrial control systems security. In: Proceedings of the International Conference on Industrial Informatics (INDIN) (2015)
10. Fovino, I.N., Carcano, A., Masera, M., Trombetta, A.: Design and implementation of a secure modbus protocol. In: Palmer, C., Shenoi, S. (eds.) ICCIP 2009. IAICT, vol. 311, pp. 83–96. Springer, Heidelberg (2009). doi:10.1007/978-3-642-04798-5_6
11. Ghosh, D., Sharman, R., Rao, H.R., Upadhyaya, S.: Self-healing systems - survey and synthesis. Decis. Support Syst. **42**(4), 2164–2185 (2007)
12. Hoekstra, M., Lal, R., Pappachan, P., Phegade, V., Del Cuvillo, J.: Using innovative instructions to create trustworthy software solutions. In: Workshop on Hardware and Architectural Support for Security and Privacy, HASP (2013)
13. Homeland Security: Recommended practice: improving industrial control systems cybersecurity with defense-in-depth strategies. Technical report, U.S. Homeland Security, October 2009. https://ics-cert.us-cert.gov/sites/default/files/recommended_practices/Defense_in_Depth_Oct09.pdf
14. Hong, Y., Chen, D., Li, L., Trivedi, K.S.: Closed loop design for software rejuvenation. In: Workshop on Self-healing, Adaptive, and Self-managed Systems (2002)
15. Kaspersky Lab: Empowering industrial cyber security. Technical report, Kaspersky Lab (2015). http://media.kaspersky.com/en/business-security/Empowering%20Industrial%20Cyber%20Security_web:pdf
16. Kuang, L., Zulkernine, M.: An intrusion-tolerant mechanism for intrusion detection systems. In: Availability, Reliability and Security, pp. 319–326. IEEE (2008)
17. Kugler, C., Müller, T.: SCADS. In: Tian, J., Jing, J., Srivatsa, M. (eds.) SecureComm 2014. LNICSSITE, vol. 152, pp. 323–340. Springer, Cham (2015). doi:10.1007/978-3-319-23829-6_23
18. Langner, R.: Stuxnet: dissecting a cyberwarfare weapon. IEEE Secur. Priv. **9**, 49–51 (2011)
19. Meduna, A., Vrabel, L., Zemek, P.: Converting finite automata to regular expressions (2012). http://www.fit.vutbr.cz/ izemek/grants.php.cs?file=%2Fproj%2F589%2FPresentations%2FPB05-Converting-FAs-To-REs: pdf&id=589
20. Paillet, D.: Defending against cyber threats to building management systems (FM Magazine), April 2016. https://www.fmmagazine.com.au/sectors/defending-against-cyber-threats-to-building-management-systems/
21. Platania, M., Obenshain, D., Tantillo, T., Sharma, R., Amir, Y.: Towards a practical survivable intrusion tolerant replication system. In: 2014 IEEE 33rd International Symposium on Reliable Distributed Systems (SRDS) [1], pp. 242–252
22. Salamat, B., Gal, A., Jackson, T., Manivannan, K., Wagner, G., Franz, M.: Multi-variant program execution: using multi-core systems to defuse buffer-overflow vulnerabilities. In: Complex, Intelligent and Software Intensive Systems (CISIS) (2008)
23. Salewski, F., Wilking, D., Kowalewski, S.: The effect of diverse hardware platforms on N-version programming in embedded systems-an empirical evaluation. In: Workshop on Dependable Embedded Sytems (WDES). Citeseer (2006)

24. Sekar, R., Gupta, A., Frullo, J., Shanbhag, T., Tiwari, A., Yang, H., Zhou, S.: Specification-based anomaly detection: a new approach for detecting network intrusions. In: Proceedings of the Conference on Computer and Communications security. ACM (2002)
25. Sousa, P., Bessani, A.N., Correia, M., Neves, N.F., Verissimo, P.: Highly available intrusion-tolerant services with proactive-reactive recovery. IEEE Trans. Parallel Distrib. Syst. **21**(4), 452–465 (2010)
26. Stouffer, K., Lightman, S., Pillitteri, V., Abrams, M., Hahn, A.: Guide to Industrial Control Systems (ICS) security. NIST Special Publication, May 2014. http://www.gocs.com.de/pages/fachberichte/archiv/164-sp.800_82_r2_draft.pdf
27. Totel, E., Majorczyk, F., Mé, L.: COTS diversity based intrusion detection and application to web servers. In: Valdes, A., Zamboni, D. (eds.) RAID 2005. LNCS, vol. 3858, pp. 43–62. Springer, Heidelberg (2006). doi:10.1007/11663812_3
28. Tu, H.y.: Comparisons of self-healing fault-tolerant computing schemes. In: World Congress on Engineering and Computer Science (2010)
29. Verissimo, P.E.: Travelling through wormholes: a new look at distributed systems models. In: ACM SIGACT News (2006). http://dl.acm.org/citation.cfm?id=1122497
30. Veronese, G.S., Correia, M., Bessani, A.N., Lung, L.C., Verissimo, P.: Efficient Byzantine fault-tolerance. IEEE Trans. Comput. **62**(1), 16–30 (2013)
31. Virvilis, N., Gritzalis, D., Apostolopoulos, T.: Trusted computing vs. advanced persistent threats: can a defender win this game? In: Proceedings of the 10th International Conference on Autonomic and Trusted Computing (ATC), pp. 396–403. IEEE (2013)
32. Weatherwax, E., Knight, J., Nguyen-Tuong, A.: A model of secretless security in N-variant systems. In: Workshop on Compiler and Architectural Techniques for Application Reliability and Security (CATARS-2) (2009)
33. Zhou, Z., Gligor, V.D., Newsome, J., McCune, J.M.: Building verifiable trusted path on commodity x86 computers. In: IEEE Symposium on Security and Privacy (SP), pp. 616–630. IEEE (2012)

Process Discovery for Industrial Control System Cyber Attack Detection

David Myers[(✉)], Kenneth Radke, Suriadi Suriadi, and Ernest Foo

Queensland University of Technology, 2 George St, Brisbane, QLD 4000, Australia
d2.myers@qut.edu.au

Abstract. Industrial Control Systems (ICSs) are moving from dedicated communications to Ethernet-based interconnected networks, placing them at risk of cyber attack. ICS networks are typically monitored by an Intrusion Detection System (IDS), however traditional IDSs do not detect attacks which disrupt the control flow of an ICS. ICSs are unique in the repetition and restricted number of tasks that are undertaken. Thus there is the opportunity to use Process Mining, a series of techniques focused on discovering, monitoring and improving business processes, to detect ICS control flow anomalies. In this paper we investigate the suitability of various process mining discovery algorithms for the task of detecting cyber attacks on ICSs by examining logs from control devices. Firstly, we identify the requirements of this unique environment, and then evaluate the appropriateness of several commonly used process discovery algorithms to satisfy these requirements. Secondly, the comparison was performed and validated using ICS logs derived from a case study, containing successful attacks on industrial control systems. Our research shows that the Inductive Miner process discovery method, without the use of noise filtering, is the most suitable for discovering a process model that is effective in detecting cyber-attacks on industrial control systems, both in time spent and accuracy.

Keywords: Industrial Control Systems · Process mining · Anomaly detection

1 Introduction

There have been several cyber-attacks on ICS devices and infrastructure. One notable recent example is the December 23, 2015 attack on three Ukrainian power companies, causing power disruption to 225,000 customers [7]. Such attacks highlight the risk of interconnecting ICS with corporate networks, most notably in terms of the inadequacy of existing IDSs for control system purposes. Corporate networks typically use Intrusion Detection Systems (IDS) to monitor for known cyber-attacks. IDSs come in two types, signature-based IDS (which compare network traffic to signatures of known cyber-attacks), and statistical anomaly based IDS, (which examines network traffic over time for unusual behaviour). However,

S. De Capitani di Vimercati and F. Martinelli (Eds.): SEC 2017, IFIP AICT 502, pp. 61–75, 2017.
DOI: 10.1007/978-3-319-58469-0_5

these IDSs do not detect attacks which exploit or disrupt the *control flow* of an ICS [6], thus, such IDSs may not be sufficient as the goal of exploiting an ICS network is the disruption of ICS system (which is achievable through disruption of the control flow of the systems), rather than exfiltration or infiltration of data as per a typical corporate network attack.

An ICS *control flow* refers to a process, i.e. sequence of events, conducted by an ICS device. These ICS processes are sometimes multiple sequential processes operating concurrently. ICS typically executes a series of steps for a given task, that modify the behaviour of physical devices. Tasks may include creating various fuels in an oil refinery, manufacturing circuit boards, or large scale food manufacturing. The order of events in an ICS process is imperative to the task being conducted, and the deviation from this sequence of events, or control flow, can disrupt the current industrial process. Using the oil refinery example, there may be a sequence of events used to burn off excess gases, such as "turn on flame" → "release gas" → "turn off flame". Changing the order of events to "turn on flame" → "turn off flame" → "release gas" could result in the gas being continually released, potentially damaging equipment. These events may all be valid ICS events, however when the events are conducted in the incorrect sequence there is potential to disrupt the industrial process being conducted.

As per the example above, in order to detect anomalies in ICS system, there is first a need to have knowledge and a model of the expected behaviour of the ICS process. ICS systems are often modelled using state or control flow diagrams, where the actual execution semantics of ICS devices are not captured. This is where techniques from the process mining domain can be of use. Process mining consists of a series of techniques used to *"discover, monitor, and improve real processes by extracting knowledge from event logs"*, and is comprised of process discovery, conformance checking, and process enhancement techniques [14].

Process discovery is the method of deriving a process model describing the control flow of a system from an event log. Using this technique there is the potential to generate process models of an ICS system showing the expected behaviour, by learning from device logs generated by ICS devices such as PLCs. Conformance checking is another technique used to compare a process model or some known business rules to an event log, in order to determine how the events in the log align with the expected behaviours as captured in a process model. In the context of ICS security, we can use conformance checking to identify deviant behaviour that does not match the expected behaviour identified in a generated process model. Thus, by using process discovery and conformance checking, we have a set of tools which can be used to identify deviations, or disruptions in an ICS control flow. In contrast, traditional IDSs which use signatures, or monitor a network for statistical anomalies, do not focus on the overall control flow of a process.

There are numerous process discovery algorithms, each of which have advantages and disadvantages. Several studies have been conducted, comparing these process discovery algorithms [10,17]. However, these comparisons have been conducted in the context of business processes. ICS is a unique environment, and as such there is a need to have an understanding of which process discovery algorithms are the most suitable for this environment.

Thus, the contributions of this paper are as follows: Firstly, we identify the ICS characteristics and ICS modeling requirements. Secondly, we evaluate process models generated using several widely used process discovery algorithms, namely the α-algorithm [13], the Fuzzy Miner [5], the ILP Miner [16], the Flexible Heuristics Miner (FHM) [18], and the Inductive Miner [11] algorithms, on our ICS process modeling requirements for process discovery. Finally, we validate the evaluation of process models with ICS modeling requirements through process mining's conformance checking activity. This conformance checking activity was conducted using ICS device logs from industry-standard ICS devices, four Siemens S7-1200s, which contain cyber-attacks from an 8-hour attacking vs defending exercise. These process discovery and conformance checking activities show that process discovery algorithms can be used to generate models, and detect cyber-attacks, within an ICS control flow.

2   Background

Industrial control systems (ICS), including supervisory control and data acquisition (SCADA) networks, consist of devices such as programmable logic controllers (PLC) which are controlled by operators through human-machine interfaces (HMI). These devices are used to control industrial facilities and critical infrastructure, such as power generation and distribution systems, and water treatment facilities [4,8].

ICS networks can spread over large geographical regions, and have been traditionally controlled through point-to-point communications such as serial links. However, these networks are increasingly migrating from dedicated communication links to switched and routed corporate networks through the use of specialised gateways, accessed via virtual private networks (VPN) or the Internet [8,9]. While exposure to corporate networks and the Internet allows for easier management of ICS devices over a large geographical distance, it also places these devices at risk of cyber-attack [8,9].

ICS devices generate device logs, which are typically stored on the PLC, or in complex ICS networks, these device logs can be aggregated to a Historian, a device for the storage and archival of device logs. There are several methods ICS devices use to generate device logs, primarily the "Cyclic" method, which records all "tags" or memory values on the PLC at some predefined interval of time, and the "On Change" method, which only records values which have changed in some way. An additional common method of event logging used by ICS devices is to log an event *only when an error occurs*. This method of recording events is not suitable for process mining based analysis, as the error logs do not log the control flow of the ICS system. From observation of the recorded device logs, we found the "on change" device logs did not measure each value of all tags as the value changed, where some tags with high variance (such as measuring pressure, or water level) were recorded in 2–3 s intervals. In this regard, the "Cyclic" method configured with a 1 s polling interval provides more complete and accurate device logs than the "on change" method. As such, in this paper, we use the Cyclic type of device log as the starting point for process mining based analysis.

Process models, generated by process discovery algorithms, capture the normative behaviour of the system being modeled. As an example of a process model, we have a sequence of events, (A, B, D). In the second iteration of the process, the sequence of events is (A, C, D). This can be represented in a process model using a Petri-net, describing the control flow of the process, as shown in Fig. 1. This method of discovering and modeling the sequence of events can be applied to ICS systems, with the potential to be used to discover a process model, and attacks on the control flow of an ICS process.

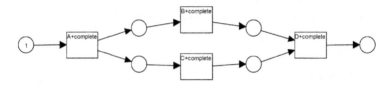

Fig. 1. Example of a process model capturing both sequential and concurrent events.

There are a wide range of process discovery algorithms, which can be identified in several types; such as abstraction-based, heuristic-based, search-based and region-based algorithms [3]. The issue of determining the "best" process mining discovery algorithm for a process discovery activity is a known issue in the process mining domain [12], and several comparisons of algorithms have previously been conducted [10,17]. While process discovery and conformance checking have previously been used in the area of security auditing of business processes to detect anomalous behaviour in various contexts [1–3], they are insufficient in the ICS context. This is because there are a number of differences between business processes, the traditional focus of process mining, and ICS processes. Business processes typically contain events which are executed by humans and recorded by an information system, such as a Workflow Management System [15]. Compared to ICS processes, these business processes are far more flexible and varied than an ICS process, which is a structured and rigid sequence of events executed by a ICS device. In addition to this difference, event logs generated from business processes are typically far more verbose when compared to device logs from ICS devices, such as PLCs. Therefore, there is a need to identify which process mining algorithm(s) are best for discovering and modeling an ICS process.

To determine which process discovery algorithms are most suitable to generate process models from ICS device logs, that can also be used as an input to a conformance checking activity, we have identified several process discovery algorithms for comparison. These discovery algorithms, namely, are the α-algorithm [13], the Integer Linear Programming (ILP) Miner [16], the Flexible Heuristics Miner (FHM) [18], and the Inductive Miner (IM) [11] algorithms.

These algorithms were selected as they appear promising for use in conformance checking to detect cyber-attacks on ICS devices. Before we can assess the algorithms, we need to identify requirements needed to create a suitable model of ICS processes.

3   ICS Modeling Requirements

In the context of ICS networks, there are two main goals for the discovery of an ICS process model. Firstly, to use as an input for a conformance checking activity for the goal of detecting cyber-attacks in an ICS event log, and secondly, to create a process model of an ICS process which is clear and understandable for human interpretation. To generate a process model to suit both of these goals, a process discovery algorithm is used. Process discovery algorithms all have several common features, including the ability to model both sequential and concurrent events, and in addition model repeating event sequences. We have identified several further characteristics for consideration when identifying the most suitable algorithm for ICS process discovery.

Usable Model Representation. For our analysis, we require a usable process model, which contains clear execution semantics, for use in the conformance checking activity. The current state-of-the-art conformance checking activities require the use of Petri-net models. As such, throughout our experiments we use Petri-net models to represent our ICS process and conduct conformance checking activities.

Accuracy. Rozinat et al. [12] outline two evaluation dimensions outline two evaluation dimensions which can be applied to determine the accuracy of a model, "Fitness", and "Precision". The first dimension, fitness, describes how well the event log matches the process model. Fitness is measured numerically, between 0 and 1, where 1 represents a perfect fit. Some process discovery techniques remove "noise" from a process model, commonly to simplify the model. Examples of this are the Fuzzy Miner, and the Inductive Miner. However, this will lower the fitness of the model. For conformance checking purposes, especially for identifying anomalous events, the fitness of the generated process model is imperative. The Precision evaluation dimensions prevents over general models, where the generated models are accurate to the process being modelled.

Simplicty. This requirement reflects the goal of creating a process model of an ICS process which is clear and understandable for human interpretation. In most ICS networks, there does not exist a process model of either individual process, or an overall model. The generated process model must be represented in a way which is understandable, avoiding overcomplicated "spaghetti" models. In the case of anomaly detection, when a process model is visually complex, it becomes difficult for a human to quickly visually validate the anomaly. Rozinat et al. [12], describe two evaluation dimensions which can apply to this simplicity requirement, "Generalisation" and "Structure". The Generalisation evaluation dimension, conversely to "Precision", prevents over precise models, where over precise models may show each path in the process and may contain duplicate events, which may be easier to understand but less fitting. The Structure dimension refers to the visual structure of the process model. Highly fitting process models may be visually complicated, and hard to read and interpret. Modeling repeating event sequences is a common feature of all process discovery algorithms, and can be modeled either directly in the model, or expressed through the use of silent (τ)-transitions (suitable when there is a choice in the model). Silent transitions are not necessary to model repeating event sequences in a process model, however make the model less complicated. These evaluation dimensions can have an effect on the accuracy of the process model, where more generalisation can reduce the overall fitness of the model.

4   Experiment

In this section, we outline our experimental methodology to evaluate process models by generated by discovery algorithms, and compare to our identified ICS characteristics and ICS modeling requirements. Firstly, we outline the experimental setup, describing the ICS devices, logging method, and dataset used throughout our experiment. Secondly, we describe our process discovery, and validation using conformance checking activities.

4.1   Experimental Setup

The experimental setup consists of four distinct scale industrial control systems, each of these controlled by industry-standard PLCs, Siemens S7-1200's. These four scale systems include a bi-directional conveyor belt system, a water pump system, and a "reactor" system, all connected to a master power meter. These four systems are controlled through the use of a HMI, which acts as a historian, collecting device logs from each of the PLCs. These four devices together with the HMI made a "Process Control Network", connecting to a multi-level corporate network through a gateway, representing a typical ICS network. The device logs recorded throughout our experiment are "Cyclic" device logs, which were configured to record with a 1 s interval, and stored in comma-separated values (CSV) format. This "Cyclic" device log method is where the value of all "tags", or addresses in a PLCs memory, are recorded every specified interval, in our configuration, every 1 s. An example of a typical, unprocessed ICS device log is shown below, in Table 1.

The scale industrial systems form one complete industrial process. This industrial process starts with the bi-directional conveyor belt system, which consists of two loops. Two sensors; one which detects the presence of a puck, and one which detects the colour of a puck, control the direction of a "paddle". As an example of the "Cyclic" device logging method, a snippet of the device log from the conveyor belt is shown in Table 1. Once every second all "tags", or memory addresses on the PLC logged. When a puck is detected, the "VarValue" of the tag "Conv_Read_Conv_Color_PE", shown in Table 1, will change from 0 to 1

Table 1. Example snippet of a typical ICS device log, obtained from the conveyor belt system.

VarName	TimeString	VarValue	Validity	Time_ms
Conv_Read_Conv_Color_PE	16/07/2015 9:31	0	1	42201396613
Conv_Read_Conv_HMI_Direction	16/07/2015 9:31	0	1	42201396613
Conv_Read_Conv_Present_PE	16/07/2015 9:31	0	1	42201396613
Conv_Read_Solenoid_Left_Direction	16/07/2015 9:31	0	1	42201396613
Conv_Read_Solenoid_Right_Direction	16/07/2015 9:31	0	1	42201396613

or -1 depending on the colour of the puck. Once a puck is detected and the colour is determined, the paddle will direct the puck onto one of the two conveyor belt loops depending on the colour.

Once the conveyor belt system has completed, the water tank system begins to operate. The water tank system consists of an upper reservoir and a lower reservoir full of water. The lower reservoir is connected to a water pump, which transfers water to the upper reservoir, which uses gravity to feed water back to the lower reservoir. The upper water reservoir contains a water sensor, which turns off the pump when the specified water level is met. This process repeats until a specified time length has elapsed.

The final stage of the industrial process is the "reactor", a pressure vessel system. The reactor is a pipe system, which is connected to an air compressor, and a solenoid with pressure sensors that measures the pressure level in the pipe system, in pounds per square inch (PSI). Once a specified pressure level has been reached, the solenoid activates and opens its valve, releasing air and lowering the pressure to a lower level. Once the lower level has been reached, the solenoid closes and the "reactor" begins to build pressure once again. This process repeats for a designated period of time, at which the remaining pressure is released and the air compressor switches off.

The device logs were generated by the PLCs throughout the operation of an 8 h exercise, in which two teams: a defending team of four people protecting the process control and corporate networks from an attacking team of six attackers with industrial experience. The attackers were tasked with disrupting the process, through exploiting the "Process Control Network", and causing the ICS devices to deviate from the programmed, expected behaviour of that device.

One example of the attacking team successfully disrupting the industrial process is the changing of the direction of the bi-directional conveyor belt. The conveyor belt sorts coloured "pucks" placed on the belt, sending each colour around a different loop on the conveyor. The attacking team successfully compromised the HMI, and changed the sorting direction of these coloured pucks. This results in the pucks being directed around the wrong direction, disrupting the expected industrial process. Throughout this exercise the attacking team were successfully able to disrupt the industrial process running on all three systems, the conveyor belt system, the water tank system, and the "reactor" system. The device logs from each ICS system were collected by the HMI on the "Process Control Network", which acted as the historian. These collected devices logs contained the cyber-attacks that were conducted by the attacking team throughout the duration of the 8 h exercise. These device logs were then aggregated and pre-processed, creating our dataset of event logs, and preparing them for process mining activities.

The dataset consisted 25 cases, with 71 event classes and a total of 1855 events. One "case" represents a complete execution of the ICS process. The PLCs, HMI, and device logging methods were programmed and configured through the use of WinCC and STEP 7, as part of the Siemens TIA Portal V11 SP2. The experiments were not conducted on production ICS networks, as attacks conducted upon these scale systems interrupt the control flow of the ICS process. These scale systems and industrial process used throughout or experiments, while not production systems, use industry-standard ICS devices, four Siemens S7-1200 PLCs.

4.2   Experimental Methodology

Using our dataset of pre-processed event logs, generated from device logs aggregated throughout the 8 h exercise, we discover 5 process models using the widely used algorithms outlined in Sect. 2. These include the α-algorithm, ILP Miner, Flexible Heuristics Miner, Inductive Miner configured with default fitness, and Inductive Miner configured with perfect fitness. The default and perfect fitness for the Inductive Miner are configuration parameters when generating a process model. The use of both Inductive Miner with default fitness and the Inductive Miner with perfect fitness to generate a process model is to compare the results of removing noise and low-varying events from a process model, and the impact this has upon conformance checking for anomaly detection. In addition to the models generated by process discovery algorithms, we use a manually-created Petri-net model of the ICS process. While the manual creation of a process model can capture an accurate picture of an ICS process, this requires specialist knowledge of the ICS systems, and process, being modeled. Using process discovery algorithms, a process model of a complicated ICS system can be created without this in-depth knowledge requirement.

To discover a process model using the outlined algorithms from our dataset, we extracted the first 10 cases, or first 10 complete process executions of the ICS process; a representative sample of the complete ICS process where the cases were *known to contain no cyber-attacks*. It is assumed while generating models of the ICS process, the event logs used in the generation contain no attack data. Using the Disco[1] tool, we converted the pre-processed event log from CSV format to XES format, for use with the Process Mining Toolkit (ProM)[2] version 6.5.1. Using the Petri-net models generated using the ProM tool, and our manually created Petri-net model, we conducted a total of 6 conformance checks, using ProM with the

---

[1] http://fluxicon.com/disco/.
[2] http://www.promtools.org/doku.php.

"Replay a Log on Petri Net for Conformance Analysis" plug-in, comparing each discovered process model against our full dataset. Both the process discovery and conformance checking activities were conducted on a Dell Optiplex 9020 desktop computer, with an i7-4770 CPU, 16 GB RAM, and 256 GB SSD.

5   Results and Analysis

We have laid out in Sect. 3 the requirements for generating process models, firstly for use in a conformance checking activity with the goal of identifying anomalies, such as cyber attacks, in an ICS event log, and secondly for human interpretation. The process models generated by the selected process mining algorithms, outlined in Sect. 2 are evaluated by these requirements, and the results of this evaluation are described under each requirement below, and summarised in Table 2.

Table 2. Comparison of models generated by selected process discovery algorithms with identified requirements of ICS process discovery.

Algorithm	Model	Accuracy	Simplicity
α-algorithm [13]	✓	✓	✗
ILP Miner [16]	✓	✓	✗
FHM [18]	✓/✗	✗	✓
IM (Default) [11]	✓	✗	✓
IM (Perfect) [11]	✓	✓	✓

All models were either generated in or can be converted to Petri-net form, making all models usable in a conformance checking activity. To test the "Fitness" of the generated process models, we conduct a conformance check on the representative sample used to generate each model. The process models generated by the ILP Miner, α-algorithm, and Inductive Miner with perfect fitness, all fit the representative example of the ICS process event log which was taken to generate the process models, and are precise. Both models generated by the Flexible Heuristics Miner with a move-log fitness of 0.27, and the Inductive Miner, configured with default fitness, with a move-log fitness of 0.95, do not fit this sample. This is due to both algorithms filtering infrequent events. The process model generated for use in conformance checking for anomaly detection must be as close to, or perfectly fitting, to the ICS process as possible. Any non fitting events during a later conformance check for anomaly detection are treated as "anomalous", resulting in "false positives" as the model is inaccurate. This can be observed in Table 3. From this "fitness" metric, we can determine that the process models generated by the Flexible Heuristics Miner and Inductive Miner with default fitness are not suitable for use in a conformance checking activity to detect anomalous events, such as cyber attacks (Fig. 2).

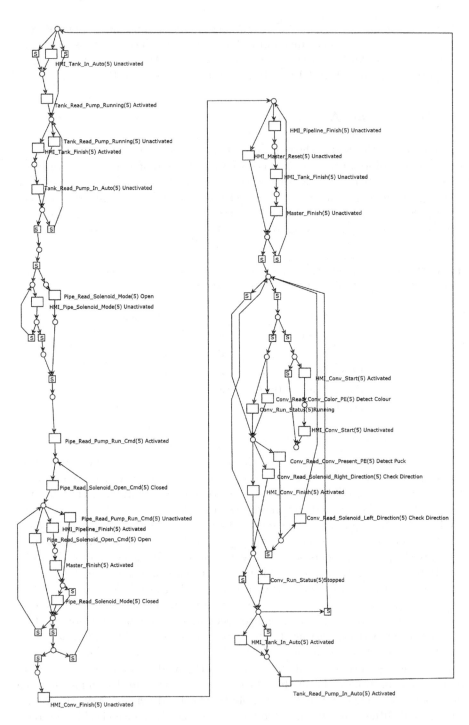

Fig. 2. Process model generated using Inductive Miner (perfect fitness).

We have identified two evaluation dimensions for the Simplicity requirement, described in Sect. 3, "Generalisation" and "Structure". Both the generalisation and structure dimensions can be evaluated through observation of the generated process models. The process models generated by the Heuristics Miner, and Inductive Miner are both structured and are at a suitable level of generalisation, showing the control flow of the ICS process without impacting on the fitness of the process model. However, the models generated by the α-algorithm and ILP Miner, although fitting, have significantly more arcs within the model, with 47 places connected by 122 arcs, and 26 places connected by 179 arcs respectively. This significant difference in arcs is shown in Fig. 3. This is compared to Inductive Miner with 30 places connected by 88 arcs for default fitness, and 34 places connected by 110 arcs for perfect fitness, resulting in the ILP and α-algorithm models being less structured and visually harder to interpret. The process models generated by the Flexible Heuristic Miner and Inductive Miner with both default fitness and perfect fitness settings model repeating event sequences through the use of silent transitions. These models with silent transitions simplify the model, resulting in the models being easier to interpret.

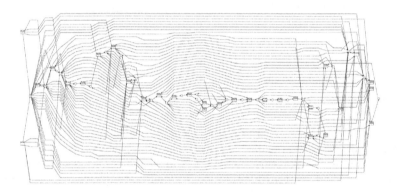

Fig. 3. Process model for illustrative purposes using the ILP Miner to show the complexity of discovered model, where there is less generalisation and structure, with and more arcs in model.

Using the process models generated from several widely used discovery algorithms, we conduct several conformance checking activities on our pre-processed ICS event log. Our dataset contained 25 cases, five of these cases contained cyber-attacks which were conducted on the experimental setup throughout the duration of the 8-hour exercise, outlined in Sect. 4.1. The results of these conformance checking activities are shown below, in Table 3, including number detected anomalous cases, Trace Fitness, and calculation time in milliseconds. The "Trace Fitness" value represents how well the event log fits the Petri-net models generated by the discovery algorithms.

The conformance checking activities were successfully able to identify the 5 anomalous cases on models generated by the α-algorithm, ILP Miner, Inductive

Miner with perfect fitness, and our existing, manually-created model, as shown in Table 3. These anomalous cases contain the cyber-attacks conducted by the attacking team throughout the 8 h exercise, showing where the event log deviates from the expected behaviour of the ICS, outlined in the generated process models. An example of this deviation can be shown with the water tank system. During one attack case, the attackers exploited the HMI and changed the operation of the water tank from "automatic" to "manual". This allows an attacker to manually control the level at which the water level sensor activates, potentially allowing the attackers to overflow one of the water reservoirs. When this event is recorded in the device log, and "replayed" over the process models during the conformance checking activity, it appears as a deviation where the event did not "fit" the process model representing the control flow of the ICS process.

Table 3. Results of conformance checking activity on discovered process models.

Algorithm	Cases	Trace Fitness	Time(ms)
α-algorithm [13]	5	0.93	25.60
ILP Miner [16]	5	0.93	2.08
FHM [18]	25	0.31	54.24
IM [11] (Perfect)	5	0.93	1.88
IM [11] (Default)	24	0.89	1.48
Manual Model	5	0.93	28.68

Both models created by the Flexible Heuristics Miner and Inductive Miner with default fitness settings failed to accurately model the ICS process, resulting in the conformance check returning both 25 and 24 anomalous cases, respectively. This was caused by both Flexible Heuristics Miner and Inductive Miner reducing "noise".

The Flexible Heuristics Miner, and Inductive Miner with default fitness, both employ methods of filtering noise and low-frequency events. While the removal of noise is a common and useful practice in process mining activities, it is not recommended in anomaly detection for identifying cyber-attacks, as the models must accurately represent the behaviour of the ICS. Removing low-frequency events or "noise" from the model can result in false positives, as shown with Flexible Heuristics Miner and Inductive Miner (with default fitness). These results suggest that the Inductive Miner algorithm, configured with perfect fitness, is the most suitable process discovery algorithm for both the creation of a process model of an ICS process for human interpretation, and for use in a conformance checking activity with the goal of identifying anomalies, such as cyber attacks, in a ICS event log. One limitation to current process discovery algorithms is the concept of a "case" in process mining. Most ICS device logs do not have an indication of "case", and require a pre-processing stage to prepare the logs for process mining activities. An area of future work is the development of a process discovery algorithm which can discover an ICS process model without the requirement for a "case".

In addition to detected cases, we found considerable differences in the time required for conducing the conformance checks. The ProM tool reported the calculation time in milliseconds(ms) taken for each full conformance check. The conformance check on the model generated by the Flexible Heuristics Miner was conducted in the largest amount of time, a total of 54.24 ms. This was followed by the existing, manually-created model in 28.68 ms, and the α-algorithm in 25.60 ms. The conformance checks using the models generated by the Inductive Miner (with perfect fitness), the Inductive Miner (with default fitness), and ILP Miner, were significantly faster. The Inductive Miner with perfect fitness completing in 1.88ms, with default fitness in 1.48 ms, and the ILP miner in 2.08 ms. The conformance check upon the manually-created model the returned same anomalous cases as process models generated by the α-algorithm, ILP Miner, and Inductive Miner configured with perfect fitness, however took more time to complete, in 28.68 ms. This indicates the process models generated by process discovery algorithms can accurately capture an ICS process.

Existing IDS used on ICS networks rely on signatures of known attacks in signature-based IDS, or long-term analysis of network traffic in statistical anomaly based IDS. For a signature of an cyber-attack to exist, there must be prior knowledge of the cyber-attack. Our process mining based process discovery and conformance checking methods used in this paper have successfully detected cyber-attacks conducted on industry standard ICS devices, the Siemens S7-1200, using process models generated by widely-used process discovery algorithms. This shows process mining can be used in supplement to traditional IDS devices to detect previously-unknown cyber-attacks.

6   Conclusion

The conformance checking activity with the α-algorithm, ILP Miner, Inductive Miner with perfect fitness all successfully identifying the five anomalous cases containing cyber attacks in the ICS event log. Experimental results show that the Inductive Miner algorithm, configured with perfect fitness, was the most suitable algorithm for use in detecting cyber attacks.

The process mining based methods presented in this paper, unlike IDS systems, are a form of offline analysis, which takes place on device logs after a process has been completed. An area of future work is to modify this method to operate in real or near-real time to improve the detection speed of ICS anomalies. Some attacks, such as Man-in-the-Middle (MITM) attacks used in the Stuxnet attack, may not be detected due to insufficient logging. One method of detecting these attacks could be to correlate device log data and low level sensor data for use in process mining based intrusion detection. Larger datasets, and assessment of the scalability of this method on larger datasets is required.

References

1. Van der Aalst, W.M.P., de Medeiros, A.K.A.: Process mining and security: detecting anomalous process executions and checking process conformance. Electron. Notes Theor. Comput. Sci. **121**, 3–21 (2005)
2. Accorsi, R., Stocker, T.: On the exploitation of process mining for security audits: the conformance checking case. In: SAC, pp. 1709–1716. ACM (2012)
3. Accorsi, R., Stocker, T., Müller, G.: On the exploitation of process mining for security audits: the process discovery case. In: SAC, pp. 1462–1468. ACM (2013)
4. Daneels, A., Salter, W.: What is SCADA. In: Bulfone, D., Daneels, A. (eds.) International Conference on Accelerator and Large Experimental Physics Control Systems, pp. 339–343. ELETTRA, October 1999
5. Günther, C.W., Aalst, W.M.P.: Fuzzy mining – adaptive process simplification based on multi-perspective metrics. In: Alonso, G., Dadam, P., Rosemann, M. (eds.) BPM 2007. LNCS, vol. 4714, pp. 328–343. Springer, Heidelberg (2007). doi:10.1007/978-3-540-75183-0_24
6. Hadžiosmanović, D., Bolzoni, D., Hartel, P.H.: A log mining approach for process monitoring in SCADA. Int. J. Inf. Secur. **11**(4), 231–251 (2012)
7. ICS-CERT. Alert (IR-ALERT-H-16-056-01) cyber-attack against ukrainian critical infrastructure. https://ics-cert.us-cert.gov/alerts/IR-ALERT-H-16-056-01, Accessed 18 Apr 2016
8. Igure, V.M., Laughter, S.A., Williams, R.D.: Security issues in SCADA networks. Comput. Secur. **25**(7), 498–506 (2006)
9. Knijff, R.V.D.: Control systems/SCADA forensics, what's the difference? Digital Invest. **11**(3), 160–174 (2014). Special Issue, Embedded Forensics
10. Leemans, M., van der Aalst, W.M.P.: Discovery of frequent episodes in event logs. In: Ceravolo, P., Russo, B., Accorsi, R. (eds.) SIMPDA 2014. LNBIP, vol. 237, pp. 1–31. Springer, Cham (2015). doi:10.1007/978-3-319-27243-6_1
11. Leemans, S.J.J., Fahland, D., van der Aalst, W.M.P.: Discovering block-structured process models from event logs containing infrequent behaviour. In: Lohmann, N., Song, M., Wohed, P. (eds.) BPM 2013. LNBIP, vol. 171, pp. 66–78. Springer, Cham (2014). doi:10.1007/978-3-319-06257-0_6
12. Rozinat, A., de Medeiros, A.K.A., Günther, C.W., Weijters, A.J.M.M., van der Aalst, W.M.P.: The need for a process mining evaluation framework in research and practice. In: Hofstede, A., Benatallah, B., Paik, H.-Y. (eds.) BPM 2007. LNCS, vol. 4928, pp. 84–89. Springer, Heidelberg (2008). doi:10.1007/978-3-540-78238-4_10
13. Van der Aalst, W.M.P., Weijters, T., Maruster, L.: Workflow mining: discovering process models from event logs. IEEE Trans. Knowl. Data Eng. **16**(9), 1128–1142 (2004)
14. van der Aalst, W.M.P., et al.: Process mining manifesto. In: Daniel, F., Barkaoui, K., Dustdar, S. (eds.) BPM 2011. LNBIP, vol. 99, pp. 169–194. Springer, Heidelberg (2012). doi:10.1007/978-3-642-28108-2_19
15. van der Aalst, W.M.P., Reijers, H.A., Weijters, A.J.M.M., van Dongen, B.F., de Medeiros, A.K.A., Song, M., Verbeek, H.M.W.E.: Business process mining: an industrial application. Inf. Syst. **32**(5), 713–732 (2007)

16. van der Werf, J.M.E.M., van Dongen, B.F., Hurkens, C.A.J., Serebrenik, A.: Process discovery using integer linear programming. In: Hee, K.M., Valk, R. (eds.) PETRI NETS 2008. LNCS, vol. 5062, pp. 368–387. Springer, Heidelberg (2008). doi:10.1007/978-3-540-68746-7_24

17. Weerdt, J.D., Backer, M.D., Vanthienen, J., Baesens, B.: A multi-dimensional quality assessment of state-of-the-art process discovery algorithms using real-life event logs. Inf. Syst. **37**(7), 654–676 (2012)

18. Weijters, A.J.M.M., Ribeiro, J.T.S.: Flexible heuristics miner (FHM). In: CIDM, pp. 310–317. IEEE (2011)

Security and Privacy in Social Applications and Cyber Attacks Defense

Secure Photo Sharing in Social Networks

Pablo Picazo-Sanchez[1]([✉]), Raúl Pardo[2], and Gerardo Schneider[1] (iD)

[1] Department of Computer Science and Engineering, University of Gothenburg,
Gothenburg, Sweden
{pablop,gersch}@chalmers.se
[2] Department of Computer Science and Engineering, Chalmers University of
Technology, Gothenburg, Sweden
pardo@chalmers.se

Abstract. Nowadays, in an ubiquitous world where everything is connected to the Internet and where social networks play an important role in our lives, security and privacy is a must. Billions of pictures are uploaded daily to social networks and, with them, parts of our private life are disclosed. In this work, we propose a practical solution for secure photo sharing on social network with independence of its architecture which can be either centralised or distributed. This solution solves the inconsistencies that appear in distributed social network as a consequence of treating photos and access policies separately. Specifically, we solve this open problem by attaching an access policy to the images and thus, each time a photo is re-shared, the access policy will travel together with the image.

Keywords: Privacy · Social networks · Applied cryptography

1 Introduction

Online Social Networks (OSNs) such as Facebook, Twitter or Instagram are only a few examples of the most used Internet applications all over the world. A recent study shows that Facebook [1] has at least 1.71 billion active users per month. Moreover, according to that study, it is estimated than more than 300 million photos per day are being uploaded.

Most OSN users have the tendency to share photos. There are several works that are focused on the reason for sharing personal information such as photos on OSNs from a sociological perspective [2–5]. These studies found out that most users share photos on OSNs to seek affection. Nevertheless, users are aware of the risks of their actions which might reveal personal aspects of their lives. Due to this, users usually weight the risks of disclosing private information against benefits of not doing it.

© IFIP International Federation for Information Processing 2017
Published by Springer International Publishing AG 2017. All Rights Reserved
S. De Capitani di Vimercati and F. Martinelli (Eds.): SEC 2017, IFIP AICT 502, pp. 79–92, 2017.
DOI: 10.1007/978-3-319-58469-0_6

Both security and privacy issues have been pointed out in several papers as unsolved and challenging problems [6]. Specifically, in the privacy domain, some authors have addressed *photo sharing*[1] as an open problem in OSN [6,7].

This problem arises when users take photos they have access to and increase the audience of the photo by re-sharing it. For instance, imagine that Alice shares a photo with her friends, and later, Bob—who is a friend with Alice—re-shares it with his own friends, thus increasing the audience to his own friends as well. Essentially, this circumstance is given because the privacy policies that Alice has previously defined are applied only to her public domain and are not attached to the objects she shares out.

OSNs can be classified into centralised and distributed social networks. In centralised OSNs there is only one instance which has a global view of the state of the system and where all information is handled. On the other hand, in *Distributed Online Social Networks (DOSNs)*, there are different servers where each one of them has its own instance of the OSN and has the ability of sharing and exchanging information between them.

Facebook, Twitter or Instagram are some examples of centralised OSNs. However, under the hood, the store infrastructure of these OSNs is geographically distributed. For instance, Facebook developers have deployed a distributed data store for the resources of the OSN [8,9]. This storage system is based on a master/slave architecture which replicates the information geographically so that it is accessed efficiently. Bronson *et al.* pointed out in [8] that their storage system explicitly favours availability and per-machine efficiency over strong consistency. They also remarked the problem of *expensive read-after-write consistency, i.e.,* the cost of forwarding writes to the master and later being replicated, and the existence of time elapses before all slaves have a consistent information. In the context of photo sharing, it might originate problems while updating the audience of a photo. Imagine that Alice initially shares a photo with her friends, but after a while she decides to restrict the audience to her family and rewrites the access control policy of the photo. Before this policy is replicated in the whole system—a few milliseconds according to [8]—there will be slaves which would show Alice's photo to the incorrect audience.

Diaspora [10] is the most popular example of DOSNs with more than 0.6 million users. Moreover, in Diaspora, each server is called a *pod* and has its own database. Thus, this architecture prevents a single party to have all the users' personal information. In a DOSN when users from different nodes of the system share information, it is replicated on each node. This highly distributed architecture makes very hard to keep consistency between pods and it directly affects the photo sharing problem we are tackling here. Furthermore, in Diaspora after a user has shared a photo, it is not possible to update its access control policies. This is because once the photo is replicated, a static access control policy is sent to specify the audience of the photo in that pod. Due to this unpleasant restriction, inconsistencies when a user updates the relationships with users from

---

[1] It is also known as *photo re-sharing* since photos can be shared many times and by different users.

different pods may appear. For instance, imagine that Alice shares a photo with her friends. Bob, who signed up in a different pod, gets access to the photo, given that it was replicated to his pod and the access control policy allows him to see it. A few days afterwards, Alice decides to end her friendship with Bob. One would expect Bob to not be able to see the photo shared with Alice's friends. However, the unfriend event is not replicated to all pods where the photo was sent, and therefore Bob continues having access to the photo.

Note that in both architectures the problem arises from having two separate entities, *i.e.*, the photo and its access control policy, and inconsistencies while updating the access control policy of a photo. Here we propose a solution where access control policies are "stuck" to the photo. Therefore when a photo is replicated in different nodes, its access policy travels together with it.

Contributions. We focus on how to share private images on DOSN in a secure way. To do so, we have developed a solution where the access policy is attached to the image by using *Attribute Based Encryption (ABE)*, instead of defining a common access control policy in the generic privacy settings, *e.g.*, "only family" or "colleagues and friends". Moreover, we have tested our proposal on Diaspora to demonstrate its viability on both modes centralised and decentralised[2]. As far as we know, this is the first solution which allows different images formats such as PNG, JPEG or TIFF. Finally, by using the centralised mode of Diaspora, we show how this could be easily deployed into real applications such as Facebook, Twitter or any other OSN.

The rest of this paper is organised as follows: Sect. 2 introduces background knowledge on ABE. In Sect. 3 we present our system design and the core of our proposal. Section 4 presents the results and the experiments we have run. In Sect. 5 we give an overview of works on OSNs from the security and privacy photo re-sharing point of view, and present a comparison with our approach. We conclude and describe future work in the last section.

2 Preliminaries

For completeness and readability, this section provides a brief overview of the cryptographic primitives and security assumptions used throughout the paper.

2.1 Access Structure

Let $\mathcal{U}$ be the attribute universe and $\mathbb{A}$ a non-empty collection of attributes $\{Att_1, Att_2, \ldots, Att_n\}$, with $Att_i \in \{0,1\}^n$. $\mathbb{A}$ is an access structure over $\mathcal{U}$ where the sets specified by $\mathbb{A}$ are called the authorised sets. Notice that each time that new users join the network, a set of attributes is assigned to them.

Moreover, an access structure $\mathbb{A} \subseteq \mathcal{U}$ is monotone if $\forall B, C \subseteq \mathcal{U}$ if $B \subseteq \mathbb{A}$ and $B \subseteq C$ then $C \subseteq \mathbb{A}$.

---

[2] Accessible online at http://ppf-diaspora.raulpardo.org.

2.2   Linear Secret Sharing Scheme

Informally, a *secret-sharing scheme* among a dealer and a set of parties is an algorithm in which a secret k is distributed to a set of i parties in such way that only authorised subsets of parties can reconstruct the secret by pooling the shares of the authorised parties, while unauthorised subsets will learn nothing about the secret. Additionally, when the secret is a random vector chosen over $\mathbb{Z}_p$ is called *linear* secret sharing scheme.

Furthermore, we assume that when an access structure $\mathbb{A}$ is given as a monotonic boolean formula over a set of attributes, there is a polynomial time algorithm that translates it to the matrix access policy [11]. Formally, let p be a prime number and $\mathcal{U}$ the attribute universe, a secret-sharing scheme Π with domain of secrets $\mathbb{Z}_p$ realising access structures on $\mathcal{U}$ is *linear* over $\mathbb{Z}_p$ if:

- The shares of a secret $k \in \mathbb{Z}_p$ for each attribute form a vector over $\mathbb{Z}_p$;
- There exists an $l \times n$ matrix $M \in \mathbb{Z}^{l \times n}$, called the *share-generating matrix*, where for all $x = 1, \ldots, l$, the *x-th* row of M is labelled by a function $\rho(x)$ (from $\{1, \cdots, l\}$ to $\mathcal{U}$). Additionally, during the shares generation, if we consider the column vector $v = (k, r_2, \ldots, r_n)^l$, where $r_2, \ldots, r_n \in \mathbb{Z}_p$ are randomly chosen, then the vector of l shares of the secret k according to the Π is $Mv \in \mathbb{Z}_p^{l \times 1}$. The share $(Mv)_x$ belongs to $\rho(x)$.

2.3   Multi-authority Attributes

Since our solution uses the *Multi Authority-Attribute Based Encryption (MA-ABE)* scheme proposed in [12], we assume that there is a computable function T which links each attribute $\mathcal{U}$ to a unique authority ϕ of the set of authorities $\mathcal{U}_\phi$ i.e., $T : \mathcal{U} \to \mathcal{U}_\phi$. Moreover, this function creates a second labelling of rows in the policy $(\mathbb{A}, \rho)$, which maps rows to attributes by $T(\rho(x))$. We additionally follow the same notation introduced in the original paper where the attributes are defined according to the next pattern: [attribute-id]@[authority-id].

2.4   Bilinear Pairings

Informally, a pairing function is a function that associates each pair of values of a given set with a single value of the set. A bilinear parting function is a pairing function that satisfy bilinear, non-degenerate, efficient and symmetric properties. More formally, let $\mathbb{G}$ and $\mathbb{G}_T$ be two multiplicative cyclic groups of the same prime order p, g a generator of $\mathbb{G}$, and $e \colon \mathbb{G} \times \mathbb{G} \to \mathbb{G}_T$ a pairing function satisfying the following properties:

- Bilinear: $\forall u, v \in \mathbb{G}$ and $a, b \in \mathbb{Z}_p$; we have $e(u^a, v^b) = e(u, v)^{ab}$.
- Non-degenerate: $e(g, g) \neq 1$, *i.e.*, the identity element of $\mathbb{G}_T$.
- Efficient: there is an efficient algorithm to compute $e(u, v), \forall u, v \in \mathbb{G}$.
- Symmetric: e is symmetric, *i.e.*, $e(g^a, g^b) = e(g, g)^{ab} = e(g^b, g^a)$.

It is important to mention that both authorities and users are provided with a unique identifier *GID* which is mapped by a function $\mathcal{H}$ to an element in the group $\mathbb{G}$, *i.e.*, $\mathcal{H} \colon GID \to \mathbb{G}$. Additionally, we define another function $\mathcal{F}$ that translates attributes to elements in a group $\mathbb{G}$, *i.e.*, $\mathcal{F} \colon Att \to \mathbb{G}$.

2.5 Security Assumptions

Similarly to [12], the security of our proposal relies on the *q-type* assumption (*q*-DPBDHE2 in short) which basically is a slight modification of the *q*-Decisional Parallel Bilinear Diffie-Hellman Exponent Assumption [13]. The following definition has been previously demonstrated in [13], so we encourage the reader to check the full security proof.

Let $a, s, b_1, \cdots, b_n \in \mathbb{Z}_p$ be randomly chosen and g a generator of $\mathbb{G}$ of prime order p. If an adversary $\mathcal{A}$ is provided with $\{\mathbb{G}, p, e, g, g^s\} \cup D$ where D is:

$$D = \left(\left\{ g^{a^i} \right\}_{\substack{i \in [2q] \\ i \neq q+1}}, \left\{ g^{a^i b_j} \right\}_{\substack{(i,j) \in [2q,q] \\ i \neq q+1}}, \left\{ g^{s/b_i} \right\}_{i \in [q]}, \left\{ g^{sa^i b_j/b_{j'}} \right\}_{\substack{(i,j,j') \in [q+1,q,q] \\ j \neq j'}} \right)$$

for any probabilistic algorithm $\mathcal{B}$, the advantage of $\mathcal{A}$ in solving the *q*-DPBDHE2 problem is negligible *i.e.*, this assumption relies on the fact that the probability of distinguishing the bilinear pairing $e(g,g)^{sa^{q+1}}$ from a random element $R \in \mathbb{G}_T$ is negligible:

$$Adv_{\mathcal{B}}^{q-DPBDHE2} = \left| Pr \left[\mathcal{B}(D, e(g,g)^{sa^{q+1}}) = 0 \right] - Pr\left[\mathcal{B}(D, R) = 0 \right] \right| \leq \epsilon$$

2.6 MA-ABE Algorithms

The MA-ABE scheme is mainly based on four different algorithms: *GlobalSetup*, *AuthSetup*, *KeyGen*, *Encrypt* and *Decrypt*. In the following we summarise the five algorithms (for a more detailed description check [12]):

- *GlobalSetup*$(1^\lambda) \rightarrow GP$. This method requires a security parameter λ. It outputs the global parameters $GP = \{p, \mathbb{G}, g, \mathcal{H}, \mathcal{F}, \mathcal{U}, \mathcal{U}_\phi\}$.
- *AuthSetup*$(GP, \phi) \rightarrow \{PK_\phi, SK_\phi\}$. This algorithm generates both a public and a private key for each one of the authorities.
- *KeyGen*$(GID, \phi, Att, SK_\phi, GP) \rightarrow SK_{GID,Att}$. This method takes as input the user's GID, the authority ϕ, the attribute Att, the secret key of the authority SK_ϕ and the general parameters GP and it outputs the user's secret key for a given attribute Att —controlled for the authority ϕ.
- *Encrypt*$(M, \mathcal{T}, \{PK_\phi\}, GP) \rightarrow CT$. This algorithm is run by the users and it receives as input the message to be encrypted M, the access policy $\mathcal{T} = (\mathbb{A}, \rho)$, the public keys of the authorities $\{PK_\phi\}$, and the general parameters GP. It outputs the ciphertext CT (ciphered under the access policy $\mathcal{T}$) together with $\mathcal{T}$.
- *Decrypt*$(CT, \{SK_{GID,Att}\}, GP) \rightarrow M$. When a user wants to decrypt a ciphertext, she runs this algorithm. The GP, the ciphertext CT and all the secret keys of that user $SK_{GID,Att}$ (to recover the shares of the access matrix) should be provided to get the plaintext.

3 System Design

In this section we explain in detail our proposed solution for re-sharing photos in DOSNs. Concretely, we describe the design we implemented in Diaspora.

3.1 Diaspora's Architecture and Assumptions

As mentioned in the introduction, Diaspora is a very popular DOSNs. The source of its popularity lies on a distributed architecture which prevents a single party to control users' data. Moreover, Diaspora can work as a centralised social network if there is only one pod in the system.

The distributed architecture of Diaspora consists of *pods*. A *pod* is a server which runs an instance of Diaspora's source code. In order for users to join Diaspora they can either join an existing pod or create their own. Every pod has its own database, therefore when users join a pod, their information is not available to everyone. Moreover, only the owner of the pod has direct access to the information of the database.

Users can connect with other users from the pod they joined as well as users who signed up in other pods. As usual in OSNs, they can define connection relations to classify their contacts such as *friends, acquaintances, family* and so on. Using these relations, users can define the audience of their information, *i.e.*, posts, photos, polls, etc. When information is shared with users from different pods it needs to be replicated. For example, when a set of photos are accessed in different pods then they are replicated in the databases of each one of the involved pods. After the photo is replicated, the access control policies (of the target pod) are updated to determine which users in the pod can access it. If the owner of the pod were to update the photo audience, the access control policies should be updated in all the pods where the photo was distributed to.

Note that this approach requires distributing the photo and (separately) the access control policy. In this way, consistency errors can easily appear, *e.g.*, if the photo is successfully distributed but there is an error while distributing the access control policy. An additional problem is updating the policies of a photo. If a user decides to update the audience of a photo from her friends to nobody, this policy must be transmitted to all the pods where the photo has been replicated. As before, it can originate inconsistencies, for instance, when a pod with a replica of the photo loses connectivity. Currently in Diaspora it is not possible to update the access control policies of a photo after sharing it. This is, probably, because of the difficulties to enforce consistency in such a distributed environment. The previous example can be seen in Fig. 1.

Finally, in our proposal we assume the following: (i) The pods of Diaspora are trustworthy; (ii) the *KeyGen* algorithm is only run by the pods; (iii) photos can be stored either in the pods or in public repositories so it is not mandatory to be secure; and (iv) there is a function named *getAtt* that given a user, it returns the set of a attributes of the user from all the pods in the network.

3.2 MA-ABE in Diaspora

In our solution we propose to attach the "access control policies" to the photo by using a decentralised version of ABE. Classical ABE approaches are based on a centralised assumption where a *Trusted Party (TP)* is in charge of distributing the keys of the scheme and sets up the system. However this is infeasible because

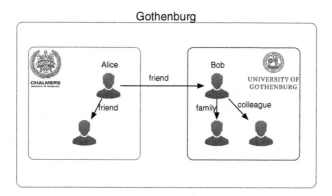

Fig. 1. DOSN example.

of two main problems: (1) the TP has the power to decrypt everything in the system and (2) there is no practical solution if there are n-different authorities running the same cryptographic schema and users from different authorities want to share information with them.

In a nutshell, our approach consists in encrypting (parts of) the photo with a policy which specifies the attributes that other users must possess in order to see the encrypted parts. In what follows we provide a detailed description of our design of photo sharing in Diaspora based on MA-ABE.

Attributes in Diaspora. We define the attribute universe, $\mathcal{U}$, to be the set of all possible connections between users. For instance, in a pod with only two users, Alice and Bob, and the *friend* relation, the universe of attributes is $\mathcal{U} = \{friend(\text{Alice}), friend(\text{Bob})\}$. The attribute *friend*(Alice) will be granted to users that Alice marked as friends. In general, given a set of users $\mathcal{US}$ and a set of connections $\mathcal{C}$, the shape of $\mathcal{U}$ is as follows: $\mathcal{U} = \{c(u) \mid \forall u \in \mathcal{US}, \forall c \in \mathcal{C}\}$.

The universe of attributes in the system is not centralised. Due to Diaspora's distributed architecture, the universe of attributes is composed by the attributes in each pod. Let $\mathcal{U}_{Chalmers}$ and $\mathcal{U}_{GU}$ be the universe of attributes of the Diaspora pods of *Chalmers University* and the *University of Gothenburg (GU)*, respectively. We say that the universe of attributes in Gothenburg is $\mathcal{U}_{GBG} = \mathcal{U}_{Chalmers} \cup \mathcal{U}_{GU}$. We use the same notation to denote the set of users $\mathcal{US}_{GBG} = \mathcal{US}_{Chalmers} \cup \mathcal{US}_{GU}$ and the set of connections in Gothenburg pods $\mathcal{C}_{GBG} = \mathcal{C}_{Chalmers} \cup \mathcal{C}_{GU}$.

In this way, diaspora pods act as authorities which grant attributes to users. Determining whether a user has an attribute can be easily checked by querying the database of the pod. Note that users might have attributes which belong to different pods, *e.g.*, Alice (from the Chalmers pod) can mark Bob (from the GU pod) as *friend*. Therefore, Bob will have attributes that come, not only from the GU pod, but also from the Chalmers pod. We use the same notation as in the original definition of MA-ABE in [12] to specify the provenance of an attribute, *e.g.*, *friend*(Alice)@Chalmers. This example can be seen in Fig. 1.

Key Generation. Initially, when users join Diaspora, they have no connection to other users. Thus, they possess no attributes. As they interact with the system they start to create new connections, and consequently, grant (and be granted with) new attributes. As we mentioned in the preliminaries section, there exists a *KeyGen* algorithm which given the attributes $Att_1, \ldots, Att_n$ of a user, her *GID* and some additional parameters, it produces the corresponding secret keys, $SK_{GID,Att_1} \ldots, SK_{GID,Att_n}$ for $n \in \mathbb{N}$. Nevertheless, note that the set of attributes that a user has is dynamic, *i.e.*, it will change as users interact with each other. Therefore, a very important question to answer is: When should the key generation step be carried out?

We chose to perform the key generation algorithm only when the set of attributes of a user changes. Checking a change in the set of attributes of a user requires performing a broadcast call to all pods in the network. We use a function $getAtt : \mathcal{US} \rightarrow 2^{\mathcal{U}}$ which given a user, it returns the set of attributes posses by the user in any pod in the network. Afterwards, we execute *KeyGen* for the new attributes of the user—in the corresponding pod—and remove the keys from attributes that might have been revoked[3]. Though executing *getAtt* is not computationally expensive, it requires communication between pods and might introduce delays, therefore it is important to minimise its use. Having an updated set of attributes is only necessary when decrypting photos since the set of attributes that a user has determines which parts of the photo that are visible.

Therefore, in order to reduce the overhead of this operation to the minimum, we only execute *getAtt*—and the corresponding calls to *KeyGen*—after receiving a set of photos to show. This occurs, for instance, every time users access their stream of posts, or whenever they access a particular photo. Encrypting a photo does not require these secrets key (see Sect. 2). It only requires having access to the plain attributes the user will use for the policy. As mentioned earlier, this attributes are easily accessible by querying the database.

Attaching policies to photos. In the same way that users can now choose the audience of a photo, in our proposal users choose the attributes that other users must have in order to access a photo. Moreover, we let users grab the area of the photo that they want to protect and the actions that can be performed with the photo *e.g.*, re-share, like, comment, etc. This information constitutes the access policy, $\mathcal{T}$. The photo to protect together with $\mathcal{T}$—and, as before, some additional parameters, see Sect. 2—are the input parameters of the encrypt algorithm, which returns a ciphertext CT. This ciphertext is distributed in the system and it contains both the picture and the access policy.

Example 1. Imagine that the department of vehicle's design from Chalmers decides to use Diaspora to share the photo shown in Fig. 2a. However, this photo contains some parts that are still pending of the patent's decision and the researchers only want their colleagues to see the final design. In our system, researchers can select the part of the photo—where some compromised

---

[3] We discuss other approaches to attribute revocation proposed in the literature in Sect. 5.

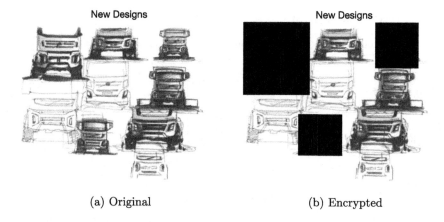

(a) Original   (b) Encrypted

Fig. 2. Sample photo with and without encrypted area.

design appears—and encrypt it with the attribute $colleague(Department_{design})$ @*Chalmers*. Later users with the attribute $colleague(Department_{design})$ @*Chalmers* will be able to decrypt the photo and see Fig. 2a and the remaining users will see Fig. 2b.

Several access policies can be attached to a photo. The only restriction we impose is that encrypted areas cannot be re-encrypted. For instance, let Alice be an engineer working at the Swedish vehicle manufacturer *Ovlov*, and also collaborating with the department of vehicle's design at Chalmers. She decides that there are some parts of the image that the researchers at Chalmers shared (Fig. 2b) that are still visible but should only be accessible by *Ovlov* employees. In other words, some areas of Fig. 2b that were not encrypted by Chalmers researchers. Therefore, she decides to encrypt some of those parts and share the photo again. The resulting ciphertext will allow users with the attribute $colleague(Department_{design})$@*Chalmers* to only see some parts of the photo, users with the attribute $employee(Ovlov)$@*Ovlov* to see others parts of the image, and users with both attributes to see the complete photo.

4   Evaluation

In this section we show different experiments that have been run in order to test our solution to demonstrate that it can be deployed in Diaspora and thus, the security of this DOSN would improve considerably. Additionally, our proposed solution is open source and can be downloaded online[4].

We have run the simulations 10 times and we have computed the time average. Additionally, we have deployed the solution in a real scenario using the *Amazon Web Services (AWS)* architecture. All AWS instances are catalogued

---

[4] https://github.com/raulpardo/ppf-diaspora/tree/abe-photos.

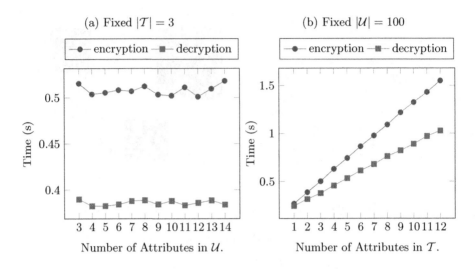

Fig. 3. Encryption and decryption time in a 800×574 image.

as *t2.xlarge* in such environment. The characteristics in term of hardware are: 4 virtual Intel Xenon CPU with 16 GB of RAM with no *Elastic Block Store (EBS)* storage system. Regarding the software, all instances are running a x64 architecture under Ubuntu 12.04 operating system. The generated JSON files of the systems are in average: 4 Kb (users' secret keys); 401 kb (ABE's global parameters); 490 Kb (authorities' keys) and for the CT some samples—which depend on the size of the photo to encrypt—are shown in Fig. 4 (in the worst case, *i.e.*, encrypting the whole area of the photo).

Figure 3 shows how ABE behaves when different amount of attributes take place when both algorithms encryption and decryption are run over an entire image of 800×574 pixels. In Fig. 3a we have fixed the number of attributes in the policy to 3, *i.e.*, $|\mathcal{T}| = 3$. On the other hand, in Fig. 3b we have fixed the number of attributes in the universe to 100, *i.e.*, $|\mathcal{U}| = 100$. From these plots, it is interesting to see that the number of attributes do not affect to the performance and thus, taking into account that we have run our experiments in the worst case (encrypting the whole image), all results under 2 s in the decryption algorithm can be considered as good results. Finally, we can conclude that our distributed solution for photo re-sharing will perform perfectly when the number of attributes in the policy $\mathcal{T}$ is no higher than 13 attributes.

We have run one more experiment to show how the size of the ciphertext CT is independent of both the numbers of attributes in the systems and the length of the access policy $\mathcal{T}$. However we have observed that the size of the CT generated is hardly dependent of both the photo's resolution and logically the selected area to be encrypted. In this experiment, we have used different images resolution and we have cyphered all the image –which rarely occurs– to be in the worst case. It is important to remark that Facebook re-sizes the

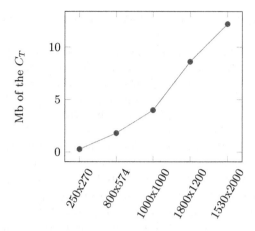

Fig. 4. C_T vs resolution image.

images, and the widest side of image does not exceed 2048 pixels. In the Fig. 4 can be seen that the generated CT depends on the resolution of the image. It was expected, because the larger the image is, the larger the area to cypher is. We have additionally tested if the size of the generated CT depends on either the number of attributes on the system $\mathcal{U}$ or on the number of attributes involved in the access policy $\mathcal{T}$ and we have realised that the size remains constant.

5 Related Work

Despite the fact that there are several works that try to guarantee both security and privacy on photos, only few proposals specifically focus on DOSNs [14–20] and only a subset where ABE is used [14,17,19].

Nilizadeh *et al.* proposed a DOSN called Cachet [17]. The main characteristic of this schema is that both ABE and a symmetric encryption are used together. Basically, the secret key is encrypted using ABE and only those users that satisfy the policy will get the secret key and decrypt the content. This architecture is similar to the one proposed by Baden *et al.* some years before in [14].

Recently, a work published by Yuan *et al.* in [19] proposed to encrypt an image under an access policy by using an ABE scheme. This proposal uses three different encryption schemes: symmetric encryption, RSA and *Ciphertext Policy-Attribute Based Encryption (CP-ABE)*. Symmetric encryption, in particular *Advanced Encryption Standard (AES)*, is used to encrypt the areas of the image. The RSA algorithm is used to encrypt a secret key for a given user. Finally, CP-ABE is used to check who can access to a given secret key in order to decrypt a given photo.

ABE it is commonly used as an encryption scheme to share the secret key of a symmetric encryption such as AES. This is especially useful because symmetric encryption performance is significantly lower than any other public encryption schema. Additionally, by using this technique the size of the ciphertext produced by the ABE remains always constant.

However, using symmetric encryption to hide some area of the picture and ABE for encrypting that secret key has one problem when it is applied to a OSN: once a user has access to decrypt that piece of information, she might share the secret key and thus no more security will be provided. So, unlike [14,17] we do not rely on symmetric encryption together with ABE.

Our proposal, in comparison to [19], contemplates both DOSNs and OSNs. We do not need to include two more parties in the architecture such as a key server and a certificate authority. We do not need to create a dedicated application on the client's side to view the encrypted photo. We support both, JPEG, PNG and TIFF files. Additionally, we have tested our proposed solution based on different attributes on both the universe $\mathcal{U}$ and in the access policy $\mathcal{T}$.

Furthermore, it is worth mentioning that classical ABE approaches are based on a centralised assumption where a TP is in charge of distributing the keys of the schema and sets up the system. However this is infeasible in DOSNs because there were no practical solution if there are n-different authorities running the same cryptographic scheme and users from different authorities want to share out private information. Nonetheless, Rouselakis *et al.* proposed in [12] a decentralised and MA-ABE where different authorities spread all over the world can share information in a secure way by using an ABE scheme.

Another still open issue in MA-ABE is how to revocate attributes, *i.e.*, how to generate again the users' secret keys once an attribute is not hold by a user anymore. In the literature there are some approaches such as using an expiration time in the access policy $\mathcal{T}$ or using specific cryptographic primitives [21]. However, in our approach we have solved it by running the *KeyGen* algorithm each time a photo is requested by a user.

6   Conclusions

In this paper we have proposed a solution for re-sharing photos securely on distributed social networks. We have used ABE to encrypt and decrypt the content of the picture that belongs to that person and thus, users can define different access control according to some policies previously defined over the same image. Moreover, as far as we know, this is the first solution that can be deployed into both decentralised and centralised social networks and we also allow different photograph's formats such as PNG, JPEG or TIFF. Finally, we have tested our solution on the distributed social network Diaspora, with one pod (centralised mode) and more than three pods (decentralised mode), a hundred of attributes each and the evaluations show that our solution can encrypt/decrypt images in less than two seconds.

ABE guarantees, by construction, that only those users having the "right" attributes can decrypt a ciphertext previously encrypted with a certain access policy aimed at users with those attributes. On the other hand, ABE does not ensure that users indeed have the attributes they claim to have. In most ABE proposed schemes researchers assume that there is a trusted party in charge of verifying that a user holds the attributes she claims to have. Though we do not explicit depend on this assumption, our proof-of-concept implementation in Diaspora comes with strong guarantees in this sense: the attributes of our policies are relationships between users and cannot be faked.[5] That said, our approach is more general and our policy description would in principle allow to define other attributes besides relationships in the OSN, like profession or location, which might be fields on a user profile and thus under control of the user. In this case we would need a trusted party to certify that the user has the attributes she claims to have.

Future Work. Currently there are no well-defined rules about who can encrypt which parts of a photo. In this work we impose the rule that no-one can re-encrypt areas of a picture that are already encrypted. This simple rule might not be enough from the point of view of usability. It might still lead to undesirable behaviours. For instance, imagine that Alice uploads a photo of herself without encryption. Later Bob—who has access to the photo—decides to encrypt some part of it so that only he can see the photo. In other words, now Alice cannot see parts of the photo that she uploaded. This authorisation problems go beyond the scope of this paper and require a detailed analysis of the interactions that can be performed in the social network together with the encryption algorithms. There are formal techniques to attack this problem, in particular to encode privacy settings of social networks and formally reason about them [22–24]. We plan to formalise our solution in order to precisely define which actions are allowed and prove that no undesirable behaviours can occur.

References

1. Statista: Facebook statistics (2016). https://www.statista.com/statistics/264810/number-of-monthly-active-facebook-users-worldwide/. Accessed 4 Oct 2016
2. Eftekhar, A., Fullwood, C., Morris, N.: Capturing personality from facebook photos and photo-related activities: how much exposure do you need? Comput. Hum. Behav. **37**, 162–170 (2014)
3. Litt, E., Hargittai, E.: Smile, snap, and share? A nuanced approach to privacy and online photo-sharing. Poetics **42**, 1–21 (2014)
4. Lobinger, K.: Photographs as things – photographs of things. A texto-material perspective on photo-sharing practices. Inf. Commun. Soc. **19**(4), 475–488 (2016)
5. Malik, A., Dhir, A., Nieminen, M.: Uses and gratifications of digital photo sharing on facebook. Telematics Inform. **33**(1), 129–138 (2016)
6. Liang, K., Liu, J.K., Lu, R., Wong, D.S.: Privacy concerns for photo sharing in online social networks. IEEE Internet Comput. **19**(2), 58–63 (2015)
7. Taheri-Boshrooyeh, S., Küpçü, A., Özkasap, O.: Security and privacy of distributed online social networks. In: 2015 IEEE 35th International Conference on Distributed Computing Systems Workshops, pp. 112–119, June 2015

---

[5] We do assume that Diaspora is correctly implemented, and that users cannot access and modify the corresponding database.

8. Bronson, N., Amsden, Z., Cabrera, G., Chakka, P., Dimov, P., Ding, H., Ferris, J., Giardullo, A., Kulkarni, S., Li, H., et al.: Tao: Facebook's distributed data store for the social graph. In: USENIX ATC 2013, pp. 49–60 (2013)

9. Nishtala, R., Fugal, H., Grimm, S., Kwiatkowski, M., Lee, H., Li, H.C., McElroy, R., Paleczny, M., Peek, D., Saab, P., Stafford, D., Tung, T., Venkataramani, V.: Scaling memcache at facebook. In: NSDI 2013, USENIX, pp. 385–398 (2013)

10. Diaspora (2016). https://joindiaspora.com

11. Lewko, A., Waters, B.: Decentralizing attribute-based encryption. In: Paterson, K.G. (ed.) EUROCRYPT 2011. LNCS, vol. 6632, pp. 568–588. Springer, Heidelberg (2011). doi:10.1007/978-3-642-20465-4_31

12. Rouselakis, Y., Waters, B.: Efficient statically-secure large-universe multi-authority attribute-based encryption. In: Böhme, R., Okamoto, T. (eds.) FC 2015. LNCS, vol. 8975, pp. 315–332. Springer, Heidelberg (2015). doi:10.1007/978-3-662-47854-7_19

13. Waters, B.: Ciphertext-policy attribute-based encryption: an expressive, efficient, and provably secure realization. In: Catalano, D., Fazio, N., Gennaro, R., Nicolosi, A. (eds.) PKC 2011. LNCS, vol. 6571, pp. 53–70. Springer, Heidelberg (2011). doi:10.1007/978-3-642-19379-8_4

14. Baden, R., Bender, A., Spring, N., Bhattacharjee, B., Starin, D.: Persona: an online social network with user-defined privacy. SIGCOMM Comput. Commun. Rev. **39**(4), 135–146 (2009)

15. Buchegger, S., Schiöberg, D., Vu, L.H., Datta, A.: Peerson: P2P social networking: early experiences and insights. In: Workshop SNS '09 (SNS 2009), pp. 46–52. ACM, New York (2009)

16. Cutillo, L.A., Molva, R., Strufe, T.: Safebook: a privacy-preserving online social network leveraging on real-life trust. IEEE Commun. Magaz. **47**(12), 94–101 (2009)

17. Nilizadeh, S., Jahid, S., Mittal, P., Borisov, N., Kapadia, A.: Cachet: a decentralized architecture for privacy preserving social networking with caching. In: CoNEXT 2012, pp. 337–348. ACM, New York (2012)

18. Ra, M.R., Govindan, R., Ortega, A.: P3: toward privacy-preserving photo sharing. In: NSDI 2013, Lombard, IL, USENIX, pp. 515–528 (2013)

19. Yuan, L., Mc Nally, D., Küpçü, A., Ebrahimi, T.: Privacy-preserving photo sharing based on a public key infrastructure. In: SPIE Optical Engineering + Applications. Applications of Digital Image Processing XXXVIII (2015)

20. Zhang, L., Jung, T., Liu, C., Ding, X., Li, X.Y., Liu, Y.: POP: privacy-preserving outsourced photo sharing and searching for mobile devices. In: 2015 IEEE 35th International Conference on Distributed Computing Systems, pp. 308–317, June 2015

21. Qian, H., Li, J., Zhang, Y., Han, J.: Privacy-preserving personal health record using multi-authority attribute-based encryption with revocation. Int. J. Inf. Secur. **14**(6), 487–497 (2015)

22. Fong, P.W.: Relationship-based access control: protection model and policy language. In: CODASPY 2011, pp. 191–202. ACM (2011)

23. Pardo, R., Kellyérová, I., Sánchez, C., Schneider, G.: Specification of evolving privacy policies for online social networks. In: 23rd International Symposium on Temporal Representation and Reasoning (TIME), pp. 70–79 (2016)

24. Pardo, R., Schneider, G.: A formal privacy policy framework for social networks. In: Giannakopoulou, D., Salaün, G. (eds.) SEFM 2014. LNCS, vol. 8702, pp. 378–392. Springer, Cham (2014). doi:10.1007/978-3-319-10431-7_30

Context-Dependent Privacy-Aware Photo Sharing Based on Machine Learning

Lin Yuan[(⊠)], Joël Theytaz, and Touradj Ebrahimi

Multimedia Signal Processing Group, EPFL, Station 11, 1015 Lausanne, Switzerland
{lin.yuan,joel.theytaz,touradj.ebrahimi}@epfl.ch

Abstract. Photo privacy has raised a growing concern with the advancements of image analytics, face recognition, and deep learning techniques widely applied on social media. If properly deployed, these powerful techniques can in turn assist people in enhancing their online privacy. One possible approach is to build a strong, automatic and dynamic access control mechanism based on analyzing the image content and learning users sharing behavior. This paper presents a model for context-dependent and privacy-aware photo sharing based on machine learning. The proposed model utilizes image semantics and requester contextual information to decide whether or not to share a particular picture with a specific requester at certain context, and if yes, at which granularity. To evaluate the proposed model, we conducted a user study on 23 subjects and collected a dataset containing 1'018 manually annotated images with 12'216 personalized contextual sharing decisions. Evaluation experiments were performed and the results show a promising performance of the proposed model for photo sharing decision making. Furthermore, the influences of different types of features on decision making have been investigated, the results of which validate the usefulness of pre-defined features and imply a significant variance between users sharing behaviors and privacy attitudes.

Keywords: Privacy protection · Online social network · Photo sharing · Access control · Decision making · Context · Machine learning

1 Introduction

Wide spread of smart mobile devices and online social networks (OSNs) make photo sharing an easy and popular activity. However, it has also raised concerns on privacy since the shared content reveals substantial sensitive information about people. Most social networking or photo sharing services provide access control for users to manage their privacy. However, users need to manually set their sharing policies in only a static manner, without the possibility to share their photos to different groups of people dependent to contexts, e.g. the location, time or even nearby people of potential viewer. Most access control mechanisms

© IFIP International Federation for Information Processing 2017
Published by Springer International Publishing AG 2017. All Rights Reserved
S. De Capitani di Vimercati and F. Martinelli (Eds.): SEC 2017, IFIP AICT 502, pp. 93–107, 2017.
DOI: 10.1007/978-3-319-58469-0_7

enforce only binary sharing options, namely "Yes" or "No", which may not provide the best experience when a user just wants to disable partial information in photo sharing. With the latest progress in image analytics, pattern recognition, and deep learning techniques, large scale information is mined from the shared multimedia content. Although seemingly compromising privacy, those techniques can in turn be used to enhance privacy, in such a way of helping people estimate the privacy value of their content or control the access of their content automatically and dynamically.

In this paper, we present a machine learning based model that can accurately predict users photo sharing decisions based on their past decisions. To make photo sharing decisions, the proposed model takes into account not only the content of an image, but also the context information about the image capture and potential requester. To validate the proposed model, we conducted a user study on 23 subjects and three sets of evaluation experiments.

The rest of the paper is structured as follows. Section 2 introduces related works. Section 3 describes in detail the proposed model. Then Sects. 4 and 5 present the user study and performance evaluation. Finally, Sect. 6 outlines some discussions and Sect. 7 summaries the paper.

2 Related Work

A number of studies have been focused on understanding users privacy concern on photo sharing, as well as the potential privacy implications via both subjective [1,2] and objective [8,13] studies. A number of approaches to privacy protection in photo sharing have been proposed, including usage control scheme in distributed OSNs [6], Secure JPEG scrambling image visual information [20,22,23], separate coding and sharing of JPEG image by P3 [14] and tag-based access control [12]. In addition, a substantial research effort has been made on estimating the privacy value or detecting privacy-sensitive objects in images. These works include private/public image classifications and privacy-sensitive visual information detection, based on not only learning low-level image features (color, edge, faces and SIFT) [24], but also deep learning approaches such as Convolutional Neural Network (CNN) [16,17].

Another branch of research has been focused on context-aware information sharing in the scenario of social networks or cloud services. Smith et al. [15] provided an early investigation on solutions to enable people to share contextual information in mobile social networks. Wiese et al. [19] investigated the impact of various factors on people's willingness to share information. Harkous et al. [10] present a conceptual framework named C3P for automatic estimation of privacy risk of data based on the sharing context. Bilogrevic et al. [4] present SPISM, an information-sharing system that predicts (semi-)automatically sharing decision, based on personal and contextual features. Despite the substantial works on contextual information sharing, very few have considered context information for privacy protection in online photo sharing. To the best of our knowledge, this paper is the first attempt to investigate the feasibility of deploying both

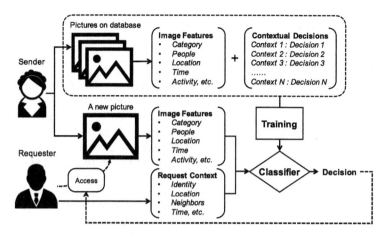

Fig. 1. Framework of a photo sharing system based on the proposed model.

content-related and contextual features of images, to automatically make or "recommend" photo sharing decisions.

3   A Model for Context-/Privacy-Aware Photo Sharing

3.1   Security Assumption and Operating Principle

First of all, we assume the photo sharing service providers are trustworthy. Users allow the service to conduct necessary analysis on their photos, and the system is granted the right to enforce access control of users photos.

Figure 1 illustrates a photo sharing architecture of the proposed model. The operating procedures of the model can be described by the following story: Alice (the *sender*, who wants to upload and share photos with online friends) uploads a set of pictures on the photo sharing service, and the service system analyzes each picture and extracts a set content and contextual features about those pictures. Meanwhile, the system asks Alice a set of questions on her willingness to share each picture to specified individuals in various scenarios. These individuals can be selected from those who visited Alice's profile recently or frequently. Each scenario describes a certain context of a possible *requester*, who attempts to visualize a picture shared by the sender. The context includes the identity (either real name or social group), location, nearby people and the time when the requester tries to visualize the image. The system then trains a classifier based on Alice's answers for different photos in different scenarios. On the other side, Bob (the requester) visits the profile page of Alice. With the help of the classifier, the system analyzes Bob's context and Alice's photo information, to decide whether or not to show certain photos to Bob, and if yes, at which granularity.

Table 1. Feature notations and definitions.

	ID	Feature	Description
What	I_C	Image: Category	Major category of the picture, selected from the eight categories identified in Instagram pictures [11]: *Friends, Activity, Selfie, Food, Pets, Gadget, Fashion* and *Captioned photo*
	I_A	Image: Activities	Activities involved in the picture, selected from 26 keywords partially defined by [5]: *working, meeting, reading, presentation, resting, chatting, socializing, family, friends, vacation, TV, cooking, eating, drinking, cleaning, shopping, exercising, traveling, walking, landscape, city, concert, sporting, gaming, gadget* and *pets*
Who	I_P	Image: # of People	The number of people in the picture
		Image: Identities	The existence of different identities in the picture. Eight types of identities were defined: *Sender him/herself, Family, Close friend, Schoolmate or Colleague, Girl or Boyfriend, Acquaintance, Celebrity* and *Stranger*
	R_I	Requester: Identity	The relationship between the requester and the sender, categorized in six types: *Family, Close friend, Schoolmate or Colleague, Girl or Boyfriend, Acquaintance* and *Stranger*
	R_G	Requester: Gender	Gender of the requester: *Female* or *Male*
	R_N	Requester: Nearby	Whether or not the requester has other people nearby at requesting time
Where	I_L	Image: Location	The semantic location where the image was captured, selected from 12 major location categories adopted from Foursquare Location Categories
		Image: Loc. Coordinates	Latitude and longitude of the image capture location
		Image: Loc. Frequency	The frequency of the sender being present in such place, selected from *Rarely, Sometimes, Often* and *Almost everyday*
	R_L	Requester: Location	Semantic location of the requester, categorized in *Unknown, Friend's home, His/her own home, Work place* and *Public place*
When	I_T	Image: Time	The time of photo capture in a float value, e.g. 14.5 denotes 2:30 PM
		Image: Day	The day (in a week) of photo capture, selected from *Monday* to *Sunday*

3.2   Feature Definition

To train such a classifier, we considered two groups of features: **Image Semantic Features (I)** and **Requester Contextual Features (R)**. Instead of using low-level image features such as color, texture, composition and SIFT, we believe higher-level semantic features have more immediate relations with privacy. These features include the image category, number/identities of people in image, activities or objects in image and the location and time of image capture. The contextual features of the requester include the requester's identity, location, nearby people and time.

A detailed description of all the features used in our experiments, grouped in different aspects of context, is shown in Table 1. Note that the time of requester is not used in the current experiment because it would be too cumbersome for subjects to read and analyze the complete information containing all contexts.

3.3   Photo Sharing Decisions

We defined three photo sharing decisions, corresponding to different levels of photo information disclosure. The three decisions and corresponding descriptions presented in the user study are listed in the following:

Decision 1 - Do NOT Share: No, I don't want to share the picture.
Decision 2 - Partially Share: Yes, but with some image region protected or/and metadata (GPS, time, etc.) removed.
Decision 3 - Entirely Share: Yes, I want to share the picture completely.

The reasons of using the specific three sharing decisions instead of conventional binary decisions ("Yes" or "No") are twofold: First, in many scenarios of online photo sharing, people may want to simply remove partial privacy-sensitive visual information in an image, such as ID card, license plate or their children faces. Second, most images shared from smart mobile devices contain metadata such as geotags, camera model and time, which could also compromise privacy. Therefore, an option should be provided for users to partially protect and share their image content.

4   User Study and Data Collection

We conducted a study that put participants in personalized photo sharing scenarios, and collected an image dataset containing manual-annotated image semantic features and contextual sharing decisions.

To conduct the user study, we developed an Android app[1], named *ProShare S*. The application allows a user to create an account, take pictures, conduct a set of surveys for each, protect privacy-sensitive image regions, and finally upload them to a dedicated server. The workflow of a user study using ProShare S is illustrated in Fig. 2. Particularly, the survey part is structured in two sets of questionnaires:

---

[1] The application is publicly available at http://grebvm2.epfl.ch/proshare-s/proShare-rd2.1.apk.

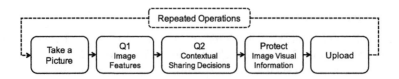

Fig. 2. Workflow of user study using ProShare S.

Q1 - Image Semantic Information. The first questionnaire (Q1) requires the user to add necessary image semantic tags. This questionnaire appears once a picture has been taken from either gallery or camera. The questions in Q1 cover all the semantic features defined in Sect. 3.2. A build-in face detector offered by Android API is applied to count the number of people in image, which can be manually modified if not correct. Location coordinates and capture time are automatically extracted from image metadata.

Q2 - Contextual Photo Sharing Decisions. Once Q1 is finished, the user is directed to the second questionnaire (Q2), where he/she is presented with 12 sharing contexts/questions. For each context, the user needs to decide how he/she would like to share the picture with the specific requester, by selecting one of the three decisions defined in Sect. 3.3. An example context is "Would you share this picture with a *close friend*, when *he* is at a *public place* with *other people*?" The 12 contexts/questions are selected in a special way such that each of the six requester identities appears twice in a random order, with the other contextual features (gender, location, nearby people) sampled at random. In the study, basic user profile is also collected through the App. We therefore present the sharing contexts adaptively based on user's profile. For instance, for a female user we present the requester as "your boyfriend" instead of "girl or boyfriend".

We recruited 23 volunteers to participate in our user study, and assigned each of them a task of uploading at least 50 daily pictures of their own and completing corresponding surveys using ProShare S. Each subject was required to complete the task within a week and to try to cover a wide range of image content[2]. Finally, 20 out of the 23 subjects successfully finished the required task. We therefore kept only the data of the 20 effective subjects for the later evaluation. A total of 1'018 images including 12'216 sharing decisions were contributed by the 20 subjects, each providing 50.9 images on average. Figure 3 shows the histogram of images in each category and the contextual sharing decisions made on all the images.

---

[2] The instruction and agreement sheet for the user study including several screenshots of the ProShare S App is available at http://grebvm2.epfl.ch/proshare-s/instruction_sheet_rd2.1.pdf.

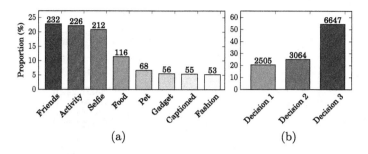

Fig. 3. Distribution of (a) images in each category and (b) subjects sharing decisions.

5 Evaluation and Analysis

5.1 Methodology

To evaluate the performance of the proposed model for decision making, we conducted three sets of experiments based on the data collected from our user study. We take the working hypothesis that users photo sharing behaviors and privacy attitudes are highly subjective and the difference in users behaviors may cause the proposed model to perform differently between subjects.

The first experiment focused on the performance of the proposed model with respect to each user, namely, within-subject analysis. In the second experiment, we explored a universal one-size-fits-all classifier trained on all users data for predicting a new user's decisions. In the third experiment, we investigated the influences of different image and requester features on the decision making performance of the proposed model.

The WEKA machine learning library [9] was used in experiments and three representative classification methods were considered: logistic regression, support vector machine (SVM) and random forest. We started with a preliminary test by running a 10-fold cross validation on each user's data using the three methods and random forest always outperformed the other two. We therefore kept using random forest for the rest of the experiment.

To evaluate the decision making performance, the following metrics are used:

- **Correct Decision rate:** The proportion of correctly predicted decisions.
- **Over-Sharing rate:** The proportion of cases where image information is shared more than what user expect to share, which compromises privacy.
- **Under-Sharing rate:** The proportion of cases where image information is shared less than what user expects to share, which may compromise usability.
- **Kappa statistic:** Cohen's kappa score [18] that measures the chance-corrected agreement between predicted and ground truth decisions.

5.2 Within-Subject Analysis

In the first experiment, we used different proportions (from 10% to 90%) of each subject's data to train a classifier, and evaluated the classifier on the rest of the

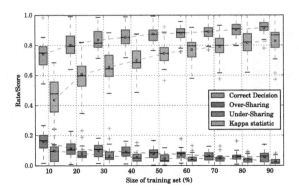

Fig. 4. Performance of sharing decision prediction at different sizes of training sets.

data (evaluation set). This is to examine the trade-off between user-burden and prediction accuracy of the proposed model. The evaluation results measured by different metrics across the 20 subjects are shown as box plots in Fig. 4. In this figure, one observes that the median correct decision rate has already reached 0.75 at a training set of only 10%, which corresponds to only 5 images in average. This means we could already build an acceptable model for half of the users using a very small number of images and their decisions. Above the training set of 50%, most users obtained the correct decision rate higher than 0.8. The median Kappa score at the training set of 10% is below 0.5 and rapidly reaches 0.6 at the training set of 20%. Above the training size of 60%, an almost perfect prediction is observed for half of the users with a median Kappa statistic greater than 0.8. On the other hand, both the over-sharing and under-sharing rates of most users are very low, even at the training set of 10%. However, we observe the over-sharing rate is always higher than the under-sharing rate. A possible explanation is that most users tend to share images and the numbers of different decisions in the dataset are imbalanced. From the results, one also observes a significant variance between users. At the training size of 10%, the maximum difference in correct decision rate between users is up to 0.44. At the training size of 80%, where the optimal performance is obtained for most of the users, such difference still remains around 0.2. Such results agree with our hypothesis made in the beginning of this section that users subjective behaviors may influence the performance of the proposed model.

Table 2. The cost matrix of the applied cost-sensitive learning.

↓ classified as →	Decision 1	Decision 2	Decision 3
Decision 1	0	$C_{1\to2} = c$	$C_{1\to3} = 2c$
Decision 2	1	0	$C_{2\to3} = c$
Decision 3	1	1	0

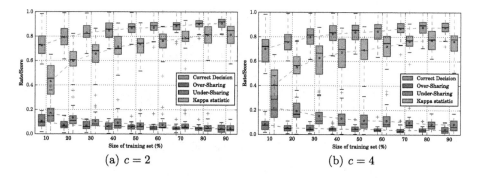

Fig. 5. Performance of cost-sensitive decision making with two different values of c.

Cost-Sensitive Decision Making. To address the issue of over-sharing, we introduced the cost-sensitive learning [7] in our decision making core. The aim is to evaluate the extent to which incorrect decisions can be biased towards the under-sharing cases instead of over-sharing, when users concern their privacy more than usability. We specified different error-penalties $C_{i \to j}$ (> 1) for over-sharing cases and the penalty of 1 for under-sharing. Therefore, the training process tries to minimize the following cost: $\sum_{1 \leqslant i < j \leqslant 3}(C_{i \to j} \times N_{i \to j} + 1 \times N_{j \to i})$, where $N_{i \to j}$ denotes the number of cases where Decision i is misclassified classified as Decision j. Specially, we assigned a double error-penalty $2c$ for the over-sharing cases $C_{1 \to 3}$ compared to the other two over-sharing cases. This is because a mistake by classifying "Do NOT Share" to "Entirely Share" may severely compromise privacy. The cost matrix for the cost-sensitive learning is shown in Table 2.

We experimented with a set of values for c (from 1.5 to 5), on each user's data using the same random forest classification. The results at $c = 2$ and $c = 4$ are shown in Fig. 5. With an error-penalty $c = 2$, the over-sharing rate is greatly reduced to a level lower than the under-sharing rate. When increasing c to 4, the over-sharing rate is further reduced, in sacrifice of a significant increase on the under-sharing rate. This indicates a significant trade-off between the capability of privacy protection and system usability. In any cases of cost-sensitive learning, the overall correct decision rate and Kappa statistic do not change much, as the introduced error-penalty mainly acts as a parameter to tune the weights of different incorrect decisions.

5.3   One-Size-Fits-All Model

In the second experiment, we evaluated a one-size-fits-all model, to examine the potential of building a global classifier trained on the data of all users, to make or "recommendation" decisions for new users. To be fair, for each subject i, we trained a classifier with random forest on the data of the remaining subjects, which was then evaluated on the data of subject i. Cost-sensitive learning was also included in this experiment for comparison. The results over all the

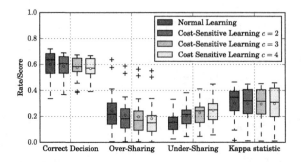

Fig. 6. Performance of a One-Size-Fits-All classifier.

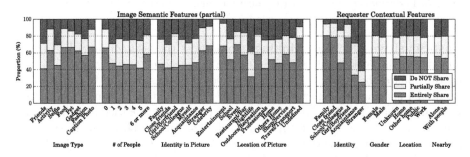

Fig. 7. Distribution of photo sharing decisions distinguished by different features.

20 subjects are shown in Fig. 6. The median correct decision, over-/under-sharing rates and the Kappa statistic without cost-sensitive learning are 0.636, 0.218, 0.155 and 0.348 respectively. With cost-sensitive learning, the over-sharing rates are reduced below under-sharing, without greatly degrading the correct decisions and Kappa score. The overall performance of such a one-size-fits-all model is not as good as the personalized classifier built on each user's own data. This again implies that users may have very different behaviors and privacy attitudes towards photo sharing. However, such a classifier could already provide an acceptable performance better than a random guess. This experiment provides the insight of building a one-size-fits-all classifier to predict or "recommend" photo sharing decisions for a new user, until the user has enough data to build a personalized classifier.

5.4   Influences of Features on Decision Making

At the end, we investigated the influences of different types of features on users photo sharing decisions and on the performance of our prediction model.

First, the histograms of three sharing decisions distinguished by different types of features are shown in Fig. 7. The variation in distributions over different feature values indicates the degree of influence of a particular type of features. One observes a significant difference in decision histograms across different requester identities, which implies that the requester identity influences users decision making the most. On the other hand, although the decision histograms do not change much between other contextual features of the requester, there is still a small decrease of the "Entirely Share" decisions at the cases where the requester is at an "Unknown" place or with "Other people" nearby. Image semantic features also influence users decision making significantly. For instance, users prefer sharing photos without people or with a lot of people (≥ 6), to sharing photos with 1–5 people. Also, users favor sharing those pictures containing strangers or celebrities, over personal photos with intimate connections like family and close friends.

We then evaluated the performance of decision making on different combinations of image and requester features, by conducting a 10-fold cross validation on each user's data. The correct decision rates of cross validation of all the 20 subjects are shown in Fig. 8. Please refer to the feature notations in Table 1. We gradually remove certain features, and the leftmost and rightmost box plots in Fig. 8 show two extreme cases where all the features ($\mathbf{I}_{All} + \mathbf{R}_{All}$) or only the requester features ($\mathbf{R}_{All}$) were used. As is shown, when reducing features, the correct decision rate of the majority of subjects decreases, which implies that all those features in general have a positive impact on decision making for most users. When reducing image-related features, a significant variance across different subjects is observed, which indicates that those image features are important for modeling many users sharing decisions. However, for two of those subjects, the prediction model still performs well (correct decision rate higher than 0.9) even using only the requester features ($\mathbf{R}_{All}$). A possible reason is that the two users made their sharing decisions mostly dependent on the context of requesters, regardless of the image content.

One also finds that by removing certain requester contextual features, like requester gender ($\mathbf{R}_G$), location ($\mathbf{R}_L$), or nearby people ($\mathbf{R}_N$), the overall accuracy does not significantly change. With merely the requester identity ($\mathbf{R}_I$) + all image features ($\mathbf{I}_{All}$), the overall decision making accuracy still remains high. This implies that the requester contextual information than the requester identity has very week or even negative influence on decision making. However, this is not always the case for every subject. Figure 9 illustrates the results of five example subjects obtained on different combinations of requester contextual features (along with all image features $\mathbf{I}_{All}$). Here, one observes that the inclusion of requester contextual features other than the requester identity influences decision making quite differently between users. For instance, the correct decision rate of User C obtained on all requester features (~ 0.8) is much higher than that on only requester identity $\mathbf{R}_I$. For User A or D, combining different requester features ($\mathbf{R}_{I,L,N}$ or $\mathbf{R}_{I,N}$ respectively) generates better accuracy than just using requester identity $\mathbf{R}_I$. However, for User B and E, using only the requester identity $\mathbf{R}_I$ provides the best performance, in which case the other contextual features of requester are considered as noise in machine learning. Such a variance between users again proved our hypothesis that users have different personalized behaviors in photo sharing.

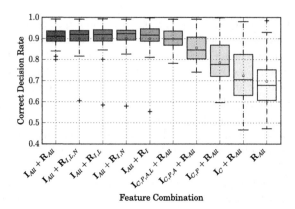

Fig. 8. Correct decision rates of all users obtained on different combinations of features.

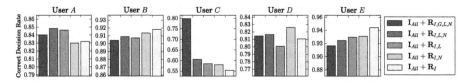

Fig. 9. Performance of five example users obtained on combination of all Image Semantic Features ($\mathbf{I}_{All}$) and different Requester Contextual Features ($\mathbf{R}$).

6   Discussions

Image Visual Information and Metadata Protection. Prior to this study, we have proposed and researched on different approaches [20–23] to protect image privacy (visual information and metadata) such that the protected photos can be publicly shown to any party (service provider and individuals) while original photos being secretly shared to authorized individuals. The principal idea of these approaches is to utilize JPEG application markers to secretly preserve partial image information or metadata, which not only enables the reversibility of the obfuscated image but also minimizes the storage burden. Such approaches are collectively named Secure JPEG. In the proposed photo sharing model, Secure JPEG can be used to create a secure version of a photo. Depending on the predicted decision, the system can release the corresponding version (protected or recovered original form) of the image to a requester.

Security Discussion. As mentioned in Sect. 3.1, we assume the service provider in proposed model is trusted. The reasons are twofold: First, it is still not possible to perform certain pattern recognition tasks on client devices efficiently, e.g. image semantic recognition; Second, the system makes sharing decisions in a dynamic way by analyzing both image content and requester context, which means the decision making core must lie on the service provider. However, as the development of pattern recognition on mobile devices, the security requirement of the proposed model can be relaxed. In another specific case of the proposed model, where only requester's identity is taken into account (no other context), the security assumption can be discarded. In this case, the photo sharing decisions are made in a static way equivalent to using an access policy. According to a privacy-preserving photo sharing architecture proposed in our previous work [23], the access policy can be integrated in a Ciphertext-Policy Attribute-Based Encryption (CP-ABE) [3] and secure photo sharing can be achieved through an "Honest but Curious" untrusted server.

Feature Extraction. In this study, most image semantic features were manually annotated. This is because we lack the access and control to a popular social network, and that the automatic tools for extraction of some semantic features (e.g. activities in image [5]) are not mature enough. In practice, with the advances in deep learning, content understanding and ubiquitous sensors, automatic extraction of different semantic or contextual features is becoming more accurate and fine-grained.

7   Conclusion

This paper presents a conceptual model for context-dependent and privacy-aware photo sharing based on machine learning. The proposed model utilizes the images semantic and requesters contextual information to predict photo sharing decisions for users, based on their previous shared photos and past decisions. To evaluate the proposed model, we first conducted a user study on 23 subjects and collected a dataset containing 1'018 manually annotated images with 12'216 personalized sharing decisions in different contexts. Evaluation experiments have been performed and show a promising performance of the proposed method. Furthermore, the influence of different content- and context-related features on decision making has been investigated, the results of which validated the importance of pre-defined features and implied a significant variance between users sharing behaviors and privacy attitudes.

As our future work, we intend to conduct larger-scale user study based on realistic social networking environment. This will further help us understand users photo sharing behaviors. In addition, we will investigate more sophisticated machine learning or even deep learning approaches to build more accurate and secure photo sharing systems. We believe machines will become intelligent enough to understand people's privacy concerns towards their photo content and this is how we define "privacy-aware".

Acknowledgement. This research was possible thanks to the Swiss National Science Foundation funded project LEADME (200020-149259). We also acknowledge Thomas Mizraji and Vincent Debieux for contributions in the development of ProShare S app. A special thank goes to all the patient subjects who participated in the user study.

References

1. Ahern, S., Eckles, D., Good, N., King, S., Naaman, M., Nair, R.: Over-exposed? Privacy patterns and considerations in online and mobile photo sharing. In: CHI, pp. 357–366. ACM (2007)
2. Besmer, A., Richter Lipford, H.: Moving beyond untagging: photo privacy in a tagged world. In: Proceedings of the SIGCHI Conference on Human Factors in Computing Systems (CHI 2010), pp. 1563–1572. ACM, New York (2010)
3. Bethencourt, J., Sahai, A., Waters, B.: Ciphertext-policy attribute-based encryption. In: Proceedings of the 2007 IEEE Symposium on Security and Privacy (SP 2007), pp. 321–334. IEEE Computer Society, Washington, DC (2007)
4. Bilogrevic, I., Huguenin, K., Agir, B., Jadliwala, M., Gazaki, M., Hubaux, J.P.: A machine-learning based approach to privacy-aware information-sharing in mobile social networks. Pervasive Mobile Comput. **25**, 125–142 (2016)
5. Castro, D., Hickson, S., Bettadapura, V., Thomaz, E., Abowd, G., Christensen, H., Essa, I.: Predicting daily activities from egocentric images using deep learning. In: ISWC (2015)
6. Cutillo, L.A., Molva, R., Önen, M.: Privacy preserving picture sharing: enforcing usage control in distributed on-line social networks. In: 5th ACM Workshop on Social Network Systems, Bern, Switzerland, April 2012
7. Elkan, C.: The foundations of cost-sensitive learning. In: Proceedings of the 17th International Joint Conference on Artificial Intelligence (IJCAI 2001), vol. 2, pp. 973–978. Morgan Kaufmann Publishers Inc., San Francisco, CA, USA (2001)
8. Friedland, G., Sommer, R.: Cybercasing the joint: on the privacy implications of geo-tagging. In: Proceedings of the 5th USENIX Conference on Hot Topics in Security (HotSec 2010), pp. 1–8. USENIX Association, Berkeley (2010)
9. Hall, M., Frank, E., Holmes, G., Pfahringer, B., Reutemann, P., Witten, I.H.: The WEKA data mining software: an update. SIGKDD Explor. Newsl. **11**(1), 10–18 (2009)
10. Harkous, H., Rahman, R., Aberer, K.: C3P: context-aware crowdsourced cloud privacy. In: Cristofaro, E., Murdoch, S.J. (eds.) PETS 2014. LNCS, vol. 8555, pp. 102–122. Springer, Cham (2014). doi:10.1007/978-3-319-08506-7_6
11. Hu, Y., Kambhampati, L.: What we Instagram: a first analysis of instagram photo content and user types. In: Proceedings of the 8th International Conference on Weblogs and Social Media (ICWSM 2014), pp. 595–598. The AAAI Press (2014)
12. Klemperer, P., Liang, Y., Mazurek, M., Sleeper, M., Ur, B., Bauer, L., Cranor, L.F., Gupta, N., Reiter, M.: Tag, you can see it! Using tags for access control in photo sharing. In: Proceedings of the SIGCHI Conference on Human Factors in Computing Systems (CHI 2012), pp. 377–386. ACM, New York (2012)
13. Pesce, J.a.P., Casas, D.L., Rauber, G., Almeida, V.: Privacy attacks in social media using photo tagging networks: a case study with facebook. In: Proceedings of the 1st Workshop on Privacy and Security in Online Social Media (PSOSM 2012), pp. 4:1–4:8, New York, NY, USA (2012)
14. Ra, M.R., Govindan, R., Ortega, A.: P3: toward privacy-preserving photo sharing. In: Presented as part of the 10th USENIX Symposium on Networked Systems Design and Implementation, pp. 515–528. USENIX, Berkeley (2013)
15. Smith, I., et al.: Social disclosure of place: from location technology to communication practices. In: Gellersen, H.-W., Want, R., Schmidt, A. (eds.) Pervasive 2005. LNCS, vol. 3468, pp. 134–151. Springer, Heidelberg (2005). doi:10.1007/11428572_9

16. Tonge, A., Caragea, C.: Image privacy prediction using deep features. In: Proceedings of the Thirtieth AAAI Conference on Artificial Intelligence (2016)
17. Tran, L., Kong, D., Jin, H., Liu, J.: Privacy-CNH: a framework to detect photo privacy with convolutional neural network using hierarchical features. In: Proceedings of the Thirtieth AAAI Conference on Artificial Intelligence (2016)
18. Viera, A.J., Garrett, J.M., et al.: Understanding interobserver agreement: the kappa statistic. Fam. Med. **37**(5), 360–363 (2005)
19. Wiese, J., Kelley, P.G., Cranor, L.F., Dabbish, L., Hong, J.I., Zimmerman, J.: Are you close with me? Are you nearby? Investigating social groups, closeness, and willingness to share. In: Proceedings of the 13th International Conference on Ubiquitous Computing, pp. 197–206. ACM (2011)
20. Yuan, L., Korshunov, P., Ebrahimi, T.: Secure JPEG scrambling enabling privacy in photo sharing. In: 11th IEEE International Conference and Workshops on Automatic Face and Gesture Recognition (FG), vol. 04, pp. 1–6, May 2015
21. Yuan, L., Ebrahimi, T.: Image transmorphing with JPEG. In: 2015 IEEE International Conference on Image Processing (ICIP), pp. 3956–3960, September 2015
22. Yuan, L., Korshunov, P., Ebrahimi, T.: Privacy-preserving photo sharing based on a secure JPEG. In: 2015 IEEE Conference on Computer Communications Workshops (INFOCOM WKSHPS), pp. 185–190. IEEE (2015)
23. Yuan, L., McNally, D., Kupcu, A., Ebrahimi, T.: Privacy-preserving photo sharing based on a public key infrastructure. In: Proceedings of SPIE, vol. 9599 (2015)
24. Zerr, S., Siersdorfer, S., Hare, J., Demidova, E.: Privacy-aware image classification and search. In: Proceedings of the 35th International ACM SIGIR Conference on Research and Development in Information Retrieval (SIGIR 2012), pp. 35–44, NY, USA. ACM, New York (2012)

3LP: Three Layers of Protection
for Individual Privacy in Facebook

Khondker Jahid Reza[1]([✉]), Md Zahidul Islam[1], and Vladimir Estivill-Castro[2]

[1] School of Computing and Mathematics, Charles Sturt University,
Panorama Avenue, Bathurst, NSW 2795, Australia
{kreza,zislam}@csu.edu.au
[2] DTIC Universitat Pompeu Fabra, Roc Boronat, 138, 08018 Barcelona, Spain
vladimir.estivill@upf.edu

Abstract. The possibility that an unauthorised agent is able to infer a user's hidden information (an attribute's value) is known as attribute inference risk. It is one of the privacy issues for Facebook users in recent times. An existing technique [1] provides privacy by suppressing users' attribute values from their profiles. However, suppression of an attribute value sometimes is not enough to secure a user's confidential information. In this paper, we experimentally demonstrate that (after taking necessary steps on attribute values) a user's sensitive information can still be inferred through his/her friendship information. We evaluated our approach experimentally on two datasets. We propose 3LP, a new three layers protection technique, to provide privacy protection to users of on-line social networks.

Keywords: Privacy enhancing technologies · Attribute inference

1 Introduction

Humans naturally keep themselves connected with friends, colleagues and families but due to geographical distances, people may not be able to meet their friends regularly. Hence, online social networks (OSNs) play a vital role to connect and share contents among people. Now, all over the world, citizens and organisations make extensive use of OSNs such as Facebook, Twitter, LinkedIn, and Google+. In recent years the usage of OSNs, particularly the usage of Facebook, has increased extensively [2,3].

Facebook is currently the third (after Google and Youtube) most viewed website [3] with 1.09 billion average active users every day [2]. Users typically store and share various personal data on Facebook resulting in the possibility of privacy breaches [4]. Privacy is a crucial element of society. Social scientists have provided several definitions. Tavani defines privacy as our ability to restrict access to our personal information and to have control over the transfer of our information [5]. Rachel [6] argues that privacy is the individuals' ability to disclose selectively personal information related to themselves. What is private for

S. De Capitani di Vimercati and F. Martinelli (Eds.): SEC 2017, IFIP AICT 502, pp. 108–123, 2017.
DOI: 10.1007/978-3-319-58469-0_8

one may not be private for some others. For example, some may consider their political affiliation to be private while some others may not consider important to disclose their political alignment.

Data stored on Facebook about other users can be analysed for link prediction and attribute value prediction to learn sensitive and private information of victim users and hence compromise their privacy [7,8]. Sophisticated data mining techniques can breach individual privacy [9] on Facebook.

It was empirically demonstrated [9] that a data set built from other users' data that do reveal what one user U considers confidential can be used by an attacker M to build a classifier that predicts U's private information with high confidence. The fundamental idea of the first techniques to guard against the attribute inference attack ($NOYB$ [10], $TOTAL\_COUNT$, and $CUM\_SENSITIVITY$ [1]) is to identify a user's publicly available attribute values which are high predictors of a sensitive attribute value and recommend to the user to obfuscate the predictors. While $NOYB$ [10] randomly selects visible attribute values to obfuscate, $TOTAL\_COUNT$ and $CUM\_SENSITIVITY$ [1] heuristically identify which public data is highly informative and very likely to be influential in any classifier built by data mining techniques; therefore, recommending to the victim to modify or suppress the visible attribute values those are high predictors. The difference between $TOTAL\_COUNT$ and $CUM\_SENSITIVITY$ is in the ranking of the predictors, but both of them are very similar, so we encapsulate them into the global name of $PrivAdv$ for short.

The protection technique $PrivAdv$ does not consider friendship links among the users as information that M can use to infer the sensitive value of U. The information from on-line social networks can often be organised as a social attribute network (SAN) [11]. The SAN model integrates both users' attribute information and their friendship network. Although $PrivAdv$ has been extended to evaluate risks of the inference attack that derive from connections in the social network [12], the easiness of such an attack was not illustrated. Moreover, no concrete suggestions of what shall users do when their privacy is at risks because of social connections. That is, in such extensions [12], the algorithms recommend to unfriend or befriend a user from the victim's friend list randomly if such friend discloses any information which is sensitive to the victim. In those methods, the number of added or deleted friends may be large, and the victim may not be interested in this frequent addition and deletion of friends. We experimentally show that friendship links can be a useful piece of information for M. We also show that naively extending the existing technique [1] may not be effective to ensure privacy protection against M usage of this information. Here, we also propose a new technique (which we name $3LP$) with three layers of protection in order to protect the sensitive value of U even if M uses the friendship links. We also experimentally demonstrate the effectiveness of $3LP$.

This paper is organised as follows. Section 2 discusses some limitations of existing techniques as evidenced by our initial experiments. Section 3 presents $3LP$, followed by Sect. 4 where experimental results are discussed. Finally, Sect. 5 gives concluding remarks.

2   The Importance of Friendship Links

We now argue that any protection technique that does not take into consideration both, the attribute values of a user and links of a social network, is not able to ensure sufficient protection. We justify our argument since a real-life attacker can try to infer the sensitive information using whichever of the two aspects (attribute values and links) is ignored by the protection technique, dodging the single focused privacy mechanism. For example, we demonstrate that a previous work [1] that does not take the link information into consideration may not be able to secure sensitive data of users when an attacker uses the connection information of a social network.

We assume that attackers have access to a large data set which has the structure of an undirected social network (or graph) G having a N number of users, each with A attributes. Here, without loss of generality, each attribute value is considered as a distinct binary attribute. This standard data representation converts a categorical attribute like *hometown* (with possible values *Sydney*, *Melbourne*, and *Brisbane*) into a characteristic vector: the value is true if and only if the user's residential city correspond to that attribute-value pair. Under the *SAN* model, not only members of the OSN are vertices, but attribute-values are also vertices. For each user-vertex u with an attribute-value pair $a = v$, the *SAN* places an edge between u and the attribute-value pair $a = v$.

The *SAN* model also places an edge between two users if they are friends.

The *SAN* data model can be used by attackers to estimate the influence of a user on another user. The idea here is that linked users who have a small number of friends are strongly connected and have a high influence on each other. For example, if a user Tom White is linked to Rob Black and each of them has only two other friends then Tom and Rob have a high influence on each other meaning that if Rob supports the Labour party, then there is a greater chance that Tom will also support the Labour party. On the other hand, if a user is linked to another user who has a huge number of friends then the two users are relatively weakly connected and have low influence on each other. For example, if Tom is linked to Mel Gibson who has thousands of friends, then the fact that Tom supports the Liberal party does not give a strong clue on whether or not Mel Gibson also supports the Liberal party. Such influence of a user on another user u can be computed through a metric that represents the strength of the connection between u and an attribute-value pair $a = v$, where the strength of a connection is proportionate to the number of common users (who are friends of u and have the attribute-value pair $a = v$) and inversely proportionate to the numbers of friends of the common users.

We first need to introduce some notations before we formally present the metric function for a user and an attribute-value pair. We denote by $\Gamma_{s+}(u)$ the set of all social users linked to a user u. Similarly, $\Gamma_{s+}(a = v)$ is the set of all users having the attribute-value $a = v$. Also, $\Gamma_{a+}(u)$ is the set of all attribute-value pairs linked to user u. Thus, the neighbourhood of u in the *SAN* is, $\Gamma_+(u) = \Gamma_{s+}(u) \cup \Gamma_{a+}(u)$. On the other hand, $w(u)$ is the weight of any social node (i.e. a user) $u \in G$. In this study, we assume the weight of each social node is constant and is set to 1. The equation [13] for the metric $m(u, a = v)$ is

$$m(u, a = v) = \sum_{t \in \Gamma_{s+}(u) \cap \Gamma_{s+}(a=v)} \frac{w(t)}{log|\Gamma_+(t)|}. \tag{1}$$

An interesting property of this metric is that, if friendship information is available, then $m(u, a = v)$ can be calculated for any attribute-value pair $a = v$ whether the user u has that value or not. A high $m(u, a = v)$ suggests that u has a high chance of having value v for attribute a since, u is connected to many other users who have $a = v$. Since $m(u, a = v)$ is computed by taking the network link information into account, we will add $m(u, a = v)$ information for each user and each attribute in a data set (having a number of users and a number of attributes for the users) [12] to demonstrate that an existing technique [1] (that does not take the network link information into account) may not provide protection against an attack using the link information.

Table 1. Attributes of Facebook data set D_{FB}.

Attribute name	Attribute values
Gender	Female; all 616 users are female aged over 18 years
Profile image	Contains 12 categories represented by 1 to 12, as follows, image shows the user: 1-alone, 2-with one or more friends, 3-at a special occasion, 4-with their special partner, 5-smiling, 6-in a unique location not in their hometown, 7-shows only face/head, 8-playing or watching sport, 9-with family, 10-depicts an object with apparent meaning to the user, 11-having a unique visual effect, 12-Reveals too much skin
Relationship status	Contains 11 categories: 1 to 10 and null, as follows. 1-single, 2-in a relationship, 3-engaged, 4-married, 5-it's complicated, 6-in an open relationship, 7-widowed, 8-separated, 9-divorced, 10-in a civil union, null
Interested in	Null, men,women,both
Family on FB	Absent, present
Hometown	Absent, present
Show sex	No, yes
High school	Absent, present
Year-graduated from High school	Absent, present
University or college	Absent, present
Year graduated from University or college	Absent, present
Timeline	Absent, present
Work	Absent, present
Friend	High, medium, low, null
Album	High, medium, low, null
Photo	High, medium, low, null
Language	English, english+, other, other+, null
Religion	Absent, present
Activities	Absent, present
Email	Absent, present
Date of birth (DOB)	1-full dob is revealed, 2-only day and month are revealed, 3-dob is not revealed
Political view	Absent, present
People who inspire	Absent, present
Class attribute	Connected, lonely

2.1   Data Sets

We use the same data set D_{FB} that was used in some previous studies [1,9]. The data set D_{FB} has 616 records where each record contains information of a female Facebook user who is either feeling *lonely* or *connected* as it is explicitly mentioned in their recent posts. Out of 616 records, 308 users are *lonely*, and 308 users are *connected*. As in the previous studies [1,9], we also assume that the *emotional status* is confidential. A malicious data miner will try to learn this information of a user who has not revealed this information. Hence, *emotional status* is the class attribute while building a classifier to learn the patterns for discovering the *emotional status* of members of the social network.

Thus, the structure of the data set D_{FB} consists of 23 non-class attributes and the class attribute *emotional status*. Table 1 provides details of these attributes.

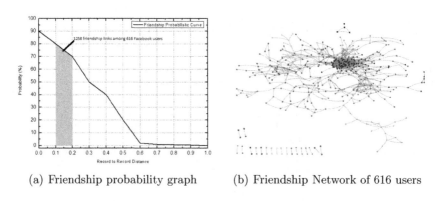

(a) Friendship probability graph   (b) Friendship Network of 616 users

Fig. 1. The friendship links simulation

For example, the *Profile Image* attribute contains 12 categories based on the image. If the image shows the user alone, then the value of the attribute is 1, if the image shows the user with one or more family members, then the value of the attribute is 2 and so on. The attribute *Hometown* contains two values *absent* and *present*. If the hometown of a user is revealed, then the value of the attribute is *present*; otherwise, *absent*. The attribute *Friend* has four possible values: *high*, *medium*, *low* and *null* depending on the user's number of friends. If the friendship information is not available, then the attribute has *null*.

However, D_{FB} does not have any information relating the social network links (i.e. friendship information). Therefore, we first simulate the connections among users to construct a data set D'_{FB} that contains information relating social network links. We set the probability of a link between two users inversely proportional to the Hamming distance between the two users. We set the record-to-record distance (or $R2RD \in [0,1]$) between two users as the Hamming distance divided by 23 (the number of non-class attributes).

Users having similar attribute values (i.e. low Hamming distance) are likely to have common interests and thus are likely to have friendship links (social links) between them [14]. A link between two users will be a Bernoulli trial with probability p where we set p as a high probability of a friendship link when the $R2RD$ is low. In particular, when the value of $R2RD$ between two users is within the range of 0.0 and 0.2, then we set the link probability p linearly between 0.9 and 0.7. When $R2RD$ is between 0.2 and 0.3, then the link probability p is linear between 0.7 and 0.5. Thus, for example, if the $R2RD$ between two users is 0.3, then we draw a link between them with probability $1/2$; that is, it is equally likely there is no connection. Figure 1(a) provides the plot that determines the link probability p as a function of $R2RD$. In this model, even if the $R2RD$ is large, between 0.6 and 1, there is still some probability that the users are linked as friends. Figure 1(a) shows that 1258 friendship links were created among users whose $R2RD$ is between 0.1 and 0.2. Figure 1(b) shows a social network drawn in the way, where the dots represent the users and the links represent the friendship between the users.

Once the friendship links are simulated we can compute the $m(u, a = v)$ for every user u and attribute-value pair $a = v$. Recall that the data set D_{FB} has 23 non-class attributes and a class attribute. A user u is represented by a record $r \in D_{FB}$ that has 24 attribute values. For each attribute value of u we compute $m(u, a = v)$. Thus, for each attribute-value pair, we create a new attribute containing $m(u, a = v)$ for each user u. Let us call these newly created attributes "link attributes" and the original 23 attributes "regular attributes". Therefore, when we consider the link information, the expanded data set D'_{FB} has now altogether $24 + 24 = 48$ attributes. That is, in the expanded data set D'_{FB}, we have 47 non-class attributes and a class attribute containing two possible values: *lonely* and *connected*.

We also utilize a synthetic data set as per those synthetic OSN data sets [15]. This data set consists of 11 non-class attributes which are given in Table 2. The data contains 1000 records (489 male users and 511 female users) and 50,397 friendship links. These are also synthetically generated friendship links [15]. We shall consider two version of this data set. In the first, we take *political orientation* as the confidential attribute of the data set and it is denoted by $D_{Political}$. In the second one, now D_{Sexor} we consider *sexual orientation* as the confidential attribute. Both of this will have 10 non-class attributes (but they exchange *sexual orientation* and *political orientation* as the class attribute).

After preparing $D_{Political}$ and D_{Sexor}, we calculate SAN metric values for each attribute as we did for D'_{FB}. This results in expanded data sets $D'_{Political}$ and D'_{Sexor} respectively with $11 + 11 = 22$ attributes one of which is the confidential class attribute.

2.2   Empirical Demonstration

We now empirically demonstrate the impact of considering social links on individual's privacy. For a data set D, in our experiments, we split the users in 10 disjoint groups: $\{D^1, D^2, D^3, \ldots, D^{10}\}$. For example, for D_{FB} $|D^i_{FB}| = 61$ for $i = 1, \ldots, 9$ and $|D^{10}_{FB}| = 67$. For the i-th iteration the users in D^i are considered those users who wish to keep their confidential attribute unpredictable from the

Table 2. Attributes of synthetic dataset.

Attribute name	Attribute values
Age	Contains 7 categories: 18–25, 26–35, 36–45, 46–55, 56–65, 66–75, 76–85
Gender	Male, female
Residence	Contains 5 categories: palo alto, santa barbara, san jose, boston, winthrop
Religion	Contains 7 categories: christian, hindu, jewish, muslim, sikh, other religions, no religious affiliation
Marital status	Contains 4 categories: single, married, divorced, widowed
Profession	Contains 7 categories: image shows the user: manager, professional, service, sales and office, student, natural resources construction and maintenance, production transportation and material moving
Political orientation	Contains 7 categories: absent sexual information, bisexual, heterosexual, homosexual
Political orientation	Contains 7 categories: far left, left, centre left,centre, centre right, right, far right
Like 1	Contains 5 categories: entertainment, music artist, drink brand, soccer club, tv show
Like 2	Contains 5 categories: entertainment, music artist, drink brand, soccer club, tv show
Like 3	Contains 5 categories: entertainment, music artist, drink brand, soccer club, tv show
Class attribute	Political orientation or sexual orientation (any one at a time)

adversary M, while the adversary has the data of the other users $\cup_{j=1}^{10} D^j \setminus D^i$ who have revealed such confidential attribute.

For each user U in D^i, we use *PrivAdv* repeatedly to identify the sensitive rules R^u. In each iteration, the primary attribute obtained from R^u is suppressed until $R^u = \emptyset$. At this stage, *PrivAdv* considers U's privacy protected. Different users in D^i have different attribute-value pairs suppressed.

How, we complement the columns of $\cup_{j=1}^{10} D^j \setminus D^i$ and D^i with the link information, essentially considering D' instead of D. We impersonate the adversary M who builds a forest from $\cup_{j=1}^{10} D'^j \setminus D'^i$. That is, we assume the adversary uses the *SAN* metric and thus obtains a new set of sensitive rules R'^u for each user U in D^i (the users in D^i and D'^i are the same, D'^i has the *SAN* link information as the metric $m(u, a = v)$ as per Eq. (1)).

The assumed strategy of the adversary for each D'^i is a decision-tree forest *SysFor* [16] with the aim of building a forest of 10 trees. Throughout the experiments, we use the standard set of parameters of *SysFor*. *SysFor* sometimes cannot build 10 trees as requested due to various reasons such as not having enough good attributes. Nevertheless, *SysFor* always builds at least 8 trees and 40 rules for D'_{FB} data set (refer to Table 3). The sensitive rules (SR) obtained by the adversary's strategy are of 3 types, SRR tests only regular attributes, SRRL tests both link attributes and regular attributes, SRL are sensitive rules made of only the link attributes.

Table 3. Analysis of sensitive rules with and without social link information

Run	Trees	Rules	SR	SRR	SRRL	SRL
1	9	40	31	1	7	23
2	8	71	41	1	8	32
3	8	50	33	0	9	24
4	8	69	42	3	6	23
5	8	83	43	3	20	20
6	8	81	44	3	13	28
7	9	60	41	3	8	30
8	8	49	35	1	13	21
9	8	61	42	3	13	26
10	8	48	37	0	5	32
Average	**8.2**	**61.2**	**38.9**	**1.8**	**10.2**	**25.9**

Table 3 contrasts the types of sensitive rules that are obtained from the link attributes from D'_{FB} versus those that do not. Those users in D^i_{FB} who have at least one sensitive rule $\in R'^u_{FB}$ for which no regular attribute value is suppressed by *PrivAdv* are at risk, and we found that the adversary always found at least 20 of these rules. That is, there are plenty of sensitive rules for which all values tested in the antecedent are *link attributes* (i.e. the attributes that contain $m(u, a = v)$ values). Note again that these values are not suppressed by *PrivAdv* since *PrivAdv* only uses *regular attributes* from D_{FB} [1]. Users are not properly secured by *PrivAdv* with respect to the social link information. For instance, consider D'^1_{FB}, any records satisfying any of the 23 SRLs for D^1_{FB} are not secured by *PrivAdv*. We can see from Table 3 that on an average there are 25.9 SRLs out of 38.9 SRs. This indicates that most of the sensitive rules obtained from D'_{FB} are not taken care of by *PrivAdv*. This should not be surprising, the vast majority of information derived in recommender systems and on-line social networks where information is represented as graph models like the *SAN* derives from the link information.

On the other hand, *SysFor* generates 9 trees in each component D_i for both $D'_{Political}$ and D'_{Sexor} data sets. The average number of SRRL is comparatively higher than SRL and SRR in each component of $D'_{Political}$. Out of 50 SR (i.e., sensitive rules), on average, the number of SRRL is 41.6 where SRL (i.e., sensitive rules with link attributes only) is approximately 0 in our experiments. In D'_{Sexor} data set, on average, 180 SR are generated in each part D_i and among these 176.4 are SRRL. Only 3.7 (on average) sensitive rules are SRL (i.e., containing both regular and link attributes).

The limitation of *PrivAdv* is further defined by the confidential attribute-value pair is revealed by rules in SRL or SRRL. If a user in D'^i has a sensitive rule in SRL or SRRL (*PrivAdv* does not suppress any of the attributes in the antecedent of the rule), then the user's information is considered to be insecure, otherwise the user's information is considered to be secure.

In our experiments, we found that among 62 users in each cross fold of D'_{FB} data set, 35 of them (56.62%) have protected information. However, 27 (43.38%) out of 62 users having insecure information. In case of $D'_{Political}$ and D'_{Sexor} data sets, out of all 10 parts D^i, on an average 41.7% and 70.5% users, respectively, are having insecure information after $PrivAdv$ has been applied. For these insecure users, the attributes suppressed by $PrivAdv$ are insufficient to protect their privacy when an adversary uses a data set with link attributes.

3   Our Technique

Our technique $3LP$ secures the confidential attribute-value pairs of users even when link attributes (obtained from social links) are taken into consideration. Our technique suggests three layers of protection: Layer 1 suggests to suppress necessary attribute values (and is equivalent to $PrivAdv$: Step 1 and 2 in Algorithm 1), Layer 2 suggests to hide some friendship information and Layer 3 suggests to add new friends.

Step 1 *Compute Sensitivity of Each Attribute for a User.* In Step 1, we invoke the function *GetSensitiveRules()* to create the set of sensitive rules R^s. The set R^s is generic, but the function *GetSensRulesForUser()* uses the attribute values of a particular user U and returns the set R^u of sensitive rules for U. The set $A_u^{r/s}$ of sensitive attributes is the union of all regular attributes in the antecedents of the rules in R^u. The $TOTAL\_COUNT$ [1] counts how many times each regular attribute A_i appears in the antecedents of set R^u.

Step 2 *Suppress Attribute Values as Necessary (Layer 1).* 3LP identifies the regular attribute A_n with the highest number of appearances in the set R^u and suggests user U shall suppress the value of attribute A_n. As in $TOTAL\_COUNT$ [1], our first layer only suggests the suppression and leaves the decision up to the user. Either way, the attribute A_n is removed from the set A_u^s of sensitive attributes. If user U suppresses attribute A_n, then all sensitive rules in R^u that have A_n in their antecedent are no longer applicable. In this case, those sensitive rules are no longer in R^u. The treatment is repeated with the next regular attribute with the highest number of appearances in the set R^u until R^u is empty (in which case the algorithm terminates) or the set $A_u^{r/s}$ of regular attributes in R^u is empty (in which case the algorithm continues with **Step 3**. We remark here that in the experiments of this study we assume that a user follows all the suggestions.

Step 3 *Hide Friendship Links as Necessary (Layer 2).* If there are still some sensitive rules $R_j^u \in R^u$, such rules must use only link attributes. We explore if there is any link attribute $m(u, A_n = v)$ whose value can be reduced by deleting or hiding some friendship links in order to reduce the number of sensitive rules in R^u. Unlike the regular attributes, the link attributes cannot be suppressed easily. Moreover, as discussed when Eq. (1) was introduced, in many cases $m(u, A_n = v)$ derives from the social links of the user and not the explicit links the user has control.

However, we can offer to the user to carefully change the social links (by deleting/hiding some friendships) and thus alter the values of the link attributes $m(u, A_n = v)$. For example, if we hide the friendship link of the user U with a friend who also shares the same attribute-value pair $A_n = v$, then we can decrease the link attribute value $m(u, A_n = v)$. Moreover, we can see from Eq. (1) that if we hide the friendship link of the friend t who has the smallest $\Gamma_+(t) = \Gamma_{s+}(t) \cup \Gamma_{a+}(t)$, then we can maximise the reduction of $m(u, A_n = v)$.

In Step 3, we first find the most sensitive link attribute $m(u, A_n = v)$ for the user U. We then check if the value of $m(u, A_n = v)$ is higher than the split point in a sensitive rule R_j^u, where one of the tests in the antecedent of R_j^u is $A_n \geq split\_point$. If it is, then we suggest user U shall hide the friendship link with a friend who has the smallest $\Gamma_+(t) = \Gamma_{s+}(t) \cup \Gamma_{a+}(t)$ in order to reduce the $m(u, A_n = v)$ value the most. If the user accepts the recommendation, we recompute $m(u, A_n = v)$.

The goal here is to reduce the value of $m(u, A_n = v)$ below the split point so rule R_j^u is no longer applicable to U. We continue the process of hiding friends until we get the a value of $m(u, A_n = v)$ lower than the split point in R_j^u. We then remove R_j^u and any other rules no longer applicable to user U from R^u and repeat the process for another sensitive rule R_j^u that tests $m(u, A_n = v) \geq some\ split\_point$ in it antecedent. At the end of Step 3, if we still have some rules $R_j^u \in R^u$ then we move to Step 4 (Layer 3).

Step 4   *Add New Friends as Necessary (Layer 3).* We again find the most sensitive link attribute $m(u, A_n = v)$ for the user. We check if there is any sensitive rule $R_j^u \in R^u$ that has an antecedent of the from $m(u, A_n = v) \leq some\ split\_point$. If there is such R_j^u, then we aim to add friends and thus increase the value of $m(u, A_n = v)$ so that it eventually becomes greater than the split point and thus R_j^u is no loner applicable to U. Our algorithm *3LP* suggests the adding approach to the user U and the user shall make the decision whether to add the friend or not. Our *3LP* retrieves the possible friend t with the smallest $\Gamma_+(t) = \Gamma_{s+}(t) \cup \Gamma_{a+}(t)$, and recommends to add a friendship link to t. This maximises the increase of the value of $m(u, A_n = v)$ and minimises the number of friendship links to be added.

4   Experimental Results and Discussion

We now present experimental results that validate our algorithm *3LP*. We apply *3LP* on the expanded data sets named D'_{FB}, $D'_{Political}$ and D'_{Sexor} separately. We again partition the data sets into 10 disjoint parts, using one part as the potential victims and 90% of the dataset as the data available for inferring confidential attributes. Table 4 shows experimental results for D'_{FB}.

Table 4. Number of insecure users after applying *3LP* on expanded dataset D'_{FB}.

Run	Number of users in test data set	Number of insecure users			
		After using *PrivAdv*	After using Layer 1 of *3LP*	After using Layer 1 and Layer 2 of *3LP*	After using Layer 1, Layer 2 and Layer 3 of *3LP*
1	61	18	18	15	0
2	61	40	40	36	0
3	61	35	35	19	0
4	61	9	9	9	0
5	61	35	35	33	0
6	61	29	29	27	0
7	61	20	20	17	0
8	61	10	10	10	0
9	61	34	34	22	0
10	67	38	38	28	0
Average	**61.6**	**27**	**27**	**22**	**0**

Earlier we saw that *PrivAdv* [1] could secure the confidential attributes of only 56.62% users from the attribute inference attack that uses link information on the D'_{FB} dataset. However, using algorithm *3LP* the remaining 43.38% users are protected. Later 1 is essentially *PrivAdv*, none of the information of the users at risk is secured further. Typically, for a group of 61 users, 27 users are still at risk after Layer 1. But, on average, 5 of them can prevent a breach of privacy by hiding friends. In percentage terms, users whose confidential attribute is secure increases to 64.52% after Layer 2, with a 7.9% increment with respect to Layer 1. Although hiding a particular friend from user profile is currently unavailable on Facebook these results suggest that the operators of OSN such as Facebook may consider adding this option to a user profile. That is, enable users to select the automatic masking of some friendships to any data analyst so their confidential attribute (already not present) can not be inferred.

Moreover, to secure the data of the remaining users, our experimental results show that on an average 22 users need to add more friends to prevent a breach of privacy. (i.e., Layer 3 of *3LP*). Of the users who are not protected by previous approaches (Layer 1), equivalently 83.84% (22 out of 27) need to do it by adding friends. While choosing the friend during addition, lower degree friends carry more impact on the metric function values.

Although adding more friends may seem unrealistic in OSNs settings, and other risks may derive from linking with strangers, we believe the operators of OSNs would be able to perform this. Certainly ensuring the privacy of their users

Algorithm 1. 3LP()

Input   : User U, attribute C that U considers confidential is the class attribute, dataset D having N records, A is the set of non-class attributes where $A^r \subset A$ is the set of regular attributes and $A^l \subset A$ is the set of link attributes, C denotes the class attribute C and G the graph information.

Output   : Recommendations for U to act on some attributes in A.

Variables   : A_n =the nth attribute
R^s = set of sensitive rules

Step 1: Compute Sensitivity of Each Attribute for a User

$\quad R^s \leftarrow GetSensitiveRules(D, C)$
$\quad R^u \leftarrow GetSensRulesForUser(R^s, U)$
$\quad Counter_i \leftarrow 0; \forall Counter_i \in Counter$ /*$Counter_i$ shall total the number of appearances of $A_i \in A^r$ in the set of sensitive rules*/;
$\quad A_u^{r/s} \leftarrow \phi$ /*Initially A^s is set to null*/;
$\quad$ **foreach** $R_j^u \in R^u$ **do**
$\quad\quad$ **foreach** attribute $A_n \in A^r$ **do**
$\quad\quad\quad$ **if** A_n is in the antecedent of R_j^u **then**
$\quad\quad\quad\quad Counter_n \leftarrow Counter_n + 1$
$\quad\quad\quad\quad A_u^{r/s} \leftarrow A_u^{r/s} \cup \{A_n\}$ /* Add the nth attribute in A^s */
$\quad\quad\quad$ **end**
$\quad\quad$ **end**
$\quad$ **end**
end

Step 2: Suppress Attribute Values as Necessary for the User

$\quad$ **while** $R^u \neq \phi$ OR $A_u^{r/s} \neq \phi$ **do**
$\quad\quad A_n \leftarrow maxarg(Counter)$ /*Indentify the attribute that appears the most in R^u*/
$\quad\quad SuggestSuppress(A_n)$ /*Suggest the user to suppress the attribute value for A_n*/
$\quad\quad A_u^{r/s} \leftarrow (A_u^{r/s} \setminus \{A_n\})$
$\quad\quad Counter \leftarrow (Counter - Counter_n)$ /*The counters are kept aligned with the attributes*/
$\quad\quad$ **if** A_n is suppressed **then**
$\quad\quad\quad R^u \leftarrow (R^u \setminus FindRules(R^u, A_n))$ /*Rules using A_n in preconditions are removed*/
$\quad\quad$ **end**
$\quad$ **end**
end

Step 3: Hide Friendship Links as Necessary for the User

$\quad A_n \leftarrow FindMostSensitive(A^l, R^u, U, G)$ /*$A_n = Val(m(u, a))$*/
$\quad$ **while** $A_n \neq null$ **do**
$\quad\quad a \leftarrow WhichAttr(A_n, A^l)$
$\quad\quad$ **foreach** $R_j^u \in R^u$ **do**
$\quad\quad\quad$ **if** $A_n \in IsTested(R_j^u)$ and $Val(A_n) \geq SplitPoint(R_j^u, A_n)$ **then**
$\quad\quad\quad\quad$ **while** $Val(A_n) \geq SplitPoint(R_j^u, A_n)$ and $MoreFriends(U, G)$ **do**
$\quad\quad\quad\quad\quad f \leftarrow FriendWithLeastDegree(G, D, U, a)$
$\quad\quad\quad\quad\quad SuggestHide(f)$
$\quad\quad\quad\quad\quad$ **if** $t \in IsHidden(f)$ **then**
$\quad\quad\quad\quad\quad\quad G \leftarrow RemoveLink(G, U, f)$
$\quad\quad\quad\quad\quad\quad Recompute(A_n, G, D, U)$
$\quad\quad\quad\quad\quad$ **end**
$\quad\quad\quad\quad$ **end**
$\quad\quad\quad$ **end**
$\quad\quad\quad R^u \leftarrow R^u \setminus \{R_j^u\}$
$\quad\quad$ **end**
$\quad\quad A_l \leftarrow A_l \setminus \{A_n\}$
$\quad\quad A_n \leftarrow FindMostSensitive(A^l, R^u, U, G)$ /*$A_n = Val(m(u, a))$*/
$\quad$ **end**
end

Step 4: Add New Friends as Necessary for the User

$\quad A_n \leftarrow FindMostSensitive(A^l, R^u, U, G)$ /*$A_n = Val(m(u, a))$*/
$\quad$ **while** $A_n \neq null$ **do**
$\quad\quad a \leftarrow WhichAttr(A_n, A^l)$
$\quad\quad$ **foreach** $R_j^u \in R^u$ **do**
$\quad\quad\quad$ **if** $A_n \in IsTested(R_j^u)$ and $Val(A_n) \leq SplitPoint(R_j^u, A_n)$ **then**
$\quad\quad\quad\quad$ **while** $Val(A_n) \leq SplitPoint(R_j^u, A_n)$ and $MoreUsers(U, G)$ **do**
$\quad\quad\quad\quad\quad f \leftarrow UserWithLeastDegree(G, D, U, a)$
$\quad\quad\quad\quad\quad SuggestAdd(f)$
$\quad\quad\quad\quad\quad$ **if** $t \leftarrow IsAdded(f)$ **then**
$\quad\quad\quad\quad\quad\quad G \leftarrow AddLink(G, U, f)$
$\quad\quad\quad\quad\quad\quad Recompute(A_n, G, D, U)$
$\quad\quad\quad\quad\quad$ **end**
$\quad\quad\quad\quad$ **end**
$\quad\quad\quad$ **end**
$\quad\quad\quad R^u \leftarrow R^u \setminus \{R_j^u\}$
$\quad\quad$ **end**
$\quad\quad A_l \leftarrow A_l \setminus \{A_n\}$
$\quad\quad A_n \leftarrow FindMostSensitive(A^l, R^u, U, G)$ /*$A_n = Val(m(u, a))$*/
$\quad$ **end**
end

Table 5. Number of insecure users after applying $3LP$ on the expanded dataset $D'_{Political}$ and D'_{Sexor}.

$D'_{Political}$		Number of insecure users			
Run	Number of users in D_i	After using $PrivAdv$	After using Layer 1 of $3LP$	After using Layer 1 and Layer 2 of $3LP$	After using Layer 1, Layer 2 and Layer 3 of $3LP$
1	100	17	0	X	X
2	100	15	0	X	X
3	100	12	0	X	X
4	100	100	99	0	X
5	100	20	0	X	X
6	100	35	0	X	X
7	100	29	0	X	X
8	100	97	95	0	X
9	100	53	39	0	X
10	100	39	0	X	X
Average	**100**	**41.7**	**23.3**	**0**	**X**
D'_{Sexor}		Number of insecure users			
Run	Number of users in D_i	After using $PrivAdv$	After using Layer 1 of $3LP$	After using Layer 1 and Layer 2 of $3LP$	After using Layer 1, Layer 2 and Layer 3 of $3LP$
1	100	69	1	0	X
2	100	69	0	X	X
3	100	67	0	X	X
4	100	75	7	0	X
5	100	86	15	0	X
6	100	77	0	X	X
7	100	60	0	X	X
8	100	74	0	0	X
9	100	63	5	0	X
10	100	65	0	X	X
Average	**100**	**70.5**	**2.8**	**0**	**X**

[X = This layer is not required]

is in the operators' best interest, Thus, our results here suggest that operators can suggest to users the addition of some synthetic friends. Alternatively, they could use such technique to sanitise the data before releasing it to data analysts. We plan to focus on this in our future work. On the other hand, in Table 5 we present respectively the experimental results with $D'_{Political}$ and D'_{Sexor}. The average

Table 6. Required number of attribute Suppression, Friend Deletion or Addition for each insecure user suggested by *3LP* in expanded data set D'_{FB}.

Run	Average number of attribute suppression (per user) in Layer 1 of *3LP*	Average number of friends needed to be hidden (per user) in Layer 2 of *3LP*	Average number of friends needed to be added (per user) in Layer 3 of *3LP*
1	0	1	2
2	0	1	1
3	0	1	1
4	0	0	1
5	1	2	2
6	0	1	2
7	1	1	1
8	0	0	1
9	1	1	2
10	0	1	2
Average	0	1	2

results show that, for a group of 100 users, about 23 and 3 (after rounding) users are still insecure after applying the first layer of *3LP* on $D'_{Political}$ and D'_{Sexor} data sets respectively.

In order to secure these users we then apply Layer 2 of *3LP* (i.e., obfuscate friends from friend lists) and we notice that no more users are at risk (after applying Layer 2 of *3LP*) in both $D'_{Political}$ and D'_{Sexor} data sets. Hence Layer 3 of *3LP* is not required in our experiments for both of these data sets.

The Column 2 of Table 6 shows the number of attributes needed suppression in Layer 1 of *3LP*. Please note that these are the suppressions made in addition to the suppressions suggested by the regular *PrivAdv*. The average number of attribute suppression (Layer 1 of *3LP*), on the other hand, is higher both in $D'_{Political}$ and D'_{Sexor} compared to D'_{FB}. The reason may be the number of generated SRR (i.e., sensitive rules with regular attributes) is much lower for D'_{FB}.

Our results also show that the burden of additions and obfuscations of friends is not that large. For example, in D'_{FB} data set, we need to hide/add at most 1–2 friends, on average, in each partition D^i to secure the confidential attribute (refer to Table 6).

In case of the data sets $D'_{Political}$ and D'_{Sexor}, we need to hide 3–4 friends, on average, in each partition whereas, Layer 3 is not required in our experiments (refer to Table 7).

Table 7. Required number of attribute Suppression, Friend Deletion or Addition for each insecure user suggested by *3LP* in expanded data sets $D'_{Political}$ and D'_{Sexor}.

$D'_{Political}$ Run	Average number of attribute suppression (per user) in Layer 1 of *3LP*	Average number of friends needed to be hidden (per user) in Layer 2 of *3LP*	Average number of friends needed to be added (per user) in Layer 3 of *3LP*
1	1	X	X
2	1	X	X
3	1	X	X
4	1	10	X
5	1	X	X
6	1	X	X
7	1	X	X
8	1	6	X
9	1	11	X
10	2	X	X
Average	**1.1**	**2.7**	**X**
D'_{Sexor} Run	Average number of attribute suppression (per user) in Layer 1 of *3LP*	Average number of friends needed to be hidden (per user) in Layer 2 of *3LP*	Average number of friends needed to be added (per user) in Layer 3 of *3LP*
1	2	11	X
2	2	X	X
3	2	X	X
4	1	9	X
5	2	7	X
6	1	X	X
7	1	X	X
8	3	X	X
9	1	14	X
10	2	X	X
Average	**2**	**4.1**	**X**

5   Conclusion

We proposed *3LP*, a privacy-preserving technique in order to protect the privacy of Facebook users from attribute inference risks. Previous works did not consider friendship network information which may create vulnerability to users' privacy. Our technique provides suggestions, to a user to suppress necessary attribute values and fabricate friendship links, in order to protect sensitive attribute values of the user. The technique can also enable a social network provider to query a user whether to fabricate such links to preserve his/her privacy. Our experimental results show that by hiding or adding a few friends in a user's profile can protect the user's sensitive information from being inferred. Though hiding a particular friend from the user's profile is currently unavailable on Facebook, the approach here suggests that such feature could be added in order to protect users' privacy.

In this paper, we have considered that only the user or few others in user's network are consumers of *3LP*. If all friends in a user's friend list continuously use and adopt the recommendations of *3LP*, then the calculation will be dynamic and different. We believe this is an exciting avenue for further research.

References

1. Estivill-Castro, V., Hough, P., Islam, M.Z.: Empowering users of social networks to assess their privacy risks. In: 2014 IEEE International Conference on Big Data, pp. 644–649 (2014)
2. Facebook stats. newsroom.fb.com/company-info/. Accessed 03 June 2016
3. The top 500 sites on the web. //www.alexa.com/topsites. Accessed 03 June 2016
4. Ho, A., Maiga, A., Aimeur, E.: Privacy protection issues in social networking sites. In: IEEE/ACS International Conference on Computer Systems and Applications, pp. 271–278 (2009)
5. Tavani, H.T.: Ethics and Technology: Controversies, Questions, and Strategies for Ethical Computing, 3rd edn. Wiley Publishing, Hoboken (2011)
6. Rachels, J.: Why privacy is important. Philos. Publ. Affairs **4**(4), 323–333 (1975)
7. Heatherly, R., Kantarcioglu, M., Thuraisingham, B.M.: Preventing private information inference attacks on social networks. IEEE Trans. Knowl. Data Eng. **25**(8), 1849–1862 (2013)
8. Ryu, E., Rong, Y., Li, J., Machanavajjhala, A.: Curso: protect yourself from curse of attribute inference: a social network privacy-analyzer. In: SIGMOD Workshop on Databases and Social Networks (DBSocial 2013), pp. 13–18, NY. ACM (2013)
9. Al-Saggaf, Y., Islam, M.Z.: Privacy in social network sites (SNS): the threats from data mining. Ethical Space Int. J. Commun. Ethics **9**(4), 32–40 (2012)
10. Guha, S., Tang, K., Francis, P.: NOYB: privacy in online social networks. In: First Workshop on Online Social Networks (WOSN 2008), pp. 49–54, NY, USA. ACM (2008)
11. Gong, N.Z., Talwalkar, A., Mackey, L.W., Huang, L., Shin, E.C.R., Stefanov, E., Shi, E., Song, D.: Joint link prediction and attribute inference using a social-attribute network. ACM Trans. Intell. Syst. Technol. **5**(2), 27 (2014)
12. Estivill-Castro, V., Nettleton, D.F.: Can on-line social network users trust that what they designated as confidential data remains so? In: 2015 IEEE Trustcom/BigDataSE/ISPA, pp. 966–973, Washington. IEEE Computer Society (2015)
13. Adamic, L., Adar, E.: Friends and neighbors on the web. Soc. Netw. **25**(3), 211–230 (2003)
14. La Fond, T., Neville, J.: Randomization tests for distinguishing social influence and homophily effects. In: 19th International Conference on World Wide Web (WWW 2010), pp. 601–610, NY. ACM (2010)
15. Nettleton, D.F.: Generating synthetic online social network graph data and topologies. In: 3rd Workshop on Graph-Based Technologies and Applications (Graph-TA 2015). UPC, Barcelona (2015)
16. Islam, Z., Giggins, H.: Knowledge discovery through SysFor: a systematically developed forest of multiple decision trees. In: 9th Australasian Data Mining Conference, vol. 121, pp. 195–204, Darlinghurst. Australian Computer Society (2011)

A Framework for Moving Target Defense Quantification

Warren Connell, Massimiliano Albanese[✉], and Sridhar Venkatesan

George Mason University, Fairfax, VA 22030, USA
{wconnel2,malbanes,svenkate}@gmu.edu

Abstract. Moving Target Defense (MTD) has emerged as a game changer in the security landscape, as it can create asymmetric uncertainty favoring the defender. Despite the significant work done in this area and the many different techniques that have been proposed, MTD has not yet gained widespread adoption due to several limitations. Specifically, interactions between multiple techniques have not been studied yet and a unified framework for quantifying and comparing very diverse techniques is still lacking. To overcome these limitations, we propose a framework to model how different MTD techniques can affect the information an attacker needs to exploit a system's vulnerabilities, so as to introduce uncertainty and reduce the likelihood of successful attacks. We illustrate how this framework can be used to compare two sets of MTDs, and to select an optimal set of MTDs that maximize security within a given budget. Experimental results show that our approach is effective.

Keywords: Moving target defense · MTD quantification · Framework

1 Introduction

Moving target defense offers a great potential in turning the typical asymmetry of the cyber security landscape in favor of the defender [9], and many techniques have been developed since the term first surfaced in the literature. However, each technique only addresses a narrow subset of potential attack vectors and different techniques tend to measure their effectiveness in different and incompatible ways. Additionally, in order to provide a comprehensive security solution, multiple techniques should be used jointly, but this requires the selection of an optimal subset of available techniques. Although several surveys note where certain MTDs might not work well together [12], or give a qualitative estimate of their effectiveness and cost [6], a quantitative framework that can accommodate any existing or future MTDs is still needed for this area of research to progress

This work was partially supported by the Army Research Office under grants W911NF-13-1-0421 and W911NF-13-1-0317, and by the Office of Naval Research under grant N00014-13-1-0703. We acknowledge Dr. George Cybenko and Dr. Sushil Jajodia for the invaluable inputs they provided in the early stages of this work.

S. De Capitani di Vimercati and F. Martinelli (Eds.): SEC 2017, IFIP AICT 502, pp. 124–138, 2017.
DOI: 10.1007/978-3-319-58469-0_9

past specialized, isolated solutions. To address this pressing need, we present a novel framework that captures the relationships between available MTDs and the information such MTDs may affect through probabilistic measures. It also captures the relationships between services, their weaknesses, and the knowledge required to exploit such weaknesses to probabilistically determine the effectiveness of any given technique or set of techniques, regardless of how they operate. Our framework presents the following desirable attributes: (i) **generality** – the relationship between MTDs and the knowledge they protect defines an interface that enables to plug any MTD into the framework; (ii) **extensibility** – the model can be extended to accommodate future MTDs by introducing new elements, such as additional knowledge blocks or classes of weaknesses; (iii) **resilience** – as the framework addresses generic classes of weaknesses rather than specific vulnerabilities, the model can address both known and unknown (zero-day) attacks; (iv) **usability** – the framework is simple and intuitive, can be used to compute utility estimates at different levels of granularity, and can incorporate cost in the estimation of utility.

The remainder of the paper is organized as follows. Section 2 discusses related work, whereas Sect. 3 covers our threat model and underlying assumptions. The framework itself is presented in detail in Sect. 4 with a simple running example, while a more complex case study is discussed in Sect. 5. Then, Sect. 6 shows two applications of the proposed model. Finally, Sect. 7 discusses potential future work and gives some concluding remarks.

2 Related Work

Many different metrics are used in the literature to measure the effectiveness of MTDs, such as attacker's success rate [3], or metrics for deception, deterrence, and detectability [8]. Still others utilize multiple metrics (productivity, success, confidentiality, and integrity) for both the attacker and the defender [16], leading to confusion over the multiple dimensions. However, all these metrics only evaluate a few select MTDs. One expert survey provides a thorough assessment of the effectiveness and cost of many techniques across the spectrum of existing MTDs [6], but the survey is qualitative in nature and potentially subject to reviewer's bias. Our work leverages existing work on attack graphs [10], particularly those approaches that evaluate security by looking at how the probability of a successful attack propagates over an attack graph [15]. The TREsPASS project[1] provides a holistic view of an organization's information security risk. It provides a visualization framework that combines the impact of vulnerability exploitation, physical security breach and social engineering on the target organization. This framework can be used to analyze several properties of multi-step attacks such as the required effort or time, and likelihood of success. However, attack graphs cannot be readily used with every MTD, as they are often tied to specific vulnerabilities. In fact, several MTDs can drastically alter a system's attack surface, requiring to generate an entirely new attack graph every time

---

[1] http://www.trespass-project.eu.

the MTD changes the system's configuration, which is not feasible in practice. Our work is also inspired by research on autonomous systems, particularly self-protecting systems [1], which autonomously change their settings to adapt to their environment, implicitly creating a *moving target*. In order to do so efficiently, they must quantify the effectiveness and cost of all possible changes.

3   Threat Model and Assumptions

The general nature of our model lets us make very broad, worst-case assumptions about the cyber threats we are trying to protect against. In particular, we assume that *attackers can exploit any possible attack vector*. Most techniques described in the literature only protect against a narrow subset of possible attacks and no single MTD can protect against all possible attack vectors. This is handled by our model by providing the ability to combine multiple MTDs in a defense-in-depth approach. We also make the worst-case assumption that *no static defense can prevent an attack*, as the attacker has virtually unlimited time to plan and execute an attack and zero-day exploits can evade static defenses. Only MTDs are considered to have an effect on the attacker's success rate, and even then, an MTD may not be perfect. We assume that *attackers can be stopped or at least delayed by preventing them from acquiring accurate knowledge* about the target system. Our primary focus here is on the reconnaissance phase, when that knowledge is gathered prior to planning and executing attacks. Our goal can be achieved by either preventing attackers from accessing that knowledge or delaying them until that knowledge is no longer useful.

Finally, we make several additional simplifying assumptions throughout the paper that we summarize here. Future work will allow us to revise many of our assumptions in order to further generalize our approach. We assume that services and weaknesses are time-invariant. We also assume that services and knowledge blocks are independent, but multiple services with dependencies could be modeled. We currently assume that each MTD has a predefined optimal configuration of its parameters, and that, if multiple MTDs affect a knowledge block, they do not interact and only the most effective one is considered.

4   Quantification Framework

In this section, we present the proposed quantification framework, which, as shown for the motivating example of Fig. 1, consists of four layers: (i) a time-invariant service layer representing the set S of services to be protected; (ii) a weakness layer representing the set W of general classes of weaknesses that may be exploited; (iii) a knowledge layer representing the set K of all possible knowledge blocks required to exploit those weaknesses; and (iv) an MTD layer representing the set M of available MTD techniques.

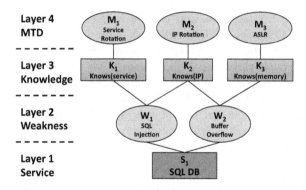

Fig. 1. Quantification framework layers

4.1 Mathematical Model

The proposed MTD quantification framework can be formally defined as a 7-tuple $(\mathcal{S}, \mathcal{R}_{SW}, \mathcal{W}, \mathcal{R}_{WK}, \mathcal{K}, \mathcal{R}_{KM}, \mathcal{M})$, where: (i) $\mathcal{S}$, $\mathcal{W}$, $\mathcal{K}$, $\mathcal{M}$ are the sets of services, weaknesses, knowledge blocks, and MTD techniques, respectively; (ii) $\mathcal{R}_{SW} \subseteq \mathcal{S} \times \mathcal{W}$ represents relationships between services and the common weaknesses they are vulnerable to; (iii) $\mathcal{R}_{WK} \subseteq \mathcal{W} \times \mathcal{K}$ represents relationships between weaknesses and the knowledge blocks required for an attacker to exploit them; and (iv) $\mathcal{R}_{KM} \subseteq \mathcal{K} \times \mathcal{M}$ represents relationships between knowledge blocks and the MTD techniques that affect them. The proposed model induces a k-partite graph (with $k = 4$) $G = (\mathcal{S} \cup \mathcal{W} \cup \mathcal{K} \cup \mathcal{M}, \mathcal{R}_{SW} \cup \mathcal{R}_{WK} \cup \mathcal{R}_{KM})$.

Layer 1: Service Layer. The first layer represents the set $\mathcal{S}$ of services we wish to protect against attacks. We assume that the services are time-invariant, i.e., the functionality of the services does not change over time, and services cannot be taken down to prevent attacks, as this action would result in a denial-of-service. We only consider one service in the case studies presented in this paper, but the model could be extended to consider multiple interdependent services, similarly to how an exploit chain might occur within attack graphs [10,15].

Layer 2: Weakness Layer. The second layer represents the set of weaknesses $\mathcal{W}$ that services are vulnerable to. We choose general classes of weaknesses rather than specific vulnerabilities because there are too many vulnerabilities to enumerate, some vulnerabilities are unknown, and, depending on the MTD used (e.g., OS rotation), specific vulnerabilities may change over time. Using general classes of weaknesses when building the model makes them time-invariant.

The examples used in this paper draw these weaknesses primarily from MITRE's Common Weakness Enumeration (CWE) project [5], particularly from those known as the *"Top 25 Most Dangerous Software Errors."* Although many of the top software errors are primarily the result of bad coding practices and better solved at development time, the top software errors enabling exploits such as *SQL Injection*, *OS Injection*, and *Classic Buffer Overflow* can be addressed at runtime by MTDs (e.g., SQLrand) and make for good general categories of weaknesses. The Microsoft STRIDE Threat Model [7] has also been used as a source of general threats in MTD research [14] and can fill in areas where CWE may be lacking. For example, *Information Disclosure* (eavesdropping) and *Denial of Service* are not specifically addressed by CWE. Our example shows two weaknesses, *SQL Injection* and *Buffer Overflow*. More weaknesses, such as *OS Injection*, might be included in a more complex example, while other weaknesses, such as *Cross-Site Scripting*, would not be applicable to this service.

Layer 3: Knowledge Layer. The third layer represents the knowledge blocks $\mathcal{K}$ required to effectively exploit weaknesses. This knowledge is required to plan an attack even when no MTD is deployed (such as a victim's IP address) or it may be an additional piece of information required due to the use of an MTD. For example, SQLrand [2] adds a keyword to SQL commands, which must be known for a malicious user to perform SQL injection. We assume that knowledge blocks are independent and must be acquired using different methods. For example, IP address and port number should not modeled as separate knowledge blocks because a method to determine one would also reveal the other.

The relationship between the knowledge and weakness layers is many-to-many. A weakness may require several pieces of knowledge to be exploited, and a knowledge block may be key to exploiting several weaknesses. This layer may also be extended as new MTDs – disrupting new and different aspects of an attacker's knowledge – are developed.

In our example, we assume that, in order to execute a SQL Injection attack, the attacker must gather information about the service (e.g., name and version of the specific DBMS) and the network configuration (e.g., IP address). In order to execute a Buffer Overflow attack, an attacker must know the IP address and some information about the vulnerable memory locations. A higher-fidelity version of this model may take a knowledge block and break it down into smaller, more specific items that are specifically targeted by available MTDs.

Layer 4: MTD Layer. The fourth layer of the model represents the set $\mathcal{M}$ of available MTDs. As MTD techniques provide probabilistic security, we model the impact of an MTD M_i on the attacker's effort to acquire knowledge K_j by associating a probability $P_{i,j}$ – representing the attacker's success rate – with the relation (K_j, M_i). As mentioned in the Sect. 3, when only static defenses (i.e., no MTD) are deployed, an attacker will acquire the necessary knowledge without significant effort, which we model by associating a probability of 1.

For example, if technique M_1 in Fig. 1 (*Service Rotation*) reduces an attacker's likelihood of acquiring knowledge block K_1 (i.e., correct version of the service) by 60%, we would label that edge with $P_{1,1} = 0.4$. If an MTD delays an attacker by some factor, we can also express that as a probability that the attacker will not gather the correct information in a timely manner. For example, an MTD that expands addressable memory by a factor of 10 might reduce the attacker's probability of success to 0.1, so $P_{i,j} = 0.1$. The exact methodology for determining the value of $P_{i,j}$ may vary from MTD to MTD, and we are investigating this problem as a separate line of research that goes beyond the scope of this paper. Specifically, we are developing a general app- roach to model the tradeoff between cost and effectiveness of MTD techniques, as we vary the values of a technique's tunable parameters and other aspects of the attacker/defender interaction. Ultimately, this approach will enable us to identify the optimal configuration for each technique. Therefore, in this paper, we assume that such optimal configuration has already been identified for each available MTD technique, along with the corresponding value of $P_{i,j}$ and the corresponding cost.

Expressing MTD effectiveness in terms of the probability an attacker will succeed in acquiring required knowledge enables us to analyze multiple tech- niques using a uniform approach that yields values in the [0,1] range, with a theoretically perfect MTD yielding $P_{i,j} = 0$, and a completely ineffective MTD yielding $P_{i,j} = 1$. In our example, we use *service rotation* to disrupt knowledge about the version of the service, and naïvely assume that rotating between 4 services reduces the attacker's probability of gathering the correct information to $P_{1,1} = 0.25$. We apply an *IP address rotation* scheme to mask the victim's IP address. It has been shown that perfect shuffling reduces the attacker's likelihood of guessing the correct IP address by 37% [3]. Using a conservative estimate, we assume $P_{2,2} = 0.75$. Finally, to protect knowledge of the memory layout, we use a dynamic ASLR scheme. Although dynamic ASLR only adds a single bit of entropy compared to typical ASLR [13], this further delays the attacker, result- ing in a probability $P_{3,3} = 0.5$ of gathering the correct information.

4.2   Computing MTD Effectiveness

We compute an MTD's effectiveness starting from layer 4 of the model and working our way down to find the overall probability of attacker's success. First, we define $P(K_j)$ as the probability that the attacker has the correct information about knowledge block K_j, and compute $P(K_j)$ for each K_j in layer 3, based on the active MTDs affecting it. If there is no active MTD, we assume that the attacker is guaranteed to obtain that information, i.e., $P(K_j) = 1$.

In our example, each knowledge block is affected by only one MTD. When multiple MTDs affect the same knowledge block, we make the simplifying assumption that the resulting effect is driven by the best-performing MTD. Thus:

$$P(K_j) = \begin{cases} 1, & \text{if } \nexists M_i \in \mathcal{M} \text{ s.t. } (K_j, M_i) \in \mathcal{R}_{KM} \wedge active(M_i) \\ \min_{M_i \in \mathcal{M} \text{ s.t. } (K_j, M_i) \in \mathcal{R}_{KM}} P_{i,j} \wedge active(M_i), & \text{otherwise} \end{cases} \quad (1)$$

A possible improvement to the model would be to capture the effect of mul- tiple MTDs acting on the same knowledge block by using a function modeling either diminishing returns or some other interaction between multiple MTDs.

Next, we determine the probability $P(W_k)$ that an attacker has gained all the knowledge required to exploit a given weakness W_k. Since each knowledge block is independent, this is simply the product of the probabilities associated with all knowledge blocks leading to it, as shown by Eq. 2.

$$P(W_k) = \prod_{K_j \in \mathcal{K} \text{ s.t. } (W_k, K_j) \in \mathcal{R}_{WK}} P(K_j) \tag{2}$$

In our example, when calculating $P(W_1)$ and $P(W_2)$ for *SQL Injection* and *Buffer Overflow*, respectively, we obtain $P(W_1) = 0.25 \cdot 0.75 = 0.1875$ and $P(W_2) = 0.75 \cdot 0.50 = 0.375$.

Finally, we determine the defender's utility U gained by deploying MTD techniques based on the reduced probability of exploit for each class of weaknesses. In this work, the utility is defined as a function of the probability $P(S_l)$ that an attacker can compromise a service S_l by exploiting any of the weaknesses leading to it. $P(S_l)$ can be computed as the probability of the union of non-mutually exclusive events, using the *Inclusion-Exclusion Principle* [4]. With respect to our running example, $P(S_1)$ can be computed as follows:

$$P(S_1) = P(W_1 \cup W_2) = P(W_1) + P(W_2) - P(W_1 \cap W_2) \tag{3}$$

As W_1 and W_2 are not necessarily independent (as shown in this example), we cannot assume $P(W_1 \cap W_2) = P(W_1) \cdot P(W_2)$. Instead, we must express each $P(W)$ in terms of its corresponding independent knowledge blocks K_j, that is $P(W_1) = P(K_1) \cdot P(K_2)$, $P(W_2) = P(K_2) \cdot P(K_3)$, and $P(W_1 \cap W_2) = P(K_1) \cdot P(K_2) \cdot P(K_3)$, and then express $P(S_1)$ as a function of probabilities $P(K_j)$:

$$P(S_1) = P(K_1) \cdot P(K_2) + P(K_2) \cdot P(K_3) - P(K_1) \cdot P(K_2) \cdot P(K_3)$$

which results in

$$P(S_1) = 0.25 \cdot 0.75 + 0.75 \cdot 0.5 - 0.25 \cdot 0.75 \cdot 0.5 = 0.469$$

For graphs with 3 or more weaknesses $\mathcal{W}^* \subseteq \mathcal{W}$, we can expand Eq. 3 to the generalized form of the *Inclusion-Exclusion Principle* [4]:

$$P\left(\bigcup_{W_k \in \mathcal{W}^*} W_k\right) = \sum_{i=1}^{|\mathcal{W}^*|} \left((-1)^{i-1} \cdot \sum_{\mathcal{W}' \in 2^{\mathcal{W}} \text{ s.t. } |\mathcal{W}'|=i} P\left(\bigcap_{W_j \in \mathcal{W}'} W_j\right)\right)$$

Computing the probability of the union of multiple events is an NP-hard problem that cannot be solved in better than $O(2^n)$ time [4]. However, the general nature of the weaknesses in layer 2 of the model limits their number – as opposed to vulnerabilities which may number in the thousands – keeping the computing time manageable.

After computing $P(S_l)$, we can easily compute the defender's utility as $U = 1 - P(S_l)$. Besides this simple approach, the utility could be a sigmoid function of $P(S_l)$ with an inflection point centered around a desired effectiveness.

Such functions are commonly used in autonomic computing [1]. The complete computation for each of the values in our example is shown in Fig. 2. Note that this choice of utility function relies upon the expectation that at least some measure of protection will be guaranteed for at least one knowledge block for each weakness, otherwise the attacker will be guaranteed to exploit that weakness and reduce the utility to 0. To handle this issue, utility can be defined as a function of the probabilities to exploit each weakness.

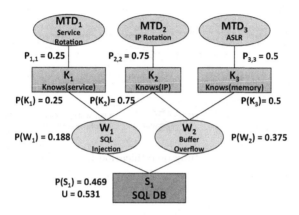

Fig. 2. Computing MTD effectiveness

5   Experimental Evaluation

We now present a more complex example to demonstrate the capabilities of our model. As seen in Fig. 3, we consider the same basic service but protect against two additional classes of weaknesses, OS Injection [5] and Eavesdropping (related to Information Disclosure from the STRIDE model [7]).

In this case study, more fine-grained knowledge blocks have been considered in order to provide more detail or to fit the specific MTDs selected for the case study. For example, knowledge block *Knows(memory)* has been broken down into separate blocks related to system call mapping, memory address, and stack direction. Similarly, SQL Injection now explicitly requires knowledge of keywords appended to SQL commands and some knowledge of the database schema, both of which are disrupted by SQLRand. Most importantly, we can now observe the many-to-many relationships between weaknesses, knowledge blocks, and MTDs, and conclude that finding the optimal solution is no longer trivial. However, using approximate yet reasonable values of $P_{i,j}$ for each MTD and cost constraints, we can determine the final utility as a function of selected MTDs using the steps previously shown and find an optimal solution using a problem solving method, such as stochastic hill climbing or evolutionary methods.

As a proof of concept, we can take the model in Fig. 3 and perform all the necessary computations programatically. As mentioned earlier, we are studying

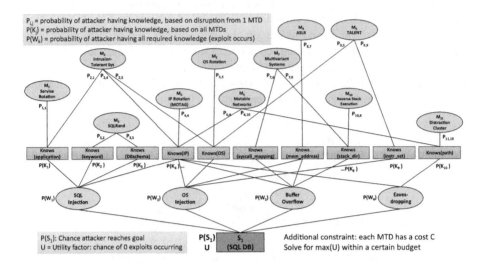

Fig. 3. Case study quantification framework

Table 1. Sample case study evaluation

MTD	$P_{i,j}$		Cost	Active?	$P_{i,j}$ (effective)	Cost (effective)
M_1 (Service Rotation)	$P_{1,1}$	0.500	15	No	1.000	0
M_2 (Intrusion Tolerant Systems)	$P_{2,1}$	0.900	25	No	1.000	0
	$P_{2,4}$	0.900			1.000	
	$P_{2,5}$	0.900			1.000	
M_3 (SQLRand)	$P_{3,2}$	0.300	20	No	1.000	0
	$P_{3,3}$	0.300			1.000	
M_4 (IP Rotation/MOTAG)	$P_{4,4}$	0.900	25	No	1.000	0
M_5 (OS Rotation)	$P_{5,5}$	0.700	15	No	1.000	0
M_6 (Mutable Networks)	$P_{6,4}$	0.500	20	Yes	0.500	20
	$P_{6,10}$	0.500			0.500	
M_7 (Multivariant Systems)	$P_{7,6}$	0.500	20	No	1.000	0
	$P_{7,8}$	0.500			1.000	
M_8 (ASLR)	$P_{8,7}$	0.500	10	Yes	0.500	10
M_9 (TALENT)	$P_{9,5}$	0.500	20	No	1.000	0
	$P_{9,9}$	0.500			1.000	
M_{10} (Reverse Stack Execution)	$P_{10,8}$	0.500	20	No	1.000	0
M_{11} (Distraction Cluster)	$P_{11,10}$	0.500	20	No	1.000	0

Knowledge:

Knows(application)	1.000
Knows(keyword)	1.000
Knows(DBschema)	1.000
Knows(IP)	0.500
Knows(OS)	1.000
Knows(syscall_mapping)	1.000
Knows(mem_address)	0.500
Knows(stack_dir)	1.000
Knows(instr_set)	1.000
Knows(path)	0.500

Chance of attack success:

SQL Injection	0.500
OS Injection	0.250
Buffer Overflow	0.250
Easvesdropping	0.250

Chance of attacker success:	0.500
Utility	**0.500**

Total Cost	30
Total Budget	120

Cost:	
High	25
Medium	15
Low	5

Effectiveness:	
High	0.3
Medium	0.5
Low	0.9

the relationship between cost and effectiveness of MTD techniques as part of another line of research. For the purpose of this paper and the evaluation we are presenting, we obtained qualitative values of $P_{i,j}$ and cost from an expert survey [6] which estimates the relative effectiveness and cost of several MTD techniques by grouping them into coarse-grained categories of Low, Medium, or High. Whether or not an MTD is active can be treated as a Boolean variable, with inactive MTDs implying an attacker's probability of success of 1 and a cost of 0. The values from a sample MTD setup are shown in Table 1. The interim calculations for the probabilities of each knowledge block being acquired and each weakness being able to be exploited are also shown.

6   Applications

In these section, we discuss two different applications of our framework.

6.1   Comparing MTDs

Given a set $\mathcal{M}$ of MTD techniques, we want to identify the one that provides the highest overall utility. With respect to the example of Fig. 3, we start from the baseline deployment, shown earlier in Table 1, including M_6 (Mutable Networks) and M_8 (ASLR) to ensure we have a utility value to compare with. We then measure the updated utility value after individually adding each of the other MTDs to our baseline deployment. From the results reported in Table 2, we find that M_3 (SQLRand) offers the greatest increase in utility, with M_1, M_2, and M_3 being the only ones offering any increase at all. To explain these results, we observe that there is a lower bound on $P(S_1)$ that translates into an upper bound on U, defined by $\max(P(W_1), P(W_2), P(W_3), P(W_4))$.

In other words, the overall defense can only be as strong as the protection against exploitation of its most vulnerable weakness, which in turn benefits from the deployment of multiple MTDs. Therefore, given the baseline conditions, only an MTD that affects the most vulnerable weakness will yield any improvement in our utility value. This procedure could be used iteratively in an attempt to find an optimal solution in a greedy manner, but there would have to be some way to handle cases where no MTD adds any utility (such as random selection).

Table 2. Improvement from adding MTDs

MTD	M_1 (Service Rotation)	M_2 (Intrusion Tolerant Systems)	M_3 (SQLRand)	All others
Utility	0.5625	0.513	0.614	0.5
Delta	0.0625	0.013	0.114	0.0

6.2 Selecting Optimal Defenses

Given a set $\mathcal{M}$ of MTDs and a budget, we would like to select the optimal set of MTDs that yield the highest utility with a total cost within the budget. As we now have a tool to evaluate the utility of any MTD deployment, we can also solve for the optimal selection of MTDs, given the constraints that the deployment of each MTD is a Boolean variable (either active or not) and that the sum of the costs of selected MTDs be under our budget. For the purpose of evaluating our framework and making the problem interesting, we selected a value of the budget (120) halfway between 0 and the total cost of deploying all available MTDs (i.e., 210). This choice ensured that a solution with utility greater than 0 would be found and that approximately half the MTDs would be chosen as part of the optimal solution. We solved using the *generalized reduced gradient non-linear algorithm* [11] with random restarts to eliminate finding local maxima. After solving, we obtain an optimal solution with the selected MTD highlighted with a thicker red outline in Fig. 4 and detailed results, including margins of error for our estimates of effectiveness, shown in Table 3.

We can observe that our choice of a utility function forces the selection of a variety of MTDs such that each weakness has at least one MTD affecting one of its knowledge blocks and that protection is evenly distributed over the 4 weaknesses. Visually, we can also observe that an MTD with the ability to affect multiple knowledge blocks is inherently more powerful than one that only affects one. However, if their cost is too high or effectiveness too low, it will still not be chosen as part of an optimal solution. Similarly, an MTD that only affects one knowledge block may be chosen if it is effective, low-cost, or affects a knowledge block that still receives relatively weak protection from other MTDs.

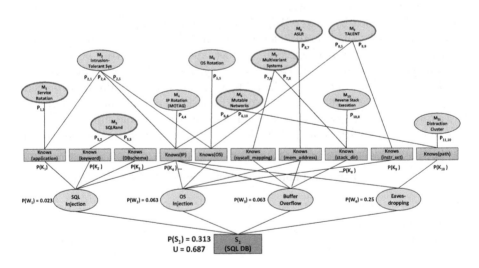

Fig. 4. Case study optimal configuration

Table 3. Case study optimal configuration

MTD	$P_{i,j}$		C	Active?	Pi,j (effective)	C (effective)
M_1 (Service Rotation)	$P_{1,1}$	0.500 ± 0.05	15	Yes	0.500 ± 0.05	15
M_2 (Intrusion Tolerant Systems)	$P_{2,1}$	0.900 ± 0.05	25	No	1.000	0
	$P_{2,4}$	0.900 ± 0.05			1.000	
	$P_{2,5}$	0.900 ± 0.05			1.000	
M_3 (SQLRand)	$P_{3,2}$	0.300 ± 0.05	20	Yes	0.300 ± 0.05	20
	$P_{3,3}$	0.300 ± 0.05			0.300 ± 0.05	
M_4 (IP Rotation/MOTAG)	$P_{4,4}$	0.900 ± 0.05	25	No	1.000	0
M_5 (OS Rotation)	$P_{5,5}$	0.700 ± 0.05	15	No	1.000	0
M_6 (Mutable Networks)	$P_{6,4}$	0.500 ± 0.05	20	Yes	0.500 ± 0.05	20
	$P_{6,10}$	0.500 ± 0.05			0.500 ± 0.05	
M_7 (Multivariant Systems)	$P_{7,6}$	0.500 ± 0.05	20	Yes	0.500 ± 0.05	20
	$P_{7,8}$	0.500 ± 0.05			0.500 ± 0.05	
M_8 (ASLR)	$P_{8,7}$	0.500 ± 0.05	10	Yes	0.500 ± 0.05	10
M_9 (TALENT)	$P_{9,5}$	0.500 ± 0.05	20	Yes	0.500 ± 0.05	20
	$P_{9,9}$	0.500 ± 0.05			0.500 ± 0.05	
M_{10} (Reverse Stack Execution)	$P_{10,8}$	0.500 ± 0.05	20	No	1.000	0
M_{11} (Distraction Cluster)	$P_{11,9}$	0.500 ± 0.05	20	No	1.000	0

Knowledge:

Knows (1,application)	0.500 ± 0.05
Knows (1,keyword)	0.300 ± 0.05
Knows (1,DBschema)	0.300 ± 0.05
Knows (1,IP)	0.500 ± 0.05
Knows (1,OS)	0.500 ± 0.05
Knows (1, syscall_mapping)	0.500 ± 0.05
Knows (1, Mem_Address)	0.500 ± 0.05
Knows (1,stack_dir)	0.500 ± 0.05
Knows (1,instr_set)	0.500 ± 0.05
Knows (1,path)	0.500 ± 0.05

Total Cost	105
Total Budget	120

Cost:	
High	25
Medium	15
Low	5

Effectiveness:	
High	0.3 ± 0.05
Medium	0.5 ± 0.05
Low	0.9 ± 0.05

Chance of attack success:

SQL Injection	0.023 ± 0.006
OS Injection	0.063 ± 0.013
Buffer Overflow	0.063 ± 0.013
Easvesdropping	0.250 ± 0.035

Chance of attacker success:	0.313 ± 0.043
Utility	**0.687 ± 0.043**

6.3 Extending the Framework

Our framework can accommodate any existing MTD as long as we can identify the knowledge blocks it affects, the extent to which it disrupts that knowledge, and how it relates to the weaknesses we plan to protect against. Another important feature of our framework is the ability to be extended to accommodate any future MTD that may be developed. A new MTD that affects existing knowledge blocks may be simply added to the MTD layer of the model, while an MTD that works in ways we have not yet considered might also require the addition of new knowledge blocks. Even a new class of weaknesses could be added to the model if the situation warrants it, making our model "future-proof" against new developments in cyber threats.

7 Conclusions and Future Work

In this paper, we have introduced a framework for quantifying moving target defenses. Our approach to quantifying the benefits of MTDs yields a single, probability-based utility measure that can accommodate any existing or future MTD, regardless of their nature. Our multi-layered approach captures the relationship between MTDs and the knowledge blocks they are designed to protect and the relationship between knowledge blocks and generic classes of weaknesses that can be exploited using that knowledge. We have shown through case studies that we can compute the joint effectiveness of multiple MTDs as a function of their individual effectiveness and, by doing so, we can make informed decisions about which MTD or set of MTDs provide better protection based on the security requirements or cost constraints.

Although the work presented in this paper represents a significant step towards effective MTD quantification, several limitations still exist and will be addressed as part of our planned future work. Specifically, limitations exist in the following areas: (i) **probability computation** – our methods for computing the probability $P_{i,j}$ of knowledge disruption provide rough estimates, so a procedure needs to be developed to accurately assess the effectiveness of any MTD; (ii) **cost modeling** – currently, we adopt a very simple notion of cost, and use cost just as an additional constraint, whereas a more sophisticated notion of cost could be introduced and taken into account in the computation of utility values; and (iii) **choice of utility function** – the proposed utility function is based on the assumption that all weaknesses need to be at least partially protected by MTDs to prevent the utility from dropping to 0, therefore, if the risk of leaving a specific weakness unprotected can be accepted, other classes of utility functions could be explored. To address these limitations and further refine our model, we plan to work on several aspects of the framework, as briefly described below.

Implementation and validation. To validate the model, we plan to deploy multiple MTDs on our computing infrastructure and then examine their effectiveness both in isolation – in order to determine the value of $P_{i,j}$ for each MTD – and jointly – in order to accurately study the combined cost and performance.

Application to multiple attack phases. Our model aims at disrupting an attacker's knowledge in the reconnaissance phase of the cyber kill chain. While this may be the most cost-effective way to approach cyber security, no defense is perfect, and we need to ensure multiple layers of defense. Some MTDs can disrupt an attacker's ability to maintain a foothold in the system, so we plan to extend our framework to model this additional class of MTDs.

Application to dependent services. Our framework currently models only independent services. Similar to attack graphs, an attacker may need to execute a sequence of exploits to reach a specific goal. Thus, we plan to extend our framework by introducing a meta-model that captures the relationships between services and the MTDs that can protect them from multi-step attacks.

Heuristics. Because of the $O(2^n)$ runtime to evaluate utility with the current model, it may be necessary to develop heuristics to speed up the evaluation in the case that the number of weaknesses grows to the point where using the model becomes infeasible.

Confidence intervals. Because of the level of uncertainty of our probabilistic values, we may not have a completely accurate utility value. With enough experimental samples, we could introduce confidence intervals into our assertion that a certain MTD or set of MTDs has a higher utility.

References

1. Alomari, F., Menascé, D.A.: An autonomic framework for integrating security and quality of service support in databases. In: Proceedings of the 6th International Conference on Software Security and Reliability (SERE 2012), Gaithersburg, MD, USA, pp. 51–60, June 2012
2. Boyd, S.W., Keromytis, A.D.: SQLrand: preventing SQL injection attacks. In: Jakobsson, M., Yung, M., Zhou, J. (eds.) ACNS 2004. LNCS, vol. 3089, pp. 292–302. Springer, Heidelberg (2004). doi:10.1007/978-3-540-24852-1_21
3. Carroll, T.E., Crouse, M., Fulp, E.W., Berenhaut, K.S.: Analysis of network address shuffling as a moving target defense. In: IEEE International Conference on Communications (ICC 2014), Sydney, Australia, pp. 701–706, June 2014
4. Chen, S.G.: Reduced recursive inclusion-exclusion principle for the probability of union events. In: Proceedings of the IEEE International Conference on Industrial Engineering and Engineering Management (IEEM 2014), Malaysia, pp. 11–13, December 2014
5. Christey, S.: 2011 CWE/SANS top. 25 most dangerous software errors (2011). http://cwe.mitre.org/top.25/
6. Farris, K.A., Cybenko, G.: Quantification of moving target cyber defenses. In: Proceedings of SPIE Defense + Security 2015, Baltimore, MD, USA, April 2015
7. Howard, M., LeBlanc, D.: Writing Secure Code. Microsoft Press, Redmond (2002)
8. Jafarian, J.H., Qi Duan, E.A.S.: Spatio-temporal address mutation for proactive cyber agility against sophisticated attackers. In: Proceedings of the 1st ACM Workshop on Moving Target Defense (MTD 2014), Scottsdale, AZ, USA, pp. 69–78. ACM (2014)
9. Jajodia, S., Ghosh, A.K., Swarup, V., Wang, C., Wang, X.S. (eds.): Moving Target Defense: Creating Asymmetric Uncertainty for Cyber Threats, Advances in Information Security, 1st edn., vol. 54. Springer, New York (2011)
10. Jajodia, S., Noel, S., O'Berry, B.: Topological analysis of network attack vulnerability. In: Kumar, V., Srivastava, J., Lazarevic, A. (eds.) Managing Cyber Threats: Issues, Approaches, and Challenges, Massive Computing, vol. 5, pp. 247–266. Springer, USA (2005)
11. Lasdon, L.S., Fox, R.L., Ratner, M.W.: Nonlinear optimization using the generalized reduced gradient method. Revue française d'automatique, d'informatique et de recherche opérationnelle. Recherche opérationnelle 8(3), 73–103 (1974)
12. Okhravi, H., Rabe, M.A., Mayberry, T.J., Leonard, W.G., Hobson, T.R., Bigelow, D., Streilein, W.W.: Survey of cyber moving targets. Technical report 1166, MIT Lincoln Laboratory, Lexington. MA, USA, September 2013
13. Shacham, H., Page, M., Pfaff, B., Go, E.J., Modadugu, N., Boneh, D.: On the effectiveness of address-space randomization. In: Proceedings of the 11th ACM Conference on Computer and Communications Security (CCS 2004), Washington DC, USA, pp. 298–307. ACM, October 2004
14. Soule, N., Simidchieva, B., Yaman, F., Watro, R., Loyall, J., Atighetchi, M., Carvalho, M., Last, D., Myers, D., Flatley, B.: Quantifying minimizing attack surfaces containing moving target defenses. In: Proceedings of the Resilience Week (RWS 2015), August 2015

15. Wang, L., Islam, T., Long, T., Singhal, A., Jajodia, S.: An attack graph-based probabilistic security metric. In: Atluri, V. (ed.) DBSec 2008. LNCS, vol. 5094, pp. 283–296. Springer, Heidelberg (2008). doi:10.1007/978-3-540-70567-3_22
16. Zaffarano, K., Taylor, J., Hamilton, S.: A quantitative framework for moving target defense effectiveness evaluation. In: Proceedings of the 2nd ACM Workshop on Moving Target Defense (MTD 2015), Denver, CO, USA, pp. 3–10. ACM, October 2015

Private Queries and Aggregations

Query Privacy in Sensing-as-a-Service Platforms

Ruben Rios[✉], David Nuñez, and Javier Lopez

Network, Information and Computer Security (NICS) Lab,
Computer Science Department, University of Málaga, Málaga, Spain
{ruben,dnunez,jlm}@lcc.uma.es

Abstract. The Internet of Things (IoT) promises to revolutionize the
way we interact with the physical world. Even though this paradigm is
still far from being completely realized, there already exist Sensing-as-a-
Service (S^2aaS) platforms that allow users to query for IoT data. While
this model offers tremendous benefits, it also entails increasingly challenging privacy issues. In this paper, we concentrate on the protection of
user privacy when querying sensing devices through a semi-trusted S^2aaS
platform. In particular, we build on techniques inspired by proxy re-
encryption and k-anonymity to tackle two intertwined problems, namely
query privacy and query confidentiality. The feasibility of our solution is
validated both analytically and empirically.

1 Introduction

The interconnection of computational and sensing devices to the Internet is
expected to transform every single aspect of our lives. This novel paradigm,
already known as the Internet of Things (IoT) [16], brings about a whole set
of innovative services and Sensing-as-a-Service (S^2aaS) [22,23] platforms play a
fundamental role as they allow querying IoT devices. In this model, the sensing devices deployed by companies, administrations or citizens can be queried
through a sensing server, which acts as gateway, as shown in Fig. 1. This model
is already a reality and there are some companies, like Amazon (cf., AWS IoT
platform [1]), which are offering the infrastructure necessary for delivering these
sort of services.

While this model offers great opportunities to both industry and citizens, it
also poses serious privacy risks. In particular, there is the possibility of exposing
user interests to honest-but-curious sensing servers since they act as intermedi-
aries for the sensing devices. Therefore, it is paramount to provide the users of
these platforms with mechanisms that allow them to remain unlinkable from the
sensing devices they are interested in querying. This is precisely the main objective of this paper, to provide a solution to query privacy in Sensing-as-a-Service
scenarios where the access to the readings of sensing devices is managed by a
semi-honest sensing server, which may be interested in profiling the users of the
platform.

© IFIP International Federation for Information Processing 2017
Published by Springer International Publishing AG 2017. All Rights Reserved
S. De Capitani di Vimercati and F. Martinelli (Eds.): SEC 2017, IFIP AICT 502, pp. 141–154, 2017.
DOI: 10.1007/978-3-319-58469-0_10

Fig. 1. Sensing-as-a-Service platform

One may think that such a solution can be achieved with traditional public key cryptography but there are some notable limitations to this approach. First, the user needs to be aware of the public key of every single sensing device, which raises evident usability and scalability issues. Moreover, it is necessary for the user to check the status of the public keys, such as whether or not they have been revoked. Moreover, if a query is intended for multiple (or all) sensing nodes, the user has to query the sensors individually. This not only implies more energy and bandwidth waste but it is also highly advisable to hide these issues from the user, so as to facilitate the development and adoption of S^2aaS platforms.

The main contribution of this paper is the QPSP (Query Privacy for Sensing Platforms) protocol. The proposed protocol is based on proxy re-encryption and k-anonymity techniques to provide both query confidentiality (i.e., hiding the query itself and the sensed data) and query privacy (i.e., hiding the nodes replying to the queries) in semi-trusted S^2aaS platforms. The proposed scheme is, to the best of our knowledge, the first solution to exploit these notions to protect query privacy issues in sensing scenarios.

This rest of this paper is organized as follows. Section 2 analyzes previous papers describing query privacy solutions in related domains. Next, in Sect. 3 we provide a detailed description of the problem addressed by the QPSP protocol and identify some general assumptions that are applicable to the rest of the paper. The various phases of the QPSP protocol are described in Sect. 4 and its privacy guarantees are analyzed in Sect. 5. In addition, we experimentally evaluate the feasibility of our solution with current sensing devices in Sect. 6. Finally, Sect. 7 presents the conclusions of the paper and outlines some potential lines of future research.

2   Related Work

Most of the research in query privacy has been done in the area of Wireless Sensor Networks. Although this problem can be trivially solved by making all sensor nodes reply to every query, it also imposes severe energy requirements on the sensor nodes. Consequently, some authors have striven to find the right balance between privacy protection and energy consumption. The authors in [13] propose reducing the amount of traffic generated by using data-aggregation. This solution is only suitable for a particular type of query. A more general approach is presented in [7], where the authors propose transmitting bogus queries to the network to hide the destination of real queries. Instead of sending bogus queries, the authors in [12] propose hiding the recipient of the queries by sending them on a particular path of nodes that contains the actual destination. Unfortunately, the user needs to define the path, which is impractical for large-scale sensor networks.

A completely different approach is to unlink the original data source from the current location of the data, which is mostly achieved by having two types of nodes: sensing and storage nodes. The authors in [14] propose having several data replicas so that user queries are forwarded to a number of random points with the hope that the query arrives at some of them. PriSecTopK [19] concentrates on enabling top-k querying with the help of order-preserving encryption. A major limitation of this scheme is the need for shared secrets between the user and each sensing node. In addition, some papers [8,24] have considered the problem of privacy-preserving range queries. Basically, the idea behind these schemes is to transform data and queries into special codes that can be processed by storage nodes without leaking information in the case they are compromised. All these solutions restrict the user to a particular type of query.

Finally, some effort has been made to protect query privacy in urban sensing scenarios. The approach followed in [11] is again based on data replication and storage devices. Their scheme is complemented with bogus replies to hide the data sources. A noteworthy difference with respect to our work is the adversarial model, which is an external attacker located at the edge of the network.

3 Problem Definition

This section deals with the definition of the problem. First, we present a general description of the system and then we illustrate the capabilities of the adversarial model. This section introduces the main assumptions applicable to the rest of the paper.

3.1 System Model

The system we are aiming for is composed of a substantial number of sensing devices which can be queried through a sensing server. Without loss of generality, we assume that the sensing devices are organized into clusters, where one node acts as the head or leader of each cluster. However, it is also reasonable to assume a more general model where the sensing server provides access to several sensing networks, like the one depicted in Fig. 2, which is a typical configuration in fully-fledged IoT scenarios. Note that the secure selection of cluster heads is beyond the scope of this paper and the interested reader is referred to [21] for a survey.

Moreover, there are at least $n > 1$ cluster heads in the sensing network. The cluster heads are considered to be able to communicate with one another and also with the sensing server. In the more general model, the cluster heads of each of the sensing networks are also necessarily interconnected. In either case, the communication with other cluster heads can be done directly through the

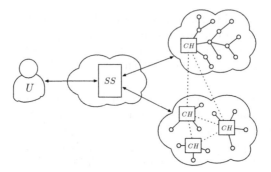

Fig. 2. General system model

Internet or by using the routing information available to them after the execution of a secure clustering protocol. The routing information also allows the cluster heads to determine how to reach any sensing device in the network.

Finally, we focus on a scenario where the readings of the sensing devices are publicly available to anyone willing to access them. This is, for example, the case of a Smart City [9]. Another important assumption is that the sensing devices, including the cluster heads, are owned and managed by an entity (e.g., the city council) other than the one that governs the access to the readings of the devices, namely the sensing server (e.g., Amazon). Moreover, the two entities are considered not to collude against the users.

3.2 Adversarial Model

The adversarial model considered in this paper is *semi-honest* (or honest-but-curious), which means that the adversary is assumed to follow the protocol but may try to benefit from a privileged role in the system to obtain information beyond what is permitted. More precisely, the adversary is interested in learning information about the interests of a particular user based on the queries he/she issues and the nodes responding to them.

We assume that the sensing server is a semi-honest adversary which has the following capabilities:

- **Content analysis:** inspects any packet it receives in order to retrieve sensitive information. The analysis is not limited to the payload of the packets but may also include the packet headers. Thus, the adversary may learn the query contents, the sensed data and the identities of the parties involved in the communication.
- **Statistical analysis:** analyzes the features of the communication flow including the distribution of messages, the time at which messages are delivered or received, the transmission rate, and so on. The goal of this type of attack is to discover patterns in the transmissions in order to infer sensitive information.

The hearing range of the adversary is also an important aspect to consider when dealing with traffic analysis attacks. Typically, a semi-honest adversary is internal and limits its actions to the traffic addressed to it or traversing it. Nonetheless, in this paper we assume a more powerful adversary, which is allowed to extend its hearing range to the sensing network. The attacker is allowed to collude with external entities located in the vicinity of the sensing devices.

Moreover, we consider that a semi-honest sensing server can try to cheat by slightly modifying its behavior as long as it does not deviate from the protocol specification. For example, the adversary can craft random numbers at will instead of using a pseudo-random number generator for that purpose. The adversary can benefit from vague protocol specifications or randomly defined operations.

4   Query Privacy for Sensing Platforms Protocol

This section provides a detailed description of the QPSP protocol. First, we present a brief overview of the protocol and then continue with the explanation of each of the phases involved in it. Prior to that, we introduce some cryptographic background.

4.1   Overview

The QPSP protocol consists of three phases: initialization, query, and response. During the initialization a *global public key*, denoted by pk_P, is generated by the cluster heads in a distributed way. This global public key corresponds to the sensing network as a whole and no single entity controls the corresponding decryption key in order to reduce the possibility of key compromise. This phase also deals with the generation of the corresponding re-encryption keys.

The global public key pk_P is used to encrypt the queries sent to the sensing server, which transforms them using techniques from proxy re-encryption into new, encrypted queries that can be decrypted by the cluster heads only. This is done using special keys called *re-encryption keys*. During this process, the content of the query remains unaltered and cannot be obtained by the sensing server. Once the query has been decrypted by a cluster head, it is forwarded to the appropriate sensing device without disclosing its identity to the gateway.

The response phase is simpler. The confidentiality of the response is secured from the user end by incorporating a fresh key into the query to be used to encrypt the content of the response. From an abstract point of view, the communications are basically a two-message exchange between a user and a sensing device but some traffic obfuscation mechanisms are introduced to prevent leaking information.

4.2   Preliminaries

This section introduces some cryptographic notions that will be used during the definition of the QPSP protocol. Due to space limitations we do not go into details.

Bilinear Pairings. Let $\mathbb{G}_1, \mathbb{G}_2$ and $\mathbb{G}_T$ be cyclic groups of prime order q. A bilinear pairing is a map $e : \mathbb{G}_1 \times \mathbb{G}_2 \to \mathbb{G}_T$ satisfying the properties of bilinearity, non-degeneracy, and computability (see [17] for more details). Depending on the characteristics of the groups involved, there are essentially three types of pairings, namely Type-1, Type-2 and Type-3. In this paper we use Type-3 pairings as they achieve the best trade-off between security and efficiency [15].

Proxy Re-encryption. From a high-level viewpoint, proxy re-encryption is a type of public-key encryption that enables a proxy to transform ciphertexts under Alice's public key into ciphertexts decryptable by Bob's secret key. In order to do this, the proxy is given a re-encryption key, generated by Alice, which makes this process possible. There are multiple proxy re-encryption proposals in the literature, the most prominent are those of Blaze et al. [6] and Ateniese et al. [4].

4.3 Initialization Phase

In this phase, the sensing platform sets up the necessary public parameters and cryptographic keys. As mentioned, we describe a distributed key generation procedure, principally performed by the cluster heads. Finally, we also present a key validation procedure in order to guarantee the correctness and validity of the key generation process.

Setup. Let $e : \mathbb{G}_1 \times \mathbb{G}_2 \to \mathbb{G}_T$ be a Type-3 pairing, and g and h generators of $\mathbb{G}_1$ and $\mathbb{G}_2$, respectively. Let Z be the result of computing $e(g, h)$. The public parameters of the system are the elements of the tuple (e, g, h, Z).

Key Generation. The main goal of this procedure is to create the global public key for the sensor domain, denoted by pk_P, with no associated private key. In parallel, it is also necessary to create re-encryption keys that enable the transformation of ciphertexts between the global public key and the cluster heads' public key.

First, each cluster head CH_i generates a key pair $(pk_i, sk_i) = (h^{x_i}, x_i)$, where x_i is sampled uniformly at random from $\mathbb{Z}_q$. The cluster heads distribute their public keys among the rest, so we can assume that after this step, the cluster heads knows each others' public key. Next, each cluster head independently generates a temporal secret value p_i sampled uniformly at random from $\mathbb{Z}_q$, and computes the values $u_i = Z^{p_i}$ and $v_{ij} = (pk_j)^{p_i} = h^{p_i x_j}$, for all $j \in \{1, ..., N\}$. Finally, it sends $(u_i, \{v_{ij}\})$ to the sensing server for aggregation.

Once the sensing server has received the inputs from all the cluster heads, it computes the global public key and corresponding re-encryption keys as follows:

$$pk_P = \prod_{i=1}^{N} u_i = \prod_{i=1}^{N} Z^{p_i} = Z^{p_1 + ... + p_N} = Z^p \tag{1}$$

$$rk_{P \to i} = \prod_{j=1}^{N} v_{ji} = \prod_{j=1}^{N} h^{x_i p_j} = h^{x_i (p_1 + \ldots + p_N)} = h^{x_i p} \qquad (2)$$

Note that this procedure guarantees that the secret $p = p_1 + \ldots + p_N$ (which is the private key associated with the global public key) is never computed explicitly and that it cannot be recovered efficiently, by the Discrete Logarithm hardness assumption.

Key Validation. Given that the sensing server aggregates the inputs from all the cluster heads in order to create the global public key and the associated re-encryption keys, it is possible (although not sensible) that it misbehaves during the aggregation process, for example, by discarding the input and publishing an alternative global public key for which it controls the corresponding decryption key. Recall that the goal of the distributed key generation process is to create a global public key with no associated private key.

In Appendix A.1 we describe a procedure for key validation, in which the cluster heads interact with each other and the sensing server. The existence of such a procedure acts as a deterrent to possible misbehavior from the sensing server, since it represents an efficient mechanism to detect any deviation from the agreed key generation process. Therefore, we can assume that the sensing server does not misbehave during key generation.

4.4   Query Phase

This phase comprises the first direction of the communication, which is from user to cluster head, via the sensing server (as shown in Fig. 3). It comprises two messages: the first between user and sensing server, and the second between sensing server and the cluster head.

Message 1 (Encryption). The first message of the protocol is constructed on the user side, and is delivered to the sensing server. The idea is that the user encrypts the query with the global public key pk_P, and the encrypted query is later re-encrypted to a cluster head of the sensing platform.

The encryption scheme[1] we propose is based on Ateniese et al.'s proxy re-encryption scheme [4], which is proven IND-CPA secure. Let us suppose that the input to be encrypted is represented by an element $m \in \mathbb{G}_T$. The user samples random $r \in \mathbb{Z}_q$ and produces the ciphertext $CT = (CT_1, CT_2)$ as follows:

$$\mathsf{Enc}_P(m) = (g^r, m \cdot (pk_P)^r) = (g^r, m \cdot Z^{pr})$$

---

[1] In practice, the proposed scheme would be used to encrypt a fresh random key, which in turn will be used to encrypt the actual message with a symmetric encryption algorithm, following a hybrid encryption approach. For simplicity in the description, we will obviate this.

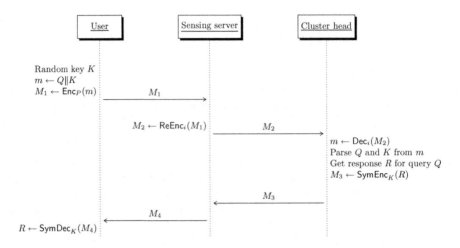

Fig. 3. Main part of the QPSP protocol

An important point when it comes to defining the actual protocol messages is that the initiator (i.e., the user) does not need to own any kind of key (either symmetric or asymmetric) to query the responder (i.e., a sensing device); that is, the initiator is unauthenticated. To the contrary, the responder has a public key, in this case, a global public key for the sensing platform. Therefore, the initiator can use this public key as a means to set up a secure channel for the response, by encrypting a fresh random key K with the public key of the sensing platform (as with the query Q). This is reminiscent of the one-pass key transport technique described in [20, Sect. 12.5.1]. Therefore, the first message of the protocol, which is named M_1 and generated by the user, is basically the encryption of the query Q and a fresh random key K to be used for securing the response, as shown in Fig. 3.

Message 2 (Re-encryption). Message M_1 is received by the sensing server, which transforms it into a ciphertext, decryptable by one of the cluster heads. Since, in principle, the encrypted query does not convey any metadata, the sensing server simply chooses some arbitrary cluster head (either at random or following some network delivery criteria). Therefore, the server is basically a blind gateway between the users and the sensing network.

Let us suppose that the sensing server chooses cluster head CH_i then, the corresponding re-encryption key is $rk_{P \to i} = h^{x_i p}$. The sensing server transforms the original ciphertext CT into a new ciphertext CT' intended for CH_i as follows:

$$\mathsf{ReEnc}_i(CT) = (e(CT_1, rk_{P \to i}), CT_2) = (Z^{pr x_i}, m \cdot Z^{pr})$$

The final message M_2 is simply the re-encrypted ciphertext.

4.5   Response Phase

This phase includes the decryption and delivery of the query to the actual recipient as well as the response to the user.

Message 3 (Decryption). The cluster head CH_i receives message M_2, containing ciphertext $CT' = (CT'_1, CT'_2)$ and decrypts it using its own secret key as follows:

$$\mathsf{Dec}_i(CT') = CT'_2 \cdot (CT'_1)^{-1/sk_i} = m \cdot Z^{pr} \cdot (Z^{pr x_i})^{-1/x_i} = m$$

The resulting output m is parsed as the original query Q and a response key K. Next, the cluster must deliver m to the actual destination but as this process is subject to traffic analysis we propose a transmission mechanism inspired by the notion of k-anonymity.

All cluster heads use a *deterministic mapping function* to choose k destinations. This function is such that it receives one identifier as input and always returns the set of k identifiers, which include the original one. Therefore, CH_i can either forward the actual query (encrypted under a shared key) to the k sensing devices output by the mapping function or simply send bogus queries to the $k-1$ cover destinations. In either case, the cluster heads must share secrets to encrypt the message and thus prevent content analysis attacks.

After reaching the k sensing devices, all of them must behave in the same way. As a result, devices receiving a (cover) query must reply to it, possibly with bogus or synthetic data. Finally, the results collected by the corresponding cluster heads are relayed to the cluster head who originally received the query, which filters out cover messages and selects the true response R. Finally, the cluster head encrypts it using the key K to produce message M_3; alternatively, the sensing device itself can encrypt the response, provided the cluster head sends the key K together with the query. Finally, message M_3 is delivered to the sensing server, which simply forwards it to the user.

Message 4 (Delivery of Response). The user receives message M_4 from the sensing server, and decrypts it using the key K in order to retrieve the response to his original query.

5   Security Analysis

The analysis presented in this section concentrates on the two security properties the QPSP protocol aims to protect, namely query confidentiality and query privacy.

5.1   Query Confidentiality

The encryption scheme we use for protecting queries from the user to the cluster heads is essentially a restricted version of Ateniese et al.'s proxy re-encryption scheme [4], adapted to a Type-3 pairing setting. This encryption scheme satisfies the security notion of indistinguishability against chosen-plaintext attacks (IND-CPA), under the External Diffie-Hellman assumption (XDH) [5]. For reasons of space, we omit the full security proof, but the rough idea is as follows.

Assuming that there is an adversary $\mathcal{B}$ that wins the IND-CPA security game, it is possible to construct an algorithm $\mathcal{A}$ that uses $\mathcal{B}$ to solve the XDH problem (which is essentially the DDH problem in $\mathbb{G}_1$ but in a pairing setting). Adversary $\mathcal{A}$ receives a DDH tuple $(g, g^a, g^b, g^c) \in \mathbb{G}_1^4$, and is asked to decide whether $c = a \cdot b$. In order to decide, it simulates the environment for the adversary $\mathcal{B}$ by taking element g^a for generating the global public key $pk_P^* = e(g^a, h) = Z^a$, and elements g^b and g^c for generating the challenge ciphertext $CT^* = (g^b, m_\delta \cdot e(g^c, h)) = (g^b, m_\delta \cdot Z^c)$. It can be seen that when $c = a \cdot b$, the challenge ciphertext is a valid encryption of m_δ under pk_P^*, and $\mathcal{B}$ guesses δ correctly with non-negligible advantage. When the guess is correct, adversary $\mathcal{A}$ outputs $c = a \cdot b$, which solves the DDH problem in $\mathbb{G}_1$ with the non-negligible advantage. To the contrary, when c is random, $\mathcal{B}$ does not have any advantage in guessing δ, and hence, neither does $\mathcal{A}$. Overall, it can be seen that $\mathcal{A}$ still solves the XDH problem with non-negligible advantage.

5.2   Query Privacy

We have just shown that the sensing server cannot obtain information from content analysis but may still perform statistical analysis. Next we show that even when the sensing server does not strictly follow the protocol specification, it learns nothing.

First, let us assume a single protocol run. After a single query, the sensing server may learn, with the help of external colluders, that the user has queried one of the k nodes responding to the query. Note that if k is sufficiently large, query privacy is ensured as long as the mapping function has been designed taking into account the properties of l-diversity and t-closeness [18]. In the case that the mapping does not respect these notions, the attacker may not know which particular device replied to the query but still learn that the user is interested in, for instance, radiation levels. We assume that this is dependent on the scenario and thus beyond the scope of this paper.

Let us now assume that the user is repeatedly issuing queries. If the queries are addressed to different sensing devices, the analysis is similar to the single execution case. However, if the user is regularly querying a particular device and the sensing server is aware of this, the adversary is incapable of determining which of the elements in the anonymity set is the actual recipient. Even if the sensing server tries to cheat by choosing the cluster heads at will, it is still unable to reduce the size of the anonymity set because all cluster heads use the same mapping function.

The sensing server's last resort is to craft its own queries and submit them to the sensing network. This is possible since we are considering a public sensing network. However, there is no incentive for it to do so since the only thing the attacker will learn is the mapping function for a particular node, which is not secret, and the data sensed by the node. These data are not sensitive since they are obtained from a query issued by the sensing server and not by a particular user. Thus, the interests of the user are not revealed.

Finally, recall that the sensing server and the sensing devices are supposed not to collaborate. This is because the former knows the identity of the user and the latter is aware of the nodes of interest to the user. To reduce the risk of privacy exposure, the identity of the user can be further protected with the help of an anonymity network, such as Crowds or Tor.

6 Experimental Evaluation

In order to experimentally evaluate the overhead of the cryptographic operations in our proposal, we implemented a proof of concept in C using the Apache Milagro Crypto Library [2]. Since we defined the cryptographic scheme over a Type-3 pairing setting, it was necessary to use an elliptic curve that supports this. We selected a 256-bit Barreto-Naehrig (BN) curve, which is suitable for said pairings and offers a good trade-off with respect to security and performance [3].

We used three different execution platforms, in order to simulate the characteristics of the entities involved in the potential use cases. For the user and sensing server, we used a laptop with an Intel Core 2 Duo processor @ 2.66 GHz and 8 GB of RAM. For the cluster heads, we performed our tests in two different platforms: a Raspberry Pi Gen 1 Model B (SoC Broadcom BCM2835, 32-bit, single core, 700 Mhz, 512 MB), and an Intel Galileo Gen 1 (SoC Intel Quark X1000 32-bit, single core, single-thread, P54C/i586 400 Mhz, 256 MB).

Table 1. Performance of the cryptographic operations for different execution platforms

Entity	Platform	Operation	Cost (ms)
User	Laptop	Encryption	7.58
Sensing server	Laptop	Re-Encryption	11.55
Cluster head	Raspberry Pi	Decryption	46.20
Cluster head	Intel Galileo	Decryption	122.20

Table 1 shows the results of our experiments, categorized by the type of operation, entity and execution platform. Both encryption and re-encryption of queries are tested on a PC-like platform, while decryption is done in a sensor-like device. Experiments were executed 100 times and the average value was taken. It can be seen that the results are of the order of 10 ms in the user- and server-side, while they range between 46 and 122 ms on the side of the cluster head, depending on the execution platform. Further optimizations include the pre-computation of pairings for re-encryption, given that re-encryption keys are fixed arguments to pairings. In this regard there are several techniques, such as [10] which reports a speed-up around 30%. It is also possible to study different curves in order to find the more efficient ones on the side of the cluster head, that is, curves that minimize the cost associated with exponentiations on $\mathbb{G}_T$.

7   Conclusions

This paper has presented the QPSP protocol. The proposed solution prevents users from being profiled by semi-trusted Sensing-as-a-Service platforms. This is achieved with the help of proxy re-encryption primitives and traffic obfuscation at the sensing network. More precisely, the user sends queries to the platform encrypted with a global public key generated by a set of cluster heads, the query is then re-encrypted by the sensing server and forwarded to one of the cluster heads, which is responsible for transmitting the query to the final destination using a privacy-preserving routing protocol.

The proposed solution is intended for Sensing-as-a-Service platforms where the data collected by the sensing devices are public and therefore anyone can query the network. We are planning to extend our solution to a scenario where the access needs to be both authenticated and respectful of privacy. Moreover, we are exploring network management issues such as the revocation of nodes and how to deal with the addition of new cluster heads once the network has been deployed.

Acknowledgements. This paper has been partially supported by the Junta de Andalucía through the project FISICCO (P11-TIC-07223) and the Spanish Ministry of Economy and Competitiveness through the PERSIST (TIN2013-41739-R) and SMOG (TIN2016-79095-C2-1-R) projects.

A   Appendix

A.1   Key Validation Procedure

The validation process has to check three requirements: (i) that the global public key is the result of aggregating the inputs from all the cluster heads, (ii) the re-encryption keys are also generated by aggregation, and (iii) the re-encryption keys are correctly associated with the global public key (i.e., they allow the transformation of ciphertexts from the global public key to the cluster heads' keys).

Validation requirement (i) can be checked simply by engaging all the cluster heads in an incremental ring-style protocol, where each of them receives an intermediate value and multiplies it by its input u_i for the public key; hence, at the end of the protocol, the global public key (which we assume is published by the system and known by all the cluster heads) should be obtained. As long as no cluster head is corrupted, this requirement can be correctly checked.

Validation requirements (ii) and (iii) involve re-encryption keys. A complication here is that, although the global public key is, indeed, public, re-encryption keys may not be (and possible should not be) public[2]. However, it is possible for each cluster head to challenge the service provider and to test if the response corresponds to a valid re-encryption key as follows. Each cluster head CH_i computes a random challenge value g^k, and sends it to the sensing server, which responds with the value $e(g^k, rk_{P \to i})$. Now the cluster head checks whether the following equation holds:

$$e(g^k, rk_{P \to i}) = (pk_P)^{x_i k}$$

It can be seen that, given $rk_{P \to i} = h^{x_i p}$ and $pk_P = Z^p$, the correct response from the service provider will be $Z^{x_i k p}$, which is indeed equal to $(pk_P)^{x_i k}$. Therefore, each cluster head can independently check requirements (ii) and (iii) and report to the others in the case there is a problem. Since, the correctness of the global public key has been checked before, and this public key is used during the validation of the re-encryption keys, it can be safely accepted that all the keys are correct.

References

1. Amazon Web Services: How the AWS IoT Platform Works. https://aws.amazon.com/iot/how-it-works/. Accessed Nov 2016
2. Milagro, A.: Apache Milagro Crypto Library. https://milagro.apache.org/
3. Aranha, D.F., Barreto, P.S.L.M., Longa, P., Ricardini, J.E.: The realm of the pairings. In: Lange, T., Lauter, K., Lisoněk, P. (eds.) SAC 2013. LNCS, vol. 8282, pp. 3–25. Springer, Heidelberg (2014). doi:10.1007/978-3-662-43414-7_1
4. Ateniese, G., Fu, K., Green, M., Hohenberger, S.: Improved proxy re-encryption schemes with applications to secure distributed storage. ACM Trans. Inform. Syst. Secur. 9(1), 1–30 (2006)
5. Ateniese, G., Camenisch, J., De Medeiros, B.: Untraceable RFID tags via insubvertible encryption. In: Proceedings of the 12th ACM Conference on Computer and Communications Security, pp. 92–101. ACM (2005)
6. Blaze, M., Bleumer, G., Strauss, M.: Divertible protocols and atomic proxy cryptography. In: Nyberg, K. (ed.) EUROCRYPT 1998. LNCS, vol. 1403, pp. 127–144. Springer, Heidelberg (1998). doi:10.1007/BFb0054122
7. Carbunar, B., Yang, Y., Shi, W., Pearce, M., Vasudevan, V.: Query privacy in wireless sensor networks. ACM Trans. Sen. Netw. 6(2), 14:1–14:34 (2010)
8. Chen, F., Liu, A.X.: Privacy- and integrity-preserving range queries in sensor networks. IEEE/ACM Trans. Networking 20(6), 1774–1787 (2012)
9. Cocchia, A.: Smart and digital city: a systematic literature review. In: Dameri, R.P., Rosenthal-Sabroux, C. (eds.) Smart City, pp. 13–43. Springer, Cham (2014). doi:10.1007/978-3-319-06160-3_2

---

[2] In the proxy re-encryption literature, knowledge of a re-encryption key and the corresponding recipient's private key can be used in some cases to derive the original private key. This is known as a "collusion attack" [4].

10. Costello, C., Stebila, D.: Fixed Argument Pairings. In: Abdalla, M., Barreto, P.S.L.M. (eds.) LATINCRYPT 2010. LNCS, vol. 6212, pp. 92–108. Springer, Heidelberg (2010). doi:10.1007/978-3-642-14712-8_6

11. De Cristofaro, E., Di Pietro, R.: Adversaries and countermeasures in privacy-enhanced urban sensing systems. IEEE Syst. J. **7**(2), 311–322 (2013)

12. De Cristofaro, E., Ding, X., Tsudik, G.: Privacy-preserving querying in sensor networks. In: 18th International Conference on Computer Communications and Networks, ICCCN 2009, San Francisco, CA, 3–6 August 2009, pp. 1–6. IEEE Computer Society, Washington, DC (2009)

13. Di Pietro, R., Viejo, A.: Location privacy and resilience in wireless sensor networks querying. Comput. Commun. **34**(3), 515–523 (2011)

14. Dimitriou, T., Sabouri, A.: Privacy preservation schemes for querying wireless sensor networks. In: IEEE International Conference on Pervasive Computing and Communications Workshops, pp. 178–183 (2011)

15. Galbraith, S.D., Paterson, K.G., Smart, N.P.: Pairings for cryptographers. Discrete Appl. Math. **156**(16), 3113–3121 (2008)

16. Gubbi, J., Buyya, R., Marusic, S., Palaniswami, M.: Internet of Things (IoT): A vision, architectural elements, and future directions. Future Gener. Comput. Syst. **29**(7), 1645–1660 (2013)

17. Kiraz, M.S., Uzunkol, O.: Still wrong use of pairings in cryptography. Cryptology ePrint Archive, Report 2016/223 (2016). http://eprint.iacr.org/

18. Li, N., Li, T., Venkatasubramanian, S.: t-closeness: Privacy beyond k-anonymity and l-diversity. In: IEEE 23rd International Conference on Data Engineering, ICDE 2007, pp. 106–115, April 2007

19. Liao, X., Li, J.: Privacy-preserving and secure top-k query in two-tier wireless sensor network. In: 2012 IEEE Global Communications Conference (GLOBECOM), pp. 335–341, December 2012

20. Menezes, A.J., Van Oorschot, P.C., Vanstone, S.A.: Handbook of Applied Cryptography. CRC Press, Boca Raton (1996)

21. Schaffer, P., Farkas, K., Horváth, Á., Holczer, T., Buttyán, L.: Secure and reliable clustering in wireless sensor networks: a critical survey. Comput. Netw. **56**(11), 2726–2741 (2012)

22. Sheng, X., Tang, J., Xiao, X., Xue, G.: Sensing as a service: challenges, solutions and future directions. IEEE Sens. J. **13**(10), 3733–3741 (2013)

23. Willard, T.: Sensors as a Service on the Internet of Things. White paper, ARM Ltd., January 2014

24. Zhang, X., Dong, L., Peng, H., Chen, H., Li, D., Li, C.: Achieving efficient and secure range query in two-tiered wireless sensor networks. In: 2014 IEEE 22nd International Symposium of Quality of Service (IWQoS), pp. 380–388, May 2014

Secure and Efficient k-NN Queries

Hafiz Asif[1], Jaideep Vaidya[1(✉)], Basit Shafiq[2], and Nabil Adam[1]

[1] MSIS Department, Rutgers University, New Brunswick, USA
jsvaidya@rutgers.edu
[2] CS Department, Lahore Univeristy of Managment Sciences, Lahore, Pakistan

Abstract. Given the morass of available data, ranking and best match queries are often used to find records of interest. As such, k-NN queries, which give the k closest matches to a query point, are of particular interest, and have many applications. We study this problem in the context of the financial sector, wherein an investment portfolio database is queried for matching portfolios. Given the sensitivity of the information involved, our key contribution is to develop a secure k-NN computation protocol that can enable the computation k-NN queries in a distributed multi-party environment while taking domain semantics into account. The experimental results show that the proposed protocols are extremely efficient.

Keywords: k-NN queries · k-NN classification · Privacy · Distributed computation

1 Introduction

Nearest neighbor (NN) queries are an extremely important data analysis tool, and have been used in numerous domains. Indeed, they have been identified (in the form of k-NN classification) as one of the top 10 algorithms in data mining [17], though they can also be used for other applications such as regression, content retrieval, and structure prediction. While the typical use of k-NN does not worry about the sensitivity of the data, k-NN is also applicable in many cases where the data may be private, and the organization interested in querying is different from the organization holding the data.

The work of Shafiq is supported by HEC grant under the PAK-US Science and Technology Cooperation Program and by HEC NRPU grant. The work of Adam is supported by the National Academies of Sciences, Engineering, and Medicine under the PAK-US Science and Technology Cooperation Program. The work of Vaidya and Asif is supported in part by the National Science Foundation Grant CNS-1422501 and the National Institutes of Health Award R01GM118574. The content is solely the responsibility of the authors and does not necessarily represent the official views of the agencies funding the research.

S. De Capitani di Vimercati and F. Martinelli (Eds.): SEC 2017, IFIP AICT 502, pp. 155–170, 2017.
DOI: 10.1007/978-3-319-58469-0_11

Consider the financial environment, wherein we have several organizations (such as Ameritrade, Charles Schwab, etc.) which possess financial data about individuals, including their current stock positions, transactional history, etc. Now, a regulating agency such as the SEC may be interested in finding individuals who have a certain stock position, or have indulged in particular type of transactional behavior. Since perfect match is often difficult, best match queries are used to find the closest individuals of interest. Alternatively, a financial advisor service might want to provide recommendations based on similar stock positions or transactional behavior. Typically, since financial data is extremely sensitive, the organizations may be unwilling or even (legally) unable to allow unfettered access to this data. However, in certain cases, there may be a lot of value associated to be obtained through computing the best match queries. For example, one can identify trading behavior of investors from their portfolio structures as shown by [3]; this kind of information is invaluable for numerous organizations e.g. State Exchange Commission (SEC) in the United States. Similar problems exist in the field of medicine, finance, and homeland security.

In this paper, we address this specific problem. We consider the scenario where several organizations possess independent portfolio databases, each record of which contains financial stock positions for a single portfolio. Together, these databases comprise the global database which contains the portfolios of all entities, though no third party exists which knows this global database in its entirety. Another organization, called the querier, would like to query this global database to retrieve the k portfolios that are the most similar to a particular query portfolio that it possesses. All of the organizations would like to protect the privacy of their information, while still enabling the computation. There has been some work addressing this problem in the past, especially in the context of outsourcing [7,16]. Our proposed solution improves on the state of the art by providing a way to incorporate the domain semantics and is significantly more efficient. Our solution is also applicable in the outsourcing environment where an organization may want to outsource its database in encrypted form and still enable best match queries. Furthermore, our solution can be extended to provide top-k results based only on private ranking criteria (without reference to a specific query point) in an even more efficient fashion. It is worth noting that while the problem has been formulated in the context of financial domain, our approach is quite general and can be used to solve k-NN and top-k query problems in any domain. Overall, our key contributions are:

1. We introduce the notion of semantic distance which is useful in taking domain semantics into account while computing k-nearest neighbor queries.
2. We propose an extremely efficient multi-party protocol to compute k-NN queries that is robust to semi-honest adversaries.
3. We show how the protocol can be adapted to the outsourced data model and used for k-NN based classification without leaking any additional information.

2   Problem Statement

In this paper, we build a protocol for overcoming the privacy problem for situations where organizations (or people) are interested in finding the best matches for a query over distributed data. As discussed earlier, we formulate the problem in the context of the financial domain i.e., finding investment portfolios from a distributed database, which best match a given query portfolio in a dynamic and semantic aware environment, while also providing confidentiality and security-privacy guarantees to the parties involved in the protocol. We consider a database $\mathcal{P} \in \mathbb{R}^{N \times M}$ is horizontally distributed among n parties $P_1, \ldots, P_n$ such that for all $i \in [n]$ and $N_i \in \mathbb{N}$ the database fragment $\mathcal{P}_i \in \mathbb{R}^{N_i \times M}$ is kept by P_i where $\sum_{i \in [n]} N_i = N$. Each party P_i collects the same features of information but for different entities. These parties could be banks, hedge-funds, mutual-funds, or other institutions. Another party Q is interested in performing a k-NN query, which also incorporates structure and semantics, on this distributed data without revealing its query, while the parties owning data being queried want to avoid disclosure of their data except for the legitimate output of the query. Thus, the problem can be formally defined as follows:

Definition 1 (Distributed Secure k-NN query: DS-kNN). *Given a database $\mathcal{P} \in \mathbb{R}^{N \times M}$, which is horizontally distributed among n parties with party P_i having fragment $\mathcal{P}_i \; \forall i \in [n]$, a querier Q wants to privately find semantic distance (Definition 3) based k-NN in $\mathcal{P}$ to its query $q \in \mathbb{R}^M$ for $N, M, n \in \mathbb{N}$, where $n \geq 2$.*

Definition 2 (Security/Privacy). *A protocol Π computes DS-kNN query securely if it reveals nothing but k-NN records to Q with leakage $\mathcal{L}$ to all other parties with negligible probability in security parameter – a function, $\mu(m)$, is negligible in m if $\mu(m) < \frac{1}{p(m)}$ for all sufficiently large m and polynomial $p(m)$.*

Hence Definition 2 ensures that data owners do not learn anything about the query beyond what they already know or infer from leakage, and Q learns nothing about $\mathcal{P}$ beyond what it already knows and can infer from the output and leakage.

Adversarial Model: We assume all parties to be non-colluding and *semi-honest* (i.e., honest-but-curious) adversaries, who communicate over a secure channel. However, *restriction on collusion among the data owners can be relaxed to the collusion of at least α data owners, where $\alpha \leq n$* (total number of data owners). We can accomplish this (without any major change in the proposed protocol) by employing additive homomorphic encryption with threshold α, which for decryption will require α parties each performing partial decryption on an encrypted message.

3   Proposed Approach

We first introduce a notion of semantic awareness for distance metrics that can capture the desired level of granularity and structure for measuring similarity. For example, standard distance metrics such as Euclidean distance fails to capture structural and semantic information such as the industry or sector a stock belongs to, market capitalization, risk and type of the stock, etc. Consider an investor who would like to find similar portfolios, while incorporating portfolio structure and/or commodity relationships with regards to a particular *categorization model* (e.g., the industry classification of stocks [1]). Such a categorization model would typically be built by domain experts. We assimilate the categorization model into the distance metric, denoted sem_dist, which we term as the semantic distance. This enables the integration of semantic information representing the true interest of the querier, while evaluating similarity among portfolios (or records). We now formalize the notion of semantic aware distance and then discuss how it will be calculated in a secure (and privacy-preserving) manner.

Definition 3. *Semantic Distance between two points* $X, Y \in \mathbb{R}^M$ *is Euclidean distance between their linear projection in space* $\mathbb{R}^l$, *where* $l, M \in \mathbb{N}$ *and the projection is guided by a given categorization model* (map, W), *and is formalized as follows.*

$$
sem\_dist(X,Y) = \sqrt{\sum_{l:c_l \in C} \left(\sum_{j:c_l \in map(s_j)} w_{lj} (x_j - y_j) \right)^2}
$$

Here, $map : S \to 2^{\mathcal{C}}$ specifies the category $c_l \in \mathcal{C}$ to which the stock $s_j \in S$ should be mapped with $\mathcal{C}$ and S being set of all the categories and set of all stocks respectively. $C \subseteq \mathcal{C}$ is the set of categories, for which sem_dist is to be calculated, whereas w_{lj} in $W = [w_{lj}]_{|C| \times M}$ gives the number of units of c_l equivalent to one unit of s_j. We also define *signed-distance(X, Y)* at a category level (c_l) to be $D_l = \sum_{j:c_l \in map(s_j)} w_{lj} (x_j - y_j)$.

Tuple (map, W) defines categorization model. map gives the relationship among commodities e.g., Industrial Classification Benchmark (ICB) [1] provides a classification for stocks based on the sector and industry; equivalently map could specify the categorization based on market capitalization or some other type. W, here, could denote a weight factor to estimate equivalent worth of a stock in an industry or sector. In general, sem_dist allows for a richer query specification, which is very helpful. For example, sem_dist allows accounting for risk and/or diversity of each portfolio, while calculating distance between a portfolio and a query portfolio. Here we show, using an example, the effectiveness of semantic distance. Consider Table 1a, which contains three portfolios p_1, p_2 and p_3. Each portfolio specifies the number of stocks of AAV, RDC, ICD, GTT and NOW held in it. The stocks in Table 1a are from Oil and IT sectors. Table 1b gives the conversion factor per share of a stock to equivalent dollar value in a sector. Now, consider an investor who wants to find a portfolio from Table 1a, which is the closest in terms of its value at sector level. If Euclidean distance is directly used, then the results are not meaningful, as can be seen from the results in Table 1c; i.e., according to Euclidean distance, p_2 and p_3 are equally

Table 1. Example illustrating semantic distance effectiveness

	AAV	RDC	ICD	GTT	NOW
p_1	0	10	0	5	0
p_2	5	0	5	0	5
p_3	0	0	0	15	0

(a) Portfolios

	AAV	RDC	ICD	GTT	NOW
OIL	80	30	50	0	0
IT	0	0	0	100	50

(b) Weights for Categories

	p_1	p_2	p_3
p_1	0	$10\sqrt{2}$	$10\sqrt{2}$
p_2	$10\sqrt{2}$	0	$10\sqrt{3}$
p_3	$10\sqrt{2}$	$10\sqrt{3}$	0

(c) Euclid distance

	p_1	p_2	p_3
p_1	0	$50\sqrt{74}$	$100\sqrt{109}$
p_2	$50\sqrt{74}$	0	$50\sqrt{794}$
p_3	$100\sqrt{109}$	$50\sqrt{794}$	0

(d) Semantic Distance

close (similar) to p_1, whereas we notice that in term of the value of portfolio at sector level, p_1 should be closer to p_2 as compared to p_3, since in contrast to p_3, where only 15 shares of stocks are held in IT sector, p_1 and p_2 both hold 10 shares of stocks in Oil sector and 5 shares of stocks in IT sector. On the other hand if we use semantic distance then the results corroborate with our intuition and the semantic meaning of the query asked by the investor; this can be seen from the calculated distances in Table 1d. Though the calculated Euclidean distance is spatially correct, it fails to capture a lot of domain, structural and semantic information.

We stress that the proposed protocol is also able to calculate secure DS-kNN query based on simple Euclidean distance measure. In semantics distance formulation, this can be accomplished by a $map : S \rightarrow C$, which is bijective, and setting W to identity matrix of dimension $|S| \times |S|$. This will essentially calculate the Euclidean distance between two points.

3.1   DS-kNN Query Protocol

Before presenting the details of the approach to compute the k closest portfolios as per the problem definition above, we first present the underlying assumptions, the notation used, and a few preliminaries. N, S and C are known to all the parties including querier. Furthermore, each data owner (P_i) knows the size $(N_j \; \forall j \in [n])$ of all databases fragments $\mathcal{P}_j$. The database can be viewed as a matrix. In rest of the paper by parties/party we mean parties/party owning data, whereas Q is referred to as querier. Additive homomorphic encryption (AHE) e.g., Paillier allows addition of two encrypted values and multiplication of encrypted value with a plain-text value. The plain text values on which AHE operates come from $\mathbb{N}$; let us say for a given security parameter λ AHE accepts plain-text values from $P(\lambda)$ such that $\forall x \in P(\lambda)$, $x < \Lambda$, where $\Lambda \in \mathbb{N}$. We divide $P(\lambda)$ into two halves where lower half is positive and upper half is negative (i.e. contains additive inverses of lower half). Whenever a text is decrypted it is converted to equivalent negative or positive value; additive inverse of an encrypted value x i.e., $E_{pk}[x]$, is $E_{pk}[x]^{\Lambda-1}$. As for the decimal values we can decide for a precision up to a decimal point d, then multiply each plain-text value with 10^d and convert it to an integer value. $\lambda \in \mathbb{N}$ is picked in such a manner that the finally computed plain-text value in encrypted form is always within the range. We also employ garbled circuit [19] for secure comparison.

The basic idea in *DS-kNN* is for data owners to encrypt the portfolio database and send it to Q, who calculates *signed-distances* w.r.t. its query, q, in encrypted form (Algorithm 1), and uses them to collaboratively calculate semantic distances in form of random shares with a data owner (Algorithm 1). A distributed rank query is then carried out to identify the indices of k portfolios with the smallest distances (Algorithm 2). Finally, Q retrieves portfolios, corresponding to the indices identified above, from the portfolio database.

We now discuss the details. In Algorithm 1 we outline the algorithm for DS-kNN, where a party P_t is picked at random from data owners to initiate the protocol. P_t can be picked by each party generating a random number r_i from $[n]$ and then calculating $\sum_{i\in[n]} r_i \mod (n+1)$ using secure sum [6]. P_t generates public-private (pk, sk) key pair of AHE and sends it to all data owners and pk to Q. P_t also picks two parties P_l and $P_{l'}$ randomly and lets all the parties know who they are. Next, every P_i first permutes its database, and creates encrypted shares $EP_i = E_{pk}[\mathcal{P}_i^{\pi_i} - \mathcal{R}_i]$ and $ER_i = E_{pk}[\mathcal{R}_i]$. Note that these are homomorphically encrypted additive random shares of $\mathcal{P}_i$. Now P_i sends EP_i to P_l and ER_i to $P_{l'}$. This ensures that every database is split into two parts and thus prevents the leakage of any information to other parties or to Q. P_l and $P_{l'}$ put all of these shares together and permute them using a common random seed $\tilde{s}$ (which can be done by having P_l and $P_{l'}$ each pick a random number and send it to the other and then compute the XOR of both random numbers). These encrypted permuted shares (denoted EP and ER) are then sent to Q. At this point, Q also randomly permutes the received shares of the database to avoid linkage attack by data owners. Q can reconstruct the database by adding together the received shares of database in encrypted form. Q then proceeds to calculate *signed-distance* in encrypted form according to its specified (map, W) and C. This steps consists of addition of encrypted values and their multiplication by values in plain-text (weights), which can be done in encrypted form thanks to the additive homomorphism.

Next, these signed distances need to be squared. This is accomplished by Q generating random numbers, r and g for each signed-distance, $v_{i,l}$. Q sets its random share for the squared signed-distance to be $v_{i,l}^1 = -r^2 + g$, and sends P_t, $E_{pk}[v_{i,l} - r]$ and $E_{pk}[2rv_{i,l} - g]$. P_t decrypts the received encrypted messages, converts them to appropriate negative or positive values as explained in preliminaries and sets its share to be $v_{i,l}^2 = (v_{i,l} - r)^2 + 2rv_{i,l} - g$. It is obvious that $(v_{i,l})^2 = v_{i,l}^1 + v_{i,l}^2$. Summing all shares of squared signed-distances of a portfolio will give the share of square of semantic distance for the portfolio. Thus Q and P_t can compute their shares for the distance for each portfolio since $\mathtt{sem\_dist}(p_i, q)^2 = \sum_{l=1}^{|C|} v_{i,l}^1 + \sum_{l=1}^{|C|} v_{i,l}^2$. At this

---

Algorithm 1. DS-kNN

Input: $(m, \mathcal{P}_i)$ at P_i $\forall[n]$, security parameter and database of portfolios
Input: At Q: q, query; (map, W), categorization model; k, number of NN; m
Output: Q gets k-NN portfolios

1: Generate random seed, s_i, at P_i $\forall i \in [n]$
2: All data owners, $P_1, \ldots, P_n$, together pick t uniformly from $[n]$
3: P_t generates (pk, sk), key pair, for AHE and shares it with all data owners, and pk with Q
4: P_t picks l from $[n]$ and l' from $[n] \setminus \{l\}$ uniformly and sends (l, l') to all data owners

5: **for** each P_i $\forall i \in [n]$ **do**
6:     Generate a matrix $\mathcal{R}_i$ of random numbers: $\mathcal{R}_i \leftarrow \mathbb{N}^{N_i \times |S|} \{N_i$ is the size of $\mathcal{P}_i\}$
7:     Permute the database $\mathcal{P}_i$: $\mathcal{P}_i^{\pi_i} = \pi(s_i, \mathcal{P}_i)$
8:     Create encrypted random shares of $\mathcal{P}_i^{\pi_i}$: $(EP_i, ER_i) = (EP_{pk}[\mathcal{P}_i^{\pi_i} - \mathcal{R}_i], EP_{pk}[\mathcal{R}_i])$
9:     Send EP_i to P_l and ER_i to $P_{l'}$
10: P_l sets $EP = \pi(\tilde{s}, (EP_1, \ldots, EP_n))\{$seed $\tilde{s}$ is picked together by P_l and $P_{l'}\}$
11: $P_{l'}$ sets $ER = \pi(\tilde{s}, (ER_1, \ldots, ER_n))$
12: P_l and $P_{l'}$ respectively send EP and ER along with t to Q
13: Q permutes EP and ER using random seed $\hat{s}$: $(EP^\pi, ER^\pi) = (\pi(\hat{s}, EP), \pi(\hat{s}, ER))$

14: Q sets $q_{enc} = E_{pk}[q]^{(\Lambda-1)}$
15: Q initializes matrices, T and D_Q, of sizes $N \times |C|$ and $N \times 1$, to have $E_{pk}[0]$'s and 0's resp.
16: P_t initializes
    D_t as matrix of 0's with size $N \times 1$
17: **for** each $i \in [N]$ **do**
18:   **for** $j \in \{1, \ldots, |S|\}$ **do**
19:       Q sets $T[i, map[j]] = T[i, map[j]] \times (EP^\pi[i][j] \times ER^\pi[i][j] \times q_{enc}[j])^{W[map[j], j]}$
20:     **for** $l \in \{1 \ldots |C|\}$ **do**
21:         Q generates random numbers r and g and sets $T_Q[i, l] = -r^2 + g$
22:         Q sets $v_r = E_{pk}[T[i, l]] \cdot E_{pk}[r]^{(\Lambda-1)}$ and $v_g = E_{pk}[T[i, l]]^{2r} \cdot E_{pk}[g]^{(\Lambda-1)}$
23:         Q sends (v_r, v_g) to P_t
24:         P_t sets $T_t[i, l] = D_{sk}[v_r]^2 + D_{sk}[v_g]\{D_{sk}$ decrypts to equivalent +ive/-ive value$\}$
25:         Q sets $D_Q[i] = D_Q[i] + T_Q[i, l]$
26:         P_t sets $D_t[i] = D_t[i] + T_t[i, l]$
27: Q and P_t interactively find indices of k-smallest distances: $I \leftarrow$ k-Smallest(D_Q, D_t, k)
28: **return** portfolios corresponding to I to Q by getting their random shares decrypted from P_t

---

point, the square of semantic distance between each portfolio and the query has been randomly split between Q and P_t. For the sake of efficiency we do not compute the square root of squared semantic distance. However, this does not impact correctness of the protocol. Henceforth, Q and P_t engage in an interactive protocol to compute the k smallest distances corresponding to k-NN portfolios.

Algorithm 2. k-Smallest(D_Q, D_t, k)

Input: At Q: D_Q, at P_t: D_t, such that D_Q and D_t are random shares of the squared distances

Input: At Q, P_t: k, the number of closest records desired

Output: At Q: I, the array containing indices of smallest elements in $D_Q + D_t$

1: At Q: $\forall i, V_Q[i] = D_Q[i] \times |D_Q|$
2: At P_t: $\forall i, V_t[i] = D_t[i] \times |D_t| + i$
3: **while** $k > 0$ **do**
4:     Q sets $(\mu_Q, \ell) = (mean(V_Q), |V_Q|)$, and P_t sets $(\mu_t, \ell) = (mean(V_t), |V_t|)$
5:     **for** $i \in 1 \ldots \ell$ **do**
6:         Q sets $U_Q[i] = (V_Q[i] - \lfloor \mu_Q \rfloor)$; P_t sets $U_t[i] = (-V_t[i] + \lfloor \mu_t \rfloor)$
7:         **if** $U_Q[i] \leq U_t[i]$ {At Q, P_t: Yao Comparison} **then**
8:             Remove i^{th} element from V_Q and V_t and add to V_Q' and V_t' at Q and P_t respectively
9:     **for** $j \in \{Q, t\}$ **do**
10:         **if** $|V_j'| > k$ **then**
11:             set $V_j = V_j'$
12:         **else**
13:             For each element in V_j', add to I the index of corresponding element in D_j
14:             $k = k - |V_j'|$
15: **return** I

To find the k-smallest entries from the split distance vectors we develop a novel protocol **k-Smallest** that can accomplish this both securely and efficiently. We first present the simple-k-smallest (SKS) protocol, that efficiently computes the k-smallest entries without worrying about security. For a given a vector V containing *unique* values, v, and $\mathcal{S} = \{\}$, the k-smallest values can be found as follows:

– **1:** Set $\mu = \sum_{v \in V} \frac{v}{|V|}$ and divide V into $V_g = \{v \in V : v > \mu\}$ and $V_{le} = V \setminus V_g$
– **2:** If $|V_{le}| > k$, set $V = V_{le}$ and go to step 1
– **3:** If $|V_{le}| \leq k$ then set $V = V_g$, $\mathcal{S} = \mathcal{S} \cup V_{le}$ and $k = k - |V_{le}|$
– **4:** if $k \neq 0$ go to step 1, terminates otherwise

SKS terminates, since each iteration reduces size of V. Note that, only the correct distances are added to the output in step 3 since the distances in V_{le} are guaranteed to be smaller than the ones in V_g. SKS works very well for our problem setting and can easily be extended to be secure. *Though any point in V instead of arithmetic mean can be used to split V without affecting correctness of the algorithm, choice of arithmetic mean as a split point is quite effective as long as subsets (of different sizes) of data are not highly skewed to the left for small values of k.* This assumption does hold in real world data. Specifically, we show through empirical analysis that portfolio distances for real world stock market data [3] are but slightly skewed to left. We used portfolio data of hundred thousand individuals, which was collected over the period of three years from Swedish stock market [3]. We calculated the mean distance and variance for the mean distance over samples of various sizes (i.e., number of portfolios).

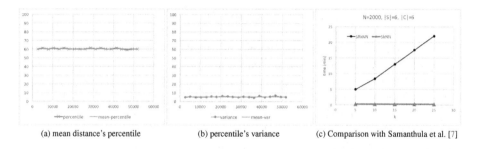

(a) mean distance's percentile   (b) percentile's variance   (c) Comparison with Samanthula et al. [7]

Fig. 1. Empirical analysis

Figure 1a depicts the percentile for mean distance and average percentiles for mean distances. It can be seen that mean distance is consistently at percentile 60. Figure 1b depicts the variance for the above calculated percentile for mean distance, and the average variance, which asserts that percentile for mean distance does not vary much. The complexity of SKS for such a distribution will be $O(|V|)$ regardless of value for k. *In the case where data is highly skewed or follows exponential distribution or leakage function is different a randomly picked data points can be used as a split point instead.*

Now we focus on devising a secure and distributed SKS so that it can be carried out on random shares of distances without violating the privacy. It is easy to see that if the first step of SKS can be performed in a secure and distributed form (note, in our case, D_Q and D_t together give V), the remaining steps can be performed locally at Q and P_t.

SKS requires the distances in vector to be *unique* i.e. $\forall i \in [N]$, $D_Q[i] + D_t[i]$ is *unique*. This is necessary, not only to guarantee that the protocol terminates but also to ensure security. In essence, if distances were non-unique, it could have been possible that all of the distances were same, thus resulting in $V_{le} = V$ for all iterations. Since, in our case, uniqueness does not generally hold; therefore, we use a perturbation mechanism to achieve uniqueness. This can be accomplished by scaling the distance of portfolio p_i by N, and translating it by i. In the protocol, k-smallest, it is carried out as follows: Q multiplies $D_Q[i]$ with N while P_t multiplies $D_t[i]$ with N and adds i to it (lines 1–2 of Algorithm 2) (Note: $|D_Q| = |D_t| = |\mathcal{P}| = N$), which will together gives us $N \times (D_Q[i] + D_t[i]) + i$. Next we need to devise a secure and distributed protocol to compute mean and identify indices of D_Q or D_t for which distances $(D_Q[i] + D_t[i])$ are greater than the mean. If we let mean distance to be $\mu = \mu_Q + \mu_t$,

where $\mu_Q = \sum_i D_Q[i]/N$ and $\mu_t = \sum_i D_t[i]/N$ then

$$D_Q[i] + D_t[i] > \mu \iff D_Q[i] - \mu_Q > -D_t[i] + \mu_Q$$

The above observation tells us that result of comparing the distance for a record against the mean distance can be equivalently obtained by comparing the difference between random share and the mean of random shares. Note that since Q and P_t can locally compute this difference, the parties can simply use a secure comparison [19] (the garbled circuit approach) to compute the first step of SKS in a secure manner. Furthermore, Since we are using a finite integer field, it is possible that μ_Q and μ_t are fractional, and hence outside the field. To avoid this we use the output of floor-function on μ_Q and μ_t and employ the following comparison instead: $D_Q[i] - \lfloor \mu_Q \rfloor > -D_t[i] + \lfloor \mu_t \rfloor$, but it does not affect the performance of Algorithm 2 since $0 \leq \mu - (\lfloor \mu_Q \rfloor + \lfloor \mu_t \rfloor) < 2$. Since the remaining steps are local, both parties can calculate k-smallest entries securely and identify their corresponding indices in D_Q or D_t.

Result Extraction: Using above found indices Q can identify and obtain k-NN portfolios from the encrypted database. Let I contain the indices of k-smallest distances and $\forall j \in I$, $\hat{t}_j$ and $\tilde{t}_j$ be the corresponding records in EP and ER then for all j, Q asks P_t for decryption of $E_{pk}[\varphi_j] = E_{pk}[\hat{t}_j] \otimes E_{pk}[\tilde{t}_j] \otimes \gamma_j$, where γ_j is uniformly picked vector of size $|S|$ from an appropriate domain and $\otimes$ gives coordinate-wise product of two vectors. It is straightforward to compute $E_{pk}[\varphi_j]$ for homomorphically encrypted values and the original record t_j from φ_j i.e., $t_j = \varphi_j - \gamma_j$. Thus completing the protocol for computing sem_dist based k-NN for horizontally fragmented database in a privacy preserving fashion.

3.2   Extensions

We can easily extend the protocol devised above to work for the outsourced data model. It can also be used for k-NN classification. Both of these are briefly described below.

Outsourcing Case: Our protocol can very simply be applied for the case where the computation of data owners is transferred to the cloud in a secure manner. Parties can pick non-colluding, semi-honest and untrusted servers C_1 and C_2 to take responsibilities of P_l and $P_{l'}$ respectively except for creation random shares of their databases and their encryption. All the responsibilities of P_t for distance and k-smallest computation along with decryption for result retrieval phase are handed to one of the servers. Once responsibilities have been assigned to C_1 and C_2, following the protocol stated in DS-kNN will compute k-NN securely in cloud.

k-NN Classification Case: The proposed protocol also has the ability to carry out k-NN classification with a very small modification. Let us say there are G classes with labels $\{1, 2, \ldots, G\}$. We append each database fragment with G new columns and name them $1, 2, \ldots, G$. For each row with class label g only column g of the appended G columns will have the value 1, and value 0 for the others. Now all the steps outlined in DS-kNN are carried on the database with appended columns, except for the result retrieval step; furthermore, appended columns are not used for k-NN computations. Once Q has identified k-NN records in encrypted database, it computes a vector $\mathcal{G}$, where $\forall g \in [G]$, $\mathcal{G}[g]$ contains k minus the sum of values in column g of k-NN records i.e., k minus the number of votes for each class; thus smaller the value $\mathcal{G}[g]$, higher the number of votes for class g. Next, Q permutes $\mathcal{G}$, creates random shares of values in $\pi(\mathcal{G})$ and send them to P_t, after which both Q and P_t follow k-smallest protocol with $k = 1$. At the end of k-smallest Q is able to identify the class of its instance q.

4   Complexity Analysis

Let N be the number of portfolios in database $\mathcal{P}$ horizontally distributed among parties $P_1, \ldots P_n$, where each record is of dimension $M = |S|$. The asymptotic computational complexity of DS-kNN is $O(N^2) = O(NM, N \times |C| + N^2)$ since in the worst case there will be $O(NM)$ encryption and $O(N \times |C|)$ decryption operations along with $O(N^2)$ secure comparison by data owners, whereas querier will perform $O(N \times |C|)$ arithmetic operations on encrypted values and $O(N^2)$ secure comparisons; furthermore, in most of the application scenarios $M, |C|, k \ll N$.

It is important to note that in real world data for portfolios require only $O(N)$ comparison to find k smallest entries as shown in Fig. 1 and is explained in Sect. 6. Moreover, $|C|$ would also be much smaller as compared to $|S|$ because thousands of stocks are traded in the market. So for all practical purposes asymptotically complexity for our problem will be $O(NM)$ Following the same reasoning as above the asymptotic communication complexity of DS-kNN will also be $O(NM)$.

With respect to the communication complexity, *it may appear that the cost of transferring the entire database over is excessive. While this is true in terms of the communication itself, both the monetary and time cost of doing this is negligible*, since currently available bandwidth and speed are quite high e.g., currently ISPs are providing 1000 Mbps connection to residential users and small businesses, which allows an encrypted database of million rows and ten attributes to be transferred in matter of few seconds. On the other hand, in many cases cost and the time required for secure operations are significantly higher than that of required for data transfer. Additionally, many of the secure protocols including [7,12] require transferring complete database between/among the parties. Therefore, we believe that this cost is reasonable.

5   Security Analysis

In this section we analyze the security of DS-kNN under the framework of Definition 2. We want to show the following:

DS-kNN is secure if probabilistic polynomial time simulators $\mathcal{S}_i(m, \mathcal{P}_i, \mathcal{L}_P)$ *and* $\mathcal{S}_Q(m, q, (map, W), \mathcal{L}_Q, \mathcal{O}_k)$ *can respectively simulate the view of* $P_i, \forall i \in [n]$ *and* Q *during the execution of DS-kNN.*

This means that if $\mathcal{S}_i$ is provided with P_i's input $(m, \mathcal{P}_i)$ and leakage $\mathcal{L}_P$ (which gives $(J, j_1, \ldots, j_J, N_1, \ldots, N_n, |C|)$), and $\mathcal{S}_Q$ with Q's input $(m, q, (map, W))$ and output ($\mathcal{O}_k$ i.e. k-NN records) along with $\mathcal{L}_Q$ (which gives $(J, j_1, \ldots, j_P, N, S)$) then these simulators will have the same view as their respective parties; thus asserting that DS-kNN reveals no extra information and does fulfill the security Definition 2. In the output of leakage functions J is the total number of iterations taken in Algorithm 2 corresponding to $\mathcal{P}$ and q, j_ℓ is the percentile of mean distance in ℓ^{th} iteration, whereas rest of the symbols are same as defined previously.

Let us analyze $\mathcal{S}_j$ for the situation where $j = t$ and also $j \in \{l, l'\}$ (l, l' and t are as per specification in Algorithm 1) since such a party, P_j, will receive the biggest set of intermediate messages, in all other cases parties receive less information. P_j's view consists of its input (m, P_j), random shares ($\mathcal{D}_i \in \mathbb{N}^{N_i \times |S|}$, $\forall i \in [n]$) of database fragments, random shares ($\mathcal{H}_R \in \mathbb{N}^{N \times |C|}$) of distances at category level, random seeds $(s_j, \tilde{s})$, random-tape ($r_j \in \{0,1\}^{p(m)}$) and $\mathcal{L}_P$. P_j's view can easily be generated by $\mathcal{S}_j$: based on m, P_j and $\mathcal{L}_P$ that are provided to $\mathcal{S}_j$, it can generate $\mathcal{D}_i^j \leftarrow \mathbb{N}^{N_i \times |S|}$, $\mathcal{H}_R^j \leftarrow \mathbb{N}^{N \times |C|}$, $(s_j', \tilde{s}_j') \leftarrow \mathbb{N}^2$ and $r_j' \leftarrow \{0,1\}^{p(m)}$, $\mathcal{L}_{P_j}$ using uniform distribution. Thus P_j's view, $(m, P_j, \mathcal{D}_1, \ldots, \mathcal{D}_n, \mathcal{H}_R, s_j, \tilde{s}_j, r_j, \mathcal{L}_P)$, is computationally indistinguishable from $\mathcal{S}_j$'s view, $(m, P_j, \mathcal{D}_1^j, \ldots, \mathcal{D}_n^j, \mathcal{H}_R^j, s_j', \tilde{s}_j', r_j', \mathcal{L}_P)$, in polynomial time, otherwise pseudo-random generator, which is assumed to be secure, can be broken which is used to create random shares and seeds. It is straightforward that for all other cases a party's view will consist of less information than that of P_j's view; hence $\forall i \in [n]$, $\mathcal{S}_i$ will be able to generate P_i's view.

The case for $\mathcal{S}_Q$, is also very similar in that respective inputs, output, and leakage is provided to $\mathcal{S}_Q$, except for the difference that Q receives encrypted database $EP \in \mathbb{N}^{N \times |S|}$ instead of random share of a database, but since AHE is (semantically) secure – meaning EP is computationally indistinguishable from $EP' \leftarrow \mathbb{N}^{N \times |S|}$ (i.e. generated uniformly) – $\mathcal{S}_Q$ can generate a view using $m, q, (map, W)$ and $\mathcal{L}_Q$ that is indistinguishable from Q's view. *Thus proving that DS-kNN is secure.*

Note that the defined leakage reveals information, usually known in our application scenario. If one wants to hide this information then following is one way to accomplish this. Instead of mean distance, randomly picked distances can be used for the purpose of comparison to find k-smallest distances; dummy portfolios with sentinel values can be added to hide size of database; extra columns can be added for dummy coordinates, mapping to which can be provided through a secure and modified bloom filter. $|C|$ can be hidden by adding dummy signed-distances with value zero. Though such measures will stop the leakage, they will significantly reduce the efficiency of the protocol.

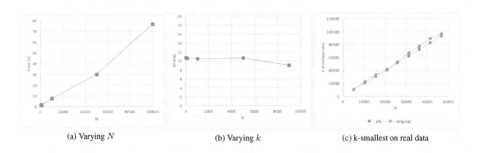

(a) Varying N (b) Varying k (c) k-smallest on real data

Fig. 2. k-smallest (Algorithm 2) computation time

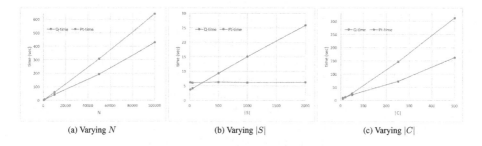

(a) Varying N (b) Varying $|S|$ (c) Varying $|C|$

Fig. 3. Distance computation time for Q and P_t

6   Experimental Evaluation

We implemented DS-kNN in Java. The platform used for testing is asymmetric in terms of its computational power. The querier machine had a 2.2 GH core-i7 processor and 16 GB RAM whereas each of the database owners was a Xeon E5-2680 v2, with 10 cores running at 2.80 GHz, and 96 GB RAM. For AHE and garbled circuit we employed the implementation available at [2] with key size 1024 and [9] with a key size of 512 respectively. The default values for parameters are set based upon domain semantics. Specifically, even though 2k-3k stocks are traded on the stock exchange, only a few hundred of them are most often traded; thus we set $|S|$ to be 100. $|C|$ is set to be 10 because ICB [1] classification taxonomy segregates stocks to 10 industries at the top level. As for k, it is set to 1, which represents the worst case for Algorithm 2. Lastly, N is set to be 1000. For each experiment, only one parameter is varied, while keeping the rest constant. Experiments described below were carried out with synthetic data. The results on real data are described later.

Figures 3a, b and c report time taken for distance computation by Q and P_t, with varying N, $|S|$ and $|C|$ respectively. Time for all of these experiments grows linearly except for P_t w.r.t. $|S|$. This is because of the fact that distance computation time for P_t depends on $|C|$ and N, but not on $|S|$. Let us now look at the performance of Algorithm 2, which only depends upon N. Figure 2a plots the computation time taken by Algorithm 2 for varying values of N. Again, the computation time scales linearly w.r.t. N. Figure 2b plots the computation time with respect to varying k. It is interesting to note that the time taken is roughly constant, and thus the time taken by our approach is actually independent of k.

We also compare our work with Elmehdwi et al. [7] for outsourcing case. Figure 1c compares the complete time taken by DS-kNN and SRkNN [7]. For the sake of fair comparison results are computed for same parameters and equivalent processing power. It can be seen that DS-kNN outperforms existing state of the art by an order of magnitude. Additionally, our implementation is in Java and uses threading only for decryption at P_t, whereas implementation in [7] uses the openMP parallelization framework. Thus with an equivalent implementation, our results can be further improved.

Performance on real data: We obtained Swiss stock market data for year 2009–2011, which is a collection of portfolios of around 100k individuals for 300 stocks; the data was previously used in [3]. We only evaluated the performance of k-smallest protocol because time for distance computation is independent of data distribution. We randomly picked a subset of the data and choose one portfolio from it as the query portfolio, and computed the number of actual comparisons required by the k-smallest protocol for $k = 1$. Figure 2c plots the number of comparisons carried out for different values of N (the number of portfolios) along with a reference line for $2N$. The two lines are almost perfectly in lock-step, which demonstrates the efficiency and suitability of our algorithm for real world data. However, in the worst case, it is still possible that in each iteration only one distance will be removed resulting in $O(N^2)$ total comparisons.

7   Related Work

Privacy-preserving data mining has received a lot of attention [15]. Given the numerous practical applications of privacy-preserving k-NN search, various protocols have been developed to address this problem. [5,14] present solutions to the problem of computing k-NN, where the data is fragmented among different parties, while also preserving privacy. [4] uses a semi-trusted third party to find best k matches. In [12] Qi et al. introduce a single-step protocol for k-NN search, whereas [8] proposed a secure k-NN searching protocol based on PIR for location-based services. However, none of the above work is appropriate for computation over encrypted data. [10] solves recommendation problem using Self-Organizing Map for clustering and k-NN based collaborative filtering, but reveals query to data owner. Zang et al. in [20] employ homomorphic encryption for finding k-NN in distributed setting, but in contrast to our work it reveals distances, partial access pattern to the parties. In [18], the query along with k-NN distances is exposed and the output is less accurate. [11] makes use of untrusted third party and reveals query to parties. Although semantic distance can be applied here, the *categorization model* will be revealed to data owners. Shaneck et al. [13] provide a solution that reveals partial access pattern while being slower than our proposed protocol. Not only is our protocol straightforwardly extensible to provide outsourcing and k-NN classification, but it also allows for incorporation of semantic distance, while still being comparatively very efficient as compared to state of the art [7].

8   Conclusion and Future Work

In this paper we have presented a secure approach to computing k-nearest neighbor queries for horizontally distributed data. Our approach is an order of magnitude faster than the existing state of the art. It is also applicable in the outsourcing environment, and can be used to compute top-k queries, as well as k-NN based classification. In the future, we plan to develop solutions that are resilient to stronger adversaries, some of which may collude as well.

References

1. Industry classification benchmark (2015). http://www.icbenchmark.com/ICBDocs/Structure_Defs_English.pdf. Accessed 06 Feb 2016
2. Pailliar encryption implementation (2015). https://code.google.com/p/thep/
3. Bohlin, L., Rosvall, M.: Stock portfolio structure of individual investors infers future trading behavior. PLoS One **9**(7), e103006 (2014)
4. Boneh, D., Gentry, C., Halevi, S., Wang, F., Wu, D.J.: Private database queries using somewhat homomorphic encryption. In: Jacobson, M., Locasto, M., Mohassel, P., Safavi-Naini, R. (eds.) ACNS 2013. LNCS, vol. 7954, pp. 102–118. Springer, Heidelberg (2013). doi:10.1007/978-3-642-38980-1_7
5. Burkhart, M., Dimitropoulos, X.: Fast privacy-preserving top-k queries using secret sharing. In: Proceedings of 19th International Conference on Computer Communications and Networks (ICCCN), pp. 1–7 (2010)
6. Clifton, C., Kantarcioglu, M., Lin, X., Vaidya, J., Zhu, M.: Tools for privacy preserving distributed data mining. SIGKDD Explor. **4**(2), 28–34 (2003)
7. Elmehdwi, Y., Samanthula, B.K., Jiang, W.: Secure k-nearest neighbor query over encrypted data in outsourced environment. In: The 30th International Conference on Data Engineering, Chicago, USA, pp. 664–675, March 2014
8. Ghinita, G., Kalnis, P., Khoshgozaran, A., Shahabi, C., Tan, K.L.: Private queries in location based services: anonymizers are not necessary. In: Proceedings of the 2008 ACM SIGMOD International Conference on Management of Data, pp. 121–132. ACM (2008)
9. Henecka, W., Schneider, T.: Faster secure two-party computation with less memory. In: Proceedings of the 8th ACM SIGSAC Symposium on Information, Computer and Communications Security, pp. 437–446. ACM (2013)
10. Kaleli, C., Polat, H.: Privacy-preserving som-based recommendations on horizontally distributed data. Knowl.-Based Syst. **33**, 124–135 (2012)
11. Kantarcıoğlu, M., Clifton, C.: Privately computing a distributed k-nn classifier. In: Boulicaut, J.-F., Esposito, F., Giannotti, F., Pedreschi, D. (eds.) PKDD 2004. LNCS (LNAI), vol. 3202, pp. 279–290. Springer, Heidelberg (2004). doi:10.1007/978-3-540-30116-5_27
12. Qi, Y., Atallah, M.J.: Efficient privacy-preserving k-nearest neighbor search. In: The 28th International Conference on Distributed Computing Systems, ICDCS 2008, pp. 311–319. IEEE (2008)
13. Shaneck, M., Kim, Y., Kumar, V.: Privacy preserving nearest neighbor search. In: Shaneck, M., Kim, Y., Kumar, V. (eds.) Machine Learning in Cyber Trust, pp. 247–276. Springer, Heidelberg (2009)
14. Vaidya, J., Clifton, C.: Privacy-preserving kth element score over vertically partitioned data. IEEE Trans. Knowl. Data Eng. **21**, 253–258 (2009)
15. Vaidya, J., Clifton, C., Zhu, M.: Privacy Preserving Data Mining. Advances in Information Security, vol. 19. Springer, Heidelberg (2006)
16. Wong, W.K., Cheung, D.W.l., Kao, B., Mamoulis, N.: Secure k-NN computation on encrypted databases. In: Proceedings of the 2009 ACM SIGMOD International Conference on Management of data, pp. 139–152. ACM (2009)
17. Wu, X., Kumar, V., Quinlan, J.R., Ghosh, J., Yang, Q., Motoda, H., McLachlan, G.J., Ng, A., Liu, B., Philip, S.Y., et al.: Top 10 algorithms in data mining. Knowl. Inf. Syst. **14**(1), 1–37 (2008)
18. Xiong, L., Chitti, S., Liu, L.: Mining multiple private databases using a k-NN classifier. In: Proceedings of the 2007 ACM Symposium on Applied Computing, pp. 435–440. ACM (2007)

19. Yao, A.C.: Protocols for secure computation. In: Proceedings of the 23rd Annual IEEE Symposium on Foundations of Computer Science, pp. 160–164 (1982)
20. Zhang, F., Zhao, G., Xing, T.: Privacy-preserving distributed k-nearest neighbor mining on horizontally partitioned multi-party data. In: Huang, R., Yang, Q., Pei, J., Gama, J., Meng, X., Li, X. (eds.) ADMA 2009. LNCS (LNAI), vol. 5678, pp. 755–762. Springer, Heidelberg (2009). doi:10.1007/978-3-642-03348-3_80

Secure and Trustable Distributed Aggregation Based on Kademlia

Stéphane Grumbach and Robert Riemann$^{(\boxtimes)}$

Inria, Lyon, France
{stephane.grumbach,robert.riemann}@inria.fr

Abstract. Aggregation of values that need to be kept confidential while guaranteeing the robustness of the process and the correctness of the result is required in an increasing number of applications. We propose an aggregation algorithm, which supports a large spectrum of potential applications including complex voting protocols. It relies on the distributed hash table Kademlia, used in BitTorrent, for pseudonymous communication between randomly predetermined peers to ensure a high degree of confidentiality which does not solely relies on cryptography. The distribution of data and computation limits the potential for data breaches, and reduces the need for institutional trust. Experimental results confirm the complexity of $\mathcal{O}\left(\log n\right)$ for n peers allowing for large-scale applications.

Keywords: Distributed aggregation · DHT · Privacy · Trust

1 Introduction

An increasing number of applications require aggregation of values that should not be revealed, for various aspects of privacy protection. They include personalized services related to domotic, smart cities, or mobility for instance that are blooming today, while revealing security breaches. Confidentiality protecting aggregation is of even greater importance for online voting. We demonstrate that peer-to-peer systems offer great promises for such aggregations, because they limit the potential for data breaches and simplify the essential question of trust.

This paper presents ADVOKAT, a distributed protocol for confidential aggregation of inputs produced by large sets of peers. It relies on the distributed hash table Kademlia [1], that offers both an overlay network to organize peers, as well as a tree structure to compute the aggregation. Kademlia is a robust and scalable technique which is used in particular by BitTorrent [2]. The proposed protocol integrates also techniques from Bitcoin [3] and BitBallot [4].

Voting is the main privacy preserving aggregation realized with pre-digital technologies. Paper-based voting protocols offer an unmatched solution to satisfy often contradicting though essential properties, such as secrecy of the ballot, correctness of the tally and verifiability. Moreover, the possibility given to voters to participate in the supervision on-site of both the casting and tallying procedures

S. De Capitani di Vimercati and F. Martinelli (Eds.): SEC 2017, IFIP AICT 502, pp. 171–185, 2017.
DOI: 10.1007/978-3-319-58469-0_12

ensures trust. No expert knowledge is required to understand the protocol and its verification procedure. Thus, no trust in organizing authorities is necessary. Paper-based voting owes its robustness to its independence from institutional trust. Our objective is to transfer as much as possible these properties in the online world, while offering new properties not available in the classical setting, such as remote participation as well as the capacity to launch a new aggregation.

The case of voting protocols is particularly interesting due to its conflicting, but essential security requirements. On one hand, the eligibility of every voter to cast a ballot must be ensured, while, on the other hand, no link can be established between a given ballot and the corresponding voter. Furthermore, the final tally must be verifiable. Distributed protocols are promising for voting since they allow to reduce the reliance on trust and open new prospects for verification. The various tasks are carried out collectively in a peer-to-peer manner by the participants, much like voters in paper-based voting.

We assume the existence of an administrator trusted to certify the eligibility of peers. Supported by a tracker, eligible peers join a Kademlia DHT that provides a tree-like overlay network in which peers are assigned to random leaves. Peers pull inputs, and later input aggregates, from other peers close to them in the tree overlay, which allows to compute aggregates for all ancestor nodes up to the root. The strategy resides on pulling versus pushing for dissemination. Cryptographic signatures are used to authorize peers to pull in different subtrees.

Although several protocols propose a distributed aggregation over tree-like overlay networks [5–8], to the best of our knowledge, the proposed algorithm is the first to consider eligibility, confidentiality, scalability and verifiability at once. The DASIS protocol [9] balances the Kademlia tree by routing joining peers to less populated subtrees. Internally, the subtree size is computed in a similar fashion to our approach, but no security measures are introduced. A distributed, Kademlia-based voting protocol to rank the quality of BitTorrent content has been proposed [10]. However, confidentiality and eligibility are not addressed.

Using distributed protocols for voting is a very natural idea to avoid concentration of power. Common building blocks, like blind signature schemes [11], Mix Networks [12] or threshold decryption [13] exercise decentralization on a small scale. Many classical online voting protocols employ already a set of authorities [14–16] to achieve privacy. However, they assume trust in the authorities and the aggregation is generally centralized, rendering the protocols vulnerable to DDoS attacks and data breaches of global impact for instance.

Various efforts[1] are ongoing to propose distributed online voting protocols, based on the Bitcoin blockchain [3], that does not require trusted authorities. Still, published results are sparse. [17] describes a protocol for a binary majority voting to determine the receiver of a voter sponsored Bitcoin payment.

---

[1] Blockchain-based voting techniques include: http://votem.com, http://cryptovoter. com, http://votosocial.github.io, http://followmyvote.com, http://bitcongress.org, http://github.com/domschiener/publicvotes.

The *SPP* protocol [18], based on Secure Multi-Party Computation, partitions the aggregation over a tree hierarchy of peers of which a random set of peers serves as authorities to carry out the final decryption step. *DPol* [19] and its extension *EPol* [20] are similar to our protocol in that the aggregation is distributed to all peers and for their renunciation of cryptography. However, their message complexity does not allow for large-scale elections.

The aggregation protocol is evaluated with respect to the security properties used for centralized voting protocols such as FOO [15], and to scalability properties used for distributed aggregation protocols such as SPP [19]. We consider eligibility, confidentiality (secrecy), completeness and correctness, verifiability, and complexity in terms of messages, memory and time.

The paper is organized as follows. In the next section, we present the general setting of the protocol. The basic aggregation is shown in Sect. 3, while the recursive process that takes advantage of the tree overlay of the Kademlia DHT is shown in Sect. 4. Then, in Sect. 5, the recursive aggregation process is extended to allow a minority of dishonest Byzantine peers. Several desirable security and complexity properties are sketched in Sect. 6. The provided confidentiality is experimentally examined in Sect. 7 by means of a simulation.

2   Aggregation Protocol

The protocol relies on *peers*, an *administrator* and a *tracker*. The administrator is entrusted to certify the eligibility of peers. For this purpose, we assume an authenticated, tamper-resistant communication channel between the administrator and each peer, e.g. using an existing public key infrastructure.

Once certified, *peers* join a distributed hash table (DHT) that is mainly used to find other peers, but allows also to retrieve and store data. We choose the Kademlia DHT [1] whose tree-like network overlay is well-suited for aggregations. Like in BitTorrent, a *tracker* is employed to provide an initial peer as an entry point. Peers communicate via pairwise channels assumed to be confidential and authenticated to the degree of a peer pseudonym, e.g. a public IP address.

We use the following notations adapted from [15]:

A	Administrator
P_i	Peer, i-th out of n
a_i	Initial aggregate of peer P_i
(pk_i, sk_i)	public and private key pair of peer P_i
$\eta(m)$	Hashing technique for message m, e.g. SHA-1
$\sigma_i(m)$	Peer P_i's signature scheme using (pk_i, sk_i)
$\sigma_A(m)$	Administrator's signature scheme
$\chi(m, r)$	Blinding technique for message m and random number r
$\delta(s, r)$	Retrieving technique of blind signature

The proposed protocol follows the following structural steps:

Preparation Peers create personal public and private key pairs and send authorization requests with their blinded public key to the administrator.

Administration Once for each peer, the administrator signs the peer's blinded public key without learning it and sends the signature to the peer.

Aggregation Supported by the tracker, peers join the tree-like overlay network of Kademlia. Then, peers assign their *initial aggregate* to their leaf node and compute collectively the *root aggregate* from all initial aggregates using the *distributed aggregation algorithm*. This requires the computation of *intermediate aggregates* for all their ancestor nodes in the Kademlia tree.

Evaluation On fulfilment of a well-defined verification criteria, peers accept their root aggregate as *final root aggregate*. The outcome (e.g. election result) is eventually derived from the final root aggregate.

In the preparation step, each peer P_i generates on it's own authority a public and private key pair (pk_i, sk_i) to sign messages with $\sigma_i(m)$. To limit the number of valid keys to one per eligible peer, the public key must have the signature of the administrator A [18]. As in FOO [15], a blind signature scheme [11] is used to ensure that A cannot recognize peers after the administration step. P_i randomly chooses a blinding factor r_i, computes its blinded public key $b_i = \chi(pk_i, r_i)$ and sends it to A using the authenticated, tamper-resistant channel.

In the administration step, A ensures to sign only a unique b_i for each P_i and responds to P_i with its signature $s_i = \sigma_A(b_i)$. Eventually, P_i can retrieve the *authorization token* $t_i = \delta(s_i, r_i)$. A does not intervene any further once all eligible peers have acquired their authorization or a time-out has elapsed.

During the aggregation step, all peers run the distributed aggregation algorithm, that is presented hereafter in Sects. 3 and 4.

3   Basic Aggregation

The aggregation algorithm allows to implement various kinds of confidential aggregations. In particular, with standard security requirements slightly weakened, it supports a large spectrum of voting systems.

Aggregates are values to be aggregated, whether initial aggregates, constituting inputs from peers, or intermediate aggregates obtained during the computation. The specification of the aggregation algebra is formulated below. We then introduce the *aggregate container* allowing to attach meta-information to aggregates that is used to position them in the tree and ensure verifiability.

We introduce an algebra whose operation applies to *aggregates*, which are aggregated during the computation of the operation. In the case of a vote, aggregates correspond to ballot boxes filled with ballots, and the operation is the union of sets. The data structure can be adapted to different applications with different aggregation functions, such as average, majority voting, etc.

We consider a set $\mathbb{A}$ of aggregates. The aggregation operation, $\oplus$, combines two *child aggregates* to a *parent aggregate* in $\mathbb{A}$. *Initial aggregates*, corresponding to peer inputs, are not computed, but provided by the peers. We assume that the operation $\oplus : \mathbb{A} \times \mathbb{A} \mapsto \mathbb{A}$ is commutative and associative.

Consider for illustrative purposes the algebra for the *Plurality Voting* (PV). Peers, or here more precisely voters, choose one out of d options, that are modeled in the algebra with initial aggregate vectors $(e_1, \ldots, e_d)$ in $\mathbb{A} = \mathbb{N}^d$, with $\sum_{x=1}^{d} e_x = 1$. The operation $\oplus$ is simply vector addition in $\mathbb{A}$. The root aggregate $a_R = (n_1, \ldots, n_d)$ with $\sum_{x=1}^{d} n_x = n$ indicates how many peers n_x have chosen each option. The option x with the highest n_x, hence plurality, corresponds to the vote outcome. The system can be easily extended to $\mathbb{A} = \mathbb{Q}_+^d$ to support vote splitting between two or more options. The Manhattan norm is used to ensure the validity of initial aggregates a_i with constant weight: $\|a_i\|$.

More complex voting systems such as for instance the *Alternative Voting* and the *Single Transferable Voting* systems can easily be encoded. In both cases, voters have to rank options. Every ranking of $d!$ possible rankings in total can be interpreted as one option in the PV algebra. The set of aggregates $\mathbb{A}$ consists of vectors $\mathbb{A} = \mathbb{N}_0^{d!}$ and the operation is again vector addition. Note that alternative, more compact encodings can be defined for efficiency reasons.

The aggregation algorithm relies on meta-information of an aggregate a that is in general not directly involved in the aggregate computation, and constitutes together with a the aggregate container of a:

h	hash $\eta(\cdot)$ of the aggregate container without h
a	aggregate
c	counter of initial aggregates in a, $c = c_1 + c_2$
c_1, c_2	counter of initial aggregates of child aggregates
h_1, h_2	container hashes of child aggregates
$\widehat{\mathbb{S}}(x, d)$	identifier of subtree whose initial aggregates are aggregated in a

The counter c allows to detect protocol deviations and to measure the number of initial aggregates in the root aggregate that can be compared to n [6].

The aggregate container hash h depends on its child aggregate hashes h_1, h_2. As such, a chain of signatures is spanned reaching from the root or any intermediate aggregate down to the initial aggregates of the peers. Also employed in the Bitcoin blockchain, this technique ensures that the sequence of aggregate containers is immutable.

4   Recursive Aggregation over the Kademlia Binary Tree

The aggregation protocol relies on the Kademlia DHT that establishes a binary tree overlay network in which each peer P_i is assigned to a leaf node. Using the aggregation operator $\oplus$, peers compute the intermediate aggregate for all the parent nodes from their corresponding leaf up to the root node of the tree. The aggregates used to compute any intermediate aggregate of a given tree node are those of its child nodes. Hence, aggregates have to be exchanged between peers of *sibling subtrees*, i.e. subtrees whose roots have the same parent. Kademlia is not used solely to discover other peers, but its internal tree overlay also provides the hierarchy for the aggregation algorithm [9]. We use in the following a notation adapted from Kademlia [1].

k	maximum number of contacts per Kademlia segment (k-bucket)
x	a Kademlia leaf node ID (KID) of size B
B	size of a KID in bits, e.g. 160
x_i	KID of peer P_i
d	node depth, i.e. number of edges from the node to the tree root
$\widehat{\mathbb{S}}(x, d)$	subtree whose root is at depth d which contains leaf node x
$\mathbb{S}(x, d)$	*sibling subtree* whose root is the sibling node of the root of $\widehat{\mathbb{S}}(x, d)$

The leaf node identifiers $x \in \{0, 1\}^B$ (B bits) span the Kademlia binary tree of height B and are denoted KID. Each peer P_i joins the Kademlia overlay network using its KID defined as $x_i = \eta(t_i)$ with the authorization token t_i and the hashing technique η. This way, x_i depends on both P_i's and A's key pair, so that x_i cannot be altered unilaterally [21]. B is chosen sufficiently large, so that hash collisions leading to identical KIDs for distinct peers are very unlikely. Consequently, the occupation of the binary tree is very sparse.

Any node in the tree can be identified by its depth $d \in \{0, \ldots, B\}$ and any of its descendant leaf nodes with KID x. A *subtree* $\widehat{\mathbb{S}}(x, d)$ is identified by the depth d of its root node and any of its leaf nodes x. We overload the subtree notation to designate as well the set of players assigned to leaves of the corresponding subtree. Further, we introduce $\mathbb{S}(x, d)$ for the sibling subtree of $\widehat{\mathbb{S}}(x, d)$, so that $\widehat{\mathbb{S}}(x, d) = \widehat{\mathbb{S}}(x, d+1) \cup \mathbb{S}(x, d+1)$. The entire tree is denoted $\widehat{\mathbb{S}}(x, 0)$. We observe that $\forall d : P_i \in \widehat{\mathbb{S}}(x_i, d)$ and $\forall d : P_i \notin \mathbb{S}(x_i, d)$.

In Kademlia, the distance $d(x_i, x_j)$ between two KIDs is defined as their bit-wise XOR interpreted as an integer. In general, a peer P_i with KID x_i stores information on peers with x_j that are close to x_i, i.e. for small $d(x_i, x_j)$. For this purpose, P_i disposes of a set denoted k-bucket of at most k players $P_j \in \mathbb{S}(x_i, d)$ for every $\mathbb{S}(x_i, d)$ with $d > 0$.[2] See Fig. 1 for an example. The size of subtrees decreases exponentially for growing depth d. Consequently, the density of known peers of corresponding k-buckets grows exponentially.

Kademlia ensures that the routing table, that is the set of all k-buckets, is populated by peer lookup requests for random KIDs to the closest already known peers. Requests are responded with a set of closest, known peers from the routing table. One lookup might require multiple, consecutive request-response cycles.

We assume that peers are either present or absent. Present peers join the Kademlia overlay network within a given time interval and stay responsive until

---

[2] Note that originally [1] the common prefix length b is used to index k-buckets/sibling subtrees while we use the depth $d = b + 1$ of the root of the subtree.

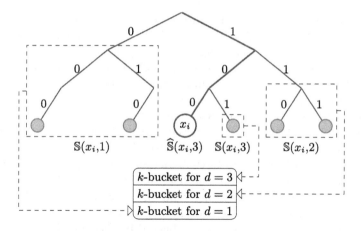

Fig. 1. Example of Kademlia k-buckets for KID $x_i = 100$ assuming $B = 3$. The sparse tree is partitioned into subtrees $\mathbb{S}(x_i, d)$ with root node at depth $d = 1, 2, 3$. The k-buckets for each d contain at most k peers $P_j \in \mathbb{S}(x_i, d)$.

their aggregation step is terminated. The aggregation is carried out in B *epochs*, one tree level at a time. Epochs are loosely synchronized, because peers may have to wait for intermediate aggregates to be computed in order to continue.

First, every peer P_i computes a container for its initial aggregate. The container is assigned to represent the subtree $\widehat{\mathbb{S}}(x_i, B)$ with only \$P_i.

In each epoch for $d = B, \ldots, 1$, every peer P_i requests from any $P_j \in \mathbb{S}(x_i, d)$ the aggregate container of subtree $\mathbb{S}(x_i, d)$. P_j responds with the demanded aggregate container. With the received container of $\mathbb{S}(x_i, d)$ and the previously obtained of $\widehat{\mathbb{S}}(x_i, d)$, peer P_i computes the parent aggregate using the aggregation operator $\oplus$. Its corresponding container is then assigned to the parent subtree $\widehat{\mathbb{S}}(x_i, d-1)$. If $\mathbb{S}(x, d) = \emptyset$ for any d, the container of $\widehat{\mathbb{S}}(x, d-1)$ is computed only with the aggregate container of $\widehat{\mathbb{S}}(x, d)$ from the previous epoch.

After B consecutive epochs, peer P_i has computed the root aggregate of the entire tree $\widehat{\mathbb{S}}(x_i, 0)$ that contains the initial aggregates of all present peers. If all present peers are honest, the root aggregate is complete and correct.

5   Robust Aggregation

The recursive aggregation introduced in Sect. 4 is very vulnerable to aggregate corruptions leading to erroneous root aggregates, and to illegitimate requests compromising the confidentiality. Following the attack model from [18], we assume a minority of dishonest, Byzantine peers entirely controlled by one adversary that aims to interrupt the aggregation, manipulate root aggregates and increase its knowledge on initial and intermediate aggregates. Byzantine peers can essentially behave arbitrarily, but are assumed to be unable to prevent their initial integration in the routing tables by honest peers.

To prevent Sybil attacks and arbitrary requests, all messages m between peers are signed by the sender P_i using $\sigma_i(m)$ [21]. For signature verification, the public key pk_i and the token t_i must be either published (in the DHT) or sent along with every signature. Henceforth, a peer P_i answers aggregate requests for $\widehat{\mathbb{S}}(x_i, d)$ only for peers $P_j \in \widehat{\mathbb{S}}(x_i, d)$ in the same subtree or $P_j \in \mathbb{S}(x_i, d)$ in the sibling subtree. Consequently, peers cannot obtain more knowledge on aggregates than strictly necessary to compute the root aggregate.

Further, player signatures are employed to detect deviations from the protocol. For every computed aggregate container of $\widehat{\mathbb{S}}(x_i, d)$ with hash h and counter c, player P_i produces an aggregate container signature $\sigma_i(h, d, c)$. A signature $\sigma_i(h, d, c)$ expresses the capacity of a peer P_i to compute the container identified by its hash h and is consequently only valid for containers of $\widehat{\mathbb{S}}(x_i, d)$ for any d.

In Fig. 2, we consider the steps of $P_j \in \mathbb{S}(x_i, d)$ to produce for any P_i a *confirmed aggregate container* of $\mathbb{S}(x_i, d)$ backed by the signatures listed below. Note that the necessary signatures depend on the subtree configuration that can be explored by P_i using peer lookup requests. Like for the recursive aggregation, P_j requests first the sibling aggregate container (①) if $\mathbb{S}(x_j, d+1) \neq \emptyset$. For $|\mathbb{S}(x_j, d+1)| < k$, the corresponding k-bucket is exhaustive [1] and the aggregate counter c must not exceed its size. k-buckets are hardened against insertion of false contacts by requiring for all P_q in lookup responses the proof of their KID (pk_q, t_q). Then, the so-called *container candidate* for $\mathbb{S}(x_i, d)$ is computed (②).

New is the *confirmation* (③ and ④) to acquire necessary signatures by otherwise redundant requests to peers in the same subtree $\mathbb{S}(x_i, d)$. Candidates are exchanged solely among peers of that subtree to allow for mutual confirmation.

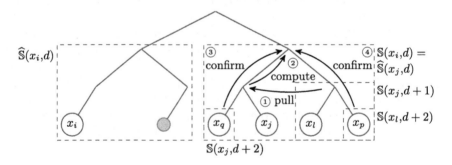

Fig. 2. P_j with x_j produces a confirmed aggregate container of $\mathbb{S}(x_i, b)$. This scheme applies to all tree levels with possibly large subtrees to request from.

P_i requires from P_j the following signatures with the container for $\mathbb{S}(x_i, d)$:

1. P_i requires the signature $\sigma_j(h, d, c)$ on container hash and counter.
2. If $c > 1$, there is at least one child aggregate with hash h_1 and counter c_1 and $\sigma_j(h_1, d+1, c_1)$ must be provided.

3. If $c > 1$ and $c_1 > 1$, a confirmation request (③) is necessary to provide $\sigma_q(h, d, c)$ from $P_q \in \mathbb{S}(x_j, d')$ with the smallest $d' > d + 1$ for a non-empty subtree, ideally in the subtree $\mathbb{S}(x_j, d + 2)$.
4. If $c > 1$ and $c_2 > 0$, P_j provides $\sigma_l(c_2, d + 1, h_2)$ acquired before (①) as 1. signature.
5. If $c > 1$ and $c_2 > 0$, a confirmation request (④) is necessary to provide $\sigma_l(h, d, c)$ if P_l for $c_2 = 1$, and otherwise $\sigma_p(h, d, c)$ from $P_p \in \mathbb{S}(x_l, d')$ with the smallest $d' > d + 1$ for a non-empty subtree, ideally in $\mathbb{S}(x_l, d + 2)$.

The 1., 2. and 4. signature listed above are required already for candidate containers and allow to detect dishonest peers during confirmation. The 3. and 5. signature promote a consensus in $\widehat{\mathbb{S}}(x_j, d + 1)$ respectively $\mathbb{S}(x_j, d + 1)$.

The requests ③ and ④ provide additional signatures, that may reveal dishonest peers deviating from the protocol. Note that dishonest peers cannot influence which peers are requested to avoid detection with certainty. For this, we focus on signatures $\sigma_e(h, d, c)$ and $\sigma_e(h', d, c)$ of the same peer P_e with equal counter c for distinct containers ($h \neq h'$) of the same subtree. In case of $c = 1$, P_e derived from the protocol with certainty, is as such detected as dishonest, and its signatures and containers are discarded. A new candidate container without it is computed. The same holds for $c = 2$, because P_e has not discarded itself two distinct containers with $c = 1$ of the same peer, and alike for $c = 3$. Without obvious proof for $c > 3$, we assume P_e to be honest. The discarded signatures form a verifiable proof that is attached to request responses for the newly computed (candidate) container and stored in the DHT under the key $\eta(x_e)$ if there was none before. Detected dishonest peers are permanently removed from the routing table.

With all required signatures, a candidate container of $\mathbb{S}(x_i, d)$ is confirmed and may be requested by peers in $\widehat{\mathbb{S}}(x_i, d)$. If the candidate cannot be confirmed by a peer P_e, a proof of former deviation is looked up, and requests to other peers continue for a limited number of tries. If P_j gathers this way a majority of signatures for a different child container than those it has computed earlier, P_j repeats the previous aggregation in order to correct or confirm again its child container. If P_j gathers instead a majority of signatures for a different child container than those it has requested, P_j repeats the current aggregation in order to request potentially a different sibling child container to use. Requests for containers with $c = 1$ are not repeated to prevent revisions of initial aggregates.

The administration step ensures that the global minority of dishonest voters is randomly distributed over the tree. Hence, the implicit majority vote on hashes is supposed to be decided by the local majority of honest peers in the subtree. Note that a vote, and thus a honest majority, is not required for subtrees with less than 4 peers, because dishonest peers are detected and removed based on signatures on containers.

If P_j can still not acquire all signatures, e.g. due to a dishonest peer P_e blocking the confirmation, P_j continues the aggregation nevertheless and compensates the missing signature by both child aggregate containers with all their signatures, so that the aggregate computation of P_j can be reproduced. The confidentiality of P_j and P_e is diminished to the same degree.

At last, the root aggregate container is confirmed by some additional signatures to increase the confidence that it has been adopted by the majority.

6   Protocol Properties

Common security properties of online voting protocols [16,18] are considered using the attack model of a dishonest minority from Sect. 5.

Eligibility. The administrator is trusted to sign one authorization request for every eligible peer. Without signature, peers cannot engage in the aggregation.

Confidentiality. The protocol does not ensure secrecy of the initial aggregate due to the necessity to share it at least once over a pseudonymous channel. However, the access to the initial aggregate is limited to randomly determined peers that acquire mostly partial knowledge, so that confidentiality is ensured to a high degree. The pseudonymous channel between peers augments further the confidentiality. The DHT is ephemeral, distributes information evenly among peers, and vanishes when peers disconnect after the aggregation. Potential data breaches are therefore local and bounded in time.

Completeness and Correctness. A local majority of dishonest peers in a subtree $\widehat{\mathbb{S}}(x,d)$ with at least 3 peers allow for manipulations of the corresponding aggregate container. Manipulations of its counter c require further at least k peers in $\widehat{\mathbb{S}}(x,d)$. Hence, for a reasonably-sized global dishonest minority, the protocol ensures that peers compute with high probability root aggregates that are with high probability correct or almost correct.

Verifiability. Using requests, P_i can determine with high probability which root aggregate has been confirmed by most peers and verify the chain of container hashes to the hash of its initial aggregate.

Robustness and Non-interruptibility. The aggregation step is entirely distributed to equipotent peers. With no weakest link, the influence of a reasonably-sized dishonest minority is locally limited. The redundancy of the aggregate computation increases exponentially in every epoch as aggregates become more meaningful.

The *protocol complexity* is mostly inherited by the properties of Kademlia, which have been studied [22] and experimentally confirmed as part of BitTorrent.

Message Complexity. For a network of n peers, a lookup requires with great probability $\mathcal{O}(\log n)$ request-response cycles. Joining the network requires a limited number of lookups and is thus as well of order $\mathcal{O}(\log n)$. With the consideration to estimate the number of empty k-buckets from [22], the average number of container requests for the basic aggregation is found to be $\mathcal{O}(\log n)$.

Memory Complexity. The memory required to store non-empty k-buckets is $\mathcal{O}(\log n)$. Further, the aggregation algorithm requires to store $\mathcal{O}(\log n)$ received aggregate containers for non-empty sibling subtrees and perhaps a limited number of alternatives in case of failing confirmations. Hence, for a constant size of aggregate containers, the total memory complexity is again $\mathcal{O}(\log n)$.

Time Complexity. Intermediate aggregates for ancestor nodes are computed in sequence. For a constant computation time per aggregate and with an upper limit to request and confirm aggregates, the time complexity is $\mathcal{O}(\log n)$.

7   Experimental Confidentiality Analysis

The protocol has been simulated on the basis of `kad`, an implementation of Kademlia[3] written in JavaScript with its extension `kad-spartacus`. For each peer P_i, key pairs (pk_i, sk_i) are generated using elliptic-curves cryptography. The KID x_i of each peer P_i is derived by hashing pk_i first with SHA-256 and the result again with RIPEMD-160. It is assumed that the use of pk_i instead of the token t_i leads to an equally random distribution of KIDs, so that the administration step can be omitted in the simulation. A simulation parameter allows to vary the generation of key pairs and consequently the KIDs, so that different tree configurations can be tested.

After all n peers are instantiated, every P_i connects to the Kademlia network using an initial contact P_{i-1}. According to the Kademlia protocol, peers update their routing table using lookup requests. In our model, peers do not join or leave during the aggregation, so that the routing table does not change hereafter. Once all routing tables are complete, peers start the aggregation step like detailed in Sect. 4. The simulation does not consider absent or dishonest peers.

If a peer receives a request for an intermediate aggregate that has not yet been computed, the response is delayed. The aggregation steps in the simulation use neither parallel requests nor timeouts for requests.

We consider the issue of confidentiality, and measure both the degree of leakage of initial aggregates, and the concentration of knowledge on initial aggregates. For that purpose, we assume that all initial aggregates are distinct.

We define the *leaked information* L_i of a peer P_i to be the sum of the inverse of the counters of all containers that P_i used to respond to aggregation requests. $1/c$ denotes the probability to correctly link the contained initial aggregate of P_i to the pseudonym of P_i, e.g. an IP address. The leaked information L_i is at least 1, because in a non-trivial aggregation with $n > 1$, P_i must respond at least once with its initial aggregate container with $c = 1$. In a perfectly balanced tree with $n = 2^B$ peers, L_i is strictly smaller than 2:

$$L_i = \sum_{n=0}^{B-1} \left(\frac{1}{2}\right)^n < 2$$

---

[3] http://kadtools.github.io/, v1.6.2 released on November 29, 2016.

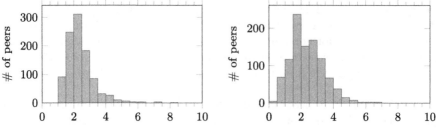

(a) Histogram of leaked information L_i.   **(b)** Histogram of received information R_i.

Fig. 3. In a simulation with $n = 1000$, peers leak (a), respectively receive (b), information on initial aggregates depending on the global distribution of peers on the binary Kademlia tree. L_i peaks close to the theoretical value 2 of an optimally balanced tree. Only few peers leak significantly more. While the mean for R_i is the same, the distribution is slightly different.

Conversely, we define the *received information* R_i of P_i as the sum of $1/c$ of all containers that P_i receives as responses to its requests. In a perfectly balanced tree, $R_i = L_i$. We further introduce relative measures $l_i = L_i/(n-1)$ and $r_i = R_i/(n-1)$ normed by the worst case that initial aggregates of all other $n-1$ peers are leaked/received. Figure 3 shows the distribution of L_i and R_i for a simulation run with $n = 1000$ peers. The simulation has been repeated with different tree configurations without notable changes. In the examined case, the relative leak to the network is $l_i = 0.24(9)\%$. The relative received information $r_i = 0.24(10)\%$ is the same with a slightly higher standard derivation.

The worst case is given by the least balanced tree configuration in which $|\mathbb{S}(x_i, d)| = 1$ for all $d \in \{B, \dots, 1\}$. That means for the given P_i, every sibling subtree contains exactly one other peer. Here, P_i learns in every epoch one initial

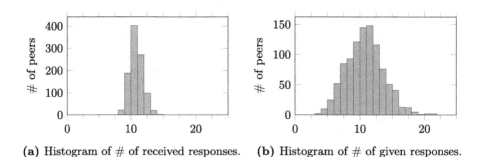

(a) Histogram of # of received responses.   **(b)** Histogram of # of given responses.

Fig. 4. In a simulation with $n = 1000$, the number of given (b) and received (a) responses has been recorded for every peer. While the distribution of received responses is very sharp, the distribution for given responses is twice as broad. In the Kademlia routing tables, some peers are more often represented than others.

aggregate with certainty. However, such a tree allows for only $B + 1$ peers and every additional peer decreases L_i.

Moreover, the load on peers measured by the number of received and given responses has been examined. The histograms in Fig. 4 indicates that no peer receives significantly more load than others—a property that has been shown for Kademlia before.

Eventually, the average number of requests per peer simulated with different numbers of peers n up to $n = 1000$ confirmed the theoretical message complexity of $\mathcal{O}(\log n)$ shown in Sect. 6.

8 Conclusion

We considered the fundamental problem of large-scale confidential aggregation, and proposed the distributed aggregation protocol ADVOKAT. It prioritizes system wide properties like scalability and robustness over perfect completeness, correctness or full secrecy of initial aggregates.

The aggregation step is distributed to entirely equipotent peers which improves the robustness in face of all sorts of attacks and reduces the reliance on institutional trust. Peers may choose their trusted protocol implementation. Cryptography is only employed to manage authorization and ensure integrity, but not to ensure secrecy, which renders the protocol easier to understand and independent of hardness-assumptions common in cryptography. Due to the even distribution of data and the ephemeral nature of the network, the risk of global or targeted leaks after the aggregation is eliminated. With its global message complexity of $\mathcal{O}(n \log n)$, it outperforms SPP with $\mathcal{O}(n \log n^3)$ [18] and DPol with $\mathcal{O}(n\sqrt{n})$ [19] which both provide instead stronger confidentiality.

We showed that the protocol offers a high level of confidentiality though at least comparable to postal voting with trusted authorities. For large n, it is very unlikely that the initial aggregate of a given peer is revealed, which might be acceptable for many applications. Completeness and correctness can be compared to paper-based voting. It is possible that few initial aggregates are manipulated or not counted, but not at a global scale and not often. An individual verification allows to detect manipulations.

The universal protocol algebra supports a wide range of applications, e.g. distributed lottery, aggregation of sensible healthcare data, or all sorts of reduce operations. Turning our protocol into a solution that can be adopted in practice will require some effort. Foremost, a formal definition of completeness and correctness must be introduced so that upper limits of their manipulations depending on the ratio of dishonest peers in the attack model from Sect. 5 can be formulated. Further, the influence of churn of Byzantine peers on the routing tables must be analysed and, if necessary, restricted to allow for Byzantine peers with no assumptions.

Acknowledgments. The authors thank Stéphane Frénot, Damien Reimert, Aurélien Faravelon, Pascal Lafourcade and Matthieu Giraud for fruitful discussions on distributed voting protocols and attack vectors.

References

1. Maymounkov, P., Mazières, D.: Kademlia: a peer-to-peer information system based on the XOR metric. In: Druschel, P., Kaashoek, F., Rowstron, A. (eds.) IPTPS 2002. LNCS, vol. 2429, pp. 53–65. Springer, Heidelberg (2002). doi:10. 1007/3-540-45748-8_5

2. Cohen, B.: The BitTorrent protocol specification (2008).http://bittorrent.org/beps/bep_0003.html

3. Nakamoto, S.: Bitcoin: a peer-to-peer electronic cash system (2008).https://bitcoin.org/bitcoin.pdf

4. Reimert, D., Frénot, S., Grumbach, S., Meyffret, S.: Machine de Vote electronique et Infrastructure comportant une telle Machine. Patent FR3037702 (FR) (2016). http://bases-brevets.inpi.fr/en/document-en/FR3037702.html

5. Zhang, Z., Shi, S.-M., Zhu, J.: SOMO: self-organized metadata overlay for resource management in P2P DHT. In: Kaashoek, M.F., Stoica, I. (eds.) IPTPS 2003. LNCS, vol. 2735, pp. 170–182. Springer, Heidelberg (2003). doi:10.1007/978-3-540-45172-3_16

6. Renesse, R., Bozdog, A.: Willow: DHT, aggregation, and publish/subscribe in one protocol. In: Voelker, G.M., Shenker, S. (eds.) IPTPS 2004. LNCS, vol. 3279, pp. 173–183. Springer, Heidelberg (2005). doi:10.1007/978-3-540-30183-7_17

7. Cappos, J., Hartman, J.H.: San Fermín: aggregating large data sets using a binomial swap forest. In: Proceedings of the 5th USENIX Symposium on Networked Systems Design and Implementation (2008)

8. Artigas, M.S., García, P., Skarmeta, A.F.: DECA: a hierarchical framework for DECentralized aggregation in DHTs. In: State, R., Meer, S., O'Sullivan, D., Pfeifer, T. (eds.) DSOM 2006. LNCS, vol. 4269, pp. 246–257. Springer, Heidelberg (2006). doi:10.1007/11907466_23

9. Albrecht, K., Arnold, R., Gähwiler, M., Wattenhofer, R.: Aggregating information in peer-to-peer systems for improved join and leave. In: Proceedings - 4th International Conference on Peer-to-Peer Computing, P2P 2004, pp. 227–234. IEEE (2004). doi:10.1109/PTP.2004.1334951

10. Evseenko, N.: New hybrid distributed voting algorithm. CoRR abs/1305.0 (2013)

11. Chaum, D.: Blind signatures for untraceable payments. In: Chaum, D., Rivest, R.L., Sherman, A.T. (eds.) Advances in Cryptology: Proceedings of Crypto 82, pp. 199–203. Springer, Boston (1983)

12. Chaum, D.L.: Untraceable electronic mail, return addresses, and digital pseudonyms. Commun. ACM **24**(2), 84–90 (1981)

13. Gennaro, R., Jarecki, S., Krawczyk, H., Rabin, T.: Secure distributed key generation for discrete-log based cryptosystems. In: Stern, J. (ed.) EUROCRYPT 1999. LNCS, vol. 1592, pp. 295–310. Springer, Heidelberg (1999). doi:10.1007/3-540-48910-X_21

14. Benaloh, J.D.C., Yung, M.: Distributing the power of a government to enhance the privacy of voters. In: Proceedings of PODC 1986, pp. 52–62. ACM, USA (1986)

15. Fujioka, A., Okamoto, T., Ohta, K.: A practical secret voting scheme for large scale elections. In: Seberry, J., Zheng, Y. (eds.) AUSCRYPT 1992. LNCS, vol. 718, pp. 244–251. Springer, Heidelberg (1993). doi:10.1007/3-540-57220-1_66

16. Ibrahim, S., Kamat, M., Salleh, M., Aziz, S.: Secure e-voting with blind signature. In: Proceedings of NCTT 2003, pp. 193–197 (2003). doi:10.1109/NCTT.2003. 1188334

17. Zhao, Z., Chan, T.-H.H.: How to vote privately using bitcoin. IACR Cryptology ePrint Archive (2015)
18. Gambs, S., Guerraoui, R., Harkous, H., Huc, F., Kermarrec, A.-M.: Scalable and secure aggregation in distributed networks. arXiv e-prints (2011)
19. Guerraoui, R., Huguenin, K., Kermarrec, A.M., Monod, M., Vigfússon, Í.: Decentralized polling with respectable participants. J. Parallel Distrib. Comput. **72**(1), 13–26 (2012). doi:10.1016/j.jpdc.2011.09.003
20. Hoang, B.-T., Imine, A.: Efficient and decentralized polling protocol for general social networks. In: Pelc, A., Schwarzmann, A.A. (eds.) SSS 2015. LNCS, vol. 9212, pp. 171–186. Springer, Cham (2015). doi:10.1007/978-3-319-21741-3_12
21. Baumgart, I., Mies, S.: S/Kademlia: a practicable approach towards secure key-based routing. In: Proceedings of ICPADS 2007, pp. 1–8. IEEE Computer Society, Washington, DC (2007). doi:10.1109/ICPADS.2007.4447808
22. Cai, X.S., Devroye, L.: A probabilistic analysis of Kademlia networks. In: Cai, L., Cheng, S.-W., Lam, T.-W. (eds.) ISAAC 2013. LNCS, vol. 8283, pp. 711–721. Springer, Heidelberg (2013). doi:10.1007/978-3-642-45030-3_66

Operating System and Firmware Security

HyBIS: Advanced Introspection for Effective Windows Guest Protection

Roberto Di Pietro[1,2], Federico Franzoni[3], and Flavio Lombardi[4(✉)]

[1] Nokia Bell Labs, Paris-Saclay, Paris, France
[2] Maths Dept., Università di Padova, Padova, Italy
[3] Pompeu Fabra University, Barcelona, Spain
[4] IAC-CNR, Rome, Italy
name.surname@cnr.it

Abstract. Effectively protecting the Windows[TM] OS is a challenging task, since most implementation details are not publicly known. Windows OS has always been the main target of malware that have exploited numerous bugs and vulnerabilities exposed by its implementations. Recent trusted boot and additional integrity checks have rendered the Windows OS less vulnerable to kernel-level rootkits. Nevertheless, guest Windows Virtual Machines are becoming an increasingly interesting attack target. In this work we introduce and analyze a novel *Hypervisor-Based Introspection System* (HyBIS) we developed for protecting Windows OSes from malware and rootkits. The HyBIS architecture is motivated and detailed, while targeted experimental results show its effectiveness. Comparison with related work highlights main HyBIS advantages such as: effective semantic introspection, support for 64-bit architectures and for recent Windows versions ($\geq$ win 7), and advanced malware disabling capabilities. We believe the research effort reported here will pave the way to further advances in the security of Windows[TM] OSes.

1 Introduction

Securing the Windows OS is a very challenging task, given its complexity and also given that its internals are not publicly known. Over time, a large set of malware has targeted vulnerabilities in Windows OSes and services. Due to the very large installed base of Windows OSes, there is a great amount of new malware produced every year, which implements advanced methods for detection avoidance. The problem is particularly interesting for recent Windows versions, which have not yet been fully analyzed/investigated by the research community.

Among the different kinds of malware, rootkits represent the most complex and dangerous threats. In fact, rootkits can alter the system's perception of itself, and conceal malicious activities over a large period of time. In particular, modern rootkits can directly manipulate memory structures to further enhance their stealthiness. As such, security tools can hardly detect them and are usually

© IFIP International Federation for Information Processing 2017
Published by Springer International Publishing AG 2017. All Rights Reserved
S. De Capitani di Vimercati and F. Martinelli (Eds.): SEC 2017, IFIP AICT 502, pp. 189–204, 2017.
DOI: 10.1007/978-3-319-58469-0_13

unable react to the infection. For this reason, rootkit detection is a vital task for protecting Windows and it is then fundamental to make it as effective as possible.

1.1 Motivation

Current monitoring approaches cannot provide an adequate level of protection against rootkits targeting Windows OSes. In fact, most solutions operate at the same level as rootkits do [8,22,28]. By tampering with the functions leveraged by security tools, rootkits are able to evade detection from within the OS. Hence, anti-rootkit tools working at the OS level cannot be trusted in case of rootkit infection. When the OS is running in a virtual machine, however, this problem can be addressed in a different way. Such a scenario, in fact, allows an external observation of the OS, from a more trustworthy and isolated environment. This capability is provided by the hypervisor, which can directly access VM components without leveraging OS functions.

Such a capability enables the adoption of virtual machine introspection (VMI [14,21]), which consists of inferring the guest OS semantics from the analysis of the status of VM components. VMI provides a valuable tool to counter rootkits since they can hardly conceal their presence to a monitoring system not dependent on OS functions.

On the one hand, VMI on Windows guest is however hard in practice, as it requires some specific OS information in order to make sense out of raw machine data [14]. This is one of the challenges of our present work, and it is also one of the main contribution of this work. On the other hand, VMI can be supported by the use of forensic memory analysis (FMA), which provides the means for extracting OS information from raw memory data. In fact, as stated above, since modern rootkits manipulate memory to avoid detection, they can be identified by inspecting the same memory contents [19]. This is a clear advantage over rootkits and allows the implementation of more reliable security systems.

Moreover, once the infection has been identified, the hypervisor also allows an effective reaction. In fact, by leveraging unfettered access to physical resources, a security tool can directly manipulate the VM and stop rootkit activities.

All these features, render the hypervisor a very attractive place where to implement security functionalities. In this work, we will leverage advanced VMI and FMA to help securing Windows OSes in virtualized environments.

1.2 Contribution

This work introduces and discusses a novel effective approach for countering rootkits on a Windows OS running in a VM. The implemented security monitor is external to the target machine, similarly to some recent literature [13,35]. By leveraging VMI and current FMA tools, we developed a novel *Hypervisor-Based Introspection System* (HyBIS) for protecting a Windows OS from stealth malware, in particular from rootkits.

The proposed system extends the hypervisor to monitor the state of the running machine, to detect rootkits, and to react to the discovered anomalies. The monitoring functionality leverages VMI techniques to infer the guest OS status. In order to detect rootkits, guest memory is scanned for kernel objects which may have been hidden. Such a scan is performed on memory dump files by means of FMA techniques and tools. Although such tools are typically used for offline analyses, the proposed system utilises them in a live way, during the system execution. To this purpose, HyBIS provides a novel dumping system which allows improving the performance of the memory acquisition task. Furthermore, a novel reaction approach is implemented that makes use of the hypervisor to manipulate memory contents while the virtual machine is running. This capability is leveraged to prevent the execution of detected rootkit processes. HyBIS allows detecting and reacting to rootkits effectively on recent Windows OSes. HyBIS successfully proves that the combination of VMI and FMA provides a valuable tool for countering rootkits on Windows OSes.

2   Related Work

This section surveys most relevant related work and stresses the main differences with respect to our solution.

Zhang et al. [33] leverage SMM, an advanced x86 execution mode, for detecting memory-based stealthy malware. Their SPECTRE framework can introspect a live operating system and supports both Windows and Linux OSes. However, this framework is vulnerable to hardware-based attacks, such as [34]. Furthermore, their work is limited to Windows XP SP3.

In [16], Hizver and Chiueh make use of Volatility for the analysis of VM execution states. Their RTKDMS system is able to perform real-time monitoring at the hypervisor level. Differently from HyBIS, such an architecture leverages an additional VM for the introspection analysis. Again, the experiments are limited to Windows XP. Furthermore, their system does not tackle the rootkit threat specifically, neither it explores any reaction possibility.

Deng et al. [9] propose the SPIDER architecture, a stealthy program instrumentation and debugging framework built upon hardware virtualization. SPIDER enables monitoring memory read/write at any address. Nonetheless, unlike HyBIS, it requires an in-guest agent which modifies the guest OS kernel.

In [20], Lengyel et al. describe DRAKVUF, a novel dynamic malware analysis system based on Xen, which improves hardware resources usage efficiency. DRAKVUF takes advantage of the hardware virtualization extensions to provide a transparent and scalable environment to enable in-depth analysis of malware samples. In this case, the target OS is Windows 7 SP1 in both 32- and 64-bit versions.

Differently from DECAF [15] which only supports introspection of 32 bit guests, our HyBIS approach also allows inspecting 64 bit Windows guests. Furthermore, Henderson et al. declare that VMI has limitations against some types of attack (due to the ability of the guest attacker to modify memory contents at will). While we agree that memory analysis can be circumvented in theory, we believe in practice continuous monitoring and effective/smart diff-deltas can render an attack much less practical.

As regards memory forensics issues, an interesting work by Balzarotti et al. [7] assesses the impact of GPU-assisted malware [10] on memory forensics. They discuss different techniques that malware can adopt to hide its presence on GPUs. Their analysis shows that, by offloading some computation to the GPUs, it is possible to successfully hide some malicious behavior.

Harrison [13] suggests an approach that is somewhat similar to HyBIS. However it aims to be integrated into other IDS solutions [11], and mostly focuses on the analysis phase. HyBIS, instead also explores the novel reaction capabilities given by the combination of VMI and FMA techniques.

3   HyBIS - Approach and Functionalities

This section describes the approach behind HyBIS, the proposed Hypervisor-Based Introspection System for Windows. HyBIS combines FMA techniques with the VMI approach. As mentioned above, the main goal of our work is to improve Windows security in virtualized environments. In particular, our research focuses on protecting such OS from rootkits. In order to protect Windows from modern rootkits, we mostly focused our studies on the RAM component. Memory, in fact, stores both code and data and is involved in almost every operation performed on the machine during OS execution. Thus, RAM can be considered the most complete source of information about the status of a running OS at a specific time. For such a reason, modern rootkits use to manipulate memory to conceal their activities and resources. Nonetheless they reside in RAM while running, thus giving the opportunity to detect their presence. Hence, memory is the best place where to look for inferring the current status of the target machine. FMA enables performing such a task in an effective and convenient way.

The basic idea we followed for the development of our security system was that the hypervisor can do more than what it is intended for. The chosen design approach was then to augment the hypervisor capabilities by means of introspection techniques. We extended the hypervisor by introducing the following functionalities: (i) *Monitoring*: the hypervisor is enabled to monitor the machine state in order to realize if something anomalous is happening; (ii) *Analysis*: the hypervisor is enabled to analyze the state of the guest OS in order to detect the presence of rootkits; (iii) *Reaction*: the hypervisor is enabled to react when a rootkit is detected and block its activities. The above functionalities leverage internal hypervisor functions as well as external libraries and tools. The internal functions provide direct access to virtual machine hardware components. In particular, they allow to monitor the VM CPU and physical memory. By checking the CPU state and reading the memory contents, it is possible to implement a transparent monitoring function. Furthermore, the write access to memory can give the ability to perform changes into a running VM.

By making use of external tools and libraries, the hypervisor can be given even more capabilities. For instance, by integrating memory forensic functions, it is possible to implement advanced analysis techniques, which may allow detecting the presence of rootkits into the system.

Monitoring - Checking The System State: the virtual machine state can be analyzed by means of VMI. As stated before, the hypervisor has the ability to access virtual hardware resources directly, allowing the monitoring of all the VM components. In particular, we chose to monitor CPU and memory as they are core components of the machine.

CPU state changes can be easily monitored by using internal hypervisor functions. Such functions allow, for instance, checking the current operating mode, or inspecting registers.

VM memory contents changes can be monitored by means of differential dumps. With this approach, memory dumps are periodically generated to check if a particular area has been modified. In order to implement such a functionality, an initial memory snapshot must be taken at a specific time. Such a snapshot can then be used as basis for the comparison with the following checkpoints.

Analysis - Detecting Rootkits: as previously explained, modern rootkits are able to manipulate memory objects at runtime to conceal their activities. Hence, in order to detect rootkits, the analysis functionality should focus on the memory contents. This kind of analysis requires advanced forensic techniques to discover an infection. A convenient approach would be then to make use of functions from an external forensic tool or library.

Memory forensic analyses are commonly based on memory dumps. Hence, a memory acquisition functionality is required to make use of the forensic tools. Fortunately, most hypervisors implement their own dumping facility which can be used to acquire guest memory. Such a facility can be easily expanded/adapted to improve the acquisition process and realize the above-mentioned differential dumping functionality.

Reaction - Countering Rootkits: in order to react when a rootkit is detected, some kind of action has to be taken to prevent it from performing further activities. As such, guest memory can be used to implement the reaction functionality.

Since rootkits, even if concealed, reside in memory, it would be a good approach to counter them into the same place. Once again, hypervisor functions can come in handy: by writing into guest memory, it could be possible to delete the detected rootkit from memory, or to block its current execution.

3.1   HyBIS Functionalities

We set up to implement four high-level functionalities in HyBIS: Automatic boot dump generation; Smart differential dumping; Detection of hidden rootkit processes; Blocking of hidden rootkit processes. In the following, we detail each functionality.

Automatic Boot Dump Generation: as explained above, the monitoring functionality should allow deciding when an analysis operation would be appropriate. Since the analysis functionality operates over memory dumps, we decided to automatically generate a dump on the basis of some hardware event. In particular, we chose to monitor the VM during the boot phase in order to produce a dump at the very beginning of the Windows loading procedure.

This choice has a twofold reason. Firstly, it aims at determining the first feasible moment for analyzing a memory dump with a forensic tool; in fact, these tools need the kernel to be loaded in order to work. Secondly, such initial dump can be used as starting point for a following monitoring of the memory; in fact, after the kernel has been loaded, most of the system areas remain fixed during the rest of OS execution.

Hence, this function should allow HyBIS to automatically generate a memory dump as soon as the Windows kernel process starts.

This objective has been chosen to demonstrate how, by means of introspection, the VM state monitoring can be effectively used for determining meaningful moments of the OS execution.

Smart Differential Dumping: besides the CPU, the monitoring functionality can check specific virtual machine memory areas for changes, in order to decide if an analysis operation is needed.

As stated above, a differential approach can be taken to perform this kind of monitoring. However, memory acquisition can be a very onerous task to perform, especially when it has to be repeated over time. So, it is important to do such an operation efficiently in order to not compromise the guest system performance. Since only some memory ranges need to be checked, there is no need to dump the whole memory at every checkpoint. Instead, it should be enough to acquire only the ranges we are interested in.

This function should allow HyBIS to update a previously created dump by acquiring selective ranges and overwriting them into the corresponding areas. Previous contents of such ranges should be backed up in separate files in order to allow the comparison between different checkpoints. With such an approach, it can be said that HyBIS uses "dynamic" dumps.

Dynamic dumps can also be used to improve the acquisition process necessary for the forensic analyses. In fact, since such analyses usually involve only some ranges of the whole dump, it is possible to use the update mechanisms described above, to perform the analyses of different checkpoints without needing to create multiple dumps of the whole memory.

This objective has been chosen to demonstrate how monitoring the VM memory can be both effective and efficient.

Detection of hidden rootkit processes: it is well-known that rootkits try to hide their processes to avoid detection. This is effectively obtained by implementing the DKOM technique [17]. In particular, a rootkit that wants to hide a process, could remove the corresponding object from the active process list. In fact, Windows uses two lists of processes: one for scheduling, and one for tracking. A process whose object is removed from the tracking list, will be invisible while still active. As such, hidden processes can be detected by means of a cross-view analysis[1]. More specifically, this can be done by scanning memory for process objects, and comparing the results with the active process list. If a scanned process is not present in this list it is likely to be a hidden rootkit process. This function should allow HyBIS to detect hidden processes by creating a memory dump and scanning it for concealed process objects.

This objective has been chosen to demonstrate how FMA can help in detecting rootkits on running guest OSes.

Blocking of hidden rootkit processes: once a hidden process has been detected, it should be blocked to prevent it from keeping performing malicious activities. This action will not clean the infection but it could be a first step to defeat the rootkit.

A good idea for blocking a hidden process would be to exclude it from scheduling, thus preventing its execution. This can be done using the DKOM technique in a similar way as that used by rootkits. More specifically, we can block a hidden process by removing the corresponding object from the scheduling list. This function should allow HyBIS to manipulate the VM memory in order to prevent the rootkit process to be executed.

This objective has been chosen to demonstrate how the hypervisor capabilities allow an effective reaction to a rootkit infection by means of memory manipulation.

4   HyBIS - Design, Architecture and Implementation

This section shows how HyBIS was designed to extend the hypervisor capabilities for securing a guest Windows OS from the rootkit threat. First, we show the overall HyBIS operation from a high-level point of view. Next, we describe the HyBIS architecture. Finally, we describe and motivate the technologies chosen to build up the first HyBIS prototype, and the most relevant implementation details.

The high-level overview of the HyBIS operating mode is depicted in Fig. 1a. The new functionalities are designed to work as a closed loop control system. The monitoring phase extracts information from a running machine and intercepts events which could reveal the presence of rootkits. The analysis phase examines the system in order to evaluate if a rootkit infection occurred. In such a case, it triggers the reaction phase, otherwise it returns to the monitoring phase. The reaction phase tries to remove the infection or block the rootkit for preventing further malicious activities.

The monitoring and reaction functionalities leverage the introspection and control capabilities of the hypervisor. The analysis functionality is based on forensic functions provided by external tools but needs some additional intervention to interpret the results and taking further actions. Since the complexity of such a task, some kind of intelligence is needed to take decisions. This

---

[1] It is worth noticing that malware able to infiltrate the task scheduling could be executed without being on process lists. Current HyBIS does not test for this. This is left as future work.

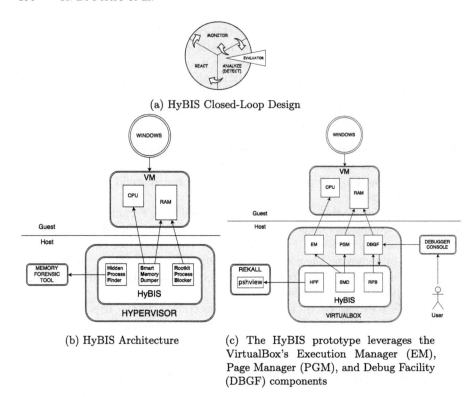

(a) HyBIS Closed-Loop Design

(b) HyBIS Architecture

(c) The HyBIS prototype leverages the VirtualBox's Execution Manager (EM), Page Manager (PGM), and Debug Facility (DBGF) components

Fig. 1. HyBIS design, architecture, and implementation details

is represented by the *evaluator*, which is an external component that can be inserted into the analysis phase. The evaluator functionality can be performed by a human examiner as well as an external plugin which implements advanced AI techniques, such as Machine Learning, Expert Systems, Human Expertise, and so on.

4.1 Architecture

The HyBIS architecture is shown in Fig. 1b. As can be seen, on the guest side, there is a Windows OS running on a virtual machine (VM). On the host side, there is the hypervisor that controls the VM, which incorporates the HyBIS component. The HyBIS component extends the hypervisor with the new security functionalities. Such functionalities are implemented by three components, described below. Outside the hypervisor, on the same side, there is the memory forensic tool, which is used by HyBIS to provide advanced analysis capabilities.

HyBIS Components: HyBIS includes three components, running in parallel with the guest OS, without interrupting/suspending its execution:

- *Smart Memory Dumper* (SMD): this component allows creating the dynamic dumps described in the previous section; it leverages the hypervisor to read the VM's RAM contents and create or update dump files on the host disk;
- *Hidden Process Finder* (HPF): this component allows detecting hidden processes running in the guest Windows OS; it leverages the external memory forensic tool to perform analyses on the dump files created by SMD;
- *Rootkit Process Blocker* (RPB): this component allows blocking a detected rootkit process on the guest OS by preventing it from being scheduled for execution; it receives from HPF the information on the detected process and leverages the hypervisor for manipulating the VM's RAM.

4.2   Technology Info

In this section we discuss the technologies selected for the development of the first HyBIS prototype. In particular, the target Windows version, the hypervisor and the forensic tool, have been chosen due to their effectiveness and wide deployment base.

The Target OS: most of the latest security-related work still focuses on Windows XP or Windows 7 OSes. However, Windows 8 introduced some internal changes (such as [18]) and security mechanisms (see [27]) which partially invalidate previous results. For instance, the removal of the `KiFastSystemCall` function makes all rootkit techniques based on this function unusable [26]. Furthermore, the latest Windows 10 OS appears to keep such changes, rendering previous work yet more obsolete.

At the time we started the development of HyBIS, Windows 10 was only available in its Technical Preview release. Hence, we selected Windows 8.1 (which is much more widespread then Windows 8) as the target of our experiments.

We initially decided to focus our tests on the 32-bit version since it is more efficient when performing extensive memory-related experiments. Furthermore, the 64-bit version which implements more advanced security mechanisms, would have limited our malware testbed. As such, extensive experimental activity on 64-bit OSes will be the target of future work.

The Hypervisor: most of the recent projects targeting Windows as guest OS, involve the qemu-kvm [1] or the Xen hypervisors [4]. Although these ones represent valid tools, we decided to make use of the VirtualBox [24] hypervisor. In fact, VirtualBox, apart from being one of the mainstream virtualization technologies, has two main advantages over qemu-kvm and Xen: firstly, it fully supports all Windows versions, including the latest Windows 10; secondly, it includes various VM-debugging functionalities, that allow controlling and manipulating VM components [24]. Such funcionalities can be very useful when implementating advanced introspection techniques. For the HyBIS prototype implementation the latest VirtualBox 5.0 version has been used.

The Memory Forensic Tool: among the available FMA tools, Volatility [3] is certainly the most widespread. It has a vast number of functionalities and it can count on a very active community. Nonetheless, it does not fully support all Windows kernel versions. In addition, its performance on memory analysis is quite low for our real-time usage requirement.

A derived project, named Rekall [2], overcomes these limits, while maintaining main Volatility features and advantages. Its novel kernel profiling system, enables Rekall to automatically upgrade its compatibility with new Windows versions [5]. Furthermore, thanks to some improved memory-scanning functions, it shows better analysis performances. This renders Rekall both more efficient and effective than Volatility. Moreover, it can be integrated as part of other software as a library. Finally, since Rekall is implemented in the Python language, it can be easily installed into a variety of host OSes (This is also an advantage of VBox over Kvm and Xen). For the HyBIS prototype implementation we made use of Rekall 1.4.

4.3   Implementation Details

We will now describe how the proposed architecture was implemented by making use of the previously-mentioned technologies. The HyBIS implementation details are depicted in Fig. 1c. As before, on the guest side we have a Windows OS, running in a VM. On the host side, we have the VirtualBox hypervisor, with its internal components: the Execution Manager (EM), the Page Manager (PGM), and the Debug Facility (DBGF). The HyBIS component is implemented as a new VirtualBox component, interacting with the other ones to perform its tasks. In particular, the SMD component leverages PGM for the memory acquisition, and EM for the automatic boot dump generation. The RPB component uses DBGF to manipulate guest memory. The HPF component makes use of the external Rekall component to perform advanced analyses over memory dumps.

The interaction with the HyBIS components is provided through a set of new commands on the VirtualBox integrated Debug Console. These commands will be described later in this section.

Extending VirtualBox. The following VirtualBox components have been involved for the HyBIS implementation:

- Virtual Machine Monitor (VMM): this is the core hypervisor;
- Execution Manager (EM): it controls the execution of guest code;
- Page Manager (PGM): it controls guest memory paging;
- Debug Facility (DBGF): it provides a built-in debugger for the VM.

Most of the VM-related components are implemented in the VMM section. Therefore, this is the most suitable place where to insert the new HyBIS component. The EM component is leveraged to monitor the CPU operation mode in order to automatically generate the boot dump. The PGM provides all guest memory management functions and is used to implement the acquisition functionalities. The DBGF provides a lot of useful debugging functions, which are used for implementing the reaction functionality. Furthermore, it provides the console devoted to the interaction with the HyBIS component.

Integrating Rekall. Since Rekall is written in Python, an interpreter must be present on the host system. For incorporating Rekall, it has been necessary to import the Python C++ library into the VirtualBox source code. The Rekall functionalities, instead, can be used by means of the provided API library, as mentioned in the previous section. In order to make use of the forensic analysis functions, a suitable session has to be set up. A Rekall session represents a specific combination of a dump file and a selected profile. When starting a session, if a valid profile for the current kernel version is found, every compatible Rekall plugin automatically becomes available to be used for a forensic analysis.

4.4 Further Details

HyBIS embodies a set of novel architectural and implementation-related features. In the following, a broad view and some relevant details are given.

Technically speaking, HyBIS is an hypervisor-based IDS which leverages Virtual Machine Introspection (VMI) to monitor a virtualized environment and exploits Forensic Memory Analysis (FMA) to bridge the semantic gap.

With respect to previous solutions, HyBIS uses a novel approach, whose differences are explained in the following.

Use of VMI: typical hypervisor-based IDSs reside on top of the hypervisor, in a Secure Virtual Machine (SVM) (see Fig. 2).

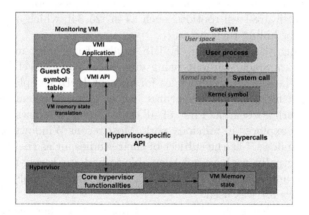

Fig. 2. A typical VMI architecture [30]

Such an approach has the advantage of isolating the security functions so to avoid corruption. However, in such a case, the IDS requires an additional VM, and its capabilities are limited by the functionalities provided through the hypervisor APIs. HyBIS, instead, is integrated into the hypervisor, as shown in Fig. 1b. As such, it is able to exploit all the hypervisor capabilities in order to have full control over the target VM.

An alternative VMI approach leverages advanced CPU features to interpose the security functions between the OS and the hardware [35]. However, this kind of hypervisor does not have the control over all the machine components. Furthermore, this approach usually requires an in-guest agent to be installed into the OS kernel. Conversely, HyBIS does not require any addition to the guest OS kernel and does not rely on any CPU feature.

So, while current VMI-based solutions have limited possibilities to exploit the hypervisor capabilities, the HyBIS novel approach gives the ability to fully exploit them by integrating into the hypervisor. By working from below the VM, it has a full overview of the whole machine state, while still being isolated from the target machine, thus avoiding both OS-level and hardware-level attacks.

Use of Memory Forensics: FMA can be a valuable means for VMI-based systems to bridge the semantic gap. However, it has not yet been fully leveraged by current solutions. This is probably due to the slowness of the memory acquisition process. In fact, FMA tools usually operate on offline dump files, whose creation may take too long for a practical real-time usage. As such, memory acquisition, represents a critical step for the implementation of a real-time FMA-based solution. Furthermore, the soundness of the acquisition process is another serious concern, given that memory is usually dumped by tools installed into the guest OS (see [29]). Such tools have the drawback of altering memory contents and to be vulnerable to OS-level attacks which may corrupt acquired data. Alternatively, memory acquisition can be hardware-based, using techniques, such as DMA, that allow bypassing the OS. Such techniques, however, can still be bypassed by hardware-level rootkits, such as in [25,34], which are able to alter acquired data for hiding their presence.

By leveraging the hypervisor, HyBIS is able to acquire memory using a novel dynamic approach, without being vulnerable to OS-level and hardware-level attacks. The chosen technologies for present HyBIS implementation was not only chosen for their useful features. All of them represent an element of novelty for security research. First of all, the chosen Windows kernel version has been poorly explored in previous work. Most recent Windows-related papers still refer to Windows 7 as the subject of their studies, or as the target for their experiments. Actually, we have not been able to find any kernel-related research on Windows 8 and Windows 8.1. Instead, in our HyBIS implementation and testing, Windows 8.1 was used.

Leveraging the Virtualbox hypervisor represents another relevant contribution of this paper. Most security and virtualization studies involved other common hypervisors, like KVM or Xen. Instead, besides a few performance analyses, we were able to find only a single work involving VirtualBox for its implementation [23]. In the development of HyBIS, VirtualBox has proved to be a great tool for our purposes. In fact, its features and functionalities have been very helpful for the exploration of VMI techniques.

A similar discussion can be made about the Rekall forensic tool. To the best of our knowledge, Rekall was rarely used as part of a security research project. The only online reference found was in [6], where Rekall was used to analyze Windows profiling. This is probably due to its relatively recent introduction (2007). Most studies and researches involved Volatility instead, from which Rekall was derived. In fact, Volatility has the advantage of being more widespread and supported. However, as previously described, Rekall presents almost the same features but introduce novel features that drastically improves performance and usability. As such, we found it a valuable tool for memory forensic research.

5   Evaluation

Experiments have been performed, testing the implemented prototype effectiveness, and the functionality of each HyBIS component described in Sect. 3.1. Some details of the evaluation are given below.

Boot Dump Generation: As previously described, this function should generate a memory dump as soon as the Window kernel has been loaded and begins to run. In order to prove the effectiveness of this function, the generated dump has been analyzed with Rekall. The analysis showed that the only running process found in memory was `System`, that is the Windows kernel image process. This proves that the dump generation actually occurs at the beginning of the Windows kernel execution. This dump also proved to be acquired in the very first moment the kernel loads. Dumps generated before this point failed to be analyzed by both Rekall and Volatility.

As for what stated above, we can claim that this function generates a dump at the very first suitable time for being analyzed by these kind of FMA tools. Moreover, we believe this functionality, if properly extended, can be helpful in detecting those rootkits that load during the very early stages of the Windows boot.

Dynamic Dumping: This function has been devised to explore new ways of making the dump creation phase faster for monitoring purposes. In order to test it, we identified a restricted memory area to update a previously created dump, while still allowing forensic analysis functionalities. In particular, we selected a range of 250MB, which empirically showed to always contain all kernel process objects. ASLR [12], does not to affect the results of our tests. In fact, the leveraged tools are able to find out the correct position for the kernel structures.

With the purpose of proving the usefulness of this functionality we first created a dump, then started a new process in the guest, and eventually updated the dump by acquiring the above mentioned memory range. Thereafter, we scanned the updated dump with Rekall, to retrieve the active processes list. As expected, the new process was correctly present in the list.

This demontrates that such a reduced memory acquisition speeds up the acquisition process, while not preventing Rekall to properly work, with respect to specific operations. This enables a new form of memory monitoring, which is not limited to single page changes, but involves larger areas. In fact, by leveraging FMA, it is possible to check memory for changes in the OS-level data (e.g. the presence a new process).

Detection and Blocking of Hidden Processes: In order to monitor guest OSes, HyBIS creates a monitoring thread for each VM. This thread periodically dumps the VM memory and analyze it with Rekall. In particular, we created an improved version of the `psxview` plugin, called `pshview`, in such a way that it could be automatically filter the suspected hidden processes. Specifically, it tries to distinguish among dead processes, which may remain in memory for a while after their termination, from those which are still present in the system lists, such as the thread list or the session list. In addition, this function avoid scanning the whole memory, as this seldomly proved to discover more processes than those found by reconstructing kernel object lists. The user also has the ability to enable or disable the scan function, as well as increment or decrement the scanning rate.

If after the analysis the `pshview` plugin returns a suspected hidden process, a pop-up message will be shown to the user, warning about the detected threat, and suggesting to block it through the `.psblock` function. This removes the hidden process object from the system scheduling list (as well as other system lists), thus preventing its execution. In order to prove the effectiveness of this action, we again dumped memory and fully analyzed it to verify the blocked process was not among the active processes lists anymore.

Testbed Setup: All experiments were conducted on a machine with 12 GB of memory and CPU Intel Core i7 2.4 GHz. Each VM had 1 GB of memory (common size on AWS), and Intel VT-x, EPT, and PAE features enabled. As stated above, the target OS was Windows 8.1 32-bit. The OS was infected with different rootkit specimens, chosen among the most widespread and dangerous, such as ZeuS [31] and ZeroAccess [32].

6   Conclusion and Future Work

In this work we shed light on some security issues of the Windows OS. Our main contribution is the design of the novel HyBIS architecture, which successfully combines VMI and FMA to build up an anti-rootkit security system for Windows. VMI is used to examine the Windows status by means of hardware monitoring, while FMA is used to carve meaningful information from raw memory data. A rich experimental campaign was performed over most relevant malware specimens, allowing us to detect and block different hidden malicious processes. Given the architectural complexity of the Windows kernel security field, the results reported in this paper — other than being interesting on their own — also pave the way for further research.

References

1. Kvm. http://www.linux-kvm.org. Accessed 20 Feb 2017
2. Rekall memory forensic framework. http://www.rekall-forensic.com. Accessed 20 Feb 2017
3. The volatilty foundation. http://www.volatilityfoundation.org. Accessed 20 Feb 2017
4. The xen project. http://xenproject.org. Accessed 20 Feb 2017
5. Rekall profiles, February 2014. http://rekall-forensic.blogspot.it/2014/02/rekall-profiles.html. Accessed 20 Feb 2017
6. Windows Virtual Address Translation (2015). http://www.rekall-forensic.com/posts/2015-08-03-address_translation.html. Accessed 20 Feb 2017
7. Balzarotti, D., Di Pietro, R., Villani, A.: The impact of GPU-assisted malware on memory forensics. Digit. Investig. **14**(S1), S16–S24 (2015)
8. Battistoni, R., Gabrielli, E., Mancini, L.V.: A host intrusion prevention system for windows operating systems. In: Samarati, P., Ryan, P., Gollmann, D., Molva, R. (eds.) ESORICS 2004. LNCS, vol. 3193, pp. 352–368. Springer, Heidelberg (2004). doi:10.1007/978-3-540-30108-0_22
9. Deng, Z., Zhang, X., Xu, D.: Spider: stealthy binary program instrumentation and debugging via hardware virtualization. In: Proceedings of the 29th Annual Computer Security Applications Conference, ACSAC 2013, pp. 289–298. ACM, New York (2013)
10. Di Pietro, R., Lombardi, F., Villani, A.: CUDA Leaks: a detailed hack for CUDA and a (Partial) fix. ACM Trans. Embed. Comput. Syst. **15**(1), 15:1–15:25 (2016)
11. Di Pietro, R., Mancini, L.V.: Intrusion Detection Systems, 1st edn. Springer Publishing Company, Incorporated (2008)
12. Gu, Y., Lin, Z.: Derandomizing kernel address space layout for memory introspection and forensics. In: Proceedings of the 6th Conference on Data and Application Security and Privacy, CODASPY 2016, pp. 62–72. ACM, New York (2016)
13. Harrison, C.B.: ODinn: An In-Vivo Hypervisor-based Intrusion Detection System for the Cloud. Ph.D. thesis, Auburn University (2014)
14. Hebbal, Y., Laniepce, S., Menaud, J.-M.: Virtual machine introspection: Techniques and applications. In: 10th International Conference on Availability, Reliability and Security (ARES), pp. 676–685, August 2015
15. Henderson, A., Prakash, A., Yan, L.K., Hu, X., Wang, X., Zhou, R., Yin, H.: Make it work, make it right, make it fast: Building a platform-neutral whole-system dynamic binary analysis platform. In: Proceedings of the International Symposium on Software Testing and Analysis, ISSTA 2014, pp. 248–258. ACM, New York (2014)
16. Hizver, J., Chiueh, T.-C.: Real-time deep virtual machine introspection and its applications. In: ACM SIGPLAN Notices, vol. 49, pp. 3–14. ACM (2014)
17. Hoglund, G., Butler, J.: Rootkits: Subverting the Windows Kernel. Addison-Wesley Professional, Boston (2005)
18. Ionescu, A.: How control flow guard drastically caused windows 8.1 address space and behavior changes (2015). http://www.alex-ionescu.com/?p=246. Accessed 20 Feb 2017
19. Kornblum, J.D.: Exploiting the rootkit paradox with windows memory analysis. Int. J. Digital Evid. **5**(1), 1–5 (2006)
20. Lengyel, T.K., Maresca, S., Payne, B.D., Webster, G.D., Vogl, S., Kiayias, A.: Scalability, fidelity and stealth in the DRAKVUF dynamic malware analysis system. In: Proceedings of the 30th Annual Computer Security Applications Conference (2014)

21. Lombardi, F., Di Pietro, R.: Secure virtualization for cloud computing. J. Netw. Comput. Appl. **34**(4), 1113–1122 (2011)
22. Mahapatra, C., Selvakumar, S.: An online cross view difference and behavior based kernel rootkit detector. SIGSOFT Softw. Eng. Notes **36**(4), 1–9 (2011)
23. Mulfari, D., Celesti, A., Puliafito, A., Villari, M.: How cloud computing can support on-demand assistive services. In: Proceedings of the 10th International Cross-Disciplinary Conference on Web Accessibility, W4A 2013, pp. 27:1–27:4. ACM, New York (2013)
24. Oracle Corp. Oracle vm virtualbox programming guide and reference (2016). http://download.virtualbox.org/virtualbox/SDKRef.pdf. Accessed 20 Feb 2017
25. Rutkowska, J.: Beyond the CPU: Defeating Hardware-based RAM acquisition. Black Hat Briefings (2006). Accessed 20 Feb 2017
26. M. Tech. Intercepting all system calls by hooking kifastsystemcall, April 2015. http://www.malwaretech.com/2015/04/intercepting-all-system-calls-by.html. Accessed 20 Feb 2017
27. M. TechNet. What's changed in security technologies in windows 8.1, July 2013. https://technet.microsoft.com/it-it/library/dn344918.aspx. Accessed 20 Feb 2017
28. Tsaur, W., Yeh, L.: Identifying rootkit infections using a new windows hidden-driver-based rootkit. In: International Conference on Security and Management, Las Vegas, USA, pp. 16–19, July 2012
29. Vömel, S., Freiling, F.C.: Correctness, atomicity, and integrity: defining criteria for forensically-sound memory acquisition. Digital Invest. **9**(2), 125–137 (2012)
30. Win, T.Y., Tianfield, H., Mair, Q., Said, T.A., Rana, O.F.: Virtual machine introspection. In: Proceedings of the 7th International Conference on Security of Information and Networks, SIN 2014, pp. 405:405–405:410. ACM, New York (2014)
31. Wyke, J.: What is Zeus? Sophos Technical report, Sophos, May 2011
32. Wyke, J.: Zeroaccess. Technical report, April 2012
33. Zhang, F., Leach, K., Sun, K., Stavrou, A.: SPECTRE: a dependable introspection framework via System Management Mode. In: Proceedings of the 43rd IEEE/IFIP International Conference on Dependable Systems and Networks (DSN), DSN 2013, pp. 1–12. IEEE Computer Society, Washington, DC (2013)
34. Zhang, N., Sun, K., Lou, W., Hou, Y.T., Jajodia, S.: Now you see me: Hide and seek in physical address space. In: Proceedings of the 10th Symposium on Information, Computer and Communications Security, ASIACCS 2015, pp. 321–331. ACM, New York (2015)
35. Zhong, X., Xiang, C., Yu, M., Qi, Z., Guan, H.: A virtualization based monitoring system for mini-intrusive live forensics. Int. J. Parallel Program. **43**(3), 455–471 (2015)

Detection of Side Channel Attacks Based on Data Tainting in Android Systems

Mariem Graa[1](✉), Nora Cuppens-Boulahia[1], Frédéric Cuppens[1],
Jean-Louis Lanet[2], and Routa Moussaileb[1]

[1] IMT Atlantique, 2 Rue de la Châtaigneraie, 35576 Cesson Sévigné, France
{mariem.graa,nora.cuppens,frederic.cuppens,
routa.moussaileb}@imt-atlantique.fr
[2] Campus de Beaulieu, 263 Avenue Général Leclerc, 35042 Rennes, France
jean-louis.lanet@inria.fr

Abstract. Malicious third-party applications can leak personal data stored in the Android system by exploiting side channels. TaintDroid uses a dynamic taint analysis mechanism to control the manipulation of private data by third-party apps [9]. However, TaintDroid does not propagate taint in side channels. An attacker can exploit this limitation to get private data. For example, Sarwar *et al.* [2] present side channel class of attacks using a medium that might be overlooked by the taint-checking mechanism to extract sensitive data in Android system. In this paper, we enhance the TaintDroid system and we propagate taint in side channels using formal policy rules. To evaluate the effectiveness of our approach, we analyzed 100 free Android applications. We found that these applications use different side channels to transfer sensitive data. We successfully detected that 35% of them leaked private information through side channels. Also, we detected Sarwar *et al.* [2] side channel attacks. Our approach generates 9% of false positives. The overhead given by our approach is acceptable in comparison to the one obtained by TaintDroid (9% overhead).

1 Introduction

Android devices account for 80.7% of the global smartphone sales in most markets in the world [8]. With the continuous demand of these systems, the user privacy threat is growing. Malicious applications aim to steal personal data stored in the device or potentially available through side channels such as timing, storage channels, etc. Side channel attacks [4,13,18] exploit the use of medium to infer private information (SMS, contacts, location, phone number, pictures...) by analyzing side channels. Sarwar *et al.* [2] proposed side channel attacks such as the bypass timing, bitmap cache, meta data, and graphical properties attacks that create taint free variables from tainted objects to circumvent the dynamic taint analysis security technique. Kim *et al.* [15] utilized screen bitmap memory attack proposed by Sarwar *et al.* to propose a collection system that retrieves sensitive

S. De Capitani di Vimercati and F. Martinelli (Eds.): SEC 2017, IFIP AICT 502, pp. 205–218, 2017.
DOI: 10.1007/978-3-319-58469-0_14

information through screenshot image. The Android security model is based on application sandboxing, application signing, and a permission framework. The side channel attack runs in its own process, with its own instance of the Dalvik virtual machine. It accesses to side channels that are a public medium. Consequently, the application sandboxing technique cannot detect these attacks. The malicious application that implements side channel attacks is digitally signed with a certificate. Therefore, it can be installed on Android systems. The standard Android permission system controls access to sensitive data but does not ensure end to end security because it does not track information flow through side channels. As the core security mechanisms of Android cannot detect side channel attacks, new approaches that extend the Android OS have been proposed. XMan-Droid [3], a security framework, extends the monitoring mechanism of Android to detect side channel attacks such as Soundcomber. However, it cannot detect subset of side channels such as timing channel, processor frequency and free space on filesystem. TaintDroid [9], an extension of the Android mobile phone platform, uses dynamic taint analysis to detect direct buffer attack. The dynamic analysis approach [9,11,19] defined in smartphones cannot detect software side channel attacks presented in [2,15]. In this paper, we modify the Android OS to detect software side channel attacks that try to bypass detection mechanisms based on dynamic taint analysis. We propagate taint in timing, memory cache and GPU channels and in meta data (file and clipboard length) using taint propagation rules. To evaluate the effectiveness of our approach, we analyzed 100 free Android applications. We found that these applications use different side channels to transfer sensitive data. We successfully detected that 35% of them leaked private information through side channels. Also, we detected Sarwar *et al.* [2] side channel attacks. Our approach generates 9% of false positives. It has a 9% overhead with respect to the TaintDroid system. The rest of this paper is organized as follows: Sect. 2 presents the dynamic taint analysis mechanism and the TaintDroid approach. Section 3 describes the threat model. Section 4 presents side channel class of attacks that TaintDroid cannot detect. Section 5 describes the proposed approach. Section 6 provides implementation details. We test the effectiveness of our approach and we study our approach overhead in Sect. 7. Section 8 describes how our approach can resist to code obfuscation attacks. We present related work about side channel attacks and countermeasures in Sect. 9. Finally, Sect. 10 concludes with an outline of future work.

2   Background

2.1   Dynamic Taint Analysis

The dynamic taint analysis technique is used for tracking information flows in operating systems. The principle of this mechanism is to tag some of the data in a program with a taint mark, then propagate the taint to other objects depending on this data when the program is executed. It is used primarily for vulnerability detection, protection of sensitive data, and more recently, for binary malware analysis. To detect vulnerabilities, the sensitive data must be monitored to ensure that they are sent through interfaces to the outside world. Many dynamic taint analysis tools are based on bytecode instrumentation to analyze sensitive data [6,16]. TaintDroid implemented similar concepts to prevent leakage of private data in Android system. We present the TaintDroid system in more details in the following section.

2.2   TaintDroid

TaintDroid improves the Android mobile phone OS to control the manipulation of users personal data in realtime by third-party applications. It analyzes application behavior to determine when privacy sensitive information is leaked. TaintDroid considers that information acquired through low-bandwidth sensors (location and accelerometer), high-bandwidth information source (microphone and camera), information databases (address books and SMS messages) and device identifiers(the phone number, SIM card identifiers (IMSI, ICC-ID), and device identifier (IMEI)) are privacy sensitive information that should be tainted. So, it uses dynamic taint analysis to track propagation of tainted data at different levels: instruction level, message-level between applications and file-level. TaintDroid defines taint sinks to detect vulnerabilities. The taint sinks present interfaces to the outside world (e.g., network interface) where tainted data are not expected to be sent. Therefore, TaintDroid, issues warning reports when the tainted data are leaked by malicious applications. One limit of TaintDroid is that it cannot propagate taint through side channels except direct memory. Therefore, it can not detect side channel attacks presented in the Sect. 4.

3   Target Threat Model

The adversary's goal is to extract sensitive data from the Android third-party system. He/She develops a malicious application that will be executed on this system and that sends sensitive data through the network to a system which the adversary controls. We assume that the smartphone user installs the malicious application on his phone. Also, we assume that he/she uses a dynamic taint tracking system such as TaintDroid to protect his private data. So, the malicious application will be executed under this system. The adversary exploits the limitation of dynamic taint analysis mechanism that it cannot propagate taint through side channels. He/She interferes in the taint propagation level and he/she removes taint of sensitive data that should be tainted. Therefore, these data will be leaked without being detected. Next, we present different examples of side channels attacks that a dynamic taint tracking system such as TaintDroid cannot detect.

4   Side Channels Attacks

Sarwar et al. [2] present side channel class of attacks such as the bypass timing, bitmap cache, meta data, and graphical properties attacks using a medium that might be overlooked by the taint-checking mechanism to extract sensitive data. They tested and evaluated the success rate and time of these attacks with the TaintDroid system. We are interested in these attacks because they are the most important attacks presented by siwar and al. and the other attacks are already detected [10]. We present in this section examples of these side channel attacks.

4.1 Timing Attack

The timing attack is an example of a side channel attack in which the attacker attempts to compromise a cryptosystem by analyzing the time taken to gain information about the keys. Similar concept can be used to leak tainted data when running a program with taint analysis approach. Algorithm 1 presents

---

Algorithm 1. Timing Attack

$X_{Tainted} \leftarrow Private\_Data$
$n \leftarrow CharToInt(X)$
$StatTime \leftarrow ReadSystemTime()$
$Sleep(n)$
$StopTime \leftarrow ReadSystemTime()$
$y \leftarrow (StopTime - StartTime)$
$Y_{Untainted} \leftarrow IntToChar(y)$
$Send\_Network\_Data(Y_{Untainted})$

---

the timing attack in the taint tracking system. This attack exploits the system clock which is not tainted. The sleep() function suspends the execution of the current program until the waiting period that depends on the value of a tainted variable has elapsed. Therefore, the difference in time readings before and after a waiting period indicates the value of sensitive data. This difference is not tainted because there is no taint propagation in the system clock. Consequently, it can be assigned to the taint-free output variable and leaked through the network without being detected.

4.2 Cache Memory Attack

The cache memory attack is another example of side channel attacks that can be used to extract sensitive data. This attack exploits the fact that graphical output can be obtained from cache of the currently displayed screen. Algorithm 2 presents the bitmap cache attack. The graphical widget contains the private data. The attacker successfully extracts it from the bitmap cache without any warning reports because the taint is not propagated in the cache memory. He/She sends the bitmap data to a cloud and uses the Optical Character Recognition (OCR) techniques [14] to read the value of sensitive data.

Bitmap Pixel Attack: An attacker can extract private data by exploiting bitmap cache pixels as shown in Algorithm 3. He/She modifies an arbitrarily

---

Algorithm 2. Bitmap Cache Attack

$X_{Tainted} \leftarrow Private\_Data$
$W \leftarrow CreateNewTextWidget()$
$B \leftarrow CreateNewBitmap()$
$WriteText(X_{Tainted} \rightarrow W)$
$B \leftarrow CaptureBitmapCache(W)$
$Y \leftarrow OpticalCharacterRecognition(B)$
$Send\_Network\_Data(Y_{Untainted})$

Algorithm 3. Bitmap Pixel Attack

$X_{Tainted} \leftarrow Private\_Data$
$B \leftarrow CreateNewBitmap()$
$SetPixel([10; 10], X_{Tainted} \rightarrow B)$
$Y_{Untainted} \leftarrow GetPixel(B; [10; 10])$
$Send\_Network\_Data(Y_{Untainted})$

---

chosen pixel to represent the private data value. Then, he/she reads the value contained in this pixel at specific coordinates.

4.3 Meta Data Attacks

Taint analysis systems such as TaintDroid associate taint to the object containing sensitive data. However, these systems do not propagate taint to object size. We present side channel attacks that exploit meta data to evade taint tracking.

File length Attack:

Algorithm 4. File Length Attack

$X_{Tainted} \leftarrow Private\_Data$
$F \leftarrow CreateNewFileHandle()$
$z \leftarrow 0$
while $z < X_{Tainted}$ **do**
  $WriteOneByte(F)$
  $z \leftarrow z + 1$
end while
$Y_{Untainted} \leftarrow ReadFileLength(F)$
$Send\_Network\_Data(Y_{Untainted})$

As the file size is not tainted, an attacker can exploit this meta data to leak sensitive data, as shown in Algorithm 4. Each character in private data is represented by an arbitrary file size. One byte is written to a file until its size equals to the character private data value. Then, the attacker obtains the file size which corresponds to the sensitive data without any warning reports.

Clipboard Length Attack: An attack similar to the file length Attack can be performed if an application required a clipboard to exchange data. In the clipboard length attack, the size of the file is replaced with the size of the content of the clipboard as shown in the Algorithm 5.

Algorithm 5. Clipboard Length Attack

$X_{Tainted} \leftarrow Private\_Data$
$z \leftarrow 0$
while $z < X_{Tainted}$ **do**
  $WriteOneByte(Clipboard)$
  $z \leftarrow z + 1$
end while
$Y_{Untainted} \leftarrow ReadFileLength(Clipboard)$
$Send\_Network\_Data(Y_{Untainted})$

4.4   Graphics Processing Unit Attacks

We are interested on a graphics processing unit class of attacks that exploits the properties of a graphical elements to evade the taint tracking mechanism.

Algorithm 6. Text Scaling Attack

$X_{Tainted} \leftarrow Private_D ata$
$T \leftarrow TextViewWidget()$
$T \leftarrow SetTextScalingValue(X_{Tainted})$
$Y_{Untainted} \leftarrow GetTextScalingValue(T)$
$Send\_Network\_Data(Y_{Untainted})$

For example, in the text scaling attack presented in Algorithm 6, the attacker sets an arbitrary property of a graphical widget (the scaling) with the value of private data. Then, he/she extracts and sends this property through the network.

5   Detection of Side Channel Attacks

Our approach is based on dynamic taint analysis to overcome side channel attacks as attacks presented in Sect. 4. We specify a set of formally defined rules that propagate taint in different side channels to detect leakage of sensitive data.

5.1   Timing Side Channel Propagation Rule

The timing attack exploits the system clock which is available without tainting. The attacker reads the system clock after the waiting period. We define the $Timing\_Context\_Taint$ which is activated when the argument (arg) of the $Sleep()$ function is tainted.

$$Sleep(arg) \wedge Is\ tainted(arg) \implies Activate(Timing\_Context\_Taint)$$

In this case, we propagate taint in timing side channel. Therefore, the system clock is tainted and the attacker cannot leak sensitive information through timing side channel.

$$Is\ activated(Timing\_Context\_Taint) \implies Taint(system\ clock)$$

5.2 Memory Cache Side Channel Propagation Rules

The bitmap cache attack exploits the cache memory of the currently displayed screen. The attacker captures the bitmap cache of a graphical object containing private data. We define the $Bitmap\_Context\_Taint$ which is activated when the graphical object is tainted.

$$Is\ tainted(graphical\ object) \implies Activate(Bitmap\_Context\_Taint)$$

In this case, we propagate taint in the bitmap cache side channel and we associate taint to the bitmap object.

$$Is\ activated(Bitmap\_Context\_Taint) \implies Taint(Bitmap)$$

For the bitmap pixel attack, the attacker exploits the bitmap cache pixels that is modified to get the private data value. We define the $Pixels\_Context\_Taint$ which is activated when the argument parameter of the set pixel function is tainted. So, an arbitrarily chosen pixel is changed to represent value of the private data

$$Set\ pixel(arg) \wedge Is\ tainted(arg) \implies Activate(Pixels\_Context\_Taint)$$

In this case, we assign taint to the return value of $getpixel()$ function.

$$Is\ activated(Pixels\_Context\_Taint) \implies Taint(return\_getpixel)$$

By using these memory cache side channel propagation rules, the attacker cannot leak sensitive information through bitmap cache memory.

5.3 Meta Data Propagation Rule

The meta data attacks exploit the size of the object which is available without tainting. We define the $Meta\_Data\_Context\_Taint$ which is activated when the application gets private data.

$$get\_private\_data() \implies Activate(Meta\_Data\_Context\_Taint)$$

In this case, we define meta data propagation rule and we associate taint to the return value of the $length()$ method.

$$Is\ activated(Meta\_Data\_Context\_Taint) \implies Taint(length\_object)$$

Therefore, by applying the meta data propagation rule, the attacker cannot leak sensitive information using meta data.

5.4   GPU Propagation Rule

The graphics processing unit class of considered attacks exploits the properties of the graphical elements (the scaling, Text size...). The attacker sets an arbitrary property of a graphical widget to the value of private data. So, we define the *GPU_Context_Taint* which is activated when the argument parameter of the Set property function is tainted.

$$Set\ property(arg) \wedge Is\ tainted(arg) \implies Activate(GPU\_Context\_Taint)$$

In this case, we assign taint to the return value of *Getproperty*() function to prevent this attack.

$$Is\ activated(GPU\_Context\_Taint) \implies Taint(return\_getproperty)$$

By using the GPU propagation rule, the attacker cannot leak sensitive information by exploiting properties of the graphical elements.

6   Implementation

We modify the TaintDroid System to implement the taint propagation rules defined in Sect. 5. Figure 1 presents the modified components (gray components) to detect side channel attacks in TaintDroid system. We modify the dalvik virtual machine to detect timing attacks. We implement the memory cache and the GPU propagation rules at the framework level to prevent bitmap cache and GPU class of attacks. We instrument the core libraries to associate taint to meta data.

6.1   Timing Attack Detection

The $VMThread\_sleep(constu4 * args, JValue * pResult)$ function in Dalvik virtual machine native code suspends the execution of the current thread until the value of a tainted variable has elapsed. Then, the attacker reads the system clock after the waiting period. We test the argument of $VMThread\_sleep()$ to implement the *Timing_Context_Taint*. We modify the $currentTimeMillis(constu4 * args, JValue * pResult)$ function in the Dalvik virtual machine native code to propagate taint in the system clock if the *Timing_Context_Taint* is activated. Therefore, the difference in time readings before and after a waiting period that indicates the value of sensitive data is tainted.

6.2   Cache Memory Attack Detection

We verify if the graphical object contains a private data to implement the *GPU_Taint_Context*. All of the graphical objects defined in the Android framework extend View. So, we check if the view is tainted. The *getDrawingCache*() function in the view class creates and returns a bitmap object that contains the private data. Therefore, we taint the return value of *getDrawingCache*() function if the *GPU_Taint_Context* is activated. For the bitmap pixel attack, the

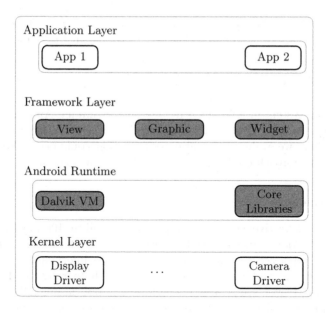

Fig. 1. The modified components (gray) to detect side channel attacks

bitmap is created in the first time and then it is modified by exploiting the bitmap cache pixels. We verify if the argument parameter of the set pixel function in Bitmap class (Graphic package) is tainted to implement *Pixels_Taint_Context*. In this case, we assign taint to the return value of *getpixel*() function in the bitmap class.

6.3   Meta Data Attacks Detection

TaintDroid implements taint source placement where privacy sensitive information types are acquired (low-bandwidth sensors, e.g. location and accelerometer; high-bandwidth sensors, e.g., microphone and camera; information Databases, e.g. address books and SMS messages; Device Identifiers, e.g. SIM card identifiers (IMSI, ICC-ID), and device identifier (IMEI)). In each taint source placement, we implement the *Meta_Data_Context_Taint* which is activated if private data is acquired. To detect the meta data class of attacks, we associate taint to the return value of the *length*() method at libcore level in File and String classes if the *Meta_Data_Context_Taint* is activated.

6.4   Graphics Processing Unit Attacks Detection

To launch the graphics processing unit class of considered attacks, the attacker sets an arbitrary property of a graphical widget with the value of private data. Therefore, we verify if the argument parameter of the Set-Property (*SetTextScalingValue* function) in graphical widget class is tainted to implement *GPU_Taint_*

Context. Then, we taint the return value of Get-Property (*GetTextScalingValue* function) if *GPU_Taint_Context* is activated to prevent this attack.

7   Evaluation

We install our system in a Nexus 4 mobile device running Android OS version 4.3. We analyze a number of Android applications to test the effectiveness of our approach. Then, we evaluate the false positives that could occur. We study our taint tracking approach overhead using standard benchmarks.

7.1   Effectiveness

To evaluate the effectiveness of our approach, we analyze 100 most popular free Android applications downloaded from the Android Market [1]. These applications are categorized in games, shopping, device information, social, tools, weather, music and audio, maps and navigation, photograhy, productivity, life style, reference, travel, sports and entertainment applications. We observe that all applications use bitmap cache channel, 50% of these applications use timing channel, 30% use GPU channel (get and set graphic properties) and 20% use meta data (file and clipboard sizes). We found that 66% of these applications manipulate confidential data. Our approach has succesfully propagated taint in side channels and detected leakage of tainted sensitive data by checking the content of network packets sent by applications.

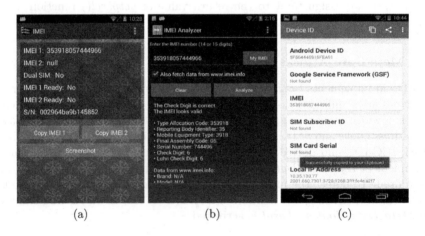

(a)   (b)   (c)

Fig. 2. Leakage private data through the bitmap cache side channels

We found that 35% of applications leaked private data through timing and bitmap cache side channels. For example, the IMEI application takes and send a screenshot of IMEI information through the network by exploiting the bitmap cache side channel (see Fig. 2(a)). Other applications copy the SIM card and device information from the screen to the clipboard and send them through the network, SMS or bluetooth using the bitmap cache side channel (see Fig. 2(c)). Some applications get the drawing cache to leak implicitly private data. For example, the IMEI Analyser application gets the drawing cache to send implicitly the IMEI outside the smartphone (see Fig. 2(b)). Games applications leaked implicitly the devices ID through the timing side channel at the time of score sharing. In addition, we successfully implement and detect side channels class of attacks presented in Sect. 4.

7.2 False Positives

We found that 35 of the 100 tested Android applications leaked sensitive data through side channels. We detected three device information (Android id, Device Serial, Device model, Phone number...) leakage vulnerability. Also, we detected that the IMEI is transmitted outside of smartphone by two different forms (digital and by another application which takes screenshot of IMEI). In addition, we detected four SIM card information (SIM provider's country, SIM Contacts, SimState...) leakage vulnerability. As the user is sent these information by email, SMS or bluetooth, we can not treat these applications as privacy violators. Therefore, our approach generates 9% of false positives.

7.3 Performance

We use the CaffeineMark [7] to study our approach overhead. The CaffeineMark scores roughly correlate with the number of Java instructions executed per second and do not depend significantly on the amount of memory in the system or on the speed of a computers disk drives or internet connection. Figure 3 presents the execution time results of a Java microbenchmark.

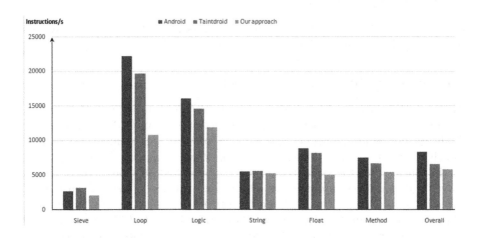

Fig. 3. Microbenchmark of Java overhead

The unmodified Android system had an overall score of 8401 Java instructions executed per second and the TaintDroid system measured 6610 Java instructions executed per second. Therefore, TaintDroid has a 21% overhead with respect to the unmodified Android system. Our approach had an overall score of 5873 Java instructions executed per second. So, our approach has a 9% overhead with respect to the TaintDroid system. It gives a slower execution speed rate because we propagate taint in side channels. However, the overhead given by our approach is acceptable in comparison to the one obtained by TaintDroid.

8   Discussion

We have proposed in a previous work [10] an enhancement of the TaintDroid approach that propagates taint along control dependencies to track implicit flows in smartphones. We have shown that our previous approach can resist to code obfuscation attacks based on control dependencies in the Android system. In addition, we have successfully detected side channel attacks exploiting control flows by combining static and dynamic analyses. However, we did not propagate taint in side channels. Consequently, we could not detect these class of attacks when they do not use control flows which generates false negatives. An attacker can obfuscate the application code by exploiting side channels to evade detection of leakage of private data in the Android system. The approach proposed in this paper propagates taint in a specific side channels. So, our approach can be used to detect code obfuscation attacks based on side channels in the Android system. We can extend our approach based on taint analysis to detect other side channel attacks such as ACCessory [17] and Soundcomber [18] attacks. To do so, we propagate taint in accelerometer and audio side channels. The limitation of our approach is that it can not be used to detect hardware side channel attacks.

9   Related Work

In this section, we present side channels attacks in Android systems. We also discuss existing countermeasures.

9.1   Software Side Channels Attacks

Memento [13] is a side-channel attack based on tracking changes in the browser's memory footprint to infer which pages the victim is browsing. Soundcomber [18] analyzes audio side channel in a user's phone conversations to infer sensitive data. TouchLogger [4] exploits different vibrations when typing on different locations on the touch screen to extract sequences of entered text on smartphones. ACCessory [17] uses the accelerometer to get the data entered by user. Chen et al. [5] exploit a shared-memory side channel to stealthily inject into the foreground a phishing activity and steal sensitive information. Kim et al. [15] utilized screen bitmap memory attack proposed by Sarwar et al. [2] to propose a collection system that retrieves IMEI and IMSI information through screenshot images. As we propagate taint in bitmap cache memory, we can detect Kim *et al.* attacks. We are interested on software side channel attacks that try to bypass dynamic taint analysis based detection technique such as timing, memory cache, GPU channels and meta data (file and clipboard length) [2,15].

9.2 Side Channels Countermeasures

Many works exist in the literature to detect side channel attacks in Android systems. App Guardian [20] thwarts a malicious app's runtime monitoring attempt by pausing all suspicious background processes, which are identified by their behaviors inferred from their side channels. In this paper, we are interested in side channel attacks running in the foreground. So, App Guardian cannot detect this category of attacks. XManDroid [3] uses dynamic taint analyses to detect side channel attacks such as Soundcomber. However, it cannot detect subset of side channels such as timing channel, processor frequency and free space on filesystem. TaintDroid [9] uses dynamic taint analysis to detect direct buffer attack. DroidBox [19] analyzes the malicious applications by using sandbox and tainting techniques based on TaintDroid. It combines static and dynamic analysis, and it uses machine learning techniques to cluster the analyzed samples into benign and malicious ones. AppFence [11] extends TaintDroid to implement enforcement policies. The dynamic analysis approach defined in smartphones like TaintDroid, AppFence and DroidBox cannot detect software side channel attacks presented in [2,15].

10 Conclusion

The dynamic taint analysis approaches implemented in the Android system can be bypassed by exploiting side channel attacks. We have improved the Taint-Droid approach to propagate taint in side channels. We have analyzed 100 free Android applications to evaluate the effectiveness of our approach. We successfully detected sensitive information leakage caused by side channels. We found that 35% of analyzed applications leaked private data through side channels. We showed that our approach generates significant false positives (9%). Our approach creates a 9% overhead with respect to the TaintDroid system. Future work will be to improve our approach for detecting other side channel attacks inferring private data. Also, we will demonstrate the completeness of the taint propagation rules.

References

1. Android market. https://play.google.com/store/apps?hl=fr
2. Babil, G.S., Mehani, O., Boreli, R., Kaafar, M.A.: On the effectiveness of dynamic taint analysis for protecting against private information leaks on android-based devices. In: 2013 International Conference on Security and Cryptography (SECRYPT), pp. 1–8. IEEE (2013)

3. Bugiel, S., Davi, L., Dmitrienko, A., Fischer, T., Sadeghi, A.R.: Xmandroid: a new android evolution to mitigate privilege escalation attacks. Technische Universität Darmstadt, Technical report TR-2011-04 (2011)
4. Cai, L., Chen, H.: Touchlogger: inferring keystrokes on touch screen from smartphone motion. In: HotSec 2011, p. 9 (2011)
5. Chen, Q.A., Qian, Z., Mao, Z.M.: Peeking into your app without actually seeing it: Ui state inference and novel android attacks. In: 23rd USENIX Security Symposium (USENIX Security 2014), pp. 1037–1052 (2014)
6. Cheng, W., Zhao, Q., Yu, B., Hiroshige, S.: Tainttrace: efficient flow tracing with dynamic binary rewriting. In: Proceedings of the 11th IEEE Symposium on ISCC 2006, pp. 749–754. IEEE (2006)
7. Corporation, P.S.: Caffeinemark 3.0 (1997). http://www.benchmarkhq.ru/cm30/
8. Egham: Gartner says worldwide smartphone sales grew 3.9 percent in first quarter of 2016, May 2016. http://www.gartner.com/newsroom/id/3323017
9. Enck, W., Gilbert, P., Han, S., Tendulkar, V., Chun, B.G., Cox, L.P., Jung, J., McDaniel, P., Sheth, A.N.: Taintdroid: an information-flow tracking system for realtime privacy monitoring on smartphones. ACM Trans. Comput. Syst. (TOCS) **32**(2), 5 (2014)
10. Graa, M., Boulahia, N.C., Cuppens, F., Cavalliy, A.: Protection against code obfuscation attacks based on control dependencies in android systems. In: 2014 IEEE Eighth International Conference on Software Security and Reliability-Companion (SERE-C), pp. 149–157. IEEE (2014)
11. Hornyack, P., Han, S., Jung, J., Schechter, S., Wetherall, D.: These aren't the droids you're looking for: retrofitting android to protect data from imperious applications. In: Proceedings of the 18th ACM Conference on Computer and Communications Security, pp. 639–652. ACM (2011)
12. Hund, R., Willems, C., Holz, T.: Practical timing side channel attacks against kernel space ASLR. In: Proceedings of the 2013 IEEE Symposium on Security and Privacy, SP 2013, pp. 191–205. IEEE Computer Society, Washington, DC (2013)
13. Jana, S., Shmatikov, V.: Memento: learning secrets from process footprints. In: 2012 IEEE Symposium on Security and Privacy, pp. 143–157. IEEE (2012)
14. Kay, A.: Tesseract: an open-source optical character recognition engine. Linux J. **2007**(159), 2 (2007)
15. Kim, Y.K., Yoon, H.J., Lee, M.H.: Stealthy information leakage from android smartphone through screenshot and OCR. In: International Conference on Chemical, Material and Food Engineering. Atlantis Press (2015)
16. Newsome, J., Song, D.: Dynamic taint analysis for automatic detection, analysis, and signature generation of exploits on commodity software. Citeseer (2005)
17. Owusu, E., Han, J., Das, S., Perrig, A., Zhang, J.: Accessory: password inference using accelerometers on smartphones. In: Proceedings of the Twelfth Workshop on Mobile Computing Systems & Applications, p. 9. ACM (2012)
18. Schlegel, R., Zhang, K., Zhou, X.y., Intwala, M., Kapadia, A., Wang, X.: Soundcomber: a stealthy and context-aware sound trojan for smartphones. In: NDSS, vol. 11, pp. 17–33 (2011)
19. Spreitzenbarth, M., Schreck, T., Echtler, F., Arp, D., Hoffmann, J.: Mobilesandbox: combining static and dynamic analysis with machine-learning techniques. Int. J. Inf. Secur. **14**(2), 141–153 (2015)
20. Zhang, N., Yuan, K., Naveed, M., Zhou, X., Wang, X.: Leave me alone: App-level protection against runtime information gathering on android. In: 2015 IEEE Symposium on Security and Privacy, pp. 915–930. IEEE (2015)

The *Fuzzing* Awakens: File Format-Aware Mutational Fuzzing on Smartphone Media Server Daemons

MinSik Shin, JungBeen Yu, YoungJin Yoon, and Taekyoung Kwon$^{(\boxtimes)}$

Information Security Lab, Yonsei University, Seoul 03722, Korea
{msshinaktl,symnoisy,youngjin339,taekyoung}@yonsei.ac.kr

Abstract. Media server daemons, running with a high privilege in the background, are attractive attack vectors that exist across various systems including smartphones. Fuzzing is a popularly used methodology to find software vulnerabilities although symbolic execution and advanced techniques are obviously promising. Unfortunately, fuzzing itself is not effective in such format-strict environments as media services. Thus, we study file format-aware fuzzing as a technical blend for finding new vulnerabilities. We present our black-box mutational fuzzing on the latest smartphone systems, Android and iOS, respectively, with manipulation of the MPEG-4 Part 14 file format and show results that affect a wide range of related systems. In our approach, we automate a seed file selection process to crawl a crowd-sourcing public website and validate arbitrary m4a/mp4 audio files according to the FOURCC atom list we gained through white-box analysis in Android. We acquired eight seed files covering all effective atoms in 2,600 s. We then performed size field mutation in a little amount and generated 1,102 test cases common to both systems. During six CPU hours of fuzzing, we identified three crash atoms in iOS 9.3.5 and 15 in Android 6.0.1, respectively. Due to format-awareness, we were able to easily locate crash points through a mutation table. It was discovered that the new crash atoms found in iOS allowed remote attackers to execute arbitrary code or cause a denial of service by memory corruption in iOS and also OS X, tvOS and watchOS.

Keywords: Mutational fuzzing · Format awareness · Media server

1 Introduction

Multimedia services are attractive attack vectors that exist across various systems and platforms. For instance, audio services, such as phone calls, ringtones, alarming sounds, audio file players, and audio streaming over mobile web browsers, are frequently requested in smartphones and related smart devices. To deal with these requests, a special daemon process having a high privilege runs in

© IFIP International Federation for Information Processing 2017
Published by Springer International Publishing AG 2017. All Rights Reserved
S. De Capitani di Vimercati and F. Martinelli (Eds.): SEC 2017, IFIP AICT 502, pp. 219–232, 2017.
DOI: 10.1007/978-3-319-58469-0_15

the background, e.g., `mediaserverd` in iOS and `mediaserver` in Android, and automatically restarts when it occasionally crashes. Unfortunately, its framework is quite complex, e.g., as a mixture of Java and native code in Android, and a wide variety of audio codecs and plugins are written by non-security-experts. Furthermore, users are likely to install third-party sounds (e.g., the Star Wars imperial march ring-tone) and perceive an audio file or streaming relatively harmless, even played without user's consent (e.g., an auto-streaming on Facebook). Indeed, many vulnerabilities [11] have been discovered in Android 6.0.x regarding the Stagefright engine that manipulates audio-video playbacks, and significantly fixed in Android 7.1.x. On the contrary, a relatively small number of media file related vulnerabilities were found in iOS, and in particular audio-related vulnerabilities of iOS were rarely discovered (e.g., CVE-2010-0036 and CVE-2015-5862). An academic study was also less presented in the literature [19,21]. Thus, it might be interesting to investigate audio-related vulnerabilities on both iOS and Android platforms because the same audio file formats are readily accepted in both smartphone platforms.

A fuzzing method, first introduced by Miller et al. in 1990 [25], is still the most widely-used tool[1] for finding software vulnerabilities in a variety of systems although symbolic execution and advanced techniques are obviously promising. Unfortunately, however, fuzzing itself is not effective in such format-strict environments as media services [33] because it needs a large amount of fuzzing work, mostly format-blocked, and it can hardly locate a crash point. To the best of our knowledge, there is no explicit literature studying the file format-aware fuzzing on the media server daemons of the smartphone systems and also for the latest versions, such as iOS 9.3.x and Android 6.0.x, when we conducted this study. Thus, it would also be interesting to investigate the file format-aware fuzzing on the latest smartphone systems.

Contributions. In this paper, concerning the problems and motivations above, we 'awaken' the file format-aware fuzzing for finding new security vulnerabilities related to media server daemons (with very little amount of fuzzing work and by easily locating the crash points under specific file formats) in the 'latest' versions of iOS and Android. For convenience, we call our methodology *TFA*, standing for 'Tiny Fuzzing on Audio' or 'The Fuzzing Awakens'. After reviewing backgrounds in Sect. 2, we describe TFA in Sect. 3 and evaluate it in Sect. 4. We discuss limitations and future work in Sect. 5 and related work in Sect. 6, and then conclude this paper in Sect. 7. We summarize our study as follows:

- TFA is *strategic*: We choose a seed file format as MPEG-4 Part 14 which is most widely played by default media players in smartphones, and confront several challenges to conduct file format-aware fuzzing. Our unique strategies to overcome such challenges are as follows: (1) To ease format-awareness, we utilize a GNU-GPL parser tool called AtomicParsley. This might be a benefit of targeting multimedia files. (2) To gain the valid MPEG-4 atom[2] list, we

---

[1] https://lcamtuf.blogspot.kr/2015/02/symbolic-execution-in-vuln-research.html.
[2] An atom is a basic data unit in MPEG-4. Readers are referred to Fig. 1 and [1].

conduct a white-box analysis to the Android 6.0.1 source code. (3) To automate a seed file crawling process, we setup selection criteria of target websites and select a crowd-sourcing public website called 4shared.com for automation. (4) To automate a mutational fuzzing process in iOS, we backward-fuzz the old jailbroken version of iOS (7.1.2) and forward-verify new crashes in the latest version (9.3.5 on conducting our study) of which a jailbreaking is impossible for now.

- TFA is *efficient*: In a seed file selection phase, we obtain eight seed files only in 2,600 s to cover all of the effective and valid atoms. In a mutational fuzzing phase, we perform mutation of the atom size fields that are likely to cause a heap overflow. We generate 1,102 test cases[3] and a mutation table having 58 records only. They are commonly applied to Android and iOS.

- TFA is *effective*: Due to format-awareness, it is possible to simply locate crash atoms[4] through a mutation table.

For six CPU hours, we found three crash atoms in iOS 9.3.5 and reported the results to Apple (CVE-2016-4702, CVSS Score 10.0). Interestingly, these new crash atoms commonly affected iOS and the related systems such as OS X, tvOS, and watchOS to allow remote attackers to execute arbitrary code or cause a denial of service by memory corruption. The new vulnerabilities were fixed in iOS 10.x.x.

For six CPU hours, we found 15 crash atoms in Android 6.0.1 but they were thrown to an exception due to the existence of CHECK() functions that signal the kernel to kill and restart a media server daemon process.

2   Background

2.1   Attack Vectors: Media Server Daemons and Multimedia Files

As for file format-aware fuzzing, our target (media server daemons) and seed (multimedia file) both have a great implication as an attack vector because of the followings.

To deal with frequent audio service requests, media server daemons always run with a high privilege in the background, commonly in modern smartphones and the related systems. For instance, an media daemon called mediaserverd aggregates the sound output of all applications and governs events such as volume and ringer-switch changes in iOS and similarly in tvOS, watchOS, and OS X [19]. Android also runs a media server daemon called mediaserver, which is responsible for starting media related services, including Audio Flinger, Media Player Service, Camera Service, and Audio Policy Service [12], and the related systems, such as Android Auto, Android TV, Android Wear, and Android Things, also share this property in their source code. Thus, if a critical vulnerability is discovered in a smartphone regarding media server daemons, the related systems and devices might be affected by the same attack that exploits it.

---

[3] Much more test cases are required in dumb fuzzing.
[4] It is technically infeasible to identify unique crash atoms by performing a random bit-flipping only.

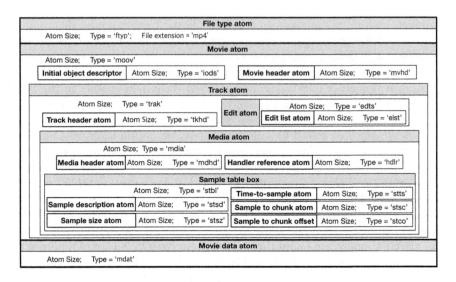

Fig. 1. MPEG-4 atom structure [1]

Furthermore, it might be highly likely to feed a corrupted multimedia file to a vulnerable system as studied in the previous work [33], particularly without specialized access conditions or authentication to exploit the vulnerability.

2.2 Seed File Format

According to www.file-extensions.org, 30 type extensions of audio and sound files, such as m4a, wma, and mp3, are most commonly used in various platforms among 1,285 file type extensions. Meanwhile, 35 type extensions of video and movie files, such as mp4, mov, and avi, are commonly used in various platforms among 659 file type extensions. All file extensions are categorized under digital container format such as Ogg, 3 GP, QuickTime.

We chose a seed file format as MPEG-4 Part 14 which is the most widely used digital multimedia container format to store video and audio, such as mp4, m4a, m4r, m4b, m4p, and m4v. As depicted in Fig. 1, m4a/mp4 files are structured hierarchically by the basic data unit called an *atom* or a *box*. An atom is called a container atom if it is not a leaf atom in the nested hierarchy. Each atom consists of a header, followed by atom data. The header contains the atom's size and type fields, giving the size of the atom in bytes and its type. Note that each atom has an 'offset' that describes the atom's position according to the size value. The size and the type fields are assigned 32-bit integers, respectively, and the size fields are the main target of our mutation in this paper because of high likeliness of raising memory collisions. Particularly, an mp4 file structure consists of three container atoms: File type atom (`ftyp`) has a certain file type of format, movie atom (`moov`) contains all meta data of corresponding media, and movie data atom (`mdat`) stores raw data. Moreover, movie atom (`moov`) involves various leaf atoms including track atom (`trak`) and media atom (`mdia`). There could be multiple track atoms (`trak`) in the same file. Note that it is very important to have a concrete strategy to select a qualified seed file because different atom structures can be made in files depending on a file generation environment, such as codec, encoder, program, and device.

3   File Format-Aware Mutational Fuzzing

3.1   Overview

We describe a general overview of TFA fuzzing procedure in Algorithm 1. The TFA fuzzing procedure consists of a seed file selection phase and a mutational fuzzing phase: We collect and choose seed files in the former, and perform mutation and fuzzing in the latter.

Let T_x and T_y denote a list of crashes and a mutation table, respectively. We assume they are initially null. In the seed file selection phase, we repeatedly perform SEED_CRAWLING through website W and verify atoms of the result S as in FORMAT_AWARENESS(S). If there exist new atoms in S, we add S to the queue T. We repeat this phase until we collect seed files that cover all atom lists. Otherwise, we abort this process (line 2–7).

In the mutational fuzzing phase, we set t as the next seed file queued in T, and identify offset addresses of atom (size) fields through FORMAT_AWARENESS(). We then generate a test case t' through ATOM_MUTATION() and add this to a mutation table T_y which contains offset addresses, atom types and file names. We set $n = 19$ in our experiment. We finally feed this test case to the target system. If the generated test case t' crashes the media server daemon, it is added

---

Algorithm 1. TFA file format-aware fuzzing algorithm

Input : Website W
1: $T_x = \emptyset$, $T_y = \emptyset$ ▷ $T_y \leftarrow \{address, atom\_type, file\_names[n]\}$
2: **repeat**
3:     $S =$ SEED_CRAWLING(W)   ▷ **Seed File Selection Phase**
4:     **if** new atom found in FORMAT_AWARENESS(S) **then**
5:         add S to T
6:     **end if**
7: **until** abort-signal
8: **repeat**
9:     $t =$ CHOOSE_NEXT(T)
10:    $t' =$ ATOM_MUTATION(t, FORMAT_AWARENESS(t))   ▷ **Mut. Fuzzing Phase**
11:    add t' to T_y
12:    **if** t' crashes **then**
13:        add t' to T_x
14:    **end if**
15: **until** abort-signal
Output: Crashing Inputs T_x, Mutation Table T_y

Table 1. System environment

Device:	Web Server	MacBook (Xcode)	iPhone 4/6s	Nexus 5
OS ver:	Ubuntu 12.0.4.5	OS X 10.11.6	iOS 7.1.2/9.3.5	Android 6.0.1

Table 2. Android FOURCC function examples

(1)	(2)
```switch(chunk_type) { case FOURCC('m','o','o','v'): case FOURCC('t','r','a','k'): ... case FOURCC('m','d','i','a'): case FOURCC('m','d','a','t'): { ... } }```	```if (chunk_type==FOURCC('t','r','a','k')) { isTrack = true; Track *track = new Track; track->next = NULL; if (mLastTrack) { mLastTrack->next = track; ...} ... }```

to the crashing input set T_x. We repeat this phase until we finish our fuzzing work with collected seed files, and otherwise abort this process (line 8–15).

Note that it is simple to locate crash atoms through T_x and T_y due to file format-awareness. We automate the whole processes and implement the system for experiments with an environmental setting as described in Table 1.

3.2 Challenges

We dealt with the following challenges in a practical sense in our fuzzing work.

Format-awareness. It is well known that format-awareness is a crucial job in the related work [13,29,34]. To ease format-awareness, we utilize a GNU-GPL parser tool called AtomicParsley. We use parsed atom types for seed validation and offset address for mutation.

An m4a/mp4 file contains many atoms that include size, type, and even data fields while the number of structural atom types that could extend data fields is 302 in total according to the atom list of www.mp4ra.org. Thus, we conducted a white-box analysis to the Android 6.0.1 source code to gain the effective MPEG-4 atom list. As shown in Table 2, the FOURCC function, composed of switch statements as in (1), processes the input file by each atom as in (2). We then collect a FOURCC atom list of 94 atoms and validate arbitrary audio and video files according to this list.

Seed Crawling. To automate a seed file crawling process, we setup selection criteria of target websites as follows.

– Avoid a robot check function
– Utilize an internal search function for audio/video files
– Aim at a sufficiently large file pool

According the criteria, we selected a crowd-sourcing public website, 4shared.com for automation.

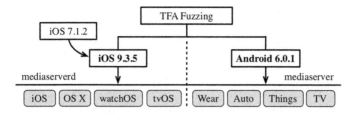

Fig. 2. Target system versions (Bold characters denote the latest versions.)

Latest Version Problem. The final challenge was a *jailbreaking* or *rooting* process required for fuzzing on the smartphone platforms, that is, for automation inside the smartphones. It was infeasible for us to jailbreak the latest version of iOS (9.3.5) while it was possible to root the latest version of Android (6.0.1). Thus, as for iOS, we decided to awaken the old version of iOS (7.1.2) running on iPhone 4. As illustrated in Fig. 2, we first performed fuzzing on iOS 7.1.2 by jailbreaking iPhone 4 and installing OpenSSH, BigBoss recommend tools, and SButils for running a fuzzer.

To verify the crashes (of iOS 7.1.2 iPhone 4) on iOS 9.3.5 in iPhone 6s, we connect iPhone 6 s to the latest version of Xcode (8.2.1) running in a MacBook and check the device console and the device logs by manually loading the crash files to mobile Safari one by one. Note that the number of crash files, i.e., the test case files that aroused crashes in iOS 7.1.2 iPhone 4, is quite lightweight for us to manually load them to the latest version.

3.3   Main Phases

Seed File Selection Phase. As we mentioned, we chose 4shared.com because it satisfies the requirements stated in our selection criteria. There was no robot check function in 4shared.com but an internal search function was provided. The pool of 4shared.com was sufficiently large with more than 1.5 million m4a/mp4 files. Note that we compare 4shared.com with the case of YouTube.com in Sect. 4.1. We implemented automation software to crawl the website through mouse/keyboard macro features in C. We described this as SEED_CRAWLING in Algorithm 1. We implemented a validation tool in Python, which has a function that utilizes AtomicParsley to parse atom types and offset addresses.

Mutational Fuzzing Phase. Given the set of test case files from seed file selection phase, we implemented format-awareness for get the offset address of atom size field. Given the mutation targets from format-awareness, i.e., the positions of the size fields of the seed file, we need to generate small test cases for fuzzing. We implemented a simple generation tool in a Python code for automation of the test case generation. We see that this actually happened due to the mutation of atom size fields with the integers highly likely to arouse memory collisions [31].

We sequentially mutate the value of the size fields with four-byte mutation values as summarized in Table 3. We don't mutate size fields of duplicate

Table 3. Mutation values for atom size fields

1: 0x000000FF	2: 0x0000FF00	3: 0x00FF0000	4: 0xFF000000	5: 0xFFFFFFFF
6: 0x7FFFFFFF	7: 0x80000000	8: 0x20000000	9–19: 0x00000000–0x0000000A	

atom types which mean the atoms already contained in another seed file. Those mutation values are highly probable integers for arousing memory collisions and actually borrowed from [31]. We construct a mutation table to contain a name of a test case file and atom types in each raw.

We need to instruct a media server daemon to consecutively load and handle each of the mutated test case files, and monitor and log possible crashes. We also automate this phase by writing a shell script to automatically open the test case files in the mobile web browsers, such as mobile Safari and mobile Chrome, one by one while monitoring the media server daemons for faults. Note that the simple shell script is very similar to that of [19]. We can easily locate the crash points effectively by file names of crash log due to the generated mutation table in test case generation phase.

4   Evaluation

4.1   General Results

Seed File Selection Phase. We performed a seed file crawling experiment in both 4shared.com and YouTube.com using our automated crawling software. Figure 3 shows the results of crawling, i.e., the percentage of covered atoms in the FOURCC atom list (total 94 atoms). The gray area implies a portion (36

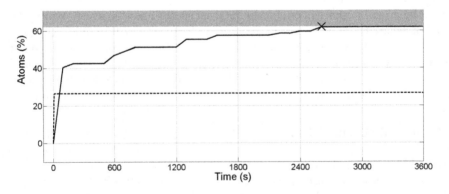

Fig. 3. #Atoms/FOURCC atom list over time for 4shared.com (solid line) vs. YouTube.com (dashed line). Shade area indicates atom types unused in MPEG-4 Part 14 format. 'X' represents the point that achieves the maximum number of effective atoms, i.e., 58 atoms in 2,600 s.

Table 4. TFA fuzzing results and comparisons. (Note: Numbers in parenthesis denote mp4 and the others m4a.)

Target	#Seed	TFA: #Atoms		Comparison: #Crash_Files	
		Mutated	Crash	ZZUF	AFL
iOS 9.3.5	4 (4)	44 (14)	3 (0)	0 (0)	–
Android 6.0.1	4 (4)	44 (14)	12 (3)	9 (1)	6 (4)

atoms including MPEG-B Part 7 atoms such as sinf, tenc, and enca) that is actually unused (i.e., ineffective) in MPEG-4 Part 14. As illustrated in a solid line in Fig. 3, we were able to cover all effective atoms (58 atoms) in 2,600 s through 4shared.com. We also made a comparison with YouTube.com. However, as shown in a dashed line in Fig. 3, the number of atom types was constant (25 atoms) in YouTube.com because all files should have been uploaded in webm type and then converted to m4a/mp4 format in the server when downloaded. On the contrary, 4shared.com downloaded crowd-sourcing files as in genuine format. Consequently, we acquired eight seed files (four m4a and four mp4 files) covering all effective atoms in 2,600 s through 4shared.com.

Mutational Fuzzing Phase. As summarized in Table 4, we found three crash atoms in iOS 9.3.5 and 15 crash atoms in Android 6.0.1 from 1,102 test cases for six CPU hours, respectively. Table 4 shows crash atom numbers according to OSs and seed types (mp4 in parenthesis). Due to the mutation table constructed on fuzzing, we were able to easily locate crash points and exploit input files.

As for crashes, we were able to discover vulnerabilities that cause memory corruption in iOS because we only mutated atom size fields related to memory assignment. The new crash atoms were mvhd, trak, and udta in iOS 9.3.5 and they were significant. However, in Android, various kinds of CHECK() and CHECK_XX() functions were used to verify size fields and then format-block (i.e., SIGABRT) a file that has unusual values in size fields. Thus, a mediaserver process which was regarded as a format error should have been killed and restarted by

Table 5. Experiment results for all FOURCC atoms. (Shade area indicates 58 fuzzed effective atoms. 17 crash atoms are in bold. Three iOS crash atoms are underlined.)

©alb	3g2b	**covr**	edts	h263	isom	meta	mp4v	s263	sinf	stz2	trex
©ART	3gp4	cpil	elst	hdlr	keys	mfra	MSNV	saio	**stbl**	tenc	trkn
©day	aART	**cprt**	enca	hev1	mdat	minf	**mvex**	saiz	stco	text	trun
©gen	**albm**	ctts	encv	hvc1	mdhd	moof	**<u>mvhd</u>**	samr	stsc	tfhd	tx3g
©nam	**auth**	d263	esds	hvcC	mdia	moov	**name**	sawb	stsd	**titl**	**<u>udta</u>**
©wrt	avc1	**data**	frma	ID32	mdta	mp41	**perf**	sbtl	stss	tkhd	**yrrc**
©xyz	avcC	**dinf**	ftyp	ilst	**mean**	mp42	pssh	schi	stsz	traf	
3g2a	co64	disk	**gnre**	iso2	mehd	**mp4a**	qt	sidx	stts	**<u>trak</u>**	

the Android kernel. Such crash atoms were `stbl`, `trak`, `mean`, `name`, `data`, `cprt`, `covr`, `albm`, `gnre`, `perf`, `titl`, `yrrc`, `auth`, `dinf`, and `mp4a` but they were only insignificantly denied in Android 6.0.1. Table 5 summarizes these results. Note that the crashes make the native daemon, i.e., the media server daemon and not only a forked server process, die and restart. As a result, the whole media server daemons and related services, such as audio, radio, and camera, were killed together. Even a simple crash could make a media server daemon and its related services go down temporarily because such a daemon process does not fork to handle individual requests.

4.2   Comparisons

We adopt open source fuzzers such as ZZUF 0.15 [20] and AFL-fuzz 2.39b [37], for comparisons with TFA regarding their fuzzing performance (#Crashes/Time). The seed files selected in TFA were commonly used for comparison experiments. In ZZUF, we set the default mutation ratio as 0.4 for generating test cases. Note that even this small ratio makes a large amount of mutation. AFL-fuzz is a coverage-based grey-box fuzzer which uses coverage information to fuzz [37]. In this study, we used original AFL-fuzz with porting for comparison of fuzzing on Android. We plan to perform a comparison of fuzzing on iOS in the future study. In AFL-fuzz, we needed a specific procedure to make a precise comparison. First, we compiled the stagefright module that uses `libstagefright.so` library with `afl-clang-fast` and `afl-clang-fast++`, and then cross-compiled afl-fuzz for armv7-a to run on Nexus 5. Subsequently, we loaded afl-fuzz binary to Nexus 5 and conducted fuzzing on libraries. Finally, we conducted fuzzing again, but on a chrome browser with crash files obtained through libraries, to verify the crash results under our experiment design.

For comparisons with TFA, we treated the same eight seed files (four m4a and four mp4 files) selected from TFA, and set the same amount of time (six CPU hours) for fuzzing in ZZUF and AFL-fuzz, as TFA. The comparison results are summarized in Table 4. We were able to exactly identify crash atoms due to format-awareness in TFA but only crash files in ZZUF and AFL-fuzz. Furthermore, we were able to find more crashes, three of which found on iOS 9.3.5 were significant. We reported the results to Apple to be archived in CVE-2016-4702 (CVSS Score 10.0).

5   Limitations and Future Work

In this Section, we review some limitations of this work and discuss promising (and our own on-going) future work.

Seed Container Type Selection. Although we selected two audio/video file types such as m4a and mp4 from the MPEG-4 Part 14 file type lines, it would be promising to expand the sort of container types for more interesting results in the future study. Note that, for example, there exist 3 audio file container, 2 image file container, and 13 audio/video container used for multimedia file types. If there does not exist a file format specification or a parser tool, it would be promising to adopt the automatic input format recovery [6,9,23] to automatically analyze the native file formats for enabling the automated file format awareness phase in general.

Coverage-based Fuzzing. It would be promising to combine file format-aware fuzzing like TFA and coverage-based fuzzing in the future study. We did not consider deeper paths and code coverage in TFA but plan to work on coverage-based fuzzers, such as libFuzzer and AFL-fuzz, by replacing the mutation strategy part with TFA-like format-awareness strategy. It might be expected to improve the performance of fuzzers significantly.

Latest Version. When we work on TFA, the latest version of iOS was 9.3.2 - 9.3.5 and we reported our result to Apple. Our result was announced as CVE-2016-4702. We confirmed that all the crashes found in TFA work was successfully blocked in the current latest version of iOS 10.2.1. In the future study, we will work on iOS 10.2.1 with the plans described above.

6   Related Work

Fuzzing. Fuzzing first appeared as technical jargon in 1990 when Miller et al. showed that randomly generated character streams, fed into UNIX utility programs, could result in significant program crashes [25]. Fuzzing is such a security test method that causes crashes and discovers potential memory corruption and vulnerabilities by feeding randomized data into target application programs [24,32]. Fuzzing is classified into Black-box fuzzing [10,19,21,28,36], white-box fuzzing [5,7,14,16,17,35], and grey-box fuzzing [2–4] according to the existence of internal information of software. Our TFA fuzzing starts with a white-box analysis to gain the FOURCC atom list but mainly runs with black-box fuzzing on both iOS and Android. Fuzzing can also be classified into generation-based fuzzing [15,18,26] and mutational-based fuzzing [21,28,36] according to the way of input data generation. Our TFA fuzzing is mutational-based fuzzing Fuzzing was actively used for protocol security test around 1999, e.g., the PROTOS test suite of the University of Oulu [29]. File fuzzing received public attention in 2004 due to Microsoft security bulletin MS04-028.

Recently, fuzzing received academic attention regarding seed selections and mutation strategies. In 2014, A. Rebert et al. [28] pointed out that there had been little systematic effort in understanding the science of how to fuzz properly and studied how best to pick seed files to maximize the total number of bugs found during a fuzz campaign. In 2015, Cha et al. [8] studied how to compute a probabilistically optimal mutation ratio when a certain program-seed pair is given. They leveraged white-box symbolic analysis on an execution trace for a given program-seed pair to detect dependencies among the bit positions of an input. In 2016, Spephens et al. [30] proposed the so-called Driller which is a hybrid vulnerability excavation tool to exercise deeper paths in executables.

They used selective concolic execution to generate inputs which satisfy the complex checks separating the compartments exercised by inexpensive fuzzing. In 2016, Bohme et al. [4] proposed the CGF (Coverage-based Greybox Fuzzing) method to explore significantly more paths with the same number of tests. They used the Markov chain model for the purpose.

File Format-awareness. Sutton et al. [31] introduced the benefits of investigating seed file formats. Due to file format-awareness, it would be possible to appropriately mutate more interesting fields in seed files. In 2007, Lewis et al. [22] used a modification of traditional format-free fuzzing techniques to identify vulnerabilities in the format-strict environment of media players. They stressed the significance of having the appearance of a valid media file on fuzzing. In 2008, Thiel presented the results of file format-aware fuzzing on 'PC' media software by investigating various media file formats [33]. It was possible to find new bugs that could not be found in simple fuzzers.

Fuzzing on Smartphone. There have been studies of fuzzing on iOS and Android related to our research but there is no file format aware fuzzing in this area [19,21,27]. In 2010, Klein et al. introduced a black-box 'byte-wise' mutational fuzzing on the previous versions of iOS 3.1.3 by selecting an m4r/m4a ring-tone file (415,959 bytes) as a seed file and discovered a unique bug regarding `mediaserverd` (CVE-2010-0036). He generated test cases by sequentially mutating offset 0 to 999 with value of 255 [19]. In 2015, Lee et al. [21] studied a qualified seed file selection strategy and adopted a mutational fuzzing to find bugs from old iOS versions (6.x–6.1.x) and Android old versions (2.3.x–4.3.x), respectively [21]. They discovered several crashes by fuzzing real world format (*gif, jpeg, png, mp3,* and *mp4*) in both iOS and Android. They used CACE (Crash Automatic Classification Engine) method to design SFAT (Seed File Analysis Tool) for a good selection of seed files and categorized the discovered crashes automatically. As a result, they achieved better results by discovering about 1900 crashes and seven (unlike) unique bugs in iOS and Android. Compared with Lee et al.'s work, our research is different in analyzing the file format to optimize the number of test cases and fuzzing time.

7   Conclusion

In this paper, we studied file format-aware fuzzing on the media server daemons running in the latest versions of smartphones, and presented a new smartphone attack that exploits the results of such a fuzz input. Our methodology was strategic to overcome fuzzing challenges, such as format-awareness, seed file crawling, format-aware fuzzing, and latest versions. It was efficient for black-box mutational fuzzing with regard to a seed file selection and a test case generation, and also effective to find critical crash atoms in iOS and related systems. Although both iOS and Android have been updated on submission of this paper, we believe our strategic, efficient, and effective methodology and the proven results (CVE-2016-4702 CVSS Score 10.0) are promising for the future study. We plan to diversify input file formats in the near future.

Acknowledgement. This work was supported by the National Research Foundation of Korea (NRF-2015-R1A2A2A01004792).

References

1. Quicktime file format specification. https://developer.apple.com/library/mac/documentation/QuickTime/QTFF/QTFFPreface/qtffPreface.html
2. Bekrar, S., Bekrar, C., Groz, R., Mounier, L.: Finding software vulnerabilities by smart fuzzing. In: Proceeding the IEEE International Conference on Software Testing, Verification and Validation (ICST), pp. 427–430 (2011)
3. Bekrar, S., Bekrar, C., Groz, R., Mounier, L.: A taint based approach for smart fuzzing. In: Proceeding the IEEE International Conference on Software Testing, Verification and Validation (ICST), pp. 818–825 (2012)
4. Böhme, M., Pham, V.T., Roychoudhury, A.: Coverage-based Greybox Fuzzing as Markov Chain. In: Proceeding the ACM SIGSAC Conference on Computer and Communications Security (CCS), pp. 1032–1043 (2016)
5. Bounimova, E., Godefroid, P., Molnar, D.: Billions and billions of constraints: whitebox fuzz testing in production. In: Proceeding the International Conference on Software Engineering (ICSE), pp. 122–131 (2013)
6. Caballero, J., Yin, H., Liang, Z., Song, D.: Polyglot: automatic extraction of protocol message format using dynamic binary analysis. In: Proceeding the ACM SIGSAC Conference on Computer and Communications Security (CCS), pp. 317–329 (2007)
7. Cadar, C., Ganesh, V., Pawlowski, P., Dill, D., Engler, D.: EXE: a system for automatically generating inputs of death using symbolic execution. In: Proceeding the ACM Conference on Computer and Communications Security (CCS) (2006)
8. Cha, S.K., Woo, M., Brumley, D.: Program-adaptive mutational fuzzing. In: Proceeding of the IEEE Symposium on Security and Privacy (S&P), pp. 725–741 (2015)
9. Cui, W., Peinado, M., Chen, K., Wang, H.J., Irun-Briz, L.: Tupni: automatic reverse engineering of input formats. In: Proceeding the ACM SIGSAC Conference on Computer and Communications Security (CCS), pp. 391–402 (2008)
10. De Ruiter, J., Poll, E.: Protocol state fuzzing of TLS implementations. In: Proceeding of the USENIX Security Symposium (2015)
11. Drake, J.: Stagefright: Scary Code in the Heart of Android. BlackHat USA (2015)
12. Drake, J.J., Lanier, Z., Mulliner, C., Fora, P.O., Ridley, S.A., Wicherski, G.: Android Hacker's Handbook. Wiley (2014)
13. Eddington, M.: Peach Fuzzing Platform. http://www.peachfuzzer.com/
14. Ganesh, V., Leek, T., Rinard, M.: Taint-based directed whitebox fuzzing. In: Proceeding of the International Conference on Software Engineering (ICSE), pp. 474–484 (2009)
15. Godefroid, P., Kiezun, A., Levin, M.Y.: Grammar-based whitebox fuzzing. In: Proceeding of the ACM SIGPLAN Conference on Programming Language Design and Implementation (PLDI), vol. 43, pp. 206–215 (2008)
16. Godefroid, P., Levin, M.Y., Molnar, D.: SAGE: whitebox fuzzing for security testing. Queue **10**(1), 20 (2012)
17. Godefroid, P., Levin, M.Y., Molnar, D.A., et al.: Automated whitebox fuzz testing. In: Proceeding of the Network and Distributed System Security Symposium (NDSS), vol. 8, pp. 151–166 (2008)

18. Holler, C., Herzig, K., Zeller, A.: Fuzzing with code fragments. In: Proceeding of the USENIX Security Symposium, pp. 445–458 (2012)
19. Klein, T.: A Bug Hunter's Diary: A Guided Tour Through the Wilds of Software Security. No Starch Press (2011)
20. Caca labs: ZZUF. http://caca.zoy.org/wiki/zzuf
21. Lee, W.H., Srirangam Ramanujam, M., Krishnan, S.: On designing an efficient distributed black-box fuzzing system for mobile devices. In: Proceeding of the ACM SIGSAC Conference on Computer and Communications Security (CCS), pp. 31–42 (2015)
22. Lewis, C., Rhoden, B., Sturton, C.: Using Structured Random Data to Precisely Fuzz Media Players. Project Report. University of UC Berkeley (2007)
23. Lin, Z., Zhang, X.: Deriving input syntactic structure from execution. In: Proceeding of the ACM SIGSOFT International Symposium on Foundations of Software Engineering (FSE), pp. 83–93 (2008)
24. Miller, B.P.: Fuzz Testing of Application Reliability. UW-Madison Computer Sciences (2007)
25. Miller, B.P., Fredriksen, L., So, B.: An empirical study of the reliability of UNIX utilities. Commun. ACM **33**(12), 32–44 (1990)
26. Miller, C., Peterson, Z.N.: Analysis of Mutation and Generation-based Fuzzing. Independent Security Evaluators (2007)
27. Mulliner, C., Miller, C.: Fuzzing the phone in your phone. In: BlackHat USA, vol. 25 (2009)
28. Rebert, A., Cha, S.K., Avgerinos, T., Foote, J., Warren, D., Grieco, G., Brumley, D.: Optimizing seed selection for fuzzing. In: Proceeding of the USENIX Security Symposium, pp. 861–875 (2014)
29. Röning, J., Lasko, M., Takanen, A., Kaksonen, R.: Protos-systematic approach to eliminate software vulnerabilities. Invited presentation at Microsoft Research (2002)
30. Stephens, N., Grosen, J., Salls, C., Dutcher, A., Wang, R., Corbetta, J., Shoshitaishvili, Y., Kruegel, C., Vigna, G.: Driller: augmenting fuzzing through selective symbolic execution. In: Proceeding of the Network and Distributed System Security Symposium (NDSS) (2016)
31. Sutton, M., Greene, A.: The art of file format fuzzing. In: BlackHat USA (2005)
32. Takanen, A., Demott, J.D., Miller, C.: Fuzzing for Software Security Testing and Quality Assurance. Artech House (2008)
33. Thiel, D.: Exposing vulnerabilities in media software. In: BlackHat EU (2008)
34. Tool: Spike Fuzzer Platform. http://www.immunitysec.com
35. Wang, T., Wei, T., Gu, G., Zou, W.: TaintScope: a checksum-aware directed fuzzing tool for automatic software vulnerability detection. In: Proceeding of the IEEE Symposium on Security and Privacy (S&P), pp. 497–512 (2010)
36. Woo, M., Cha, S.K., Gottlieb, S., Brumley, D.: Scheduling black-box mutational fuzzing. In: Proceeding of the ACM SIGSAC Conference on Computer and Communications Security (CCS), vol. 9 (2013)
37. Zalewski, M.: American Fuzzy Lop (AFL) fuzzer. http://lcamtuf.coredump.cx/afl/

Towards Automated Classification of Firmware Images and Identification of Embedded Devices

Andrei Costin[1]([✉]), Apostolis Zarras[2], and Aurélien Francillon[3]

[1] University of Jyväskylä, Jyväskylä, Finland
andrei.costin@jyu.fi
[2] Technical University of Munich, Munich, Germany
zarras@sec.in.tum.de
[3] EURECOM, Biot, France
aurelien.francillon@eurecom.fr

Abstract. Embedded systems, as opposed to traditional computers, bring an incredible diversity. The number of devices manufactured is constantly increasing and each has a dedicated software, commonly known as *firmware*. Full firmware images are often delivered as multiple releases, correcting bugs and vulnerabilities, or adding new features. Unfortunately, there is no centralized or standardized firmware distribution mechanism. It is therefore difficult to track which vendor or device a firmware package belongs to, or to identify which firmware version is used in deployed embedded devices. At the same time, discovering devices that run vulnerable firmware packages on public and private networks is crucial to the security of those networks. In this paper, we address these problems with two different, yet complementary approaches: firmware classification and embedded web interface fingerprinting. We use supervised Machine Learning on a database subset of real world firmware files. For this, we first tell apart firmware images from other kind of files and then we classify firmware images per vendor or device type. Next, we fingerprint embedded web interfaces of both physical and emulated devices. This allows recognition of web-enabled devices connected to the network. In some cases, this complementary approach allows to logically link web-enabled online devices with the corresponding firmware package that is running on the devices. Finally, we test the firmware classification approach on 215 images with an accuracy of 93.5%, and the device fingerprinting approach on 31 web interfaces with 89.4% accuracy.

1 Introduction

In the wake of the Internet of Things (IoT), embedded devices are becoming increasingly present in many computing and networked environments. In fact, multiple reports estimate an increase in the number of embedded devices in the next few years [16,24]. These devices often rely on *network connectivity*, are

© IFIP International Federation for Information Processing 2017
Published by Springer International Publishing AG 2017. All Rights Reserved
S. De Capitani di Vimercati and F. Martinelli (Eds.): SEC 2017, IFIP AICT 502, pp. 233–247, 2017.
DOI: 10.1007/978-3-319-58469-0_16

administrated through *web interfaces*, and *firmware packages* are made available with new features and bug fixes. In addition, many firmware releases are available for each device leading to a large number of firmware images [12]; this number will likely grow with the increasing number of newly deployed devices. Therefore, it is challenging to apply manual analysis, classification and fingerprinting, as it does not scale. Hence, novel, scalable, and automated approaches are needed.

Usually, a firmware image is custom made for a specific device. Although, it is relatively easy for a human to find the vendor, the version, and the device for which the firmware is intended, because embedded devices are very diverse, it is difficult to automatically link a device model and a firmware image without a learning system that supports them. At the same time, it is extremely hard for an automated system to categorize firmware files from unstructured download sites by device class or by vendor. While this can be automated for a few well-defined file categories, this becomes hard when crawling thousands of firmware images from a wide diversity of devices. Similarly, when administrating an embedded device, a human can have contextual clues about its firmware version, however, an automated system requires a different approach to device identification.

Within this context we formulate the following problems: (*i*) how to automatically label the brand and the model of the device for which the firmware is intended and (*ii*) how to automatically identify the vendor, the model, and the firmware version of an arbitrary web-enabled online device. File classification and (*web*) fingerprinting might seem trivial problems, however, such problems are not trivial and were addressed in different contexts, for file classification [5,26,27,32], device fingerprinting [6,14,19], and web fingerprinting [1,2,29,33]. Moreover, these problems need to be addressed in a reliable and scalable manner which is independent of device, vendor, or custom protocols running on the device.

In this paper, we apply *Machine Learning* (ML) to classify firmware files according to their vendor or device type. First, we explore several feature sets derived from the characteristics of firmware images. Then, we recommend a feature set for this type of classification problems that we found to be optimal and show that our approach achieves high accuracy. Next, using sound statistical methods, such as confidence intervals, we estimate the performance of our classifiers for large scale datasets. Complementary to the previous approach, we build a fingerprinting database of web interfaces using emulated firmware images (similar to [11,13]) and physical devices. We show that it is feasible to match an unknown embedded web interface to the list of known web fingerprints in our database by using multiple features such as the web interface sitemap or the HTTP protocol Finite-State Machine (FSM). Finally, we use multiple scoring systems to rank the web fingerprint matches. The outcomes reveal that we are able to accurately classify firmware and fingerprint embedded web interfaces.

In summary, we make the following main contributions:

- We are the first to apply ML in the context of firmware classification. For this we propose and study the firmware features and the ML algorithms that makes the classification effective, accurate, and feasible.

– We research the fingerprinting and identification of web-enabled embedded devices and their firmware version, and introduce fingerprinting features for the embedded web interfaces of physical and emulated devices.
– We present and discuss direct practical applications for both techniques.

2   Firmware Classification and Identification

In this section we show how we classify the firmware files at vendor or at device-type level. Specifically, we present the details of our classifier for which we use supervised ML. In supervised ML, the algorithms must be trained with a set of annotated (e.g., manually, computer-aided) samples before it can classify unknown or new samples. In our experiments we use *Decision Trees (DT)* and *Random Forests (RF)* algorithms that are able to handle better non-linear features, and are easier and faster to train. The supervised ML algorithms also require *features* that are used to partition and distinguish the learned classes of data. Feature selection is usually specific to the domain to which the ML is applied and thus it must be carefully performed and evaluated. Therefore, we first present a set of "naive" attempts and their limitations. Then, we present our dataset, the features we explore, and the motivations behind our selection. Finally, we measure the performance of our classifiers trained for firmware files.

2.1   Discussion on "Naive" Attempts

One "naive" attempt could be the use of the firmware filenames as the source of various information (e.g., vendor and device name, firmware version). In practice, there are several problems with such an attempt. First, there is no standard that specifies if and how the filenames should carry metadata information. In fact, many firmware images are released with generic names such as `firmware.bin` or `upgrade.fw`. Second, extracting information from filenames is domain specific and is non-trivial [4]. Third, often the filenames can be fake and not related to their content. This is a known problem in "free-riding" on P2P and file sharing networks [17]. It also constitutes a problem in malware and spam distribution, where a filename can be used to disguise the real function of the file [21]. Therefore, we consider the filenames to be an untrustworthy source of information, but it could *optionally* be used at later stages for cross-validation of the information.

Another "naive" attempt could be the compilation of a dictionary of hashes based on *all* firmware files. One could query this dictionary when trying to obtain information (e.g., vendor, product, version) for a previously obtained firmware image. Such an attempt could face several challenges. First, there is no database that provides a list of *all* the firmware images that were created and are available to date: firmware releases and updates are not standardized or never publicly released. Second, even if such a database would hypothetically exist and the hashes of all the firmware files to date would be known, the problem remains for the firmware released in the future. It would be hard, if not impossible, to classify future firmware releases with such an attempt. In fact, this is one of the main reasons why malware file classification techniques do not use it, and rather propose alternative ways to detect and classify malware samples [5,32], including techniques based on ML [26,27]. Finally, it could still be possible to use fuzzy hashing to classify unseen or future firmware images with the right firmware category (i.e., label) according to fuzzy hash similarity. However, fuzzy hashing has its own limitations and is not viable in practice.

2.2 Dataset

From a dataset of firmware images we collected over time, we select 215 images from 13 vendors that manufacture several type of devices [13]. We will refer to these vendors as *classification categories*. Each of these categories contains a varying number of firmware images. In fact, this is a realistic scenario since firmware release cycles and the numbers of released firmware are diverse and vary across vendors, and even across devices from the same vendor. Each classification category contains between 5 and 54 firmware images, with an average of 16 images per vendor. Finally, we create a special classification category of files for which we know that they are not firmware images. For example, such files include drivers and PDF or text documents, which are often released along with firmware updates at a common download location or in a common file archive [12].

2.3 Features Selection

The classification of a firmware file can be performed at vendor or at device-type level, depending on the granularity objectives. For consistency, we will refer to both vendor and device-type categorization as *classification categories*.

Firmware File Size. The file size of a full firmware upgrade for an embedded device is directly related to the hardware design and the functionalities of the device. At the same time, a firmware upgrade file cannot exceed the limited memory available in the particular device types which it targets. This motivates us to use *firmware file size* as a good feature to discriminate between firmware images of devices from different classification categories.

Firmware File Content. Most vendors use custom procedures to build and package their firmware upgrades. This makes the firmware images to have specific distribution and density of the information they contain. Therefore, we use information theory properties as features for ML. In this sense, we leverage the following characteristics of the firmware files as ML features: (*i*) file entropy (i.e., the informational density of bits per byte), (*ii*) arithmetic mean of file bytes, (*iii*) file compressibility percentage (i.e., an empirical value that is an upper bound of the Kolmogorov complexity), (*iv*) serial correlation value, (*v*) monte-carlo value and its estimation error, and (*vi*) chi-square distribution and its excess error. We will refer to the file entropy as *entropy* feature and to the rest of the features from the above list as the *entropy extended* features set.

Firmware File Strings. Many software packages, including firmware files, contain strings. These strings may embody copyright, debugging, or other information. They often also contain vendor or device specific information. Hence, the strings in a given firmware file represent a fingerprint of the corresponding firmware, device, and vendor. Consequently, the intersection of strings of each file within a particular classification category is a strong classification feature for that category. Suppose that an unknown firmware sample contains a string that is found within strings intersection of a *classification category A*. There are high chances that this sample is related to the files in the *classification category A*.

Unfortunately, many firmware files contain strings that are common across multiple classification categories. This may happen if the firmware uses common Free Open Source Software (FOSS) code such as Linux kernel or OpenSSL libraries. In this case, an unknown sample can match several different classification categories and can mislead the ML classifier. To overcome this, for each trained classification category we also build a dictionary that contains only strings *unique* to that category. Therefore, each classification category in the training set adds two different features: the *Category Strings Feature* (CSF) and the *Category Unique Strings Feature* (CUSF). Unfortunately, the CUSF feature derivation comes with a drawback which can limit the scalability of our techniques with larger datasets. Whenever a new firmware file is added to a given classification category, the entire CUSF process has to be re-run on the labeled dataset.

Fuzzy Hashing of Firmware File Content. Fuzzy hashing is a technique which provides the ability to compare two different items and determine a fundamental level of similarity between them. While the cryptographic hashing is used to determine if two different items are *identical*, the fuzzy hashing is used to decide if two different items are *homologous* (i.e., similar but not exactly the same). In our approach, we use *Context Triggered Piecewise Hashes* (CTPH) [20]. Intuitively, firmware files from a given classification category should be more "fuzzy hash similar" among themselves than cross-category. As such, for each trained classification category we build a list containing fuzzy hashes of files within the category. For a training or an unknown file, we compare its fuzzy hash with the fuzzy hashes in the list of each category. If there is at least one fuzzy hash match with similarity above an empiric threshold, the fuzzy hash feature of that category is set to 1; otherwise, is set to 0. Surprisingly, including the fuzzy hash similarities as features proved to result in worse classification accuracy as discussed in Sect. 2.4.

2.4   Evaluation

Running supervised ML experiments requires training sets. Since our dataset has the classification categories of varying lengths, we create the training sets by taking a constant percentage from each category as training samples. We start with 10% as *training set percentage* and then increment it by 10% until training set percentage reaches 90%. For each training set percentage, we run 100

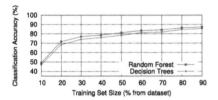

Fig. 1. Firmware classification performance using [size, entropy] features set.

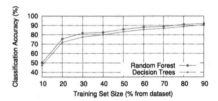

Fig. 2. Firmware classification performance using [size, entropy, entropy extended] features set.

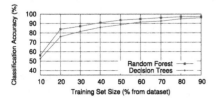

Fig. 3. Firmware classification performance using [size, entropy, entropy extended, strings, strings unique] features set.

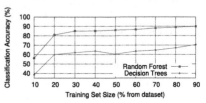

Fig. 4. Firmware classification performance using [size, entropy, entropy extended, strings, strings unique, fuzzy hash] features set.

experimental runs by randomly sampling the given percentage of files as training samples and running the training and classification. Finally, for each *training set percentage*, we compute its average classification accuracy and error based on results of each of the 100 experimental runs. For any experiment run, we use both the DT and RF algorithms so that we can compare their performance under various conditions. Since we use DT and RF algorithms, we do not perform cross-validation because these algorithms do it internally. The firmware classification performance for various ML algorithms, feature sets, and training sets size is summarized in the Figs. 1, 2, 3, and 4. For each algorithm and features sets, the figures depict the average accuracy per 100 experimental runs for *training set size* increasing with 10% increments.

First, we observe that the classification accuracy improves with the increased size of the training set. Although this appears to be trivial, is not always the case as there exist scenarios where larger datasets lead to worse results [30]. Second, contrary to the intuitive expectation, the addition of the fuzzy hash similarity features reduced the accuracy. Interestingly, these features made both the RF and the DT classifiers perform worse. The DT classifier also performed much worse compared to the DT classifiers with very basic feature sets, such as [size, entropy] or [size, entropy, entropy extended]. In parallel, the RF classifier in this setup failed to perform at least marginally better than the RF classifiers based on basic feature sets mentioned above. One explanation could be the fact that a fuzzy hash is not an accurate file match. Such hashing can return high similarity scores even for pair of files that are totally unrelated. The accuracy of the fuzzy hashing can be influenced by the file size and various other factors.

Based on the previous observations, we conclude that the feature set of [size, entropy, entropy extended, category strings, category unique strings] constitutes the best choice. It also provides best accuracy when used with the RF classifiers; more than 90% classification accuracy when the training set is based on at least 40% of the known firmware files. Another observation is that both the RF and the DT classifiers using other feature sets reach the 90% accuracy only for training set sizes of 80%–90% of the known firmware files, which is not practical in real-life. Also, the RF and the DT classifiers with the most basic feature set [size, entropy] does not even reach 90% classification.

We try to identify the most reliable feature set and learning classifier, however, the *generalization of learning* is an open problem in the ML field [7,8,15]. The ML algorithms performance cannot be guaranteed on another dataset (e.g., bigger). We compensate this limitation with statistical methods such as confidence intervals. In this context, we use statistical confidence intervals [10] to evaluate the accuracy of our technique when applied to real-world populations of firmware images. For example, by taking any firmware in a dataset of 172 K firmware images [12], with an accuracy of 99% we can compute the confidence interval for our best feature set and a training based on 50% of the dataset. In this case, our RF firmware model can correctly classify the firmware in 93.5% ± 4.3% of the cases. Manually annotating 50% of a dataset with 172 K firmware images is not trivial and does not scale. However, this challenge can be solved using alternative approaches. First, many files could be automatically annotated based on the metadata that was acquired by the crawler, assuming that the metadata from the vendor is reliable. Second, building in an incremental manner a clean training set can be achieved by using services like Amazon's Mechanical Turk.

3   Device Fingerprinting and Identification

Often firmware fingerprinting is not sufficient and thus it required to fingerprint the device itself. Many approaches exist for fingerprinting and identification of computing device and sensors [6,14,19]. However, the fingerprinting features used by these techniques are strongly linked to the real hardware or the way the live devices operate. Such strong dependencies can make these techniques less effective, for example, when dealing with emulated devices and virtualized appliances. In addition, these techniques do not necessarily take advantage of the devices' firmware packages. Often firmware packages can be emulated and can provide additional information for a reliable device identification.

At the same time, the embedded devices often lack the user interfaces of desktop computers, such as keyboard, video, and mouse. Nevertheless, these devices need somehow to be administrated. Even though some devices alternatively rely on custom protocols such as "thick" clients or even legacy interfaces (e.g., telnet), the web became the universal administration interface. Thus, the firmware of these devices often embed a web server providing a web interface and these web applications range from quite simple to fairly complex.

These observations suggest that higher level approaches are required, regardless the way the devices operate. As such, we propose an approach that fingerprints the devices at high level as possible, which in our case is the *embedded web interface* level. Our solution benefits from the firmware contents and the device emulation based on the firmware images alone. Previous works touched some aspects of our fingerprinting techniques, however, either they suggest manual approaches [22] or do not provide enough insights and evaluations [29]. The well recognized project such as ZMap/ZTag also include a device/service fingerprinting feature. However, their efforts in this regard have been mostly manual so far as seen in their GitHub and Travis-CI logs.

3.1   Discussion on "Naive" Attempts

One "naive" attempt to create or verify fingerprints of embedded web interfaces is to use physical devices in a private network or devices connected to the Internet with public IPs. In practice, there are several problems with such an attempt. First, it is unfeasible to operate physical devices in a private network for all the embedded devices that exist to date. Second, it could be unethical, or even sometimes illegal, to scan the devices connected to the Internet with public IPs for the purpose of analysis or fingerprinting without prior authorization. Another "naive" attempt could be to check the existence of unique files/URLs, or specific strings in the web interface pages or HTTP authentication prompts. However, in our view such an attempt cannot deal very well with false positives that can be produced by fake web pages created by web traffic generators, and fake services produced by rather simple honeypots [23]. Therefore, we suggest that more elaborate approaches must be designed and proposed.

3.2   Dataset

We used the emulated web interface of 27 firmware images originating from 3 vendors that split across 7 functional categories. 9 of these images where also part of the firmware ML classification: they were classified by our ML firmware model with an accuracy of 100% using RF (and around 99.5% using DT). There are practical reasons why we could not use the entire dataset of 215 images from the firmware classification experiment: (*i*) emulating a large number of diverse firmware images is a challenging problem [13] and (*ii*) it is unfeasible and expensive to acquire many devices such that their number is large enough to produce convincing and representative results. We also used 4 physical devices from 2 vendors that cover 4 functional categories. We consider that the dataset has a sufficient size and enough intramodel similarity to provide a conclusive estimation of the effectiveness and the accuracy of our technique.

3.3   Features for Web Interface Fingerprinting

We propose six different features that are computed for each training or unknown embedded web interface, which present them below and motivate the choice.

Web Sitemap. A sitemap is a list of pages of a website which are publicly or privately accessible. Files and URLs that exist in one website do not necessarily exist in another, even if they run on the same web server. We leverage this fact and create a fingerprint based on this assumption. In detail, to categorize the web interface of an unknown embedded device, we access URLs and files which exist in our trained dataset and represent the sitemap of a known web application. If the sitemap of the unknown web interface matches with a known one in our database, we classify it as belonging to an embedded device running a specific firmware version. This sitemap approach however would not work for single-page web applications that use JavaScript router scripts. This could be addressed by fingerprinting the Document Object Model (DOM) of those interfaces.

HTTP Finite-State Machine. The HTTP protocol, is a stateless application-level protocol for distributed, collaborative, and hypermedia information systems. For our fingerprinting and detection purposes we focus only on the server responses. HTTP is a liberal protocol which means that the structure of a response message is diversified among the different web server implementations. Each web server implements the response messages differently in terms of the headers it uses, the sequence of these headers inside the message, and the value of each header. Hence, it is possible to fingerprint them by extensively analyzing the messages they exchange [31, 34]. We leverage these differences to identify the type of server involved in a specific HTTP conversation. Therefore, we create a model which is able to learn the headers' order of an HTTP response and then use this order to classify an unknown HTTP conversation. In essence, we have implemented an HTTP FSM in which the headers represent the states of this FSM and the order of the headers the transitions from one state to another.

Cryptographic Hashing of HTML Content and HTTP Headers. We expand the FSM approach by using also the HTTP response values. Although some headers will always display the same information (e.g., the header *Server*) few other headers will not remain constant over time (e.g., the header *Date*). Such small variations in responses results in significant changes in the cryptographic hashes of the headers. For example, the cryptographic hashes of headers of two consecutive responses to exactly the same static web resource will result in two different values and will generate a false mismatch. To overcome this type of "noise", instead of retrieving the actual value of such a header, we dynamically create a regular expression. As a consequence, headers such as *Date* do not affect our features and matching. We create two cryptographic hash values from a complete HTTP response. The first contains the hashed headers of the message as explained above and the second the hashed message body. If we have a match between an unknown response and a response contained in our database, we can successfully fingerprint the device that sent this response. However, many times an HTTP response from an unknown device will match a list of devices that can reply back with responses that hash to the same values. In those cases, we can use this approach to minimize the number of devices that match this response.

Fuzzy Hashing of HTML Content and HTTP Headers. It is not always possible to have a fingerprint based on a cryptographic hash value even if it comes from the same device. This happens because the modification of a single byte in a large byte stream causes the cryptographic hash function to generate a completely different hash value. To counter this behavior we use fuzzy hashing. In our approach we use *Context Triggered Piecewise Hashes* (CTPH) [20]. Using fuzzy hashing, we compute the similarity between an unknown HTTP response (HTTP headers, HTML content) and a list of HTTP responses in our database for which we know the fuzzy hash values. The procedure we follow is quite similar to the one we followed in the case of the cryptographic hashing, but in this approach we are using a completely different hashing function. If the similarity between the unknown and a known HTTP response exceeds an empirically calculated threshold, we can successfully classify this unknown device.

3.4   Scoring Systems for Features

Scoring is the way each feature contributes to the final rank of a given match. We propose three different scoring systems and briefly present them below.

Majority Vote Scoring. Each feature of each fingerprint match is ranked in decreasing order. The fingerprint match that ranks highest on most of its features is considered to be the most accurate match to the unknown sample.

Uniform and Non-Uniform Weighs Scoring. Each feature value of a fingerprint is assigned a weight. Then, for each feature of each fingerprint all the weighted values are summed into a total value of the fingerprint. Finally, all the total values are ranked in decreasing order. The match whose total value ranks highest is considered as the most accurate match to the unknown sample. For our evaluation, we used the uniform weights of 16.6% (i.e., a uniform devision of 100% match to each of the six features). For the non-uniform scoring, we used the following empirically found weights: 4% for `web sitemap`, 4% for `HTTP FSM`, 1% for `fuzzy hash HTTP header`, 1% for `fuzzy hash HTML content`, 10% for `crypto hash HTTP header`, 80% for `crypto hash HTML content`.

Score Fusion. In our evaluation, we used the *score fusion* technique to improve the accuracy of identification. The score fusion technique is widely and actively used in various research fields, such as biometrics and sensors data [18]. It is used to increase the confidence in the results and to counter the effect of imprecisely approximated data (e.g., fingerprints in biometrics) and unstable data readings (e.g., sensors data). We take as input the decreasingly ordered rankings from each of the scoring systems described above. Then, we apply majority voting to each ranking from these three scoring systems. This allows our system to decide which match is the most accurate based on its scores computed using the three different scoring systems presented above.

3.5 Evaluation

We start by connecting up the 4 physical devices and emulating the 27 firmware images. Then we create one fingerprint for the embedded web interface of each of these 31 devices. Subsequently we create a list of IP addresses based on the IP address of each of the 31 running devices. We feed sequentially each IP address to the identification module which acts like an *oracle* and has to "guess" to what fingerprint to assign the web-interface at this particular IP address. For this, the identification module loads the previously created fingerprinting database, computes the features' scores for each URL and accumulates them, runs the scoring systems and finally outputs the most accurate fingerprint match by applying the score fusion method. The list of these steps constitutes an experimental run. We execute the above steps for 100 experimental runs at various points in time, under varying network conditions and varying IP address assignments. We also vary the number of threads used for web interface crawling and the speed at which they crawl. Finally, we compute the average successful and erroneous identification rates based on results from each experimental run.

Summarized, our tests on average resulted in 89.4% accuracy in device identification. The tests were run using a database containing 31 fingerprints of embedded web interfaces. Also, the dataset provided enough intramodel similarity, because around a third of the fingerprinted web interfaces consist of similar or consecutive firmware versions (e.g., Brickcom). Our evaluations show that the cryptographic hash of the content is the most stable and accurate feature. On average, it provided an accuracy of more than 85%. On the other end, the fuzzy hash of headers and content were the most unstable. One reasons for this is that fuzzy hashing does not perform well with short data (e.g., HTTP headers). Another reason, as discussed also in Sect. 2.4, could be the fact that fuzzy hash is not an accurate data match and can introduce noise rather than useful similarity information. These empirical observations lead us to choose the non-uniform scoring weights as presented in Sect. 3.4. Finally, the most accurate scoring system in our tests was the majority voting, followed by the non-uniform. As expected, the uniform weights scoring system performed the worst with more than 50% of classification errors. This could be explained by the high weight values assigned to the fuzzy hash features which can be noisy and inaccurate.

4 Usage Scenarios

While taking a research-oriented approach to the open problems, with this work we also aim at providing practical results and usability. Thus, we consider that providing real-life examples and applications is equally important.

4.1 Firmware Classification

Correct identification and classification of a firmware could be extremely useful. First, it could allow easy and fast clustering and navigation of firmware files according to their vendor or device type. Subsequently, this more granular separation could be used to apply more refined techniques on each category, such as version or release date ordering within the category. With all the files in one huge cluster, such refined techniques would be more challenging, if not impossible. Second, it could allow to build a database of firmware images associated with inputs that trigger their vulnerabilities. Finding such vulnerabilities is an interesting topic itself, but is outside the scope of this paper and were addressed in [12,13]. Subsequently, for new firmware releases labeled into a category, the vulnerability triggering inputs from older firmware releases could be automatically tested. This could be used to test if a specific vulnerability was fixed in the last version or it is still present. Third, for well classified firmware files only a specific set of firmware effective unpackers are run. Unpacking firmware files is known to be resource and time consuming [12]. Applying a specific set of effective unpackers skips the brute force unpacking, thus saving processing time and providing faster and more accurate results. Finally, once the vendor is known, as a result of a successful firmware classification, vendor-specific analysis techniques and tools may be applied. The specifics can be tuned based on the knowledge of vendor's development practices and technologies used.

4.2   Device Fingerprinting and Identification

Defensive use. Our technique may be used to scan a network and fingerprint the detected embedded web interfaces. The fingerprint information may be used to identify the device model and vendor, and its firmware version. This information can also be used to offer a firmware upgrade if the identified firmware version running on the device is obsolete. The remaining unidentified devices in the network could be easily annotated by the user with attributes such as vendor, device model, and firmware version.

Offensive use. A penetration tester performing a black-box test may use our device fingerprinting and identification technique to identify the device model and the firmware version of an unknown embedded device encountered during the test. With this information, CVEs or exploits could be automatically retrieved for the particular device model and firmware version. This may help increase the test's success rate and decrease the required test time. Recent evidence shows that a similar but simplified technique was used for offensive use by a malvertising campaign targeting home routers and similar embedded devices [25].

4.3   Automated End-to-End Scenario

It is practical to have a system that can address the *firmware vulnerability discovery* and the *vulnerable device discovery* in an end-to-end autonomous process. The proposed techniques are an ideal complement for the firmware vulnerability discovery techniques [11–13]. First, the crawlers collect firmware images. Then, the ML techniques from Sect. 2 classify the firmware. Using static and dynamic analysis as well as emulation techniques on both generic and firmware-specific processing, we can discover vulnerabilities within the firmware. Once the emulator of the firmware is functional, the techniques from Sect. 3 create a fingerprint for the emulated device and firmware version. Finally, using scanning tools such as Shodan.io and Censys.io (Internet), or nmap and Nessus (Intranet), we can identify devices based on their fingerprint, and immediately label and isolate them according to discovered vulnerabilities. This way, we can cover the entire vulnerability life-cycle in an automated manner.

5 Related Work

Kohno et al. [19] introduced the area of remote physical device fingerprinting. Desmond et al. [14] proposed a fingerprinting technique that differentiates between unique devices through timing analysis of 802.11 probe request frames. Shah [29] presented early techniques to fingerprint and identify web applications at the HTTP level. Similar, the BlindElephant [1] attempts to discover the version of a web application. While, Wapplyzer [33] uses regular expressions to uncover the technologies used on websites, WhatWeb [2] uses more than 900 plugins to recognize the web technologies used within a website. Alvarez [3] used the Extended File Information (EXIF) metadata in JPEG files to generate fingerprints, and Bongard [9] studied the implementation differences among the PNG codecs used with the most popular web application platforms. Samarasinghe and Mannan [28] used TLS/SSL certificate details to fingerprint embedded devices.

6 Conclusion

In this paper we presented two complementary techniques, *embedded firmware trained classification* and *embedded web interface fingerprinted identification*. We proposed ML for the firmware classification challenge, and explored features and score fusion to address the web interface fingerprinting and identification problem. With high confidence for real-world large scale datasets, our tests demonstrated that the classifiers and features we proposed achieved 93.5% accuracy in firmware classification and 89.4% accuracy in device identification. Finally, we presented practical use cases of our techniques which motivated our work. The datasets and scripts will be available at http://firmware.re project page.

Acknowledgments. The research was partially supported by the German Federal Ministry of Education and Research under grant 16KIS0327 (IUNO).

References

1. BlindElephant Web-App Fingerprint. http://blindelephant.sourceforge.net
2. WhatWeb. http://morningstarsecurity.com/research/whatweb
3. Alvarez, P.: Using Extended File Information (EXIF) file headers in digital evidence analysis. Int. J. Digital Evid. **2**(3), 1–5 (2004)

4. Anquetil, N., Lethbridge, T.: Extracting concepts from file names: a new file clustering criterion. In: International Conference on Software Engineering (1998)
5. Bailey, M., Oberheide, J., Andersen, J., Mao, Z.M., Jahanian, F., Nazario, J.: Automated classification and analysis of internet malware. In: Kruegel, C., Lippmann, R., Clark, A. (eds.) RAID 2007. LNCS, vol. 4637, pp. 178–197. Springer, Heidelberg (2007). doi:10.1007/978-3-540-74320-0_10
6. Bates, A., Leonard, R., Pruse, H., Lowd, D., Butler, K.: Leveraging USB to establish host identity using commodity devices. In: ISOC Network and Distributed System Security Symposium (NDSS) (2014)
7. Bishop, C.M.: Pattern Recognition and Machine Learning. Machine Learning (2006)
8. Blum, A.L., Langley, P.: Selection of relevant features and examples in machine learning. Artif. Intell. **97**(1), 245–271 (1997)
9. Bongard, D.: Fingerprinting web application platforms by variations in PNG implementations. Blackhat (2014)
10. Le Boudec, J.-Y.: Performance Evaluation of Computer and Communication Systems. EPFL Press (2011)
11. Chen, D.D., Egele, M., Woo, M., Brumley, D.: Towards automated dynamic analysis for linux-based embedded firmware. In: ISOC Network and Distributed System Security Symposium (NDSS) (2016)
12. Costin, A., Zaddach, J., Francillon, A., Balzarotti, D.: A large-scale analysis of the security of embedded firmwares. In: USENIX Security Symposium (2014)
13. Costin, A., Zarras, A., Francillon, A.: Automated dynamic firmware analysis at scale: a case study on embedded web interfaces. In: ACM Symposium on Information, Computer and Communications Security (ASIACCS) (2016)
14. Desmond, L.C.C., Yuan, C.C., Pheng, T.C., Lee, R.S.: Identifying unique devices through wireless fingerprinting. In: Wireless Network Security (2008)
15. Domingos, P.: A few useful things to know about machine learning. Commun. ACM **55**(10), 78–87 (2012)
16. Intel. Rise of the Embedded Internet (2009)
17. Karakaya, M., Korpeoglu, I., Ulusoy, Ö.: Free riding in peer-to-peer networks. IEEE Internet Comput. **13**(2), 92–98 (2009)
18. Klein, L.A., Sensor, D.F.: A Tool for Information Assessment and Decision Making. SPIE Press Bellingham (2004)
19. Kohno, T., Broido, A., Claffy, K.C.: Remote physical device fingerprinting. IEEE Trans. Dependable Secure Comput. **2**(2), 93–108 (2005)
20. Kornblum, J.: Identifying almost identical files using context triggered piecewise hashing. Digital Invest. **3**, 91–97 (2006)
21. Li, F., Lai, A., Ddl, D.: Evidence of advanced persistent threat: a case study of malware for political espionage. In: International Conference on Malicious and Unwanted Software (MALWARE) (2011)
22. Niemietz, M., Schwenk, J., Network, owning your home: router security revisited. In: Web 2.0 Security and Privacy (W2SP) (2015)
23. Pa, Y.M.P., Suzuki, S., Yoshioka, K., Matsumoto, T., Kasama, T., Rossow, C.: IoT-POT: analysing the rise of IoT compromises. In: USENIX Workshop on Offensive Technologies (WOOT) (2015)
24. Postscapes. Internet of Things Market Forecast (2014)
25. Proofpoint Inc., Home Routers Under Attack via Malvertising on Windows, Android Devices. https://www.proofpoint.com/us/threat-insight/post/home-routers-under-attack-malvertising-windows-android-devices

26. Rieck, K., Holz, T., Willems, C., Düssel, P., Laskov, P.: Learning and classification of malware behavior. In: Detection of Intrusions and Malware, and Vulnerability Assessment (DIMVA) (2008)
27. Sahs, J., Khan, L.: A machine learning approach to android malware detection. In: European Intelligence and Security Informatics Conference (2012)
28. Samarasinghe, N., Mannan, M., Paper, S.: TLS ecosystems in networked devices vs. web servers. In: International Conference on Financial Cryptography and Data Security (FC) (2017)
29. Shah, S.: HTTP Fingerprinting Advanced Assessment Techniques. Blackhat (2003)
30. Shalev-Shwartz, S., Ben-David, S.: Understanding Machine Learning: From Theory to Algorithms. Cambridge University Press (2014)
31. Stringhini, G., Egele, M., Zarras, A., Holz, T., Kruegel, C., Vigna, G.: B@bel: Leveraging Email Delivery for Spam Mitigation. In: USENIX Security (2012)
32. Tian, R., Batten, L.M., Versteeg, S.: Function length as a tool for malware classification. In: Conference on Malicious and Unwanted Software (2008)
33. Wappalyzer. Identify Technology on Websites. https://wappalyzer.com
34. Zarras, A., Papadogiannakis, A., Gawlik, R., Holz, T.: Automated generation of models for fast and precise detection of HTTP-based malware. In: International Conference on Privacy, Security and Trust (PST) (2014)

Runtime Firmware Product Lines Using TPM2.0

Andreas Fuchs, Christoph Krauß$^{(\boxtimes)}$, and Jürgen Repp

Fraunhofer Institute for Secure Information Technology SIT, Darmstadt, Germany
{andreas.fuchs,christoph.krauss,juergen.repp}@sit.fraunhofer.de

Abstract. Runtime firmware product lines enable the generation of unified firmware images, i.e., a single firmware with several features can be used on several models. The device itself "decides" whether to unlock a feature or not. However, an attacker could alter their model and upgrade it to a higher-level model. In this paper, we propose an approach for secure runtime firmware product lines. Unified firmware images can be provisioned to a whole series of products while preventing unauthorized feature activation. Our approach is based on a Trusted Platform Module (TPM) 2.0, acting as security anchor using several new TPM 2.0 functionalities. The feasibility is shown in a proof-of-concept implementation.

1 Introduction

The development of Information Technology (IT) products has shifted drastically from separate and designated designs per model to unified hardware architectures with different software versions. Different products of similar kind nowadays only differ by their casing and firmware – and sometimes additional interfaces. For example, an Original Equipment Manufacturer (OEM) may produce routers and firewalls that only differ in the casing, firmware, and number of network ports. The firmware, however, differentiates a router from a firewall.

To improve the software production process, *software product lines* [11] were introduced for generating similar software versions at compile-time from a shared set of software components using conditional compilation techniques, e.g., #ifdef in the C programming language or flags such as --enable-feature[=arg] in the GNU Autoconf package [17]. *Firmware product lines* are used for generating unified firmware source code for (embedded) systems, e.g., by using the OpenEmbedded software framework [7] to generate a customized Linux distribution.

The next iteration of device product lines will go even beyond this and we refer to this step as *runtime firmware product lines*. Instead of compiling and packaging different firmware images from the same code collection, a unified firmware image will be delivered for a whole product series. The product customization will happen on the device itself. Hence, one firmware image contains several features and the device itself "decides" whether to unlock a certain feature or not. We use *overlay mounting* for the unlocking of features. This approach is particularly attractive due to its cost efficiency and simplifies the maintenance

© IFIP International Federation for Information Processing 2017
Published by Springer International Publishing AG 2017. All Rights Reserved
S. De Capitani di Vimercati and F. Martinelli (Eds.): SEC 2017, IFIP AICT 502, pp. 248–261, 2017.
DOI: 10.1007/978-3-319-58469-0_17

of devices drastically. However, it poses the risk that attackers could alter their model and upgrade it to a higher-level model.

In this paper, we propose an approach for *secure runtime firmware product lines* enabling the provisioning of unified firmware images to a whole series of products while preventing unauthorized feature activation by an attacker. Our approach uses the Trusted Platform Module (TPM) 2.0 to protect the intellectual property and model feature sets while still enabling refurbishment by changing the concrete model assignment. The general idea is using the TPM as a security anchor to individually encrypt the different features and controlling access to these features using some of the new TPM 2.0 functionalities such as enhanced authorization. Using our approach, development and firmware update processes are eased drastically by enabling unified firmware provisioning for complete model series which is also shown by our proof-of-concept implementation.

2   General Idea

In our approach, a device is equipped with a TPM 2.0 that can be a dedicated hardware chip but also a software implementation to save costs. The TPM acts as security anchor by providing secure storage, secure execution, and additional features for controlling access (cf. Sect. 3.3).

The general idea of our approach is as follows. A *unified firmware image* for a product line consists of several separate read-only *feature filesystems*. Each feature filesystem contains a specific feature set and is encrypted using a unique cryptographic *feature key*. For each model of a product line, a different model number is stored inside the devices' TPM. This TPM-resident model number serves as a basis of the runtime configuration of the firmware image to be booted. By verifying a TPM-Policy, only the allowed features for a specific model of a product line are unlocked, i.e., decrypted. Note that accessing the unified firmware image is only possible on an original OEM device containing the preconfigured TPM. If required, additional read-write filesystems for local data *localdataFS* (e.g., for /etc, /home, /srv) and temporary files *tmpFS* (e.g., for /var) can be mounted. The protection of the *localdata* filesystem against manipulation is out of scope of this paper, but can be easily realized, for example, using the approach presented in [16].

Figure 1 shows an example to illustrate our approach in more detail. The unified firmware image is structured by the means of overlay read-only filesystems. A base file system *BaseFS* contains those parts that are shared between all models. It includes the operating system (OS) kernel and a multitude of basic libraries and services. Each model then comes with its feature filesystems *FeatureFS-X*. In the example, we have four of these filesystems, *FeatureFS-0* to *FeatureFS-3*. They contain the differences of this feature compared to the underlying filesystem. This may be additional files, removed files, or even altered files. For any given model, a stack can then be built that includes the base filesystem and a series of feature filesystems that are overlayed in order to provide the actual final boot system. The TPM decides, based on the model number,

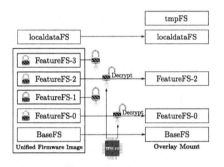
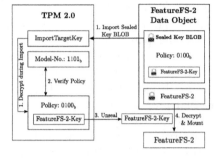

Fig. 1. General idea   **Fig. 2.** Runtime feature unlocking

which features to unlock, i.e., unseal the respective *feature key* which was used to encrypt the feature filesystem to decrypt it.

The unlocking of individual features during runtime configuration is illustrated by the example shown in Fig. 2. The model number is used to denote a specific combination of encrypted feature filesystems for a model of the product line. In the example, the model number has a length of 4 bits to be able to encode the four different feature filesystems. The binary model number of 0101_b will enable the feature filesystems *FeatureFS-0* and *FeatureFS-2* to be loaded, since the respective bits were set within the model number's feature bitmask. The figure shows the unlocking of *FeatureFS-2*. As mentioned above, *FeatureFS-2* is encrypted using *FeatureFS-2-Key*. This key is encrypted using the TPM-resident *ImportTargetKey* and stored together with the *Policy: 0100_b* in an integrity-protected *Sealed Key BLOB*. The integrity of the BLOB can be verified using also the *ImportTargetKey*. The BLOB and the encrypted *FeatureFS-2* form the *FeatureFS-2 Data Object*. In step 1, the TPM imports the sealed key blob, decrypts the *FeatureFS-2-Key*, and checks the integrity of the key BLOB. The TPM verifies the policy in step 2, by checking that the third bit from the right of the policy 0100_b equals 1 (since it was also set to 1 in the model number 1101_b). If this is true, the decrypted *FeatureFS-2-Key* is unsealed and transfered to the host CPU (step 3), which uses it to decrypt and mount *FeatureFS-2* as part of the overlay mount (step 4).

In the example, the entire model number was used to encode the used features. It is also possible to define certain parts of the model number for encoding the used features. The remaining parts can be used for other purposes, e.g., to encode the color of the casing. In principle, the modeling of the model number can be arbitrary complex to realize certain policies (cf. Sect. 5.2).

3   Related Work

3.1   Secure Runtime Product Lines

The work in this paper extends the idea and concept of compile-time firmware product lines based upon unified software repositories to run-time firmware product lines based upon unified firmware images. The most prominent example for compile-time firmware product lines are the Yocto [14], OpenEmbedded [7], and BitBake [22] projects. The BitBake project provides the build-chain and environment for a compile-time firmware product line. OpenEmbedded and Yocto provide the core and application level software recipes to build a multitude of firmware images for a multitude of devices. The Docker project [2] performs some form of packaging-time product lines by using overlay filesystems in their images similarly to our approach in order to stack feature filesystems. We use the same concept but for device boot of the basic operating system and additionally preventing activation and decryption of any unauthorized feature layer.

Another closely related case of product lines are so-called (feature oriented) software product lines, e.g., [8]. A lot of research has been conducted on software product lines [9,12,18,29] and even their security [10], practical implementations exist and given the inclusion in mainstream build systems, such as autotools [17], they are at the core of modern software engineering. The presented approach, just as the Yocto and OpenEmbedded projects, facilitate these capabilities and use them for realizing firmware product lines.

Other related technologies that are designed with a closely related focus are called feature activation. This term refers to the activation of features on devices (similar to the presented approach), but based on additional fees payed by the device owner. Though much research has been conducted on securing feature activation [24] and many more patents were filed, such as [15,20], these works have focused on the secure transfer of activation codes; i.e., on providing the evidence for an activated feature into the device. The actual securing of the feature-relevant programs on the device were to the best of the authors knowledge not yet solved. Also note that feature activation is not the focus of the presented approach and would require a rework of the model number deployment process (cf. Sect. 5.2).

Finally, it is known that many firmwares today are already partially self-reconfiguring upon startup due to their model by activating or deactivating certain software services. However, the security of these features remains yet to be solved, and a plausible approach is presented in this paper.

3.2   Overlay Filesystems

Overlay filesystems combine multiple filesystems into one single virtual filesystem and directories with equal paths are merged to one path. A typical application is the combination of read only devices (e.g., a CD) with writable devices, where all changes in the read only filesystem are stored on the writable device. This example use case could be realized under Windows with the Unified Write Filter [3]. For Linux the overlay filesystems AUFS [21] and OverlayFS [23] are available. AUFS is a reimplementation of UnionFS [6] the first available implementation of an overlay filesystem for Linux. UnionFS is also available for Free BSD and Net BSD. AUFS was the first device driver used in Docker [2] to layer Docker images and is very stable. OverlayFS is included in the mainline kernel and is potentially faster than AUFS. Despite this fact, we used AUFS in our prototypical implementation to present our concept since the structuring of the data was more simple, and AUFS did match better the requirements for the integration of encrypted SquashFS [5] read only filesystems into the virtual overlay filesystem.

3.3   TPM 2.0

The second iteration of the Trusted Platform Module (TPM), namely the TPM 2.0 Library Specification [25] has been released by the Trusted Computing Group (TCG) in October 2014. It provides a catalog of functionalities that can be used to build TPMs for different platforms. Accompanying the TPM specifications, the TCG has developed the specification of a TPM Software Stack (TSS) 2.0 for this new generation of TPMs. It consists of multiple Application Programming Interfaces (APIs) for different application scenarios [26,28].

Difference of TPM 2.0 to TPM 1.2. Compared with TPM 1.2, TPM 2.0 is a complete rewrite. Many of the new features were not compatible with the data type and function layout of TPM 1.2. The new features of TPM 2.0 in comparison to TPM 1.2 include:

- Cryptographic Agility: placeholders for cryptographic algorithms, e.g. RSA, ECC, AES, SHA1, and SHA256 (cf. TCG Algorithm Registry [27]).
- Support of Symmetric Algorithms: AES and HMACs.
- Enhanced Authorization: TPM 1.2 provided only limited authorization mechanisms: SHA1 hashes of passwords and binding a single set of PCR values for key use and sealing. TPM 2.0 included the concept of Enhanced Authorization, that allows the forming of arbitrary policy statements based on a set of policy commands. This provides a high flexibility requiring multiple factors to be fulfilled but also to allow different paths for policy fulfillments.
- Non-Volatile Memory: With TPM 2.0 the capabilities of the TPM's integrated non-volatile memory (NV-RAM) were enhanced. They can now be used as counters, bitmaps, and even extended PCRs.
- Flexibility: the TPM can be realized as dedicated hardware chip but also in software, e.g., as a firmware TPM or software protected by a Trusted Execution Environment (TEE). In addition, TPM profiles can be defined to specify required functionalities of the TPM and TSS.
- Many more enhancement were made. A lot of those are outline in [13].

TPM 2.0 Features. In the following, those TPM 2.0 features and command relevant for the proposed solution are briefly introduced.

- **TPM Sealed Objects** The TPM 2.0 can seal data. The purpose of sealing is to encrypt data with the TPM and to ensure that only this TPM can unseal the data again. In order to unseal the data, an authentication secret can be provided or a policy session that follows the scheme for Enhanced Authorization can be used. The commands used for working with sealed objects are TPM2_Create, TPM2_Import, and TPM2_Unseal.

- **TPM2_Create** This command is used to create all kinds of objects for the TPM. This includes sealed object as well as keys usable as import targets. During creation, a usage policy can be provided that restricts usage of the created object.
- **TPM2_Import** In addition to the local creation of objects inside the TPM, the TPM2_Import command further allows the external creation and importing of all kinds of objects, including keys and sealed objects. The creation of such an import blob is denoted as *create_Import*.
- **TPM2_Unseal** In order to retrieve the content of an encrypted, sealed object, the TPM2_Unseal command can be used. If the object was created or imported with a certain usage policy, this policy needs to be fulfilled for usage. This is done using so-called policy sessions.
- **TPM2_EvictControl** Since the TPM only has limited persistent internal memory, objects are usually stored externally, encrypted with a TPM-resident key. Any object can be made persistent inside the TPM on request by the owner. The TPM2_EvictControl command is used to store an object persistently in the TPM or to delete an object from persistent storage.
- **TPM NV Storage** A TPM comes with an internal non-volatile memory. This memory can be used to make keys of the TPM persistent but can also be allocated by applications. Classes of NV-Indices are Extendable NV-Indices, NV-Counters, and BitMasks. The latter can be used to individually set bits of an NV index's or to test bits within Enhanced Authorization policies.
- **TPM2_NV_DefineSpace** The TPM2_NV_DefineSpace command is used to define an NV index. Depending on the assigned index number, the NV index is either part of the user-owned (storage hierarchy) or of the platform-/OEM-owned (platform hierarchy) areas of the TPM. For the sake of this paper, only OEM-owned indices are used.
- **TPM2_NV_Read/TPM2_NV_Write** The TPM2_NV_Read/TPM2_NV_Write command is used to read/write data to a TPM NV index.
- **Enhanced Authorization** With Enhanced Authorization, any object that requires authorization can either be authorized using a secret value assigned during creation (similar to TPM 1.2) or using a policy scheme. Enhanced Authorization consists of a set of policy elements that are each represented via a TPM command. Currently, eighteen different policy elements exist that can be concatenated to achieve a logical *and* in arbitrary order and unlimited number. Two of these policy elements – PolicyOr and PolicyAuthorize – act as logical *or*. Due to implementation requirements, policy statements are, however, neither commutative nor distributive. Once defined they need to be used in the exact same order. In this paper, we use the following notation: $Policy_{abc} := PolicyX_1() \wedge PolicyX_2() \wedge \ldots PolicyX_n()$ where $Policy_{abc}$ is the "name" for this policy, such that it can be referred to from other places and $PolicyX_i()$ describes the n concatenated TPM2 Policy commands that are required to fulfill this policy.
- **TPM2_StartAuthSession** In order to fulfill any authorization policy, the application needs to start a policy session using the TPM2_StartAuthSession

command. Then the actual policy statements are subsequently satisfied by invoking the corresponding TPM commands.

- **TPM2_PolicyNV** The PolicyNV element provides the possibility to include NV-indices in the evaluation of a policy. Amongst other operations, it can be used to test whether a certain bit is set or clear within the value of a specified NV-index: $Policy_{abc} := PolicyNV(NVindex, operation, value)$. For the operation of testing where the third bit $0x0004$ is set in the NV index NV_{abc} the following statement can be used: $Policy_{abc} := PolicyNV(NV_{abc}, BITSET, 0x0004)$. This policy will only succeed, if the equation $value \& 0x0004 == 0x0004$ evaluates to true.
- **TPM2_PolicyNVWritten** This policy statement evaluates to true, if a given NV index has not been written to before.
- **sim_PolicyXYZ** In order to precalculate so-called policy digests – the representation of a policy used during creation – certain calculations need to be performed. To refer to these calculations, the notion of sim_PolicyXYZ is used, e.g. sim_PolicyNV.

4   Concept

Our concept for implementing *Secure Runtime Firmware Product Lines* consists of three parts: (1) configuration of the device during production, (2) creation of the firmware image, and (3) booting a model-specific firmware.

4.1   Device Production

During device production, two steps need to be taken. A key must be deployed to the device, that is used for importing the sealed key blobs, and the model type number must be stored inside the device's TPM. The following TPM commands are used to realize this:

```
// Set model number
TPM2_NV_DefineSpace(modelIdx, policyWritten, UserRead PolicyWrite)
// Create policy session
sess = TPM2_StartAuthSession(PolicySession)
TPM2_PolicyNVWritten(modelIdx, false, sess)
TPM2_NV_Write(modelIdx, modelNo, sess)
// Deploy (import) ImportTargetKey
ImportKeyBlob := TPM2_Import(ImportTargetKey)
tmpHandle := TPM2_Load(ImportKeyBlob)
TPM2_EvictControl(tmpHandle, ImportKeyHandle)
```

Model Number. The model number is stored inside the NV-storage of the TPM and can be read by anybody but cannot be altered. The number will subsequently be used to test whether a certain software feature shall be decrypted and activated at boot time for the given device. It is even possible to store the model number as part of the serial number, since the TPM-operations also allow the testing of only parts of a number stored in NV memory.

The purpose of the TPM2_PolicyNVWritten is to disallow subsequent writes by anybody to the model number NV index. Only as long as the NV index has not been written, can it be written. This also enables partial pre-production of products, where for example the board is assembled and fit into a chassis and the TPM is partially pre-provisioned but the model number is not yet set.

ImportTargetKey. The anchor for the decryption operations during boot is the ImportTargetKey. This key needs to be deployed to all devices of a product line. It is stored persistently inside the TPM for the lifetime of the device. This key is imported into the TPM and stored persistently using the TPM2_EvictControl command. When booting a firmware, the keys used for each of the features are imported underneath this key before being unsealed for actual usage during firmware decryption and activation.

4.2   Firmware Creation

Two additional steps are required for building a firmware image: the product line elements must be created by means of an overlay filesystem and the filesystems must be encrypted with a sealed TPM key bound to the corresponding model number bit. The process involving the TPM can be realized as follows:

```
firmware = createBaseImage()
for fs=overlay_1 to overlay_N do
    tmpfs = createFeatureLayer()
    fs.bitmask = createFeatureBitmask()
    key = TPM2_GenRandom()
    fs.data = encrypt(key, tmpfs)
    policyDigest = sim_PolicyNV(modelIdx, fs.bitmask, BITSET)
    fs.seal = create_Import(importTargetKey, featureKey, policyDigest)
    firmware.add(fs)
end for
release(firmware)
```

Filesystem Creation. The firmware for Secure Runtime Firmware Product Lines needs to be constructed in a specific way. For this example, we assume to have a base firmware image that is common to all models of the given product line. Note though that even different base images can be provisioned, this requires more space in the resulting firmware image. For the sake of explanation, we consider the construction of a firmware image for two models ModelA and ModelB with two mutually exclusive features FeatureA and FeatureB.

A base image is constructed as file image on the build PC. For a Linux system, this would include things such as libc, base-tools, init-system, etc. Next, a second (empty) image file is created and mounted as overlay to the base image. Then the software for FeatureA is installed into the overlay filesystem. This step can also include the rewriting or even the deletion of files. Some overlay filesystems represent deletion as entries to the 0-inode for example. When unmounting the filesystem, the differences from base image to ModelA are stored inside the

FeatureA filesystem. Now, a second file image can be created for FeatureB and the process of overlay mounting and installation can be repeated.

The approach can be further generalized by, e.g., mounting the images for base, FeatureA, and FeatureC versus base, FeatureB, and FeatureC if models differ for example in some intermediate layer, but not in the highest layer.

Filesystem Encryption. For each of the feature filesystem layers, a bitmask is created regarding which bits inside the model number represent the activation of the corresponding feature. For example, any model number with bit 0 set (i.e., uneven numbers) will include the filesystem for FeatureA. With this information, a corresponding TPM2_PolicyNV statement can be constructed that represents the test for this bit inside the model number NV index. It can also test for multiple bits or even the complete model number. This depends on the architecture for assignment of features to model numbers. The result of the policy statement creation is a policyDigest, i.e., a hash value that represents this policy.

Then a symmetric key is created that is used for encrypting the feature filesystem image. This key is then embedded within an import blob for the target TPM. This import blob is of type keyedHash, which means that it can be unsealed on the target TPM. It includes the key for the filesystem and also the policyDigest that restricts the unsealing of the key to those devices that have a model number corresponding to the policy's requirements. Finally, this import blob is encrypted using the ImportTargetKey as decryption key.

The bitmask, the encrypted key seal blob for TPM import, and the encrypted filesystem are then provided with the firmware image as a package *FeatureFS-X Data BLOB*. Note that the order of mounting the overlay images plays an important role, especially if file alterations or removals exist. This can be represented by naming of the files that contain the feature packages (if they are stored as files inside the firmware image) or by the order in which they are stored, if e.g., a partition table is used, where each package is contained inside its own partition.

4.3 Booting a Model-Specific Firmware

During firmware boot, the specific firmware for the given model of the product line is unlocked and mounted. This process uses the following algorithm:

```
current = mount(basefs)
modelNo = TPM2_NV_Read(modelIdx)
for fs=overlay_1 to overlay_N do
    if fs.bitmask == modelNo & fs.bitmask then
        seal = TPM2_Import(importKeyHandle, fs.seal)
        pSess = TPM2_StartAuthSession(PolicySession)
        TPM2_PolicyNV(modelIdx, fs.bitmask, BITSET, pSess)
        key = TPM2_Unseal(seal, pSess)
        overlay = decrypt(key, fs.data)
        current = overmount(current, overlay)
    end if
end for
```

current = overmount(current, localdatafs, localdata-directory)
current = overmount(current, tmpfs, runtime-directory)
chroot_and_boot(current)

Basic Preparations. During boot, the first step is to perform some basic operations. During this step, the basefs image is mounted and the model number is read from the TPM. This reading of the model number is not restricted in any way and can be performed by any running software. Only writing is restricted to the vendors production step.

Feature Loop. The loader will loop over all features that are provided within the unified firmware image and test for each of these, whether they are activated for the given model number. Those that are not active will be skipped. For all activated features, the loader will import the sealed feature key into the TPM under the ImportTargetKey. Then it will provide a policy session that proofs to the TPM that the policy for this sealed feature key is fulfilled by the model number stored inside the TPM. Then it will request the unsealing of the feature key from the TPM, based on the policy session that proofs the correctness of this attempt. With the unsealed feature key, the loader can decrypt the feature filesystem and mount it on top over the currently mounted system – either over the basefs or over the stack of basefs and previously mounted feature overlays.

Local Configuration and Runtime Data. Before switching into the final stack of overlay filesystems, the loader mounts two final filesystems. The runtime overlay is a temporary filesystem held only in RAM for the current boot cycle. This is necessary for the firmware in order to create sockets for local IPC connections, storing process identifiers, or to create temporary files for locking to schedule access to certain resources. The configuration overlay is an additional filesystem that contains local configuration data of the device. The reason for performing an overlay mount for this filesystem instead of a regular mount is that the feature filesystems can provide default configurations within their images. Thus, only changed configuration files are actually stored on local storage.

5   Discussion

5.1   Security

To upgrade his device to a higher-level model, an user/attacker can try the following attacks.

Attacking the TPM. The attacker can try to read out the feature keys of the TPM. The secrecy of the feature keys depends directly on the secrecy of the ImportTargetKey stored inside the TPM. An extraction of this key is unlikely if a hardware TPM certified by Common Criteria (usually using EAL4+) targeting the TCG's defined Protection Profile for TPMs is used. To further mitigate the impact of a successful key extraction from the TPM, the vendor could also rotate the import key with every production batch. This will, however, require the vendor to provide import-blobs of the sealed feature keys for all of these rotated import keys. In order to compensate for the latter, the vendor can instead choose to deploy an additional intermediate key together with the firmware blobs. In this approach, every production batch would have its own import target key. Each firmware version would then include a specific intermediate import key that is prepared for importing under all import target keys. The sealed feature keys would then be encrypted for import under the intermediate keys. Given a realization with n import target keys, i.e., production batches, and m sealed feature keys, this would mean that each firmware blob includes one (unique) intermediate key that is packaged n times for the different import target keys and m sealed feature keys that are encrypted for the intermediate import key. This is a significant simplification compared to the $n \cdot m$ sealed feature key that would be required without an intermediate import key.

Attacking the Unsealed Feature Keys. To decrypt and mount a feature filesystem, the required feature key is decrypted by the TPM and transferred to the host CPU. An attacker could sniff on the transmission. This threat can be mitigated either by physically securing the bus between TPM and main CPU or by using the TPM protocols built-in encryption capabilities. For this, the boot-code of the device could include the public portion of the import key and use this to encrypt a salt value during session establishment. Attacks against the host CPU are not addressed by the presented approach. This includes attacks against the OS kernel or even cold boot attacks. To address the latter, mechanisms such as full memory encryption could be applied [19].

Attacking a Feature-Rich Model. An attacker could attack a feature-rich model and try to extract an unencrypted firmware image and inject it into a low-feature device. This attack would require access to the raw RAM during runtime via a software exploit. To cope with potentially unknown vulnerabilities, appropriate mechanisms for secure code update should be applied [16].

Manipulation of the Model Number. An attacker could try to change the model number to a number of a device with more features. The integrity of the model number depends on the inability of the user to write to the model number NV index. This needs to be ensured by disallowing TPM2_UndefineSpace and TPM2_UndefineSpaceSpecial with Platform-Authorization, which is supposed to be under vendor-control anyways. In order to mitigate attack potential even further, the vendor can set TPM2_NV_WriteLock on model number explicitly on each boot.

5.2   Extensions

Refurbishment of Devices. In many environments with device product lines, there exists the necessity to refurbish devices that are e.g. produced but never delivered. This can occur due to canceling of orders or because a certain hardware feature is defect that is required for a certain version of the device. In such scenarios, the vendor will refurbish the device to a new model by exchanging the chassis or a model number sticker on the chassis and reconfigure the firmware on the device to the new device type.

In order to support this process with the presented scheme, the policy for the model number NV index on the device can be set to a policy that allows the vendor (and only the vendor) to perform write operations on this index. Such a case can be achieve using a TPM2_PolicySigned. This policy requires an external entity to sign a challenge from the TPM in order to perform a certain operation.

Model Number Attestation. Many devices nowadays are provided with the inclusion of additional services, such as cloud integration. This may, however, be a premium feature that is only activated for premium devices. The presented scheme of storing the model number inside the TPM supports such scenarios using the TPM2_NV_Certify command. Using this command, the vendor's cloud service can send a challenge to the device and the TPM will certify that the device has a given model number.

Model Numbering Schemes. The presented approach uses a very simplistic scheme for activation of feature filesystem for a given model number by querying whether certain bits in the model number are set. In addition, it is possible to extend these schemes further using a combination of AND and OR in the policy statements. For example, it is possible to require a (set of) bits to be zero using the TPM2_PolicyNV with the operation TPM_EO_BITCLEAR. These policies can then be extended using the TPM2_PolicyOR to enable a certain feature filesystem for other bit combinations as well.

6   Implementation

We implemented our concept on an Intel NUC D34010WYK equipped with a TPM 2.0 implementation running Ubuntu 16.04 with kernel version 4.4. An Apache and a Samba server were used as PLE (PLE) examples. For accessing the TPM, a TSS implementation of the TPM 2.0 System API was used together with accompanying bash tools for rapid prototyping [4].

In the device production phase, the storage root key (SRK) of the TPM is generated, and the model number is written to the NV-Storage. The firmware creation need to construct the overlay filesystems. For this purpose, we used the AUFS [21]. For every product line, an encrypted SquashFS filesystem [5] is created for overlay mounting. This filesystem is encrypted using dm-crypt [1] container files. Dm-crypt is a Linux module used for transparent disk encryption. The AES encryption keys of the encrypted SquashFS filesystem is encrypted with a private asymmetric key. The created TPM object is protected by a policy testing the flag corresponding to the PLEin the TPM's NV model number.

For booting a model-specific firmware, the mounting of these filesystems is integrated into the boot process by using initramfs which make necessary preparations before switching to the systemd init process. A shell script for the creation of the overly filesystem is added to the bottom stage of initramfs. Scripts in this stage are executed before procfs and sysfs are moved to the real rootfs and execution is turned over to the init binary of the rootfs. The command 'mount -t aufs -o br=/r/tmps=rw:/r/02_apache:/r/ none /r/chr/' mounts the overlay filesystem with a temporary top filesystem /r/tmps, the mounted Apache Squash filesystem /r/02_apache, and the Ubuntu base system root directory /r to the mount point /r/chr. This overlay is finally mounted over the root filesystem /r/tmps and the init process is started to boot the system. Since the top filesystem of the current overlay system is a temporary filesystem, all file changes of the running system will be temporary. In this example, only the Apache SquashFS is mounted because the flag for enabling the Samba container was not set. Only the key for the encrypted Apache SquashFS file system could be unsealed because the corresponding flag was set. The booted system then produces the same state as during the firmware creation after the installation of the apache packages. This also includes correct configurations, since no overrides are provided via a local configuration overlay.

A first performance analysis showed only a negligible delay in the boot process introduced by using or concept for runtime firmware product lines.

7   Conclusion and Future Work

In this paper, we propose an approach for secure runtime firmware product lines. Unified firmware images can be provisioned to a whole series of products while preventing unauthorized activation of features that belong to a different model instance. Using the features of TPM 2.0 Enhanced Authorization, Sealing, and Importing we show that this scheme can be implemented by using CotS hardware. We also present an implementation, to show the feasibility of this approach and its integration with a Linux-based system. Future work includes the extension of the presented approach to include unified images for hardware product lines, similar to the OpenEmbedded's Board Support Packages and the tight integration with the build process of unified firmware images as well as a thorough performance evaluation using different embedded platforms.

Acknowledgment. The work presented in this paper has been partly funded by the German Federal Ministry of Education and Research (BMBF) under the project "SURF".

References

1. dm-crypt: Linux kernel device-mapper crypto target. https://gitlab.com/cryptsetup/cryptsetup/wikis/DMCrypt
2. Docker. http://www.docker.com/what-docker
3. Overlay for Unified Write Filter (UWF). https://msdn.microsoft.com/en-us/library/windows/hardware/mt571992(v=vs.85).aspx
4. Software Platform for TPM 2.0. https://www.sit.fraunhofer.de/en/tpm/
5. SQUASHFS. http://squashfs.sourceforge.net/
6. Unionfs: A Stackable Unification File System. http://unionfs.filesystems.org/
7. OpenEmbedded (2016). http://www.openembedded.org/wiki/Main_Page

8. Apel, S., Batory, D., Kästner, C., Saake, G.: Feature-Oriented Software Product Lines. Springer, Heidelberg (2013)
9. Atkinson, C., Bayer, J., Muthig, D.: Component-based product line development: the kobra approach. In: Donohoe, P. (ed.) Software Product Lines: Experience and Research Directions, vol. 576, pp. 289–309. Springer, Heidelberg (2000)
10. Bodden, E., Tolêdo, T., Ribeiro, M., Brabrand, C., Borba, P., Mezini, M.: SPL LIFT: statically analyzing software product lines in minutes instead of years. ACM SIGPLAN Not. **48**, 355–364 (2013)
11. Carnegie Mellon Software Engineering Institute Web Site: Software Product Lines (2016). http://www.sei.cmu.edu/productlines/
12. Clements, P., Northrop, L.: Software Product Lines. Addison-Wesley, Boston (2002)
13. Challener, D., Arthur, W.: A Practical Guide to TPM 2.0: Using the Trusted Platform Module in the New Age of Security. Apress, New York (2015)
14. Flanagan, E.: The Yocto project. In: The Architecture of Open Source Applications, vol. 2, pp. 347–358 (2012)
15. Fountian, T.: Secure feature activation (Aug 25 2003), US Patent Ap. 10/526,252
16. Fuchs, A., Krauß, C., Repp, J.: Advanced remote firmware upgrades using TPM 2.0. In: Hoepman, J.-H., Katzenbeisser, S. (eds.) SEC 2016. IAICT, vol. 471, pp. 276–289. Springer, Cham (2016). doi:10.1007/978-3-319-33630-5_19
17. GNU: Autoconf (2016). http://www.gnu.org/software/autoconf/
18. Gomaa, H.: Designing software product lines with UML. In: SEW Tutorial Notes, pp. 160–216 (2005)
19. Henson, M., Taylor, S.: Memory encryption: a survey of existing techniques. ACM Comput. Surv. **46**(4), 1–53 (2014)
20. Ishii, A., Parthasarathy, N.: SIM-based automatic feature activation for mobile phones (Apr 23 2004), US Patent Ap. 10/830,755
21. Okajima, J.R.: Advanced multi layered unification Filesystem AUFS. http://aufs.sourceforge.net/
22. Lauer, M.: Building embedded linux distributions with bitbake and openembedded. In: Free and Open Source Software Developers' European Meeting (2005)
23. Brown, N.: Overlay filesystem. https://www.kernel.org/doc/Documentation/filesystems/overlayfs.txt
24. Schramm, K., Wolf, M.: Secure feature activation. SAE Int. J. Passenger Cars Electron. Electr. Syst. **2**(2009–01-0262), 62–67 (2009)
25. Trusted Computing Group: Trusted Platform Module Library Specification, Family 2.0, Level 00, Revision 01.16 edn., October 2014
26. Trusted Computing Group: TSS Feature API Specification, Family 2.0, Level 00, Revision 00.12 edn., November 2014
27. Trusted Computing Group: Algorithm Registry, revision 01.22 edn. (2015)
28. Trusted Computing Group: TSS System Level API and TPM Command Transmission Interface Specification, Family 2.0, Revision 01.00 edn., January 2015
29. Van Gurp, J., Bosch, J., Svahnberg, M.: On the notion of variability in software product lines. In: Conference on Software Architecture, pp. 45–54. IEEE (2001)

User Authentication and Policies

On the Use of Emojis in Mobile Authentication

Lydia Kraus[1]([⊠]), Robert Schmidt[1], Marcel Walch[2]([⊠]), Florian Schaub[3],
and Sebastian Möller[1]

[1] Quality and Usability Lab, Technische Universität Berlin, Berlin, Germany
`lydia.kraus@qu.tu-berlin.de, mail@robschmidt.de,`
`sebastian.moeller@tu-berlin.de`
[2] Institute of Media Informatics, Ulm University, Ulm, Germany
`marcel.walch@uni-ulm.de`
[3] School of Information, University of Michigan, Ann Arbor, USA
`fschaub@umich.edu`

Abstract. Mobile authentication methods protect smartphones from
unauthorized access, but also require users to remember and frequently
enter PINs, passwords, or graphical patterns. We propose the EmojiAuth
scheme with which we study the effects of Emoji use on the usability and user experience of mobile authentication. We conducted two
between-subjects studies (lab study: $n = 53$; field study: $n = 41$) comparing EmojiAuth to standard PIN entry. We find that EmojiAuth provides
good memorability for short passwords and reasonable memorability for
longer passwords. Moreover, we identify diverse Emoji-password selection
strategies and provide insights on the practical security of Emoji-based
mobile authentication. Our results suggest that Emoji-based authentication constitutes a practical alternative to traditional PIN authentication.

Keywords: Mobile authentication · Security · Usability · User experience · Emoji

1 Introduction

Usability of mobile authentication is an active research topic [1–3], given
that users spend a considerable amount of time unlocking their phones [2].
Knowledge-based authentication mechanisms, such as PIN and unlock pattern
(on Android), have been widely deployed for smartphone locking; alphanumer-
ical passwords are also a common option. While PINs, especially 4-digit PINs,
are susceptible to user choice [4] and shoulder surfing [5], they balance short
log-in time and good memorability with sufficient protection against casual
attackers [5]. Biometric authentication, such as fingerprint and face recognition
emerged recently as alternatives, but still rely on knowledge-based authentication as a fallback [6]. Therefore, knowledge-based authentication remains relevant for smartphones and is unlikely to be replaced soon. However, if users
need to spend mental effort and time to protect their smartphone, the required
interactions should be as pleasant and positive as possible.

S. De Capitani di Vimercati and F. Martinelli (Eds.): SEC 2017, IFIP AICT 502, pp. 265–280, 2017.
DOI: 10.1007/978-3-319-58469-0_18

Designing positive interactions has gained considerable attention in user experience research. Concepts such as hedonic (product) qualities, joy of use, and stimulation evolved as important aspects of user experience design [7]. We argue that considering positive interaction aspects is also relevant in the design of usable security mechanisms. An interesting direction for positive interaction in mobile authentication is the use of Emojis as password characters. Emojis are largely used in positive contexts [8] and are popular among users. Thus, providing potential for offering positive user experiences. Emoji-based passwords have recently been introduced by a commercial application [9].

In this paper, we study opportunities of Emojis for creating a positive mobile authentication experience. We further study how Emoji-based authentication influences password selection and shoulder surfing. To gather insights, we developed an Emoji-based authentication scheme (EmojiAuth) and evaluated it in a lab study ($n = 53$) and a field study ($n = 41$), including a shoulder-surfing experiment ($n = 38$). Our contributions include (1) the identification of five main Emoji-password selection strategies; (2) a comparative evaluation of PIN- and Emoji-based passwords regarding their susceptibility to shoulder surfing, indicating a slight improvement with Emojis; and (3) an analysis of the user experience of Emoji-based passwords. While Emoji and PIN show similarly high usability, users indicated that they would prefer Emoji over PIN as a screen lock.

2   Related Work

Mobile authentication has received considerable research attention [1–3,10]. A multi-national survey showed that 50.4% (Italy) to 76.4% (UK) of users use a screen lock on their phone [10]. Authentication schemes can be divided into knowledge-based, token-based, and biometric schemes [11]. The Emoji-based password scheme belongs to the class of graphical authentication schemes which is a subclass of knowledge-based authentication. In the following we detail related work on these two areas.

PINs and passwords are commonly deployed knowledge-based authentication schemes. While PINs can be entered quickly and accurately [3,5], they lack entropy. With a 4-digit PIN the password space is constrained to about 14 bit. Users tend to weaken PINs by choosing easy-to-remember numbers, e.g., birth dates [4]. Random passwords are more secure but harder to remember [12]. PINs generated under a security policy are more secure, but also harder to remember than freely-chosen PINs [13].

Graphical authentication schemes are motivated by the fact that graphics are easier to remember than alphanumeric passwords [14]. As for PINs and passwords, major issues of graphical passwords arise from the susceptibility to capture and guessing attacks [14]. For instance, image-based cued-recall schemes are prone to hotspots [14], i.e., image regions users are likely to select, which can be used in guessing attacks. Graphical passwords can also take longer to enter. A study with Android pattern unlock found that participants needed twice as long to enter a pattern and made more mistakes compared to a PIN [3]. Yet, users tend to rate pattern usability and likability similar to PIN, likely due to easy error recovery [3]. However, to be practical, a login attempt should not take longer than for a PIN or a pattern lock mechanism [2]. Patterns have a smaller theoretical password space as PINs and their security is considered low in general [15].

Icon-based graphical authentication schemes are a promising approach enabling fast log-in times [5], while potentially providing a theoretical password space similar to PIN or larger. The Story scheme [16] is somewhat similar to our proposed Emoji-based scheme as users create a password from a 3x3 set of photo icons from different categories (objects, food, people). An interesting finding is that Story did not result in a skewed password probability distribution [16]. Emoji-based authentication has been recently suggested [9]. Shortly after our lab study was conducted, Golla et al. conducted an online study to investigate the susceptibility of Emoji-based passwords to guessing attacks [17]. Their Emoji-based authentication scheme features a keyboard with 20 Emojis. With their scheme, they found that the distribution of Emoji-passwords is skewed, but 4-digit user-chosen Emoji-passwords were still more resistant to guessing attacks than 4-digit user-chosen PINs.

User experience and authentication should be considered together. To create a positive user experience, psychological needs, such as stimulation and popularity, should be addressed in the interaction design of mobile authentication mechanisms [18]. Also, while mobile and graphical authentication schemes have been investigated intensively in terms of usability and security, user experience evaluations beyond usability, have received little attention [19].

While Emojis have been used in authentication, we are the first to study usability and user experience of an Emoji-based scheme in the lab and in the wild, as well as its resistance to shoulder-surfing attacks.

3 EmojiAuth: Emoji-Based Authentication Scheme

The use of Emojis may lead to a positive and pleasing user experience and positive perception of EmojiAuth: Emojis have been shown to enable the expression of moods, emotions and nuances in written text [20]. Thus, Emojis may also make authentication more (personally) meaningful for users. Emojis further have positive associations which may lead to authentication being perceived positively as well. The most frequently used Emojis are rated significantly more positive than the remaining Emojis [8].

Similar to PIN entry, our EmojiAuth scheme features twelve buttons (cf. Fig. 1(a)). We further designed a PIN lock as a baseline comparison (cf. Fig. 1(b)). In both schemes, if users enter their password correctly, the entry field turns green and the screen unlocks automatically. If the password is incorrect, the phone vibrates and a respective message appears above the entry field. The use of a keyboard with twelve Emoji buttons is grounded in the advantages of PIN keyboards: PIN entry is easy and fast [3]. Simple keyboards have further been linked to authentication usability [21].

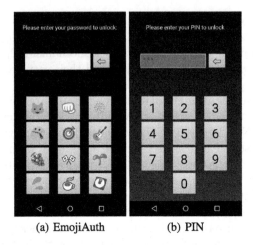

(a) EmojiAuth   (b) PIN

Fig. 1. EmojiAuth and PIN user interfaces. The original UIs were in German. Emojis are depicted in the Noto Emoji Font by Google Inc. https://github.com/googlei18n/noto-emoji.

In EmojiAuth's keyboard generation, three Emojis are randomly selected from each of four categories (Person and Face: 226 Emojis, Object: 287 Emojis, Nature: 204 Emojis, and Activity: 44 Emojis) to support easy assembly of passwords. Once a user-specific keyboard has been initialized, the Emojis and their position remain static to reduce search time and thus enable shorter login times [5, 22].

The theoretical password space of EmojiAuth is more than two times larger than the password space of PINs for 4-digit passwords (EmojiAuth: 20,736; PIN: 10,000), and almost three times larger than PIN for 6-digit passwords (EmojiAuth: 2,985,984; PIN: 1,000,000). However, that users favor certain Emojis is evident from rankings of currently popular Emojis [23] and has been also shown as an issue in related work on Emoji-based authentication [17]. To mitigate the issue of hotspot Emojis, EmojiAuth generates an individual keyboard for each user during password enrollment. Keyboards generated from a large set of Emojis may increase the practical password space as specific Emojis have low probability to appear on individual keyboards, thus decreasing the probability that certain Emojis are favored across the whole user population.

We conducted a lab study and a field study, both between subjects, to evaluate EmojiAuth (treatment) in comparison to PIN entry (control). In the lab study, we evaluated memorability, selection strategies, and user experience of Emoji-passwords. In the field study, we validated our findings in the wild. We further conducted a shoulder-surfing experiment at the end of the field study.

4   Lab Study

4.1   Methodology and Procedure

In the lab study, the Emoji and PIN conditions were further divided into two subgroups to investigate effects of varying password length (4 and 6 digits). Groups are subsequently referred to as Emoji-4, Emoji-6, PIN-4 and PIN-6. The lab study was conducted in two sessions. The first session started with participants signing the consent form and completing an entry questionnaire on demographics and smartphone use. They were informed that passwords they create in the study will be stored in plain text to enable scientific analysis, but will not be linked to their identity. Participants were then assigned round-robin to an Emoji or PIN group. Participants who currently used a PIN (or fingerprint and PIN combination) on their smartphone were assigned to the Emoji group, in order to reduce the impact of prior habituation to PIN entry.

After a training task with randomly generated passwords, participants were asked to choose their own password and instructed that they will have to remember it. After creating their password, they had to enter it three times with a mental rotation task (MRT) between attempts. The MRTs served to distract participants and clear their short-term memory between login attempts [5, 24]. Participants then completed a usability and user experience questionnaire (AttrakDiff 2 mini [25]) and a five-minute semi-structured interview, in which they were asked to describe how they selected their password and their level of confidence in remembering their password. AttrakDiff 2 mini measures different aspects of user experience [25, 26]: pragmatic quality (PQ), hedonic quality (HQ), and attractiveness (ATT). Each dimension is measured on a semantic differential with 7 rating levels between differentials. Pragmatic quality is related to usability, i.e., functional aspects of a product [27]. Hedonic Quality (HQ) relates to the capability of a product to address aspects of *personal relevance* [27, p. 38]. The hedonic quality scale is further divided into the sub-dimensions *Stimulation* and *Identity* [26]. Stimulation refers to a products' capability to provide stimulating experiences (e.g. in terms of providing *new impressions, opportunities, insights*), whereas identity refers to a products' capability to communicate identity [27, p. 35]. Attractiveness is related to the overall judgment of a product [26].

One week after the first session, participants returned to the lab for the second session. Participants had to enter the password they created in the first session and completed the same usability and UX questionnaire. They were also asked in a short interview how they memorized their password and whether they had written it down. All participants conducted the study on the same smartphone (LG Nexus 5, Android 5.1.1). The interviews were recorded and transcribed verbatim for further analysis. Participants received 4€ compensation for the first study session, and 8€ for the second one in order to incentivize participants to return and thus reduce drop-outs. Participants were recruited through a participant panel of TU Berlin, classified ads posted on an online service similar to Craigslist, flyers, and e-mail.

4.2 Results

In total, 53 smartphone users participated in the lab study: 14 in the Emoji-4 group, 13 in each of the other three groups. Participants were 18 to 70 years old ($M = 31$, $Mdn. = 27$); 28 were male, 25 female. The average time between sessions was 7 days ($SD = 1.2$ days; range 3–12 days due to scheduling). Over half the participants were students (58.5%), despite not targeting campus populations. Other participants were employees (15.1%), self-employed (7.5%), retired (5.7%), and others (13.2%). Most (75.5%) did not have a professional or educational IT background. In the sample were 69.8% Android users, 22.6% iOS users, and 7.6% other smartphone users. Most participants (69.8%) reported to use authentication on their phone; most common were PIN (28.3%), unlock pattern (22.6%), and fingerprint with PIN as fallback (11.3%).

Password Memorability. The lab study results indicate high memorability of both EmojiAuth passwords and PINs. After one week all participants (EmojiAuth and PIN) were able to successfully authenticate within three attempts. Long Emoji-passwords seem to be slightly harder to remember after a week of non-use, as a lower number of participants managed to enter their password correctly for all three trials in week 2 (Emoji-4: 92.9% in both weeks; Emoji-6: 100% in week 1 and 69.2% in week 2; PIN-4: 100% in both weeks; PIN-6: 100% in week 1 and 92.3% in week 2). A Fisher's exact test did not reveal statistically significant differences between groups. Only four PIN participants reported writing down their passwords after the first session.

Password Selection. Interviews on password selection strategies were first coded openly by one coder, who created separate code books for Emoji and PIN with some overlapping codes. Two coders then independently re-coded all interviews with the code books. Multiple codes could be assigned. Interrater agreement was high for both groups (Emoji: Cohen's $\kappa = .83$; PIN: $\kappa = .72$). Coders subsequently reconciled the remaining cases. Participants in the PIN group relied on predictable password selection strategies, e.g., birth dates as PIN [4]. The selection strategies of the Emoji participants overlapped only partially with the PIN strategies. Emoji participants often selected passwords based on a preference for certain Emojis and remembered them by creating stories, memorizing spatial patterns or repeating characters. We identified five main password selection strategies each for Emoji passwords and PINs (frequencies are provided in Table 1):

- **Emoji preference (Emoji):** Emojis are selected based on personal preference, e.g., "Well I clicked those Emojis I was interested in" (P33).
- **Association & story (Emoji):** Participants leverage an association between Emojis and their own knowledge or experience, and/or a password is selected or memorized by creating a story connecting the Emojis, e.g., "[I selected the password] after a song. [...] each Emoji stands for one word and depending on the song which words came first, I typed [the Emojis] in." (P22); "I just thought about the weekend [laughing]" (P3).

- **Pattern & position (Emoji):** A spatial pattern is used to create or remember the password and/or the position on the keyboard is used to remember certain Emojis, e.g., "And then I went from the upper left down to the bottom right" (P16).
- **Repetition & similarity (Emoji):** Either single characters or character sequences are repeated to create a password and/or a password is assembled from Emojis which are (subjectively) similar to each other, e.g., "[I chose the password so] that the pictures look similar" (P39).
- **Color & Shape (Emoji):** A Password is selected based on color or shape of Emojis, e.g., "Well... first I chose four symbols with the same color." (P16); "I chose [the Emojis] according to circular shape" (P18).
- **Date (PIN):** A date of personal importance (birthday, anniversary, etc.) is used to create a PIN.
- **Repetition & sequence (PIN):** Single numbers or number sequences are repeated to create a PIN and/or a PIN is created with consecutive numbers.
- **Re-use (PIN):** A PIN is selected by re-using a current or former PIN.
- **Pattern & position (PIN):** A spatial pattern is used to create or remember the PIN and/or the keyboard position is used to remember certain numbers.
- **Association (PIN):** An association between numbers and the user's knowledge or experience is used to select the password (e.g., choosing a name that contains a number or a phone number as PIN).

The PIN selection strategies are consistent with findings in related work. For instance, dates as PINs or parts of passwords are commonly observed [4,28] and were also the most frequent selection strategy in our study. We further observed spatial patterns as PIN selection strategies, which are known user strategies to improve memorability [4,28]. The re-use of passwords is another well-known issue [28] that also surfaced in our study. Participants reported that they used former or current PINs.

The emergence of the Emoji-password selection strategy "Preference" suggests that passwords generated with EmojiAuth may also follow a skewed password distribution. We analyzed the set of Emoji-passwords created in both our studies to further explore this issue (cf. Sect. 5.3).

User Experience. Pragmatic Quality (PQ) for Emoji was medium-high in week 1 ($M = 4.5$, $SD = 1.4$), but lower compared to PIN ($M = 5.9$, $SD = 0.77$). A Kruskal-Wallis test revealed a significant difference between the groups, $H(3) = 16.25$, $p = .001$, with PQ for Emoji-4 and Emoji-6 being significantly lower than for PIN-4. In week 2, PQ increased for Emoji ($M = 5.5$, $SD = 1.2$) and approximated the ratings for PIN ($M = 5.9$, $SD = 0.71$). The Kruskal-Wallis test did not reveal significant differences in PQ between groups in week 2. Hedonic Quality in terms of Stimulation was medium-high for Emoji (week 1: $M = 4.8$; $SD = 1.36$; week 2: $M = 4.9$; $SD = 1.38$) and medium-low for PIN (week 1: $M = 3.8$; $SD = 1.19$; week 2: $M = 4.0$; $SD = 1.13$). Differences were significant in both weeks (Mann-Whitney U; week 1: $U = 185$; $p = .003$; week 2: U, $U = 209$; $p = .018$). This suggests that Emoji users found the authentication more stimulating in both weeks compared to PIN.

5 Field Study

5.1 Methodology and Procedure

The field study consisted of a pre-study questionnaire, an introductory session, a field phase of 15–17 days, and an exit session. In order to ensure meaningful use of the authentication methods during the study, we deployed EmojiAuth and PIN as a protection mechanism for the participants' email app on their own phone. E-mails have been shown to often contain sensitive information [1] worth protecting. Consequentially, we recruited only Android users who use an email app on their device and verified this in a screening survey. Participants were recruited through a participant panel of TU Berlin and classified ads posted on an online service similar to Craigslist. Participants from the first study could not participate. Participants received 25€ compensation of which 5€ were paid at the introductory session and 20€ at the end.

During the introductory session participants received information about the study and were asked for consent. Then, either EmojiAuth or PIN was installed as a lock for their email app on their own devices. We used Android accessibility services to monitor whether the e-mail app is currently in the foreground. In order to activate this service, the participants had to select one or more e-mail apps which they currently use from the list of installed apps. After they created an Emoji-password or PIN (depending on the group), opening their email app required participants to authenticate with their password/PIN. Our apps had a 30 second time-out for an authentication session, i.e., if participants left their e-mail app for 30 s or more, they had to re-authenticate. Participants were asked to pick their password/PIN at home. It had to be at least 4 digits. For the PIN group, only meta-data of the user-chosen PINs was collected (PIN length and number of differing characters).

Directly after creating the password, participants received a questionnaire asking about the importance of different password/PIN selection criteria, which were derived from the lab study results. Participants could change their password or PIN during the study (within our app) and EmojiAuth users could further generate a new Emoji-keyboard. In case that they had forgotten their password or PIN, users could enter a pre-defined backup-password in our app and select a new password/PIN. If the password/PIN was entered five times incorrectly in a row, users also had to provide their backup-password to unlock their e-mail app and to select a new password.

The field phase lasted 15–17 days, depending on when participants scheduled their exit session. Similar to Wechsung et al.'s study [29], participants received a daily reminder to complete a daily feedback questionnaire, which asked participants to rate on a Smiley-scale how they liked interacting with EmojiAuth or PIN that day. Participants could further explain their rating in a free-text field. On days 2, 8, and 14, participants further received the AttrakDiff2 mini-questionnaire to assess user experience.

After the field phase, participants returned to the lab for the exit session in which they completed an exit survey (on paper) followed by the shoulder-surfing experiment. Furthermore, EmojiAuth/PIN was uninstalled from their devices.

5.2 Shoulder-Surfing Experiment

The field study's exit session contained a shoulder surfing experiment, modeled after similar experiments in related work [5,30], in which the threat model is a casual observer. Participants acted as shoulder surfers for either EmojiAuth or PIN (based on their field study condition), whereas the experimenter served as the observation target. In contrast to related work, our shoulder surfers were experienced with the authentication scheme they tried to observe after two weeks of use. Participants could position themselves either left, right or behind the experimenter who sat at a table to enter the password. Participants were provided with pen and paper for note taking. To ensure that passwords are entered with similar speed and in the same position, the experimenter trained password entry beforehand.

To test shoulder surfing susceptibility for passwords created with different password selection strategies, the procedure was repeated with five passwords in counterbalanced order. Emoji- and PIN-passwords used the same spatial position of keys on the keyboard in order to facilitate direct comparison between the two schemes. The first and second passwords were random 6-digit ('341779') and 4-digit passwords ('1706'). The third ('134679') and fourth passwords ('5802') were patterns lab study participants had created. The fifth password was an association based on the Christmas Eve date ('2412') for the PIN users and a Christmas-related story created by a lab study participant for the Emoji users ('bear - Christmas tree - snowman - heart' or '23#4' on a numerical keyboard). After a password was entered by the experimenter, the participant had three trials to enter the observed password on a LG Nexus 5 smartphone (Android 5.1.1).

5.3 Results

In total, 41 smartphone users participated in the field study: 21 in the Emoji group, 20 in the PIN group. Three PIN users had to be excluded (2 due to issues with participants' phones; one due to out of scope/inappropriate responses in almost all daily feedback questions). Thus, the PIN group decreased to 17.

Participants were 19–63 years old ($M = 34$, $Mdn. = 28$, $SD = 12.1$); 24 were female (59%). Most were students (22), although we did not target students. The second largest group were employees (8), followed by job seekers (5), self-employed (2), and others (4). Most (80.5%) did not have a professional IT background. 19 participants currently used a PIN, 3 a password, 9 an Android pattern, and 11 did not use any locking method.

Success Rates. In both groups, few incorrect unlocks were recorded during the field study (Emoji: 3% of total unlocks; PIN: 1.5%). In total, 3,514 correct and 83 incorrect unlocks were recorded. EmojiAuth accounted for 1,924 correct ($M = 91.6$, $SD = 66.1$) and 58 incorrect unlocks ($M = 2.8$, $SD = 4.2$); PIN accounted for 1,590 correct ($M = 93.5$, $SD = 70.4$) and 25 incorrect unlocks ($M = 1.5$, $SD = 1.6$). Fisher's exact tests did not reveal significant differences in the number of correct and incorrect unlocks between the groups.

Success rates for PIN were high, suggesting that PIN performs well in the wild. This confirms related work that found PIN to be a practical authentication method with low error rates [3]. Emoji success rates were also high, suggesting that EmojiAuth is a practical authentication method, too.

Password Length and Changes. The majority of participants in the Emoji group (19) initially picked a 4-digit password, whereas 2 participants picked a 5-digit password. Participants in the PIN group initially picked diverse PIN lengths: 10 picked a 4-digit PIN, 2 picked a 5-digit PIN, 3 picked a 6-digit PIN, and 2 an 8-digit PIN. A Mann-Whitney U test did not indicate significant differences in the mean password length between groups (Emoji: $M = 4.1$, $SD = 3$; PIN: $M = 4.9$, $SD = 1.4$).

Four Emoji participants changed their password once, 3 changed their password twice. In the PIN group, 4 participants also changed their PIN once, 1 changed their PIN twice. A Mann-Whitney U test did not indicate significant differences in the mean number of password changes between groups (Emoji: $M = .48$, $SD = .75$; PIN: $M = .35$, $SD = .61$).

Password Selection. The same password selection strategies identified in the lab study also surfaced in the field study (cf. Table 1). Figure 2 provides examples of Emoji-passwords created by study participants in the lab and in the field study.

Fig. 2. EmojiAuth passwords created by lab and field study participants. Passwords are grouped according to password selection strategies.

Based on the results of the lab study, we asked questions (available online at: http://bit.ly/2imyb2H) about Emoji and PIN password selection in the field. For EmojiAuth, the questionnaire contained 17 5-point items (1 = 'does not apply at all'; 5 = 'completely applies'), with 2–4 items to measure each selection strategy. For PIN, the questionnaire contained 15 items, with 1–6 items per selection strategy. Lab study frequencies for Table 1 were calculated by counting the occurrences of each interview code. Field study frequencies were calculated as the number of participants who rated at least half of the items of a scale (selection strategy) as important or very important.

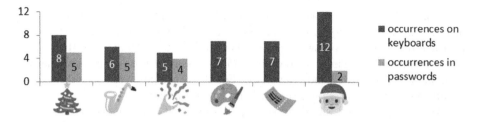

Fig. 3. Password-Emojis examples of the most popular (*left*) and unpopular (*right*) password-Emojis together with their occurrences on the keyboards.

The overlaps between selection strategies in both studies suggest reasonable validity of the identified strategies. The PIN selection strategies in both studies align with findings in related work [4]. For Emoji-password selection, *Preference*, *Pattern & Position*, and *Association & Story* played an important role in both studies.

The importance of the *Preference* selection strategy for Emoji passwords is also visible from the distribution of selected Emojis across passwords. Figure 3 depicts three examples of the most popular and three examples of the most unpopular Emojis together with their occurrences on the keyboards (lab and field study). Due to the different sizes of the category lists from which Emojis were selected in EmojiAuth, some Emojis appear more often on the keyboard than others. Although we expected the individual keyboards to decrease the probability of hotspots, Fig. 3 suggests that the distribution of password-Emojis is skewed.

Shoulder Surfing. We calculated the minimal Levenshtein distance for each user ("attacker") and each password, i.e., the number of deletions, insertions, or substitutions, needed to obtain the correct password from the entered

Table 1. Frequencies of password selection strategies. Note that some participants used multiple strategies.

Strategy	Emoji		PIN	
	Lab ($n=27$)	Field ($n=20$)	Lab ($n=26$)	Field ($n=17$)
Color and Shape	2 (7%)	9 (43%)	-	-
Icon Preference	10 (37%)	12 (60%)	-	-
Repetition	9 (33%)	4 (20%)	7 (27%)	7 (42%)
Pattern and Position	12 (44%)	8 (40%)	5 (19%)	3 (18%)
Association and Story	10 (37%)	8 (40%)	5 (19%)	12 (71%)
Password re-use	1 (4%)	-	7 (27%)	4 (24%)
Date	-	-	13 (50%)	8 (47%)

password [21,31]. There was a significant difference in the minimal Levenshtein distance between Emoji ($M = 2.45$, $SD = 1.64$) and PIN ($M = .72$, $SD = .83$) for the 6-digit random password (Mann-Whitney-U, $U = 289.0$; $p = .001$; $r = .53$) with medium effect. Thus, the 6-digit random password was significantly harder to shoulder surf on the Emoji keyboard. For the other passwords, there were no significant difference between the authentication methods.

We also compared shoulder surfing susceptibility of passwords from the same scheme. For Emoji, a Friedman's test revealed significant differences in the minimal Levenshtein distance between passwords ($\chi^2 = 40.44$; $p < .001$). Post-hoc analysis with Bonferroni correction revealed that the 6-digit random password was significantly harder to shoulder surf than the 4-digit random password ($M = .75$, $SD = .93$; $Z = 1.45$, $p = .037$, $r = .46$), the 6-digit pattern ($M = .15$, $SD = .67$; $Z = 2.75$, $p < .001$, $r = 0.72$), and the 4-digit pattern ($M = .15$, $SD = .37$; $Z = 2.2$; $p < .001$, $r = .70$). All post-hoc results for Emoji had medium to large effect sizes. For PIN, a Friedman's test revealed significant differences between passwords ($\chi^2 = 10.78$; $p < .029$), but post-hoc tests were not significant.

The post-experiment questionnaires revealed four different strategies attackers used to observe the password: paying attention to the numbers on the keyboard ("numbers"), the password's spatial pattern ("pattern"), a mix of both strategies ("mix"), or they reported observing password entry with high concentration ("observation"). The frequencies of strategies significantly differed between Emoji and PIN ($p = .026$; Fisher's exact). "Attackers" in the Emoji group were more likely to use the pattern observation strategy (Emoji: 16; PIN: 8). Not surprisingly, "attackers" in the PIN group were more likely to use the numbers observation strategy (Emoji: 0; PIN: 4).

In summary, the 6-digit random password was harder to shoulder surf with the Emoji keyboard compared to PIN and was also harder to shoulder surf with the Emoji keyboard compared to the 4-digit random password and the 4- and 6-digit pattern passwords on the Emoji keyboard. The casual "attackers" in the Emoji group largely relied on the pattern observation strategy which may make Emoji passwords that are based on spatial patterns more susceptible to shoulder surfing attacks.

User Experience. The daily feedback questionnaires answered during the field study indicate that the user experience of EmojiAuth and PIN was perceived similarly well. This is supported by the AttrakDiff 2 mini ratings, with the difference that EmojiAuth users perceived the authentication method more stimulating at the beginning of the study. In total, participants reported 342 (Emoji: 184) positive experiences, 99 neutral experiences (Emoji: 51), and 14 negative experiences (Emoji: 10). A Mann-Whitney U test did not reveal significant differences between distribution of positive, neutral, and negative experiences between groups.

To further analyze users' experiences, the free-text answers of the daily feedback were open-coded by one coder. This led to a code list of 17 codes. The qualitative data was then independently coded with the code list by another coder. Inter-rater agreement was high (Cohen's $\kappa = .83$). The coders jointly reconciled the remaining cases. A third of participants' comments (35%) expressed that everything was well (e.g., "everything's ok," "fine," "works"). The second most common comments (10%) concerned good usability of the methods (e.g., "really easy and not annoying", "fast [PIN] entry, no problems, I don't have concerns regarding memorability as long as the positions of the numbers don't change"). Six percent of comments indicated participants got familiar with the methods (e.g., "I've became accustomed to it," "it [the authentication] already belongs to my daily routine"). Thereby, Emoji participants reported this twice as much as PIN participants (14 vs. 7 comments). Four percent of codes concerned hedonic aspects. Hedonic aspects were mostly mentioned by Emoji users (11 out of 14, e.g., "I liked choosing the Emojis as I could select them on my own without restrictions," "it was fun to open the e-mail app with the Emojis while sitting next to my friends," "I changed my password twice today as I was curious which other Emojis are available"). A few comments (2.5%) also concerned perceived security vulnerabilities of the schemes ("when I open the app in quick succession, EmojiAuth didn't work properly" [participant was likely corollary not aware of 30 s time-out]; "it's relatively easy for others to find out the [Emoji] combination").

The AttrakDiff 2 mini ratings align with the daily feedback: Pragmatic quality was perceived as high ($M > 5$) for both methods at all measurement points (day 2, 8, and 14). Emoji users rated hedonic quality in terms of stimulation higher than PIN users on day 2 (Emoji: $M = 4.62$, $SD = 0.89$; PIN: $M = 3.22$, $SD = 0.60$; Mann-Whitney U, $U = 34$; $p < .001$; $r = .70$). However, this effect disappeared over time: there were no significant differences in stimulation between the groups for day 8 and 14.

Despite negligible quantitative differences in user experience, 17 of 20 Emoji users reported in the exit questionnaire that they would prefer using Emojis over PIN as a screen lock, mainly due to the high perceived memorability of Emoji-passwords (12 answers) and the appeal of the Emoji-based method (six answers).

6   Discussion and Conclusion

Limitations. Our study has a few potential limitations. Participants self-selected to participate in a study on mobile authentication, thus our participants may have higher technology affinity than the general population. As the sample size in both studies was limited, generalizations should be made with caution. However, our results facilitate a meaningful comparison of EmojiAuth to the current baseline: PIN entry. Furthermore, the consistency between lab and field study findings indicates a reasonable validity of our results.

Practical Emoji authentication. We have gained valuable insights into the practical aspects of Emoji-based mobile authentication. The results suggest that EmojiAuth may be a practical authentication method with a good password memorability of short passwords and a reasonable memorability of longer passwords.

Study participants created their Emoji-based passwords with five different strategies: *Emoji preference, association & story, pattern & position, repetition & similarity,* and *color & shape.* The results suggest that the distribution of Emoji passwords may be skewed, even with individual keyboards. We plan to conduct further studies to quantify the frequency of each selection strategy and its contribution to the practical password space. Results from the shoulder-surfing experiment suggest that EmojiAuth performs better for longer passwords that do not follow distinct spatial patterns. As the "attackers" in this experiment mostly focused on the *pattern* strategy, we recommend that spatial patterns should not be used for password creation. We also plan to conduct further studies to investigate whether password creation policies could help users create Emoji passwords that are resistant to guessing and capture attacks, as well as memorable. For example, such policies could blacklist most popular Emojis or spatial patterns.

The role of UX in mobile authentication. Both, EmojiAuth and PIN, were perceived as highly usable and as providing a good user experience in the lab and the field study. In the field study, EmojiAuth users mentioned hedonic aspects slightly more often in their daily feedback. However, for both methods, the overall number of experiences related to hedonic aspects was rather low. The Hedonic Quality/Stimulation ratings indicate that EmojiAuth users perceived their authentication method as more stimulating in the beginning of the field study compared to PIN users. The majority of EmojiAuth users (field) also indicated that they would prefer EmojiAuth over PIN as a screen lock, which is a promising result. We plan to conduct further studies to investigate how hedonic quality could be further increased and maintained in authentication methods and whether it contributes to long-term user "relationships" with the authentication method.

Acknowledgement. The authors thank Christopher Krügelstein and Felix Kaiser for their assistance to this research. This work was partially funded by the German Federal Ministry of Education and Research (BMBF) under the project Softwarecampus, grant no. 01IS12056.

References

1. Egelman, S., Jain, S., Portnoff, R.S., Liao, K., Consolvo, S., Wagner, D.: Are you ready to lock? In: Proceedings of CCS, pp. 750–761 (2014)
2. Harbach, M., von Zezschwitz, E., Fichtner, A., De Luca, A., Smith, M.: It's a hard lock life: a field study of smartphone (un)locking behavior and risk perception. In: Proceedings of SOUPS, pp. 213–230 (2014)
3. Von Zezschwitz, E., Dunphy, P., De Luca, A.: Patterns in the wild: a field study of the usability of pattern and pin-based authentication on mobile devices. In: Proceedings of MobileHCI, pp. 261–270 (2013)
4. Bonneau, J., Preibusch, S., Anderson, R.: A birthday present every eleven wallets? The security of customer-chosen banking pins. In: Keromytis, A.D. (ed.) FC 2012. LNCS, vol. 7397, pp. 25–40. Springer, Heidelberg (2012). doi:10.1007/978-3-642-32946-3_3

5. Schaub, F., Walch, M., Könings, B., Weber, M.: Exploring the design space of graphical passwords on smartphones. In: Proceedings of SOUPS, p. 11 (2013)
6. Bhagavatula, C., Ur, B., Iacovino, K., Kywe, S.M., Cranor, L.F., Savvides, M.: Biometric authentication on iPhone and Android: usability, perceptions, and influences on adoption. In: Proceedings of USEC (2015)
7. Bargas-Avila, J.A., Hornbæk, K.: Old wine in new bottles or novel challenges: a critical analysis of empirical studies of user experience. In: Proceedings of CHI, pp. 2689–2698 (2011)
8. Novak, P.K., Smailović, J., Sluban, B., Mozetič, I.: Sentiment of emojis. PloS one 10(12), e0144296 (2015)
9. Intelligent Environments: Now you can log into your bank using emoji. http://www.intelligentenvironments.com/info-centre/press-releases/now-you-can-log-into-your-bank-using-emoji-1. Accessed 2 Mar 2017
10. Harbach, M., De Luca, A., Malkin, N., Egelman, S.: Keep on lockin' in the free world: a multi-national comparison of smartphone locking. In: Proceedings of CHI, pp. 4823–4827 (2016)
11. O'Gorman, L.: Comparing passwords, tokens, and biometrics for user authentication. Proc. IEEE 91(12), 2021–2040 (2003)
12. Yan, J., et al.: Password memorability and security: empirical results. IEEE Secur. Priv. 2(5), 25–31 (2004)
13. Kim, H., Huh, J.H.: Pin selection policies: are they really effective? Comput. Secur. 31(4), 484–496 (2012)
14. Biddle, R., Chiasson, S., Van Oorschot, P.C.: Graphical passwords: learning from the first twelve years. ACM Comput. Surv. (CSUR) 44(4), 19 (2012)
15. Elenkov, N.: Android Security Internals: An In-Depth Guide to Android's Security Architecture. No Starch Press, San Francisco (2015)
16. Davis, D., Monrose, F., Reiter, M.K.: On user choice in graphical password schemes. In: USENIX Security Symposium, vol. 13, p. 11 (2004)
17. Golla, M., Detering, D., Dürmuth, M.: EmojiAuth: quantifying the security of emoji-based authentication. In: Proceedings of the Usable Security Mini Conference (USEC) (2017)
18. Kraus, L., Wechsung, I., Möller, S.: Exploring psychological need fulfillment for security and privacy actions on smartphones. In: Proceedings of EuroUSEC (2016)
19. Kraus, L., Antons, J.N., Kaiser, F., Möller, S.: User experience in authentication research: a survey. In: Proceedings of PQS, pp. 54–58 (2016)
20. Cocozza, P.: Crying with laughter: how we learned how to speak emoji. http://www.theguardian.com/technology/2015/nov/17/crying-with-laughter-how-we-learned-how-to-speak-emoji. Accessed 2 Mar 2017
21. Schaub, F., Deyhle, R., Weber, M.: Password entry usability and shoulder surfing susceptibility on different smartphone platforms. In: Proceedings of MUM, p. 13 (2012)
22. Stobert, E., Biddle, R.: Memory retrieval and graphical passwords. In: Proceedings of SOUPS, pp. 15:1–15:14 (2013)
23. Rothenberg, M.: Emojitracker: realtime emoji use on twitter. http://emojitracker.com/. Accessed 2 Mar 2017
24. Chiasson, S., Oorschot, P.C., Biddle, R.: Graphical password authentication using cued click points. In: Biskup, J., López, J. (eds.) ESORICS 2007. LNCS, vol. 4734, pp. 359–374. Springer, Heidelberg (2007). doi:10.1007/978-3-540-74835-9_24
25. Hassenzahl, M., Monk, A.: The inference of perceived usability from beauty. Hum. Comput. Interact. 25(3), 235–260 (2010)

26. Diefenbach, S., Hassenzahl, M.: Handbuch zur Fun-ni Toolbox (2011)
27. Hassenzahl, M.: The thing and i: understanding the relationship between user and product. In: Blythe, M.A., Overbeeke, K., Monk, A.F., Wright, P.C. (eds.) Funology: From Usability to Enjoyment. Human-Computer Interaction Series, vol. 3, pp. 31–42. Springer, Heidelberg (2003)
28. Fahl, S., Harbach, M., Acar, Y., Smith, M.: On the ecological validity of a password study. In: Proceedings of SOUPS, p. 13 (2013)
29. Wechsung, I., Jepsen, K., Burkhardt, F., Köhler, A., Schleicher, R.: View from a distance: comparing online and retrospective ux-evaluations. In: MobileHCI, pp. 113–118. ACM (2012)
30. Tari, F., Ozok, A., Holden, S.H.: A comparison of perceived and real shoulder-surfing risks between alphanumeric and graphical passwords. In: Proceedings of SOUPS, pp. 56–66 (2006)
31. Levenshtein, V.I.: Binary codes capable of correcting deletions, insertions and reversals. Soviet Phys. Doklady **10**, 707 (1966)

EmojiTCHA: Using Emotion Recognition to Tell Computers and Humans Apart

David Lorenzi[1], Jaideep Vaidya[1]($^{(\boxtimes)}$), Achyuta Aich[2], Shamik Sural[2], Vijayalakshmi Atluri[1], and Joseph Calca[3]

[1] MSIS Department, Rutgers University, Newark, NJ, USA
`jsvaidya@rbs.rutgers.edu`
[2] CSE Department, IIT Kharagpur, Kharagpur, WB, India
[3] Cloud Creative Group, Tempe, AZ, USA

Abstract. Any successful CAPTCHA design must creatively balance the three competing criteria of usability, scalability, and robustness to achieve widespread deployment in public facing web services. We propose a novel CAPTCHA called EmojiTCHA which utilizes symbolic representations of human emotions in the form of emojis correlated to an image of real humans expressing the same emotion on their face. By leveraging the Project Oxford Emotion API from Microsoft's cognitive services platform, which provides automated detection of human emotion expressions on human faces, we generate a tagged dataset in an automated fashion. Through the use of image warping and distortion techniques, we can significantly increase the robustness of the CAPTCHA against automated attacks, without compromising on usability, as confirmed by our user study.

Keywords: CAPTCHA · Emotion recognition · Online security · Usability

1 Introduction

The Completely Automated Public Turing test to tell Computers and Humans Apart (CAPTCHA) was invented by von Ahn et al. [2] to enable discrimination between humans and computers online. CAPTCHAs are reverse Turing tests administered by computers designed to keep bots from abusing web services and online forms made for human users. CAPTCHAs rely on hard AI problems to provide the challenge question asked to the user (human or bot). This ensures that the challenge question is one that is difficult for a computer to perform with a high degree of success, yet still remains easy for a human to perform quickly.

Designing effective CAPTCHA challenges has been an ongoing subject of research for more than a decade. Since the widespread introduction of the traditional text based CAPTCHA challenge where the user is asked to enter a string of characters to demonstrate they are human, CAPTCHAs have evolved significantly in style, design and complexity over time as they respond to advancements

© IFIP International Federation for Information Processing 2017
Published by Springer International Publishing AG 2017. All Rights Reserved
S. De Capitani di Vimercati and F. Martinelli (Eds.): SEC 2017, IFIP AICT 502, pp. 281–295, 2017.
DOI: 10.1007/978-3-319-58469-0_19

in attacks from image processing, computer vision and attacker creativity. The greatest challenge in designing a successful CAPTCHA that serves its intended purpose to distinguish between human users and bots is managing the tradeoffs between the competing requirements of usability, scalability and robustness with regard to design.

While text based CAPTCHAs have been the *de facto* style for CAPTCHA implementations on public websites that need protection from bot abuse, their usage is quickly falling out of favor as more advanced attacks and deep learning models have evolved that can solve the challenge at ever more accurate rates in an automated fashion. As image processing and computer vision algorithms become increasingly more adept at solving traditionally complex problems such as object and text recognition (and even attempts at scene recognition and identifying contextual information contained in an image) [21], the standard text based CAPTCHA has increasingly become obsolete.

Newer models for CAPTCHA that are replacing traditional text based challenges rely on strong image identification/object recognition tasks as their primary challenge method. One example of this is Google's new image based version of reCAPTCHA, which asks users to select all images that relate to a particular category (e.g., select all images that contain street signs) from a grid of nine images.

Behavior based models that focus on unique traits and actions of the target user such as websites visited, user agent of browser, geographic location of IP address, browser cookies, etc., to determine a probabilistic score as to whether or not the target user is legitimate are also gaining traction as a new way to distinguish between bot and human. Although these models are not like text/image based CAPTCHAs, they represent a new risk-calculation based approach to this problem. While these image based models are emerging as the preferred alternative to text based CAPTCHAs, they require extensive investments in back-end infrastructure and data gathering capabilities (typically at Google scale) to operate in a secure and effective manner. Thus, although the these traditional methods eventually will be broken (such as text vs. deep learning models), for the time being, image based CAPTCHAs can still withstand sophisticated attacks.

In this paper, we demonstrate our design and implementation for a new image based CAPTCHA – one that meets all the three criteria of usability, scalability and robustness. The CAPTCHA is constructed entirely from freely available online tools, open source software and emojis. The central challenge question revolves around the task of asking the user to match an emoji whose expressed emotion corresponds to the face contained in the image(s) displayed. Utilizing the Microsoft Cognitive Services Platform's Project Oxford Emotion API [1], human faces and the emotions they are expressing can be detected in an automated fashion from images. This information is subsequently stored and used for preparing a CAPTCHA challenge. However, to prevent the tool itself as well as other image lookup services from being used against the challenge, image warping, noise and distortions are introduced to the image, thus providing security.

2   Preliminaries

In this section, we cover the core components and tools used to construct the CAPTCHA challenge that allows for the design to be usable, scalable and robust – i.e., providing a reasonable level of security for the online form it is protecting.

2.1   Microsoft Project Oxford

Microsoft's Project Oxford is a collection of easy to use artificial intelligence based vision, speech and language APIs that are cloud accessible and can be used in applications by developers. In our CAPTCHA design, we utilize the Face API and the Emotion API. The Emotion API takes an image as an input, and returns the confidence score across a set of emotions for each face in the image, as well as the bounding box for the face, using the Face API. The emotions detected are anger, contempt, disgust, fear, happiness, neutral, sadness, and surprise. These emotions are understood to be cross-culturally and universally communicated with particular facial expressions.

Project Oxford's Emotion API is a REST API provided by Microsoft and can be interacted with online. This tool is what provides the critical functionality that delivers the scalability capabilities for our CAPTCHA design. It supports an automated method to accurately and consistently identify and tag emotions within images that contain people's faces. Indeed, we store the output of the Emotion API in a database along with the image and subsequently use it in a challenge served to a user, which asks the user to identify the emotions depicted in the image. The power of this service is that the algorithm can easily scale with demand on the CAPTCHA challenge service, e.g., instances can be run in parallel to produce the requested volume of tagged output as required by the challenge service, i.e., number of unique challenges that need to be served at a particular rate. In order to prevent the use of this and other similar tools against the CAPTCHA, noise is added to the original face image, thereby ensuring failure to identify emotion or faces on images used in challenges. The process of using and applying image noise is described in more detail in the Methodology Section. More details of the Emotion API can be found at https://www.projectoxford. ai/emotion.

2.2   Emoji Character Set

The emoji character set is a UNICODE character set designed to convey complex ideas and emotions in the form of small and simple ideograms and/or pictograms. The cross-cultural nature of emojis enhances the usability as it removes specific language and alphabets as a barrier to usability. Our challenge asks a user to match emotions of people in an image with an emoji that conveys the same emotion, providing a solid basis for a simple CAPTCHA challenge task that is easy for humans to understand. Furthermore, since this character set consists of images instead of text, techniques used to provide noise to the images will also work on the emoji characters, which can be scaled based on font size and noised to thwart attackers further, though we do not do so right now. Widespread availability of the emoji UNICODE character sets on smartphone and tablet operating systems ensures high portability on mobile devices that use touchscreens. A list of emoji characters is available at http://apps.timwhitlock. info/emoji/tables/unicode. In our particular implementation for experimentation, we have chosen to use the Twitter emoji set which is open sourced by Twitter for public use. Note that in the current implementation we do not use the UNICODE characters, we simply use the image, since this is easier and does not impact the CAPTCHA itself. UNICODE integration is deferred to future work.

3   Related Work

Text based CAPTCHA challenges have been under attack by various computer vision and image processing tools since their release via services hosted online. Segmentation attacks, pixel count attacks, filtration attacks and more have all proven effective against certain implementations. Bursztein et al. provide an overview of the strengths and weaknesses of text based CAPTCHA and demonstrate the need to continue to advance the field of CAPTCHA research [3]. As of 2016, text CAPTCHAs are not being used to a great extent due to deep learning models being able to decipher characters, even distorted and obfuscated ones, at an accuracy of close to 99.8% [10]. The security field is moving forward with new designs to supersede text based CAPTCHA. For example, Google has developed reCAPTCHA to use images from its image search library and streetview images gathered by its Maps program to provide challenges for the user to solve (categorization task and text entry tasks, respectively) [10].

While the concept of image CAPTCHAs has been known for a while, their designs have certain inherent properties that make them strong candidates for communicating complex ideas to humans in a quick and efficient manner. Most versions use some form of object/image recognition [11,15] or categorization task [6,7,16] as their primary challenge. The most common shortcoming of existing image based CAPTCHAs, however, is their inability to scale - due to the fact that the images used need to be manually collected, edited, tagged and indexed, be unique, etc. Also, attackers have had some degree of success beating them using image processing and computer vision tools [22] together with novel machine learning [9] techniques to solve the challenges. Three-Dimensional models [14,19] and spatial/depth perception [13,18] are gaining popularity in the image CAPTCHA space as strong use cases for challenges. This style represents an interesting avenue of research as they present challenges that are not singularly straightforward for a machine to solve, as the primary task asked of the user requires multiple subtasks, such as image manipulation by the user or using a mouse instead of a keyboard [4], that must be completed in conjunction to solve the challenge. The Puzzle Only Solvable by Humans (POSH) [5] is another approach to exploit human interaction for discrimination between humans and computers. A POSH can be generated by a computer, can be consistently answered by a human, and a human answer cannot be efficiently predicted by a computer. However, a POSH does not even have to be verifiable by a computer at all. Usability of CAPTCHAs is also a key issue [20] and new solutions are being devised to provide a fair trade-off between security and usability [8].

Although human face image based CAPTCHAs have been studied before [15,17], our work requires multiple subtasks, such as identifying the face in the image, determining their expression, and subsequently matching the appropriate emoji to the correct face. Our key contribution is to develop a scalable and usable image based CAPTCHA that is difficult for a machine to solve.

4 Methodology

In this section, we discuss the design choices that were made in order to ensure the usability, scalability, and robustness of the proposed CAPTCHA while demonstrating the security it provides from potential attacks.

Figure 1 provides an example of the Microsoft Emotion API output. Using a sample face that is smiling (a depiction of the emotion "happiness"), the API provides the coordinates for a faceRectangle, which is a bounding box based on the area in the image (in pixels) where the Face API detected a human face. It also gives a confidence score for each of the eight emotions that it can detect. For the example image shown in the figure, it is seen that the emotion "happiness" was identified with very high confidence. These two pieces of information provide the ability to generate a CAPTCHA challenge where the user is asked to answer what emotion the face in the presented image is expressing. Note that we could also ask the user to identify the face in the image, though this is correspondingly easy for automated attackers to do. In our implementation, a python script is used to interact with the API online and save the results it returns to a local SQL database, along with the image.

Figure 2 depicts an example of the test image served without noise or filters into Google's reverse image search. Note that the results of the search include the

Fig. 1. Example output from Emotion API

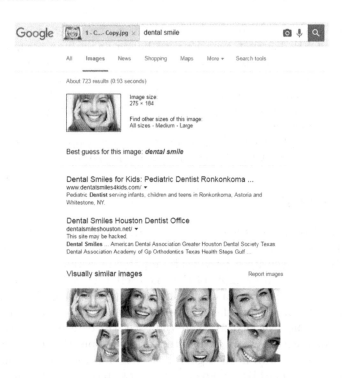

Fig. 2. Useful information can be produced from default image

image at other dimensions, a keyword guess for what is depicted in the image (e.g. "dental smile"), and a number of visually similar images that all depict "dental smiles", which if one were to ask a person what emotion was being expressed, most likely "happiness" would be the response. Without introducing noise, distortions and filters to the image, an attacker will be able to answer the challenge question without much difficulty. Another straightforward attack would have been to submit it to the same Emotion API application that was used to annotate the challenge image and get the answer.

Figure 3 depicts an example chain of filters applied in a specific order to achieve the goal of altering the image enough that reverse image search (RIS), Google image search service (ISS), and computer vision based attacks cannot determine what is depicted in the image. The key is to introduce the minimal amount of distortion such that the tools used to create the challenges are stopped from returning meaningful results. Note that each filter often has multiple parameters that can be adjusted along a range to introduce variability into their output and how they affect the image. For testing, we have determined a series of fixed values for the filters that provide the level of distortion we required to stop the Computer Vision (CV) attack while still maintaining a reasonable level of usability/ease of understanding of the image.

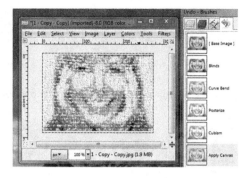

Fig. 3. Example of a series of filters applied to the image of Fig. 1

Figure 4 demonstrates how the appropriate level of distorts causes the ISS engines to return results that cannot be meaningfully used to attack the proposed CAPTCHA. Notice that the addition of the "canvas" filter effect influenced the ISS results towards needlepoint/grid based images - none of which focus on facial features. Also, no keyword is returned as well as no images of other sizes. For all intents and purposes, this distorted image is unique to the search engine, despite the original being indexed and tagged by it.

Fig. 4. No useful information can be extracted from noised image

Figure 5 is an example of the Twitter emoji set we used to map to the eight emotions provided by the Microsoft Emotion API. The initial build of our CAPTCHA included all these eight emotions. Microsoft noted that contempt and disgust were experimental emotions, and thus were usually not read

Fig. 5. Twitter Emojis used to represent the 8 emotions

Fig. 6. Reduced emotion version of EmojiTCHA challenge

as accurately as the other six emotions. After an initial round of user testing, we decided to reduce the number of emotions that could be selected to the five emotions depicted in Fig. 6 in an effort to remove confusion and increase usability.

5   CAPTCHA Challenge Generation

This section focuses on the process flow within the toolchain that is used to generate the CAPTCHA challenges. Figure 7 shows the step by step process used to generate a unique challenge. Specifically, the following process is undertaken:

1. Gather images involving one or more people whose faces are clearly visible expressing one of the following eight emotions: anger, contempt, disgust, fear, happiness, neutral, sadness, or surprise. These images can be gathered from anywhere, e.g., using image search engine, downloaded from a camera, etc. They do not need to be manually tagged as the Emotion API will provide that information.
2. Each image is run through the Microsoft Project Oxford Emotion API to detect the number of faces expressing emotions in the image and the facial expressions that fall into one of the eight emotional categories. If at least one clear face is not found or no emotion can be read from the face by the algorithm, the image is discarded. If at least one clear face expressing one of the eight emotions is found, the image is kept and stored in a database.
3. The output of the Emotion API is recorded in the database along with the stored image. The output from the algorithm includes the face bounding box # (which face in the image the emotion information is from), the emotion expressed by the face, and the level of confidence as a percentage for the emotion expressed by the face.
4. The image is next run through a series of filters and manipulations from GNU Image Manipulation Program (GIMP) [12] to distort the image for protecting it against reverse image search attacks and computer vision tool

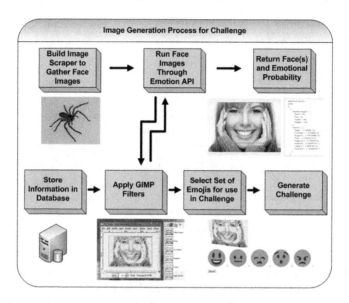

Fig. 7. Captcha generation process flow

based attacks. The number, type, and values for each of the filters used can be varied at random for each individual image produced to make it very difficult for attackers to filter the alterations. This step is important as it prevents using the tools that generate the challenge from being exploited by attackers. The output image is tested against the Emotion API to ensure that no emotion is meaningfully detected. The final altered image, now ready to be used as challenge, is stored in the database with the corresponding information used to create it. Figure 8 shows how filters used in a chain can successively distort an image until it meets the needed security criteria.

5. A set of emojis is selected such that one of them matches the emotion recorded from the Emotion API, and the remaining not matching the emotion, i.e., they would be incorrect/nonexistent responses.
6. The challenge is generated and the user is presented with one or more images of distorted faces and a corresponding set of emojis. The user simply needs to match the correct emoji with the facial expression in the image to complete the challenge. The correctness of the response is evaluated against the ground truth stored in the database.

6 EmojiTCHA Usability Study

The goal of this section is to evaluate the effectiveness and ease of use of EmojiTCHA. We conducted user trials with 30 participants and asked them to solve as many challenges as they could in 10 min. The first run included all eight emotions from the emotion engine. The user was served a challenge at random and

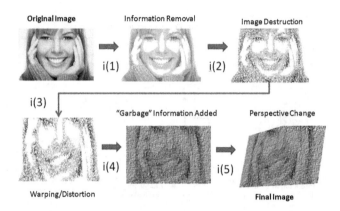

Fig. 8. Filter based distortion

asked to match the corresponding emoji to the emotion depicted on the face displayed. Each of the emotion categories had 10 images that were tagged and identified by the Emotion API. The image filters were applied at random until the image no longer returned a match from the Emotion API, thus some images were more distorted than others.

Emotional Guess Matrix

	Happiness	Neutral	Sadness	Disgust	Fear	Surprise	Contempt	Anger	
Happiness	125	1	1	0	0	0	11	0	138
Neutral	1	148	0	1	3	0	1	0	154
Sadness	2	16	83	15	16	0	3	2	137
Disgust	3	12	13	51	0	0	3	26	108
Fear	2	9	5	5	93	25	0	1	142
Surprise	9	0	0	0	7	117	0	1	134
Contempt	5	14	11	26	1	0	87	3	147
Anger	4	3	3	15	1	5	2	106	139
Totals	151	203	116	113	123	147	107	139	1099

Fig. 9. Confusion matrix for complete set of emotions

Figure 9 depicts the confusion matrix (i.e., the emotion guess results) for the first run with the complete set of eight emotions. The totals on the horizontal axis represent the number of times a challenge with the correct response being the emotion in green was served whereas the totals on the vertical axis represent the number of times that a particular emotion was given as a response for a challenge with the correct answer in green. Figure 10 gives the results for the second run with the reduced set of five emotions as options.

To make it easier to analyze the results we plot the precision and recall results for the different emotions in both runs. Figures 11a and b give the recall and precision for each emotion when all 8 emotions are used. The recall gives the percentage of images of each emotion correctly identified with that emotion whereas precision gives the percentage of images identified with a particular emotion that do actually have that emotion. The emotions from best performing to

Emotional Guess Matrix

	Happiness	Neutral	Sadness	Surprise	Anger	
Happiness	219	5	0	1	0	225
Neutral	0	209	12	0	1	222
Sadness	1	34	187	1	9	232
Surprise	10	0	2	201	1	214
Anger	3	3	3	1	205	215
Totals	233	251	204	204	216	1108

Fig. 10. Confusion matrix for reduced set of emotions

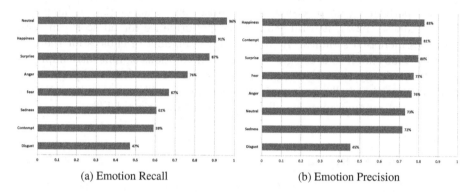

(a) Emotion Recall   (b) Emotion Precision

Fig. 11. Results with all 8 emotions

worse performing on recall are: neutral (96%), happiness (91%), surprise (87%), anger (76%), fear (67%), sadness (61%), contempt (59%) and disgust (47%). The emotions from best to worse performing on precision are: happiness (83%), contempt (81%), surprise (80%), fear (77%), anger (76%), neutral (73%), sadness (72%) and disgust(45%). Note that disgust was the worst performing emotion in both cases. It was expected that the more abstract of the universal emotions might be more difficult to discern for humans, namely, disgust and contempt. For recall, these emotions performed the worst, scoring significantly lower than the top three emotions. Interestingly, for precision, contempt was the second best emotion recognized, although the scores for the challenges were somewhat lower than the scores for recall, they were much more consistent across emotions, with disgust being the outlier. One aspect is the overlap of emotions that are consistently mistaken for another emotion that may appear similar. For example, we see that disgust was mistaken for anger 26 times. It is easy to imagine that a disgusted face can take a similar shape to an angry one. We also see this in contempt and anger being mistaken for disgust as well for 26 and 15 times respectively. More user testing will need to be conducted so that any set of emotions served to the user in a challenge will be ones that are not easily mistaken for each other. However, this can also provide a way to make it more difficult for machines – if a competing emotion detection algorithm is ranking a facial expression it is possible that it will score and categorize it differently than the Microsoft Emotion API.

Furthermore, most users were able to solve challenges in a very short duration. Additionally, after solving a few challenges, users are able to significantly increase their subsequent accuracy. To summarize, our study shows that EmojiTCHA in its current form is quite accessible to a wide range of users, with respondents coming from different continents. Figures 12a and b give the recall and precision when only 5 emotions are used in the challenges. The emotions from best performing to worse performing on recall are: happiness (97%), anger (95%), neutral (94%), surprise (94%), sadness (81%). The emotions from best to worse performing on precision are: surprise (99%), anger (95%), happiness (94%), sadness (92%), neutral (83%). The performance for all scores in both categories increased significantly in limiting the number of choices for the user to select. This shows that using a smaller set of emotions significantly improves usability of the system. Note that this does not significantly compromise on security since the challenge image still does not provide any results, and the probability of random guess is still 1/5 instead of the original 1/8.

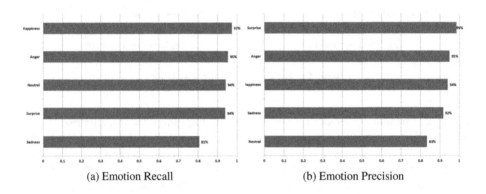

(a) Emotion Recall   (b) Emotion Precision

Fig. 12. Results when only 5 emotions are used

We have also experimented with an alternative design which improves usability, but provides equivalent security to the original version. For example, Fig. 13 shows an example where only two emotions are used, but users are asked 3 challenges instead of 1. This keeps the security of random guessing to $(1/2)^3 = 1/8$ giving us equivalent security to the original single challenge with 8 emotions, but potentially is significantly easier for humans to answer.

7   Design Limitations and Security Analysis

The images that were chosen for use in the challenges were hand curated to ensure that the desired emotion was demonstrated in the image. Work is currently in progress to tune the image scraper and the Emotion API checker to

Fig. 13. Example with 3 challenges using 2 emotions each

accept an "emotion" threshold score as a percentage to ensure that there is a high degree of confidence in any particular emotion expressed in a face. Any images that have emotions that register below the threshold can be discarded accordingly. Additional work must be done to determine the optimal "co-emotions" to display with one another to ensure there is minimal mixup by between the emotions displayed on the screen. These will all be addressed in future iterations of the study.

Furthermore, in our current implementation, we only use a single emotion from a single face per challenge. Multi-face, multi emotion challenges are currently under development. We are also currently developing ordinality rules for filter application to minimize the number of rounds of filter applications that are required to ensure the security guarantees that CV attacks and RIS attacks will not be successful. The test images used in the experiments for the user study only provide the security guarantee for emotion API attacks - they do not ensure RIS or ISS attacks are not successful, although many of the images do indeed stop these attacks in their current form.

Note that the security of the EmojiTCHA depends on two different factors. First, is the ability of the attacker to successfully de-obfuscate the image, and then use the Emotion API to solve the challenge. Second, is the ability of the attacker to randomly guess the correct response. Regarding the first, the image is obfuscated using lossy filters which result in information loss which cannot be reversed. This provides a layer of security. Furthermore, we ensure that the obfuscated image is robust against reverse image search attacks, which are based on image similarity. Note, that this process can be adjusted as required, if improvements are made in cracking techniques, or in filtering techniques. Regarding the ability to randomly choose the correct response, the current 8-emotion version has a fixed probability of $1/8$ for a correct random guess. However, as we have discussed above, reducing the number of emotions improves usability. At the same time, we can ask for a higher number of challenges. Similar to Fig. 13, if we ask three challenges, where the number of emotions is increased to three, then the probability reduces to $1/27$, which is significantly stronger. We have actually implemented this, and are currently carrying out comparative usability testing. Note that since a fresh CAPTCHA is provided on every refresh, the possibility of a brute force attack is limited as long as sufficient images are included in the CAPTCHA database. Furthermore, since the noise addition is randomly carried out, noise can be added to the same image multiple times, resulting in fresh challenges.

8   Conclusions and Future Work

In this paper, we have designed a new CAPTCHA that is based on emotion recognition that has the advantage of being scalable and usable while providing good security. In the future, additional work around new form types and challenge questions will be experimented with. For example, testing out multiple emotions in a single image and having a user identify all of the emotions – a multi-answer CAPTCHA. Another example would be asking the user to identify the opposite emotion of that depicted in an image (e.g. pick sad if the image is showing a happy face). Additional work around creating a challenge with an "emotional mix" where a random set of 4 or 5 choices are selected for the challenge from the 8 possible choices. Finally, experimenting with a "not here" answer may be worthwhile to increase the security against a random guess being correct. We plan to work on these extensions in the future.

References

1. Microsoft Cognitive Services Emotion API (2016). https://www.microsoft.com/cognitive-services/en-us/emotion-api
2. Ahn, L., Blum, M., Hopper, N.J., Langford, J.: CAPTCHA: using hard AI problems for security. In: Biham, E. (ed.) EUROCRYPT 2003. LNCS, vol. 2656, pp. 294–311. Springer, Heidelberg (2003). doi:10.1007/3-540-39200-9_18
3. Bursztein, E., Martin, M., Mitchell, J.: Text-based CAPTCHA strengths and weaknesses. In: Proceedings of the 18th ACM Conference on Computer and Communications Security (CCS 2011), pp. 125–138. ACM, New York (2011)
4. Chow, R., Golle, P., Jakobsson, M., Wang, L., Wang, X.: Making CAPTCHAs clickable. In: Proceedings of the 9th Workshop on Mobile Computing Systems and Applications (HotMobile 2008), pp. 91–94. ACM, New York (2008)
5. Daher, W., Canetti, R.: Posh: A generalized CAPTCHA with security applications. In: Proceedings of the 1st ACM Workshop on Workshop on AISec (AISec 2008), pp. 1–10. ACM, New York (2008)
6. Datta, R., Li, J., Wang, J.Z.: Imagination: a robust image-based CAPTCHA generation system. In: Proceedings of the 13th Annual ACM International Conference on Multimedia (MULTIMEDIA 2005), pp. 331–334. ACM, New York (2005)
7. Elson, J., Douceur, J.R., Howell, J., Saul, J.: Asirra: a CAPTCHA that exploits interest-aligned manual image categorization. In: Proceedings of the 14th ACM Conference on Computer and Communications Security (CCS 2007), pp. 366–374. ACM, New York (2007)

8. Fidas, C., Hussmann, H., Belk, M., Samaras, G.: ihip: Towards a user centric individual human interaction proof framework. In: Proceedings of the 33rd Annual ACM Conference Extended Abstracts on Human Factors in Computing Systems (CHI EA 2015), pp. 2235–2240. ACM, New York (2015)
9. Golle, P.: Machine learning attacks against the Asirra CAPTCHA. In: Proceedings of the 15th ACM Conference on Computer and Communications Security (CCS 2008), pp. 535–542. ACM, New York (2008)
10. Goodfellow, I.J., Bulatov, Y., Ibarz, J., Arnoud, S., Shet, V.: Multi-digit number recognition from street view imagery using deep convolutional neural networks. arXiv preprint arXiv:1312.6082 (2013)
11. Gossweiler, R., Kamvar, M., Baluja, S.: What's up CAPTCHA? A CAPTCHA based on image orientation. In: Proceedings of the 18th International Conference on World Wide Web (WWW 2009), pp. 841–850. ACM, New York (2009)
12. Lecarme, O., Delvare, K.: The Book of GIMP: A Complete Guide to Nearly Everything. No Starch Press, San Francisco (2013)
13. Nejati, H., Cheung, N.M., Sosa, R., Koh, D.C.I.: DeepCAPTCHA: an image CAPTCHA based on depth perception. In: Proceedings of the 5th ACM Multimedia Systems Conference (MMSys 2014), pp. 81–90. ACM, New York (2014)
14. Ross, S.A., Halderman, J.A., Finkelstein, A.: Sketcha: a CAPTCHA based on line drawings of 3D models. In: Proceedings of the 19th International Conference on World Wide Web (WWW 2010), pp. 821–830. ACM, New York (2010)
15. Rui, Y., Liu, Z.: Artifacial: automated reverse turing test using facial features. In: Proceedings of the Eleventh ACM International Conference on Multimedia (MULTIMEDIA 2003), pp. 295–298. ACM, New York (2003)
16. Shirali-Shahreza, S., Shirali-Shahreza, M.: Categorizing CAPTCHA. In: Proceedings of the 4th ACM Workshop on Security and Artificial Intelligence (AISec 2011), pp. 107–108. ACM, New York (2011)
17. Sim, T., Nejati, H., Chua, J.: Face recognition CAPTCHA made difficult. In: Proceedings of the 23rd International Conference on World Wide Web (WWW 2014), pp. 379–380. ACM, New York (2014)
18. Wei, T.E., Jeng, A.B., Lee, H.M.: Geocaptcha: A novel personalized CAPTCHA using geographic concept to defend against 3rd party human attack. In: 2012 IEEE 31st International on Performance Computing and Communications Conference (IPCCC), pp. 392–399, December 2012
19. Woo, S.S., Kim, B., Jun, W., Kim, J.: 3DOC: 3D object CAPTCHA. In: Proceedings of the 23rd International Conference on World Wide Web (WWW 2014), pp. 397–398. ACM, New York (2014)
20. Yan, J., El Ahmad, A.S.: Usability of CAPTCHAs or usability issues in CAPTCHA design. In: Proceedings of the 4th Symposium on Usable Privacy and Security (SOUPS 2008), pp. 44–52. ACM, New York (2008)
21. Ye, Q., Doermann, D.: Text detection and recognition in imagery: a survey. IEEE Trans. Pattern Anal. Mach. Intell. **37**(7), 1480–1500 (2015)
22. Zhu, B.B., Yan, J., Li, Q., Yang, C., Liu, J., Xu, N., Yi, M., Cai, K.: Attacks and design of image recognition CAPTCHAs. In: Proceedings of the 17th ACM Conference on Computer and Communications Security (CCS 2010), pp. 187–200. ACM, New York (2010)

Assisted Authoring, Analysis and Enforcement of Access Control Policies in the Cloud

Umberto Morelli[(✉)] and Silvio Ranise

Fondazione Bruno Kessler, via Sommarive 18, 38123 Trento, Italy
{umorelli,ranise}@fbk.eu

Abstract. The heterogeneity of cloud computing platforms hinders the proper exploitation of cloud technologies since it prevents interoperability, promotes vendor lock-in and makes it very difficult to exploit the well-engineered security mechanisms made available by cloud providers. In this paper, we introduce a technique to help developers to specify and enforce access control policies in cloud applications. The main idea is twofold. First, use a high-level specification language with a formal semantics that allows to answer access requests abstracting from an access control mechanism available in a particular cloud platform. Second, exploit an automated translation mechanism to compute (equivalent) policies that can be enforced in two of the most widely used cloud platforms: AWS and Openstack. We illustrate the technique on a running example and report our experience with a prototype implementation.

Keywords: Policy translation and validation · Attribute-based Access Control · Amazon AWS · OpenStack

1 Introduction

Cloud computing platforms offer companies the opportunity to create applications that have global reach and can scale rapidly to meet sudden spikes in demand without requiring massive investments by adopting a pay-as-you-go approach. The cost of this extra flexibility is a loss of control over the software components deployed in the cloud and the data manipulated by applications, since part of the responsibility and control is transferred from Cloud Customers (CCs) to Cloud Providers (CPs); consider, e.g., the "Amazon Web Service Shared Responsibility Model"[1]. When using a cloud platform, it is crucial for CCs to understand and distinguish between security measures implemented and operated by CPs (called, security *of* the cloud) and those offered by them (called, security *in* the cloud), for which the CPs are accountable. Failure to understand the boundaries of this separation of concerns and responsibilities may lead to leave sensitive assets unprotected with the potential of disclosing sensitive information, thereby incurring in extra costs and potential loss of business,

---

[1] https://aws.amazon.com/compliance/shared-responsibility-model.

© IFIP International Federation for Information Processing 2017
Published by Springer International Publishing AG 2017. All Rights Reserved
S. De Capitani di Vimercati and F. Martinelli (Eds.): SEC 2017, IFIP AICT 502, pp. 296–309, 2017.
DOI: 10.1007/978-3-319-58469-0_20

and eliminating many of the benefits of cloud computing. Even if the separation of responsibilities is clear, CCs may find it difficult to use effectively the large array of security mechanisms provided by the specific CP. This hinders one the most important opportunities offered by CPs to CCs, namely the exploitation of the cornucopia of well-engineered security mechanisms made available by CPs.

In order to alleviate this situation, we propose a technique capable of assisting CCs in designing and deploying access control systems in two of the most widely popular cloud platforms: AWS[2] and OpenStack[3]. Access Control (AC) is one of the most important security mechanisms for the protection of data and services against unauthorized disclosure (confidentiality) and intentional or accidental unauthorized changes (integrity), while ensuring their accessibility by authorized users whenever needed (availability). The development of an AC system requires the definition of the regulations according to which access is to be controlled and their implementation as functions executable by a computer system. This development process is usually carried out with a multi-phase approach based on the concepts of policy, model, and enforcement mechanism [4]. A policy defines the (high-level) rules according to which access control must be regulated. A model provides a formal representation of the AC policy and its working. The formalization allows the proof of properties on the security provided by the AC system being designed. An enforcement mechanism defines the low level functions that implement the controls imposed by the policy and formally stated in the model. In a cloud computing platform, several enforcement mechanisms are available, ranging from access control lists to those based on roles [4]. Many of these enforcement mechanisms are of a low level nature or are variant of the standards as they are tightly coupled with the resources and operations that services made available by the CP support. For application developers, it is not easy to grasp how all the different enforcement mechanisms work and how they can be used to mediate access to the data and services that the application under development is using. In many cases, even security experts may have difficulties in expressing high-level AC constraints related to an application (e.g., Separation of Duties) by means of the enforcement mechanisms available by CPs.

The main contribution of the paper is a technique that allows application developers and security experts to design the application and the AC policies by using an abstract model of a cloud platform without committing to a particular cloud solution. Since the language in which the AC policies are written has a formal semantics, it is possible to re-use automated tools for the security analysis of policies to understand whether the written policies correspond to the designer expectations. When this is the case, the tool automatically translates the high-level AC rule into concrete policies that can be enforced by the mechanisms available in AWS and Openstack.

Plan of the paper. Section 2 introduces a scenario that illustrates the main problems underlying the development of secure applications in the cloud. Section 3 describes our high-level policy specification language and its formal semantics

---

[2] https://aws.amazon.com.

[3] https://www.openstack.org.

by using a logical framework. Section 4 explains how the policies written in the high-level language can be translated to the policies that can be enforced by the AC mechanisms available in AWS and Openstack. Section 5 shows how a prototype implementation of our techniques (called SECUREPG) solves the problems arising in the running example of Sect. 2. Section 6 presents some concluding remarks and a short comparison with related work.

2   A Running Example

The ACME shipping company wants to develop a cloud application to support a customer loyalty program (SpecialDiscounts). The idea is to reward e-payments made via a mobile application (PromoApp) with virtual credits that can be spent for additional ACME services or discounts on selected products offered by ACME Partners. To this end, ACME wants to grant the partners of the loyalty program access to a restricted set of information through the application, while maintaining control over customers' data; thereby configuring two different domains in the data storage services available in the cloud.

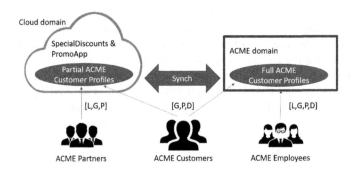

Fig. 1. Simplified architecture of the SpecialDiscounts and PromoApp cloud apps

Figure 1 shows the ACME and the cloud domains, together with three groups of users: ACME Customers, ACME Employees and ACME Partners. ACME Employees, using a system in the ACME domain, can list customers profiles (label L), extract the information they contain (label G), add new profiles (label P) or delete existing ones (label D); those operations are represented by the labelled solid arrow from ACME Employees to the ellipse named 'Full ACME Customer Profiles'. ACME Customers, by using PromoApp, can get, add or delete the information stored in the partial customer profiles (labels G, P and D linked to the arrow connecting ACME Customers to the ellipse named 'Partial ACME Customer Profiles'). The same operations are performed on their full profiles by using a system in the ACME domain. ACME Partners, using the SpecialDiscounts application, can list the partial ACME customer profiles (label L on the arrow connecting ACME Partners to the ellipse named 'Partial

ACME customer profiles') and can get or add information to the profile (labels G and P linked to the arrow connecting ACME Partners to the ellipse named 'Partial ACME Customer Profiles'). Since the full and partial ACME customer profiles can be updated independently (by using the cloud application or the system in the ACME domain), it should be possible to synchronize the information stored in both profiles (double arrow named 'Synch') so as to keep them up-to-date. The goal is to deploy the two applications, SpecialDiscounts and PromoApp, on a cloud computing platform while guaranteeing that the members of the various groups can perform only the actions discussed above. It may be also important to consider public or private cloud solutions, depending on the fact that sensitive information in the customer profiles must be stored also in the partial profiles managed by the cloud applications. For instance, it must be possible to deploy the applications on a public cloud—such as an Amazon AWS Platform-as-a-Service (PaaS) implementation, using the Simple Storage S3 service to manage customer profiles—or on a private cloud—such as an OpenStack Infrastructure-as-a-Service (IaaS) installation within ACME, that uses Swift as the data container. The main requirement is to do all this by supporting a cloud provider-agnostic specification of the access control policies that permit the automated verification of basic security properties (e.g., a member of a certain group can/cannot perform a certain action on a given resource) and their automatic instantiation to the access control mechanisms available in a particular cloud solution. In this way, it is possible to manage the heterogeneity of the multitude of IaaS and PaaS solutions currently available by increasing interoperability and avoiding vendor lock-in while exploiting to the full the well-engineered security mechanisms available in different cloud solutions. While there exist approaches in the literature that allow to manage cloud applications across different platforms (see, e.g., [6]), none of these address security issues (and in particular access control policies) as we do in this paper. For this reason, in the following, we discuss only the issues related to access control while we point the interested reader to, e.g., [6] for an approach abstracting away from the functionalities and storage capabilities of a particular cloud provider.

3 An Abstract Access Control Model for the Cloud

Since Attribute-Based Access Control (ABAC) [7] offers a powerful and unifying extension to several access control models in the literature (see [8] for a thorough discussion about the expressive power of ABAC with respect to other models), we have chosen it as the framework in which to develop our policy language and access control model for cloud applications. In ABAC, requesters are permitted or denied access to a resource based on the properties, called *attributes*, that may be associated to subjects, resources, and contextual information. Suitably defined attributes can represent identities, access control lists, or roles; in this sense, ABAC supplements rather than supplant traditional access control models [8]. Abstractly, policies in ABAC are conditions on the attribute values of the entities involved in an access decision. Our policy language for the cloud is based on the following construct:

Listing 1.1. Abstract policy specification construct

```
Grant|Deny SUBJECTS [ATTRIBUTES] the permission to ACTIONS on RESOURCES
    [ATTRIBUTES] if CONDITIONS;
```

where the parts in black are mandatory and those in gray are optional. Intuitively, the meaning is to grant or deny to a subject (described by an identifier plus, optionally, some simple conditions on its attributes) the permission to perform some action on a resource (also described by an identifier plus some simple conditions on its attributes) provided that all the complex authorization conditions on the attributes of subjects, resources, or the context are satisfied (the meaning of simple and complex conditions will be made precise below).

A subject, a resource, or an action are identified by a unique name. The attributes of a subject, a resource, or the context are also identified by a unique name and each one is associated to a type, such as the Booleans, the Integers, or an enumerated data type. Formally, a subject, a resource, or the context can be seen as records whose (typed) fields are the attributes; a type defines a set of values plus some functions and predicates (including at least the equality = operator) that can be applied to the values. A *simple condition* on a subject or on a resource can be expressed as a list (intended conjunctively) of equalities of the form $att = val$ where att is an attribute and val is one of its possible values. A *complex condition* is a Boolean combination of atomic expressions containing attributes of subjects, resources, or the context together with values and operators of the appropriate type (notice that we forbid quantifiers in complex conditions; this restriction in expressiveness was never a hindrance to specify policies in our experience). An example of a policy specification relevant to the example of Sect. 2 is provided below:

Listing 1.2. Example of an abstract rule that translates to a role policy

```
Grant ACME_employees the permission to add user to group and remove user
    from group on ACME_customers
```

This grants the ACME employees (identified by the role ID ACME_employees) the right to add and remove users from the group of ACME customers (ACME_customers). As another example, consider the following user policy:

```
Grant ACME_user_1 the permission to get object on ACME_user_1_profile if
    access time greater than 1451606400 and if access time less than
    1451779200
```

that grants the ACME user identified by the ID ACME_user_1 the permission to access his profile (ACME_user_1_profile), e.g. to check the number of virtual credits, provided that this is done in a given period of (Unix) time, namely from the first to the third of January 2016.

Following [1], it is possible to formalize the meaning of the policy constructs in Listing 1.1 by using first-order logic formulas. For this, we preliminary introduce the notion of query as a tuple (sl, a, rl, cl) where a is an action and sl, rl, cl are simple conditions involving the attributes and values of a subject, a resource, and the context, respectively. We write $\langle sl \rangle$, $\langle rl \rangle$, $\langle cl \rangle$ to denote the conjunction of equalities in the simple conditions sl, rl, and cl, respectively. A complex authorization condition in a policy construct can be considered as a first-order formula in which quantifiers does not occur. We assume the availability of the attributes sid and rid of subjects and resources, respectively, that range over their sets of identifiers.

Given a finite set Π of policy constructs of the form Listing 1.1 and a theory T formalizing the types of the attributes in P (it is well-known how to do this, we point the interested reader to [1] for details), we say that a query (sl, a, rl, cl) is granted (with respect to Π) iff there exists a policy construct

```
Grant s [sA] the permission to a on r [rA] if C
```

in Π such that the formula $sid = \mathsf{s} \wedge \langle \mathsf{sA} \rangle \wedge rid = \mathsf{r} \wedge \langle \mathsf{rA} \rangle \wedge \mathsf{C}$ in conjunction with $\langle sl \rangle \wedge \langle rl \rangle \wedge \langle cl \rangle$ is satisfiable in T (i.e. there exists a first-order structure which is a model of T and satisfies both formulae) and there is no policy construct

```
Deny s' [sA'] the permission to a on r' [rA'] if C'
```

in Π such that the formula $sid = \mathsf{s'} \wedge \langle \mathsf{sA'} \rangle \wedge rid = \mathsf{r'} \wedge \langle \mathsf{rA'} \rangle \wedge \mathsf{C'}$ in conjunction with $\langle sl \rangle \wedge \langle rl \rangle \wedge \langle cl \rangle$ is satisfiable in T. Otherwise, we say that the query is denied.

The decidability and NP-completeness of the satisfiability checks with respect to the theory T follow from results in [1] when the types of the attributes are Booleans, Integers or enumerated data types. We do not elaborate the details here for lack of space; we just observe that complex conditions with arbitrary Boolean structure makes the problem already NP-hard because the Boolean satisfiability problem is subsumed. Indeed, NP-completeness of the induced satisfiability problems implies that also answering queries is NP-complete. This should not be seen as a hindrance to the usability of our approach. SMT engines solving the generated satisfiability problems guarantees the practical viability of the technique at policy design-time with queries solved in few seconds. One reason for the good practical performances is the relative simplicity of the Boolean structure of complex conditions.

4   From Abstract to Enforceable Policies in the Cloud

Cloud providers are not able to fully support the complexity of the ABAC model and the granularity required for handling an arbitrary list of attributes: the ability to scale while maintaining data integrity and authorizations evaluation performance allows for simple AC policies based only on the identity of subjects (that request a cloud resource). Those uses a basic set of user attributes, i.e. his name, role or the group he belongs and, if supported, further restrict requester permissions with a set of environment conditions.

Table 1. Authorization patterns and cloud attributes that identify the entity types

Authorization patterns		AWS	OpenStack
Subject component	UserID [type = user_subject]	ID and ARN	ID and email
	GroupID [type = group]	ARN	ID
	RoleID [type = role]	ID and ARN	ID and email
	ServiceID [type = service]	URL	Missing
	FederatedID [type = federated]	URL or ARN	Missing
Resource component	ObjectID[type = object]	ARN	ID
	FolderID[type = folder]	ARN	ID
	ResourceID[type = keys]	ARN	Missing
	ResourceID[type = trust]	ARN	Missing

Using the model introduced in Sect. 3 it is possible to extend the identity-centric approach using generic conditions and providing attributes for the subjects and the resources. Table 1 shows the authorization patterns to explicitly suggest our prototype implementation the entity types (using their identifier and the type attribute) and the cloud attributes that uniquely identify them in Amazon and OpenStack: a subject identifier (ID), the URL or the Amazon Resource Name (ARN) code for the former and the ID or email of the subject for the latter. The current version supports three types of subjects (users, groups, roles) and two types of resources (objects and folders). Other components refer to the ability to authorize a service (handled as a role), support the identity federation features or create special policies (*type* keys or trust). If the end-user provides only the entity name, its type is retrieved querying a database; if the type is not supported (missing cases in the table) the information is instead ignored. Similarly, the attributes of subjects and resources, together with the environment conditions, are identified (using their name) and processed only if supported by the specific CP. This process, although not expanding the AC model of the supported CPs, greatly simplifies the task of writing AC policies. Moreover it allows the tool to create valid AC rules and easily supports the pure RBAC model of OpenStack and the RBAC-oriented implementation of AWS, with the possibility of future developments when more complex AC models will be made available by CPs.

4.1 Reconstruction of the Amazon and OpenStack AC Model

Figure 2 links the elements associated to the subjects in Amazon and OpenStack AC models, highlighting with dashes those that belong only to OpenStack and with the crosses those of AWS; solid lines represent instead common components and are among the ones supported by our prototype implementation.

The picture shows that both solutions present an administrative boundary, called *domain* in OpenStack and *root account* in AWS, that contains all the supported entities: Users, Groups, Roles and, exclusively for OpenStack, *projects* and *tokens*. Users may belong to a group (*User-Group* assignment) or be linked

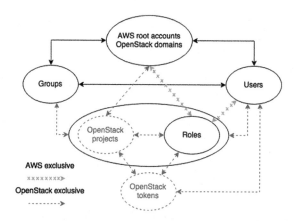

Fig. 2. Amazon AWS and OpenStack AC models. Adapted from [12,13]

to a role (*User-Role* assignment), that AWS considers as a separate complex entity (with its own set of permissions) while OpenStack as a mandatory simple property of U. OpenStack requires the user to interact with a set of resources with specific roles (*User-Project* assignment) and providing a valid authentication *token*; the same process allows the interaction for all the entities that belong to a group (*Group-Project* assignment).

4.2 Policy Support in Amazon and OpenStack

Our AC solution for the cloud supports six categories of authorization policies: assigned to the subject (User Policy or **UP**), to a users group or a role (respectively Group Policy or **GP** and Role Policy or **RoP**) and to the resources on which the subjects perform their actions (Resource Policy or **ReP**). The GP and RoP policies can also be specialized to apply only to a single user belonging to the specified group or role; in the following, these will be called special GP (**sGP**) and special RoP (**sRoP**). Two other types of permissions refer to the ability to offer the identity federation feature, which requires a trust relationship between users (Trust Policy or **TP**), and the possibility to assign permissions together with login credentials (Credential Policy or **CredP**). Those are supported only in Amazon and, when generating the OpenStack AC rules, are handled as UPs.

Table 2 provides an outline of our policy types and their support in the two CPs, including the required attributes or the services that enforce them. Amazon implement almost all types of authorization through the Identity and Access Management (IAM) service, while the Security Token Service (STS) is used for handling the CredP and three other services allow the user to specify ReP directly associated with the resource involved: S3 and the notification and queue services (respectively Simple NS and Simple QS). OpenStack instead manages permissions only through Keystone, using a set of rules related to the action performed (API actions) or the OpenStack service involved (such as *identity*,

Table 2. Policy types supported in our model, Amazon AWS and OpenStack

Policy types	Amazon AWS implementation	OpenStack implementation
UP	IAM UP	API-Service:API UP
GP	IAM GP	API-Service:API GP
sGP	Restricted GP (AWS username or user_ID)	Restricted GP (OpenStack user_id)
RoP	IAM RoP	API-Service:API RoP
sRoP	Restricted RoP (AWS username or user_ID)	Restricted RoP (OpenStack user_id)
ReP	AWS ReP for the S3, SNS and SQS services	Swift ACL or temporary URLs
TP	IAM TP	Missing
CredP	STS-AWS CredP	Missing

network or *compute*). The concept of TP and CredP is not supported in Open-Stack and the only way to implement ReP, in the case of Swift, is to provide an Access Control List (ACL) or generate a URL that allows the owner temporary access; unlike the ACL, the latter can distinguish between a folder and an object. The special GP and RoP are supported in both cloud platforms using the ID associated to an user.

5   SecurePG

To implement our AC model for the cloud according to Sect. 3, we developed a prototype implementation called SECUREPG (also referred to as *the tool*) that integrates a graphical user interface and a policy engine, both written in Java, and is supported by a MySQL database. The policy engine is responsible to analyse the authorization sentences using version 4.5.3 of the framework ANother Tool for Language Recognition (ANTLR) and identify, with the support of a general purpose grammar, the tuple < Policy Decision, Subjects, Actions, Resources, Conditions > according to our abstract policy language; it also investigates the absence of ambiguities such as the use of the same subject, resource or action in the positive and negative form or errors as the usage of a wrong operator or values when specifying the actions or the conditions names. The MySQL component contains a database schema that replicate the CPs data model and link cloud compliant names with the ones used for the authorization formulas, i.e. the subject name with its Amazon identifiers. By design, this component will interactively ask the user whether to continue if no value or more than one value are retrieved from the database tables. In the first case it also gives the possibility to generate a random value.

Figure 3 provides the architecture of the tool in the default use-case scenario. Using the subjects, actions and resources (referred as the triple $<S, A, R>$) supported by the tool and agreed with the SA, the application developers can easily deploy cloud resource and features on the CP that best meets the requirements. To demonstrate the use of the tool on the reference scenario, we analyse the processing of two authorizations: the sRoP obtained by replacing the subject pattern in Listing 1.2 with "ACME_employee_1 [role = ACME_employees]",

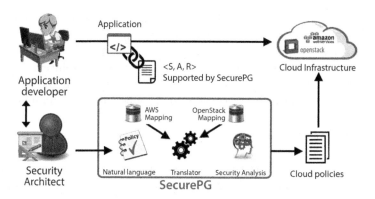

Fig. 3. SECUREPG architecture

reported in Table 3, and the CredP listed below. The latter allows the subject identified by the ID *ACME_user_1* to assume the role with ID *ACME_Customers* to access his profile and is structured in compliance with the Amazon AC model: one role policy (referred as the Role-component in Listing 1.3) assigned to the role *ACME_Customers* and one policy (referred as the Credential-component in Listing 1.3) provided to the *ACME_user_1* subject when authenticating. This policy, uniquely associated to the user's credentials, cannot define new permissions or extend pre-existing authorizations; i.e. the sRoP associated to *ACME_Customers*.

Listing 1.3. Example of an abstract rule that translates to a CredP

```
Role-component: Grant ACME_user_1 [role = ACME_customers] the permission
    to get object and put object on ACME/User_profiles/* [type = keys];

Credential-component: Deny ACME_user_1 [role = ACME_customers] the
    permission to get object and put object on not ACME_user_1_profile
    [type = keys];
```

5.1 Policy Generator Engine

Processing the sRoP and the CredP authorizations, SECUREPG is able to determine the correct policy types and suggest the creation of all the necessary entities. For the sRoP, the tool may suggest the creation of one AWS root account, one IAM user and one IAM role (both belonging to the same root account); regarding OpenStack, it recommends the use of a domain and the KeyStone user *ACME_employee_1* (created providing the KeyStone role *ACME_employees*). In both cases SECUREPG reports the skipping of the components not supported/recognized within the specific CP. Although some information may be stored, for example as metadata if the interaction refers to a Swift or a S3 resource, it can not be indicated as part of the AC rule.

When specifying a Swift resource, as in the CredP, the user can choose between two solutions: a generated URL that allows the owner temporary access to the Resource or a Swift ACL for the Keystone user that is assigned with a role on a project associated to the resource. In the example, the *user_id* 111 of *ACME_user_1* must be linked with the *role_id* 222 of *ACME_customers* and the *project_id* 333 of *P_ACME_user_1*. To implement the first solution, the system requires (or randomly generate) a duration, the resource path and a cluster key *sig* (that acts as a signature), according to the following URL template:

```
https://{host}/{path}?temp_url_sig={sig}&temp_url_expires={expires}
```

Regarding the Swift ACL instead, the SA needs to manually create a *User-Project* assignment using the Keystone interface (in the example, the triple <111, 222, 333>). Since OpenStack does not support the CredP type, SECUREPG will ignore the resource attribute *keys* and create a user policy; lacking the support of negative ACLs either, the tool will be able to generate only an authorization associated to the permit component.

5.2   Abstract Policy Analysis Engine

To allow the validation of the AC policies before the enforcement, we integrated the support of the Java Content-Based Protection and Release Language tool (JCPRL) [1] to analyse the AC rules provided by the SA. This required a bridge component to translate from the language in Sect. 3 to first-order logic formulas taken in input by the JCPRL tool. A CPRL document is then created retrieving all the necessary data from a MySQL database and the output is analysed with an SMT solver.

Table 3. Example of a sRoP processing

Auth. components	AWS policy

Policy decision:
< Grant >
Subjects:
< ACME_employee_1 >
Actions:
< add user
to group, true>
< remove user
from group, true>
Resources:
< ACME_customers,
true>
	`[{"Role Policy": {`
	`"ACME_employee": {`
	`"Version": "2012-10-17",`
	`"Statement": {`
	`"Sid": "1",`
	`"Effect": "Allow",`
	`"Action": [ "iam:AddUserToGroup,`
	`iam:RemoveUserFromGroup"],`
	`"Resource":`
	`["arn:aws:iam::xx:group/ACME_customers"]`
	`"Condition": {`
	`"StringEqualsIgnoreCase": {`
	`"aws:userid": "AIDAIYHF5BVYLMF36IKZY`[4]`" }`
	`}}}}}]`

	OpenStack policy
	"identity:add_user_to_group": "role:ACME_employees and 'ACME_customers':%(target.group.name)s and user_id:123"

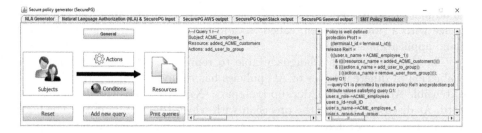

Fig. 4. SECUREPG query output using JCPRL

Fig. 5. SECUREPG AWS output from the Amazon web UI and OpenStack output

Figure 4 shows the output after the authorization query with the GUI (frame list on the left), while Fig. 5 presents the AWS output from the official Amazon web interface when manually adding the rule and the OpenStack output that will be saved in the Keystone *policy.json* file. The former prevents the Amazon java SDK from showing the following error message: *"User: arn:aws:iam::4146402582-23:user/ACME_employee_1 is not authorized to perform: iam:AddUserToGroup on resource: group ACME_customers ..Error Code: AccessDenied."*.

6   Discussion

We have presented a technique supporting the authoring of high-level AC policies for cloud applications, the capability of answering queries independently of a particular cloud platform, and the automated translation of the high-level authorizations to policies that can be enforced in two of the most widely adopted cloud platforms, namely AWS and Openstack. We have also reported our experience with a prototype tool, called SECUREPG, of the technique on a typical cloud application scenario.

The development of a language able to represent, share and facilitate the evaluation of different types of AC policies has received a lot of attention. The eXtensible Access Control Markup Language (XACML) [3] is the *de facto* standard. As discussed in [10], the precision with which this standard works is both a weakness and a strength. The solution proposed in [10] to overcome the difficulties of writing XACML is a graphical tool to display and edit the rules. Our approach is to avoid the difficulties of using XACML by employing a simple and abstract (but expressive) specification language to enforce user requirements in the cloud and easily exploit the JCPRL tool proposed in [1]. This allows to validate the AC policies before their deployment on a particular cloud platform by using a logical semantics and automated reasoning tools to mechanize the authorization query answering process. Similarly to [10], our prototype tool employs a graphical user interface to guide the generation and definition of the AC requirements hiding the complexities of the particular AC model and enforcement mechanism adopted by the cloud platform.

The abstract language we propose is similar to a structured natural language albeit simplified by using syntactic constructs to express ABAC authorization conditions in a way similar to Java Boolean conditions. A lot of work on the use of structured natural language has been done to express AC policies. For instance, the work in [9] analyzed the possibility to express user requirements using a domain dependent grammar and a restricted vocabulary of English sentences. We believe that this constitutes an interesting line of future work that can be integrated in our approach to make our abstract language even more intuitive, expressive, and friendly. Another interesting extension is to integrate a component that allows to import XACML policies in SECUREPG, and therefore to compare our tool with other policy generators; following the ABAC policy mining process presented in [11], we tested (although not integrated in SECUREPG) a component that processes the Amazon RBAC policies to generate expressions compliant with our abstract policy language. This allows to load pre-existing AWS policies (in the native JSON format) and generate, when supported by the OpenStack AC model, equivalent OpenStack authorization rules.

To the best of our knowledge, our technique is the first that is capable of generating enforceable policies in AWS and Openstack from a high-level description of the AC requirements. Our research is now trying to expand the support of our prototype tool to other cloud platforms; such as Microsoft Azure or Google Cloud in order to gain further experience with the automatic translation of high-level policies. We also intend to enrich the abstract policy languages with more constructs to express, for instance, the purpose of access—a feature which is becoming of paramount importance to ensure the privacy of the processing. This will also require the automatic synthesis of monitors to guarantee the satisfaction of purpose constraints. To this end, we envisage to integrate the approaches in, e.g., [2,5].

References

1. Armando, A., Ranise, S., Traverso, R., Wrona, K.: SMT-based enforcement and analysis of NATO content-based protection and release policies. In: Proceedings of the 2016 ACM International Workshop on Attribute Based Access Control, pp. 35–46. ACM (2016)
2. Bertolissi, C., Dos Santos, D.R., Ranise, S.: Automated synthesis of run-time monitors to enforce authorization policies in business processes. In: Proceedings of the ASIACCS, pp. 297–308. ACM (2015)
3. Committee, O.X.T., et al.: eXtensible Access Control Markup Language (XACML) Version 3.0. Oasis standard, OASIS (2013)
4. De Capitani Di Vimercati, S., Foresti, S., Samarati, P., Jajodia, S.: Access control policies and languages. Int. J. Comput. Sci. Eng. **3**(2), 94–102 (2007)
5. Masellis, R., Ghidini, C., Ranise, S.: A declarative framework for specifying and enforcing purpose-aware policies. In: Foresti, S. (ed.) STM 2015. LNCS, vol. 9331, pp. 55–71. Springer, Cham (2015). doi:10.1007/978-3-319-24858-5_4
6. Ferry, N., Song, H., Rossini, A., Chauvel, F., Solberg, A.: CloudMF: applying MDE to tame the complexity of managing multi-cloud applications. In: IEEE/ACM 7th International Conference on Utility and Cloud Computing (UCC), pp. 269–277. IEEE (2014)
7. Hu, V.C., Ferraiolo, D., Kuhn, R., Friedman, A.R., Lang, A.J., Cogdell, M.M., Schnitzer, A., Sandlin, K., Miller, R., Scarfone, K., et al.: Guide to attribute based access control (ABAC) definition and considerations (draft). **800**(162) 1–52 (2013). NIST Special Publication
8. Jin, X., Krishnan, R., Sandhu, R.: A unified attribute-based access control model covering DAC, MAC and RBAC. In: Cuppens-Boulahia, N., Cuppens, F., Garcia-Alfaro, J. (eds.) DBSec 2012. LNCS, vol. 7371, pp. 41–55. Springer, Heidelberg (2012). doi:10.1007/978-3-642-31540-4_4
9. Perry, J., Arkoudas, K., Chiang, J., Chadha, R., Apgar, D., Whittaker, K.: Modular natural language interfaces to logic-based policy frameworks. Comput. Stand. Interfaces **35**(5), 417–427 (2013)
10. Stepien, B., Felty, A., Matwin, S.: A non-technical user-oriented display notation for XACML conditions. In: Babin, G., Kropf, P., Weiss, M. (eds.) MCETECH 2009. LNBIP, vol. 26, pp. 53–64. Springer, Heidelberg (2009). doi:10.1007/978-3-642-01187-0_5
11. Xu, Z., Stoller, S.D.: Mining attribute-based access control policies from RBAC policies. In: 2013 10th International Conference and Expo on Emerging Technologies for a Smarter World (CEWIT), pp. 1–6. IEEE (2013)
12. Zhang, Y., Patwa, F., Sandhu, R.: Community-based secure information and resource sharing in AWS public cloud. In: 2015 IEEE Conference on Collaboration and Internet Computing (CIC), pp. 46–53. IEEE (2015)
13. Zhang, Y., Patwa, F., Sandhu, R., Tang, B.: Hierarchical secure information and resource sharing in OpenStack community cloud. In: 2015 IEEE International Conference on Information Reuse and Integration (IRI), pp. 419–426. IEEE (2015)

Capturing Policies for BYOD

Joseph Hallett[✉] and David Aspinall

School of Informatics, University of Edinburgh, Edinburgh, Scotland
j.hallett@sms.ac.uk

Abstract. BYOD policies are informally specified using natural language. We show how the SP4BYOD language can help reduce ambiguity in 5 BYOD policies and link the specification of a BYOD policy to its implementation. Using a formalisation of the 5 policies written in SP4BYOD, we make comparisons between them, and explore the delegation relationships within them. We identify that whilst policy acknowledgement is a key part of all 5 policies, this is not managed by existing MDM tools.

1 Introduction

Employees bring their own devices to work. In the past employees might have had a dedicated company device. Today around 70% of companies have a BYOD scheme [1]. In some fields, 85% of staff use their personal devices to look up work-sensitive information [2]. Controlling employee's devices is a challenge for IT departments. Failure to manage devices can lead to employees accidentally leaking confidential information. Unfortunately companies have limited control over the devices inside their networks if they do not own them.

One solution to controlling devices is requiring users follow BYOD policies. A BYOD policy takes the form of a user agreement, written in natural language, which describes how devices should be used and configured. Various guides are available for companies wishing to implement a policy from governments, standards bodies, and organizations seeking to advise [3–5]. On top of user agreements, companies may also use Mobile Device Management (MDM) software which can help enforce policies. MDM software can configure a device's security settings, and add security APIs, helping enforce some aspects of the policies. But the use of MDM software does not guarantee compliance. One survey from a leading MDM vendor found over 50% of companies using their MDM software still had devices that did not comply with the policy [6]. Reasons for non-compliance included out-of-date MDM configurations that hadn't been updated, and employees tampering with the MDM software.

BYOD policies are becoming more intricate. Prior work has looked at developing MDM software to enforce some aspects [7–9]. The MDM encoding of a policy is only part of the problem, however. BYOD policies are specified informally

D. Aspinall—Work supported by EPSRC App Guarden grant (EP/K032666/1) and the Alan Turing Institute.

S. De Capitani di Vimercati and F. Martinelli (Eds.): SEC 2017, IFIP AICT 502, pp. 310–323, 2017.
DOI: 10.1007/978-3-319-58469-0_21

using natural language, and they contain more than just access control decisions. They describe trust relationships inside the company between IT departments, users, and HR, who each may be delegated to provide rules and make decisions. Policies contain rules that require employees to acknowledge risks, and regulations. An antivirus or MDM program may be used to *implement* part of the policy. But it is the policy that *specifies* which software to use and when. There is no automatic way to check how the policy has been implemented and by what.

Companies lack visibility as to how well they implement their policies. When considering what tools a company may use Morrow notes *"particularly with the BYOD trend IT professionals do not know if anti-virus software is installed or if it's current"* [10]. Even when devices can implement policies correctly, it is hard to configure devices that are not owned by the company [11]. Our work aims to address these problems directly: by using formal languages we can link the policy to the implementation.

To describe the BYOD policies we present SP4BYOD: a formal language for linking policies to the tools used to implement them, and distributing decisions to relevant parties. Using a formalization of five BYOD policies written using SP4BYOD we identify different idioms and common delegation patterns present in BYOD policies. Our formalizations pick out the common concerns and trust relationships in these policies. We look at what decisions and trust relationships are used in BYOD policies. We identify BYOD idioms that capture frequently seen decisions in BYOD policies. These give a guide for where future work implementing MDM tools should focus their efforts to cover more aspects of policies.

SP4BYOD is not designed to replace existing static and dynamic analysis and enforcement tools. A company might use multiple tools, app stores, or contractual agreements with employees to enforce their policies. We aim to help clarify the meaning of ambiguous natural language policy documents, and provide a rigorous means for following them. A company can use any MDM tool, curated app store or user agreement to enforce their policy. SP4BYOD links the specification of the policy to its implementation, showing exactly how a policy is implemented and giving a rigorous means to enforce it.

We show how SP4BYOD can be used to encode policies and describe precisely the different trust relationships. SP4BYOD is an instantiation of the SecPAL authorization language [12] for mobile device policies and implemented atop of AppPAL [13], which adds mobile device specific predicates to SecPAL, for example, capturing app permissions. SecPAL is also a useful tool for describing other policies surrounding mobile ecosystems [14]. Our SP4BYOD implementation can be easily extended to support new types of policies. It also gives us access to tooling we have developed to check SP4BYOD policies for completeness and redundant statements. For this work additional tooling was developed to help visualise policies and describe their contents. This was helpful for making comparisons between policies and checking our formalisation for mistakes.

In summary, our work makes the following contributions:

- We present a formalisation of five different BYOD policies in SP4BYOD: a new instantiation of SecPAL for describing BYOD policies (Sect. 2).
- Using our formalisation of the policies we make comparisons between the different policies. Unlike previous work which looks at individual policies [15], our work looks at policies across a variety of domains (Sect. 4).
- We identify that delegation and acknowledgements are an important aspect of BYOD policies that current MDM software does not look at (Sect. 6).

1.1 Related Work

Martinelli et al.'s work looks at creating a dynamic permissions manager, called UC-Droid. Their tool can alter what an app's Android permissions are at run time based on policies [8]. The tool allows companies to reconfigure their apps depending on whether the employee is at work, in a secret lab, or working out-of-hours. These kinds of policies are more configurable than the geofenced based policies some MDM tools provide. Other work has looked at enforcing different policies based on what roles an employee holds [7]. The work allowed a company to verify the devices within their network and what servers and services they could access. It also describes a mechanism for providing different users with different policies.

Armando et al. developed BYODroid as a tool for enforcing BYOD policies through a secure marketplace [16]. Their tool allows companies to distribute apps through a secure app store [9]. The store ensures apps meet policies through a combination of static analysis and app rewriting with dynamic enforcement. Their policies are low level, based on ConSpec [17], allowing checks based on Dalvik VM's state. Using their tool, they implemented parts of a NATO Communications and Information Agency policy relating to personal networks and data management [15]. Their work shows how the app-specific sections of a BYOD policy can be check and enforced using tools. They did not look at where the checks or policies come from, however.

An SP4BYOD policy might use BYODroid to ensure that parts of a policy are enforced (as well as other tools for other parts). Using SP4BYOD, we can distribute policies by sharing signed statements from different principals. We can delegate to other marketplaces to decide if an app meets different parts of policies. We can even create new stores by composing their policies and using multiple store's statements about the apps. Distributing checks like this is useful when using some static analysis tools which can take a long time to run (e.g. TaintDroid [18]).

Tools, such as Dr. Android and Mr. Hyde [19] and Aurasium [20], have suggested app wrapping (where an app is recompiled to use guarded APIs) as a possible way to enforce policies. App rewriting has the advantage that the device's underlying OS needn't be modified as the apps are changed at the source code level. However app wrapping alone without additional analysis is insufficient to enforce policies effectively [21].

Our approach taken with SP4BYOD is similar to work on safety cases. A safety case is an argument made to say a system is acceptably safe to be used in a given scenario. Industrial safety cases are often described in natural language, which can be ambiguous and unclear. Goal Structuring Notation (GSN) [22] is one approach to make the safety cases explicit. It is a graphical formal notation that lets engineers argue that a system is safe by linking safety goals to the arguments made for a system's safety. Similarly, work developing a formal language for specifying how medical staff should collaborate in a healthcare scenario [23] again helps clarify how roles are filled in a medical context on the basis of staff and different healthcare providers.

It is interesting to examine how leading [24] MDM tools such as IBM's MaaS360, or Blackberry Enterprise Services (BES), enforce *BYOD* policies. These tools support enforcing and checking compliance policies. They do not, however, use policy languages to specify policies; rather they provide a limited number of checkboxes that admins can tweak (an excerpt of a policy from MaaS360 is shown in Fig. 1). These tools allow administrators to configure a device's settings and provision the devices with company apps. Some support app wrapping, which enables them to encrypt app data locally, use a VPN within the app, or prevent apps not being used when the device isn't compliant. But because the policies are inflexible and tightly coupled to the device's OS, intervention by an administrator is often required. Whilst MDM software is good at configuring devices, selecting which policies to apply is typically a manual

Network Settings

Allow Wi-Fi On a Wi-Fi only device, unchecking this option will not block Wi-Fi.	Yes	Android 2.2+
Enforce Wi-Fi is always on	No	Android 2.2+
Bluetooth	User Controlled	Android 2.2+
Allow Data Network	User Controlled	Android 2.2+
Enable Background Data Synchronization Allows applications to sync, send or receive data any time.	User Controlled	Android 2.X & 3.X
Auto-Sync	User Controlled	Android 2.2+
Allow user to Mobile Data limit	Yes	SAFE 4.0+
Allow VPN Allow or disallow use of the native VPN functionality. If disabled, the user cannot establish a VPN session and the UI for using VPN through the Settings application is inaccessible.	Yes	SAFE 2.2+

Fig. 1. Excerpt of a policy showing network settings from MaaS360.

process performed by an administrator. Removing blacklisted apps is a common feature, but the selection process of which apps to remove is manual.

2 Capturing BYOD Policies

As mobile devices have become more common in the workplace, BYOD policies have been written to help control them. Part of their policies are prescriptive: if you configure your device in this way, you will mitigate that threat. The policies contain more than just configuration, however. Consider this rule taken from the *Security Policy for the use of handheld devices in corporate environments* by SANS [3].

> **SANS**: *Digital camera embedded on handheld devices* might *be disabled in restricted environments, according to* ⟨*COMPANY NAME*⟩ *risk analysis. In sensitive facilities, information can be stolen using pictures and possibly sent using MMS or E-mail services.*
>
> *In high-security facilities such as R&D labs or design manufacturers, camera MUST be disabled. Furthermore, MMS messages should be disabled as well, to prevent malicious users from sending proprietary pictures.*

A company could use an MDM program to enforce this. Some MDM tools can use geofencing to apply a policies in the area around a lab. Techniques like this would implement the recommendation within the rule, but the rule itself contains more than just configuration. It talks of *restricted environments* decided by *company risk analysis*. How is this communicated to the device? Does it access the list of restricted environments once from a server, are they fixed or can a device decide them for itself? Can it judge using a policy if a location is restricted? The rule also gives a security objective: *prevent malicious users from sending proprietary pictures*. The guidelines are given, however, for the case of a legitimate user using MMS or email. It may not be sufficient to stop a sufficiently motivated *malicious* user.

Our approach does not try to enforce the policy by checking the app's code for programming errors. Rather we act as a *"glue-layer"* between the high-level policy and the tools and trust relationships used to implement them. We capture the goals of the policy rules so that the delegations of trust, tools implementing the policy and their configuration are made explicit. This gives us greater clarity as to which tool is being trusted to implement what policy. It allows us to see who is being trusted to make which decisions, and use automatic-tools to uncover problematic aspects of the policy [14]. Continuing with the example above, we can encode this in SP4BYOD as:

```
'company' says 'risk−analyst' can−say
  Location:L isHighSecurityFacility.

'company' says Device:D mustDisableIn(Location, 'camera')
  if Location isHighSecurityFacility.

'company' says Device:D mustDisableIn(Location, 'mms')
  if Location isHighSecurityFacility.

'company' says User:U hasSatisfied('proprietary_pictures_policy')
  if U hasDevice(D),
     D mustDisableIn(Location, 'camera'),
     D mustDisableIn(Location, 'mms'),
     Location isHighSecurityFacility.
```

After checking the policy we generate a proof tree that shows how the policy was satisfied. These proof trees not only show how the policy was followed but also provide an audit trail. In a company decisions may be delegated to different departments. Auditors can see what happened when things go wrong. They know who made what decision, and whether they made it through following policy rules or as a stated fact.

3   Instantiating SecPAL

SecPAL was developed as a distributed access control language [12]. It is designed to be have a clear readable syntax, and intuitive semantics. It is also designed to be extensible, which makes it ideal for extending to create new languages. All SecPAL statements are *said* by an explicit authority. The authority can say a fact (that something is described by a predicate), a delegation (that someone else *can-say* a fact), or a role assignment (that something *can-act-as* something else). This statement optionally contain conditional facts, and constraints that must be satisfied before the authority will say the statement.

To create SP4BYOD we instantiate SecPAL with four kinds of facts common in BYOD policies: *can, has, is* and *must*. Like other SecPAL-based instantiations [25,26] we extend the syntax of facts to support these constructs.

Fact	Meaning
subject can*Action*	The subject is permitted to perform the action
subject has*Action*	The subject has performed the action
subject is*Type*	The subject is a member of the type
subject must*Action*	The subject must perform the action

Facts of the *must*-kind represent obligations, actions to complete if a particular scenario presents itself. For these facts, we add a rule to check we perform the obligation. This rule should be checked periodically to ensure compliance. Our implementation contains tooling to generate these rules automatically, by parsing the policy.

```
⟨speaker⟩ says ⟨subject⟩ hasSatisfiedObligation⟨Action⟩
  if ⟨subject⟩ must⟨Action⟩,
     ⟨subject⟩ has⟨Action⟩.
```

Facts using *is* predicates give types to variables. SP4BYOD inherits from SecPAL's (and Datalog's) safety condition that the body of a statements must reference all the variables in the head. This can lead to some *boilerplate* code in policies that may obscure their meaning. To simplify the policies, we add syntactic sugar for facts giving variables their type (*variable* is *Type*). Variables in the head of the statement of the form *Type* : Variable are replaced by the variable and a condition Variable is *Type* is added to the condition. The two statements shown below (taken from the SANS policy) are equivalent, however we feel the example on the right is easier to read.

```
'company' says Device
    canConnectToAP(X)
 if X isOwnedByCompany,
    Device isDevice,
    X isAP.
```

```
'company' says Device:D
    canConnectToAP(AP:X)
 if X isOwnedByCompany.
```

4   BYOD Policies

We examined 5 policies and encoded them into SP4BYOD looking for common idioms. We selected these policies as they came from a variety of domains.

- The first is the *Security Policy Template: Use of Handheld Devices in a Corporate Environment*, published by the SANS Institute [3]. This policy is a hypothetical policy published to help companies mitigate the threats to corporate assets caused by mobile devices. Companies are expected to modify the document to suit their needs. The policy is general; not specific to any particular industry, device, or country's legislation.
- The second is taken from the Healthcare Information Management System Society (HiMSS) [27]; a US non-profit company trying to improve healthcare through IT. The HiMSS policy is relatively short and contains concerns specific to healthcare scenarios. It is written as a contract the users agree to follow. In contrast, every other policy we looked at is written as an organisation imposing rules on users they should follow to ensure compliance. The policy is designed as a sample agreement for a system trying to manage personal mobile devices in a healthcare environment.
- The third is taken from a British hospital trust [28] and describes the BYOD scheme used in practice at the hospital.

Table 1. Summary of the contents of each of the BYOD policies.

	SANS	HiMSS	NHS	Edinburgh	Sirens
Number of rules	33	15	56	20	25
SP4BYOD statements	71	21	58	10	39
Policy coverage	33 (100%)	14 (93%)	40 (71%)	10 (100%)[a]	22 (88%)
Rules using Acknowledgement	2	10	11	1	6
Rules using Delegation	23	5	33	2	13
Rules describing a restriction	18	3	8	1	5
Principal Speaker	Company	User	nhs-trust	Records-management	Department

[a]The Edinburgh policy contains a large number of rules that whilst marked as such are in fact just descriptions of the document. All the policy rules that described restrictions or relationships were implemented in SP4BYOD.

- Finally, we looked at two simpler policies from The University of Edinburgh [29] and a company specialising in emergency sirens [30]. These policies are simpler, and shorter than the other policies we looked at comprised of much more general rules.

We summarise the policies in Table 1. Each policy contains a series of *rules*, which we implemented by one or more *SP4BYOD statements*. The *policy coverage* represents the number of rules that have an SP4BYOD description attached.

All five of the policies make use of acknowledgements. The use of an acknowledgements could be because enforcing that rule in a policy through technical means is undesirable. It could indicate policy authors care more that the subjects are aware of the rules than they do for rigorous enforcement. All but the HiMSS policy have rules that include locking down a device by disabling features. All but the Edinburgh policy have rules that look at what should happen if a user loses their device. The rest have rules that require employees inform someone when something happens. Common concerns, such as these, suggest where future MDM software should focus their efforts.

Only the NHS and SANS policies, the two most complex policies, describe when a device can install an app and what kinds of apps are installable. In both policies this expressed as a delegation to the appropriate groups to authorize an app. For example, in the SANS policy the IT-Department are responsible for deciding what apps can be installed. The NHS policy, however, is significantly more complicated. Apps have to be approved by three different groups (the IGC, the Employee's manager, and the relevant group for either clinical or business cases) before the Trust will say that an employee can install an app.

NHS: *Apps for work usage must not be downloaded onto corporately issued mobile devices (even if approved on the NHS apps store) unless they have been approved through the following Trust channels: Clinical apps; at the time of writing there are no apps clinically approved by the Trust for use with patients/clients. However, if a member of staff believes that there are clinical apps or other technologies that could benefit their patients/clients, this should be discussed with the clinical lead in the first instance and ratification should be sought via the Care and Clinical Policies Group. A clinical app should not be used if it has not been approved via* *this group. Business apps; at the time of writing there are no business (i.e., non-clinical) apps approved by the Trust for use other than those preloaded onto the device at the point of issue. However, if a member of staff believes that there are apps or other technologies that could benefit their non-clinical work, ratification of the app must be sought via the Management of Information Group (MIG). An app should not be used if it has not been approved via this group. Following approval through Care and Clinical Policies and/or MIG, final approval will be required through Integrated Governance Committee. Use of paid apps must be agreed in advance with the device holder's line manager and there should be a demonstrable benefit.*

```
'nhs-trust' says App isUsable if App hasMet('clinical-use-case').
'nhs-trust' says App isUsable if App hasMet('business-use-case').
'nhs-trust' says 'cacpg' can-say App:A hasMet('clinical-use-case').
'nhs-trust' says 'mig' can-say App:A hasMet('business-use-case').
'nhs-trust' says App isInstallable
  if App hasMet('final-app-approval'), App isUsable.
'nhs-trust' says 'igc' can-say App hasMet('final-app-approval').
'nhs-trust' says Device canInstall(App)
  if App isInstallable, App isApprovedFor(Device).
'nhs-trust' says Employee:Manager can-say
  App:A isApprovedFor(Device)
  if Manager isResponsibleFor(Device).
```

We might expect corporate policies to describe what apps can be installed in terms of the apps functionality. This does not appear to be the case, however. As part of selecting the apps, an IT department or group may choose to use advanced instrumentation and policies [9]. Alternatively, they may manually chose apps to form a curated app store as some MDM vendors allow. From the perspective of the policy, it is more important *who* makes the decision rather than *what* they chose, however.

5   Authorization Example

As a worked-example consider the NHS rules for finding approved apps (Sect. 4). Suppose an employee, *Alice*, wished to get an app, *com.microsoft.office*, installed on their device. To do so, Alice would have to convince the device that:

'nhs-trust' *says* 'alices-phone' canInstall('com.microsoft.office').

Alice wishes to use the app for business so to satisfy the policy Alice must collect the following statements:

- 'nhs-trust' *says* 'com.microsoft. office ' isInstallable.
  For this, she needs a statement from the Management of Information Group that it has a business use-case. She also needs approval from the Integrated Governance Committee.
  1. 'mig' *says* 'com.microsoft. office ' hasMet('business-use-case').

2. 'igc' *says* 'com.microsoft. office ' hasMet('final −app−approval').
- 'nhs−trust' *says* 'com.microsoft. office ' isApprovedFor('alices−device'). To get this she needs a statement from the manager responsible for Alice's device (*Bob*) approving the app.
  3. 'bob' *says* 'com.microsoft. office ' isApprovedFor('alices−device').
  4. 'nhs−trust' *says* 'bob' isResponsibleFor('alices−device').
- Additionally, she needs the following typing statements.
  5. 'nhs−trust' *says* 'com.microsoft. office ' isApp.
  6. 'nhs−trust' *says* 'bob' isEmployee.

Alice obtains the statements by contacting each of the speakers. Each may either give her the statement she needs or may give her additional rules. For example, the MIG and IGC may be happy to state their statements (after a review). When checking if the app is an App in Item 5, the NHS trust may be instead inclined to delegate further. They could reply that if the App is in the Google Play store then they are convinced it is an app. Alice would then have to obtain additional statements if she wanted to prove this statement. As with SecPAL, all statements should have a signature from their speaker proving they said the statement. Alternatively, the speaker could refuse to give the statement, either because they do not believe it to be true, or they cannot give an answer. In this case, Alice would have to look for an alternative means to prove the statement or accept that they cannot install the app.

When the statements have been collected Alice can use a SecPAL inference tool (such as AppPAL[1]) to check the policy has been satisfied. The generated proof from the tool lets auditors review how the decision was made, and verify the decision-making process.

6   BYOD Idioms

When examining the policies, we noticed two particular idioms in many policies: acknowledgements and delegation. We describe both idioms in greater detail, and show how they can be implemented in SP4BYOD, below. MDM tools and research have focussed so far on implementing restrictions on apps and devices [8,31,32]. Implementing these controls is a vital aspect of BYOD policies and all 5 of the policies we looked at had rules that described restrictions (Table 1). Every policy also contained rules that required employees acknowledgements, however. Only the SANS policy (which is configuration focussed) contained more rules that required restrictions than acknowledgements. All the policies contained more rules featuring delegation relationships than functionality restrictions.

Delegation and Roles Within Policies. Delegation is an important part of each of the policies. Each of the policies describes through rules how separate entities may be responsible for making some decisions. These rules can be a

---

[1] https://github.com/apppal/libapppal.

delegation to an employee's manager to authorize a decision (as in the NHS policy). It could be to technical staff to decide what apps are part of a standard install (as in the sirens and SANS policies).

SP4BYOD requires an explicit speaker for each statement. Speakers can delegate to others by making a statement about what they *can-say*. When translating the policies, the author of the policy is used as the primary speaker of the policy's rule (Table 1). For the HiMSS policy, where the user states what they will do rather than the company stating what they must, the user is the primary speaker. All the policies describe multiple entities that might make statements and delegate. With SP4BYOD policies any speaker can delegate a decision to another speaker (with restrictions on re-delegation). The delegation might be to a user to acknowledge a policy, or it might be to other groups in the company who are responsible for certain decisions.

In all the policies we looked at the majority of the decisions are made by three groups of speakers: the company, the IT-department, and the users or employees. All the policies also delegate to a user (apart from HiMSS where the user is the primary speaker). The user is typically responsible for providing information, such as agreements to policies, reporting devices missing, and updating passcodes. In the Sirens, SANS and NHS policy each describe an IT-department who are delegated to make some decisions. The HiMSS policy describes an *xyz-health-system* who act similarly to an IT-department. These decisions are more varied and can overlap with the responsibilities of the company. In the NHS and SANS policies, the IT department is responsible for maintaining lists of activated devices. In the Sirens and SANS policies, the IT department maintains a list of what is installable on a device or not.

When a policy decision requires input from a third-party delegation is used. For example, an employee's manager has to authorise an app install. The SecPAL *can-say* statement is the basis for a delegation. We can ask the HR department to state who is someone's manager.

```
'company' says 'hr—department' can-say
  Employee:E hasManager(Employee:M).
```

If we wish to delegate to someone, we can add conditionals to the can-say statement that enforces any relationship between the delegating and delegated parties.

```
'company' says Manager can-say
  Employee canInstall(App:A)
  if Employee hasManager(Manager).
```

7 Conclusions

We have presented SP4BYOD: an instantiation of SecPAL for BYOD policies. Using an SP4BYOD formalization of 5 BYOD policies we have identified that whilst delegation and acknowledgement form a large part of written BYOD policies, existing BYOD tools ignore them. BYOD policies contain delegation and trust relationships that define who is responsible for making different decisions in a company. Sometimes that is administrators and technical staff deciding what to permit inside the company, and sometimes it is the user's themselves agreeing to follow a policy. Previous work has focussed on the technical staff's decisions and developing new ways to automate their decisions. Our work looks at the policies at a higher level tracking, managing and authorizing policies based on what people have said and what tools were run.

SP4BYOD improves upon existing MDM tools by allowing sophisticated delegation relations and by providing a declarative language for expressing policies. The language gives greater flexibility to policy authors and allows them to write policies that depend on other policies rather than predefined settings and groups. It lets us track what users have agreed to, what their policies are, how they are specified, and how they are satisfied.

Acknowledgements were used in all the policies, but were not a part of MDM tools. A purely speculative explanation for this might be that the people using the MDM software (the IT department) do not care about the acknowledgements, and that another department (HR perhaps) are responsible for tracking what corporate policies employees have agreed to and have their own methods for dealing with that. Future work will aim to further explore how these acknowledgements are used within a company and how to manage them in a practical manner.

Related systems, such as GSN described in Subsect. 1.1, use a graphical notation. Whilst SecPAL-based languages are designed to be readable, diagrams can help make authors write policies and auditors understand them. Future work will look at extending SecPAL's notation to create such diagrams and further aid readability.

Acknowledgement. All the policies we looked at require their subjects to be aware and acknowledge certain rules or policies, and that the company may perform certain actions. For example, the NHS and HiMSS policies state that the organisation will wipe devices remotely to protect confidential information a user loses their device. Both policies also say that employees would lose personal information if they had it on the device and the company needed to erase it. The employee is required to be aware of this, and in the case of the HiMSS policy, agree to hold the company harmless for the loss.

Both the SANS and the siren-company policies use acknowledgements to link to other sets of rules that employees should follow. These policies are not further specified, and in the case of an acceptable use policy may be hard to enforce automatically. The SANS policy requires that all employees follow an email security, acceptable use, and an eCommerce-security policy. The Sirens policy expects an employee to use their devices ethically and abide by an acceptable use policy.

When there is a (usually separate) set of rules and concerns employees should be aware of acknowledgements are used. The company may not wish to enforce these separate rules automatically, however. For instance, a company may have an ethics policy that says employees should not use devices for criminal purposes. The company is not interested in, or capable of, defining what is criminal. They trust their employees to make the right decision and to be aware of the rules.

To implement these in SP4BYOD, a policy author creates two rules: the first stating their employees must have acknowledged the policy, the second delegating the acceptance of the policy to the employee themselves.

```
'company' says Employee:E mustAcknowledged('policy').
'company' says Employee:E can-say
  E hasAcknowledged('policy').
```

References

1. Schulze, H.: BYOD & Mobile Security 2016 Spotlight Report. Technical report. LinkedIn Information Security (2016). http://static.tenable.com/whitepapers/byod-and-mobile-security-report-2016.pdf
2. Patel, R.K., et al.: A UK perspective on smartphone use amongst doctors within the surgical profession. Ann. Med. Surg. **4**(2), 107–112 (2015)
3. Guerin, N.R.C.: Security Policy for the use of handheld devices in corporate environments. Technical report, SANS, May 2008
4. Souppaya, M., Scarfone, K.: Guidelines for managing and securing mobile devices in the enterprise: NIST Special Publication 800–124 Revision 1 (Draft). National Institute of Standards and Technology (2012)
5. CESG. BYOD Guidance. Good Technology. Technical report, CESG, March 2015
6. MobileIron Security Labs. Q4 Mobile Security and Risk Review. Technical report, MobileIron Security Labs, December 2015
7. Costantino, G., et al.: Towards enforcing on-the-y policies in BYOD environments. In: International Conference on Information Assurance and Security, December 2013
8. Martinelli, F., Mori, P., Saracino, A.: Control, enhancing android permission through usage: a BYOD use-case. In: Symposium on Applied Computing (2016)
9. Armando, A., et al.: Enabling BYOD through secure meta-market. In: ACM Conference on Security and Privacy in Wireless & Mobile Networks, August 2014
10. Morrow, B.: BYOD security challenges: control and protect your most sensitive data. Netw. Secur. **2012**, 5–8 (2012)
11. Tokuyoshi, B.: The security implications of BYOD. Netw. Secur. **2013**(4), 1213 (2013)
12. Becker, M.Y., Fournet, C., Gordon, A.D.: SecPAL: design and semantics of a decentralized authorization language. J. Comput. Secur. **18**(4), 619–665 (2010)
13. Hallett, J., Aspinall, D.: AppPAL for android. In: Caballero, J., Bodden, E., Athanasopoulos, E. (eds.) ESSoS 2016. LNCS, vol. 9639, pp. 216–232. Springer, Cham (2016). doi:10.1007/978-3-319-30806-7_14
14. Hallett, J., Aspinall, D.: Specifying BYOD policies with authorization logic. In: PhD Symposium at iFM 2016 on Formal Methods. Reykjavik University, June 2016
15. Armando, A., et al.: Developing a NATO BYOD security policy. In: International Conference on Military Communications and Information Systems, May 2016
16. Armando, A., Costa, G., Merlo, A.: Bring your own device, securely. In: Proceedings of the 28th Annual ACM Symposium on Applied Computing (SAC 2013), pp. 1852–1858. ACM, New York (2013)

17. Aktug, I., Naliuka, K.: ConSpec–a formal language for policy specification. Electron. Notes Theor. Comput. Sci. **197**, 45–58 (2008)
18. Enck, W., et al.: TaintDroid: an information-flow tracking system for realtime privacy monitoring on smartphones. ACM Trans. Comput. Syst. **32**, 5 (2014)
19. Jeon, J., et al.: Dr. Android and Mr. Hide: fine-grained permissions in android applications. In: Proceedings of the Second ACM Workshop on Security and Privacy in Smartphones and Mobile Devices (2012)
20. Xu, R., Sadi, H., Anderson, R.: Aurasium: practical policy enforcement for android applications. In: Usenix Security Symposium (2012)
21. Hao, H., Singh, V., Du, W.: On the effectiveness of API-level access control using bytecode rewriting in Android. In: ACM Asia Conference on Computer and Communications Security (2013)
22. Kelly, T., Weaver, R.: The goal structuring notation – a safety argument notation. In: Proceedings of the Dependable Systems and Networks Workshop on Assurance Cases (2004). http://www-users.cs.york.ac.uk/tpk/dsn2004.pdf. Accessed 19 Dec 2016
23. Papapanagiotou, P., Fleuriot, J.D.: Formal verification of collaboration patterns in healthcare. Behav. Inf. Technol. **33**(12), 1278–1293 (2014)
24. Smith, R., et al.: Magic quadrant for enterprise mobility management suites. Technical report, G00279887. Gartrer, June 2016. https://www.gartner.com/doc/reprints?id=1-390IMNG&ct=160608&st=sb
25. Becker, M.Y., Malkis, A., Bussard, L.: A framework for privacy preferences and data-handling policies. Technical report, MSRTR2009128. Microsoft Research (2009)
26. Aziz, B., Arenas, A., Wilson, M.: SecPAL4DSA: a policy language for specifying data sharing agreements. In: Park, J.J., Lopez, J., Yeo, S.-S., Shon, T., Taniar, D. (eds.) STA 2011. CCIS, vol. 186, pp. 29–36. Springer, Heidelberg (2011). doi:10.1007/978-3-642-22339-6_4
27. Healthcare Information Management Systems Society. Mobile Security Toolkit: Sample Mobile Device User Agreement. Healthcare Information and Management Systems Society (2012)
28. Kennington, G., et al.: Mobiles devices policy. Technical report, Torbay, Southern Devon Health, and Care NHS Trust, March 2014
29. Williamson, D., Grzybowski, A., Graham, S.: Bring your own device policy. Policy 15. University of Edinburgh, February 2015. http://www.ed.ac.uk/files/imports/fileManager/BYODPolicy.pdf. Accessed 14 Oct 2016
30. Code3PSE.org. Sample BYOD Policy. http://www.code3pse.com/public/media/22845.pdf. Accessed 14 Oct 2016
31. IBM MaaS360 - Enterprise Mobility Management (EMM). http://www-03.ibm.com/security/mobile/maas360.html. Accessed 12 Oct 2016
32. Armando, A., et al.: Formal modeling and automatic enforcement of bring your own device policies. Int. J. Inf. Secur. **14**, 123–140 (2014)

Applied Cryptography and Voting Schemes

Improving Blind Steganalysis in Spatial Domain Using a Criterion to Choose the Appropriate Steganalyzer Between CNN and SRM+EC

Jean-Francois Couchot, Raphaël Couturier, and Michel Salomon$^{(\boxtimes)}$

FEMTO-ST Institute, CNRS - Univ. Bourgogne Franche-Comté (UBFC),
Belfort, France
{jean-francois.couchot,raphael.couturier,michel.salomon}@univ-fcomte.fr

Abstract. Conventional state-of-the-art image steganalysis approaches usually consist of a classifier trained with features provided by rich image models. As both features extraction and classification steps are perfectly embodied in the deep learning architecture called Convolutional Neural Network (CNN), different studies have tried to design a CNN-based steganalyzer. This work proposes a criterion to choose either the CNN designed by Xu et al. or the combination Spatial Rich Models (SRM) and Ensemble Classifier (EC) for an input image. Our approach is studied with three steganographic spatial domain algorithms: S-UNIWARD, MiPOD, and HILL, and exhibits detection capabilities better than each method alone. As SRM+EC and the CNN are only trained with MiPOD the proposed method can be seen as an approach for blind steganalysis.

Keywords: Steganalysis · Spatial domain · CNN · SRM+EC

1 Introduction

During this past decade many steganographic algorithms have been proposed to hide a secret message inside a cover image. Such embedding schemes can operate in the spatial domain, like for example MiPOD [20], S-UNIWARD [7], HILL [15], WOW [8], HUGO [16], or STABYLO [3] but also in the frequency domain as J(PEG) counterpart of S-UNIWARD. When designing such an algorithm the objective is to provide an approach that changes the cover image as little as possible. The less the cover is modified, the less likely the stego image containing the message is to be detected and thus the more secure the steganographic scheme is. Obviously, assessing the security of steganographic tools has given rise to the dual challenge of detecting hidden information, also called steganalysis.

The wide majority of image steganalysis approaches are two-step. The first stage exhibits useful information on image content by computing a set of features and the second one uses them to train a machine learning tool to distinguish cover images from stego ones. For the first step, different Rich Models (RM) have been proposed for the spatial domain (SRM) [5] and the JPEG one [10], while

Published by Springer International Publishing AG 2017. All Rights Reserved
S. De Capitani di Vimercati and F. Martinelli (Eds.): SEC 2017, IFIP AICT 502, pp. 327–340, 2017.
DOI: 10.1007/978-3-319-58469-0_22

for the second step the most common choice is Ensemble Classifier (EC) [12]. This combination RM+EC is used in many state-of-the-art image steganalysis tools. As an illustration, in [5] stego images obtained with the steganographic algorithm HUGO have been detected with errors of 13% and 37%, respectively, for embedding payloads of 0.4 and 0.1 bpp. These errors were slightly reduced (12% and 36%) in [9] thanks to an improved rich model.

Deep learning [14,19] has led to breakthrough improvements in various challenging tasks in computer vision, becoming the state-of-the-art for many of them. A key reason for this success is the current availability of powerful computing platforms, and more particularly GPU-accelerated ones. Among the different network architectures belonging to this family of machine learning methods, Convolutional Neural Networks (CNN) [13] are very efficient to solve image classification problems. As steganalysis is a similar problem, since the objective is to classify an input image as either a cover or a stego, the design of a CNN-based steganalyzer has received increasing attention for the past few years.

From an architecture point of view, a CNN is a feedforward network composed of two parts matching exactly the two steps used in conventional steganalysis. The first part, called the convolutional part, consists of one or several layers trained to extract feature maps becoming smaller with the layer depth. The second one is composed of some fully-connected layers trained simultaneously to perform the classification task. Hence, CNN does not only learn how to classify, but also how to automatically find a set of features giving a better representation of the input image thanks to 2D convolution kernels. A feature map is usually produced by a three-step process: a combination of filtered maps of the previous layer (or the input image for the first layer), a nonlinear processing by a neuron, and finally a size reduction through pooling (see [13] for more details).

The remainder of this paper proceeds as follows. Section 2 presents related works. The next section first recalls the CNN architecture designed by Xu *et al.* [23]. After an experimental study, we focus on why it sometimes fails to detect some stego images. Section 4 is devoted to our proposal: a criterion to choose the best suited method between CNN and SRM+EC. The paper ends with a section that summarizes the contributions and outlines suggestions for future work.

2   Related Works

2.1   Steganography

To be self-sufficient, this article recalls the key ideas of the three most secure steganographic tools, namely S-UNIWARD [7], MiPOD [20], and HILL [15]. For each of these algorithms, a distortion function ρ associates to each pixel the cost of modifying it. More formally, for a given cover X, let $\rho(X)$ be the matrix whose elements represent the cost of increasing or decreasing by 1 the corresponding pixels. By ranking pixels according to their value in $\rho(X)$, one can compute the set of pixels whose modification induces the smallest detectability. For instance the distortion function ρ_U of S-UNIWARD is defined by:

$$\rho_U(X) = \sum_{k=1}^{3} \frac{1}{|X \star K^k| + \sigma} \star |K^k|^{\curvearrowleft}, \tag{1}$$

where $\star$ is a convolution mirror-padded product, $Y^{\curvearrowleft}$ is the result of a 180°rotation of Y, K^k, $1 \leq k \leq 3$ are Daubechies-8 wavelet kernels in the three directions, and σ is a stabilizing constant. It should be noticed that the multiplicative inverse is element-wise applied. An element of $\rho_U(X)$ is small if and only if there are large variations of large cover wavelet coefficients in the three directions.

In MiPOD, the distortion function ρ_M is obtained thanks to a probabilistic approach. More precisely, let β be the matrix defined as the probabilities to increase by 1 the image pixels. The objective of such a scheme is then to find probabilities which minimize a *deflection coefficient*, $\Sigma\sigma^{-4}\beta^2$, where σ is the residual variance matrix of image pixels. Notice that the product is element-wise applied and the sum concerns all the elements of the matrix. Thanks to a Wiener filter and a Lagrangian method, β can be computed. Considering such pixel probabilities, the distortion cost ρ_M is defined by:

$$\rho_M(X) = \ln\left(\frac{1}{\beta} - 2\right). \tag{2}$$

Finally, the distortion function ρ_H of the HILL steganographic scheme is based on combinations of convolution products. However, contrary to the distortion function ρ_U of S-UNIWARD, this one combines a high-pass filter H_1 and two low-pass filters L_1 and L_2. More precisely, ρ_H is defined by:

$$\rho_H(X) = \frac{1}{|X \star H_1| \star L_1} \star L_2, \text{ where } H_1 = \begin{bmatrix} -1 & 2 & -1 \\ 2 & -4 & 2 \\ -1 & 2 & -1 \end{bmatrix} \tag{3}$$

and L_1 (resp. L_2) is a 3×3 (resp. 5×5) mean matrix.

In all aforementioned schemes, the distortion function reflects the underlying image model. To summarize, ρ returns a large value in a easy-defined or smooth area, whereas in a textured "chaotic" area, *i.e.*, with no model, it returns a small value.

2.2 CNN-Based Steganalysis

The first attempt at designing a CNN-based steganalyzer for image steganalysis is due to Tan *et al.* [21]. Their proposal, a stacking of convolutional autoencoders, yielded for HUGO a detection error more than twice as bad as the one given by SRM+EC: 31% compared to 14% for a payload of 0.4 bpp.

Qian *et al.* [18] have proposed for 256×256 input images a CNN consisting of a convolutional part of 5 layers producing at the end 256 features, which are then processed by a fully-connected part of two hidden layers and a final output one of two softmax neurons. The preliminary high-pass filtering is done using a 5×5 kernel, called F_0, similar to the 5×5 kernel predictor obtained in [6]. As noticed by Fridrich and Kodovský in [6], this kernel is inspired by a specific embedding algorithm, namely HUGO, but it worked well for the other steganographic algorithms they tested. The detection performance of this CNN was still slightly lower than the state-of-the-art SRM+EC steganalyzer, but Pibre et al. [17] improved it thanks to a CNN with a different shape.

In comparison with the work of Pibre et al., the CNN we designed in [2] being shallow, was quite different and calling into question some assumptions previously made. On the one hand, we proposed a convolutional part of two layers: a first layer reduced to a single 5×5 kernel trained to replace F_0, followed by a layer using large kernels (almost as large as the image size). On the other hand, the resulting set of 256 features (for an input image of 512×512 pixels) was so discriminating that the fully-connected network doing the classification task could be shortened to the two final softmax neurons. Unfortunately, our work, as well as the one of Pibre et al., suffers from a crippling drawback: stego images were always obtained by using the same embedding key. The work by Qian et al. might suffer from the same drawback too.

More recently, the works [22,23] by Xu et al. have shown that CNN-based steganalysis remains competitive with conventional steganalysis. In [23] they first proposed a structural design of CNNs for steganalysis that is neither large, nor deep, and learns from noise residuals, since they considered as input image the one issued from high-pass filtering using the kernel F_0. The architecture of such convolutional networks, which is the basis of our work presented thereafter, will be described in detail in the next section. The experiments they completed have considered two spatial content-adaptive steganographic algorithms: S-UNIWARD and HILL. They have shown that the performance gained by an ensemble of five CNNs is comparable to the one of SRM+EC. In the following work [22], Xu et al. decided to study the merging of CNNs and ensemble classifier. The background idea is to train a second level classifier using information provided by CNNs. Furthermore, they also sligthly modified the architecture of the original CNN designed in [23]. This new CNN architecture has one more layer and changed pooling sizes in the previous ones. In addition to the ensemble method [23], called PROB, where EC will use the output of 16 CNNs instead of five, they defined two further ensemble methods. The first one, called PROB_POOL, is supposed to lower the loss of information induced by the pooling operation. Indeed, when the stride value is larger than one, some sampling operations are dropped. For a stride value $p > 1$, applying the pooling on a block of $p \times p$ pixels gives a single value, whereas for a stride of 1 the same block would have been replaced by $p \times p$ values. The idea is thus to also consider independently each remaining $p \times p - 1$ possible sampling. The second new ensemble method, called FEA, is simpler: it uses an architecture merging the convolutional part and the ensemble classifier. From the experiments done with these 6 ensemble scenarios (two possible sizes for the final vector of features and three methods), Xu et al. concluded that it might be interesting to replace the fully-connected part of the CNN by EC for image steganalysis.

Finally, we can notice the latest work [24] by Zeng *et al.* dealing with JPEG domain steganalysis. They propose to start by manually applying to the input image the first two phases of DCTR [10], namely a convolution followed by *Quantization & Truncation (Q&T)*. They use 25 residual images, where each is obtained by using a 5×5 DCT basis pattern, and three $Q\&T$ combinations. Then, for each group of residual maps for a given $Q\&T$ combination, a subnetwork corresponding to a simplified version of the convolutional part proposed by Xu *et al.* in [23] is trained to produce a feature vector of 512 components. To obtain the final prediction, the three vectors are concatenated and given as input to a three-layer fully connected network, which is trained together with the three subnets. Based on the experiments performed on more or less large databases of images issued from ImageNet, the authors claim that their proposal outperforms all other existing steganalysis approaches.

3 Convolutional Neural Networks for Image Steganalysis

3.1 The CNN Architecture Proposed by Xu *et al.* [23]

Like almost all the previous research works on CNNs for image steganalysis in the spatial domain, Xu *et al.* proposed an architecture that takes as input a high-pass filtered (HPF) version of the input image as shown in Fig. 1(a). Therefore, they used the kernel denoted by F_0 in [6, 17, 18] to highlight noise residuals. This filtering is obviously of great importance, since it provides the input information to the CNN, and thus must be suited to the classification task. The relevance of this kernel comes from its design for rich models. A classification part reduced to output neurons means that a linear classification is able to distinguish covers from stegos using the features produced by the final convolutional layer.

Starting with a HPF image of 512×512 pixels, the convolutional part results in 128 features, as shown in Fig. 1(b). Each of the four first layers successively halves the image size by generating feature maps using an average pooling, while the fifth one replaces each feature map by a single value obtained through a global average pooling. Layers 1 and 2 learn 5×5 kernels, and the remaining layers 1×1 ones, the idea being to avoid an overfitting of the CNN to image content and/or stego noise. Layer 1 has also a specific function applied onto the outcome of the convolution, namely the absolute function (ABS), supposed to ensure that the model takes care of the symmetry in noise residuals like in rich models [6]. Batch normalization (BN) [11] is performed in every convolutional layer. A mixing of *Tanh* and *ReLU* non-linear activation offered the best performance.

3.2 Detection Performance Evaluation of the CNN

To study and assess the performance of Xu *et al.* proposal, which was originally evaluated using a modified version of Caffe toolbox, the corresponding CNN has been implemented with the open source software library TensorFlow. The implementation is available on download from GitHub[1]. All the experiments are

---

[1] https://github.com/rcouturier/steganalysis_with_CNN_and_SRM.git.

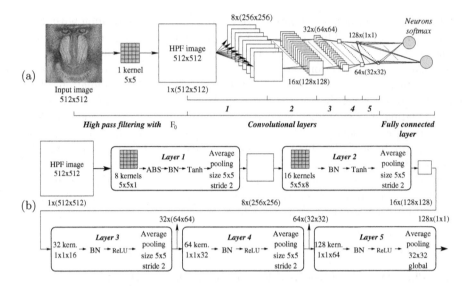

Fig. 1. CNN proposed by Xu *et al.* [23]: (a) overall architecture and (b) detailed view.

performed on a NVIDIA Tesla Titan X GPU, using as cover database the well-known BOSSBase [1]. Six stego images are associated to each cover image. They are obtained by embedding a message with S-UNIWARD, MiPOD, and HILL schemes considering two different payload values: 0.1 and 0.4 bpp. During a training execution a CNN is trained on a set of 5,000 cover-stego pairs and its detection performance assessed on a the remaining 5,000 pairs. Both training and testing sets are built by randomly picking pairs of images.

Notice that even if we implemented exactly a CNN according to the proposal, there is a major difference in comparison with the original work in the way the final prediction is obtained. In [23] Xu *et al.* generated from a training set five different non-overlapping 4,000/1,000 splits and each of them is used to train separately a CNN occurrence. The final prediction for a given test image is then obtained by averaging the five output probabilities.

Let us explain how the final prediction is computed with a set of T trained CNNs which are denoted as $\mathrm{CNN}_1, \mathrm{CNN}_2, \ldots, \mathrm{CNN}_T$. First of all, each CNN_i, $1 \le i \le T$, memorizes its L last versions provided by the L last training epochs obtained all along the program execution. These internal CNNs are denoted as $\mathrm{CNN}_i^1, \mathrm{CNN}_i^2, \ldots \mathrm{CNN}_i^L$. Each of these internal CNNs gives an answer, which is 0 if the tested image I is declared as cover and 1 otherwise. Finally, the average of all the values is computed, and a discrete answer is returned by each CNN depending on whether this average is greater or equal to 0.5 or not. This is formalized for each i, $1 \le i \le T$, by:

$$\mathrm{is\_stego}(I, \mathrm{CNN}_i) = \left\lfloor \frac{1}{L} \sum_{j=1}^{L} \mathrm{is\_stego}(I, \mathrm{CNN}_i^j) + 0.5 \right\rfloor . \tag{4}$$

The aggregation of these results must take into consideration the fact that an image I we want to classify is used in training step in some CNN_i or not. Let us consider the set $T_I = \{i | 1 \leq i \leq T$ and I is used in testing step of $CNN_i\}$ and T_I be its cardinality. The number T_I counts the number of times I is used as a testing image by some CNNs. The final answer is then the discrete answer of the average of all the CNNs that have used I as testing image. This is formalized by:

$$\text{is\_stego\_CNN}(I) = \left\lfloor \frac{1}{T_I} \sum_{i \in T_I} \text{is\_stego}(I, CNN_i) + 0.5 \right\rfloor. \tag{5}$$

Indeed, as both training and testing sets are built by randomly picking images, the number of times an image I is in a test set varies.

Due to the huge computation cost we have only trained CNNs using MiPOD dataset and tested them directly on the S-UNIWARD and HILL ones. Hence, we can assess whether a CNN is competitive in a blind steganalysis approach.

The key training parameters for reproducible experiments are discussed thereafter. First, a CNN is trained for a maximum number of training epochs $E_{\max}$ set to $1,000$ and 300, respectively, for embedding payloads of 0.1 and 0.4 bpp, without any overfitting control with a validation set. To compute the prediction given by a network CNN_i, $L = 20$ occurrences are used. Second, the network parameters are optimized by applying a mini-batch stochastic gradient descent, a typical choice in deep learning. We have used a mini-batch size of 64 samples. The gradient descent parameters are: a learning rate initialized to 0.001, but with no weight decay, and a momentum set to 0.9.

The obtained average detection errors are reported in Table 1. The first line labelled with "Caffe [23]" recalls values given in [23]. It should be noticed that "X" means that HILL has not been evaluated with the Caffe framework. The second line gives the average error rates from $T = 12$ independent training runs of the TensorFlow implementation for embedding payload of 0.4 bits per pixel. The third gives the average error rates for 200 runs with classical SRM+EC. In this latter context maxSRMd2 [4] has been used as a feature set. Finally, the last line gives the results obtained when the training stage is executed with images modified by MiPOD, whereas the testing stage is executed with images modified with another embedding scheme (SRM+EC and maxSRMd2 are still used).

From the values given in this table we can draw several conclusions. First, despite the differences highlighted previously, for a payload of 0.4 bpp the Tensor-Flow implementation produces nearly the same performance for S-UNIWARD and HILL than the original Caffe one, while for 0.1 bpp the performance is worse due to the blind context. Second, we observe that SRM+EC results in the best performances for S-UNIWARD in case of non-blind steganalysis. Third, for MiPOD the CNN approach is still competitive with SRM+EC. Fourth, the CNNs trained by only making use of the MiPOD dataset can provide a similar detection accuracy for S-UNIWARD and HILL, even if for the payload of 0.1 bpp a larger degradation of the accuracy can be noticed. Obviously, the lowest detection error is gained for the embedding scheme which has provided the training data. Fifth, CNNs outperform SRM+EC in blind steganalysis context

Table 1. Average detection error as a function of classifier (original Caffe by Xu *et al.*, our TensorFlow trained only with MiPOD at 0.4 bpp, and SRM+EC) and of payload.

	S-UNIWARD		MiPOD		HILL	
	0.1	0.4	0.1	0.4	0.1	0.4
Caffe [23]	42.67	19.76	X	X	41.56	20.76
TensorFlow	47.38	20.52	43.72	19.36	46.79	20.25
SRM+EC	39.84	18.06	41.18	21.42	42.96	23.31
SRM+EC (blind)	40.57	20.85	41.18	21.42	43.35	23.99

with a payload of 0.4 bpp, which means that CNNs allow a better generalization to different steganographic algorithms.

3.3   Characterizing the Mis-CNN-Classified Images

Let us start with some illustrative examples of images describing the typical behavior of the CNN in the case of MiPOD with payload 0.4 bpp. Figure 2 presents four case examples where for each we have the cover image and the corresponding differences between it and the stego one. From the images showing the differences we can distinguish two groups of images according to the pixels modified by the embedding process. It clearly appears that for both images shown on the upper line, 1388.pgm and 8873.pgm, MiPOD mainly modifies pixels corresponding to edges. For 1911.pgm and 3394.pgm, changes are scattered without obviously highlighting any underlying image edge. Consequently, since a CNN mainly learns to detect underlying edges, one can easily guess that the CNN-steganalyzer is able to detect both cover and stego for 1388.pgm and 8873.pgm, whereas it fails for the two other images. We are then left to provide a metric on images which reflects the difficulty to perform the CNN classification task.

Since the aforementioned steganographic schemes have their own distortion function ρ, we decided to study whether a metric can be deduced from it. Therefore, for each image I of the BossBase we have performed 200 classification procedures with SRM+EC (thanks to maxSRMd2) for the embedding algorithm MiPOD at payload 0.4 bpp. Figure 3(a) presents the resulting scatter plot of $(\overline{\rho_U}(I), \overline{e_{SRM+EC}}(I))$ pairs and the curve linking the mean error of each class, whereas the bar displays its corresponding standard deviation. This figure is obtained for S-UNIWARD, while Fig. 3(c) and (e) are the corresponding ones for HILL and MiPOD. Similarly, Fig. 3(b), (d), and (f) show the scatter plots, curve, and error bars, for the CNN. In that case, $(\overline{\rho_U}(I), \overline{e_{CNN}}(I))$, $(\overline{\rho_H}(I), \overline{e_{CNN}}(I))$, and $(\overline{\rho_M}(I), \overline{e_{CNN}}(I))$ are the average testing error obtained after training 12 independent networks. This low number explains why in comparison with the SRM+EC steganalysis context the points are less vertically spread. The scalar $\overline{\rho_U}(I)$ is the mean of all the matrices $\rho_U(X)$ presented in Eq. (1), where U means S-UNIWARD. $\overline{\rho_M}(I)$ has a similar definition for MiPOD. Finally $\overline{\rho_H}(I)$ is not directly the mean of all the matrices $\rho_H(X)$ of HILL. Due to

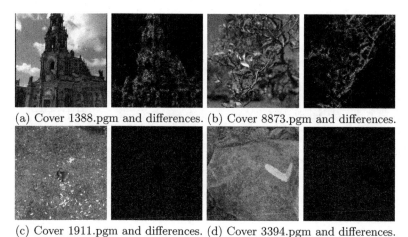

(a) Cover 1388.pgm and differences. (b) Cover 8873.pgm and differences.

(c) Cover 1911.pgm and differences. (d) Cover 3394.pgm and differences.

Fig. 2. Examples of differences images between cover and corresponding stego when embedding is performed using MiPOD with a payload of 0.4 bpp.

its definition (Eq. (3)), some extremely large values may result from an extremely small denominator and lead to a meaningless mean value. To avoid this behavior, extremely large values are excluded from the computation.

By focusing on Fig. 3(a), (c), and (e), it can be first deduced that the detection error of SRM+EC is quite independent of $\overline{p}$. Secondly, considering Fig. 3(b) and (d), we can deduce that the CNN testing error continuously decreases with respect to $\overline{\rho_U}(I)$ and with $\overline{\rho_H}(I)$. The good correlation between the prediction accuracy of the CNN for a given image I and the value of $\overline{p}(I)$ can be observed in the two former cases but not in the last one. The functions $\overline{\rho_U}$ and $\overline{\rho_H}$ are thus an indicator of the CNN accuracy. For instance, in Fig. 2, for the misclassified images we obtain $\overline{\rho_U}(1911) = 2.1$ and $\overline{\rho_U}(3394) = 3.06$; on the other hand for the well detected images we get $\overline{\rho_U}(1388) = 7.05$ and $\overline{\rho_U}(8874) = 7.39$. Thus $\overline{\rho_U}$ and $\overline{\rho_H}$ enable to cluster the images in two groups which are in accordance with those noticed at the beginning of the section.

4   Taking the Best from CNN and SRM+EC Predictions

4.1   Choosing the Best Method for a Given Input Image

We have shown that the lower the distortion function mean $\overline{\rho_U}$ of an input image is, the more difficult it will be for the CNN to correctly detect whether the image is a cover or a stego. Conversely, SRM+EC gives rather regular detection errors, without showing too much sensitivity to $\overline{\rho_U}$, being robust against the image structure. A look at Fig. 3(a) and (b) shows that we can take advantage from these different behaviors to improve the detection performance on the BossBase.

In fact, SRM+EC and the CNN can be combined due to complementary purposes. As can be seen in Fig. 4, from the largest $\overline{\rho_U}$ value up to the point

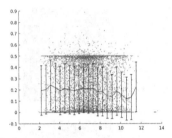

(a) Detection error w.r.t image $\overline{\rho_U}$ value for SRM+EC.

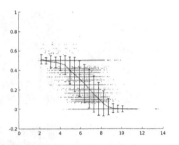

(b) Detection error w.r.t image $\overline{\rho_U}$ value for the CNN by *Xu et al.*

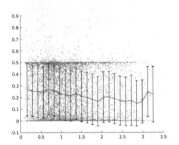

(c) Detection error w.r.t image $\overline{\rho_H}$ value for SRM+EC.

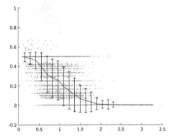

(d) Detection error w.r.t image $\overline{\rho_H}$ value for the CNN by *Xu et al.*

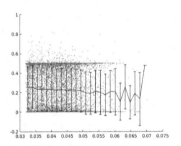

(e) Detection error w.r.t image $\overline{\rho_M}$ value for SRM+EC.

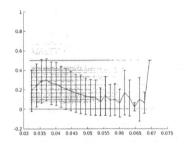

(f) Detection error w.r.t image $\overline{\rho_M}$ value for the CNN by *Xu et al.*

Fig. 3. Relation between testing errors and distortion function mean.

where both curves intersect the CNN is the most competitive, whereas after, towards the lowest $\overline{\rho_U}$ value, it is SRM+EC which is the most accurate. Formally, this can be expressed as follows for an input image I, once $\overline{\rho_U}(I)$ is computed:

$$\text{if } \overline{\rho_U}(I) < \overline{\rho_U^\cap} \text{ use SRM+EC prediction, otherwise use CNN prediction} \quad (6)$$

where $\overline{\rho_U^\cap}$ corresponds to the intersection abscissa. For Fig. 4, we have obtained $\overline{\rho_U^\cap} = 6.6$. Let us emphasize that the same approach can be applied to S-UNIWARD and HILL algorithms, leading to different values for $\overline{\rho_U^\cap}$.

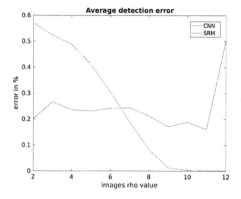

Fig. 4. Average error of CNN and SRM+EC for MiPOD 0.4 bpp w.r.t $\overline{\rho_U}$.

Overall, the feature set generated by a spatial rich model is so large and diverse that it is able to give predictions yielding almost the same level of accuracy, regardless of the pixels modified by the embedding process. Moreover, the computing of the features is precisely defined. Conversely, the CNN learns to extract a set of features to fulfill its classification task according to the data given during the training step. Therefore, it will be well-suited to process images having the same kind of embedding than the main trend in the training set. In other words, images having low $\overline{\rho_U}$ values are so underrepresented in the BossBase that they have a limited influence during the training process.

4.2 Detection Performance Evaluation of the Proposal

Table 2 presents in its last column the average detection error obtained for the three steganographic algorithms. The first column gives the performance of SRM+EC computed on images I such that $\overline{\rho_U} < \overline{\rho_U^\Omega}$, this last value is shown in the second column, while the third column shows the results gained from CNN for the remaining images. The proposal improves the detection performance for each embedding algorithm. For a payload of 0.4 bpp, S-UNIWARD has the lowest error rate with 14.82%, whereas for MiPOD and HILL we have values slightly below 17%. The lines labelled as non blind correspond to situations where SRM+EC was trained with the same algorithm than the one used to perform the embedding. Conversely, the lines denoted as blind mean that SRM+EC was trained with MiPOD and then used to detect S-UNIWARD or HILL. This also explains why for both blind and non blind situations the CNN gives the same error when both cases use the same value for $\overline{\rho_U^\Omega}$. For the lower payload of 0.1 bpp, the improvements provided by our method are also clearly visible. These results are also somewhat surprising, since they are obtained by training only CNNs using images embedding hidden messages with MiPOD. This means that even if each steganographic algorithm has its own distortion function, there is certainly a high redundancy among the modifications they made on the same cover image.

Table 2. Average detection error according to $\overline{\rho_U^\cap}$ for different embedding payloads.

Payload (bpp)	SRM+EC		$\overline{\rho_U^\cap}$		CNN		CNN+SRM+EC	
	0.1	0.4	0.1	0.4	0.1	0.4	0.1	0.4
S-UNIWARD non blind	40.08	20.01	9.2	7.1	23.36	8.25	38.06	14.82
S-UNIWARD blind	41	22.05	9.2	6.9	23.36	9.5	38.88	15.87
MiPOD non blind	42.13	23.89	8	6.6	25.84	9.26	37.82	15.65
HILL non blind	43.48	24.51	8.9	6.6	21.88	9.78	40.24	16.22
HILL blind	44.30	25.41	8.3	6.6	27.72	9.78	40.64	16.61

A closer look on the performances of each steganalyzer on the subset of images it has to classify according to $\overline{\rho_U^\cap}$ explains why our proposal is relevant. Indeed, in comparison with the performances shown in Table 1 we can remark that the SRM+EC error rate is slightly worse than on the whole dataset. Thus we take advantage from the low error rate of the CNN at a price of a slightly worse misclassification by SRM+EC. Another point to notice is the evolution in opposite directions of $\overline{\rho_U^\cap}$ and payload values, which means that, as expected, the scatterness of the modified pixels increases and thus is more difficult to detect with the current CNN architecture. Nevertheless, our approach allows us to build a competitive blind steganalyzer, which gives lower detection errors than CNN based only or SRM+EC based only approaches.

5 Conclusion and Future Work

Over the past two years the design of deep learning based approaches for image steganalysis in spatial domain, using more particularly convolutional neural networks, has received an increasing attention due to their impressive successes on many classification tasks. Recently, Xu *et al.* have introduced a CNN architecture, which, to the best of our knowledge, is the most competitive one compared to rich models with ensemble classifier. In this paper, we have investigated when this CNN architecture fails in order to propose a method improving the detection performance on the BossBase for different spatial steganography algorithms.

Thanks to a TensorFlow implementation of the CNN, giving nearly the same detection performance than the original Caffe one for S-UNIWARD and HILL, we have found a metric strongly correlated with the CNN classification performance. This metric consists in the mean of all the elements in the cost matrix provided by the distortion function ρ of the considered steganographic algorithm for the input image. We have shown that the lower this latter value $\overline{\rho_U}$ for S-UNIWARD is, the more the CNN fails to correctly detect if the image is a cover or a stego. Fortunately, the CNN and SRM+EC detection errors evolve in different ways according to the metric function. By computing the intersection of the corresponding curves we are then able to define a reliable criterion allowing to decide, for an input image, when to use the CNN or SRM+EC to obtain the most accurate prediction. The experiments done considering the steganographic algorithms S-UNIWARD, HILL, and MiPOD, have validated the proposed criterion, since it has always led to improved detection performance, regardless of the embedding payload value. Another contribution of this work is to have designed a steganalyzer insensitive to the embedding process (blind detection).

Our future work will focus on two aspects. First, it might be interesting to subdivide the BossBase in disjoint subsets according to the average distortion function value and to train several CNNs on them. However, to be able to train a CNN for low $\overline{\rho_U}$ values, the database should be expanded to include more images corresponding to this case. Second, CNNs dealing with spatial domain steganalysis work on a single high-pass filtered version of the input image. Therefore, we plan to replace the single filter by a filter bank, an approach which in the case of the JPEG domain steganalysis seems to be successful according to [24].

Acknowledgments. This article is partially funded by the Labex ACTION program (ANR-11-LABX-01-01 contract) and the Franche-Comté regional council. We would like to thank NVIDIA for hardware donation under CUDA Research Center 2014 and the Mésocentre de calcul de Franche-Comté for the use of the GPUs.

References

1. Bas, P., Filler, T., Pevný, T.: "Break our steganographic system": the ins and outs of organizing BOSS. In: Filler, T., Pevný, T., Craver, S., Ker, A. (eds.) IH 2011. LNCS, vol. 6958, pp. 59–70. Springer, Heidelberg (2011). doi:10.1007/978-3-642-24178-9_5

2. Couchot, J.F., Couturier, R., Guyeux, C., Salomon, M.: Steganalysis via a convolutional neural network using large convolution filters for embedding process with same stego key. ArXiv e-prints, May 2016

3. Couchot, J., Couturier, R., Guyeux, C.: STABYLO: steganography with adaptive, bbs, and binary embedding at low cost. Annales des Télécommun. **70**(9–10), 441–449 (2015). http://dx.doi.org/10.1007/s12243-015-0466-7

4. Denemark, T., Sedighi, V., Holub, V., Cogranne, R., Fridrich, J.J.: Selection-channel-aware rich model for steganalysis of digital images. In: 2014 IEEE International Workshop on Information Forensics and Security (WIFS 2014), Atlanta, GA, USA, 3–5 December 2014, pp. 48–53. IEEE (2014). http://dx.doi.org/10.1109/WIFS.2014.7084302

5. Fridrich, J., Kodovsk, J.: Multivariate gaussian model for designing additive distortion for steganography. In: 2013 IEEE International Conference on Acoustics, Speech and Signal Processing (ICASSP), pp. 2949–2953, May 2013

6. Fridrich, J.J., Kodovský, J.: Rich models for steganalysis of digital images. IEEE Trans. Inf. Forensics Secur. **7**(3), 868–882 (2012). http://dx.doi.org/10.1109/TIFS.2012.2190402

7. Holub, V., Fridrich, J., Denemark, T.: Universal distortion function for steganography in an arbitrary domain. EURASIP J. Inf. Secur. **2014**(1), 1 (2014). http://dx.doi.org/10.1186/1687-417X-2014-1

8. Holub, V., Fridrich, J.J.: Designing steganographic distortion using directional filters. In: WIFS, pp. 234–239. IEEE (2012)

9. Holub, V., Fridrich, J.J.: Random projections of residuals for digital image steganalysis. IEEE Trans. Inf. Forensics Secur. **8**(12), 1996–2006 (2013). http://dx.doi.org/10.1109/TIFS.2013.2286682

10. Holub, V., Fridrich, J.J.: Low-complexity features for JPEG steganalysis using undecimated DCT. IEEE Trans. Inf. Forensics Secur. **10**(2), 219–228 (2015). http://dx.doi.org/10.1109/TIFS.2014.2364918

11. Ioffe, S., Szegedy, C.: Batch normalization: accelerating deep network training by reducing internal covariate shift. arXiv preprint (2015). arXiv:1502.03167

12. Kodovský, J., Fridrich, J.J., Holub, V.: Ensemble classifiers for steganalysis of digital media. IEEE Trans. Inf. Forensics Secur. **7**(2), 432–444 (2012). http://dx.doi.org/10.1109/TIFS.2011.2175919

13. Krizhevsky, A., Sutskever, I., Hinton, G.E.: Imagenet classification with deep convolutional neural networks. In: Advances in Neural Information Processing Systems, pp. 1097–1105 (2012)

14. LeCun, Y., Bengio, Y., Hinton, G.: Deep learning. Nature **521**(7553), 436–444 (2015)

15. Li, B., Wang, M., Huang, J., Li, X.: A new cost function for spatial image steganography. In: 2014 IEEE International Conference on Image Processing (ICIP), pp. 4206–4210. IEEE (2014)

16. Pevný, T., Filler, T., Bas, P.: Using high-dimensional image models to perform highly undetectable steganography. In: Böhme, R., Fong, P.W.L., Safavi-Naini, R. (eds.) IH 2010. LNCS, vol. 6387, pp. 161–177. Springer, Heidelberg (2010). doi:10.1007/978-3-642-16435-4_13

17. Pibre, L., Jérôme, P., Ienco, D., Chaumont, M.: Deep learning is a good steganalysis tool when embedding key is reused for different images, even if there is a cover source-mismatch. In: Media Watermarking, Security, and Forensics, EI: Electronic Imaging (2016)

18. Qian, Y., Dong, J., Wang, W., Tan, T.: Deep learning for steganalysis via convolutional neural networks. In: IS&T/SPIE Electronic Imaging, pp. 94090J–94090J. International Society for Optics and Photonics (2015)

19. Schmidhuber, J.: Deep learning in neural networks: an overview. Neural Netw. **61**, 85–117 (2015)

20. Sedighi, V., Cogranne, R., Fridrich, J.: Content-adaptive steganography by minimizing statistical detectability. IEEE Trans. Inf. Forensics Secur. **11**(2), 221–234 (2016)

21. Tan, S., Li, B.: Stacked convolutional auto-encoders for steganalysis of digital images. In: 2014 Annual Summit and Conference on Asia-Pacific Signal and Information Processing Association (APSIPA), pp. 1–4. IEEE (2014)

22. Xu, G., Wu, H.Z., Shi, Y.Q.: Ensemble of CNNs for steganalysis: an empirical study. In: ACM Workshop on Information Hiding and Multimedia Security (2016)

23. Xu, G., Wu, H.Z., Shi, Y.Q.: Structural design of convolutional neural networks for steganalysis. IEEE Signal Process. Lett. **23**(5), 708–712 (2016)

24. Zeng, J., Tan, S., Li, B., Huang, J.: Large-scale JPEG steganalysis using hybrid deep-learning framework. ArXiv e-prints, November 2016

BinSign: Fingerprinting Binary Functions to Support Automated Analysis of Code Executables

Lina Nouh[✉], Ashkan Rahimian, Djedjiga Mouheb, Mourad Debbabi,
and Aiman Hanna

Concordia University, Montreal, Canada
lina.nouh@gmail.com

Abstract. Binary code fingerprinting is a challenging problem that requires an in-depth analysis of binary components for deriving identifiable signatures. Fingerprints are useful in automating reverse engineering tasks including clone detection, library identification, authorship attribution, cyber forensics, patch analysis, malware clustering, binary auditing, etc. In this paper, we present BINSIGN, a binary function fingerprinting framework. The main objective of BINSIGN is providing an accurate and scalable solution to binary code fingerprinting by computing and matching structural and syntactic code profiles for disassemblies. We describe our methodology and evaluate its performance in several use cases, including function reuse, malware analysis, and indexing scalability. Additionally, we emphasize the scalability aspect of BINSIGN. We perform experiments on a database of 6 million functions. The indexing process requires an average time of 0.0072 s per function. We find that BINSIGN achieves higher accuracy compared to existing tools.

Keywords: Code fingerprinting · Static analysis · Reverse engineering

1 Introduction

1.1 Reverse Engineering and Function Fingerprinting

Fingerprinting binary functions can be of paramount importance in reverse engineering. Function fingerprinting has many applications including compiler identification [3], authorship analysis, clone detection, vulnerability detection, provenance analysis, malware detection, malware classification [2], etc. One benefit of function fingerprinting is tagging a suspicious binary as malicious or benign. The number and complexity of malware attacks have been growing significantly. In 2015, around 431 million new malware variants were uncovered [6]. Contrary to conventional signature-based detection, heuristic-based techniques are more effective and robust in detection and classification of new variants [35].

S. De Capitani di Vimercati and F. Martinelli (Eds.): SEC 2017, IFIP AICT 502, pp. 341–355, 2017.
DOI: 10.1007/978-3-319-58469-0_23

1.2   Approach

An effective fingerprinting approach produces a unique and compact representation of the functionality of a binary function. Functions that perform similar functionalities should be assigned similar fingerprints. It must also be robust to minor byte-level discrepancies and differences in the structure of the Control-Flow-Graph (CFG). The probability of a fingerprint collision must be negligible. In this paper, we present BINSIGN, a fingerprinting framework for binary functions, which consists of two main components: (1) Scalable fingerprint generation and indexing of a large dataset, (2) Fingerprint matching. Our fingerprint generation approach relies on a set of features that are extracted from assembly functions combined with structural information from partial CFG traces.

To avoid pairwise comparison of a large volume of fingerprints, we use three mechanisms to facilitate achieving a scalable matching process. First, we leverage Locality-Sensitive Hashing (LSH) [34] and min-hashing [11] for selecting candidates. Second, we apply a filter based on the number of basic blocks of the CFG. Finally, BINSIGN system is distributed on multiple machines using Rabbit MQ [32] in order to further improve the performance and scalability. In addition, BINSIGN utilizes the Jaccard similarity to compute similarity scores between the target function and each candidate. To improve accuracy, features are ranked according to their significance while calculating the similarity score.

1.3   Contributions

Our contributions can be summarized as follows:

- We propose a fingerprinting approach for binary functions using features that capture syntactic, semantic and structural information of a function.
- We design and implement an efficient and scalable matching framework to match a target function fingerprint against a large repository of fingerprints.
- We evaluate BINSIGN in several use cases, including function reuse, malware analysis, obfuscation resilience, and function indexing scalability.

1.4   Paper Organization

This paper is structured as follows. Section 2 presents the underlying algorithmics of the components of our fingerprinting methodology, including the details of the fingerprint generation and matching algorithms. Experimental results are discussed in Sect. 3. Section 4 reviews the state-of-the-art approaches. Concluding remarks are ultimately presented in Sect. 5.

2   BINSIGN Methodology

BINSIGN utilizes meaningful features for function fingerprinting, which comprises of two main steps: fingerprint generation and fingerprint matching.

2.1   Threat Model

We design BINSIGN to help in the reverse engineering process. It is designed to be resilient to changes in the code such as those introduced by different compilers. The fingerprints are designed to be resilient to light obfuscation including register replacement, register reassignment, dead-code insertion, code substitution, name stripping, and removal of symbolic information. BINSIGN is not intended to replace the reverse engineering process, but merely to support it. Unpacking and de-obfuscation lie outside the scope of our threat model.

2.2   Feature Extraction

It is important to select the right features that characterize the semantics of programs. The semantics of code operations can be captured by analyzing mnemonic groups and operand types even if the symbols are stripped. Each function's fingerprint includes a feature vector $v_{f_i} \in V$ in the form of key/value pairs (k_i, v_i).

Features are extracted at two levels: global and tracelet features. Features that describe each basic block (such as the constants in that block) are combined into tracelet features. The structure of the CFG is captured in the function's fingerprint through the tracelet features (Table 1). The global features occur once per function and describe the function as a whole, such as the return type and function size (Table 2). The symbols "#" and "*" denote "number of" and

Table 1. Tracelet features

Data Constants	Constants, Strings, #Constants, #Strings
Functionality Tags	#API Tags, #Library Tags, #Mnemonic Groups
Tracelet Info.	#Instructions, #Operands, Code Refs., #Code Refs., Function Calls, #Function Calls, Imported Functions, #Imported Functions

Table 2. Global features

Data Constants	#Constants, #Strings
Prototypes	Return Type, Arguments, #Arguments, *Arguments
Functionality Tags	#API Tags, #Library Tags, #Mnemonic Groups
Function Info.	*Function, *Local Variables, Function Flags, Tracelets, #Tracelets, #Instructions, #Code Refs., #Out Calls, #Basic Blocks

"size of", respectively. Some features are common to both tracelet features and global features. We take into consideration the following groups of information.

Characterization of Function Prototype: Each prototype carries valuable information, such as the return type, the number and types of arguments.

Composition of CFG Instructions: These features capture the number of basic blocks and types of instructions in each block. The mnemonics and operands are extracted and normalized. The normalized mnemonics list contains a generalized representation of the instructions, with operands numbered according to their types. General registers are replaced with 1, memory references are coded as 2, etc. After that, a simple frequency analysis is performed: the number of occurrences of each instruction, and the total number of calls to registers and memory addresses are determined. Then, the instruction mnemonics are classified into 15 groups based on the type of operation. Next, the total number of instructions and the number of instructions per group are computed.

Types of Local, System, and API Calls: Functions can be categorized according to the execution outcome on a system. System calls are interaction points with the operating system and provide valuable information on the runtime behavior. These calls are used to assign functionality tags. A functionality tag is an annotation assigned to code fragments that provides a high-level description of the context and side effects. Tags are useful for fast identification of specific groups of operations. As described in [33], a function is assigned multiple tags if it encloses several system calls. Moreover, combinations of functionality tags can describe the overall functionality of the code regions and highlight the sequence of actions carried out for performing them (e.g., CRY+FIL+NET is translated to crypto-operations on a file, followed by network communication).

2.3 Fingerprint Generation

The fingerprint generation process is depicted in Fig. 1. The approach consists of: (1) Disassembling and CFG extraction, (2) tracelet generation and feature extraction, and (3) feature hashing. In the following, we detail these steps.

Disassembling and CFG Extraction: Given a binary file, the first step is to disassemble it using the industry-standard disassembler *IDA Pro* [8]. In order to capture the structural information of a function, we take into consideration its CFG because it captures syntactic elements (assembly instructions) and relationships (jumps/calls) between blocks.

Tracelet Generation: One of the objectives of BinSign is to generate fingerprints that capture not only the syntactic information of a function, but also its structure. The intent is to capture all execution traces of a function. However, extracting all paths from a CFG is computationally expensive, especially for large functions. Moreover, it would be redundant to consider the common nodes between different paths multiple times. To counter this issue, we adopt

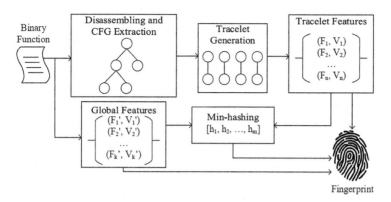

Fig. 1. Fingerprint generation

the idea presented in [17], by decomposing function CFGs into partial traces of execution, namely tracelets. In BINSIGN, tracelets are comprised of two basic blocks. This means that each edge in the CFG results in one tracelet. Considering a larger number of basic blocks per tracelet results in redundant information without offering additional benefits. This solution allows us to generate execution traces more efficiently and without losing in functionality since all CFG nodes and edges are visited. After disassembling the function, extracting its CFG, and generating tracelets, the features described in Sect. 2.2 are extracted.

Signature Hashing: We apply *min-hashing* [11] in order to produce a compact representation of the signature. In essence, min-hashing is a technique that reduces the dimensionality of a set using a number of hash functions. Min-hashing is applied to the normalized instructions. The function's normalized instructions constitute a suitable representation of the functionality and can be used effectively in the fingerprint matching process. Each instruction is normalized by replacing the operands with a number that represents the operand's type. Then, every normalized instruction is hashed using all hash functions and the minimum hash value is selected. The collection of the minimum hash values represents the signature hash. Multiple random numbers (seeds) are used in order to generate many different hash functions. The seeds are generated randomly beforehand, and remain constant every time a new fingerprint is generated.

2.4   Fingerprint Matching

Through the matching process (Fig. 2), a candidate set is selected. After that, the similarity between each candidate and the target is computed.

Fingerprint Candidate Selection: Two filters are implemented. First, the functions are filtered by the number of basic blocks. Second, LSH [34] is used. The idea is to divide the hash values of the min-hash signature into bands.

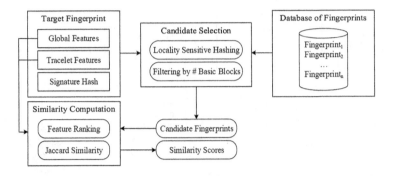

Fig. 2. Fingerprint matching

Each band consists of multiple hash values. A fingerprint from the dataset is considered as a candidate if all hash values match in at least one band. The values of each band in the target min-hash signature is used to create a query to obtain candidates from the database. The results of all the queries are combined into the candidate set. Through multiple experiments, we find that a band size of *seven* hash values and a total of *thirty* bands constitute a suitable signature. Since LSH approximates the Jaccard similarity, this choice of band size and number of bands sets the similarity threshold to about 60%. According to [34] an approximation of the threshold is calculated as $(\frac{1}{b})^{\frac{1}{r}}$, where b represents the number of bands and r the size of band. To further reduce false positives, we also filter the fingerprints based on the number of basic blocks. It is unlikely for a function with a small number of basic blocks to match a function with a significantly larger number of blocks. Through experiments, we find that a threshold of 30% for the difference in the number of basic blocks is appropriate.

Fingerprint Similarity Computation: A similarity score between the target fingerprint and each fingerprint in the candidate set is calculated using the Jaccard similarity. More precisely, the Jaccard similarity between the global features is calculated then combined with the Jaccard similarity between the tracelet features. Each feature in the fingerprint has a different effect on the similarity score, as some features are more significant than others. Therefore, each feature that influences the similarity score has a different weight. The weights are assigned using the gain ratio attribute evaluation algorithm provided by Weka [10] for ranking the features. Weka is a tool that offers implementations of several machine learning algorithms. This is performed through a supervised machine learning process where the names of the functions are known.

3   Experimental Results

We perform several experiments to evaluate BINSIGN in terms of accuracy, performance, and scalability. We also compare the accuracy with existing tools.

3.1 Dataset Description

To evaluate the scalability, we include fingerprints of 6 million functions generated from well-known libraries, malware samples, and system dynamic library files from Microsoft Windows. Additionally, we focus our matching experiments on slightly more than 23,000 functions of our dataset for a more precise evaluation of the accuracy. These functions are from different versions of the libraries: libpng, sqlite, and zlib. These files are compiled using Visual Studio (MSVC) 2010 and 2013. Zeus and Citadel malware samples are also included in the dataset. In our experiments, function names are not used during the matching process, but only for verification. If the candidate with the highest similarity score does not have the same name as the target function, we examine both functions manually. Manual examination is only performed for verification to calculate the accuracy, but it is not required by BinSign.

3.2 Comparison with Existing Tools

This experiment compares the accuracy of BinSign against Diaphora [7] and PatchDiff2 [9]. The tools Diaphora and PatchDiff2 are both IDA Pro plugins that can be used for comparing binary files. Diaphora offers different options when matching binary functions. We deactivate the option of using unreliable methods. We also activate the option of ignoring the function names.

We use the libraries libpng, sqlite, and zlib compiled using two compilers. We then compare the two binary files of each library resulting from the compilation using MSVC 2010 and MSVC 2013. By using two different compilers, we introduce some noise into the binary functions so that there are some differences introduced by the compilers. We attempt to match the functions in the file compiled by MSVC 2010 as the target set against the functions in the file compiled by MSVC 2013. We match each function in the target set using BinSign by finding the function in the candidate set with the highest similarity score.

Table 3. Function matching comparison between tools

Tool name	Library	#Target functions	#Correct matches	Accuracy
Diaphora	libpng	620	408	65.81%
	sqlite	1489	657	44.12%
	zlib	156	79	50.64%
PatchDiff2	libpng	620	510	82.26%
	sqlite	1489	937	62.92%
	zlib	156	122	78.21%
BinSign	libpng	620	553	89.19%
	sqlite	1489	1391	93.42%
	zlib	156	134	85.90%

Table 3 displays the results of the comparison. The accuracy is calculated by finding the percentage of the correctly matched functions to the total number of functions in the binary file. BinSign consistently achieves the highest accuracy between the tools being compared. This is due to the fuzziness of the method BinSign is using to perform the matching. This allows BinSign to be more lenient when dealing with the modifications presented by different compilers. The difference in accuracy is due to the types of features considered by these tools and that they require an exact match for some of the features.

3.3 Function Reuse Detection

We attempt to detect reused functions between versions 1.2.5, 1.2.6, 1.2.7, and 1.2.8 of the `zlib` library, as well as between the libraries `zlib` and `libpng`.

Each version is used to match the corresponding functions in its consecutive version. We also attempt to match reused functions from zlib library in libpng. After manual inspection, we identify 52 reused functions. The function is considered to be matched correctly if the corresponding function in the other version of the library is ranked first with the highest similarity score.

Table 4. Function reuse detection results

Library versions	#Functions	Threshold	Accuracy	#Candidates	Time
`zlib1.2.5-zlib1.2.6`	169	60%	89.47%	24970	3.9 s
		65%	78.11%	11372	2.8 s
`zlib1.2.6-zlib1.2.7`	183	60%	94.67%	30881	3.7 s
		65%	90.71%	14947	2.5 s
`zlib1.2.7-zlib1.2.8`	178	60%	98.79%	26965	4.5 s
		65%	88.76%	12003	3.7 s
`zlib1.2.8-libpng1.6.17`	52	60%	100%	4474	4.7 s
		65%	100%	2147	4.4 s

The results are shown in Table 4. The LSH similarity threshold is set once to 60% and once to 65%. The number of candidates presented in Table 4 is the sum of the size of the candidate sets for all target functions. Figure 3 plots the number of target functions against the total number of candidates. Increasing the number of functions increases the total number of candidates. There are other factors that affect the total number of candidates such as the size of the target functions. Smaller functions contain fewer distinctive features. As a result, they tend to have a larger candidate set. Therefore, the total number of candidates does not only depend on the number of target functions, but also on their characteristics and size. Figure 4 shows how the number of basic blocks of the functions affects the matching time. Most of the time is spent on computing the similarity scores.

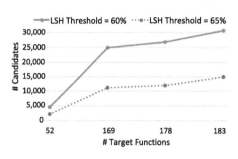

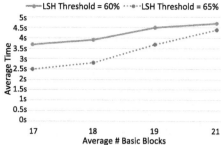

Fig. 3. Number of Target Functions vs. number of Candidates

Fig. 4. Number of Basic Blocks vs. Matching Time

Therefore, the number of candidates and the size of the functions are important factors that affect the matching time.

The difference in accuracy when the LSH threshold is set to 60% against 65% is more significant in the first and third rows of Table 4. This is due to more functions with LSH similarity scores lying between 60% and 65% in these cases. When we compare the second and third rows of the table, we see that the third row has a better accuracy score when the threshold is set to 60%. However, this is not the case when it is set to 65%. This is because the comparison displayed in the third row includes more functions with similarity scores between 60% and 65%, which are filtered out when the threshold is increased.

3.4 Scalability Evaluation

We index 6 million fingerprints and measure the time it takes. On average, the indexing process requires around 0.0072 s per function. This includes the time for fingerprint generation and database communication.

Fingerprint Methodology Scalability: Using min-hashing and LSH, we enhance the scalability by selecting a candidate set through the banding technique. To speed up the process, only candidates that are selected through our filters are considered instead of brute force matching.

Implementation Scalability: We implement a distribution mechanism (Fig. 5) using RabbitMQ [32]. It is an open source messaging software based on the international standard Advanced Message Queuing Protocol (AMQP) [5]. Thanks to its simplicity, we find that it is more suitable to our purposes than other distribution frameworks that require a lot of processing for data analysis and synchronization with the server, leading to a lot of overhead, and thus slowing the process. To index several files, the binaries are distributed to different workers. The distribution is done depending on the power of each worker machine. Each worker runs multiple instances of IDA Pro simultaneously to process the files, generate the fingerprints, and store them in the database. Note that RxPY (reactive extension) is used to run the code in an asynchronous manner. The

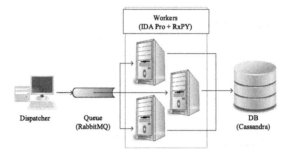

Fig. 5. Architecture of the distribution process

distribution is performed on a server machine with an Intel Xeon CPU E5-2630 v3 @2.40 GHz (2 processors) and 128 GB of RAM running Microsoft Windows Server 2008 64-bit, along with a PC with an Intel Core i7 CPU 920 @2.67 GHz and 12 GB of RAM running Microsoft Windows 7 64-bit.

3.5   Resilience to Different Compiler Optimization Levels

We use MSVC 2013 to compile version 1.2.8 of zlib with four optimization levels. MSVC 2013 offers the optimization levels: disabled optimization (Od), minimize size (O1), maximize speed (O2), or full optimization (Ox). We compile the zlib library with full optimization (Ox) and use the resulting binary functions as the target to match functions compiled using other optimization levels.

The results are presented in Table 5. The lowest accuracy score of 65.05% occurs when matching the fully optimized (Ox) functions against disabled optimization (Od). Compiling with optimization level O1 produces more similar functions to the fully optimized functions, which results in 87.85% accuracy. We find that compiling with the optimization levels Ox and O2 seem to produce identical assembly code in this case. Therefore, comparing the code compiled with O2 against O1 would produce similar results to Ox against O1.

After taking a closer look, we find that the size of the target functions has an effect on the accuracy. The accuracy of matching functions with different

Table 5. Results of matching different optimization levels

Optimization levels	Overall accuracy	Average time
Ox vs. Od	65.05%	4.2 s
Ox vs. O1	87.85%	4.3 s
Ox vs. O2	100.00%	0.26 s

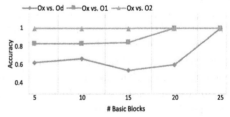

Fig. 6. Number of Basic Blocks vs. Accuracy

number of basic blocks is displayed in Fig. 6. The functions with higher number of basic blocks are matched with higher accuracy. This is due to the fact that larger functions tend to contain more distinctive features. Small functions usually have features and structures that are fairly common. Therefore, there is a higher probability of mismatching smaller functions than larger ones.

When comparing the optimization levels Ox and Od, we notice a dip in the graph, which might seem counter-intuitive. This is because smaller functions (with 5 to 10 basic blocks) may have less room for optimization. However, larger functions (with 10 to 20 basic blocks) contain higher possibilities for optimization. Functions that are even larger (with around 25 basic blocks) tend to have more distinctive features, which increases the accuracy of the matching process.

3.6 Malware Similarity Analysis

Since the functions in Citadel are derived from the functions in Zeus [30], we match one of these functions, namely the RC4 function. Citadel reuses the RC4 stream cipher function from Zeus with minor modifications [33]. IDA Pro identifies 642 functions in Zeus and 896 functions in Citadel. We then generate fingerprints for all the functions and attempt to match the RC4 function. The time it takes to match the RC4 function is 0.463 s.

We find that the top match was in fact the modified RC4 function with a similarity score of 0.68787. The other matches with lower similarity scores are from different library files. The CFG of RC4 functions in Zeus and Citadel can be seen in Fig. 7a and b respectively. Although the number of basic blocks in the two CFG's is different, the RC4 function is still identified because the difference in the number of basic blocks is less than 30%.

Since many of the functions in Citadel are derived from the functions in Zeus, we attempt to match all the functions in Zeus. BinSign matches 591 out of 642 functions in Zeus to functions in Citadel. Out of the matched functions, 517 functions are matched with a high similarity score above 90% (Table 6).

3.7 Obfuscation Resilience

Although heavy obfuscation is out of the scope of our threat model, we provide some insight into its effects. We use the Obfuscator-LLVM [25] for this purpose.

Table 6. Candidates of RC4 function from Citadel

Function	Similarity score
sub_42E92D	0.68787
sub_10034D0A	0.40042
png_set_sCAL	0.35377

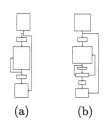

(a)   (b)

Fig. 7. CFG of RC4 function in (a) Zeus and (b) Citadel

It offers three obfuscation techniques: control flow flattening, instruction substitution, and bogus control flow. After applying the three obfuscation techniques to a piece of code in C++, we add the three different obfuscated functions to the dataset. The function that results from instruction substitution is identified as a match with a high similarity score of 0.84399, which shows resilience to this type of obfuscation. However, the obfuscated functions resulting from control flow flattening and bogus control flow are not identified. The number of basic blocks increased by more than 30%. Therefore, the fingerprints are filtered out by our filter that considers the number of basic blocks.

4   Related Work

This section reviews research on binary fingerprinting and related domains.

4.1   Exact and Inexact Fingerprint Matching

Several studies focus on fingerprinting library functions in binary files (e.g., [12, 22, 23]). Some approaches use exact matching and apply byte-level sequence patterns. *IDA Pro* is an industry-standard disassembler that is widely used by reverse engineers [23, 28]. It provides a built-in capability for recognizing standard library functions and hex code sequences that are generated by common C-family compilers through *IDA F.L.I.R.T* [22]. Although *F.L.I.R.T* is a useful mechanism, it has limitations. Library functions with small byte-level discrepancies are not recognized. The inability to perform inexact matching is a major limitation. Other studies examine flexible signature matching techniques alongside graph-based analysis to measure the similarity between programs [12, 13, 18, 23]. Such approaches show higher recall in comparison to exact matching.

4.2   Graph-Based Binary Fingerprinting

The BINDIFF algorithm [18] inspired some works that use graph matching for various purposes (e.g., [4, 13–15, 21, 23, 27, 28]). One limiting factor is placing the attention on structural similarity, ignoring the instruction semantics of each basic block. Instruction hash comparison is a simple, fast technique to fingerprint functions and assembly instructions [24]. A hash value can represent the semantics of basic blocks. The work in [29] terms such values as semantic juice.

4.3   Source and Binary Clone Detection

Research on source code clone detection investigates four types of clones [16, 26]. Type I clones are exact clones. Type II clones preserve the syntactic structure with changes in identifiers, layout, comments, and types. Type III clones have altered fragments. Type IV clones are semantic clones. Applying source code clone detection techniques to disassemblies is challenging due to limited source-level information. The research on binary clone detection measures the similarity between binary files [1,12,15,19,20,31]. The approach presented in [15] measures the provenance similarity of binaries using symbolic execution. Morphological analysis and static code synchronization is another solution for binary clone detection [12]. These approaches are good candidates for detecting types III and IV clones. The dynamic analysis techniques that monitor input/output behavior of functions result in lower false positive rates in detection of type IV clones [24].

5   Conclusion

In this paper, we defined the main components of function fingerprinting, described the algorithms, and the processes of fingerprint generation and matching. The methodology was evaluated in terms of function matching, malware analysis, obfuscation resilience, and scalability. We showed that the methodology is effective and can improve the accuracy of exact and inexact fingerprint matching. BINSIGN outperformed existing tools and achieved a higher accuracy score. We also described different measures undertaken to ensure BINSIGN's scalability. BINSIGN performed efficient fingerprint generation of 6 million functions such that the indexing process required 0.0072 s per function on average.

Acknowledgments. This work is supported by a research grant under the Department of National Defence/Natural Sciences and Engineering Research Council of Canada (NSERC) in collaboration with Google. In addition, the authors acknowledge the contribution of Nhat Nguyen in assisting with the implementation of the distribution mechanism and the web interface.

References

1. Huang, H., Youssef, A., Debbabi, M.: BinSequence: Fast, Accurate and Scalable Binary Code Reuse Detection. Accepted for publication in the ACM Asia Conference on Computer and Communications Security (ASIACCS). ACM Press (2017)
2. Alrabaee, S., Shirani, P., Debbabi, M., Lingyu, W.: On the feasibility of malware authorship attribution. In: International Symposium on Foundations and Practice of Security, pp. 256–272. Springer, Cham (2016)
3. Rahimian, A., Shirani, P., Alrabaee, S., Lingyu, W., Debbabi, M.: BinComp: a stratified approach to compiler provenance attribution. Digital Invest. **14**, S146–S155 (2015)
4. Alrabaee, S., Shirani, P., Lingyu, W., Debbabi, M.: Sigma: a semantic integrated graph matching approach for identifying reused functions in binary code. Digital Invest. **12**, S61–S71 (2015)
5. Advanced Message Queuing Protocol (AMQP). https://www.amqp.org/
6. Internet Security Threat Report 2016. https://www.symantec.com/content/dam/symantec/docs/reports/istr-21-2016-en.pdf
7. Diaphora: A Program Diffing Plugin for IDA Pro. https://github.com/joxeankoret/diaphora
8. Hex-Rays IDA Pro. https://www.hex-rays.com/products/ida/
9. Diffng Plugin for IDA. https://code.google.com/p/patchdiff2/
10. Weka: Machine Learning Software. https://weka.wikispaces.com/

11. Andoni, A., Indyk, P.: Near-optimal hashing algorithms for approximate nearest neighbor in high dimensions. Commun. ACM. **51**, 117–122 (2008)
12. Bonfante, G., Marion, J., Sabatier, F., Thierry, A.: Code synchronization by morphological analysis. Malicious Unwanted Softw. **7**, 112–119 (2012)
13. Bourquin, M., King, A., Robbins, E.: Binslayer: accurate comparison of binary executables. In: Proceedings of the 2nd ACM SIGPLAN Program Protection and Reverse Engineering Workshop, vol. 13, pp. 4:1–4:10 (2013)
14. Cesare, S., Xiang, Y., Zhou, W.: Control flow-based malware variant detection. IEEE Trans. Dependable Secure Comput. **11**, 307–317 (2014)
15. Chaki, S., Cohen, C., Gurfinkel, A.: Supervised learning for provenance-similarity of binaries. In: Proceedings of the 17th ACM SIGKDD International Conference on Knowledge Discovery and Data Mining, KDD 2011, pp. 15–23 (2011)
16. Cordy, J.R., Roy, C.K.: Efficient Checking for Open Source Code Clones in Software Systems. In: 19th IEEE ICPC, pp. 217–218 (2011)
17. David, Y., Yahav, E.: Tracelet-based code search in executables. In: Proceedings of the 35th ACM SIGPLAN Conference on Programming Language Design and Implementation, PLDI 2014, pp. 349–360 (2014)
18. Dullien, T., Rolles, R.: Graph-based comparison of executable objects (English Version). SSTIC **5**, 1–3 (2005)
19. Elva, R., Leavens, G.: Semantic clone detection using method IOE-behavior. In: 6th International Workshop on Software Clones (IWSC), pp. 80–81 (2012)
20. Farhadi, M.R., Fung, B.C.M., Charland, P., Debbabi, M.: Binclone: detecting code clones in malware. In: International Conference on Software Security and Reliability, vol. 8, pp. 78–87 (2014)
21. Gascon, H., Yamaguchi, F., Arp, D., Rieck, K.: Structural detection of android malware using embedded call graphs. In: Proceedings of the ACM Workshop on Artificial Intelligence and Security, AISec 2013, pp. 45–54 (2013)
22. Hex-Rays. Fast Library Identification and Recognition Technology: In-Depth. https://www.hex-rays.com/products/ida/tech/flirt/in_depth.shtml
23. Jacobson, E.R., Rosenblum, N., Miller, B.P.: Labeling library functions in stripped binaries. In: Proceedings of the 10th ACM SIGPLAN-SIGSOFT Workshop on Program Analysis for Software Tools, PASTE 2011, pp. 1–8 (2011)
24. Jin, W., Chaki, S., Cohen, C., Gurfinkel, A., Havrilla, J., Hines, C., Narasimhan, P.: Binary function clustering using semantic hashes. In: 11th International Conference on Machine Learning and Applications (ICMLA), vol. 1, pp. 386–391 (2012)
25. Junod, P., Rinaldini, J., Wehrli, J., Michielin, J.: Obfuscator-LLVM: software protection for the masses. In: Wyseur, B. (ed.) Proceedings of the IEEE/ACM 1st International Workshop on Software Protection, SPRO 2015, vol. 3–9 (2015)
26. Keivanloo, I., Rilling, J., Charland, P.: Internet-scale real-time code clone search via multi-level indexing. In: 18th Working Conference on Reverse Engineering (WCRE), pp. 23–27 (2011)
27. Khoo, W.M., Mycroft, A., Anderson, R.: Rendezvous: a search engine for binary code. In: Proceedings of the 10th Working Conference on Mining Software Repositories, MSR 2013, pp. 329–338 (2013)
28. Kinable, J., Kostakis, O.: Malware classification based on call graph clustering. J. Comput. Virol. **7**, 233–245 (2011)
29. Lakhotia, A., Preda, M.D., Giacobazzi, R.: Fast location of similar code fragments using semantic 'Juice'. In: Proceedings of the 2nd ACM SIGPLAN Program Protection and Reverse Engineering Workshop, PPREW 2013, pp. 5:1–5:6 (2013)
30. Milletary, J.: Citadel Trojan Malware Analysis. Technical report, Dell SecureWorks Counter Threat Unit Intelligence Services (2012)

31. Ng, B.H., Prakash, A.: Expose: discovering potential binary code re-use. In: COMP-SAC, IEEE 37th Annual, pp. 492–501 (2013)
32. Pivotal Software. RabbitMQ Web Site. https://www.rabbitmq.com/
33. Rahimian, A., Ziarati, R., Preda, S., Debbabi, M.: On the reverse engineering of the citadel botnet. In: Danger, J.-L., Debbabi, M., Marion, J.-Y., Garcia-Alfaro, J., Zincir Heywood, N. (eds.) FPS -2013. LNCS, vol. 8352, pp. 408–425. Springer, Cham (2014). doi:10.1007/978-3-319-05302-8_25
34. Rajaraman, A., Ullman, J.D.: Mining of Massive Datasets. Cambridge University Press, New York (2014)
35. Ye, Y., Wang, D., Li, T., Jiang, Q.: An intelligent pe-malware detection system based on association mining. J. Comput. Virol. **4**, 323–334 (2008)

Decoy Password Vaults:
At Least as Hard as Steganography?

Cecilia Pasquini[1,2]($\boxtimes$), Pascal Schöttle[1,2], and Rainer Böhme[1,2]

[1] Department of Computer Science, Universität Innsbruck, Innsbruck, Austria
Cecilia.Pasquini@uibk.ac.at
[2] Department of Information Systems, University of Münster, Münster, Germany

Abstract. Cracking-resistant password vaults have been recently proposed with the goal of thwarting offline attacks. This requires the generation of synthetic password vaults that are statistically indistinguishable from real ones. In this work, we establish a conceptual link between this problem and steganography, where the stego objects must be undetectable among cover objects. We compare the two frameworks and highlight parallels and differences. Moreover, we transfer results obtained in the steganography literature into the context of decoy generation. Our results include the infeasibility of perfectly secure decoy vaults and the conjecture that secure decoy vaults are at least as hard to construct as secure steganography.

1 Introduction

User-chosen passwords are still the most common authentication standard in online services and users likely cumulate a high number of passwords for different domains. To alleviate the memory effort and possibly let users choose stronger passwords, IT security professionals recommend the use of password vaults (also called "password managers"), which store a user's set of passwords in a container generally encrypted using a single master password.

This encrypted container, stored together with domains and usernames in plaintext, allows users to access websites by just remembering a single password. Furthermore, it can be stored on several (potentially) insecure devices and be backed up in the cloud. Thus, an attacker might get hold of such a container [13, 16] and mount an offline attack against the master password. In comparison to online attacks, which are likely blocked by websites detecting multiple failed login attempts, the effectiveness of an offline attack is only limited by the attacker's computational power. Brute-force attacks are likely successful, as it was shown that human-chosen master passwords have limited entropy and are relatively easy to guess [3, 7].

Although current password-based encryption (PBE) schemes (e.g., PKCS#5 [12]) adopt countermeasures (like the use of a key-derivation function to increase the encryption key entropy, salting to prevent rainbow attacks, or iterative hashing to slow down brute-force attacks), none of these methods can prevent a successful offline attack, as an attacker will always be able to recognize the correctly

S. De Capitani di Vimercati and F. Martinelli (Eds.): SEC 2017, IFIP AICT 502, pp. 356–370, 2017.
DOI: 10.1007/978-3-319-58469-0_24

decrypted result. In fact, all wrong master password candidates will provide a response that clearly does not resemble user-chosen passwords.

To circumvent this problem, so-called *cracking-resistant password vaults* (CRPVs) have been proposed [2,5,10]. The purpose of all CRPVs is to provide an attacker with *honey* or *decoy* vaults even if she decrypts the vault under a wrong master password. These decoy vaults have to be (statistically) indistinguishable from the real vault, so that the real vault is *undetectable* among decoys and the attacker is forced to mount additional online login attempts to identify it.

Another area in information security that shares the protection goal of undetectability is steganography [9]. A *steganographer* wants to communicate a secret message over a communication channel monitored by a *warden* (the attacker in that scenario). The steganographer covertly communicates by modifying a so-called *cover object* (e.g., a digital image) and obtaining a *stego object* that is sent to the intended recipient, and she wants stego objects to be undetectable among cover objects by the warden.

We can summarize the contributions of our paper as follows:

1. we point out the parallels of CRPVs and steganography (Sect. 2);
2. we present a unified model of password vaults and CRPVs (Sect. 3);
3. we transfer established results and security definitions from steganography to the domain of CRPVs, show that perfect security for CRPVs is infeasible and propose the notion of ε-security instead (Sect. 4);
4. we highlight the differences between CRPVs and steganography, conjecturing that secure CRPVs are *at least as hard* to construct as secure steganography (Sec. 5).

Finally, we give an overview of the results obtained and future directions in Sect. 6.

2 Merging Two Streams of Related Work

The already highlighted protection goal of object undetectability represents a clear parallel between CRPVs and steganography, and both communities have made strikingly similar advances.

To overcome security weaknesses of the first CRPV system proposed in [2], the authors of [5] propose the NoCrack system, where decryption under *any* master password yields a plausible decoy vault. The instant creation of decoy vaults is achieved by applying the mechanism of Honey Encryption and Decryption [11]. Despite the name, this approach does not change the encryption/decryption itself, but rather adds another encoding/decoding layer. In particular, a so-called *distribution transformation encoder* (DTE) encodes a plaintext into a bit string and decodes bit strings to plaintexts. The DTE is designed in such a way that random bit strings are decoded to plaintexts following a target statistical distribution, which is hard-coded into the DTE [11]. For instance, an application proposed in [11] is a DTE that mimics the distribution of RSA secret primes and outputs synthetic primes when decoding a uniform bit string. As we will describe in Sect. 3.2, a specific DTE is used in the NoCrack system to generate decoy vaults when a wrong master password is used to decrypt the container. A similar approach in steganography has been proposed in 1992, where so-called *mimic functions* [17] are used. Here, Huffman encoding is employed to create text that is statistically indistinguishable from human written text while embedding the secret message. The technique was then extended to arithmetic encoding in model-based steganography [15], where parts of the cover object are replaced by other parts that follow an estimated distribution, similarly to DTEs.

To demonstrate the security of NoCrack, the authors of [5] show that a machine-learning based ranking attack cannot detect the real vault among decoys. A further improvement to the NoCrack system is proposed in the most recent work on CRPVs [10], where the target distribution of the DTE is empirically mixed with the one of the real vault (thus decreasing the statistical difference between real and decoy vaults), and it is also tested against machine-learning classifiers. A relevant similarity to steganography exists, where machine-learning based attacks are used and the results obtained by this are employed to influence "design principles leading to more secure steganography" [8, p. 69].

The NoCrack system [5] with the extension proposed in [10] currently represents the state-of-the-art for CRPVs. In fact, [10] first shows a weakness of the NoCrack system, arguing that the correct vault can be statistically distinguished from the decoys. To achieve this, they use the *Kullback-Leibler divergence* (KLD) between real and decoy vault distribution, which was proposed as an information-theoretical security measure in steganography in 1998 [4].

Due to the high dimensionality of cover and stego objects, steganographers often design their embedding strategies according to *projections* of the whole objects, which are typically simplified models with lower dimensionality [15]. On her side, the warden can employ a different projection that enables her to detect stego objects [9]. This triggered a cat-and-mouse race towards the best projection. In the same way, the DTE in CRPVs reproduces the distribution of a specific projection and the authors of [10] identify the security weaknesses of NoCrack by adopting a different one.

Summarizing, the shared protection goal of undetectability has also led to the use of similar approaches and tools, although, to the best of our knowledge, this link has not been established in the literature yet. This further motivates us to exploit known results in steganography for CRPVs regarding security issues.

3   Password Vault Model

In this section, we formalize a unified model for CRPV systems. In Sect. 3.1 we first introduce a general definition for vault objects and identify potential influencing factors. Then, we describe the main components of a CRPV in Sect. 3.2, focusing on the Honey Encryption and Decryption scheme used.

3.1 Defining Password Vaults

Password vaults essentially contain credential data. We can formalize credentials as triples (d,u,pw), where d is the domain, u is the username employed and pw is the secret password chosen by the user. Then, a vault $\mathbf{v}$ is a tuple of N credential triples that can be arranged as

$$\mathbf{v} = (d_1, \ldots, d_N, u_1, \ldots, u_N, pw_1, \ldots, pw_N). \tag{1}$$

In practice, $d_1, \ldots, d_N$ and $u_1, \ldots, u_N$ are plaintext while the vector

$$\mathbf{x} \doteq [pw_1, \ldots, pw_N] \tag{2}$$

containing the passwords is encrypted to a ciphertext C under a master password mpw (also user-chosen). We explicitly consider the case where domains and usernames are not encrypted, as in [5,10], and thus the object to be modeled is given by the vector $\mathbf{x}$. Then, with a slight abuse of notation, in the rest of the paper we will use the term "vault" to indicate only $\mathbf{x}$ instead of the entire tuple $\mathbf{v}$. We can see $\mathbf{x}$ as a realization of a random vector $\mathbf{X}$ with sample space χ^L (χ is the alphabet of symbols used and L is the sum of the N password lengths) and joint probability distribution $\mathcal{P}_{real}$.

The first part of $\mathbf{v}$, composed by domains and usernames, can have influence on $\mathbf{x}$. It is known that different websites usually adopt specific policies forcing the user to follow certain constraints in choosing the password [2], for instance by requiring a minimum number of symbols, a minimum number of digits and special characters, or the use of both upper- and lower-case letters. Moreover, usernames are often also human-chosen and correlation between the choice of username and password could exist. Thus, the distribution $\mathcal{P}_{real}$ should be conditioned on the knowledge of domains and usernames, although existing approaches do not always exploit this information. For instance, one of the attacks in [10] specifically uses nonconformity to password policies to successfully detect the real vault among the decoys produced by NoCrack [5].

Even if we discard the dependency on domains and usernames, estimating $\mathcal{P}_{real}$ is a challenging task, since the statistical behaviour of human-chosen passwords in a vault is highly complex and hard to model. In fact, the partition of $\mathbf{x}$ into independent components (for instance, modeling single password distribution and assuming independence among domains) is highly questionable, as passwords of the same user are typically strongly correlated [2].

Thus, we deal with a joint distribution of L symbols which is hardly observable. However, existing approaches [5,10] employ a projection $\mathrm{Proj}(\mathbf{x})$ of the entire vector $\mathbf{x}$ and estimate the distribution $\mathcal{P}_{\mathrm{Proj}(\mathbf{X})}$ from available datasets, which is then used to generate synthetic vaults.

3.2 Mimicking Vault Distribution

CRPVs extend conventional PBE schemes, where a successful or unsuccessful decryption is perfectly recognized, by introducing the use of decoy vaults. We

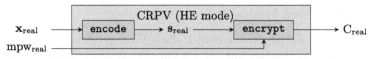

(a) Honey Encryption of the user-chosen password vault.

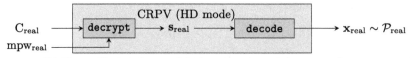

(b) Honey Decryption under the correct master password.

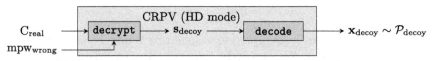

(c) Honey Decryption under a wrong master password.

Fig. 1. Honey Encryption and Decryption mechanisms in CRPVs.

now describe how the state-of-the-art CRPV (NoCrack [5]) works and specify which changes are proposed in [10].

NoCrack is a CRPV system that consists of a specific Honey Encryption and Decryption scheme. As introduced in Sect. 2, the peculiarity of such a mechanism is the use of a DTE, which is a pair of functions (encode, decode) with the following properties:

- the input of encode is a password vault x and the output is a binary string s. Conversely, decode takes as input any bit string s and outputs a vault x. It is required that a DTE is *correct*, that is, decode(encode(x)) = x.
- If applied to uniformly distributed bit strings, decode should output vaults whose projections follow a known distribution $\mathcal{P}_{\mathrm{Proj}(X)}$.

The authors of [5] devise strategies based on different projections and assumptions, e.g., considering ℓ-*gram* and *Probabilistic Context Free Grammar (PCFG)* models, but the details of DTE design are out of the scope of this section.

The resulting system works as depicted in Fig. 1. For the sake of clarity, we represent the Honey Encryption (HE) and Honey Decryption (HD) modes of the CRPV separately, and for the latter we further distinguish the case of HD with the correct and wrong master password. As mentioned in Sect. 2, Fig. 1 shows that the DTE (encode, decode) is used in combination with a pair of functions (encrypt, decrypt), which are based on standard techniques and will not be discussed in detail (we refer the reader to [5] for a thorough description).

When the user chooses the password vault x_{real} and the master password mpw_{real}, the HE mode is activated (see Fig. 1(a)). The vault x_{real} is processed by the encode function to obtain the string s_{real}, which is then encrypted under mpw_{real} into a ciphertext C_{real} by means of encrypt.[1]

In order to get access to x_{real}, the user has to decrypt the ciphertext C_{real} by submitting to the system the master password mpw_{real}, thus activating the HD mode. If C_{real} is decrypted under the correct master password mpw_{real}, the user gets as output the real vault x_{real} as shown in Fig. 1(b).

If an attacker trial-decrypts C_{real} under a wrong master password, decrypt outputs a random bit string s_{decoy}. This string is then given to decode that transforms it into a decoy password vault x_{decoy}, which is delivered to the attacker (see Fig. 1(c)). From her side, the attacker receives a set of password vaults (as many as the number of trial-decryptions), which includes x_{real} if and only if mpw_{real} has been used for trial-decrypting.

Regardless of the quality of the algorithm decode (i.e., how accurately it transforms random strings into vaults following $\mathcal{P}_{Proj(X)}$), the use of a DTE will result in a joint distribution $\mathcal{P}_{decoy}$ of the decoded vaults that is an approximation of $\mathcal{P}_{real}$. They should be as similar as possible, but the quality of $\mathcal{P}_{decoy}$ as approximation of $\mathcal{P}_{real}$ depends on the projection chosen and the database used for the training. In fact, in the attack in [10] the authors identify the correct vault among all the decoys by exploiting a different projection $\mathcal{P}_{Proj(X)}$ enabling a better distinction. Their improvement then consists exactly in designing the DTE by taking into accounts some statistical properties of the real vault.

4 Security of CRPV Systems

In this section we discuss the security of CRPV systems. First, we compare and translate the definition of perfect security from steganography to the domain of CRPVs in Sect. 4.1, arguing that this is fundamentally related to the knowledge of the distribution $\mathcal{P}_{real}$. Then, in Sect. 4.2 we analyze the computational bounds encountered in studying $\mathcal{P}_{real}$, giving insights on the practical difficulties in estimating this distribution. Finally, we extend the definition of ε-security to the domain of CRPVs in Sect. 4.3.

4.1 Perfect Security

In steganography, the goal of the steganographer is to transform cover objects $x^{(0)}$ to stego objects $x^{(1)}$ containing the secret message, in such a way that the resulting distribution of stego objects $\mathcal{P}_{stego}$ is close to the distribution of cover objects $\mathcal{P}_{cover}$. The setup of an attack against a general steganographic system is depicted in Fig. 2(a): depending on the position of the switch (red), cover or stego objects appear on the communication channel. The warden does not control the switch but monitors the channel and applies detect to every object $x^{(i)}$ that she observes. The output of detect is either 0 indicating that the object

---

[1] In case of password addition or updating, x_{real} is modified and encoded to a new string s_{real}, which is then encrypted under mpw_{real} to obtain a new ciphertext.

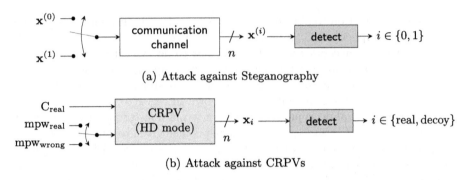

(a) Attack against Steganography

(b) Attack against CRPVs

Fig. 2. Comparison of attacks against steganography and CRPVs (Color figure online)

is assumed to be a cover object or 1 if the warden classifies it as stego. The warden wants to identify a secret communication, so her goal is to detect the stego objects among covers.

Attacks against CRPVs can be translated to a very similar setup, as depicted in Fig. 2(b). Here, the attacker has an encrypted password vault C_{real} and chooses a set of n master passwords for trial-decryption that might contain the real master password mpw_{real} but will be mostly composed of wrong passwords mpw_{wrong}. Again, the switch (red) indicating whether the chosen password was real or wrong is not under the control of the attacker, although she can decide which and how many master passwords to submit. By this, she ends up with n different password vaults x_i and she also applies detect to every object x_i she observes. The output of detect is either real, indicating that x_i was generated by inputting mpw_{real} or decoy, if a mpw_{wrong} was chosen. The goal of the attacker is to detect the real vault among the decoys.

Figure 2 opens the way for a formal relationship between $\mathcal{P}_{cover}$ and $\mathcal{P}_{stego}$ from steganography and $\mathcal{P}_{real}$ and $\mathcal{P}_{decoy}$ in CRPVs. Intuitively, we can view the distribution of real vaults $\mathcal{P}_{real}$ as the counterpart of the cover distribution $\mathcal{P}_{cover}$, as both are given by nature and cannot be influenced by either the attacker nor the defender. Both, the distribution of the decoy vaults $\mathcal{P}_{decoy}$ and the stego distribution $\mathcal{P}_{stego}$ somehow depend on $\mathcal{P}_{real}$ and $\mathcal{P}_{cover}$, respectively.

Based on this analogy, we can recall the definition of perfectly secure steganographic system given in [4] and extend it to CRPVs. According to [4], perfect security in steganography is achieved if and only if the Kullback-Leibler divergence (KLD) between $\mathcal{P}_{cover}$ and $\mathcal{P}_{stego}$ is zero, i.e.:

$$\mathrm{KLD}(\mathcal{P}_{cover}||\mathcal{P}_{stego}) = 0. \tag{3}$$

Accordingly, perfect security in CRPV systems is achieved iff:

$$\mathrm{KLD}(\mathcal{P}_{real}||\mathcal{P}_{decoy}) = 0. \tag{4}$$

In light of that, the action of the detect function in the CRPV domain can be formulated in an hypothesis testing framework, where the null and alternative hypotheses are given by:

H_0: the observed object follows $\mathcal{P}_{\text{real}}$ (i.e., it is a real vault)

H_1: the observed object follows $\mathcal{P}_{\text{decoy}}$ (i.e., it is a decoy vault) (5)

The identification of the real vault is achieved by repeatedly performing the hypothesis test on the n vaults by means of detect. Having zero KLD between two distributions essentially means that they are exactly the same distribution. Thus, with perfect security, the hypotheses in (5) are undecidable.

A fundamental question is whether perfect security in the sense of (4) is possible at all and under which assumptions. In steganography, it is commonly agreed upon by now that this is only possible for so-called *artificial cover sources*, i.e., sources for which the joint distribution $\mathcal{P}_{\text{cover}}$ is fully known, including any conditional dependencies. However, artificial sources do rarely exist in practice. In contrast to that, we deal with *empirical cover sources*, whose distribution is obtained outside the steganographic system from a finite set of observations.

The difference between artificial and empirical cover sources has been proposed in [1], where it is observed that perfect security defined as in (4) generally exists for artificial sources but is impossible for empirical sources. This is related to the fact that in the latter case $\mathcal{P}_{\text{cover}}$ is arguably *incognisable*, and statistical representations by means of proper projections of the sample space will never achieve a zero KLD.

As mentioned in Sect. 3.2, existing datasets with a finite number of vaults are used to train the DTEs, which then replicate specific statistical properties observed (for instance, ℓ-gram statistics or PCFG statistics). In the next section, we show how hard it is to provide a full characterization of $\mathcal{P}_{\text{real}}$, arguing that $\mathcal{P}_{\text{real}}$ belongs to the class of empirical distributions and is indeed incognisable.

4.2 Computational Bounds for the Estimation of $\mathcal{P}_{\text{real}}$

As we introduced in Sect. 3, in order to fully represent real vaults $\mathbf{x}$, we should consider them as vectors of L symbols regardless of the actual partitioning in different passwords. Thus, each $\mathbf{x}$ is the realization of a L-dimensional discrete random vector $\mathbf{X} = [X_1, \ldots, X_L]$ and the corresponding distribution function $\mathcal{P}_{\text{real}}$ is a joint distribution of L random variables with sample space χ.

Then, $\mathcal{P}_{\text{real}}$ can be expressed by means of the chain rule as follows:

$$\mathcal{P}_{\text{real}}(\mathbf{x}) = \prod_{\ell=1}^{L} P_{X_\ell | \mathbf{X}_{1:\ell-1} = \mathbf{x}_{1:\ell-1}}(x_\ell), \tag{6}$$

where $\mathbf{X}_{i:j}$ is the random vector composed of the random variables (r.v.) in $\mathbf{X}$ from index i to index j and $\mathbf{x}_{i:j}$ is its realization, $P_{X|\mathbf{Y}=\mathbf{y}}(\cdot)$ is the conditional probability mass function (cpmf) of a r.v. X given the realization $\mathbf{y}$ of a random vector $\mathbf{Y}$ and we define $P_{X_1 | \mathbf{X}_{1:0}}(x_1) \doteq P_{X_1}(x_1)$.

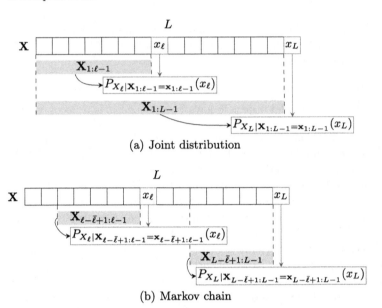

(a) Joint distribution

(b) Markov chain

Fig. 3. Representation of the joint and Markov chain distributions.

Let us now suppose to estimate $\mathcal{P}_{\text{real}}$ starting from an available dataset of password vaults, i.e., to approximate each cpmf by means of relative frequencies. In the following, we perform a simple feasibility analysis where we compute the minimum numerosity of the dataset that is necessary to estimate the cpmfs. In doing that, we first consider the joint distribution $\mathcal{P}_{\text{real}}$ in (a) and then the case of a specific projection (Markov models) in (b) and (c):

(a) **Joint distribution.** We want to have an approximation of every cpmf in (6). Thus, we need $P_{X_\ell|\mathbf{X}_{1:\ell-1}=\mathbf{x}_{1:\ell-1}}(\cdot)$ for each possible realization $\mathbf{x}_{1:\ell-1}$ of $\mathbf{X}_{1:\ell-1}$, and this holds for $\ell = 1,\dots,L$. A pictorial representation is reported in Fig. 3(a). For each ℓ a number of $|\chi|^{\ell-1}$ cpmfs are then involved. Thus, even assuming that each cpmf is estimated by one single observation (i.e., the support of each cpmf will consist in a single character) the number of necessary vaults is given by $|\chi|^{\ell-1}$. If $\gamma = \log_{10}(|\chi|)$, it is then $\mathcal{O}(10^{\gamma(\ell-1)})$. Let us consider an optimistic setup where a vault contains 10 passwords with average length of 5 characters [2,7], so that we can reasonably fix $L = 50$. Moreover, let us assume an alphabet corresponding to the printable ASCII characters, thus $|\chi| = 95$ and $\gamma \approx 1.97$. The number of vaults required for the estimation of every $P_{X_{50}|\mathbf{X}_{1:49}=\mathbf{x}_{1:49}}(\cdot)$ with one observation would have a decimal order of magnitude at least equal to $\gamma(50-1) = 96.5$. The number of protons in the universe is estimated by the Eddington number and it is assumed to have on order of magnitude equal to 79. It is worth pointing out that password policies could reduce this number as not the whole alphabet should be used. However, even supposing a restrictive policy where only digits are allowed, this would still result in 10^{49} necessary vaults.

(b) **Markov chain of order $\bar{\ell}-1$.** In [5] and [10], DTEs based on $\bar{\ell}$-gram models are trained on an external corpus. As an example, they consider $\bar{\ell} = 4$ and estimate the cpmf $P_{X_4|\mathbf{X}_{1:3}=[\text{H},\text{e},\text{l}]}(\text{l})$ as the number of occurrences of the substring "Hell" divided by the number of occurrences of the substring "Hel" in the corpus. Then, by repeating this for each 3-grams, they estimate a cpmf for each of them and use it to design the DTE.[2]

This is equivalent to considering Markov chains of order $\bar{\ell} - 1$, that is, it is assumed that the probability of a character in a certain position depends only on the previous $\bar{\ell}-1$ characters in the vault. As represented in Fig. 3(b), expression (6) is then approximated as

$$\mathcal{P}_{\text{real}}(\mathbf{x}) \approx P_{X_1}(x_1) \cdot \ \dots \ \cdot P_{X_{\bar{\ell}-1}|\mathbf{X}_{1:\bar{\ell}-2}=\mathbf{x}_{1:\bar{\ell}-2}}(x_{\bar{\ell}-1})$$
$$\cdot \prod_{\ell=\bar{\ell}}^{L} P_{X_\ell|\mathbf{X}_{\ell-\bar{\ell}+1:\ell-1}=\mathbf{x}_{\ell-\bar{\ell}+1:\ell-1}}(x_\ell). \tag{7}$$

Again, to obtain each cpmf in expression (7) we would need to observe at least once each possible realization of each $\mathbf{X}_{i:j}$ such that $j - i = \bar{\ell} - 1$, and we can again consider a lowerbound of the minimum number of necessary vaults to be $\mathcal{O}(10^{\gamma(\bar{\ell}-1)})$. We report in Table 1 the exponent $\gamma(\bar{\ell} - 1)$ as a function of $\bar{\ell}$ in the same setup as before ($|\chi| = 95$).

A proper length of the Markov chain is hard to determine and the choice relies on heuristic considerations. However, as we optimistically assumed an average password length equal to 5 symbols, in order to capture the dependencies between different passwords in the vault we should at least consider a Markov chain of order 5 ($\bar{\ell} = 6$), so that the probability of the 6-th symbol (likely the first character of the second password) depends also on the realization of the first one. From Table 1, we have that a dataset of at least 7.7 billion ($\approx 10^{9.89}$) vaults would be necessary for this purpose. As of December 2016, the world population was estimated at 7.5 billion, thus implying that the dataset should contain at least one vault for every human being on earth.

(c) **Markov model of order $\bar{\ell}-1$ with relaxed assumptions.** We can assume that, for a fixed $\bar{\ell}$, only a fraction p of the cpmfs is actually relevant and the remaining ones can be considered as uniform or estimated via smoothing techniques, as suggested in [5] when building the Markov-based DTE. Then, we can assume that a number of observations $T > 1$ is required for each cpmf in order to have a more accurate approximation. By doing so, the number of vaults is lower bounded by $p \cdot |\chi|^{\bar{\ell}-1} \cdot T$, thus it is $\mathcal{O}(10^{\delta+\gamma(\bar{\ell}-1)})$ where $\delta = \log_{10}(pT)$. The order of magnitude $\delta + \gamma(\bar{\ell} - 1)$ is tabulated in Table 2 for different values of p and T and $\bar{\ell}$ fixed to 6. The values show that even considering as relevant the 0.1% of the realizations of $\mathbf{X}_{1:5}$ and accepting a single

---

[2] It is to be noted that the authors estimate the cmpfs from datasets of single passwords instead of entire vaults.

Table 1. Order of magnitude of the minimum number of vaults necessary to the estimation of all the cpmf's when considering a Markov chain of order $\bar{\ell} - 1$.

$\bar{\ell}$	2	3	4	5	6	7	8	9	10
$\gamma(\bar{\ell} - 1)$	1.97	3.96	5.93	7.91	9.89	11.89	13.84	15.82	17.80

Table 2. Lowerbound of the minimum number of vaults for the estimation of all the cpmfs when considering a Markov chain of order 5.

p/T	1	5	10	20
0.001	6.85	7.55	7.85	8.15
0.2	9.15	9.85	10.15	10.45
0.4	9.45	10.15	10.45	10.75
0.6	9.63	10.33	10.63	10.93
0.8	9.75	10.45	10.75	10.05

observation of each related cpmf ($T = 1$) would require a number of vaults that almost equals the population of Austria (around 8.5 million).

In this framework, we should consider that, while the popular RockYou dataset contains more than 32 million passwords in total, the only database of vaults available at the moment (PBvault, see [5]) consists of 276 vaults only. Coupled with the analysis above, which already relies on simplifying assumption like the independence of password from domains and usernames, this strongly motivates our concern on the observability of the full distribution $\mathcal{P}_{\text{real}}$, or even an approximated version of it. So, we can safely say that $\mathcal{P}_{\text{real}}$ is incognisable.

4.3 ε-security

According to our observations in the last subsection, the equality in (4) expressing perfect security is hardly achievable in practice, thus suggesting to consider a non-zero statistical distance between $\mathcal{P}_{\text{real}}$ and $\mathcal{P}_{\text{decoy}}$. In [4], the definition of ε-*security* is introduced, where a system is called ε-secure if

$$\text{KLD}(\mathcal{P}_{\text{real}}||\mathcal{P}_{\text{decoy}}) \leq \varepsilon. \tag{8}$$

If we recall the hypothesis testing framework in (5), we can encounter two different kind of errors:

Type I error: classifying the real vault as a decoy.

Type II error: classifying a decoy vault as the real one.

Denoting with α and β the probabilities of Type I and Type II errors, respectively, inequality (8) is relevant to derive bounds for α and β. With this respect, the Type I error is more relevant than the Type II error for an attacker, since once the real vault is discarded there is no other possibility to successfully obtain the correct passwords. If we accept non-zero KLD, and thus, that α and β cannot be minimized at the same time, we can reasonably think that an attacker would try to achieve $\alpha = 0$ to the detriment of β. It can be shown [4,14] that, if (8) holds and $\alpha = 0$, the Type II error probability is subject to the lower bound.

$$\beta \geq 2^{-\varepsilon}. \tag{9}$$

Inequality (9) provides an interesting link to the required number of online login attempts. In fact, in performing brute force attacks, the attacker will be provided with a set of n vaults, supposedly including the real one. If she enforces $\alpha = 0$ (i.e., the real vault is not misclassified), the number ϕ of plausible candidate vaults identified by detect will be approximately at least:

$$\phi = 1 + (n - 1)2^{-\varepsilon}. \tag{10}$$

Assuming no further refinements of the candidate selection, $\phi/2$ represents the expected number of online login attempts the attacker is forced to execute. This also addresses an issue that was not explicitly discussed in [10], i.e., the relationship between the ability of detecting the real vault and the total number of decoy vaults. In fact, the authors of [10] consider $n = 1000$ (including the real vault), while an attacker will have to deal with a dramatically higher value of n (equal to the number of trial decryptions) and the performance of the ranking operation in this case is not studied.

5 Differences Between Steganography and CRPVs

Previous sections concentrated on the similarities of steganography and CRPVs, neglecting obvious differences. In this section, we highlight the main differences and point out their influence on the security of both systems.

(i) **Message embedding.** The most obvious difference between steganography and CRPVs is that in steganography we want to embed a message, which has no direct counterpart in CRPVs. But, in accordance with steganography literature, message embedding can be either seen as a randomization of encode or naturally implemented in an adapted version of the DTE. The message encoding problem in steganography is mainly solved, due to the existence of asymptotically perfect codes [6]. So, this difference will not affect the security comparison.

(ii) **Attacker's influence.** Another evident difference is the role of the attacker: in steganography, the warden passively monitors the communication channel and has little influence on the total number n of objects she observes or the relative amount of cover or stego objects. In contrast to that, an attacker against a CRPV can choose (up to her computational bound) how often she samples $\mathcal{P}_{\text{decoy}}$ and, thus, might refine her model of $\mathcal{P}_{\text{decoy}}$ as accurately as her computational power allows. Even with knowledge of the steganographic algorithm, this is not possible for a warden. Furthermore, with CRPVs the attacker knows that there is at most one real vault. This additional knowledge of an attacker against CRPVs, most likely will have a negative influence on the achievable security of CRPVs.

(iii) **Guessing strategy.** Another degree of freedom that is available to an attacker against CRPVs but not to a steganographic warden is the guessing strategy for the master passwords. If we assume that master passwords are human-chosen, every strategic attacker will choose master passwords in decreasing order of probability, following some model about the *prior* distribution of master passwords $\mathcal{P}_{\mathrm{mpw}}$. For the same arguments explored in Sect. 4.2, $\mathcal{P}_{\mathrm{mpw}}$ is incognisable. But, the lower dimensionality with respect to $\mathcal{P}_{\mathrm{real}}$ and the higher number of (single) passwords available, e. g., Rock-You, would allow for a more accurate estimate of the joint distribution.

(iv) **Oracle queries.** Finally, the possibility of confirming or disproving a vault candidate identified by detect with an online login is probably the highest advantage an attacker against a CRPV has over a warden in steganography. Each online login acts like an oracle query, and the number is only limited by the number of passwords in the vault and the maximum number of wrong login attempts allowed by the different websites. The attacker against a CRPV not only exactly knows when she has the real vault, even negative oracle responses can be used to further refine her estimate of $\mathcal{P}_{\mathrm{decoy}}$ and thus possibly further decreasing β. A warden can only dream of such an oracle in steganography.

Summarizing the above, we conjecture that secure CRPVs are *at least as hard* to construct as secure steganography. Although far away from a formal proof, the existing differences between steganography and CRPVs suggest that the advantage in knowledge an attacker against any CRPV possesses over a warden in steganography will make security of CRPVs ever harder to achieve.

Ultimately, achievable security depends on the evolution of the real distributions. If a cover channel consisting of noise is plausible, then secure steganography reduces to cryptography with the protection goal of indistinguishability of ciphertexts from random sequences. If the users of password vaults choose truly random passwords, constructing secure CRPVs reduces to the generation of random looking sequences. But then, we do not need CRPVs anymore.

6   Conclusion

In this paper we have shown that the parallels between CRPVs and steganography go deeper than the protection goal of undetectability: both fields experienced a similar development, starting from encoding schemes and ending with the employment of machine learning to influence the design of more secure schemes. While research on CRPVs only started in 2010, the field of digital steganography can look back on more than 25 years of scientific research, thus allowing us to transfer known results to the domain of CRPVs. We believe that leveraging established results in steganography will increase the awareness of researchers when designing new approaches to CRPVs.

Specifically, we argued that the joint distribution of real vaults $\mathcal{P}_{real}$ is incognisable, due to the data requirements for its full estimation. Even for an approximated version, a dataset containing one password vault for every human being currently living on earth would be needed. The incognisability of $\mathcal{P}_{real}$ implies that achieving perfect security in CRPVs is *as hard* as constructing perfectly secure steganographic systems in case of empirical sources, thus infeasible in practice. We follow up by arguing that we should rather consider ε-security instead of perfect security. Again, we can leverage established results in steganography and show that we can lower bound the expected amount of online login attempts an attacker is forced to execute when attacking an ε-secure CRPV.

Finally, we conjecture that security in CRPVs is *at least as hard* to achieve as security in steganography due to the differences in both domains' setup. An attacker against a CRPV has several advantages when mounting an attack over a warden in steganography: she can choose the number of trial-decryptions, thus getting a very accurate estimate of the distribution of decoy vaults; she can apply an advanced guessing strategy against the master password, following recent research on how humans choose passwords; and, last but not least, every online login attempt acts as an oracle query, giving the attacker a certain response on whether the vault she faces is the real one or a decoy.

Future work should include formal proofs regarding the effects of the attacker's knowledge on the security of CRPV systems. Moreover, we believe that the conceptual link between steganography and CRPVs is based on the employment of Honey Encryption. Thus, our observations could be extended to other applications of Honey Encryption in practical systems.

Acknowledgments. This research was funded by Deutsche Forschungsgemeinschaft (DFG) under grant "Informationstheoretische Schranken digitaler Bildforensik" and by Archimedes Privatstiftung, Innsbruck, Austria.

References

1. Böhme, R.: An epistemological approach to steganography. In: Katzenbeisser, S., Sadeghi, A.-R. (eds.) IH 2009. LNCS, vol. 5806, pp. 15–30. Springer, Heidelberg (2009). doi:10.1007/978-3-642-04431-1_2

2. Bojinov, H., Bursztein, E., Boyen, X., Boneh, D.: Kamouflage: loss-resistant password management. In: Gritzalis, D., Preneel, B., Theoharidou, M. (eds.) ESORICS 2010. LNCS, vol. 6345, pp. 286–302. Springer, Heidelberg (2010). doi:10.1007/978-3-642-15497-3_18

3. Bonneau, J.: Guessing human-chosen secrets. Ph.D. thesis, University of Cambridge, May 2012

4. Cachin, C.: An information-theoretic model for steganography. In: Aucsmith, D. (ed.) IH 1998. LNCS, vol. 1525, pp. 306–318. Springer, Heidelberg (1998). doi:10.1007/3-540-49380-8_21

5. Chatterjee, R., Bonneau, J., Juels, A., Ristenpart, T.: Cracking-resistant password vaults using natural language encoders. In: IEEE Security and Privacy, pp. 481–498 (2016)
6. Filler, T., Judas, J., Fridrich, J.: Minimizing additive distortion in steganography using syndrome-trellis codes. IEEE Trans. Inf. Forensics Secur. **6**(3), 920–935 (2011)
7. Florencio, D., Herley, C.: A large-scale study of web password habits. In: ACM International Conference on World Wide Web, pp. 656–666 (2007)
8. Fridrich, J.: Feature-based steganalysis for JPEG images and its implications for future design of steganographic schemes. In: Fridrich, J. (ed.) IH 2004. LNCS, vol. 3200, pp. 67–81. Springer, Heidelberg (2004). doi:10.1007/978-3-540-30114-1_6
9. Fridrich, J.: Steganography in Digital Media: Principles, Algorithms, and Applications. Cambridge University Press, New York (2009)
10. Golla, M., Beuscher, B., Dürmuth, M.: On the security of cracking-resistant password vaults. In: ACM Conference on Computer and Communications Security, pp. 1230–1241 (2016)
11. Juels, A., Ristenpart, T.: Honey encryption: beyond the brute-force barriers. In: Advances in Cryptology - EUROCRYPT, pp. 293–310 (2014)
12. Kaliski, B.: PKCS# 5: Password-based cryptography specification version 2.0. RFC 2289 (2000)
13. Li, Z., He, W., Akhawe, D., Song, D.: The emperor's new password manager: security analysis of web-based password managers. In: USENIX Security Symposium, pp. 465–479 (2014)
14. Maurer, U.M.: A unified and generalized treatment of authentication theory. In: Puech, C., Reischuk, R. (eds.) STACS 1996. LNCS, vol. 1046, pp. 387–398. Springer, Heidelberg (1996). doi:10.1007/3-540-60922-9_32
15. Sallee, P.: Model-based steganography. In: Kalker, T., Cox, I., Ro, Y.M. (eds.) IWDW 2003. LNCS, vol. 2939, pp. 154–167. Springer, Heidelberg (2004). doi:10.1007/978-3-540-24624-4_12
16. Silver, D., Jana, S., Boneh, D., Chen, E.: Password managers: attacks and defenses. In: USENIX Security Symposium, pp. 449–464 (2014)
17. Wayner, P.: Mimic functions. Cryptologia **16**(3), 193–214 (1992)

Election-Dependent Security Evaluation of Internet Voting Schemes

Stephan Neumann[1($\boxtimes$)], Manuel Noll[2], and Melanie Volkamer[1,3]

[1] Technische Universität Darmstadt, Darmstadt, Germany
{stephan.neumann,melanie.volkamer}@secuso.org
[2] Université de Liège, Liège, Belgium
mnoll@student.ulg.ac.be
[3] Karlstad University, Karlstad, Sweden

Abstract. The variety of Internet voting schemes proposed in the literature build their security upon a number of trust assumptions. The criticality of these assumptions depends on the target election setting, particularly the adversary expected within that setting. Given the potential complexity of the assumptions, identifying the most appropriate Internet voting schemes for a specific election setting poses a significant burden to election officials. We address this shortcoming by the construction of an election-dependent security evaluation framework for Internet voting schemes. On the basis of two specification languages, the core of the framework essentially evaluates election-independent security models with regard to expected adversaries and returns satisfaction degrees for security requirements. These satisfaction degrees serve election officials as basis for their decision-making. The framework is evaluated against requirements stemming from measure theory.

1   Introduction

Significant research efforts have been made to establish security requirements for Internet voting schemes [8,9,14,15]. Amongst the most prevalent requirements, there are vote secrecy (also referred to as vote privacy [6,21]), *i.e.* an adversary must not be able to establish the link between the voter and her cast vote, vote integrity, *i.e.* an adversary must not be able to undetectably manipulate votes, and eligibility, *i.e.* an adversary must not be able to cast votes for abstaining voters. The numerous Internet voting schemes proposed in the literature, *e.g.* [1,3,5,11,21], implement these requirements by making certain assumptions. For example, the JCJ/Civitas [5,11] scheme builds vote secrecy upon the assumption that the device used to cast a vote is trustworthy. Pretty Good Democracy [21] enforces vote secrecy in the presence of malicious voting devices, yet the scheme assumes that the voter can cast her vote without adversarial influence. The criticality of these assumptions, and therefore the security of Internet voting in general, differs within different election settings. To face this reality, our goal is to construct an election-dependent security evaluation framework for Internet

© IFIP International Federation for Information Processing 2017
Published by Springer International Publishing AG 2017. All Rights Reserved
S. De Capitani di Vimercati and F. Martinelli (Eds.): SEC 2017, IFIP AICT 502, pp. 371–382, 2017.
DOI: 10.1007/978-3-319-58469-0_25

voting schemes that measures to what extent an Internet voting scheme satisfies security requirements within concrete election settings.

Related Work. Several works have addressed the assessment of risks for electronic voting systems [2,4,12,17,19,20] by deriving threats trees for these systems. The fine-grained threats considered in these works require decision makers to assign probabilities to specific threats. Reviewing threat trees for Internet voting systems poses a significant burden on election officials, *e.g.* [7] provides a 18-page threat tree for Internet voting. While this approach facilitates the interpretation of large and complex threat trees, the approach is tailored towards system analysts. Hence, the approach does not foresee the incorporation of election settings by election officials. Volkamer and Grimm [24] propose the concept of resilience terms to capture complex trust distributions of Internet voting schemes and to express which central entities have to be trusted in order to fulfill security requirements. These trust distributions do, however, not incorporate the election setting into the security evaluation and expression. Furthermore, adversaries might consider other attack targets to violate security requirements, for instance voting devices or influencing voters throughout the vote casting process. On the foundation of resilience terms, Schryen *et al.* [23] develop a quantitative trust metric upon propositional logic. As foundation for their quantification, the authors determine resilience terms for security requirements in distributed systems. Thereafter, they compute the probability that security requirements might be violated on the basis of failure probabilities of individual entities. The approach inherits one essential shortcoming of the resilience term evaluation, namely the fact that the evaluation focuses on central entities of the voting system.

Contribution. We build the election-dependent security evaluation framework upon two specification languages: The language of *qualitative security models* enables system analysts to specify the security of Internet voting schemes in an election-independent manner, *i.e.* system analysts specify canonical assumptions about adversarial capabilities under which the scheme enforces security requirements. Intuitively, these canonical assumptions indicate the *weakest successful adversary* (refer to Pamula *et al.*'s notion [18]) in terms of abstract capabilities. The language of *election settings* allows election officials to specify their election settings in terms of expected adversaries and the number of voters. Upon the specification of qualitative security models and an election setting, the framework computes *satisfaction degrees* of Internet voting schemes with regard to the security requirements within the concrete election setting. Before its actual construction, the requirements for the security evaluation framework are determined. Ultimately, the framework is evaluated against these requirements.

2   Requirements for the Security Evaluation Framework

By its nature, the envisioned framework closely relates to the mathematical concept of a *measure* (refer for instance to Salamon [22]). We therefore base the requirements for the construction upon the properties of a measure and adapt them to our context. The first property a measure possesses is that it must assign the *empty set* of the σ-algebra in the measure space, to the measurement 0. Transferring this property to our context, two requirements are derived:

First, if the Internet voting scheme under investigation faces an adversary that has no capabilities, then the scheme's satisfaction degrees must be 1 with regard to all security requirements, unless the security requirement can be violated without any adversarial capabilities[1]. We refer to this requirement as *no capabilities – perfect security*. Second, if the Internet voting scheme under investigation proves to be resistant against a specific adversarial capability, then in the presence of any two adversaries that differ only with regard to that capability, the scheme's satisfaction degrees are equal. We refer to this requirements as *capability resistance*.

The second property a measure possesses is *continuity*. In measure theory, the property of continuity is defined by stating that (1) the measurement of the union of a countable infinite sequence of increasing sets $(E_n)_{n \in \mathbb{N}}$ is equal to the measurement of the last set of the infinite sequence and (2) the measurement of the intersection of an infinite sequence of decreasing sets $(E_n)_{n \in \mathbb{N}}$ is equal to the measurement of the last set of the infinite sequence. Transferring this property, we require that if the Internet voting scheme under investigation faces a sequence of adversaries, of which the capabilities converge towards the capabilities of a fixed adversary, then also the scheme's satisfaction degrees in the presence of the sequence of adversaries converges towards the scheme's satisfaction degree in the presence of the fixed adversary.

The third property a measure possesses is *monotonicity*. In terms of measure theory, the property ensures that the measurement of a subset of another set from the σ-algebra must be smaller than the measurement of the set. The fourth property a measure shall must possess is σ-*additivity*. In terms of measure theory, the property requires that the measurement of a union of disjoint subsets of the σ-*algebra* equals the sum of the measurement of the disjoint subsets. Both properties are transferred to the context of security evaluation for Internet voting schemes. Hence, we require that if the Internet voting scheme under investigation faces two adversaries, of which one is stronger than the other, then the scheme's satisfaction degrees must not be larger when facing the stronger adversary as compared to the weaker adversary.

3   Construction of the Security Evaluation Framework

The section is dedicated to the construction of the security evaluation framework. We emphasize that the herein presented construction mainly builds upon our previous construction published in 2016 [16]. Before diving into the details of the construction, we provide the necessary definitions. We subsequently show how

---

[1] This holds for instance true if vote secrecy is not required and the Internet voting scheme under investigation publishes the relation between a voter and her vote.

the security of Internet voting schemes is assessed by evaluating the election-independent security within the concrete election settings.

3.1 Definitions

Before presenting the construction of the security evaluation framework, we recall several definitions [16] while we slightly adapted the notations for this paper.

Definition 1 (Qualitative Adversary Model). *Let an Internet voting scheme A with the set of instantiated capabilities C^A be given. An adversary model $\mathcal{A}^A$, or simply adversary, against scheme A is defined by a subset of instantiated capabilities C^A, i.e. $\mathcal{A}^A \subseteq C^A$.*

Definition 2 (Qualitative Security Model). *Let an Internet voting scheme A with the set of instantiated capabilities C^A be given. We say that*

$$\mathcal{M}^{A,r,i} = (\alpha_1^{A,r,i} \vee \cdots \vee \alpha_{\xi^{A,r,i}}^{A,r,i})$$

$$\text{with } \alpha_j^{A,r,i} = (c_{j,1}^{A,r,i} \wedge \cdots \wedge c_{j,\lambda_j^{A,r,i}}^{A,r,i}) \text{ and } c_{j,k}^{A,r,i} \in C^A$$

is a qualitative security model of A with regard to security requirement r and impact level i if there exists a set of adversaries $\mathcal{S} = \{\mathcal{A}_1, \ldots, \mathcal{A}_{\xi^{A,r,i}}\}$ where $\mathcal{A}_j$ is specified by capabilities $\{c_{j,1}^{A,r,i}, \ldots, c_{j,\lambda_j^{A,r,i}}^{A,r,i}\}$, such that

1. *all adversaries $\mathcal{A} \in \mathcal{S}$ are capable of causing impact i on r, and*
2. *for all adversaries $\mathcal{A} \in \mathcal{S}$, there is no adversary $\mathcal{A}' \subset \mathcal{A}$ such that $\mathcal{A}'$ is capable of causing impact i on r, and*
3. *for all adversaries $\mathcal{A}'$ capable of causing impact i on r, there is an adversary $\mathcal{A} \in \mathcal{S}$, such that $\mathcal{A} \subseteq \mathcal{A}'$.*

Definition 3 (Resistance Against Abstract Capability). *Let an Internet voting scheme A with the set of instantiated capabilities C^A and the qualitative security models $\mathcal{M}^{A,r,1}, \ldots, \mathcal{M}^{A,r,n}$ be given. We say that the scheme A is resistant against capability $C_o \in C$ with regard to requirement r, if for all impact levels $1 \leq i \leq n$ and for all $c_{j,k}^{A,r,i}$ in all $\alpha_j^{A,r,i}$, capability $c_{j,k}^{A,r,i} \in C^A$ is not an instantiation of C_o.*

Definition 4 (Election Setting). *Given probability distributions $\mathbb{P}_{C_1}, \ldots, \mathbb{P}_{C_l}$ for all abstract capabilities $C_o \in C$, the number of eligible voters n_{el}, and the number of expected voters n_{ex}, a tuple of the form*

$$E = (\mathbb{P}_{C_1}, \ldots, \mathbb{P}_{C_l}, n_{el}, n_{ex})$$

is referred to as an election setting.

While being generous in definition, we simply require election officials to provide uniform distributions $U(a, b)$ for adversarial capabilities probabilities.

3.2   Determination of Satisfaction Degrees in Election Settings

As baseline of the framework, we show how to evaluate qualitative security models within specific election settings. Therefore, it is first shown how the probability of an adversary violating a qualitative security model can be calculated. Thereafter, it is outlined how Monte-Carlo simulations [13] are adapted for the quantitative evaluation of qualitative security models against probabilistic adversaries. The herein described algorithms build upon our previous work [16, Sect. 7.3]. As we noticed that this description is difficult to understand, we present, in the following paragraphs, the algorithm in a more readable manner. We abbreviate the probability of the event that the adversary $\mathcal{A}$ satisfies a security model X or possesses a specific (abstract or instantiated) capability, $i.e.$ $P_{\mathcal{A}}(X = 1)$, by $P(X)$.

Determination of Satisfaction Degrees with Given Probabilities. To determine the satisfaction degree of an Internet voting scheme A with qualitative security models $\mathcal{M}^{A,r,i}$ under given probabilities $P(C_o)$ for all $C_o \in C$ and under n impact levels (the instantiation of impact levels will be explained in the following paragraph), the following function $f(P(C_1), \ldots, P(C_l))$ is defined:

1. For each instantiated impact level $1 \leq i \leq n$, the probability formula of the qualitative security model is evaluated based on the given probabilities. Note, we show in [16, Sect. 7.1] how to transform qualitative security models into probability formulas.
2. For each instantiated impact level $1 \leq i \leq n$, a risk value is calculated by multiplying the normalized impact $\frac{i}{n}$ with the evaluated probability formula of the respective qualitative security model.
3. The largest risk value is identified.
4. The satisfaction degree estimator is the inverse of the largest risk value.

Extension Towards Probabilistic Adversaries. Rather than precise probabilities, election officials assign probability distributions to adversarial capabilities. While we currently assume that instantiated capabilities are independent, the framework is generated in a way that also caters for dependent instantiated

---

Algorithm 1. Satisfaction Degree Estimation (SDE)

Input: Level size n, probabilities $\{P(C_i)\}_{i=1}^{l}$
Output: Satisfaction degree estimator e

1 for $i \leftarrow 1, 2, \ldots, n$ do $p_i \leftarrow P(\bigvee_{j=1}^{\xi^{A,r,i}} \alpha_j^{A,r,i})^{P(C_1),\ldots,P(C_l)}$

2 for $i \leftarrow 1, 2, \ldots, n$ do $r_i \leftarrow p_i \cdot \frac{i}{n}$

3 $r_{\max} \leftarrow \max_{1 \leq i \leq n} r_i$.

4 $e \leftarrow 1 - r_{\max}$

5 return e

capabilities. Therefore, to determine the satisfaction degree of an Internet voting scheme A with regard to a security requirement r within a specified election setting E, we build upon Monte-Carlo simulations [13]. Therefore, the following process is defined:

Instantiation of Impact Levels. The number of impact levels and probability formulas are instantiated by the number of eligible voters n_{el} and the number of expected voters n_{ex}.

Generation of Monte-Carlo based Satisfaction Degree Estimators. The following steps are conducted m times (number Monte-Carlo iterations). The process steps are shown for the j-th Monte-Carlo iteration.

1. For each abstract adversarial capability $C_o \in C$, an estimator of the probability $P(C_o)$ is sampled according to the probability distribution $\mathbb{P}_{C_o}$.
2. For each vector of probability estimators $p_1^{(j)}, \ldots, p_l^{(j)}$, f is called.

Conducting these two steps yields samples of the following random variable:

$$M := f(P(C_1), P(C_2), \ldots, P(C_l))$$

Processing of Satisfaction Degree Estimators. We define the *statistical satisfaction degree* of scheme A with regard to requirement r and election setting E as the expected value of random variable M, *i.e.* $\mathbb{E}(M)$.

3. To approximate $\mathbb{E}(M)$ by the m satisfaction degree estimators generated in step 2, namely $e_1, \ldots, e_m$, the average of these estimators is calculated. Hence, the *empirical satisfaction degree* $\overline{M^m}$ (in the remainder simply referred to as satisfaction degree) of scheme A with regard to requirement r and election setting E is defined as:

$$\overline{M^m} := \frac{1}{m}(e_1 + \cdots + e_m) = \frac{1}{m}\sum_{k=1}^{m} f(p_1^{(k)}, p_2^{(k)}, \ldots, p_l^{(k)})$$

By the weak law of large numbers, it holds that the empirical satisfaction degree converges in probability towards the statistical satisfaction degree, *i.e.* $\overline{M^m} \xrightarrow{m \to \infty} \mathbb{E}[M]$.

To evaluate the quality of the empirical satisfaction degree with regard to the statistical satisfaction degree, a confidence interval is calculated. Within this work, we focus on the core of the framework and omit the confidence interval from further consideration (see [16] for further details).

4   Evaluation of the Security Evaluation Framework

After its construction, the security evaluation framework is evaluated with regard to the requirements determined in Sect. 2. The following proofs build upon the weak law of large numbers and hold therefore for a sufficiently large number of Monte-Carlo iterations.

Algorithm 2. Monte-Carlo based Satisfaction Degree Computation (MCSDC)

Input: Iterations m, probability distributions $\{\mathbb{P}_{C_i}\}_{i=1}^{l}$
Output: Satisfaction degree $\overline{M^m}$
1   for $j \leftarrow 1, 2, \ldots, m$ do $p_1^{(j)} \leftarrow P(C_1) \sim \mathbb{P}_{C_1}, \ldots, p_l^{(j)} \leftarrow P(C_l) \sim \mathbb{P}_{C_l}$
2   for $j \leftarrow 1, 2, \ldots, m$ do $e_j \leftarrow SDE(n, p_1^{(j)}, \ldots, p_l^{(j)})$
3    $\overline{M^m} \leftarrow \frac{1}{m} \sum_{j=1}^{m} e_j$.
4   return $\overline{M^m}$

No Capabilities – Perfect Security. The first requirement that the security evaluation framework shall possess is that the satisfaction degree of all schemes must be 1 with regard to all security requirements, if the adversary has no capabilities, unless the security requirement can be violated without any adversarial capabilities. This void of capabilities is equivalent to the absence of randomness as the adversary's capability is determined. Hence the probability distributions that are passed by the election official, degenerate to deterministic functions. Within a probabilistic framework, such deterministic functions are called constant random variables. Their distribution function is the *Dirac delta function* δ_x, where $x \in \mathbb{R}$ denotes the point of mass [10]. In particular, it holds $U(a, a + 1/n) \xrightarrow{n \to \infty} \delta_a$. Hence, for each $C_o \in C$ the Dirac delta function δ_0 is passed, as there is only one probability that can be assigned to the event that an adversary has capability C_o, namely *zero*.

Theorem 1. *Let δ_0 be the distribution function for all abstract capabilities $C_o \in C$. The satisfaction degree of scheme A is 1 for all security requirements r, unless the security requirement can be violated without any adversarial capabilities.*

Proof. If the probability of having an abstract capability $C_o \in C$ is 0 for all $C_o \in C$, then all instantiated capabilities $c_{j,k}^{A,r,i}$, with $1 \leq k \leq \lambda_j^{A,r,i}$ for the impact level i have probability 0, i.e. $P(c_{j,k}^{A,r,i}) = 0$. This leads to $P(\alpha_j^{A,r,i}) = 0$ and thus

$$P\left(\bigvee_{j=1}^{\xi^{A,r,i}} \alpha_j^{A,r,i} \right) \leq \sum_{j=1}^{\xi^{A,r,i}} P(\alpha_j^{A,r,i}) = 0.$$

As this holds true for all impact levels, the maximum risk of all impact levels equals 0. Consequently, the satisfaction degree estimator results in 1. Given the fact that the random variables for capability probability have their entire density at 0, each Monte-Carlo iteration assigns the value 0 to all capability probabilities. Hence, the resulting random variable M has its entire density on the value 1, such that $\mathbb{E}(M) = 1$. □

Capability Resistance. The second requirement refers to the resistance of Internet voting schemes against specific abstract adversarial capabilities.

Theorem 2. *Let Internet voting scheme A be resistant against abstract capability C_o with regard to requirement r. Let $P(C_1), P(C_2), \ldots, P(C_o), \ldots, P(C_l)$ denote random variables for the probabilities of adversarial capabilities $C_1, C_2, \ldots C_o, \ldots C_l$. If random variable $P(C_o)$ is replaced by a differently distributed random variable $P(C_o)'$, then the resulting satisfaction degrees of scheme A with regard to requirement r do not differ.*

Proof. For the random variables $P(C_1), P(C_2), \ldots, P(C_o)', \ldots, P(C_l)$, we denote the random variable generated by the Monte-Carlo simulations by:

$$M' := f(P(C_1), P(C_2), \ldots, P(C_o)', \ldots, P(C_l))$$

Due to A's resistance, it holds for all $c_{j,k}^{A,r,i}$ in all $\alpha_j^{A,r,i}$ that $c_{j,k}^{A,r,i}$ is no instantiation of C_o. Consequently, function f is neither affected by random variable $P(C_o)$ nor by $P(C_o)'$. As a consequence, it holds

$$\begin{aligned} M &= f(P(C_1), P(C_2), \ldots, P(C_o), \ldots, P(C_l)) \\ &= f(P(C_1), P(C_2), \ldots, P(C_o)', \ldots, P(C_l)) = M', \end{aligned}$$

and hence $\mathbb{E}(M) = \mathbb{E}(M')$.   □

Continuity. Election officials provide uniform probability distributions for capability probabilities, *e.g.* distributions $P(C_i) \sim U(a_i, b_i), i = 1, 2, \ldots, l$. To prove continuity of the framework with regard to the expected adversary, we study the framework's result under sequences of random variables $(P(C_{i,n}))_{n \in \mathbb{N}}$ where $P(C_{i,n}) \sim U(a_i, b_i + 1/n)$ for $i = 1, 2, \ldots, l$. We say that continuity is given if the framework's results are identical under the random variables $P(C_i) \sim U(a_i, b_i)$ and $P(C_{i,n}) \sim U(a_i, b_i + 1/n)$ for n converging to infinity. Formally, this is expressed as follows:

$$\begin{aligned} \mathbb{E}(M_n) &= \mathbb{E}(f(P(C_{1,n}), P(C_{2,n}), \ldots, P(C_{l,n}))) \\ &\overset{n \to \infty}{\longrightarrow} \mathbb{E}(f(P(C_1), P(C_2), \ldots, P(C_l))) = \mathbb{E}(M) \end{aligned}$$

Before proving the main theorem, we define two lemmata. Due to space limitations, we omit proofs of the lemmata herein[2].

Lemma 3. *The satisfaction degree estimator for requirement r in scheme A is continuous with regard to a sample probability $P(C_o)$ for any $C_o \in C$.*

Definition 5. *A sequence of random variables $(X_n)_{n \in \mathbb{N}}$ weakly converges to a random variable X, if for every continuous function f, it holds*

$$lim_{n \to \infty} \int_{X_n} f(x) d\mathbb{P}_{X_n} = \int_X f(x) d\mathbb{P}_X,$$

where $\mathbb{P}_{X_n}$ denotes the probability distribution of X_n and $\mathbb{P}_X$ the probability distribution of X, shortly $X_n \overset{d}{\longrightarrow} X$.

---

[2] These proofs will be published in a technical report.

Lemma 4. *Let $X \sim U(a,b)$ be a uniformly distributed random variable and let $(X_n)_{n \in \mathbb{N}} \sim U(a, b + 1/n)$ be a sequence of random variables. Then it holds $X_n \xrightarrow{d} X$.*

Theorem 5. *Let $P(C_i) \sim U(a_i, b_i), i = 1, 2, \ldots, l$ denote uniformly distributed random variables for the probabilities of adversarial capabilities C_i. The satisfaction degree of A with regard to requirement r is continuous with regard to any weakly convergent sequence of random variables $(P(C_{i,n}))_{n \in \mathbb{N}}$ where $P(C_{i,n}) \sim U(a_i, b_i + 1/n)$ for $i = 1, 2, \ldots, l$.*

Proof. Let M_n denote a framework's satisfaction degree calculation for a given sample of random variables $p_{i,n} \leftarrow P(C_{i,n}), i = 1, 2, \ldots l$. For the random variables $P(C_{1,n}), P(C_{2,n}), \ldots, P(C_{l,n})$, we denote the resulting random variable generated by f as:

$$M_n := f(P(C_{1,n}), P(C_{2,n}), ..., P(C_{l,n})).$$

Analogously to $\overline{M^m}$, we define the satisfaction degree calculated by the framework as $\overline{M_n^m} = \frac{1}{m} \sum_{k=1}^m f(p_{1,n}^{(k)}, p_{2,n}^{(k)}, \ldots, p_{l,n}^{(k)})$. By the law of large numbers, $\overline{M_n^m} \xrightarrow{m \to \infty} \mathbb{E}[M_n]$ holds. Given the weak convergence of $P(C_{i,n}) \xrightarrow{n \to \infty} P(C_i)$ (refer to Lemma 4) and the fact that the satisfaction degree estimator is continuous (refer to Lemma 3), it holds:

$$M_n = f(P(C_{1,n}), P(C_{2,n}), \ldots, P(C_{l,n})) \xrightarrow{d} f(P(C_1), P(C_2), \ldots, P(C_l)) = M$$

For the sequence of expected values $(\mathbb{E}[M_n])_{n \in \mathbb{N}}$, it consequently holds:

$$|\mathbb{E}[M_n] - \mathbb{E}[M]| = |\mathbb{E}[M_n - M]| \xrightarrow{n \to \infty} 0$$

$\square$

Monotonicity. We study the framework's result under the random variables $P(C_i) \sim U(a_i, b_i), i = 1, 2, \ldots, o, \ldots l$, when $P(C_o)$ is exchanged by a random variable $P(C_o)' \sim U(a_o', b_o')$ with $a_o' \geq a_o$ and $b_o' \geq b_o$. We say that monotonicity is given if the framework's result is larger under $P(C_i) \sim U(a_i, b_i), i = 1, 2, \ldots, c, \ldots l$ than under the same set where $P(C_o)$ is exchanged by a random variable $P(C_o)'$. Formally, this is expressed as follows:

$$\mathbb{E}(M') = \mathbb{E}(\ f(P(C_1), P(C_2), \ldots, P(C_o)', \ldots, P(C_l))\ )$$
$$\leq \mathbb{E}(\ f(P(C_1), P(C_2), \ldots, P(C_o), \ldots, P(C_l))\ ) = \mathbb{E}(M)$$

Before proving the main theorem, we define two lemmata. Due to space limitations, we omit proofs of the lemmata herein.

Lemma 6. *The satisfaction degree estimator for requirement r in scheme A is non-increasing with regard to a sample probability $P(C_o)$ for any $C_o \in C$.*

Lemma 7. *Let two random variables $X \sim U(a, b)$ and $Y \sim U(c, d)$ with $c \geq a$ and $d \geq b$ be given. For any non-decreasing function f, it holds:*

$$\mathbb{E}[f(X)] \leq \mathbb{E}[f(Y)]$$

Theorem 8. *Let $P(C_i) \sim U(a_i, b_i), i = 1, 2, \ldots, c, \ldots, l$ denote uniformly distributed random variables for the probabilities of adversarial capabilities C_i. The satisfaction degree of A with regard to requirement r is non-increasing with when random variable $P(C_o)$ is exchanged by $P(C_o)' \sim U(a_o', b_o')$, with $a_o' \geq a_o$ and $b_o' \geq b_o$.*

Proof. For $P(C_1), \ldots, P(C_o)', \ldots, P(C_l)$, we denote the resulting random variable generated by f by M', and the respective expected value by $\mathbb{E}[M']$.

By Lemma 7 and the fact that the satisfaction degree estimator is non-increasing (refer to Lemma 6), we are able to conclude that

$$\mathbb{E}(M') = \mathbb{E}(\ f(P(C_1), P(C_2), \ldots, P(C_o)', \ldots, P(C_l))\ )$$
$$\leq \mathbb{E}(\ f(P(C_1), P(C_2), \ldots, P(C_o), \ldots, P(C_l))\ ) = \mathbb{E}(M). \qquad \square$$

5   Conclusion

We constructed an evaluation framework for Internet voting schemes that incorporates the expertise of system analysts and election officials to evaluate schemes within concrete election settings. The framework's internal consistency was evaluated against requirements derived from measure theory.

We summarize limitations of the constructed framework as basis for future research: The framework's generic nature requires election officials to estimate probability distributions for abstract adversarial capabilities. Estimating presence probabilities on this level of abstraction might be more challenging than estimating probabilities of concrete capabilities for election officials and should be investigated in the future. Currently, the framework does not incorporate varying adversary motivations, *i.e.* probability distributions remain invariant over different election types and sizes. We assume adversaries specified by qualitative security models to always succeed. One might consider refining the constructed framework towards assigning success probabilities to qualitative security models.

In the future, the framework will be generalized further: Among these generalizations, the framework will be extended towards the case in which instantiated capabilities might be considered dependent. Based upon its actual concept, the framework will be extended to handle non-uniform probability distributions for abstract capabilities, *i.e.* normal distributions. Furthermore, we plan to publish the framework as collaborative platform: There, security experts are invited to discuss and jointly determine qualitative security models of Internet voting schemes. After specifying their election setting, the platform should support election officials to determine the most adequate voting scheme(s) for their setting.

Acknowledgment. The research that led to these results has been funded from a project in the framework of Hessen Modell Projekte (HA project no. 435/14-25), financed with funds of LOEWE Landes-Offensive zur Entwicklung Wissenschaftlich-ökonomischer Exzellenz, Förderlinie 3: KMU-Verbundvorhaben (State Offensive for the Development of Scientific and Economic Excellence). The second author is grateful to the F.R.S.- FNRS for a doctoral grant (1.A.320.16F).

References

1. Adida, B.: Helios: web-based open-audit voting. In: USENIX Security Symposium, pp. 335–348 (2008)
2. Bannister, F., Connolly, R.: A risk assessment framework for electronic voting. Int. J. Technol. Policy Manag. **7**(2), 190–208 (2007)
3. Budurushi, J., Neumann, S., Olembo, M.M., Volkamer, M.: Pretty understandable democracy-a secure and understandable internet voting scheme. In: 2013 Eighth International Conference on Availability, Reliability and Security (ARES), pp. 198–207. IEEE (2013)
4. Buldas, A., Mägi, T.: Practical security analysis of e-Voting systems. In: Miyaji, A., Kikuchi, H., Rannenberg, K. (eds.) IWSEC 2007. LNCS, vol. 4752, pp. 320–335. Springer, Heidelberg (2007). doi:10.1007/978-3-540-75651-4_22
5. Clarkson, M.R., Chong, S., Myers, A.C.: Civitas: a secure voting system. Technical report, Cornell University (2007)
6. Delaune, S., Kremer, S., Ryan, M.: Verifying privacy-type properties of electronic voting protocols. J. Comput. Secur. **17**, 435–487 (2009)
7. EAC Advisory Board and Standards Board: Threat trees and matrices and threat instance risk analyzer (TIRA) (2009)
8. Grimm, R., Krimmer, R., Meißner, N., Reinhard, K., Volkamer, M., Weinand, M., Helbach, J., et al.: Security requirements for non-political internet voting. Electron. Voting **86**, 203–212 (2006)
9. Lambrinoudakis, C., Gritzalis, D., Tsoumas, V., Karyda, M., Ikonomopoulos, S.: Secure electronic voting: the current landscape. In: Gritzalis, D.A. (ed.) Secure Electronic Voting. Advances in Information Security, vol. 7. Springer, New York (2012)
10. Hazewinkel, M.: Encyclopedia of Mathematics. Springer, Dordrecht (2001)
11. Juels, A., Catalano, D., Jakobsson, M.: Coercion-resistant electronic elections. In: Proceedings of the 2005 ACM Workshop on Privacy in the Electronic Society, pp. 61–70. ACM (2005)
12. Kim, H.M., Nevo, S.: Development and application of a framework for evaluating multi-mode voting risks. Internet Res. **18**(1), 121–135 (2008)
13. Metropolis, N., Ulam, S.: The Monte Carlo method. J. Am. Stat. Assoc. **44**(247), 335–341 (1949)
14. Mitrou, L., Gritzalis, D., Katsikas, S.: Revisiting legal and regulatory requirements for secure e-Voting. In: Ghonaimy, M.A., El-Hadidi, M.T., Aslan, H.K. (eds.) Security in the Information Society. IAICT, vol. 86, pp. 469–480. Springer, Boston (2002). doi:10.1007/978-0-387-35586-3_37
15. Neumann, S., Volkamer, M.: A holistic framework for the evaluation of internet voting systems. In: Design, Development, and Use of Secure Electronic Voting Systems, pp. 76–91 (2014)

16. Neumann, S., Volkamer, M., Budurushi, J., Prandini, M.: Secivo: a quantitative security evaluation framework for internet voting schemes. Ann. Telecommun. **71**(7–8), 337–352 (2016)
17. Nevo, S., Kim, H.M.: How to compare and analyse risks of internet voting versus other modes of voting. EG **3**(1), 105–112 (2006)
18. Pamula, J., Jajodia, S., Ammann, P., Swarup, V.: A weakest-adversary security metric for network configuration security analysis. In: Proceedings of the 2nd ACM Workshop on Quality of Protection, QoP 2006, pp. 31–38. ACM, New York (2006)
19. Pardue, H., Landry, J.P., Yasinsac, A.: E-voting risk assessment: a threat tree for direct recording electronic systems. Int. J. Inf. Secur. Priv. (IJISP) **5**(3), 19–35 (2011)
20. Pardue, H., Yasinsac, A., Landry, J.: Towards internet voting security: a threat tree for risk assessment. In: 2010 International Conference on Risk and Security of Internet and Systems (CRiSIS), pp. 1–7. IEEE Computer Society (2010)
21. Ryan, P.Y.A., Teague, V.: Pretty good democracy. In: Christianson, B., Malcolm, J.A., Matyáš, V., Roe, M. (eds.) Security Protocols 2009. LNCS, vol. 7028, pp. 111–130. Springer, Heidelberg (2013). doi:10.1007/978-3-642-36213-2_15
22. Salamon, D.A.: Measure and Integration. EMS Textbook series (2016, to appear)
23. Schryen, G., Volkamer, M., Ries, S., Habib, S.M.: A formal approach towards measuring trust in distributed systems. In: 2011 Annual ACM Symposium on Applied Computing (SAC), pp. 1739–1745. ACM (2011)
24. Volkamer, M., Grimm, R.: Determine the resilience of evaluated internet voting systems. In: 2009 International Workshop on Requirements Engineering for e-Voting Systems (RE-VOTE), pp. 47–54. IEEE Computer Society (2009)

Software Security and Privacy

Combating Control Flow Linearization

Julian Kirsch[1]([✉]), Clemens Jonischkeit[1], Thomas Kittel[1], Apostolis Zarras[1],
and Claudia Eckert[2]

[1] Technical University of Munich, Munich, Germany
{kirschju,jonischk,kittel,zarras}@sec.in.tum.de
[2] Fraunhofer AISEC, Munich, Germany
claudia.eckert@aisec.fraunhofer.de

Abstract. Piracy is a persistent headache for software companies that try to protect their assets by investing both time and money. Program code obfuscation as a sub-field of software protection is a mechanism widely used toward this direction. However, effectively protecting a program against reverse-engineering and tampering turned out to be a highly non-trivial task that still is subject to ongoing research. Recently, a novel obfuscation technique called *Control Flow Linearization* (CFL) is gaining ground. While existing approaches try to complicate analysis by artificially increasing the control flow of a protected program, CFL takes the exact opposite direction: instead of *increasing* the complexity of the corresponding *Control Flow Graph* (CFG), the discussed obfuscation technique *decreases* the amount of nodes and edges in the CFG. In an extreme case, this means that the obfuscated program degenerates to one singular basic block, while still preserving its original semantics. In this paper, we present the DeMovfuscator, a system that is able to accurately break CFL obfuscation. DeMovfuscator can reconstruct the control flow, making only marginal assumptions about the execution environment of the obfuscated code. We evaluate both the performance and size overhead of CFL as well as the feasibility of our approach to deobfuscation. Overall, we show that even though CFL sounds like an ideal solution that can evade the state of the art deobfuscation approaches, it comes with its own limitations.

1 Introduction

Software protection (i.e., obfuscation) is a technique used to transform code to make it harder for a human to analyze and understand. In an ideal scenario, obfuscated software maintains its original functionality but it becomes impenetrable to reverse engineering. Therefore, obfuscation offers all the necessary protection mechanisms to software authors that want to protect the internal operations of their programs from the prying eyes of reverse engineers. Here, we can define two groups of software authors: (*i*) software vendors who want to protect sensitive and confidential data shipped together with a piece of software and (*ii*) malware authors who want to evade detection by anti-virus scanners or to hinder inspection by security analysts. Both groups seek software obfuscation for their own purposes.

© IFIP International Federation for Information Processing 2017
Published by Springer International Publishing AG 2017. All Rights Reserved
S. De Capitani di Vimercati and F. Martinelli (Eds.): SEC 2017, IFIP AICT 502, pp. 385–398, 2017.
DOI: 10.1007/978-3-319-58469-0_26

Over the years, there has been proposed a wide range of obfuscation techniques that were mostly focused on hiding the original control flow by artificially increasing complexity [3,8,24]. For instance, *O-LLVM* achieves this by employing Control Flow Flattening *(CFF)*, a technique that conceals the execution sequence of basic blocks [16]. This can also be achieved by employing *virtualization-based* obfuscation techniques. A recent example of such an obfuscator is *Matryoshka* [15] which nests multiple layers of virtualization to cloak the functionality of a protected program.

Although obfuscation appears as an optimal solution, it has its own weaknesses. There exist solutions, called deobfuscators, that are centered around a symbolic execution engine and are able to penetrate various obfuscation techniques [26]. KLEE [7] is an example of such a state of the art symbolic execution engine that, however, requires the presence of the source code. ANGR [21,22] and BAP [6] are symbolic execution solutions that do not have a similar requirement. Nevertheless, current approaches for symbolic execution depend on the presence of instructions that explicitly modify the control flow during path enumeration.

Recently, a novel technique, called *Control Flow Linearization* (CFL), makes all control flow changes implicit. In fact, jump free programming is entirely feasible without loosing Turing completeness [11]. CFL constitutes a way of preventing symbolic execution engines from enumerating all satisfiable paths through a program. Therefore, deobfuscation relying on symbolic execution fails to recover the full *Control Flow Graph* (CFG) of a program protected by CFL. This is extremely useful for the software authors that desire to hide the internal operations of their programs. In essence, the MOVFUSCATOR [2], which is to the best of our knowledge the only real world implementation of CFL, helps software to defend itself from reverse engineering.

However, as with any other solution, CFL is not bulletproof. In this paper, we show that it is possible to construct a generic deobfuscator, called DEMOVFUSCATOR, that can reconstruct the control flow, making only marginal assumptions about the execution environment of the obfuscated code. In addition, we evaluate both the performance and size overhead of CFL as well as the feasibility of DEMOVFUSCATOR. Overall, we show that even though CFL sounds like an ideal solution that can evade the state of the art deobfuscation approaches, it is not impenetrable.

In summary, we make the following main contributions:

- We describe the concept of CFL as a novel obfuscation technique and evaluate it in terms of performance and size overhead.
- We propose a generic deobfuscation algorithm to counter CFL and show the effectiveness of our approach.
- We evaluate our approach by recovering the CFGs of various obfuscated binaries, including those of several third-party programs that emerged during past computer security competitions (*Capture-the-Flag contests*).
- We exhibit the advantages of our deobfuscation approach when compared with state of the art symbolic execution techniques.
- We show that CFL, although promising, is far from being perfect.

2   Background

In this section, we describe the concepts of CFL and instruction substitution before we shortly describe the MOVFUSCATOR [2], an existing example of an obfuscator that implements both CFL and instruction substitution.

2.1   Control Flow Linearization

We call a program *linearized* if it consists of only one singular basic block (excluding initialization of the environment) that ends in a jump targeting itself. Figure 1 shows an example of such a program. CFL makes the control flow of a program implicit by removing all control flow changing instructions without loosing Turing completeness [11].

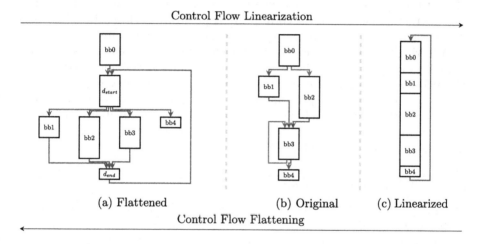

Control Flow Linearization

(a) Flattened   (b) Original   (c) Linearized

Control Flow Flattening

Fig. 1. Classification of CFL related to CFF and the original program.

The central idea of CFL is to duplicate all writable program variables in memory and to re-route all write accesses to either a real set of data or SCRATCH data. This enables the processor to formally execute all instructions in the program while only a subset of instructions affects the current program state. This effect is used to simulate the execution sequence of the basic blocks of the original program and consequently to simulate jumps without the need for branch instructions. In the following paragraphs, we structure this approach to provide a generic transformation strategy to construct linearized programs.

Without the availability of conditional jumps, all instructions of a program need to be executed. We can simulate (un)conditional jumps by mitigating the side effects of memory writes that are not caused by the currently intended basic block. If the effects of the instruction writing to memory should not be visible to the program, we need the code to write to the SCRATCH version of a variable in memory; otherwise the write operation should target the REAL version of the variable.

Next, we assign a unique LABEL to each basic block of the original program. For simplicity, we use each basic block's virtual address in memory as its LABEL. We also introduce a global STATE variable that during each point in execution holds the LABEL of the *currently executing* basic block. Thus, during execution of the linear program, the program is at all times able to calculate if the current block should write to the real program state or to the SCRATCH version.

Jumps connecting the basic blocks are realized as transitions of the global STATE variable. This is achieved by appending code that updates the STATE variable to each basic block. Note that the STATE variable itself also consists of a REAL and a SCRATCH location, as basic blocks that are not targeted by the current STATE also have to discard their updates to the STATE variable. Based on this construction, any jump predicate can be re-written as the base address of the STATE variable plus the Boolean result of the jump predicate, where TRUE equals 1 and FALSE equals 0. This allows to unconditionally execute each instruction but only if the corresponding predicate is TRUE, the side-effects of the instruction will become visible to the global program state.

Adhering to this construction, it is possible to merge all basic blocks of the original program into one linear basic block without any branch instruction. This effectively mitigates the use of symbolic execution engines to analyze and deobfuscate the generated program as we will see in Sect. 4. To re-trigger the execution of the program and to give other basic blocks the possibility to execute their payload, a final jump transferring control from the end to the start of the linearized program is appended.

2.2   CFL on the x86 Platform

When implemented for the Intel x86 architecture, CFL faces several challenges. To begin with, while a hypothetical Turing Machine operates on an infinite amount of memory, contemporary von-Neumann systems typically provide only a finite number of addressable bytes in memory. Thus, with finite memory, dereferences of unmapped memory regions can occur if the non-linearized version of the program assigns an invalid value to a index variable (e.g., a pointer in C) *at the global scope*. Even though the dereference with an out-of-bounds index might not be reachable from the point where the new value is assigned in the original program, the linearized version *will* execute the dereference and throw away the side effects later, which might lead to an instant program crash. To mitigate this issue, CFL can be extended to *guard* memory dereferences by adding an instruction that sets dereferenced operands to a known good value if the basic block containing the instruction is *not* active during execution.

Another problem of linearized programs is their ability to call into other functions, as a function call effectively introduces branches into a linearized program. Such high-level primitives can be adopted in two ways. Either the call to a function can be replaced by the called function itself, a process usually referred to as *inlining*, or local variables holding function pointers can be introduced. In the latter case, a variable would point to either the correct call target or to a single `ret` instruction depending on if the basic block containing the call is marked for execution. The two presented ways of handling function calls lead to two different results of the linearization: In the latter case, each function is linearized to one block, whereas in the former case the whole program including all functions is transformed to one block.

2.3   Instruction Substitution

While not directly related to CFL, the MOVFUSCATOR [2] employs instruction substitution to obfuscate a given binary. In context of obfuscation, instruction substitution refers to the process of replacing one or more instructions by an computationally equivalent sequence of instructions that is more difficult to understand for an analyst. Common instructions that are used for instruction substitution are: ADD, ROR, and XOR. Note however, that even restricting substitution to transform to only MOV instructions can reach Turing completeness.

Literature discusses instruction substitution in terms of increasing instruction diversity [16] for obfuscation, steganographic applications [13] or in form of case studies of malware [5]. However, *decreasing* the variety of instructions contained in a program is a relatively new idea that, to the best of our knowledge, has first been proposed by Dolan in a formal way [11]. Dolan shows that in an extreme case, instruction substitution can be performed such that the transformed program consists of at most one instruction type: the MOV instruction. We adhere to Domas' terminology and call the process of substituting a program with exclusively MOV instructions *movfuscation*. It is evident that instruction substitution implies CFL, if instructions explicitly changing the control flow are replaced. Both techniques are, however, applicable orthogonally to each other.

2.4   Formalizing the MOVFUSCATOR

Using the concepts introduced above, we describe the MOVFUSCATOR, which is to the best of our knowledge, the only public implementation of CFL and instruction substitution. The MOVFUSCATOR is implemented as a compiler back end of the *Little C Compiler* (LCC) [14], capable of compiling programs written in ANSI C. The MOVFUSCATOR is organized as a virtual machine whose instructions are implemented by only MOV instructions.

The MOVFUSCATOR VM consists of four byte-addressable general purpose registers with a machine word size of 32 bits. A stack pointer register points to a full descending stack consisting of 32 bit words. The MOVFUSCATOR VM uses an instruction pointer (IP) that addresses the program at a basic block granularity (we will use the terms IP and TARGET interchangeably). That is, the instruction pointer always points to the beginning of the currently executing basic block. A status register storing comparison results with zero-, signed-, overflow-, and carry-flag works analogously to the x86 status register.

The basic execution is governed by the virtual instruction pointer TARGET and the ON flag. The former contains a LABEL, the virtual address of the basic block that should be executed. It is updated at the end of each basic block of the original program, effectively implementing jump instructions. The ON register is a performance optimization: instead of predicating each memory write access with the result of the comparison LABEL == IP, the comparison is done only at the beginning of each basic block and the result is stored in ON. At the end of each basic block, ON is set to FALSE and TARGET reflects the outgoing edge of the current basic block.

Arithmetic operations are performed by an ALU that is capable of 32 bit integer computations. All computations are performed using look up tables. This constitutes a challenge as the machine word size is equal to the number of addressable bits in the address space. As such, look up tables for all arithmetic and logical instructions grow bigger than the addressable memory space. To circumvent this problem, the inputs for computations are split up into smaller values on which computations are performed using two-dimensional look up tables.

The execution of the generated linearized basic block is re-scheduled infinitely during program execution. To restart execution, the MOVFUSCATOR generates code that transfers the control flow to the beginning of this code. To do so, the code configures itself to be its own, nestable SIGILL handler; execution can be re-triggered at the end of the instruction stream using an illegal mov-instruction.

To interface with the OS, the MOVFUSCATOR follows the application binary interface as defined by external libraries. This means that the obfuscated program sets a special memory location EXTERNAL to the target function's entry in the plt section. Afterwards, it prepares the function arguments on the stack pointed to by the esp register prior to writing the correct return address on the stack and triggering a segfault by a NULL pointer dereference. This enables the MOVFUSCATOR to call external functions only if execution is enabled by ON. As a matter of fact, there exists a FAULT memory location that contains a valid pointer (no segfault) followed by a NULL pointer that can be accessed similar to other variables. The reason for triggering the segfault is that it provides a mov-only way of directing the execution towards a signal handler (SIGSEGV) that calls the actual library function contained in EXTERNAL.

To prevent generating code with a 1:1 relationship between the original x86 and the MOVFUSCATOR VM's instructions and to defend against pattern recognition, the MOVFUSCATOR employs two hardening techniques. The first is *register shuffling*. Instead of statically assigning registers, the generated code randomly uses one of the EAX, EBX, ECX, EDX general purpose registers for computations. The second is *instruction re-ordering*. The MOVFUSCATOR does a primitive, "overly restrictive" data-dependency analysis on the generated code. This analysis identifies independent pairs of instructions that can be re-ordered without destruction of the program's semantics.

3   Deobfuscation—Control Flow Recovery

In this section we introduce the DEMOVFUSCATOR.[1] Our deobfuscation algorithm is a linear-sweep algorithm that operates in four stages. All assumptions

---

[1] https://kirschju.re/demov.

we make are generic for every binary generated by the MOVFUSCATOR. Note that while this might seem to be very specific to the MOVFUSCATOR, we argue that all obfuscators that implement CFL are per design required to contain similar building blocks. Therefore, our approach is general for different CFL implementations. Our algorithm consists of the four steps introduced in the following.

Finding Key Structures. In this phase we infer the location of *critical data structures* such as the global variable ON indicating whether execution is enabled. Our assumptions are carefully tailored to be applicable to invariants that all linearized programs generated by the MOVFUSCATOR satisfy. We also reconstruct the semantic meaning of the respective look up tables that are later used to recover arithmetic computations performed by the code.

Identifying Labels. From instructions that enable execution (i.e., set ON to TRUE), we employ a backward data-flow analysis. Reconstruction of the LABEL is performed by an automatic theorem prover. As a side-effect, this step also reconstructs the location of the global state variable TARGET.

Identifying Jumps and Calls. From instructions that disable execution (i.e., set ON to FALSE), we infer jumps and thus basic block boundaries.

Reconstructing the CFG. Using the gained information, we patch the original binary to make the control flow explicit again.

In the first step, we are required to find critical management data structures of the state machine that were generated by the obfuscator. We first derive the location of the ON data structure from the static initialization code. Note that while a simple pattern matching approach would be sufficient (the static initialization code is approximately the same for all binaries generated by the MOVFUSCATOR modulo special compiler flags that omit parts), we improve resilience against changes and further applicability of our approach by reconstructing the location of ON using taint analysis. At a high level, our algorithm determines the location of an instruction that has the shape of instruction β as seen in Fig. 2. In the following we write $r\{N\}$ to denote an arbitrary x86 general purpose register. From instruction β, we start a backward taint analysis to infer the origin of register r1. If a construction like the above is found, and b points to data that has been statically initialized to TRUE, we assume a to be the location of SEL_ON, an array whose first entry contains a pointer to the global SCRATCH location and secondly a pointer to ON.

After having identified the location of SEL_ON, we continue by identifying the LABELs of the basic blocks contained in the original program. This is achieved by scanning for an instruction that uses SEL_ON as a base address for an indirect

```
1  mov  r1, [b]                ;  α
2  ; instructions not targeting r1
3  mov  r0, [a + r1 * 4]       ;  β
```

Fig. 2. Finding SEL_ON

```
1  mov  r0, [sel_on + r1 * 4]  ;  γ
2  ; instructions not targeting r0
3  mov  [r0], 1
```

Fig. 3. Usage of SEL_ON

memory access (instruction γ in Fig. 3). From this location we employ forward taint analysis to find the point where ON is set to 1 (TRUE). In such a case, we know that the detected instruction is responsible for selecting the ON variable or the SCRATCH variable depending on the result of the predicate stored in r1.

We perform a backward taint analysis from γ to reconstruct the predicate that evaluated to the value in r1. The backward analysis continues until: (i) the beginning of the program is reached, (ii) we find another instruction modifying ON, or (iii) all taint is sanitized. We then reconstruct the syntax tree of the predicate that evaluates to the truth value contained in r1 from the tainted instructions. To obtain the original semantic meaning of the operations, we use a-priori knowledge about the look up tables that implement the operations of the MOVFUSCATOR ALU: whenever an instruction accesses a look up table in static memory, we determine the result of the operation for two preselected arguments which are known to evaluate to distinct values for each computation that the virtual ALU is capable of. This approach enables us to reason about the arithmetic and logical operations contained in the reconstructed predicates.

The result of the above step is a Boolean formula that represents the equality check of the basic block's LABEL and the virtual instruction pointer IP indicating whether the current basic block should be executed. From this formula the algorithm obtains the location of the virtual IP as well as the LABEL of the current basic block. The latter is obtained by constraining the predicate to 1 (TRUE) and solving the formula for IP. In this step, our implementation uses the automatic theorem prover z3 [10]. By repeating the above procedure, the algorithm is able to determine the labels of all basic blocks of the program.

In the third step we use the knowledge gained in the second step to evaluate jump and call instructions. Jumps and calls are identified using an approach very similar to the identification of labels. The algorithm performs a second linear sweep and identifies instruction sequences that disable execution by setting ON to 0 (FALSE), which is illustrated in Fig. 4. This is needed to determine whether the control flow change is performed conditionally or unconditionally. We use the same technique as explained earlier involving backward taint analysis starting at instruction δ to compute the syntax tree of the predicate contained in r1. Using z3 we can decide whether the predicate evaluates to either a constant value, in which case the control flow change occurs unconditionally or alternatively to a formula containing symbolic values, which indicates an conditional jump.

To recover the target basic block label, we need to identify modifications of the virtual IP (instruction ε in Fig. 5). In this example, if r0 is the memory

```
1   mov r0, [sel_on + r1 * 4]   ; γ
2   ; instructions not targeting r0
3   mov [r0], 1
```

```
1   mov r0, [sel_on + r1 * 4]   ; δ
2   ; instructions not targeting r0
3   mov [r0], 0
```

Fig. 4. Distinguishing conditional and unconditional jumps

Fig. 5. Distinguishing direct and indirect control flow changes

location of IP then consequently c is the memory location of SEL_TARGET, an array holding the global SCRATCH location at index 0 and TARGET at index 1.

After deriving the location of SEL_TARGET we have to distinguish indirect jumps from direct jumps and calls. This is done by analyzing not only the value of r1 but also the source of the predicate contained in r2 for each access of SEL_TARGET. Table 1 lists the different decision rules used to determine the type of the control flow change. A basic block never targeted by a jump succeeding an unconditional direct jump is assumed to be a return target. Consequently, we assume the preceeding basic block to end with a call. Note that we do not infer outgoing edges for indirect jump targets, as this is a difficult problem which is heavily discussed by literature. A promising way of resolving indirect jumps is for example using value set analysis [4]. However we want to underline that our algorithm finds the basic blocks that constitute the indirect jump targets.

Table 1. Control flow changes depending on predicate sources and values written.

Predicate source	Value written	Recovered control flow change
Immediate	Constant	Unconditional direct jump
Immediate	Formula	Conditional direct jump
Stack	Ignored	Return from call
Other memory	Ignored	Indirect jump

Following all steps explained above, the algorithm constructs a list of nodes and edges that form the control flow graph of the original program. We use this information to generate images depicting the control flow as well as a patched executable. We do this by ordering all jumps and labels by their respective virtual address and interpreting them as nodes. We iterate over all nodes once. If the current node is a call label, we add an edge to the next element, if it is a conditional jump we add a node in between the current and the next node and add edges between the current and the intermediate node as well as between the intermediate and the next node. In case of an unconditional jump we just add an edge to the target of the particular jump instruction. After this step, all weakly connected nodes form a function and can be merged. By analyzing the calls made from each function, we can then reconstruct the call graph of the analyzed obfuscated binary.

4   Evaluation

To estimate the cost of the obfuscation in terms of size and run-time overhead, we obfuscated three sample programs *Primes*, *Factorial*, and *SHA-256*. Primes is an implementation of the *Sieve of Eratosthenes* calculating all prime numbers smaller than $5 \cdot 10^7$, while Factorial calculates the factorial 20! using a one-dimensional loop. To understand the overhead of programs that are closer to real-world applications, we also evaluated an implementation of the secure hashing algorithm using program SHA-256.

Table 2. Overhead in terms of run-time (seconds) and code size (bytes).

	Primes		Factorial		SHA-256	
	Non-lin.	Lin.	Non-lin.	Lin.	Non-lin.	Lin.
Non-sub.	0.88 s	5.03 s	<0.01 s	<0.01 s	0.02 s	0.4 s
	240 B	928 B	1884 B	1936 B	5672 B	8564 B
Sub.	62.82 s	289.47 s	<0.01 s	<0.01 s	8.09 s	60.57 s
	16, 957 B	16, 957 B	10, 684 B	10, 684 B	213, 740 B	213, 740 B

Every program produced eight data points: size and run-time for the non-linearized, non-substituted unobfuscated version as generated by *gcc* version 5.3.1, the linearized and substituted version as generated by the MOVFUSCATOR version 2.0 and two versions that were obfuscated using only one of the mechanisms. The linearized, non-substituted version was generated by rewriting the C source code according to MOVFUSCATOR while the non-linearized, substituted version is the output of our deobfuscator applied to the movfuscated version. All run times are averaged over ten runs as measured on a Intel Core i7-4770 clocked at 3.4 GHz. For the aforementioned combinations of obfuscation techniques we also added the net size of the generated code in bytes excluding overhead introduced by the executable format. The results can be seen in Table 2.

The measurements show that the linearization itself already leads to a notifiable increase in both run-time overhead and binary size. For example, the SHA-256 program runs about 20 times slower after linearization, while code size increases by roughly a factor of two. This magnitude of overhead makes the obfuscation unsuitable for real-time applications, but could still be used to protect critical parts of an algorithm's implementation. Instruction substitution however leads to a significant overhead both in run-time as well as in binary size. As the calculation of a hash for one megabyte of data takes more than one minute, we argue that this kind of obfuscation is not usable in practice. Note that the size values for the linear and the non-linear version in Table 2 are the same as they differ only by the patched bytes that our deobfuscation algorithm introduced. As relative distances need to remain the same, the size overhead does not change.

To determine the correctness of our deobfuscation algorithm, we compared the CFG of the pre-obfuscated version with the control flow graph of the deobfuscated version of four sample programs: *Primes, Factorial, AES-128,* and *SHA-256.* Table 3 shows the time required to run our deobfuscation algorithm on the tested binaries. In all cases, except with the simple factorial algorithm, it was faster to deobfuscate the obfuscated binary and to execute the deobfuscated result, than to execute the obfuscated version.

Table 3. Deobfuscation times of the implementation of our algorithm.

Primes	Factorial	SHA-256	AES
0.47 s	0.213 s	0.824 s	3.68 s

We chose SHA-256 and AES-128 to show that DeMovfuscator works on programs performing complex operations. For AES-128, we followed the official NIST specification on standardized AES vectors and verified that the results of encryption and decryption matched the expected outcomes [12]. To understand the qualitative behavior of our algorithm, we compared the CFG generated from the obfuscated Primes program with its known, unobfuscated C source code. The reconstructed CFG closely matches the original program. This proves that even if a program has been obfuscated with CFL, deobfuscation is still possible.

A good way to show the generality of our approach is to create a pool of binaries, obfuscate them, and then try to reconstruct their CFGs. Internet is obviously the best existing pool to collect binaries. Another source we used to harvest binaries is computer security competitions (Capture-the-Flag contests). These contests often contain clever-crafted binaries which are ideal for our evaluation. To this end, we used both sources and indeed our algorithm was able to reconstruct the control flow for all collected binaries. Our algorithm already became handful in previous Capture-the-Flag contests where it helped us to find an input accepted by the binary and therefore solving the task.

To study the impact of movfuscation on a symbolic execution engine, we reproduced the results of *Firmalice* [21] and measured execution times for the clean, the movfuscated, and the deobfuscated version of the *Fauxware* example backdoor. We used ANGR from the official repository at commit fe3027 and configuring it to prevent ANGR from concretizing symbolic memory accesses during the operation of the Movfuscator ALU. As ANGR currently does not implement the `sigaction` syscall used by the Movfuscator, we adjusted the obfuscated version to call library functions using the PLT rather than the SIGSEGV handler. We also patched out the calls to `sigaction` and replaced the final illegal instruction with a proper jump to re-trigger execution of the basic block. The *Fauxware* executable asks for a username and a password and compares them against a database of legitimate credentials. There also exists an execution path that checks the input against hard coded credentials and thus effectively bypasses the authentication step. To find the existence of the backdoor, the original work proposes to use path exploration to check whether there exists an satisfiable path to the code that should only be reachable for legit users without entering credentials from the user database. We applied the script performing the detection to the original, the obfuscated, and the deobfuscated version of the binary and measured execution times. As Table 4 shows, the backdoor can be found in short time before obfuscation. As the executable is intentionally kept simple, already the second explored path triggers the backdoor condition. Nevertheless, analyzing the same executable in its obfuscated version, ANGR times out after reaching the maximum number of executed basic blocks. Note that even though the Movfuscator generates code consisting of only one basic block, ANGR counts multiple basic blocks due to the invocation of library functions and a maximum number of instructions that one basic block can contain. Internally the path exploration seems to be unable to reason about symbolic values, as the number of paths (1) shows. We tried to re-run the experiment without a threshold and let it continue for 6 h without being presented with a result.

Table 4. Execution times of the ANGR symbolic execution engine to detect a backdoor in an example executable.

	Clean	Obfuscated	Deobfuscated
# basic blocks executed	37	99,999	87
Execution time (s)	5.1	1704.3	17.9
Explored paths	2	1	3
Executable size (bytes)	5400	5,962,776	5,962,776

After applying our deobfuscation algorithm to the obfuscated binary we let symbolic execution explore the binary and ANGR was able to find the backdoor in less than 20 s. One interesting observation is that ANGR needed to explore one additional path. We suppose this to be founded in internal path scheduling discrepancies. The run-time of our deobfuscation algorithm to generate a patched version of this example with reconstructed control flow amounted about 0.18 s (averaged over 10 runs).

5   Related Work

The topic of obfuscation to protect software is subject of active research in the academic community. Junod et al. propose *O-LLVM* [16], an obfuscator operating on LLVM intermediate representation. Offering a capricious variety of obfuscation techniques we only highlight *CFF* in context of our work. *CFF* [24] is an obfuscation technique targeting the concealment of a protected software's control flow. Ghosh et al. proposed *Matryoshka* [15], which serves exemplary for the class of *process-level-virtualization* (or *emulation*)-based obfuscation. This obfuscation technique works analogous to *CFF*, except that basic block scheduling is governed dynamically by an arbitrarily chosen byte code of a virtual CPU. Several commercial state of the art obfuscators in the industry such as VMProtect [1], EXECryptor [23], and Themida [17] also employ virtualization-based obfuscation to complicate analysis. It is noteworthy that all of the aforementioned obfuscation techniques aim to increase the complexity of the control flow by inserting additional nodes and edges into the CFG. CFL, on the other hand takes the opposite direction by decreasing the complexity of the CFG. Linear obfuscation was introduced by Wang et al. [25]. The authors propose to obfuscate trigger conditions by using unsolved conjectures such as the Collatz sequence to attack symbolic execution. This concept is orthogonal to CFL and can be combined when the ON or the TARGET registers are read or updated.

The problem of emulation-based obfuscation has been studied for more than a decade. Rolles [18] proposes to use templating languages to generate a compiler that is capable of translating a VMProtect protected sample back to the x86 architecture. Sharif et al. [20] propose a deobfuscation technique for emulators based on execution traces and dynamic taint analysis. Coogan et al. [9]

compute the relevance of instructions within an instruction trace based on data-flow towards system calls. This approach allows to further reduce the number of assumptions about the obfuscator used but as a drawback only considers parts of the program covered by the trace. Yadegari et al. [26] overcome this limitation by combining instruction traces with concolic execution [19]. Their results heavily rely on the quality of the symbolic execution engine—an assumption that does not hold for instance for programs obfuscated using the MOVFUSCATOR.

6   Conclusion

In this work, we evaluated to the best of our knowledge the only publicly available implementation of CFL. Our evaluation shows that instruction substitution is not applicable in real world scenarios due to its high overhead in terms of execution time and code size. However, the significant overhead and the concealment of explicit control flow changes poses a major challenge to dynamic symbolic execution. We have shown a state of the art symbolic execution engine to fail at path enumeration when analyzing a linearized executable. We have also shown that this problem can be recovered by employing our deobfuscation algorithm and applying symbolic execution to the deobfuscated version. In addition to the run-time overhead, which might be acceptable for the obfuscation of a small but critical part of an algorithm, CFL has a major drawback due to its structure. It depends on the existence of both a block selection register, like the TARGET register within the MOVFUSCATOR, and a global ON flag governing execution. Our investigation revealed that these registers are relatively easy to detect, as they have to be initialized within the static initialization part of the obfuscated binary and are accessed at the beginning and the end of each basic block of the original program during execution. To harden future CFL implementations the locations of those registers have to be concealed such that static analysis cannot reason about the basic blocks of the program.

Acknowledgements. The research was supported by the German Federal Ministry of Education and Research under grant 16KIS0327 (IUNO).

References

1. VMProtect - New-Generation Software Protection. https://vmpsoft.com/
2. The M/O/Vfuscator (2015). https://github.com/xoreaxeaxeax/movfuscator
3. Aucsmith, D.: Tamper resistant software: an implementation. In: Anderson, R. (ed.) IH 1996. LNCS, vol. 1174, pp. 317–333. Springer, Heidelberg (1996). doi:10.1007/3-540-61996-8_49
4. Balakrishnan, G., Reps, T.: Analyzing memory accesses in x86 executables. In: Duesterwald, E. (ed.) CC 2004. LNCS, vol. 2985, pp. 5–23. Springer, Heidelberg (2004). doi:10.1007/978-3-540-24723-4_2
5. Borello, J.-M., Mé, L.: Code obfuscation techniques for metamorphic viruses. J. Comput. Virol. 4(3), 211–220 (2008)

6. Brumley, D., Jager, I., Avgerinos, T., Schwartz, E.J.: BAP: a binary analysis platform. In: Gopalakrishnan, G., Qadeer, S. (eds.) CAV 2011. LNCS, vol. 6806, pp. 463–469. Springer, Heidelberg (2011). doi:10.1007/978-3-642-22110-1_37

7. Cadar, C., Dunbar, D., Engler, D.R., et al.: KLEE: unassisted and automatic generation of high-coverage tests for complex systems programs. In: USENIX Symposium on Operating System Design and Implementation (OSDI) (2008)

8. Collberg, C., Thomborson, C., Low, D.: A taxonomy of obfuscating transformations. Technical report (1997)

9. Coogan, K., Lu, G., Debray, S.: Deobfuscation of virtualization-obfuscated software: a semantics-based approach. In: Conference on Computer and Communications Security (CCS) (2011)

10. Moura, L., Bjørner, N.: Z3: an efficient SMT solver. In: Ramakrishnan, C.R., Rehof, J. (eds.) TACAS 2008. LNCS, vol. 4963, pp. 337–340. Springer, Heidelberg (2008). doi:10.1007/978-3-540-78800-3_24

11. Dolan, S.: Mov is turing-complete. Technical report (2013)

12. Dworkin, M.: Recommendation for block cipher modes of operation (2001)

13. El-Khalil, R., Keromytis, A.D.: Hydan: hiding information in program binaries. In: Lopez, J., Qing, S., Okamoto, E. (eds.) ICICS 2004. LNCS, vol. 3269, pp. 187–199. Springer, Heidelberg (2004). doi:10.1007/978-3-540-30191-2_15

14. Fraser, C., Hanson, D.: A Retargetable C Compiler: Design and Implementation. Addison-Wesley, Reading (1995)

15. Ghosh, S., Hiser, J.D., Davidson, J.W.: Matryoshka: strengthening software protection via nested virtual machines. In: International Workshop on Software Protection (2015)

16. Junod, P., Rinaldini, J., Wehrli, J., Michielin, J.: Obfuscator-LLVM: software protection for the masses. In: International Workshop on Software Protection (2015)

17. Oreans Technologies: Themida: advanced windows software protection systems. http://www.oreans.com/themida.php/

18. Rolles, R.: Unpacking virtualization obfuscators. In: Workshop on Offensive Technologies (WOOT) (2009)

19. Sen, K., Marinov, D., Agha, G.: CUTE: a concolic unit testing engine for C. In: European Symposium on Research in Computer Security (2005)

20. Sharif, M., Lanzi, A., Giffin, J., Lee, W.: Automatic reverse engineering of malware emulators. In: IEEE Symposium on Security and Privacy (2009)

21. Shoshitaishvili, Y., Wang, R., Hauser, C., Kruegel, C., Vigna, G.: Firmalice - automatic detection of authentication bypass vulnerabilities in binary firmware. In: ISOC Network and Distributed System Security Symposium (NDSS) (2015)

22. Shoshitaishvili, Y., Wang, R., Salls, C., Stephens, N., Polino, M., Dutcher, A., Grosen, J., Feng, S., Hauser, C., Kruegel, C., Vigna, G.: SoK: (State of) the Art of War: offensive techniques in binary analysis. In: IEEE Symposium on Security and Privacy (2015)

23. StrongBit Technology: EXECryptor - Bulletproof Software Protection. http://www.strongbit.com/execryptor.asp

24. Wang, C., Hill, J., Knight, J., Davidson, J.: Software tamper resistance: obstructing static analysis of programs. Technical report (2000)

25. Wang, Z., Ming, J., Jia, C., Gao, D.: Linear obfuscation to combat symbolic execution. In: European Symposium on Research in Computer Security (2011)

26. Yadegari, B., Johannesmeyer, B., Whitely, B., Debray, S.: A generic approach to automatic deobfuscation of executable code. In: IEEE Symposium on Security and Privacy (2015)

Ghost Patches: Fake Patches for Fake Vulnerabilities

Jeffrey Avery$^{(\boxtimes)}$ and Eugene H. Spafford

Computer Science Department and CERIAS,
Purdue University, 305 N. University St., West Lafayette, IN 47907, USA
{avery0,spaf}@purdue.edu
https://www.cs.purdue.edu/

Abstract. Offensive and defensive players in the cyber security sphere constantly react to either party's actions. This reactive approach works well for attackers but can be devastating for defenders. This approach also models the software security patching lifecycle. Patches fix security flaws, but when deployed, can be used to develop malicious exploits.

To make exploit generation using patches more resource intensive, we propose inserting deception into software security patches. These *ghost patches* mislead attackers with deception and fix legitimate flaws in code. An adversary using ghost patches to develop exploits will be forced to use additional resources. We implement a proof of concept for ghost patches and evaluate their impact on program analysis and runtime. We find that these patches have a statistically significant impact on dynamic analysis runtime, increasing time to analyze by a factor of up to $14x$, but do not have a statistically significant impact on program runtime.

1 Introduction

Software developers release programs to the public every day, but this code is not perfectly written. As stated by Mosher's Law of Software Engineering: *"Don't worry if it doesn't work right. If everything did, you'd be out of a job"* [18]. Thus developers release code that has flaws and subsequently provide the necessary patches to fix the flawed code.

These patches are released with varying frequency, depending on the severity of the flaw as well as developer resources. Software security patches have a higher severity rating than non-security patches because these vulnerabilities could negatively impact other programs and services present on the machine. Thus, when a security flaw is discovered, a patch to fix this flaw usually follows shortly after. This trend is shown by a report released in 2016 where the average time the top five most frequently exploited zero-day vulnerabilities remained undetected once an attack was released was 7 days and the average time to install a patch for these vulnerabilities once the patch was released was 1 day [23].

Despite the speed with which these flaws are detected and updated, patches also inherently have a negative impact on the software: revealing the location of

© IFIP International Federation for Information Processing 2017
Published by Springer International Publishing AG 2017. All Rights Reserved
S. De Capitani di Vimercati and F. Martinelli (Eds.): SEC 2017, IFIP AICT 502, pp. 399–412, 2017.
DOI: 10.1007/978-3-319-58469-0_27

vulnerabilities and the type of security vulnerability being patched. This provides a blueprint for attackers as they develop exploits for vulnerable systems. Exploit generation research shows that attackers can use patches to find vulnerabilities and use these results to develop exploits for unpatched code [6, 10].

One solution to make this blueprint more difficult to understand is to obfuscate the traditional patch [4, 9, 25]. This approach will make the patch more difficult to statically analyze, but dynamic analysis tools exist that can analyze obfuscated code [24] and the location of the patch is not masked. Therefore, additional techniques must be applied to software patching to enhance its security.

Thus, an additional technique we propose is to apply deception to software security patching to enhance its security. One method we propose to deceive attackers injects a faux patch, composed of one or more fake patches into traditional patches. These misleading updates could influence attackers' ability to identify a legitimate patch, making exploit generation using patches more resource intensive. While not an absolute solution to the problem of patch-based exploit generation, these misleading updates could increase the resources needed to reverse-engineer patches, which is the first step in exploit generation and along with other deceptive and detection techniques could make these attacks more cost intensive. We call the combination of a faux patch and a legitimate patch(es) for a single program a *ghost patch*.

Definition. Ghost patches are composed of two components: a legitimate patch, made of traditional patches, and a faux patch, made of fake patches. The legitimate patch component fixes any vulnerability or vulnerabilities that may exist in the program. These traditional patches are actual fixes for vulnerable code. The faux patch component is additional code meant to mislead attackers. Each fake patch within a faux patch suggests a fake vulnerability.

Ghost patches provide the same level of security as traditional patches, but could confuse attackers analyzing the code. This extra time and effort attackers spend analyzing the code would increase the time between a patch release and an exploit release. This could provide end-users more time to patch their vulnerable systems, causing fewer attacks to succeed.

Related Work. Researchers have applied deceptive techniques to software patches, but we believe our work is the first full treatment that applies, implements and analyzes fake code to software security patches, specifically patches for input validation vulnerabilities. Araujo et al. [2, 3] apply deception to security vulnerabilities such as Heartbleed and Conflicker. Their work focuses on fixing a patch by detecting an attack and diverting the runtime environment to a sanitized virtual environment that appears vulnerable. Researchers though have developed techniques to reliably distinguish sandbox environments from real user machines [27]. Thus, an attacker can identify when they are being monitored and deceived. This technique also does not camouflage legitimate patches, thus, an adversary can easily identify these patches using a diff between a patched and unpatched program. Ghost patches do mask the location of legitimate patches among other plausible code updates, making an adversary's task of identifying the legitimate patch more resource intensive.

Fake patches have also been mentioned by Bashar et al. [4] and Oh [19] as ways to deceive attackers. Our work differs from these by implementing a compiler solution using LLVM [15] to add fake patches to code and evaluating their impact on program analysis and runtime. Adding false code to improve code stealth and make reverse engineering of an entire program more difficult has been explored [14].

Work by Collberg et al. also discuss *bogus control flow* statements [8]. Bogus control flow statements are control flow statements that mislead reverse engineering techniques and static analysis tools. This technique focuses on making legitimate paths in a program more difficult to identify to prevent attackers from bypassing sections of code (i.e. registration, validation, DRM, etc.). This work is similar to our approach, as both attempt to add additional statements making code more difficult to understand. Bogus control flow mainly attempts to prevent bypassing critical code segments, while ghost patches attempt to increase the resources necessary to develop patch-based exploits. Our approach differs as dynamic and static analysis tools will be influenced by our approach (i.e. increase analysis runtime) while applying dynamic analysis to bogus control flows will expose the legitimate path in the code. Researchers also have presented the idea of inserting beaconing code traps where return-oriented-programming (ROP) gadgets would be expected by adversaries [11]. Our work differs as we implement an automated technique to enhance the security of patches for input validation vulnerabilities. Coppens et al. suggest code diversification can be introduced using patches to increase the effort necessary for exploit generation [10]. This approach would force attackers to generate multiple exploits to achieve widespread compromise, increasing the effort and resources needed to exploit a program compared to everyone having the same code with the same vulnerability. This work though does not attempt to mask the legitimate patch, thus an attacker could easily identify and analyze legitimate patches to code that fix legitimate vulnerabilities.

Our contributions from this work are as follows:

– Presentation of a novel methodology to develop and insert fake patches.
– Implementation of a proof-of-concept to inject fake patches in code with input validation vulnerabilities that could result in integer over/under-flows.
– Experimentation with dynamic analysis tool to analyze impact of fake patches.

The rest of this work is organized as follows: Section 2 discusses background information, Sect. 3 introduces our approach to applying deception to put validation patches, Sect. 4 explains how we evaluate a faux patch, Sect. 5 presents results from evaluating our proof of concept, Sect. 6 reviews limitations and challenges of ghost patches as well as discusses potential solutions, and Sect. 7 concludes this work.

2 Background

Deception. Deception has been used in computing since the 1970s [12,16,21,22]. Since its introduction, a variety of deceptive tools have been developed to bolster computer defenses. Examples of deceptive tools are those that generate decoy documents [20] and honeyfiles [29]. These documents are planted to attract attention away from critical data or resources and alert defenders of potential intrusions or exfiltration attempts.

Our research will use decoy document properties to develop fake patches. The definition of deception in computation states that any intentional act of misleading to influence decision making classifies an act as deception [1, 28]. Thus, *ghost patches* are intentionally placed in code to mislead attackers. Deception can also be broken into two components, simulation, showing the false, and dissimulation, hiding the real. Simulation and dissimulation are broken down into three separate components. Simulation is comprised of mimicking, inventing, and decoying and dissimulation is comprised of masking, repackaging, and dazzling [26].

Fake patches are an application of showing the false by *mimicking* and *decoying* and hiding the real by *dazzling*. They show the false by including characteristics of real patches, mimicking a real patch and attracting attention away from traditional patches as a decoy. Fake patches hide the real by reducing the certainty of which patches are real and which are decoys.

Exploiting Patches. Attackers can use patches to develop exploits. One approach statically reverse-engineers the patched code to determine the vulnerability being fixed. Another approach dynamically analyzes patched code to determine new paths that have been added compared to unpatched code. These new paths suggest that a vulnerability can be exploited in the unpatched program by generating input that follows the new path in the patched program.

Using either approach, attackers can view the actual lines of code being changed among program versions. With our approach, fake patches will be presented along with traditional patches, forcing adversaries using static analysis to distinguish between each type of patch before generating malicious input. The fake patches that we add can be executed by benign input without altering the program's semantics, forcing adversaries using dynamic analysis to distinguish which paths are legitimate and which are deceptive. Research has also shown that exploits can be generated automatically and quickly based on detecting new "checks" in patched code [6].

Input Validation Vulnerabilities. This work targets input validation vulnerabilities. A common patch to these types of vulnerabilities is to add boundary checks in the form of if-statements [6]. Thus, given a patch and unpatched program, a diff between the two programs will show additional branch statements in the patched version. These branch statements can be used to then determine input values that will exploit an unpatched program.

3   Approach

This research studies how a fake patch can be implemented in conjunction with a traditional patch and measures its impact on program analysis and runtime.

These fake patches should alter the control flow of a program, but not the data flow of information. Thus, given two programs, one with a ghost patch and the other with a traditional patch, the final output should be identical.

Our approach is based on the trend that input validation vulnerabilities are patched by adding conditional statements that validate the value of variables that can be tainted by malicious input [6]. Thus, to deceive attackers, we add fake patches to code that mimic these input validation conditional statements, making exploit generation using patches more resource intensive.

3.1   Threat Model

We consider attackers who are using patches to develop exploits and have access to both patched and unpatched versions of a program, and can control and monitor the execution of both as our threat model.

Ghost patching is designed for input validation vulnerabilities that have not been discovered by the public or do not have a widely available exploit. If there are scripts that already exploit a well known vulnerability, ghost patches can still be applied but with less effectiveness. Public exploit databases[1] or "underground" forums could be monitored to determine if exploits have been developed.

We specifically look at input validation vulnerabilities that involve integers. These vulnerabilities can be exploited because of a lack of boundary checking and can cause subtle program misbehavior through integer overflows or underflows.

Finally, ghost patches target input validation vulnerabilities in enterprise scale systems. Due to performance constraints, embedded or real time systems do not present a suitable environment for ghost patches.

3.2   Properties of Ghost Patches

This work applies concepts from decoy documents to deceptive patches. Decoy documents are fake documents inserted into a file system or on a personal computer and are meant to intentionally mislead attackers. These documents also *mimic* real documents and are *decoys* meant to attract attention away from critical data. Bowen et al. and Stolfo et al. have conducted research on decoy documents [5, 20] and created a list of properties that decoy documents should embody. We slightly modify these properties and present in Table 1 our list of fake patch properties as well as whether the property is trivial to implement or requires further experimentation.

3.3   Implementation Properties

The implementation of fake patches applies deception to patching because it attracts attention away from a traditional patch, but does not impact the data flow of the function being patched. Fake patches should be designed such that they are not marked as *dead-code* and removed from the binary as a result of

---

[1] https://www.exploit-db.com/.

Table 1. Fake patch properties

Property	Explanation	Implementation effort
Non-interfering	Fake patches should not interfere with program output nor inhibit performance beyond some threshold determined on a case to case basis	Experimentation
Conspicuous	Fake patches should be "easy" to locate by potential attackers	Easy
Believable	Fake patches should be plausible and not immediately detected as deceptive	Easy
Differentiable	Traditional and fake patches should be distinguishable by developers	Experimentation
Variability	Fake patches should incorporate some aspect of randomness when implemented	Easy
Enticing	Fake patches should be attractive to potential attackers such that they are not automatically discarded	Experimentation
Shelf-life	Fake patches should have a period of time before they are discovered	Experimentation

compiler optimization nor should they be trivial to identify by attackers. These patches should also address the properties outlined in Sect. 3.2. Implementation components of a fake patch should at a minimum include at least one randomly generated value and a conditional statement. Other implementation specifics depend on the actual program being patched.

Control Flow. Fake patches having conditional statements that alter control flow will make them apparent to attackers using static and dynamic analysis tools. This addresses the *conspicuous* property. This also mimics the trend of patches for input validation vulnerabilities.

Mimicking this trend could deceive attackers by showing changes that are expected but fake, addressing the *enticing* property. Experimentation will show how fake patches effect overall program runtime, addressing the *non-interfering* property. We implement fake patch conditional statements such that they include the destination or left-hand-side of an LLVM intermediate representation *store* instruction in the original program mathematically compared to a randomly generated value. The use of a random value address the *variability* property.

We form the body of if-statements by adding code that solves different mathematical expressions with the original program's value as input. These expressions do not alter the value of the legitimate variable; thus, data flow is preserved. The body of fake patch statements should be plausible for the program being patched. This suggests that the body of a fake patch should be developed based on the behavior of the program being patched.

3.4   Post Testing

After applying a ghost patch to software, further testing should be conducted for the following:

1. Evaluating ghost patch impact on software runtime and program memory (i.e. lines of code).
2. Verifying ghost patch does not introduce incompatibilities by applying unit testing.

   A ghost patch should be evaluated for its impact on the program's performance to determine if it is feasible. This determination is dependant upon each program and the execution environment of the program. The memory impact of a ghost patch should also be considered. The size of a ghost patch should be reasonable for end-users to download and apply to vulnerable systems. Developers should establish an upper threshold such that the feasibility is measurable and can be validated. Conjectures about patch size and acceptable runtime are outside of the scope of this research. We do analyze the statistical impact of ghost patches on program runtime and program analysis.

3.5   LLVM Workflow

The workflow of our LLVM prototype begins with a traditionally patched file (we assume developers have previously created a traditional patch). First, this traditionally patched file is compiled using *clang*. This creates intermediate representation bytecode of the traditionally patched program. Next, this file is compiled a second time, applying our ghost patch LLVM pass. This pass adds one or more fake patches to the traditionally patched file. The fake patches are also implemented in intermediate representation bytecode. This stage creates a new ghost patched program. Next, this ghost patched program is compiled into binary using the *clang* compiler. If the file being patched is part of a larger project, the build tool for the project should be mapped to clang to ensure the project gets compiled with the correct flag(s). After the ghost patched code is compiled, the patched and unpatched (this file is before any traditional patch has been applied) binaries are supplied to a binary diff tool, such as *bsdiff*, to create a patch file that can be distributed and applied to unpatched programs. A work flow diagram of this process is shown in Fig. 1.

3.6   Implementation

We implemented a proof of concept that addresses input validation vulnerabilities involving integer variables. We believe our approach can be extended to other variable types and data structures without loss of generality. Our implementation uses LLVM and is about 300 lines of C++ code.

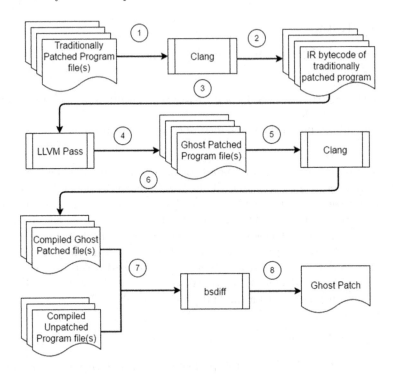

Fig. 1. Complete flow to create a ghost patch using LLVM and bsdiff

4   Evaluation

The prototype of an LLVM program was developed on an Ubuntu 14.04 x86_64 virtual machine. We used LLVM (version 3.4) to develop our pass because its front end compiler allows optimizations to be developed that can be applied to programs agnostic of the language they are written in. We use KLEE [7] (version 1.3) to dynamically analyze our vulnerable code because it evaluates paths through a program using symbolic execution, which can efficiently analyze programs without enumerating every possible input value. Thus, results from Klee represent a best case scenario for attacker resource utilization. The VM has 2 cores and 4 GB RAM. All experiments were also run on this virtual machine.

4.1   Simple Example

We evaluated our approach using the example below, which allows a user to enter two values and then copies each value into an integer variable and lacks input validation code. Then some, operations are performed and the results returned.

```
int calculate(int alpha, int beta);

int main(){
        int a,b,c;
        int d = 9;

        printf("Enter a value: \n");
        scanf("%d", &a);
        printf("Enter another value: \n");
        scanf("%d", &b);

        c = calculate(a,b);
        printf("Value of C: %d\n",c);

        a = b + d;
        if(a > 27)
                c = c * d;
        else
                b = a - b;

        d += d;
        return a;
}

int calculate (int alpha, int beta){
        if(alpha > 88)
                return (alpha + beta);
        else
                return (alpha * beta);
}
```

Experimentation. To evaluate our approach, we compare the length of time for Klee [7], a symbolic execution, dynamic analysis tool, to analyze a legitimately patched and faux patched version of the code. We use the runtime of Klee to measure the impact of a faux patch on exploit generation. We exploit the fact that each new branch will be analyzed because fake patches are indistinguishable from traditional patches from a software perspective.

To show the effect of our approach on program analysis, we evaluate whether the time to dynamically analyze traditionally patched code is significantly different statistically when compared to dynamically analyzing fake patched code using a t test. We also evaluated program runtime using this same experimental structure to determine fake patch's effect on program performance.

5   Results

5.1   Runtime Analysis

Using our simple code example, we collected runtime values using the *time* command for both the original program and a faux patched program. Figure 2 shows the difference in program runtime between a fake patched program and the unpatched program across 100 executions. Using this data, we determined the statistical significance of this difference in runtime using a *t* test. We concluded that there was no statistical significance between the runtimes for the original program and the faux patched program.

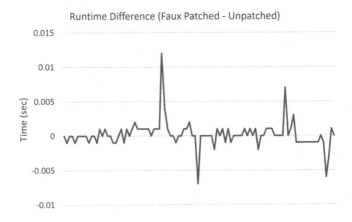

Fig. 2. Difference in faux patched vs. unpatched program runtime

5.2   Program Analysis

We collected values for the runtime of Klee using the *time* command as it analyzed an unpatched, traditionally patched and faux patched version of our simple code example. Figure 3 represents the runtime for each program across 100 executions. A *t* test using these values reveled that there is a statistical significance in Klee's runtime between a traditionally patched program and a faux patched program. This suggests that it is more resource intensive to analyze a faux patched program compared to a traditionally patched program, thus analyzing ghost patches would also require more resources.

6   Discussion

Our proof of concept implementation shows that the application of deception, in the form of fake patches, to software patching is feasible. Our evaluation shows that a faux patch does have an impact on exploit generation, increasing the number of branches in a program, by increasing the resources necessary

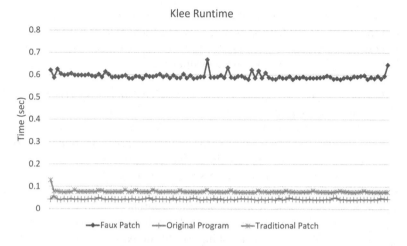

Fig. 3. Klee runtime analysis

to analyze a program. These same patches also impact a program's runtime, but this effect is not statistically significant. This suggests that deception can be used to make exploit generation using patches more resource intensive, enhancing the security of software patches. We believe that with additional research and testing, this approach, either as a standalone technique or in conjunction with other deceptive and detection methods, could impose an exponential increase in program analysis, making exploit generation based on patches an expensive operation, while only adding a minimal increase in program runtime. Our proof of concept implemented and analyzed above supports this claim.

Patch Obfuscation. There are limitations associated with ghost patches that could provide attackers an advantage in identifying fake patches or minimizing their impact on program analysis. Attackers could use exploit generation tools that perform analysis in parallel [6] to distribute the analysis load across multiple machines and optimize exploit generation. One solution is to develop fake patches that increase the length of each path in a program such that tools are unable to develop an exploit. Another solution is to implement polymorphic patches. Ghost patches can utilize randomization to create polymorphic patches that can be distributed based on different heuristics (i.e. based on region, OS version, or staggered by time). The non-deterministic nature of a polymorphic ghost patch could make exploit development more difficult because the same patch would not be applied to each end system. In this case, the traditional patch would also have to be altered for each patch instance to prevent attackers who utilize multiple instances of a patch to expose the legitimate vulnerability.

Based on our observations, traditional patches for input validation vulnerabilities detect malicious input and *return gracefully* from the function. This prevents a compromise, but when viewing a binary diff, searching for differences that add *return* commands could be an identification technique. Applying obfuscation to fake and legitimate patches or to the function being patched could increase the difficulty in distinguishing between each type of patch. Future work will explore obfuscation techniques to make code more difficult to understand [13] and control flow more difficult to evaluate [17].

Active Response Patches. Based on the *non-interfering* property, faux patches should not alter the semantics of the program; the verify step will expose that fake patches do not alter program behavior. Thus, at worst, a brute force approach could expose the vulnerability by analyzing program behavior for each path in a program and identifying which change a program's behavior.

One solution is to use the active response technique for legitimate patches. Active response patches prevent a vulnerability from being exploited but respond to exploits using the same response as an unpatched program. The response could return sanitized data from the actual machine or transfer execution to a honeypot environment [2]. This masking would increase the resources necessary for dynamic analysis tools to identify unpatched systems. Further research will develop techniques that hinder or prevent exploit verification.

Approach Limitation. Another limitation is that based on our experiments, ghost patches only have a dynamic analysis impact when there are multiple *store* operations within a program's intermediate representation (i.e. operations that includes an = sign). Programs that use standard functions (i.e. *memmov*, *memcpy*) to assign values semantically perform the same operation, but are represented differently syntactically, and thus a fake patch cannot be applied.

Adding new lines of code also could add unexpected vulnerabilities. The faux patch code is like any other code that could have a vulnerability. Ghost patched code could also be attacked. Providing attackers with additional paths that could be attacked could result in a denial of service type of attack that slows overall program runtime which could impact the machine's performance.

Future work will extend our tool to compile and add fake patches to more complex code. Additional testing will give insight into the effectiveness of ghost patches. We believe because of the simplistic nature of our approach (i.e. adding conditional statements using the store instruction), its' statistically significant increase in program analysis time will not be lost. We also believe that because of the fake patch if-statement body's code, the difference in runtime will not be statistically significant.

7   Conclusion

This work proposed, implemented and evaluated ghost patching as a technique to mislead attackers using patches to develop exploits against input validation vulnerabilities. We discuss fake patch properties as well as analyze a proof of concept using LLVM. Through experimentation, we found that fake patches add latency to program runtime that is not statistically significant while adding a statistically significant amount of latency to program analysis. If used by program developers as they develop patches for security flaws, we believe faux patches could disrupt the exploit generation process, providing more time for end users to update their systems.

Acknowledgements. The authors would like to thank the anonymous reviewers for their comments and suggestions and specially thank Breanne N. Wright, Christopher N. Gutierrez, Oyindamola D. Oluwatimi and Scott A. Carr for their time, discussion and ideas. The National Science Foundation supported this research under award number 1548114. All ideas presented and conclusions or recommendations provided in this document are solely those of the authors.

References

1. Almeshekah, M.H., Spafford, E.H.: Planning and integrating deception into computer security defenses. In: Proceedings of the 2014 Workshop on New Security Paradigms Workshop, pp. 127–138. ACM (2014)
2. Araujo, F., Hamlen, K.W., Biedermann, S., Katzenbeisser, S.: From patches to honey-patches: lightweight attacker misdirection, deception, and disinformation. In: Proceedings of the 2014 ACM SIGSAC Conference on Computer and Communications Security, pp. 942–953. ACM (2014)
3. Araujo, F., Shapouri, M., Pandey, S., Hamlen, K.: Experiences with honey-patching in active cyber security education. In: 8th Workshop on Cyber Security Experimentation and Test (CSET 2015) (2015)
4. Bashar, M.A., Krishnan, G., Kuhn, M.G., Spafford, E.H., Wägstäff, Jr., S.S.: Low-threat security patches and tools. In: International Conference on Software Maintenance, pp. 306–313. IEEE (1997)
5. Bowen, B.M., Hershkop, S., Keromytis, A.D., Stolfo, S.J.: Baiting inside attackers using decoy documents. In: Chen, Y., Dimitriou, T.D., Zhou, J. (eds.) SecureComm 2009. LNICSSITE, vol. 19, pp. 51–70. Springer, Heidelberg (2009). doi:10.1007/978-3-642-05284-2_4
6. Brumley, D., Poosankam, P., Song, D., Zheng, J.: Automatic patch-based exploit generation is possible: techniques and implications. In: IEEE Symposium on Security and Privacy, pp. 143–157, May 2008
7. Cadar, C., Dunbar, D., Engler, D.R., et al.: KLEE: unassisted and automatic generation of high-coverage tests for complex systems programs. OSDI **8**, 209–224 (2008)
8. Collberg, C., Nagra, J.: Surreptitious Software. Addision-Wesley Professional, Upper Saddle River (2010)
9. Collberg, C.S., Thomborson, C.: Watermarking, tamper-proofing, and obfuscation-tools for software protection. IEEE Trans. Softw. Eng. **28**(8), 735–746 (2002)
10. Coppens, B., De Sutter, B., De Bosschere, K.: Protecting your software updates. IEEE Secur. Priv. **11**(2), 47–54 (2013)
11. Crane, S., Larsen, P., Brunthaler, S., Franz, M.: Booby trapping software. In: Proceedings of the 2013 Workshop on New Security Paradigms Workshop, pp. 95–106. ACM (2013)
12. Dewdey, A.K.: Computer recreations, a core war bestiary of virus, worms and other threats to computer memories. Sci. Am. **252**, 14–23 (1985)
13. Dolan, S.: mov is turing-complete. Technical report 2013 (cit. on p. 153) (2013)

14. Kanzaki, Y., Monden, A., Collberg, C.: Code artificiality: a metric for the code stealth based on an n-gram model. In: Proceedings of the 1st International Workshop on Software Protection, pp. 31–37. IEEE Press (2015)
15. Lattner, C.: The LLVM Compiler Infrastructure. University of Illinois, Urbana-Campaign (2017)
16. Mitnick, K.D., Simon, W.L.: The Art of Deception: Controlling the Human Element of Security. Wiley, New York (2011)
17. Moser, A., Kruegel, C., Kirda, E.: Limits of static analysis for malware detection. In: Twenty-Third Annual Computer Security Applications Conference, 2007. ACSAC 2007, pp. 421–430. IEEE (2007)
18. Mosher's Law of Engineering: Top 50 Programming Quotes of All Time. TechSource (2010)
19. Oh, J.: Fight against 1-day exploits: diffing binaries vs anti-diffing binaries. Black Hat (2009)
20. Ben Salem, M., Stolfo, S.J.: Decoy document deployment for effective masquerade attack detection. In: Holz, T., Bos, H. (eds.) DIMVA 2011. LNCS, vol. 6739, pp. 35–54. Springer, Heidelberg (2011). doi:10.1007/978-3-642-22424-9_3
21. Spafford, E.: More than passive defense. CERIAS (2011)
22. Stoll, C.: The Cuckoo's Egg: Tracking a Spy Through the Maze of Computer Espionage. Simon and Schuster, New York (2005)
23. Symantec: Internet security threat report. Technical report, Symantec (2016)
24. Udupa, S.K., Debray, S.K., Madou, M.: Deobfuscation: reverse engineering obfuscated code. In: 12th Working Conference on Reverse Engineering, p. 10. IEEE (2005)
25. Wang, C., Suo, S.: The practical defending of malicious reverse engineering. University of Gothenburg (2015)
26. Whaley, B.: Toward a general theory of deception. J. Strateg. Stud. 5(1), 178–192 (1982)
27. Yokoyama, A., et al.: SandPrint: fingerprinting malware sandboxes to provide intelligence for sandbox evasion. In: Monrose, F., Dacier, M., Blanc, G., Garcia-Alfaro, J. (eds.) RAID 2016. LNCS, vol. 9854, pp. 165–187. Springer, Cham (2016). doi:10.1007/978-3-319-45719-2_8
28. Yuill, J.J.: Defensive computer-security deception operations: processes, principles and techniques. ProQuest (2006)
29. Yuill, J., Zappe, M., Denning, D., Feer, F.: Honeyfiles: deceptive files for intrusion detection. In: Proceedings from the Fifth Annual IEEE SMC Information Assurance Workshop, pp. 116–122. IEEE (2004)

SIMBER: Eliminating Redundant Memory Bound Checks via Statistical Inference

Hongfa Xue, Yurong Chen, Fan Yao, Yongbo Li, Tian Lan, and Guru Venkataramani(✉)

The George Washington University, Washington, DC, USA
guruv@gwu.edu

Abstract. Unsafe memory accesses in programs written using popular programming languages like C and C++ have been among the leading causes of software vulnerability. Memory safety checkers, such as Softbound, enforce memory spatial safety by checking if accesses to array elements are within the corresponding array bounds. However, such checks often result in high execution time overhead due to the cost of executing the instructions associated with the bound checks. To mitigate this problem, techniques to eliminate redundant bound checks are needed. In this paper, we propose a novel framework, SIMBER, to eliminate redundant memory bound checks via statistical inference. In contrast to the existing techniques that primarily rely on static code analysis, our solution leverages a simple, model-based inference to identify redundant bound checks based on runtime statistics from past program executions. We construct a knowledge base containing sufficient conditions using variables inside functions, which are then applied adaptively to avoid future redundant checks at a function-level granularity. Our experimental results on real-world applications show that SIMBER achieves zero false positives. Also, our approach reduces the performance overhead by up to 86.94% over Softbound, and incurs a modest 1.7% code size increase on average to circumvent the redundant bound checks inserted by Softbound.

1 Introduction

Many software bugs and vulnerabilities in applications (that are especially written using C/C++) occur due to unsafe pointer usage and out-of-bound array accesses. Security exploits, that take advantage of buffer overflows or illegal memory reads/writes, have been a major concern over the past decade. Some of the recent examples include: (i) In February 2016, a Google engineer discovered a stack overflow bug in the glibc DNS client side resolver inside getaddrinfo() function that had the potential to be exploited through attacker-controller domain names, attacker-controlled DNS servers or man-in-the-middle attack [10]; (ii) In 2016, Cisco released security patches to fix a buffer overflow vulnerability in the Internet Key Exchange (IKE) version 1 (v1) and IKE version 2 (v2) code

© IFIP International Federation for Information Processing 2017
Published by Springer International Publishing AG 2017. All Rights Reserved
S. De Capitani di Vimercati and F. Martinelli (Eds.): SEC 2017, IFIP AICT 502, pp. 413–426, 2017.
DOI: 10.1007/978-3-319-58469-0_28

of Cisco ASA Software that could allow an attacker to cause a reload of the affected system or to remotely execute code [5].

In order to protect software from spatial memory/array bound violations, tools such as Softbound [12] have been developed that maintains metadata such as array boundaries along with rules for metadata propagation when loading or storing pointer values. By doing so, Softbound makes sure that pointer accesses do not violate boundaries through runtime checks. While such a tool offers protection from spatial safety violations in programs, we should also note that they often incur high performance overheads due to the following reasons. (a) Array bound checking incurs extra instructions in the form of memory loads and stores for pointer metadata and the propagation of metadata between pointers during assignments. (b) In pointer-intensive programs, such additional memory accesses can introduce memory bandwidth bottleneck, and further degrade system performance.

To mitigate runtime overheads, static techniques to remove redundant checks have been proposed, e.g., ABCD [3] builds and solves systems of linear inequalities among bound and index variables, and WPBound [14] statically computes the potential range of target pointer values inside loops to avoid Softbound-related checks. As the relationship among pointer-affecting variables (i.e., variables, whose values can influence pointers) and array bounds become more complex, static analysis is less effective and usually cannot remove a high percentage of redundant array bound checks.

In this paper, we propose SIMBER, a novel approach that verifies conditions for eliminating bound checks on the fly by harnessing runtime information instead of having to rely on discovering redundant checks solely during compile-time or using static code analysis. SIMBER is effective in removing a vast majority of redundant array checks while being simple and elegant. The key idea is to infer the *safety of a pointer dereference based on statistics from prior program executions*. If prior executions show that the access of array A with length L at index i is within bound, then it is safe to remove the checks on any future access of A with length no smaller than L and an index no larger than i.

In summary, this paper makes the following contributions:

1. Instead of solely relying on static code analysis, SIMBER utilizes runtime statistics to check whether array bound checks can be eliminated. Our experimental results show that SIMBER can discover a high number of redundant bound checks through analyzing the variables that can affect the pointer values.
2. We determine a bound check as redundant only if previous executions deem the checks to be unnecessary and current execution satisfy the condition derived from such prior execution history. This helps SIMBER to guarantee zero false positives.
3. We evaluate using applications from SPEC2006 benchmark suite [1] that have the highest performance overheads in Softbound: bzip2, lbm, sphinx3 and hmmer. In these experiments, we observe that our approach reduces the

performance overheads of spatial safety checks by over 86.94% compared to Softbound.

2 Background

Softbound stores the pointer metadata (array base and bound) when pointers are initialized, and performs array bound checks (or validation) when pointers are dereferenced. For example, for an integer pointer ptr to an integer array $intArray[100]$, Softbound stores $ptr\_base = \&\ intArray[0]$ and $ptr\_bound = ptr\_base + size(intArray)$. When dereferencing pointers, Softbound obtains the base and bound information associated with the target pointer ptr, and does the following check: if the value of ptr is less than ptr_base, or, if $ptr+size$ is larger than ptr_bound, the program terminates. A disadvantage with this approach is the high runtime performance overheads associated with metadata tracking and bound checks especially on pointers that are largely benign or safe. Figure 1 shows the runtime overhead incurred by Softbound-instrumented applications over un-instrumented application as baseline in SPEC2006 benchmarks [1].

We note that some prior works [3,14] have proposed static analysis techniques to eliminate redundant bound checks. In SIMBER, we propose a novel framework where the redundant bound check elimination is performed with the guidance of runtime statistics. Our results show that even limited amounts of runtime statistics can be a quite powerful tool to infer the safety of pointer dereferences, and eliminate unnecessary pointer bound checks.

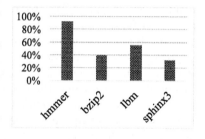

Fig. 1. Runtime performance overhead incurred by Softbound

Consider the example shown in Fig. 2, where $foo(dest, src, n)$ copies the first n characters in string src to $dest$, and replaces remaining characters with blocks of 4-character pattern '0000'. To guarantee safe pointer usage, Softbound checks (denoted by $CHECK\_SB$) will be added before each pointer dereference, e.g., in lines 8, 9, and 20. Thus, bound checks are performed for each iteration of the *for* and *while* loops, resulting in high execution time (performance) overhead.

A static approach such as ABCD [3] relies on building constraint systems for target pointers and programs to remove redundant bound checks. In particular, it identifies that indices i and j in $foo()$ must satisfy $i \leq j$ from the conditions in line 18. Therefore, bound checks on $*(dest+i)$ in line 8 is deemed redundant given the checks performed on $*(dest + j)$ in line 20. However, such static approaches cannot be effective in eliminating other bound checks where such static inferences cannot be made (e.g., in lines 9 and 20). Further, bound information for both pointers $dest$ and src needs to be kept and propagated inside $foo()$ at runtime.

In this paper, we show that (conditionally) removing all the bound checks in $foo()$ is indeed possible using SIMBER. Our solution stems from two key

```
1   foo_SB                                for (j=i; j<i+4; j++)           18
2   (char *dest,char *src,int n)          {                              19
3   {                                       CHECK_SB(dest+j);            20
4     int i, j;                             *(dest+j) = '0';             21
5                                         }                              22
6     for (i=0; i<n; i++)                 i+=4;                          23
7     {                                 }                                24
8       CHECK_SB(dest+i);                                                25
9       CHECK_SB(src+i);                main()                          26
10      *(dest+i) = *(src+i);           {                                27
11    }                                                                  28
12                                        char *dest, *src;             29
13                                        int n;                        30
14    int len=strlen(src);                ...                           31
15                                        foo_SB (dest, src, n);        32
16    while (i<len-4)                     ...                           33
17    {                                 }                                34
```

Fig. 2. Example code illustrating bound checks performed by SoftBound

observations. First, redundant bound checks can be effectively identified by examining different runs of $foo()$. Consider pointer dereference $*(src + i)$ in line 10 as an example. Let $i_{(k)}$ and $src\_bound_{(k)}$ denote the value of index i and the bound of array src in the kth run, which is already determined to be bound-safe, i.e., $i_{(k)} \leq src\_bound_{(k)}$. It is easy to see that any future runs of $foo()$ satisfying $i \leq i_{(k)}$ and $src\_bound \geq src\_bound_{(k)}$ will also be bound-safe, due to the following chain of inequalities $i \leq i_{(k)} \leq src\_bound_{(k)} \leq src\_bound$, implying $i \leq src\_bound$. Second, through a simple dependency analysis, we find that the value of index i is only positively affected by input variable n. Due to this positive dependency, the redundant-check condition $i \leq i_{(k)}$ is guaranteed if we have $n \leq n_{(k)}$. Thus, bound checks for $*(src + i)$ in line 9 can be determined as redundant by comparing input variables n and src_bound with that of previous runs, which entirely removes all checks and bound propagation in $foo()$ at function-level.

3   Overview of System Design

SIMBER consists of five modules: Dependency Graph, Statistical-guided Inference, Knowledge Base, Redundant checks removal and Check-HotSpot Identification. Figure 3 presents our system diagram. Given a target pointer, SIMBER aims to determine if the pointer dereference needs to be checked. First, SIMBER collects values of pointer-affecting variables which can affect the target pointer. It constructs multi-dimensional safe regions where the values of such pointer-affecting variables do not result in bad program behavior (e.g., program crash, buffer overflow). In the current program execution, if the data point representing pointer-affecting variables is inside the safe region, then this pointer dereference is determined to be safe.

3.1   Dependency Graph Construction

Dependency Graph (DG) is a bi-directed graph $\mathcal{G} = (\mathcal{V}, \mathcal{E})$ that represents program variables as vertices in $\mathcal{V}$, and models the dependency between the variables

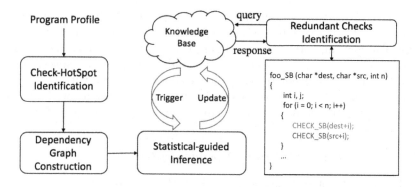

Fig. 3. SIMBER overview and key modules

and array indices/bounds through edges in $\mathcal{E}$. We construct a DG for each function by including all if its pointers and the pointer-affecting variables that could affect the value of pointer. We add trip count (number of times a branch is taken) as auxiliary variables to assist the analysis of loops.

Definition 1 (DG-Node). *The nodes in dependency graphs are the variables that can affect the pointers such as (a) the variables that determine the base of pointers through pointer initialization, assignment or casting; (b) variables that affect the offset and bound of pointers like array index, pointer increment and variables affecting memory allocation size; (c) Trip Count (TC): the number of times a branch (in which a target pointer value changes) is taken.*

Definition 2 (DG-Edge). *DG-Node v_1 will have an out-edge to DG-Node v_2 if v_1 can affect v_2.*

Abstract Syntax Tree (AST) is commonly used by compilers to represent the structure of program code, and to analyze the dependencies between variables and statements. We use Joern tool [18] to generate AST for each function.

Algorithm 1. Dependency graph construction for a given function $foo()$

1: Input: source code of function $foo()$
2: Construct AST of function $foo()$
3: Initialize $\mathcal{V} = \phi$, $\mathcal{E} = \phi$
4: **for** each variable v in AST **do**
5:     $\mathcal{V} = \mathcal{V} + \{v\}$
6: **for** each statement s in AST **do**
7:     **for** each pair of variables j, k in s **do**
8:         add edge $e(j, k)$ to $\mathcal{E}$ according to Remark 1
9: Output: Dependency-Graph $\mathcal{G} = (\mathcal{V}, \mathcal{E})$

Algorithm 1 shows the pseudocode of Dependency Graph (DG) construction for a given function, $foo()$. First, we obtain all of the pointers and their corresponding pointer-affecting variables, and represent them as DG-Nodes. Second, we traverse dependency graph and identify adjacent DG-Nodes that represent the pointer-affecting variables associated with each target pointer. Each target pointer will have an entry in the form of $(func : ptr, var_1, var_2, ..., var_n)$ where $func$ and ptr are the names of the function and target pointer respectively, with var_i being the name of pointer-affecting variables associated with ptr. Through logging the values of these variables during program executions, we build conditions to determine safe regions that help eliminate redundant bound checks.

Remark 1. **Edges added into Dependency Graph:**

E1 Assignment statements	A := B	$B \rightarrow A$	
E2 Function parameters	Func(A,B)	$B \leftrightarrow A$	
E3 Loops	for.../while...	*Add TC to Loops*	
(1) Assignment inside Loops	A := B	$TC \rightarrow A$	
E4 Array Indexing	A[i]	$i \rightarrow A$	

3.2 Statistical-Guided Inference

This module builds safe regions based on the pointer-affecting variables identified by DGs, and updates the safe region through statistical inference from previous execution. Once the pointer-affecting variables for the target pointer are determined, SIMBER collects the values of pointer-affecting variables from runtime profile, and produces a **data point** (or a vector) in Euclidean space with the coordinates of data point being the actual values of pointer-affecting variables. The dimension of the Euclidean space is the number of pointer-affecting variables for the target pointer.

The inference about pointer safety (for pointer-affecting variables that are positively-correlated with the array bound) can be derived as follows: Let us say that a data point $p = (vp_1, vp_2, \ldots, vp_d)$ from prior execution is checked and deemed as safe. Consider another data point $q = (vq_1, vq_2, \ldots, vq_d)$ for the same target pointer from current execution. If each element of q is no larger than that of p, i.e., $vq_1 \leq vp_1$, $vq_2 \leq vp_2$, ..., $vq_d \leq vp_d$, then the bound checks on the target pointer can be removed in the current execution. To extend this inference to pointer-affecting variables that are negatively-correlated with array bound, we unify the representation by converting the variable *bound* into $C - bound$ for sufficiently large constant C (such as the maximum value of an unsigned 32-bit integer). Thus $C - bound$ is also positively correlated, and $C - bound_q \leq C - bound_p$ implies $bound_q \geq bound_p$.

Definition 3 (False Positive). *A false positive occurs if a bound check, that is identified as redundant, is indeed necessary and should have not been removed.*

Definition 4 (Safe Region (SR)). *Safe region is an area that is inferred and built from given data points, such that for any point within the region, the corresponding target pointer is guaranteed to have only safe memory access, e.g., all* *bound checks related to the pointer can be removed with zero false positive, under the assumption that point-affecting variables have monotonic linear relationships with pointer bound.*

Thus, the Safe Region derived from a single data point p is the enclosed area by projecting it to each axis. In other words, it includes all vectors that have smaller (pointer-affecting variable) values and are dominated by p. For example, the safe region of a point $(3, 2)$ is all of the points in the euclidian space with the first coordinate smaller than 3 and the second coordinate smaller than 2 in $\mathbb{R}^2$, namely $q = (q_1, q_2) : q_1 \leq 3, q_2 \leq 2$. We can obtain the Safe Region of multiple data points by taking the union of the safe regions generated by each data point.

Given a set S which consists of N data points in $\mathbb{R}^D$, where D is the dimension of data points, we first project point $p_i, i = 1, 2, \ldots, N$, to each axis and build N-surface enclosed area in $\mathbb{R}^D$, e.g., building a safe region for each data point. The union of these N safe regions is the safe region of S, denoted by $SR(S)$. *Thus, if a new data point q falls inside $SR(S)$, we can find at least one existing point $p \in S$ that dominates q, i.e., $q \leq p$. That is to say, the enclosed projection area of p covers that of q, which means for every pointer-affecting variable in p is larger than that of q.*

There are data points that cannot be determined as safe based on existing (current) safe region when $q \notin SR(S)$. In this case, SIMBER performs bound checks to determine memory safety of such data points and adaptively updates the safe region based on the outcome. More precisely, given current safe region $SR(S)$ and the new coming data point $q \notin SR(S)$, $SR(S)$ will expand to $SR(S)'$ by:

$$SR' = SR(S \cup q) = SR(S) \cup SR(q) = SR(S) \cup \{x : x \leq q\}, \qquad (1)$$

where $\{x : x \leq q\}$ is the set of safe points dominated by vector q. It expands the safe region if (i) there are pointer-affecting variables in the new input q that have a larger value than all points in current safe region $SR(S)$, or (ii) there are array lengths or negatively-correlated variables that have smaller values than all points in $SR(S)$, allowing higher degree of redundant bound check elimination in future executions.

3.3   Knowledge Base

SIMBER stores the safe regions for target pointers in a disjoint memory space - Knowledge Base. The data in Knowledge Base, in the format of (*key, value*), represents the position and the sufficient conditions for removing the redundant bound checks for each target pointer. Statistical Inference is *triggered* to compute the Safe Region whenever the Knowledge Base is updated with newer data points and new execution logs.

We use SQLite [2] to store our Knowledge Base. We create a table to store conditions derived from pointer values and the corresponding pointer-affecting variables.

3.4   Redundant Checks Identification

SIMBER instruments functions within the program with a call to *SIMBER*(), that collects *pointer-affecting input parameters* inside a target function, and queries the knowledge base to obtain the conditions for eliminating array bound checks. In particular, if the all of the data points (formed using function parameters) are within the safe region, the propagation of bound information and the array bound checks can be safely removed from this target function entirely.

We maintain two versions of Check-Hotspot functions: the original version (which contains no bound checks) and the Softbound-instrumented version (that has bound checks and bound meta-data propagation). Based on the result of *SIMBER*() outcome, we can either skip all bound checks inside the function (if the condition holds) or proceed to call the Softbound-instrumented function (if the condition is not satisfied) where bound checks would be performed as shown in Fig. 2. The instrumentation of SIMBER() condition verification inside functions leads to a small increase in code size (by about 1.7%), and we note that such extra code is added only to a small subset of functions with highest runtime overhead for Softbound (see Sect. 3.5 for details).

3.5   Check-HotSpot Identification

To minimize the effect of runtime bound checks, we choose Check-Hotspots functions that have high levels of pointer activity. We identify Check-HotSpots as follows: (a) We use Perf profiling tool [6] to profile two versions of programs: non-instrumented version and softbound-instrumented source code. (b) We compute the difference in absolute execution time spent on different functions between non-instrumented source programs and softbound-instrumented programs to capture the extra time spent on softbound-related code. For every function, we calculate the function-level overhead as the ratio of the time spent on softbound-related code to the total execution time spent in the original version. (c) We list all of the functions with function-level overhead of at least 5% as the Check-HotSpots.

```
1   //original foo() function
2   foo
3   (char *dest,char *src,int n)
4   {...}
5
6   //softbound instrumented foo()
7   foo_SB
8   (char *dest,char *src,int n)
9   {...}
10  main()
11  {
12    char *dest, *src;
13    int n;
```

```
14    ...
15    /*determine whether it is
16     inside the safe region*/
17    if(SIMBER(dest,src,n))
18    {
19      foo(dest, src, n);
20    }
21    else
22    {
23      foo_SB (dest, src, n)
24    }
25    ...
26  }
```

Fig. 4. SIMBER optimized code that determines if bound checks can be removed at function-level granularity

3.6 SIMBER-Optimized Softbound Code

SIMBER instruments the program by adding two branches as shown in Fig. 4. Function *SIMBER()* verifies whether the input variables of *foo()* satisfy the condition to eliminate array bound check, and chooses one of the two possible branches accordingly. Recall the Softbound-instrumented *foo()* function in Fig. 2. The dependency graph contains edges from n to i (due to the *for* loop in line 6), from *src_len* to *len* (due to the assignment in line 14), from *len* to i (due to the *while* loop in line 16), from i to j (due to the second *for* loop in line 18), and from i, j to pointers *src* and *dest* (due to pointer dereference in lines 10 and 21).

We focus on bound checks for $*(dest + j)$ in line 20 to illustrate SIMBER. From the dependency graph, we find bound-affecting variables *len* and n, and form a 3-dimensional vector $(len, n, C - dest\_bound)$ (for large enough, constant C) to represent the safe region corresponding to bound checks for $*(dest + j)$. Assume that C is 1024 and that three previous data points are available: $P_1 = (200, 160, 1024-256)$, $P_2 = (180, 120, 1024-256)$ and $P_3 = (150, 140, 1024-512)$, respectively. Per our discussion in Sect. 3.2, a safe region can be derived from the three data point vectors in a $\mathbb{R}^3$ space, i.e., $SR = \{x : x \leq P_i, \forall i = 1, 2, 3\}$, where inequality $x \leq P_i$ between two vectors is component-wise.

In future executions, new input variables $y = (len, n, C - dest\_bound)$ are verified by $SIMBER()$ to determine if vector x is inside this safe region, i.e., $y \in SR$. As long as we can find one vector from P_1, P_2 and P_3 that dominates y, then the memory access of $*(dest + j)$ in line 20 is safe, allowing us to remove all bound checks and propagation.

4 Evaluation

We use Softbound as the baseline to evaluate the effectiveness of SIMBER in removing redundant bound checks. All measurements are made on a 2.54 GHz Intel Xeon(R) CPU E5540 8-core server with 12 GByte of main memory. The operating system is ubuntu 14.04 LTS.

We select several applications from SPEC 2006 benchmark suite [1] with high performance overheads, including *bzip2*, *hmmer* from SPECint and *lbm*, *sphinx3* from SPECfp. In the evaluation, we first instrument the applications using Softbound, and use Perf [6] to identify the Check-HotSpot functions. Similar to ABCD [3], we consider the optimization of upper- and lower-bound checks as two separate problems. In the following, we focus on eliminating redundant upper-bound checks, and we note that this approach can be adapted to the dual problem of lower-bound checks. We use *reference* inputs provided with SPEC benchmarks. For applications that do not provide developer-supplied representative test cases, we note that fuzzing techniques [11,16] can be used to generate test cases. The policies considered in our evaluation are (a) Softbound-instrumented version (denoted as **Softbound**). (b) SIMBER-Optimized Softbound (denoted as **S.O.S**), where redundant bounds check are removed.

Based on our Check-HotSpot identification results, we study 8 functions shown in Table 1. We note that some Check-HotSpot functions may contribute to high runtime overhead mainly because they are executed frequently, e.g., *bzip2::mainGtU* is called more than 8 million times, despite having small code footprint.

4.1 Redundant Checks

To illustrate SIMBER's efficiency in eliminating redundant bounds checks, Table 1 shows the number of array bound checks required by Softbound, and the number of redundant checks removed by SIMBER along with rate of false positives reported under S.O.S. Our results show that Softbound-related checks can be completely eliminated by S.O.S in three out of eight cases.

Table 2 shows the execution time incurred by Check-Hotspot functions in Softbound and S.O.S. Our experiments show that upto 86.94% improvement in execution time overhead can be achieved by S.O.S through eliminating redundant array bound checks inserted by Softbound. In a few functions, despite totally

Table 1. Redundant array bound checks in Check-HotSpot functions

Benchmark::Function name	# Bounds checks	# Redundant checks	False positives
bzip2::generateMTFValues	2,928,640	1,440,891 (49.2%)	0 (0.0%)
bzip2::mainGtU	81,143,646	81,136,304 (99.9%)	0 (0.0%)
bzip2::BZ2_decompress	265,215	196,259 (74.0%)	0 (0.0%)
hmmer::P7Viterbi	176,000,379	124,960,267 (71.0%)	0 (0.0%)
lbm::LBM_performStreamCollide	128277886	128277886 (100.0%)	0 (0.0%)
sphinx3::vector_gautbl_eval_logs3	2,779,295	2,779,295 (100.0%)	0 (0.0%)
sphinx3::mgau_eval	725,899,332	725,899,332 (100.0%)	0 (0.0%)
sphinx3::subvq_mgau_shortlist	24,704	4,471 (18.1%)	0 (0.0%)

Table 2. Execution time improvement for Check-HotSpot functions

Function name	Time spent in		Execution time reduction
	Softbound	S.O.S	
bzip2::generateMTFValues	77.21 s	39.46 s	48.89%
bzip2::mainGtU	47.94 s	6.26 s	86.94%
bzip2::BZ2_decompress	35.58 s	9.10 s	74.42%
hmmer::P7Viterbi	3701.11 s	812.91 s	78.04%
lbm::LBM_performStreamCollide	1201.79 s	407.06 s	66.13%
sphinx3::vector_gautbl_eval_logs3	1580.03 s	318.10 s	79.87%
sphinx3::mgau_eval	1582.68 s	473.10 s	70.11%
sphinx3::subvq_mgau_shortlist	270.84 s	221.81 s	18.1%

eliminating Softbound-instrumented array bound checks, a small runtime overhead is still incurred due to the extra code added by SIMBER to circumvent redundant bound checks at the function-level.

4.2   Memory Overhead and Code Increase

We note that SIMBER's memory overhead for storing Knowledge Base and additional code instrumentation are modest. Our experiments show that the worst memory overhead is only 20 KB, and the maximum code size increase is less than 5%. Across all applications, SIMBER has an average 5.28 KB memory overhead with an average 1.7% code increase. Overall, we reduce memory overhead by roughly 50% compared to that of Softbound.

4.3   Case Studies

bzip2. *bzip2* is a compression program to compress and decompress inputs files, such as TIFF image and source tar file. We use the function *bzip2::mainGtU* as an example to illustrate how SIMBER removes redundant bound checks. Using Dependency Graph, we first identify *nblock*, i_1, and i_2 as the pointer-affecting variables for the target buffer pointer. For each execution, the Statistical Inference module computes and updates the Safe Region, which results in the following (sufficient) conditions for identifying redundant bounds checks in *bzip2::mainGtU*:

$$nblock > i_1 + 20 \ or \ nblock > i_2 + 20 \qquad (2)$$

Therefore, every time this check-hotspot function is called, SIMBER will eliminate bound checks if the inputs variables' values: *nblock*, i_1, and i_2 satisfy the conditions above. Because its safe region is one-dimensional, the condition checks have low runtime overhead. If satisfied, the conditions guarantee a complete removal of bounds checks in *bzip2::mainGtU* function.

As a second example in *bzip2::generateMTFValue*, we study the conditions to remove bound checks on five different target pointers inside of the function. We observed that three out of five target pointers, with constant array length, are relatively safe from out-of-bound accesses that may also be handled through static (pre-runtime) methods. The array bounds for the other two target pointers are not constant, and eliminating redundant checks on these pointer require a more careful consideration of runtime statistics and conditions formed using pointer-affecting variables. We note that *bzip2::BZ2_decompress* also has similar behavior.

hmmer. *hmmer* is a program for searching DNA gene sequences, and involves many double pointer operations. There is only one Check-HotSpot function, *P7Viterbi*, which contributes over 98% of the performance overhead.

Inside of the *hmmer::P7Viterbi* function, there are four double pointers: *xmx*, *mmx*, *imx* and *dmx*. To cope with double pointers in this function, we consider the row and column array bounds separately, and construct safe regions for each dimension. Besides the four double pointers, we also identify conditions for identifying redundant bound checks for another 14 one-dimensional arrays and pointers. In this case, SIMBER is able to eliminate most of the redundant checks for these 14 one-dimensional arrays with relatively simple conditions for bound check removal. However, for the four double pointers, SIMBER is slightly more conservative due to higher number of dimensions in the conditions.

lbm. lbm is developed to simulate incompressible fluids in 3D, and has only one Check-HotSpot function: *lbm::LBM_performStreamCollide*. The function has two pointers (as input variables) with pointer assignments and dereferencing inside of a *for* loop. Using SIMBER, we obtain the bound conditions for each pointer dereferencing. Using runtime profile, we observed that the pointer dereferences to the same set of memory addresses repeatedly, providing an opportunity to remove all of the bound checks after successfully verifying bound conditions in the first iteration.

sphinx3. Sphinx3 is a well-known speech recognition system. For the first Check-HotSpot function *sphinx3::vector_gautbl_eval_logs3*, there are four target pointers inside this function. Due to the identical access pattern, once we derive the bound check removal conditions for one single pointer, it can also be used for all others, allowing for the redundant checks to be eliminated simultaneously in this function. We observed a similar behavior for a second Check-HotSpot function *sphinx3::mgau_eval*.

The last function *sphinx3::subvq_mgau_shortlist* also has four target pointers. For this function, SIMBER only removed 18.1% redundant checks. On further investigation, we found that a pointer, named *vqdist*, inside of this function had indirect memory access with its index value derived from another pointer: *map*. To handle such situations, we note that our DGs can be extended to include dependencies resulting from such indirect pointer references. Since we do not handle indirect memory accesses in the current version, we are unable to eliminate any redundant bound check that Softbound may perform for this pointer.

5   Related Work

Static code analysis and tools has been widely studied for discovering program vulnerabilities and bugs [8,20]. Nurit et al. [7] have studied techniques that target string-related bugs in C programs with conservative pointer analysis using abstract constraint expressions for pointer operations. Such static approaches require extensive program modeling and analysis (e.g., by constructing constraint solver systems) and may offer limited scope in dealing with certain vulnerabilities that occur only at runtime (e.g., due to user input-related bugs). Wurthinger et al. [17] use dominator tree to maintain the conditions for code blocks in Java-based programs. CCured [13] is a type-safe system that classifies pointers to three types: safe, sequence, dynamic, and then applies different rules to check them. Different from these prior works, SIMBER leverages runtime profile to determine safe pointer accesses.

Statsym [9] proposes a novel framework to combine statistical and formal methods to discover for vulnerable paths in program, and can dramatically reduce the search space for vulnerable paths compared to symbolic executors such as KLEE [4]. Additionally, some works employ machine learning to improve the efficiency of static code analysis, and use the similarity of code patterns to facilitate discovery of bugs and errors [19,20]. We note that the accuracy of such methods rely on the choice of machine learning algorithms. Hardware support to identify malicious information outflows [15] and code reuse-based attacks [21] through buffer overflows have also been studied by prior works. SIMBER can work synergistically with these approaches to improve the security of applications.

6 Conclusions and Future Work

In this paper, we propose SIMBER, a framework integrating with statistics-guided inference to remove redundant array bound checks based on runtime profile. Its statistical inference adaptively builds a knowledge base using program execution logs containing variables that affect pointer values, and then uses this information to remove redundant array bound checks inserted by popular array bound checkers such as Softbound. SIMBER reduces performance overhead of Softbound by up to 86.94%, and incurs a modest 1.7% code size increase on average to circumvent redundant bound checks inserted by Softbound. Currently, SIMBER works at function-level granularity. For future work, we will study ways to deploy SIMBER at a finer granularity to remove redundant bound checks.

Acknowledgments. This work was supported by the US Office of Naval Research (ONR) under Award N00014-15-1-2210. Any opinions, findings, conclusions, or recommendations expressed in this article are those of the authors, and do not necessarily reflect those of ONR.

References

1. SPEC CPU (2006). https://www.spec.org/cpu2006/
2. SQLite. https://www.sqlite.org
3. Bodík, R., Gupta, R., Sarkar, V.: ABCD: eliminating array bounds checks on demand. ACM SIGPLAN Not. **35**, 321–333 (2000). ACM
4. Cadar, C., Dunbar, D., Engler, D.R., et al.: KLEE: unassisted and automatic generation of high-coverage tests for complex systems programs. In: OSDI, vol. 8, pp. 209–224 (2008)
5. Cisco. CVE-2016-1287: Cisco ASA software IKEv1 and IKEv2 buffer overflow vulnerability (2016). https://goo.gl/QCPvut
6. de Melo, A.C.: The new linux 'perf' tools. In: Slides from Linux Kongress, vol. 18 (2010)
7. Dor, N., Rodeh, M., Sagiv, M.: CSSV: towards a realistic tool for statically detecting all buffer overflows in C. ACM SIGPLAN Not. **38**, 155–167 (2003). ACM

8. Evans, D., Larochelle, D.: Improving security using extensible lightweight static analysis. IEEE Softw. **19**(1), 42–51 (2002)
9. Fan, Y., Yongbo, L., Yurong, C., Hongfa, X., Venkataramani, G., Tian, L.: StatSym: vulnerable path discovery through statistics-guided symbolic execution. In: Proceedings of 2017 47th IEEE/IFIP International Conference on Dependable Systems and Networks (DSN). IEEE (2017)
10. Google: CVE-2015-7547: glibc getaddrinfo stack-based buffer overflow (2015). https://security.googleblog.com/2016/02/cve-2015-7547-glibc-getaddrinfo -stack.html
11. McNally, R., Yiu, K., Grove, D., Gerhardy, D.: Fuzzing: the state of the art. Technical report, DTIC Document (2012)
12. Nagarakatte, S., Zhao, J., Martin, M.M., Zdancewic, S.: SoftBound: highly compatible and complete spatial memory safety for C. In: Proceedings of the 30th ACM SIGPLAN Conference on Programming Language Design and Implementation, pp. 245–258. ACM (2009)
13. Necula, G.C., McPeak, S., Weimer, W.: CCured: type-safe retrofitting of legacy code. ACM SIGPLAN Not. **37**, 128–139 (2002). ACM
14. Sui, Y., Ye, D., Su, Y., Xue, J.: Eliminating redundant bounds checks in dynamic buffer overflow detection using weakest preconditions. IEEE Trans. Reliab. **65**(4), 1682–1699 (2016)
15. Venkataramani, G., Chen, J., Doroslovacki, M.: Detecting hardware covert timing channels. IEEE Micro **36**(5), 17–27 (2016)
16. Woo, M., Cha, S.K., Gottlieb, S., Brumley, D.: Scheduling black-box mutational fuzzing. In: Proceedings of the 2013 ACM SIGSAC Conference on Computer & Communications Security, pp. 511–522. ACM (2013)
17. Würthinger, T., Wimmer, C., Mössenböck, H.: Array bounds check elimination for the Java HotSpot client compiler. In: 5th International Symposium on Principles and Practice of Programming in Java, pp. 125–133. ACM (2007)
18. Yamaguchi, F.: Joern: a robust code analysis platform for C/C++ (2016). http:// www.mlsec.org/joern/
19. Yamaguchi, F., Lottmann, M., Rieck, K.: Generalized vulnerability extrapolation using abstract syntax trees. In: Proceedings of the 28th Annual Computer Security Applications Conference, pp. 359–368. ACM (2012)
20. Yamaguchi, F., Wressnegger, C., Gascon, H., Rieck, K.: Chucky: exposing missing checks in source code for vulnerability discovery. In: Proceedings of the 2013 ACM SIGSAC Conference on Computer & Communications Security, pp. 499–510. ACM (2013)
21. Yao, F., Chen, J., Venkataramani, G.: Jop-alarm: detecting jump-oriented programming-based anomalies in applications. In: Proceedings of IEEE 31st International Conference on Computer Design (ICCD), pp. 467–470 (2013)

Towards Systematic Privacy and Operability (PRIOP) Studies

Rene Meis[✉][iD] and Maritta Heisel

paluno - The Ruhr Institute for Software Technology,
University of Duisburg-Essen, Duisburg, Germany
{`rene.meis,maritta.heisel`}`@paluno.uni-due.de`

Abstract. The assessment of privacy properties of software systems gains more and more importance nowadays. This is, on the one hand because of increasing privacy concerns of end-users due to numerous reported privacy breaches, and on the other hand due to stricter data protection regulations, e.g., the EU General Data Protection Regulation that prescribes an assessment of the privacy implications that a project possibly has. The lack of systematic methods to assist a comprehensive and detailed privacy analysis makes it hard for analysts to address the end-users' and legal requirements. In this paper, we adopt the principles of the hazard and operability (HAZOP) studies, which have successfully been used for safety analyses, to privacy to provide a systematic method to identify the relevant privacy threats for a software to be developed. We propose a method called privacy and operability (PRIOP) studies that allows to systematically analyze the potential privacy issues that a software to be developed might raise, based on the software's functionality at the requirements level.

1 Introduction

Privacy is a software quality that gains more and more attention these days. On the one hand end-users are more concerned about privacy and call for more transparency on how their personal information[1] (PI) is processed [1]. On the other hand different legislators prescribe that data protection/privacy impact assessments ((D)PIAs) are performed, e.g., the European Union in the new EU General Data Protection Regulation. A (D)PIA has to be performed for all kinds of projects that involve the processing of PI. Its goal is to assess the implications of the project on the data subjects' privacy.

A central element of a (D)PIA is the identification and evaluation of privacy threats to estimate the privacy risks implied by the considered project. In this paper, we focus on software projects and want to assist analysts to identify

---

[1] We consider any information that is related to a natural person as personal information. We call this natural person *data subject*.

© IFIP International Federation for Information Processing 2017
Published by Springer International Publishing AG 2017. All Rights Reserved
S. De Capitani di Vimercati and F. Martinelli (Eds.): SEC 2017, IFIP AICT 502, pp. 427–441, 2017.
DOI: 10.1007/978-3-319-58469-0_29

and evaluate the privacy threats of a software project as early as possible during the development process, namely in the requirements engineering phase. To do so, we adopt the Hazard and Operability (HAZOP) [2] studies, which have successfully been used to assess the safety implications of a system, to a systematic methodology called Privacy and Operability (PRIOP) studies. We illustrate how PRIOP can be applied based on artifacts produced by the Problem-based Privacy Analysis (ProPAn) method [3].

The rest of the paper is structured as follows. Section 2 introduces a small eHealth scenario as running example, and HAZOP and ProPAn as background of this work. PRIOP is introduced in Sect. 3. Section 4 discusses related work and Sect. 5 concludes the paper.

2   Background

Running Example. We illustrate how a PRIOP study is performed using an electronic health system (EHS) scenario provided by the industrial partners of the EU project *Network of Excellence (NoE) on Engineering Secure Future Internet Software Services and Systems (NESSoS)*. This scenario is based on the German health care system which uses health insurance schemes for the accounting of treatments. The functionalities of the considered system cover the management of electronic health records (EHRs) (functional requirements R1 and R2), the interaction with mobile devices of patients (R5 and R6), the accounting and billing of patients (R3 and R4), and providing anonymized medical data for clinical research (R7).

In this paper, we focus on the functional requirement R3. R3 is concerned with the problem that doctors shall be able to perform the accounting of treatments that patients received from them. For this, the treatments, diagnoses, and insurance number of the patient are passed to an external insurance application that provides the connection to the patient's insurance company. This insurance application then returns the information which treatments are beared by the patient's insurance contract and the software-to-be shall create an invoice for the treatments that are not covered by the patient's insurance contract. For this, the doctor additionally enters the costs for the treatments.

Hazard and Operability Studies. The international standard IEC 61882 [2] defines what a Hazard and Operability (HAZOP) study is and a process to perform a HAZOP study. HAZOP aims at identifying potential hazards and operability problems. A hazard is defined as the potential source of *"physical injury or damage to the health of people or damage to property or the environment"* [2] and an operability problem is any *deviation* from the intended behavior of the system that leads to non-conformance with its (functional) requirements. During a HAZOP study small parts of a system are analyzed in isolation. To systematically identify the potential hazards or operability problems of these parts, HAZOP proposes the eleven guide words NO, MORE, LESS, AS WELL AS, PART OF, REVERSE, OTHER THAN, EARLY, LATE, BEFORE, and

AFTER. These guide words are interpreted in the context of the behavioral characteristics of the part under consideration and lead to deviations of the intended behavior. The derived deviations for a part are documented together with the *possible causes* of the described situation, its *consequences*, and *safeguards* that shall prevent the occurrence of this situation, or reduce the consequences the deviation may have in a template.

In this paper, we adapt HAZOP to be used in the context of a privacy threat analysis. Next, we introduce the Problem-based Privacy Analysis (ProPAn) method that can be used as a starting point for a PRIOP study.

Problem-Based Privacy Analysis. To perform a privacy threat analysis, first, the *system*, consisting of the *machine* (software to be developed) and the *environment* it shall be integrated in (cf. [4]), has to be analyzed. To be more precise, it has to be known (1) which PI of which data subjects is processed by the machine, (2) how is this PI collected by the machine, (3) where and how is the PI stored, and (4) to which other entities the machine provides the PI it processes.

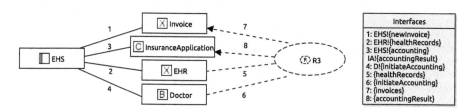

Fig. 1. Problem diagram for functional requirement R3

In this paper, we demonstrate PRIOP based on inputs provided by the Problem-based Privacy Analysis (ProPAn). ProPAn is a systematic and tool-supported[2] method to perform a privacy analysis starting with a set of functional requirements. The functional requirements represent a decomposition of the overall problem of building the machine and they have to be modeled as problem diagrams following Jackson's problem frame approach [4]. Figure 1 shows the problem diagram for requirement R3 of the EHS example.

It shows on the left the machine EHS (box on the left) and its *interfaces* (lines between the boxes) to the environment (boxes in the middle). The environment of the machine consists of *domains*. Jackson distinguishes three types of domains. Biddable domains (B) are usually people, lexical domains (X) are physical representations of data, and causal domains (C) are objects that behave according to a given specification. The relevant environment for R3 consists of the lexical domains EHR (representing the electronic health records) and Invoice (representing the invoices for treatments that the patient's insurance contracts do not cover), the causal domain InsuranceApplication (which is the interface

---

[2] http://www.uml4pf.org/ext-propan.

to the patients' insurances to perform the accounting of treatments patients received), and the biddable domain Doctor (who initiates the accounting).

On the right, the problem diagram shows the *functional requirement* R3 (dashed oval on the right) and its references to the environment. Jackson distinguishes two kinds of references from functional requirements to domains. First, a requirement can *refer to* (dashed line) an event, action, or state of a domain due to which the environment shall behave in the desired way. This desired behavior of the environment is expressed using the second kind of reference. That is, a requirement can *constrain* (dashed line with filled arrow head) events, actions, or states of a domain. R3 refers to the event that the Doctor initiates the accounting and to the EHRs of the involved patients, which contain the PI treatments, diagnoses, insurance number, and the patients billing information. Additionally, R3 constrains that the InsuranceApplication provides the feedback which treatments are covered by the patients' insurance contracts and that a corresponding invoice is created for treatments not beared by the patient's insurance.

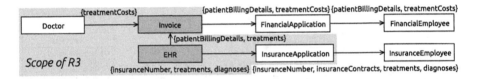

Fig. 2. Excerpt of a graph that visualizes how PI of patients is processed

ProPAn helps an analysis team that incorporates expertise in requirements engineering, privacy, and the application domain to (1) elicit privacy-relevant domain knowledge [5], (2) identify the PI processed by the system and how it flows through it [6], and (3) derive the relevant privacy requirements for the machine [3]. Figure 2 shows an excerpt of a graph that visualizes the flow of patient's PI due to the functional requirements. This graph is a result of ProPAn's steps to identify the PI that is processed by the system and how it is processed by the system. The gray highlighted part of the graph shows the information flows that were elicited due to R3. The flows outside of the gray part originate from other functional requirements or domain knowledge. The gray printed domains represent designed domains, and the white domains represent given domains. According to Jackson, designed domains are part of the machine and hence, part of the development problem. In contrast, given domains are the parts of the machine's environment that have to be considered as they are, i.e., their specified behavior is not under the control of the development team and cannot be changed. The graph shows that due to R3 treatmentCosts are collected from Doctors (flow from a given domain to a designed domain) and stored in an Invoice together with patientBillingDetails and treatments (flows to a designed domain). In other words, during the privacy analysis with ProPAn, we identified and documented that an invoice contains the previously mentioned

PI. Furthermore, insuranceNumber, treatments, and diagnoses flow to the InsuranceApplication (flow from a designed domain to a given domain), due to the machine because of R3. Due to requirement R4 and elicited privacy-relevant domain knowledge, the information provided to the InsuranceApplication flows further to InsuranceEmployees and the patientBillingDetails and treatmentCosts are sent to a FinancialApplication (R4) and further to its employees to perform the billing.

The privacy requirements considered by ProPAn are based on the six protection goals for privacy proposed by Hansen et al. [7]. These consists of the classical security requirements confidentiality (SC), integrity (SI), and availability (SA) and the privacy goals unlinkability, transparency, and intervenability. We refined the privacy goal unlinkability based on the work of Pfitzmann and Hansen [8] to the privacy requirements anonymity (UA), pseudonymity (UP), undetectability (UU), and data unlinkability (UD). The privacy goal transparency was refined by us in [9] into information requirements for the collection (TC), storage (TS), and flow (TF) of PI, and informing about exceptional cases (TE) concerning the processing of PI. In [10] we refined the privacy goal intervenability into intervention requirements for data subjects (ID) and authorities (IA).

In this paper, we consider the artifacts produced by ProPAn as input for PRIOP, but any method supporting points (1)–(3) (mentioned above) can be used.

3   Privacy and Operability Studies

PRIOP aims at a systematic privacy and operability analysis of a software project. Figure 3 visualizes the central steps (arrows) of a PRIOP study and the created artifacts (boxes). First, the software project has to be *decomposed* into subproblems. PRIOP does not prescribe how the decomposition is achieved. For example, Jackson's problem frame approach can be used to derive the project's subproblems. For each of these subproblems, we create a *table* for further analysis. This table should contain a short summary of the subproblem that is considered and should mention who is involved in the PRIOP study of the subproblem. Then each subproblem is *categorized* based on its functionality, as discussed later in this section. For each identified category of the subproblem a *block* is added to the subproblem's table. Finally, the PRIOP guide words have to be *considered* for every combination of subproblem and category. The consideration of a

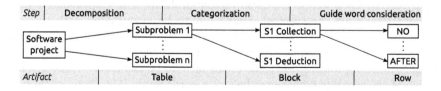

Fig. 3. Steps and artifacts of a PRIOP study

guide word results in a *row* in the block of the considered category in the table of the considered subproblem. In the following, we provide more details on the categorization of subproblems and the consideration of guide words.

PRIOP Operation Categories. During the analysis of the identified subproblems, we distinguish four categories of how PI can be processed by the machine. These categories are *collection, storage, flow,* and *deduction* of PI. An operation is in the category *collection,* if it describes that information is collected by the machine from a given domain. Operations in the category *storage* are concerned with the storage of PI at designed domains. If an operation causes a flow of PI from the machine to a given domain, then it is in the category *flow.* Operations in the category *deduction* are concerned with the deduction or computation of PI based on other information.

An operation can be in none (i.e., it does not process PI) or multiple of these categories, depending on the characteristics of the operation. This differentiation of operation categories helps to systematically assess the characteristics of a subproblem in order to identify privacy threats that it possibly causes. To refer to all of these categories simultaneously, we will use the term *processing.*

If the PRIOP study is performed based on ProPAn, then we consider the functional requirements as subproblems and can perform their categorization automatically based on the artifacts created by this method. For requirement R3 of the EHS example, we can see from Fig. 2 that it is concerned with the collection of PI from Doctors, the storage of PI at the domain Invoice, and sending PI to the InsuranceApplication. Figure 2 also shows which PI is collected, stored, and flows. Furthermore, the ProPAn model documents (not shown in this paper) that the PI treatmentCosts is derived from the PI treatments, diagnoses, and insuranceContracts by doctors based on the feedback provided by the insurance application. Hence, R3 belongs to all operation categories.

PRIOP Guide Words. We consider all HAZOP guide words as useful to identify privacy threats, because these guide words describe in general the deviations that can occur in all kinds of operations a subproblem may be concerned with. We add one additional guide word, namely INCORRECT. This guide word shall cover the cases in which operations are performed incorrectly or with incorrect information as an input. Table 1 shows all PRIOP guide words and our deviation patterns for the four previously introduced operation categories. If these deviation patterns are used for a concrete subproblem, then the terms in angle brackets (< >) have to be instantiated for the subproblem (cf. column deviations in Table 2). The term <PI> is instantiated with the PI that is collected/stored/flown/deduced due to the subproblem. If a subproblem is in the category *flow,* then the term <target> has to be instantiated with the given domains to which the PI flows. Furthermore, there are some terms in *italics.* While the other terms can be instantiated based on the combination of operation category and subproblem, the italic terms have to be instantiated under consideration of the concrete deviations the guide words imply. The terms *<other PI>* and *<additional PI>* have to be instantiated with the PI that is considered to be unintendedly collected/stored/flown/deduced. *<other domain>, <other*

target>, and *<additional target>* have to be instantiated with the domains to which information flows unintendedly.

The PRIOP Template. The previously introduced guide words shall help to identify deviations of the intended behavior of the operations a subproblem is concerned with. These deviations can lead to violations of privacy requirements and the subproblem's operability. In the case that such an identified deviation leads to a violation of a privacy requirement, the deviation is a privacy threat. We developed a template that is based on the templates proposed to be used in HAZOP studies in [2], but enhanced with additional fields to allow to elicit and document attributes that are needed for a later risk evaluation of the identified privacy threats.

An excerpt of the PRIOP template instance for R3 of the EHS example is shown in Table 2. We omit the general information about the subproblem and the people involved in the PRIOP study. In Table 2, we see for each operation category a block (introduced with a row with black background). We selected one or two guide words for each operation category block to illustrate how the proposed template could be filled. For each operation category it is documented from, at, to, or by which domain which PI is collected, stored, flows, or is deduced, respectively. The columns are separated into three areas.

The first two columns show the considered guide word for the row and the deviations it can lead to for the operation category and the considered subproblem. Our deviation patterns shown in Table 1 can be used as starting point for the derivation of the deviations implied by a guide word. The terms <PI> and <target> can be instantiated with the corresponding information provided in the operation category block. Nevertheless, the deviation pattern instances need to be modified to fit into the context of the subproblem. The deviations possibly represent privacy threats or operability issues.

The second area consists of the third and fourth column. In this area, the analysis team has to document the identified causes that possibly lead to the deviations. Additionally, the likelihood of each cause shall be documented. The analysis team should agree on a common likelihood scale, be it qualitative or quantitative. A common scale will make it easier to homogeneously evaluate the risks implied by the identified privacy threats.

The third area consists of the last three columns. This area is concerned with the consequences the deviations may have on the privacy requirements or the operability of the subproblem. The consequences are first documented as free text, then the harmed privacy requirements are explicitly listed, and it is documented to which degree the described consequences impact the listed privacy requirements. Similar to the likelihood scale, the analysis team has also to agree on a consequence scale.

If the analysis team identified possible causes for a guide word and consequences that harm privacy requirements, then the deviation represents a privacy threat. Whether and how this threat has to be further assessed is in most cases determined using a risk matrix that defines which combinations of likelihood and consequence of a threat are acceptable and which are not. Our template already

Table 1. Deviation patterns for the all combinations of proposed guide words and operation categories

Guide word	Deviation patterns for operation category			
	Collection	Storage	Flow	Deduction
NO	\<PI\> is not collected	\<PI\> is not stored	\<PI\> does not flow to \<target\>.	\<PI\> is not deduced
MORE	More \<PI\> is collected than intended, including collection of \<PI\> with additional methods, with higher linkability, in higher amount, or with higher availability.	More \<PI\> is stored than intended, including storage of \<PI\> with higher linkability, in higher amount, with higher availability, or with longer duration.	More \<PI\> flows to \<target\> than intended, including flow of \<PI\> with higher linkability, in higher amount, or with higher availability.	More \<PI\> is deduced than necessary, including deduction of \<PI\> with higher linkability, in higher amount, or with higher availability.
LESS	Less \<PI\> is collected than intended, including collection of \<PI\> with less methods, with lower linkability, in lower amount, or with lower availability.	Less \<PI\> is stored than intended, including storage of \<PI\> with lower linkability, in lower amount, with lower availability, or with shorter duration.	Less \<PI\> flows to \<target\> than intended, including flow of \<PI\> with lower linkability, in lower amount, or with lower availability.	Less \<PI\> is deduced than necessary, including deduction of \<PI\> with lower linkability, in lower amount, or with lower availability.
AS WELL AS	In addition to \<PI\> \<additional PI\> is collected or in addition to the software-to-be \<other domains\> collect the \<PI\>.	In addition to \<PI\> \<additional PI\> is stored.	In addition to \<PI\> \<additional PI\> flows to \<target\>, or\<PI\> flows to an \<additional target\>.	In addition to \<PI\> \<additional PI\> is deduced.
PART OF	Only a part of \<PI\> is collected.	Only a part of \<PI\> is stored.	Only a part of \<PI\> flows to \<target\>, or \<PI\> flows to fewer targets.	Only a part of \<PI\> is deduced.
INCORRECT	The collected \<PI\> is incorrect.	The stored \<PI\> is incorrect.	The \<PI\> flowing to \<target\> is incorrect.	The deduced \<PI\> is incorrect.
REVERSE	\<PI\> flows from machine to source of collection.	\<PI\> is deleted.	\<PI\> or \<other PI\> flows from \<target\> to the machine.	\<original PI\> is or can be deduced from \<PI\>.
OTHER THAN	\<other PI\> is collected instead of \<PI\>.	\<other PI\> is stored instead of \<PI\>.	\<other PI\> flows to \<target\> instead of \<PI\> or \<PI\> flows to \<other target\>.	\<other PI\> is or can be deduced instead of \<PI\>.
EARLY	\<PI\> is collected earlier than intended relative to clock time.	\<PI\> is stored earlier than intended relative to clock time.	\<PI\> flows earlier than intended to \<target\> relative to clock time.	\<PI\> is deduced earlier than intended relative to clock time.
LATE	\<PI\> is collected later than intended relative to clock time.	\<PI\> is stored later than intended relative to clock time.	\<PI\> flows later than intended to \<target\> relative to clock time.	\<PI\> is deduced later than intended relative to clock time.
BEFORE	\<PI\> is collected before another prior operation. E.g., collection before gaining consent.	\<PI\> is stored before another prior subsequent operation. E.g., storing before gaining consent, or before anonymization.	\<PI\> flows before another prior operation to \<target\>. E.g., sending before gaining consent, or before anonymization.	\<PI\> is or can be deduced before another prior operation. E.g., deduction before gaining consent, or before anonymization.
AFTER	\<PI\> is collected after another subsequent operation. E.g., collection of up-to-date information after it was needed or the data subject withdrew consent.	\<PI\> is stored after another subsequent operation. E.g., storage of after another operation would have needed \<PI\>, or data subject has withdrawn consent.	\<PI\> flows after another subsequent operation to \<target\>. E.g., operation on \<target\> is performed before the up-to-date \<PI\> was provided, or data subject has withdrawn consent.	\<PI\> is or can be deduced after another subsequent operation. E.g., deduction after another operation would have needed \<PI\>, or data subject has withdrawn consent.

Table 2. Excerpt of the instantiated template for functional requirement R3

Guide word	Deviations	Possible causes	Likelihood	Consequences	Harmed Privacy Requirements	Impact
Operation category: Collection	**from: Doctor**			**PI: treatmentCosts**		
NO	treatmentCosts are not collected	Doctor forgets to enter the costs of his/her treatments or does not save the changes made.	Unlikely	Doctor will not get paid and Patients not billed.	-	-
MORE	Higher treatmentCosts are collected than intended.	Doctors incidentially enter costs for treatments not performed or too high treatment costs	Unlikely	Patients will get too high bills or are billed for treatments that they did not receive.	1) SI, 2) TE, 3) ID, and 4) IA for treatmentCosts	1) Major 2), 3), and 4) Moderate
Operation category: Storage	**at: Invoice**			**PI: treatments, patientBillingDetails, treatmentCosts**		
BEFORE	treatments, patientBillingDetails, and treatmentCosts are stored in Invoice before it is known which treatments are beared by the Patient's insurance contract.	a) Doctor explicitly initiates the creation of an invoice without knowing whether the concerned treatments are beared by the Patient's insurance contract b) A software error causes the creation of the invoice without before having the necessary information	Unlikely	Patients will get too high or too low bills.	1) SI, 2) TS, 3) TE, 4) ID, and 5) IA for treatments, patientBillingDetails, treatmentCosts	Moderate
Operation category: Flow	**to: InsuranceApplication**			**PI: insuranceNumber, diagnoses, treatments**		
LESS	Less diagnoses and treatments flow than the patients received, or it is not possible for the insurance application to link the diagnoses and treatments to the Patient's insuranceNumber.	a) Software error b) Insurance Application is temporary unreachable	a) Unlikely b) Possible	i) If too few diagnoses are transmitted to the InsuranceApplication or if diagnoses and insuranceNumber are not linkable to the treatments, then the Insurance Application is not able to perform the accounting. This will result in higher bills. ii) If treatments that are not beared by the Patient's insurance contract are not transmitted to the InsuranceApplication, then no invoice will be created for them.	i) 1) SI, 2) TF, 3) TE, 4) ID, and 5) IA for treatments, diagnoses and insuranceNumber ii) -	i) Major
INCOR-RECT	The insuranceNumber, diagnoses, or treatments flowing to InsuranceApplication are incorrect.	a) Software error b) Incorrect data in EHR	a) Unlikely b) Rare	Patients will get too high bills or are billed for treatments that they did not receive.	i) 1) SI, 2) TF, 3) TE, 4) ID, and 5) IA for treatments, diagnoses and insuranceNumber	Major
Operation category: Deduction	**by: Doctor and InsuranceApplication**			**PI: treatmentCosts**		
RE-VERSE	healthInsurances, diagnoses, and treatments can be deduced from treatmentCosts.	TreatmentCosts may allow to deduce the treatments performed, diagnoses, or insuranceContracts if observed over a longer time especially if to some extent the date of deduction is known.	Rare	Financial employees that are able to observe the treatment costs over a longer time might be able to deduce the treatments, diagnoses, or insuranceContracts of specific Patients.	1) SC against Financial Employees, 2) TF, 3) TE, 4) ID, and 5) IA for treatments, diagnoses, and insuranceContracts.	Major

provides this information such that a risk matrix can easily be filled based on an instantiated template.

We only discuss the last row of the template instance for R3 in Table 2. The row is concerned with the deduction of the treatment costs for treatments not covered by the patients' insurance contracts which is performed by doctors based on the result of the accounting provided by the insurance application. The deviation that is derived for the guide word REVERSE is that the patient's PI healthInsurances, diagnoses, and treatments can be deduced from treatment-Costs. This deviation could be possible if the treatment costs are observed over a longer time, e.g., because specific diagnosed illnesses could imply a series of treatments that lead to specific treatment costs allowing to conclude from the treatment costs the diagnosed illness and received treatments. The analysis team decided that this is rarely possible. As a consequence the financial employees who are able to observe the treatment costs over a longer time might be able to deduce the treatments, diagnoses, or insuranceContracts of specific patients. The analysis team identified that this consequence harms a confidentiality requirement saying that the deducable PI shall not be disclosed to financial employees. Furthermore, the transparency requirements that are concerned with informing the patient about the flow of and exceptional cases for the deducable PI and the related intervenability requirements for the patient and authorities are harmed. From the documented consequence a major impact on all listed privacy requirements is expected.

The shown template can be enriched with further columns. For example, it can be helpful to provide additional columns to document rationales, e.g., why a specific likelihood was selected for a possible cause, why a possible cause has a documented consequence, or why a consequence impacts the stated privacy requirements in the defined way. Furthermore, already existing safeguards or possible treatments could be documented that shall either reduce the likelihood of a possible cause or the consequence on a privacy requirement.

Relation of Guide Words to Privacy Requirements. If the taxonomy of privacy requirements used by ProPAn (see Sect. 2) is used, we can provide additional support to instantiate the template. Based on the deviation patterns (see Table 1), we identified the privacy requirements that are expected to be harmed by a deviation. Table 3 shows the relations that we identified. An "X" in the table means that a deviation implied by the guide word for the operation category, could harm the respective privacy requirement. If a cell is empty or a privacy requirement is not mentioned, then we do not expect a violation of this privacy requirement for deviations implied by the respective guide word and operation category. In Table 3, we use the abbreviations for the privacy requirements that were introduced in Sect. 2 and we introduce three groups (Gn) of privacy requirements that share the combinations of guide words and operation categories for which they are relevant. This mapping of combinations of guide words and operation categories to privacy requirements shall help to identify the privacy requirements that are harmed by an identified deviation, but it could also

Table 3. Privacy requirements that might be harmed by guide words' deviations

Guide words	Collection			Storage		Flow			Deduction	
	G1, TC	G3	TF	G1, TS	G3	G1, TF	G3	TC	G1, G2	G3
NO, LESS, PART OF, INCORRECT	×			×		×			×	
MORE, AS WELL AS, EARLY, LATE, BEFORE, AFTER	×	×		×	×	×	×		×	×
REVERSE	×	×	×	×		×	×	×	×	×
OTHER THAN	×	×	×	×	×	×			×	×

G1 = {SI, SA, TE, ID, IA}, G2 = {TC, TF, TS}, G3 = {SC, UU, UA, UD, UP}

serve as a starting point to elicit scenarios that violate the privacy requirements under consideration of the guide word and operation category.

We identified that for all combinations of guide words and operation categories the privacy requirements integrity (SI), availability (SA), exceptional information (TE), data subject intervention (ID), and authority intervention (IA), which all belong to group G1, might be harmed. This is, because every change in the behavior of an operation could damage the integrity and availability of the processed information, and every change of the way that the PI is processed by the machine could lead to exceptional cases about which the data subject has to be informed and that could violate intervention options the data subject or authorities have. Additionally, all modifications of how PI is collected, stored, or flows can lead to a violation of the transparency requirements collection, storage, and flow information, respectively. A change in the deduction of information might affect collection, storage, and flow information requirements (G2).

Group G3 consists of the privacy requirements confidentiality (SC), undetectability (UU), anonymity (UA), data unlinkability (UD), and pseudonymity (UP). These requirements might be relevant for the guide words MORE, AS WELL AS, OTHER THAN, EARLY, LATE, BEFORE, and AFTER in all operation categories, because the guide words imply either that more, additional or other information is processed by the machine, or in a different order, earlier, or later as expected, which could lead to a violation of these requirements. Note that for the guide words MORE, EARLY, LATE, BEFORE, and AFTER, the requirements about the PI that is processed are affected. In contrast, for the guide words AS WELL AS and OTHER THAN, the requirements about the additional or other PI that is processed in addition to or instead of the PI that originally should be processed could be harmed. The guide words NO, LESS, PART OF, and INCORRECT are not implying a violation of the privacy requirements in group G3, because they only concern that fewer or incorrect PI is processed, which does not harm the privacy requirements contained in G3. The guide word

REVERSE is interpreted differently depending on the operation category (cf. Table 1). Hence, for the categories collection, flow, and deduction it might harm the requirements in G3, but for the category *storage* it does not.

The transparency requirement flow information (TF) might be harmed by deviations for the guide words REVERSE and OTHER THAN in the operation category *collection*, because they possibly imply a flow from the machine to another domain that is not intended. Similarly, collection information requirements (TC) might be harmed by deviations for the guide word REVERSE in the operation category *flow*. This is, because these scenarios would consider that instead of sending information to other domains, the machine would receive (collect) this or even other information which might be unintended.

Discussion. The procedure described in [2] to perform a HAZOP study stresses that for an analysis, the team has to carefully select the guide words that are considered for the system under consideration. Similarly, it can be the case that only a subset of the proposed guide words is relevant for a PRIOP study of a specific software project and that even additional guide words are identified as important. Hence, we do not claim that our selection of guide words represents a complete set of guide words relevant for the identification of privacy threats of a software project, but expect that it provides a good foundation.

Similarly, the operation categories could be extended. For example, Gürses [11] mentions that information can be collected, used, processed, distributed, or deleted. Collection and distribution (flow to other domains) are covered by our proposed categories. Usage contains from our point-of-view deduction and storage, but other kinds of usage might be identified for a concrete system as additional operation categories. Processing is considered by us as a high-level term describing that something is done with the PI, be that collection, storage, etc. Deletion is an additional category that is worth to analyze in future work, because it is only partly covered by PRIOP. The HAZOP standard does not categorize operations in a way that we propose in this work, but we think that making these operation categories explicit can help analysts to identify scenarios that lead to a harm of privacy requirements. Nevertheless, it can also be valuable to consider the guide words for a given subproblem without considering the operation categories, because this could prevent that the scope of the considered deviations is unnecessarily limited to the operation categories.

Anyway, no method for the identification of any kind of threats can guarantee to elicit a complete set of relevant threats [12]. Nevertheless, we think that our proposed systematic analysis will help analysts to identify, evaluate, and document the privacy threats relevant for their software projects.

An important point that always needs to be assessed critically is the scaleability of a proposed analysis method. If we perform a PRIOP study, then we have to fill in a template for every subproblem. For each operation category a subproblem is assigned to, we have to consider the 12 guide words. That means that in the worst case, we have to fill in 48 rows of the proposed template for each subproblem. Our observation is that this maximum is rarely reached. If it is reached, this is an indicator that the subproblem could be further decomposed into simpler subproblems, because it includes collection, storage, flow, and deduction of PI. Overall, we expect that the effort that has to be spent to perform a PRIOP study scales linearly with the complexity of the software project. The central attributes describing the complexity of the software project for a PRIOP study are the number of subproblems, data subjects, and PI that shall be processed by the machine. For the EHS example, we filled out 168 rows in total. This took us 28 h in total and 10 min per row in average.

Limitations of PRIOP are that (1) the analysis of the subproblems in isolation may not be sufficient if threats arise from the combination of different functionalities, (2) the analysis is limited to the documented subproblems and hence, PRIOP will not help in identifying privacy threats if subproblems are missing or lack important details, and (3) the success of a PRIOP study depends on the analysis team. To address limitation (3), we encourage that the analysis team has to incorporate expertise in requirements engineering, privacy, and the application domain.

4   Related Work

Deng et al. [13] propose a privacy threat analysis framework called LINDDUN. LINDDUN considers the high-level privacy threats linkability, identifiability, non-repudiation, detectability, information disclosure, content unawareness, and policy/consent noncompliance, which are negations of popular privacy goals. For the considered system, a DFD (data flow diagram) is created. For each combination of privacy threat and DFD element kind, a threat graph is provided. These are used to derive the possible concrete privacy threats that have to be handled. Based on the high-level privacy threats, the authors also suggest PETs (privacy enhancing technologies) that shall help to mitigate the concrete threats. In comparison to our work, the threat graphs of LINDDUN provide more detailed information that may help to identify whether a high-level privacy threat is relevant or not. But it is possible that the usage of these threat graphs unnecessarily limits the scope of the privacy threat analysis. In future work, we want to elaborate how LINDDUN and PRIOP could be combined to provide better support for the identification of privacy threats.

Several authors investigated the needs of (D)PIAs and methodologies that can be followed in order to perform a (D)PIA. Wright [14] gives an overview of the state of the art in PIA. Oetzel and Spiekermann [15] describe a methodology to support a complete process for a PIA, and Bieker et al. [16] describe a methodology for a DPIA under the EU General Data Protection Regulation. The proposed methodologies describe which steps have to be performed in which order to perform a (D)PIA, but they do not describe concrete techniques that can be used to systematically identify privacy threats. PRIOP can be used to realize the threat identification and risk evaluation steps of the proposed methods. Alnemr et al. [17] propose a DPIA methodology for clouds. They support the identification of privacy threats based on an exhaustive questionnaire. This questionnaire is complementary to PRIOP, and we want to investigate in future work how the questionnaire can be integrated into PRIOP.

5   Conclusions

In this paper, we present with PRIOP a systematic method to identify and document privacy threats and operability issues of software projects. During a PRIOP study, possible deviations of the software project's subproblems are examined under consideration of the four operation categories collection, storage, flow, and deduction. The deviations of a subproblem in the context of the relevant operation categories are derived using the twelve proposed PRIOP guide words. Deviation patterns are provided by PRIOP for all combinations of guide words and operation categories to support an analysis team. The identified deviations for the guide words then have to be further analyzed for possible causes and consequences they might have on the privacy requirements of the software project or the operability of the subproblem. To further support the execution of a PRIOP study, we provide a mapping that shows which privacy requirements could be harmed by a deviation for a combination of guide word and operation category. The documentation created using PRIOP can be used to further assess the risks implied by the identified privacy threats. We illustrated PRIOP using an EHS example and artifacts produced with the ProPAn method.

In future research, we will integrate PRIOP into the ProPAn tool to benefit from the artifacts created using the ProPAn method. Furthermore, we want to investigate how generic threats, e.g., in the form of threat patterns as introduced by Uzunov and Fernandez [18] for security, can be related to the operation categories and guide words to further assist the identification of privacy threats. The evaluation of PRIOP using a real case study is also future work.

References

1. GSMA: MOBILE PRIVACY: consumer research insights and considerations for policymakers. http://goo.gl/pAcvAm. Accessed 1 Mar 2017
2. IEC: IEC 61882: 2001 Hazard and Operability Studies (HAZOP Studies) - Application Guide (2001)
3. Meis, R., Heisel, M.: Computer-aided identification and validation of privacy requirements. Information **7**(2), 28 (2016)
4. Jackson, M.: Problem Frames. Analyzing and Structuring Software Development Problems. Addison-Wesley, Boston (2001)
5. Meis, R.: Problem-based consideration of privacy-relevant domain knowledge. In: Hansen, M., Hoepman, J.-H., Leenes, R., Whitehouse, D. (eds.) Privacy and Identity 2013. IAICT, vol. 421, pp. 150–164. Springer, Heidelberg (2014). doi:10.1007/978-3-642-55137-6_12
6. Meis, R., Heisel, M.: Supporting privacy impact assessments using problem-based privacy analysis. In: Lorenz, P., Cardoso, J., Maciaszek, L.A., Sinderen, M. (eds.) ICSOFT 2015. CCIS, vol. 586, pp. 79–98. Springer, Cham (2016). doi:10.1007/978-3-319-30142-6_5
7. Hansen, M., Jensen, M., Rost, M.: Protection goals for privacy engineering. In: IEEE Symposium on Security and Privacy Workshops, SPW, pp. 159–166. IEEE Computer Society (2015)

8. Pfitzmann, A., Hansen, M.: A terminology for talking about privacy by data minimization: anonymity, unlinkability, undetectability, unobservability, pseudonymity, and identity management v0.34, August 2010

9. Meis, R., Wirtz, R., Heisel, M.: A taxonomy of requirements for the privacy goal transparency. In: Fischer-Hübner, S., Lambrinoudakis, C., Lopez, J. (eds.) TrustBus 2015. LNCS, vol. 9264, pp. 195–209. Springer, Cham (2015). doi:10.1007/978-3-319-22906-5_15

10. Meis, R., Heisel, M.: Understanding the privacy goal intervenability. In: Katsikas, S., Lambrinoudakis, C., Furnell, S. (eds.) TrustBus 2016. LNCS, vol. 9830, pp. 79–94. Springer, Cham (2016). doi:10.1007/978-3-319-44341-6_6

11. Gürses, F.S.: Multilateral privacy requirements analysis in online social network services. Ph.D. thesis, Katholieke Universiteit Leuven (2010)

12. Young, W., Leveson, N.G.: An integrated approach to safety and security based on systems theory. Commun. ACM **57**(2), 31–35 (2014)

13. Deng, M., Wuyts, K., Scandariato, R., Preneel, B., Joosen, W.: A privacy threat analysis framework: supporting the elicitation and fulfillment of privacy requirements. Requir. Eng. **16**, 3–32 (2011)

14. Wright, D.: The state of the art in privacy impact assessment. Comput. Law Secur. Rev. **28**(1), 54–61 (2012)

15. Oetzel, M., Spiekermann, S.: A systematic methodology for privacy impact assessments: a design science approach. Eur. J. Inf. Syst. **23**(2), 126–150 (2014)

16. Bieker, F., Friedewald, M., Hansen, M., Obersteller, H., Rost, M.: A process for data protection impact assessment under the European general data protection regulation. In: Schiffner, S., Serna, J., Ikonomou, D., Rannenberg, K. (eds.) APF 2016. LNCS, vol. 9857, pp. 21–37. Springer, Cham (2016). doi:10.1007/978-3-319-44760-5_2

17. Alnemr, R., Cayirci, E., Corte, L.D., Garaga, A., Leenes, R., Mhungu, R., Pearson, S., Reed, C., Oliveira, A.S., Stefanatou, D., Tetrimida, K., Vranaki, A.: A data protection impact assessment methodology for cloud. In: Berendt, B., Engel, T., Ikonomou, D., Le Métayer, D., Schiffner, S. (eds.) APF 2015. LNCS, vol. 9484, pp. 60–92. Springer, Cham (2016). doi:10.1007/978-3-319-31456-3_4

18. Uzunov, A.V., Fernandez, E.B.: An extensible pattern-based library and taxonomy of security threats for distributed systems. Comput. Stan. Interfaces **36**(4), 734–747 (2014)

Data Minimisation: A Language-Based Approach

Thibaud Antignac[1]([✉]) [ID], David Sands[1] [ID], and Gerardo Schneider[2] [ID]

[1] Chalmers University of Technology, Gothenburg, Sweden
thibaud.antignac@cea.fr,dave@chalmers.se
[2] University of Gothenburg, Gothenburg, Sweden
gerardo@cse.gu.se

Abstract. Data minimisation is a privacy-enhancing principle considered as one of the pillars of personal data regulations. This principle dictates that personal data collected should be no more than necessary for the specific purpose consented by the user. In this paper we study data minimisation from a programming language perspective. We define a data minimiser as a pre-processor for the input which reduces the amount of information available to the program without compromising its functionality. We give its formal definition and provide a procedure to synthesise a correct data minimiser for a given program.

1 Introduction

According to the Article 5 of the EU *General Data Protection Regulation* proposal "Personal data must be [...] limited to what is necessary in relation to the purposes for which they are processed" [12]. This principle is called *data minimisation*. From a software perspective, data minimisation requires that the input data not *semantically* used by a program should neither be collected nor processed. The *data processor* could be seen in this context as to be the *adversary* (or *attacker*), as she knows all the information available after the input is collected (before the program execution) and thus can exploit the inputs.[1]

The goal of the *data minimisation process* is to minimise the input data so only what is necessary is given to the program. Whenever the input data exactly matches what is necessary we may say that the minimisation is the *best*. Best minimisation is, however, difficult to achieve in general since it is not trivial to exactly determine what is the input needed to compute each possible output.

```
1  input(salary)
2  benefits := (salary < 10000)
3  output(benefits)
```

Fig. 1. Program P_{bl} computes benefit level.

---

[1] In other scenarios the adversary only has access to the outputs (cf. [27]).

© IFIP International Federation for Information Processing 2017
Published by Springer International Publishing AG 2017. All Rights Reserved
S. De Capitani di Vimercati and F. Martinelli (Eds.): SEC 2017, IFIP AICT 502, pp. 442–456, 2017.
DOI: 10.1007/978-3-319-58469-0_30

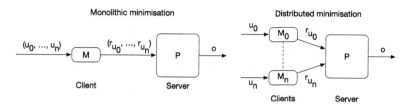

Fig. 2. Monolithic and distributed minimisation architectures.

As an example of minimisation let us consider the program P_{bl} shown in Fig. 1, whose purpose is to compute the *benefit level* of employees depending on their salary (that we assume to be between \$0 and \$100000). For the sake of simplicity, in what follows we drive our analysis on worst-case assumptions. A quick analysis shows that the range of the output is {false, true}, and consequently the data processor does not need to precisely know the real salaries to determine the benefit level. Each employee should be able to give any number between 0 and 9999 as input if eligible to the benefits, and any number between 10000 and 100000 otherwise, without disclosing real salaries.

In other words, data minimisation is the process of ensuring that the range of inputs provided to a program is reduced such that when two inputs result in the same response, then one of them can be considered redundant. Minimality is an information-flow property related to the notions of *required information release* [9], and of *strong dependency* (a.k.a. *non-interference*) [10]. Minimality can also be seen as one relating *cardinalities*: ideally, a program satisfying data minimisation should be one such that the cardinality of the possible output is equal to the cardinality of the input domain.

In a distributed setting the concept of minimisation is more complex since the minimisation process is not *monolithic* anymore as the data may be collected from multiple independent sources (users). Figure 2 gives an illustration of this difference in the case of a static minimiser run by the client.

We will see that in general we cannot decide whether a program is minimal, or compute in the general case a "best" minimiser. In order to statically compute a minimiser for a program we need to compute its *kernel*. In the monolithic case this is just a partition of the input domain so that all the inputs in a partition get mapped to the same output. A minimiser in this case can be constructed by choosing a representative for each partition, and mapping all elements in that partition to the chosen representative. The distributed case is more complex. Though producing the coarsest possible partition is uncomputable, in practice it may be computed for specific cases. This is true for programs not having complex loops, mutual recursive calls, nor using libraries for which we have neither access to the code nor the specification. Our analysis does not completely exclude such programs as it might still be done in practice if suitable *invariants* are given, by providing formal specifications about libraries, or by sacrificing complete automation and allowing a man-in-the-loop to guide the analysis.

In this paper we address *data minimisation* with the following contributions: (i) We provide a formal definition of the concept of *minimisers for a program* used to achieve data minimisation (Sect. 3) with respect to an explicit attacker model (Sect. 2); (ii) We show how we can compare minimisers, leading to the definition of *best minimiser* for a given program (Sect. 4); (iii) We propose a (semi-)procedure to generate minimisers and prove its soundness and termination (Sect. 5); (iv) We provide a proof-of-concept implementation (*DataMin*) to compute minimisers, based on symbolic execution and the use of a SAT solver in order to exemplify our approach.

The accompanying technical report [1] contains an application of our proof of concept to different prototypical programs, as well as more detailed examples and the proofs of the theorems and lemmas presented in the rest of the paper.

2   Attacker Model

In order to define data minimisation we consider an explicit attacker model. In practice a malicious server may have a *secondary use* for the data (defined as "using personal data in a different way than the primary reason why they were collected" [8]). We define here an attacker model having the following components: (i) an explicit model of a hidden secondary use of the data, and (ii) an explicit model of what the attacker learns about the data from observing the result of processing the data. We will develop a definition of minimisation which guarantees that an attacker learns no more about the private data than he can deduce from the legitimate output of the program.

To model the hidden secondary use, we suppose the attacker uses a second program denoted by a function $h \in \mathcal{I} \to \mathcal{O}'$. Thus the attacker is defined by a pair of functions p and h (the legitimate use and the hidden use of the data, respectively), and the attacker's computation is given by the function $\langle p, h \rangle \in \mathcal{I} \to \mathcal{O} \times \mathcal{O}'$ defined by $\langle p, h \rangle(i) \stackrel{\text{def}}{=} (p(i), h(i))$.

If the goal of the attacker is to learn something about the inputs by observing the output of $\langle p, h \rangle$ then it is easy to see that the worst case is when h is the identity function. In the following section we will show that if the input is first minimised using a best possible minimiser m, then what the attacker learns from $\langle p, h \rangle \circ m$ is no more than what is learned by p alone (with $\circ$ being the standard function composition operator). Here we assume that the attacker knows the minimiser m. To do this we model the attacker knowledge explicitly, as has become more common recently (e.g. [4,5,7]).

Definition 1 (Knowledge). *Let $u \in \mathcal{I}$ be an input, and f a function in $\mathcal{I} \to \mathcal{O}$. The* knowledge *about u obtained through f by observing $f(u)$, written $K(f, u)$, is defined to be the set $\{v \mid f(u) = f(v), v \in \mathcal{I}\}$.*

Thus $K(f, u)$ is the largest set of possible input values that could have led to the output value $f(u)$. This corresponds to an attacker who knows the function f and the output $f(u)$ and makes perfect logical deduction about the possible values of the input. Note that the smaller the knowledge set, the less uncertainty the observer has over the possible value of the input. The knowledge relation induces an order on programs: the bigger the knowledge set for a given input, the less a program will disclose information about the input. This is reasonable given that if more input values are mapped to the same output, more difficult it will be to guess what is the exact input when observing the output of a computation. We have then the following order between programs:

Definition 2 (Disclosure ordering). *We say f discloses less or as much information as g, written $f \sqsubseteq g$, iff for all $u \in \mathcal{I}$ we have $K(g, u) \subseteq K(f, u)$.*

If f and g are knowledge equivalent, we write $f \equiv g$. For example, functions denoted by $(\cdot \bmod 2)$ and $(\cdot \bmod 4)$ (with postfix notation) are related by $(\cdot \bmod 2) \sqsubseteq (\cdot \bmod 4)$ (knowing the last bit discloses less information than knowing the last two bits). However, $(\cdot > 0)$ is incomparable to either of them.

3   Data Minimisers

We will consider two types of minimiser depending on how the data is collected: *monolithic* and *distributed*. Monolithic collection describes the simple case when personal data is collected from a single location. In the distributed case, inputs from multiple subjects, we assume that we cannot minimise one input using knowledge of the other inputs in the setting of Fig. 2. The aim now is to defined a notion of data minimiser – a program to be deployed at a data source (one per source in the distributed case) – which can remove information from data in a way that (in the best case) the remaining information is enough for the server to compute the intended function p, and (in the best case) nothing more.

Semantics of Minimisation. Let us consider the program in Fig. 3 to discuss the need for a semantic definition of minimisation. In this program, x2 is syntactically needed to evaluate the condition ($\ell.3$). However, this condition always evaluates to true. In the same way, x3 is not semantically needed to compute the value of y since it is both added and substracted ($\ell.4$). As a consequence, it would be possible to get the same result by rewriting the program with only the input x1 without modifying its behavior. If x2 and x3 are personal data, then the semantic approach is better likely to help us to limit the collection than the syntactic approach. So, the program could be refactored by taking only the input x1 while retaining the same output behaviour. Though this would work, it requires a change in both the data collected and in the interface of the program.

Instead, we propose to keep the program unchanged and we rely on the idea that the information behind x2 and x3 (in this specific example) can be protected by providing *fixed arbitrary* values for them, instead of refactoring the program. This means the program does not need to be modified for the data processor to propose better guarantees. This approach allows a better modularity and a better integration in the software development cycle. To see this, let us consider the program shown in Fig. 1. In this case, any employee earning less than \$10000 can disclose any figure between 0 and 9999 and any employee earning at least \$10000 can disclose any figure between 10000 and 100000 without affecting the output of the program. Thus a corresponding *data minimiser* could be as shown in Fig. 4, where the representative values are taken to be 0 and 10000.

The value output by this minimiser, which is the value of `repr_salary`, can then be provided as input to the corresponding program (standing for the variable `salary`). The behaviour of the program will remain the same while the actual salary of the employee is not needlessly passed to the program.

```
1  input(x1, x2, x3);
2  y := 0;
3  if (x2 == x2;)
4        then (y := (x3 + x1 - x3);)
5  output(y);
```

Fig. 3. Example of a semantically unnecessary syntactic necessity.

This holds even when an employee earns exactly the amount of `repr_salary` since the data processor receiving this value cannot distinguish when it is the case or not.

Following this approach, we study both monolithic and distributed cases as shown in Fig. 2 where M and $\bigotimes_{i=0}^{n} M_i$ are a monolithic and a distributed minimiser respectively (each M_i is a local minimiser), P is the program, u_i are input values, r_{u_i} are input representatives, and o are outputs.

```
1  input(salary)
2  repr_salary := 0
3  if (10000 <= salary)
4        then (repr_salary := 10000)
5  output(repr_salary)
```

Fig. 4. Minimiser for P_{bl} (see Fig. 1).

3.1 Monolithic Case

Let us assume a program P constituting a legitimate processing of personal data for which the data subject had consented to the purpose. We abstract it through a function p which ranges over $\mathcal{I} \to \mathcal{O}$. Since we aim at building *pre-processors* for the program, we consider a minimiser m with type $\mathcal{I} \to \mathcal{I}$.

Definition 3 (Monolithic minimiser). *We say m is a monolithic minimiser for p iff (i) $p \circ m = p$ and (ii) $m \circ m = m$.*

Condition (i) states correctness: using the pre-processor does not change the result of the computation. Condition (ii) ensures that m chooses representative inputs in a canonical way, i.e., m removes information from the input in one go.

3.2 Distributed Case

In general a computation over private data may require data collected from several independent sources. We will thus extend our definition to the distributed setting. This is the general case where a program dp is a function of a product of input domains, $dp \in \prod_{i=0}^{n} \mathcal{I}_i \to \mathcal{O}$. The idea for the distributed minimiser will be to have a *local minimiser* $m_i \in \mathcal{I}_i \to \mathcal{I}_i$ for each source $\mathcal{I}_i$, combined into an input processor as $dm = \bigotimes_{i=0}^{n} m_i$, where for $f \in A \to A'$ and $g \in B \to B'$ we have $f \otimes g \in A \times B \to A' \times B'$. This is based on the assumption that each argument of dp is provided by a different data source.

Definition 4 (Distributed minimiser). *We say dm is a* distributed minimiser *for dp iff (i) dm is a monolithic minimiser for dp and (ii) dm has the
form $\bigotimes_{i=0}^{n} dm_i$ (with dm_i being $\mathcal{I}_i \to \mathcal{I}_i$ functions—called* local minimisers, *for
$i \in \{0, \ldots, n\}$).*

The first condition ensures that *dm* is actually a minimiser while the second
one ensures that each input is treated independently. The latter is the key dif-
ferentiator between monolithic and distributed minimisers. Each function dm_i
is only provided with an input from $\mathcal{I}_i$. Intuitively, this means that if two input
values at a given position belong to the same equivalence class, then this must
hold for all possible values provided for the other positions. For example, if the
values 0 and 1 from $\mathcal{I}_0$ belong to the same equivalence class, then each pair of
input tuples $\langle 0, x, y \rangle$ and $\langle 1, x, y \rangle$ for all $(x, y) \in \prod_{i=1}^{2} \mathcal{I}_i$ have to belong to the
same equivalence class (two by two, meaning these can be different classes for
each pair: $\langle 0, 1, 2 \rangle$ and $\langle 1, 1, 3 \rangle$ may not belong to the same equivalence class,
though $\langle 0, 1, 2 \rangle$ and $\langle 1, 1, 2 \rangle$ have to). This is formally stated in Proposition 1
below, which relies on the definition of the *kernel* of a function, which induces a
partition of the input set where every element in the same equivalence class is
mapped to the same output.

Definition 5 (Kernel of a function). *If $f \in \mathcal{I} \to \mathcal{O}$ then the* kernel of f *is
defined as* $\ker(f) = \{(u, v) \mid f(u) = f(v)\}$.

Proposition 1. *If m is a monolithic minimiser for p, then m is a distributed
minimiser for p iff for all $(\boldsymbol{u}, \boldsymbol{v}) \in \ker(m)$, for all input positions i, and all input
vectors $\boldsymbol{w}$, $(\boldsymbol{w}[i \mapsto u_i], \boldsymbol{w}[i \mapsto u_i]) \in \ker(m)$ where the notation $\boldsymbol{w}[i \mapsto u_i]$ denotes
a vector like $\boldsymbol{w}$ except at position i where it has value u_i.*

This proposition gives a data-based characterisation of *data minimisation*,
which will be useful when building minimisers in Sect. 5. Before building minimisers, we explain how to compare them in the next section.

4   Best Minimisers

Now that we defined minimisers as pre-processors modifying the input, we see
that there may exist many different minimisers for a given program. Thus we
are interested in being able to compare these minimisers. Indeed, since the identity function is a minimiser for all programs *p*, then it is clear that the simple
existence of a minimiser does not guarantee any kind of minimality. One way
to compare minimisers is to compare the size of their ranges – a smaller range
indicates a greater degree of minimality (cf. Proposition 2 below). A more precise way to compare them is by understanding them in terms of the *lattice of
equivalence relations* [24]. The set of equivalence relations on $\mathcal{I}$ forms a complete
lattice, with the ordering relation given by set-inclusion of their defining sets of
pairs. The identity relation (denoted by $\mathrm{Id}_{\mathcal{I}}$) is the bottom element, and the
total relation (denoted by $\mathrm{All}_{\mathcal{I}}$) is the top.

The following proposition provides some properties about the order relation
between programs (cf. Definition 2), including its relation with the kernel.

Proposition 2 (Disclosure ordering properties). *(1) $f \sqsubseteq g$ iff $\ker(f) \supseteq \ker(g)$ (2) $f \circ g \sqsubseteq g$ (3) $f \sqsubseteq \langle f, g \rangle$ (4) $\langle f, f \rangle \sqsubseteq f$ (5) $f \sqsubseteq g$ implies $|\mathrm{range}(f)| \leq |\mathrm{range}(g)|$*

where $\langle f, g \rangle$ is the function $x \mapsto (f(x), g(x))$ (see Sect. 2).

4.1   Monolithic Case

The disclosure ordering allows us to compare the minimisers of a given program, defining a *best* minimiser to be one which discloses no more than any other.

Definition 6 (Best monolithic minimiser). *We say that m is a best monolithic minimiser for p iff (i) m is a monolithic minimiser for p and (ii) $m \sqsubseteq n$ for all minimisers n for p.*

In this simple (monolithic) form, minimisation is easily understood as injectivity.

Proposition 3 (Monolithic best minimiser injectivity). *A monolithic minimiser m for a program p is a best one iff $p|_{\mathrm{range}(m)}$ is injective (with $p|_{\mathrm{range}(m)}$ the restriction of the program p over the range of m).*

Now we can show that using a minimiser m at the client guarantees that the attacker $\langle p, h \rangle$ learns no more about the input than which can be learned by observing the output of the legitimate use p (the proof follows from the ordering between minimisers and Proposition 2).

Theorem 1. *If m is a best monolithic minimiser for p then for all hidden uses h we have $\langle p, h \rangle \circ m \equiv p$.*

The proof of the following theorem proceeds by building a best monolithic minimiser from kernel of p.

Theorem 2. *For every program p there exists a best monolithic minimiser.*

4.2   Distributed Case

As for the monolithic case, we have an ordering between distributed minimisers. We define the notion of a best minimiser for the distributed case as follows ($\sqsubseteq$ is the order between functions, i.e. the inverse of the kernel set inclusion order).

Definition 7. (Best distributed minimiser). *We say dm is a best distributed minimiser for dp iff (i) dm is a distributed minimiser for dp and (ii) $dm \sqsubseteq dn$ for all dn distributed minimisers for dp.*

In the following we show that there always exists a best distributed minimiser.

Theorem 3. *For every distributed program dp there exists a best distributed minimiser.*

Note that there is a price to pay here: the best distributed minimiser may reveal more information than the best monolithic minimiser. An example is the OR function where the identity function is a best distributed minimiser, but in the monolithic case we can minimise further by mapping $(0,0)$ to itself, and mapping all other inputs to $(1,1)$. Similarly to Proposition 1, we give a data-centric characterisation of best distributed minimisers as follows.

Proposition 4 (Data-based best distributed minimisation). *If dm is a* best *distributed minimiser for dp, then for all input positions i, for all v_1 and $v_2 \in \mathcal{I}_i$ such that $v_1 \neq v_2$, there is some $\boldsymbol{u} \in$ range(dm) such that $dp\,(\boldsymbol{u}[i \mapsto v_1]) \neq dp\,(\boldsymbol{u}[i \mapsto v_2])$.*

5   Building Minimisers

We describe here how data minimisers are built. This (semi-)procedure is not complete for the best minimisers since obtaining a best minimiser is not computable in general. Besides, and more pragmatically, our procedure is built on top of a theorem prover and a symbolic execution engine, and it is thus limited by the power of such tools. Our procedure follows the toolchain depicted in Fig. 5. Before describing the procedure in detail, we briefly recall concepts related to *symbolic execution*.

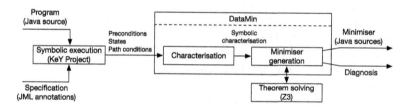

Fig. 5. Toolchain of the (semi-)procedure to generate minimisers.

5.1   Symbolic Execution

This step corresponds to the two leftmost boxes of the toolchain shown in Fig. 5. Symbolic execution has been pioneered in [17] as a way to reason about symbolic states reached by a program execution. A *symbolic execution* of a program is an execution of the program against symbolic inputs. Expressions are symbolically evaluated and assigned to variables. The state of this execution includes the values of the program (modelled as a mapping called *store*), and *path conditions* (boolean expressions ranging over the symbolic inputs, specifying the conditions to be satisfied for a node to be reached). Assignments modify the symbolic value of variables, whereas conditions and loops create branches distinguished by their path conditions. This execution generates a *symbolic execution tree* where each node is associated to a statement and each arc to a transition of the program. A state is associated to each node and the root node corresponds to the input of

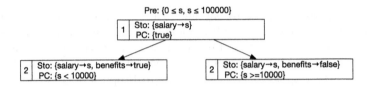

Fig. 6. Symbolic execution tree of P_{bl} (see Fig. 1).

the program. Each leaf in the tree corresponds to a completed execution path, and no two leaves have the same path condition.

Let us consider again program P_{bl} from Fig. 1. A representation of the possible paths for P_{bl} is shown in Fig. 6 where the digits 1 and 2 correspond to the lines of the program, Sto is the corresponding store, and PC is the path condition at this point (ℓ.3 of the program does not have any effect in this representation). The possible execution paths for this program lead to two main outputs, where either `benefits == true` or `benefits == false`. Thus the best minimiser should distinguish the two cases and return a representative value leading to the same output as if the program were to be executed with the "real" value assigned to `salary`. This is the case for the data minimiser described in Fig. 4. Moreover, any change of value for `repr_salary` leads to a change in the `salary` computed by the main program: this minimiser is indeed a best minimiser.

Loops in programs require an invariant. Failing to provide good invariants results in weaker path conditions failing to capture all of what is theoretically knowable about the states of the symbolic execution. To find the best invariant is a difficult problem and still an active field of research [13].

In our approach the program P is symbolically executed along with the assertions coming from the specification S. We assume that we have a global *precondition* for the program P, given in the specification S of the program, denoted $\mathrm{Pre}\langle P, S \rangle$. In our example, the conditions $0 \leq s$ and $s \leq 100000$ are part of the preconditions as shown in Fig. 6. This produces a symbolic execution tree equipped with the corresponding path conditions PC and Sto attached to its nodes. In what follows we define a symbolic characterisation of the program P under specification S capturing the conditions at the end of the execution.

Definition 8 (Symbolic characterisation of a program). *We say Γ is a symbolic characterisation of a program P under specification S, written $\Gamma_{\langle P,S \rangle}$, iff Γ collects the preconditions, stores, and path conditions to be satisfied for each possible output of P: $\Gamma_{\langle P,S \rangle} \triangleq \mathrm{Pre}\langle P, S \rangle \wedge \left(\bigvee_{l \in \mathrm{Leaves}\langle P,S \rangle} (\mathrm{PC}(l) \wedge \mathrm{Sto}(l)) \right)$, where $\mathrm{Leaves}\langle P, S \rangle$ returns the leaves of the symbolic execution tree of P under specification S, and $\mathrm{PC}(\cdot)$ and $\mathrm{Sto}(\cdot)$ return the path condition and the state associated to a leaf, respectively.*

For the example in Fig. 1, the (simplified) symbolic characterisation is:
$\Gamma_{\langle P_{bl},S_{bl} \rangle} = (0 \leq s \wedge s \leq 100000) \wedge ((s < 10000 \wedge salary = s \wedge benefits = true) \vee (s \geq 10000 \wedge salary = s \wedge benefits = false))$.

The symbolic characterisation induces an equivalence class giving a partition of the state space according to the different possible outputs. A solver uses this to get a representative for each class, which is the next step in our procedure.

5.2   Static Generation of Minimisers

We show here how best minimisers are generated from the symbolic execution tree. The monolithic case is a particular case of the distributed one. The construction spans over the *DataMin* box shown Fig. 5.

The input domain of the semantic function dp having $n+1$ inputs is $\prod_{i=0}^{n} \mathcal{I}_i$ and the corresponding input variables of dp are denoted as x_i. A local function dm_i is generated for each input $x_i \in \text{Input}(DP)$. We are still interested in the different possible outputs of dp but we cannot directly use its kernel as in the monolithic case since this would require all the minimisers to have access to the data at other data source points. Instead of this, each data source point assumes that the data to be disclosed by other points could take any possible value in their domain. Thus we need to compute, for each input variable x_i, the equivalence classes over its domain such that the value o of the output of the program remains the same for all possible assignments to the other inputs variables x_j for all $j \in (\{0, \ldots, n\} \setminus \{i\})$.

The algorithm of Fig. 7 shows how the distribution of the inputs is taken into account. Here, min ($\ell.1$) stands for the minimiser being built (as a map containing the local minimiser $min[i]$ ($\ell.5$) for each input i ($\ell.3$)), *Inputs* ($\ell.3$) denotes the inputs of the program, and Γ ($\ell.4$) denotes the formula of the symbolic characterisation of the program. The notation $\phi[y/x]$ denotes the formula ϕ in which y replaces x and $==$ the logical equality ($\ell.8$).

```
1:  min = {}                                    ▷ initialise minimiser
2:  decl logical_variable i'                    ▷ declare a new logical variable
3:  for all i ∈ Inputs do                       ▷ iterate over the inputs
4:      γ = Γ                    ▷ copy the program symbolic characterisation to γ
5:      min[i] = {}                              ▷ initialise minimiser for input i
6:      while γ.check() do        ▷ call solver to loop as long as γ is satisfiable
7:          model = γ.model()       ▷ call solver to get a valid assignment for γ
8:          formula = ((i' == model[i]) ∧ Γ ∧ Γ[i'/i])    ▷ build distributed min.
        formula
9:          wp = formula.quantif_elim()    ▷ call solver to eliminate quantifiers
10:         min[i]+= (wp, model[i]) ▷ add weakest precond. with representative to
        min.
11:         γ = γ ∧ ¬wp ▷ conjunct negation of the weakest precond. to γ to limit
        the loop
12:     end while
13: end for
```

Fig. 7. Distributed data minimiser generation (excerpt).

Primitives depending on a theorem prover are called at three locations in the algorithm. The first one, check() (ℓ.6) checks whether or not a logical formula is satisfiable. Then, model() (ℓ.7) applied to a formula returns a satisfying valuation. These two primitives are linked as it is only possible to find such a valuation for satisfiable formula. Finally, quantif_elim() (ℓ.9) is a procedure to eliminate (both universal and existential) quantifiers in a formula, thus simplifying a formula by removing the corresponding symbols.

After initialising min, holding the minimisers as a map from inputs i to tuples (*weakest precondition, representative*) (ℓ.1), a new logical variable i' is declared (ℓ.2). At this point, all the inputs (ℓ.3) and the output o of the program already exist as logical variables (implicitly introduced with Γ which is an input of this algorithm). The new logical variable i' is used to control variations on one input during the procedure (ℓ.8). Then, the algorithm iterates over all the inputs (ℓ.3). The symbolic characterisation Γ is assigned to the variable γ (ℓ.4) (which will be reinitialised at each iteration of the loop of ℓ.3). The original Γ will be used to build formulas to be solved while the fresher γ will be used to control the loop (ℓ.6). The minimiser min is then initialised for the current input i (ℓ.5). The algorithm loops over all equivalence classes for the current input i. This is ensured by (i) representing each equivalence class by its weakest precondition wp (ℓ.7–10), (ii) conjuncting the negation of the weakest precondition wp found to the symbolic characterisation γ (ℓ.10), and (iii) looping as long as there is another equivalence class to be covered by checking the satisfiability of γ conjuncted with the negation of all previous conditions (ℓ.6).

We now explain in more detail how the weakest preconditions are found (ℓ.7–10). A satisfying valuation of the characterisation γ is requested from the solver and assigned to the variable $model$ (ℓ.7). The valuation of variable x can be called by $model[x]$. A formula (assigned to the variable $formula$) is then built in two steps. First, we conjunct Γ, $\Gamma[i'/i]$, and the formula $i' == model[i]$ (ℓ.8). This fixes $\Gamma[i'/i]$ to the case where i' is equal to the satisfying valuation found previously (ℓ.7). Once the formula has been built, the quantifiers are eliminated by calling a solver (ℓ.9). This gives the weakest precondition corresponding to an equivalence class of the inputs (the one corresponding to the value of $model[i]$). This equivalence class wp is then added to the minimiser $min[i]$ along with its representative $model[i]$ (ℓ.10) before being excluded from the control γ (ℓ.11) before a new iteration, until exhaustion of the equivalence classes (ℓ.6).

This algorithm builds a map function min which is used to generate the code for the atomic minimisers in a post-processing step (not shown here).

Theorem 4 (Soundness). *The algorithm of Fig. 7 builds a best distributed minimiser dm for program dp.*

Soundness of this algorithm relies on Proposition 4, on the fact that the representative assigned to each equivalence class is fixed, on the proof of existence from Theorem 3, and on the soundness of the external procedures called.

Theorem 5 (Termination). *The algorithm of Fig. 7 terminates when the number of inputs and the number of equivalence classes on these inputs are finite, and the calls to the external solver terminate.*

This is proven by showing that all the loops in the algorithm iterate over sets built from inputs and equivalence classes. The set of inputs is not modified in the loops while the condition of (ℓ.6) strictly decreases in terms of the number of times it is satisfiable. However, it terminates only if there is a finite number of equivalence classes for the current input. Since we depend on external procedures, termination of our algorithm also depends on the termination of such procedures.

5.3   *DataMin* Implementation

The (semi-)procedure described in this section has been implemented in Python as a proof of concept named *DataMin*.[2] We rely on the Symbolic Execution Engine of the *KeY* Project [16]. This symbolic executor is run against a program P written in Java for which a minimiser should be generated. *DataMin* generates the symbolic characterisation $\Gamma_{\langle P,S \rangle}$ and builds the partitioning $k_{\langle P,S \rangle}$ and the sectioning $r_{\langle P,S \rangle}$ functions. The theorem prover *Z3* [23] is called through its API to solve constrains as needed. We currently support only a limited range of data structures but could be extended thanks to the many theories on which *Z3* relies.

Finally, *DataMin* generates the minimiser as a set of Java files to be run by the data source points before disclosing the data. These files are directly compilable and ready to be exported as Java libraries to ease their use. This whole process runs in reasonable time for the examples provided in the archive (less than a second, given that Python is run in its interpreted mode). For the first example (monolithic with a loop) the solver used (*Z3*) was not able to totally eliminate quantifiers. We thus manually eliminated quantifiers by using the *Redlog* system [11]. This limitation comes from the external tools and not from the procedure proposed. The second example (distributed) does not suffer from this limitation and shows how multiple atomic minimisers are generated.

6   Final Discussion

We provided a formal definition of *data minimisation* in terms of strong dependency and derived concepts, and introduced the concept of a *data minimiser* defined as a pre-processor to the data processor. We considered both the monolithic and distributed cases. Finally, we provided a proof-of-concept implementation to obtain data minimisers for a given program. Our approach is semantics-based, so finding a distributed minimiser is undecidable in general.

Formal and rigorous approaches to privacy have been advocated for some time [28], but the data minimisation principle has not been precisely defined in the past, as stated in [15]. A related work is the notion of *minimal exposure* [3], which consists in performing a preprocessing of information on the client's side

---

[2] http://www.cse.chalmers.se/research/databin/files/datamin.zip.

to give only the data needed to benefit from a service. In this setting, if the requested service can be modeled as $a \vee b$, then if a is true then only a will be disclosed: they reduce the *number* of inputs provided, but do not reason on the domain of the inputs as we do.

Minimality is closely related to information flow, and we have used several ideas from that area [10,18,26]. A semantic notion of dependency has been introduced in [22], where it is used to characterise the variables in an expression that are semantically relevant for the evaluation of the expression. Our notion is related to this but much more fine-grained. A notable difference in the formalisation of minimality compared to usual definitions of information flow is that the former is a necessary and sufficient condition on information flow, whereas most security formulations of the latter are sufficient conditions only (e.g., noninterference: public inputs are sufficient to compute public outputs). An exception is Chong's *required information release* [9] which provides both upper and lower bounds on information flows. For this reason many static analysis techniques for security properties (e.g. type systems) are not easy to use for minimality—an over-approximation to the information flows is not sound for minimality. The necessary and sufficient conditions embodied in minimisers appear to be closely related to the notion of *completeness* in abstract interpretation [14], where a minimiser m plays the role of a *complete abstraction*. Some work on quantitative information flow aiming at automated discovery of leaks also rely on analysis of equivalence classes [6,20]. We could use several of the ideas in [6] to improve our implementation.

Equivalence partitioning by using symbolic execution was first introduced for test case generation in [25], and later used by the *KeY* theorem prover [2]. Symbolic execution has limitations, especially when it comes to handling loops. Though being a main concern in theory and for some applications, *while* loops do not seem to be as widespread as *for* loops in practice. For instance, Malacaria et al. have been able to perform a symbolic execution-based verification of non-interference security properties from the C source of the real world *OpenSSL* library [21]. Different other techniques relying on symbolic execution and SAT solvers are presented in [29] to form *nsqflow*, a tool dedicated at measuring quantitative information flow for large programs. They also target realistic programs and thus show the feasibility to decide about non-interference properties in programs.

Acknowledgements. This research has been supported by the Swedish funding agency SSF under the grant *DataBIn: Data Driven Secure Business Intelligence*.

References

1. Antignac, T., Sands, D., Schneider, G.: Data minimisation: a language-based approach (long version) (2016). eprint arXiv:1611.05642
2. Ahrendt, W., Baar, T., Beckert, B., Bubel, R., Giese, M., Hähnle, R., Menzel, W., Mostowski, W., Roth, A., Schlager, S., Schmitt, P.H.: The KeY tool. Soft. Sys. Model. **4**, 32–54 (2005)

3. Anciaux, N., Nguyen, B., Vazirgiannis, M.: Limiting data collection in application forms: a real-case application of a founding privacy principle. In: PST (2012)
4. Askarov, A., Sabelfeld, A.: Gradual release: unifying declassification, encryption and key release policies. In: Proceedings IEEE Symposium on Security and Privacy (2007)
5. Askarov, A., Chong, S.: Learning is change in knowledge: knowledge-based security for dynamic policies. In: IEEE Conferences on CSF (2012)
6. Backes, M., Kopf, B., Rybalchenko, A.: Automatic discovery and quantification of information leaks. In: IEEE Security and Privacy (2009)
7. Balliu, M., Dam, M., Le Guernic, G.: Epistemic temporal logic for information flow security. In: PLAS (2011)
8. Bussard, L.: Encyclopedia of cryptography and security. In: Secondary Use Regulations (2011)
9. Chong, S.: Required information release. In: IEEE Conferences on CSF (2010)
10. Cohen, E.: Information transmission in computational systems. SIGOPS Oper. Syst. Rev. **11**(5), 133–139 (1977). ACM Conferences
11. Dolzmann, A., Sturm, T.: Redlog: computer algebra meets computer logic. SIGSAM Bull. **31**(2), 2–9 (1997). ACM Conferences
12. European Commission: General Data Protection Regulation. Codecision legislative procedure for a regulation 2012/0011
13. Flanagan, C., Qadeer, S.: Predicate abstraction for software verification. In: POPL (2002)
14. Giacobazzi, R., Ranzato, F.: Completeness in abstract interpretation: a domain perspective. In: Johnson, M. (ed.) AMAST 1997. LNCS, vol. 1349, pp. 231–245. Springer, Heidelberg (1997). doi:10.1007/BFb0000474
15. Gurses, S., Troncoso, C., Diaz, C.: Engineering privacy by design reloaded. In: Amsterdam Privacy Conference (2015)
16. Hentschel, M., Bubel, R., Hähnle, R.: Symbolic Execution Debugger (SED). In: Bonakdarpour, B., Smolka, S.A. (eds.) RV 2014. LNCS, vol. 8734, pp. 255–262. Springer, Cham (2014). doi:10.1007/978-3-319-11164-3_21
17. King, J.C.: Symbolic execution and program testing. CACM **19**(7), 385–394 (1976)
18. Landauer, J., Redmond, T.: A lattice of information. In: IEEE Conferences CSFW (1993)
19. Leavens, G.T., Baker, A.L., Ruby, C.: JML: a Java Modeling Language. In: Formal Underpinnings of Java Workshop (1998)
20. Lowe, G.: Quantifying information flow. In: IEEE Conferences on CSFW (2002)
21. Malacaria, P., Tautchning, M., DiStefano, D.: Information leakage analysis of complex C Code and its application to OpenSSL. In: Margaria, T., Steffen, B. (eds.) ISoLA 2016. LNCS, vol. 9952, pp. 909–925. Springer, Cham (2016). doi:10.1007/978-3-319-47166-2_63
22. Mastroeni, I., Zanardini, D.: Data dependencies and program slicing: from syntax to abstract semantics. In: PEPM (2008)
23. Moura, L., Bjørner, N.: Z3: an efficient SMT solver. In: Ramakrishnan, C.R., Rehof, J. (eds.) TACAS 2008. LNCS, vol. 4963, pp. 337–340. Springer, Heidelberg (2008). doi:10.1007/978-3-540-78800-3_24
24. Oystein, O.: Theory of equivalence relations. Duke Math. J. **9**, 573–627 (1942)
25. Richardson, D.J., Clarke, L.A.: A partition analysis method to increase program reliability. In: ICSE (1981)
26. Sabelfeld, A., Sands, D.: A per model of secure information flow in sequential programs. Higher-Order Symbolic Comput. **14**(1), 59–91 (2001). Springer Publication

27. Smith, G.: On the foundations of quantitative information flow. In: Alfaro, L. (ed.) FoSSaCS 2009. LNCS, vol. 5504, pp. 288–302. Springer, Heidelberg (2009). doi:10. 1007/978-3-642-00596-1_21

28. Tschantz, M.C., Wing, J.M.: Formal methods for privacy. In: Cavalcanti, A., Dams, D.R. (eds.) FM 2009. LNCS, vol. 5850, pp. 1–15. Springer, Heidelberg (2009). doi:10.1007/978-3-642-05089-3_1

29. Val, C.G., Enescu, M.A., Bayless, S., Aiello, W., Hu, A.J.: Precisely measuring quantitative information flow: 10k lines of code and beyond. In: IEEE Conferences on EuroS&P (2016)

Privacy

Differentially Private Neighborhood-Based Recommender Systems

Jun Wang[1]([⊠]) and Qiang Tang[2]

[1] University of Luxembourg, Esch-sur-Alzette, Luxembourg
jun.wang@uni.lu
[2] Luxembourg Institute of Science and Technology, Esch-sur-Alzette, Luxembourg
tonyrhul@gmail.com

Abstract. In this paper, we apply the differential privacy concept to neighborhood-based recommendation methods (NBMs) under a probabilistic framework. We first present a solution, by directly calibrating Laplace noise into the training process, to differential-privately find the maximum a posteriori parameters *similarity*. Then we connect differential privacy to NBMs by exploiting a recent observation that sampling from the scaled posterior distribution of a Bayesian model results in provably differentially private systems. Our experiments show that both solutions allow promising accuracy with a modest privacy budget, and the second solution yields better accuracy if the sampling asymptotically converges. We also compare our solutions to the recent differentially private matrix factorization (MF) recommender systems, and show that our solutions achieve better accuracy when the privacy budget is reasonably small. This is an interesting result because MF systems often offer better accuracy when differential privacy is not applied.

Keywords: Recommender · Collaborative filtering · Differential privacy

1 Introduction

Recommender systems, particularly collaborative filtering (CF) systems, have been widely deployed due to the success of E-commerce [25]. There are two dominant approaches in CF. One is matrix factorization (MF) [12] which models the user preference matrix as a product of two low-rank user and item feature matrices, and the other is neighborhood-based method (NBM) which leverages the *similarity* between items or users to estimate user preferences [7]. Generally, MF is more accurate than NBM [25], while NBM has an irreplaceable advantage that it naturally explains the recommendation results. In reality, industrial CF recommender and ranking systems often adopt a client-server model, in which a single server (or, server cluster) holds databases and serves a large number of users. CF exploits the fact that similar users are likely to prefer similar products, unfortunately this property facilitates effective user de-anonymization and

S. De Capitani di Vimercati and F. Martinelli (Eds.): SEC 2017, IFIP AICT 502, pp. 459–473, 2017.
DOI: 10.1007/978-3-319-58469-0_31

history information recovery through the recommendation results [5,18]. To this end, NBM is more fragile (e.g. [5,16]), since it is essentially a simple linear combination of user history information which is weighted by the normalized *similarity* between users or items. In this paper, we aim at preventing information leakage from the recommendation results, for the NBM systems. Note that a related research topic is to avoid the server from accessing the users' plaintext inputs, and many solutions exist for this (e.g. [19,26]). We skip the details here.

Differential privacy [9] provides rigorous privacy protection for user information in statistical databases. Intuitively, it offers a participant the possibility to deny his participation in a computation. Some works, such as [14,33], have been proposed for some specific NBMs, which adopt correlations or artificially defined metrics as *similarity* [7] and are less appealing from the perspective of accuracy. It remains as an open issue to apply the differential privacy concept to more sophisticated NBM models, which automatically learn *similarity* from training data (e.g. [22,27,29]). Particularly, probabilistic NBM [29] models the dependencies among observations (ratings) which leads user preference estimation to a penalized risk minimization problem to search optimal unobserved factors (In our context, the unobserved factor is *similarity*). It has been shown that the instantiation in [29] outperforms most other NBM systems and even the MF or probabilistic MF systems in many settings.

1.1 Our Contribution

Due to its accuracy advantages, we focus on the probabilistic NBM systems in our study. Inspired by [4,13], we propose two methods to instantiate differentially private solutions. First, we calibrate noise into the training process (i.e. SGD) to differential-privately find the maximum a posteriori *similarity*. This instantiation achieves differential privacy for each rating value. Second, we link the differential privacy concept to probabilistic NBM, by sampling from scaled posterior distribution. For the sake of efficiency, we employ a recent MCMC method, namely Stochastic Gradient Langevin Dynamics (SGLD) [32], as the sampler. In order to use SGLD, we derive an unbiased estimator of *similarity* gradient from a mini-batch. This instantiation achieves differential privacy for every user profile (rating vector). Our experimental results show that differentially private MFs are more accurate when privacy loss is large (extremely, in a non-private case), but differentially private NBMs are better when privacy loss is set in a more reasonable range. Even with the added noises, both our solutions consistently outperform non-private traditional NBMs in accuracy. Despite the complexity concern, our solution with posterior sampling (i.e. SGLD) outperforms the other from the accuracy perspective.

2 Preliminary

Generally, NBMs can be divided into user-user approach (relies on *similarity* between users) and item-item approach (relies on *similarity* between items) [7].

Probabilistic NBM can be regarded as a generic methodology, to be employed by any other specific NBM system. Commonly, the item-item approach is more accurate and robust than the user-user approach [7,16]. In this paper, we take the item-item approach as an instance to introduce the probabilistic NBM concept from [29]. We also review the concept of differential privacy.

2.1   Review Probabilistic NBM

r_{ui}	The rating that user u gave item i
s_{ij}	The similarity between item i and j
$R \in \mathbb{R}^{N \times M}$	Rating matrix
$R^{>0} \subset R$	All the observed ratings or training data
$S \in \mathbb{R}^{M \times M}$	Item similarity matrix
$S_i \in \mathbb{R}^{1 \times M}$	Similarity vector of item i
$R_u^- \in \mathbb{R}^{M \times 1}$	u's rating vector without the item being modeled
α_S, α_R	Hyperparameters of S_i and r_{ui} respectively
$f(S_i, R_u^-)$	Any NBM which takes as input the S_i and R_u^-
$p(*)$	Prior distribution of $*$
$p(S_i|\alpha_S)$	Likelihood function of S_i conditioned on α_S
$p(r_{ui}|f(*), \alpha_R)$	Likelihood function of r_{ui}

Suppose we have a dataset with N users and M items. Probabilistic NBM [29] assumes the observed ratings $R^{>0}$ conditioned on historical ratings with Gaussian noise. Some notation is summarized in the above table. The likelihood function of observations $R^{>0}$ and prior of *similarity* S are written as

$$p(R^{>0}|S, R^-, \alpha_R) = \prod_{i=1}^{M} \prod_{u=1}^{N} [\mathcal{N}(r_{ui}|f(S_i, R_u^-), \alpha_R^{-1})]^{I_{ui}}; \quad p(S|\alpha_S) = \prod_{i=1}^{M} \mathcal{N}(S_i|0, \alpha_S^{-1}\mathbf{I})$$

$$(1)$$

where $\mathcal{N}(x|\mu, \alpha^{-1})$ denotes the Gaussian distribution with mean μ and precision α. R^- indicates that if item i is being modeled then it is excluded from the training data $R^{>0}$. $f(S_i, R_u^-)$ denotes any NBM which takes as inputs the S_i and R_u^-. In the following, we instantiate it to be a typical NBM [7]:

$$\hat{r}_{ui} \leftarrow f(S_i, R_u^-) = \bar{r}_i + \frac{\sum_{j \in \mathcal{I} \setminus \{i\}} s_{ij}(r_{uj} - \bar{r}_j) I_{uj}}{\sum_{j \in \mathcal{I} \setminus \{i\}} |s_{ij}| I_{uj}} = \frac{S_i R_u^-}{|S_i| I_u^-} \quad (2)$$

$\hat{r}_{ui}$ denotes the estimation of user u's preference on item i, $\bar{r}_i$ is item i's mean rating value, I_{uj} is the rating indicator $I_{uj} = 1$ if user u rated item j, otherwise, $I_{uj} = 0$. Similar with R_u^-, I_u^- denotes user u's indicator vector but set $I_{ui} = 0$ if i is the item being estimated. For the ease of notation, we will omit the term $\bar{r}_i$

and present Eq. (2) in a vectorization form in favor of a slightly more succinct notation. The log of the posterior distribution over the *similarity* is

$$-\log p(S|R^{>0}, \alpha_S, \alpha_R) = -\log p(R^{>0}|S, R^-, \alpha_R) p(S|\alpha_S) =$$

$$\frac{\alpha_R}{2} \sum_{i=1}^{M} \sum_{u=1}^{N} (r_{ui} - \frac{S_i R_u^-}{|S_i| I_u^-})^2 + \frac{\alpha_s}{2} \sum_{i=1}^{M} (\|S_i\|_2) + M^2 \log \frac{\alpha_s}{\sqrt{2\pi}} + \log \frac{\alpha_R}{\sqrt{2\pi}} \sum_{i=1}^{M} \sum_{u=1}^{N} I_{ui} \tag{3}$$

Thanks to the simplicity of the log-posterior distribution (i.e. $\sum_{i=1}^{M} \sum_{u=1}^{N} (r_{ui} - \frac{S_i R_u^-}{|S_i| I_u^-})^2 + \sum_{i=1}^{M} (\|S_i\|_2)$, where we omit the constant terms in Eq. (3)). We can have two approaches to solve this risk minimization problem.

- *Stochastic Gradient Descent (SGD).* In this approach, $\log p(S|R^{>0}, \alpha_S, \alpha_R)$ is treated as an error function. SGD can be adopted to minimize the error function. In each SGD iteration we update the gradient of *similarity* $(-\frac{\partial \log p(S|R^{>0}, \alpha_S, \alpha_R)}{\partial S_{ij}})$ with a set of randomly chosen ratings Φ by

$$S_{ij} \leftarrow S_{ij} - \eta \left(\sum_{(u,j) \in \Phi} (\hat{r}_{ui} - r_{ui}) \frac{\partial \hat{r}_{ui}}{\partial S_{ij}} + \lambda S_{ij} \right) \tag{4}$$

  where η is the learning rate, $\lambda = \frac{\alpha_S}{\alpha_R}$ is the regular parameter, the set Φ may contain $n \in [1, N]$ users. In Sect. 3, we will introduce how to build the differentially private SGD to train probabilistic NBM.
- *Monte Carlo Markov Chain (MCMC).* We estimate the predictive distribution of an unknown rating by a Monte Carlo approximation. In Sect. 4, we will connect differential privacy to samples from the posterior $p(S|R^{>0}, \alpha_S, \alpha_R)$, via Stochastic Gradient Langevin Dynamics (SGLD) [32].

2.2 Differential Privacy

Differential privacy [9], which is a dominate security definition against inference attacks, aims to rigorously protect sensitive data in statistical databases. It allows to efficiently perform machine learning tasks with quantified privacy guarantee while accurately approximating the non-private results.

Definition 1 (*Differential Privacy [9]*). *A random algorithm $\mathcal{M}$ is (ϵ, σ)-differentially private if for all $\mathcal{O} \subset Range(\mathcal{M})$ and for any of all $(\mathcal{D}_0, \mathcal{D}_1)$ which only differs on one single record such that $\|\mathcal{D}_0 - \mathcal{D}_1\| \leq 1$ satisfies*

$$Pr[\mathcal{M}(\mathcal{D}_0) \in \mathcal{O}] \leq exp(\epsilon) Pr[(\mathcal{M}(\mathcal{D}_1) \in \mathcal{O}] + \sigma$$

And $\mathcal{M}$ guarantees ϵ-differential privacy if $\sigma = 0$.

The parameter ϵ states the difference of algorithm $\mathcal{M}$'s output for any $(\mathcal{D}_0, \mathcal{D}_1)$. It measures the privacy loss. Lower ϵ indicates stronger privacy protection.

Laplace Mechanism [8] is a common approach to approximate a real-valued function $f : \mathcal{D} \rightarrow \mathbb{R}$ with a differential privacy preservation using additive noise sampled from Laplace distribution: $\mathcal{M}(\mathcal{D}) \triangleq f(\mathcal{D}) + Lap(0, \frac{\Delta \mathcal{F}}{\epsilon})$, where the $\Delta \mathcal{F}$ indicates the largest possible change between the outputs of the function f which takes as input any neighbor databases $(\mathcal{D}_0, \mathcal{D}_1)$. It is referred to as the L_1-sensitivity which is defined as: $\Delta \mathcal{F} = \underset{(\mathcal{D}_0, \mathcal{D}_1)}{max} ||f(\mathcal{D}_0) - f(\mathcal{D}_1)||_1$.

Sampling from the posterior distribution of a Bayesian model with bounded log-likelihood, recently, has been proven to be differentially private [30]. It is essentially an *exponential mechanism* [15]. Formally, suppose we have a dataset of $\mathcal{L}$ i.i.d examples $\mathcal{X} = \{x_i\}_{i=1}^{\mathcal{L}}$ which we model using a conditional probability distribution $p(x|\theta)$ where θ is a parameter vector, with a prior distribution $p(\theta)$. If $p(x|\theta)$ satisfies $sup_{x \in \mathcal{X}, \theta \in \Theta} |\log p(x|\theta)| \leq B$, then releasing one sample from the posterior distribution $p(\theta|\mathcal{X})$ with any prior $p(\theta)$ preserves $4B$-differential privacy. Alternatively, ϵ differential privacy can be preserved by simply rescaling the log-posterior distribution by a factor of $\frac{\epsilon}{4B}$, under the regularity conditions where asymptotic normality (Bernstein-von Mises theorem) holds.

3 Differentially Private SGD

When applying the differential privacy concept, treating the training model (process) as a black box, by only working on the original input or finally output, may result in very poor utility [1,4]. In contrast, by leveraging the tight characterization of training data, NBM and SGD, we directly calibrate noise into the SGD training process, via Laplace mechanism, to differential-privately learn *similarity*. Algorithm 1 outlines our differentially-private SGD method for training probabilistic NBM.

Algorithm 1. Differentially Private SGD

Require: Database $R^{>0}$, privacy parameter ϵ, regular parameter λ, rescale parameter β, learning rate η, the total number of iterations K, initialized *similarity* $S^{(1)}$.

1: $S^{(1)} = S^{(1)} \cdot \beta$ ▷ rescale the initialization
2: **for** $t = 1 : K$ **do**
3:     • uniform-randomly sample a mini-batch $\Phi \subset R^{>0}$.
4:     $\Delta \mathcal{F} = 2e_{max} \frac{\tau}{C}$ ▷ $e_{max} = 0.5 + \frac{\varphi - 1}{t+1}$; $|S_i|I_u \geq C$
5:     $e_{ui} = min(max(e_{ui}, -e_{max}), e_{max})$ ▷ $e_{ui} = \hat{r}_{ui} - r_{ui}$
6:     $\mathcal{G} = \sum_{(u,i) \in \Phi} e_{ui} \frac{\partial \hat{r}_{ui}}{\partial S_i} + Laplace(\frac{\gamma K \Delta \mathcal{F}}{\epsilon})$ ▷ $\gamma = \frac{L}{\mathcal{L}}$
7:     $S^{(t+1)} \leftarrow S^{(t)} - \eta(\beta \mathcal{G} + \lambda S^{(t)})$ ▷ up-scale the update
8: **end for**
9: **return** $S^{(t+1)}$

According to Eqs. (3) and (4), for each user u (in a randomly chosen mini-batch Φ) the gradient of *similarity* is

$$\mathcal{G}_{ij}(u) = e_{ui} \frac{\partial \hat{r}_{ui}}{\partial S_{ij}} = e_{ui}(\frac{r_{uj}}{S_i I_u^-} - \hat{r}_{ui} \frac{I_{uj}}{S_i I_u^-}) \qquad (5)$$

where $e_{ui} = \hat{r}_{ui} - r_{ui}$. For the convenience of notation, we omit $S_{ij} < 0$ part in Eq. (5) which does not compromise the correctness of bound estimation.

To achieve differential privacy, we update the gradient $\mathcal{G}$ by adding Laplace noise (Algorithm 1, line 6). The amount of noise is determined by the bound of gradient $\mathcal{G}_{ij}(u)$ (sensitivity $\Delta\mathcal{F}$) which further depends on $e_{ui}, (r_{uj} - \hat{r}_{ui}I_{uj})$ and $|S_i|I_u^-$. We reduce the sensitivity by exploiting the characteristics of training data, NBM and SGD respectively, by the following tricks.

Preprocessing is often adopted in machine learning for utility reasons. In our case, it can contribute to privacy protection. For example, we only put users who have more than 20 ratings in the training data. It results in a bigger $|S_i|I_u^-$ thus will reduce sensitivity. Suppose the rating scale is $[r_{min}, r_{max}]$, removing "paranoid" records makes $|r_{uj} - \hat{r}_{ui}I_{uj}| \leq \varphi$ hold, where $\varphi = r_{max} - r_{min}$.

Rescaling the value of similarity allows a lower sensitivity. NBM, see Eq. (2), allows us to rescale the *similarity* S to an arbitrarily large magnitude such that we can further reduce the sensitivity (by increasing the value of $|S_i|I_u$). However, the initialization of *similarity* strongly influences the convergence of the training. Thus, it is crucial to balance the convergence (accuracy) and the value of *similarity* (privacy). Another observation is that the gradient downscales when enlarging the *similarity*, see Eq. (5). We can up-scale the gradient monotonically during the training process (Algorithm 1, lines 1 and 7).

The prediction error $e_{ui} = \hat{r}_{ui} - r_{ui}$ decreases when the training goes to convergence such that we can clamp e_{ui} to a lower bound dynamically. In our experiments, we bound the prediction error as $|e_{ui}| \leq 0.5 + \frac{\varphi-1}{t+1}$, where t is the iteration index. This constraint trivially influences the convergence under non-private training process.

After applying all the tricks, we have the dynamic gradient bound at iteration t as follows: $max(|\mathcal{G}^{(t)}|) \leq (0.5 + \frac{\varphi-1}{t+1})\frac{\varphi}{C}$. The *sensitivity of* each iteration is $\Delta\mathcal{F} = 2max(|\mathcal{G}^{(t)}|) \leq 2(0.5 + \frac{\varphi-1}{t+1})\frac{\varphi}{C}$.

Theorem 1. *Uniform-randomly sample L examples from a dataset of the size $\mathcal{L}$, Algorithm 1 achieves ϵ-differential privacy if in each SGD iteration t we set $\epsilon^{(t)} = \frac{\epsilon}{K\gamma}$ where K is the number of iterations and $\gamma = \frac{L}{\mathcal{L}}$.*

Proof. In Algorithm 1, suppose the number of iterations K is known in advance, and each SGD iteration maintains $\frac{\epsilon}{K\gamma}$-differential privacy. The privacy enhancing technique [3,11] indicates that given a method which is ϵ-differentially private over a deterministic training set, then it maintains $\gamma\epsilon$-differential privacy with respect to a full database if we uniform-randomly sample training set from the database where γ is the sampling ratio. Finally, combining the privacy enhancing technique with composition theory [9], it ensures the K iterations SGD process maintain the overall bound of ϵ-differential privacy.   □

4   Differentially Private Posterior Sampling

Sampling from the posterior distribution of a Bayesian model with bounded log-likelihood has free differential privacy to some extent [30]. Specifically, for probabilistic NBM, releasing a sample of the *similarity* S,

$$S \sim p(S|R^{>0}, \alpha_S, \alpha_R) \propto exp(\sum_{i=1}^{M} \sum_{u=1}^{N} (r_{ui} - \frac{S_i R_u^-}{|S_i| I_u^-})^2 + \lambda \sum_{i=1}^{M} ||S_i||_2) \qquad (6)$$

achieves $4B$-differential privacy at user level, if each user's log-likelihood is bounded to B, i.e. $\max_{u \in R^{>0}} \sum_{i \in R_u} (\hat{r}_{ui} - r_{ui})^2 \leq B$. Wang et al. [30] showed that we can achieve ϵ-differential privacy by simply rescaling the log-posterior distribution with $\frac{\epsilon}{4B}$, i.e. $\frac{\epsilon}{4B} \cdot \log p(S|R^{>0}, \alpha_S, \alpha_R)$.

Posterior sampling is computationally costly. For the sake of efficiency, we adopt a recent introduced Monte Carlo method, Stochastic Gradient Langevin Dynamics (SGLD) [32], as our MCMC sampler. To successfully use SGLD, we need to derive an unbiased estimator of *similarity* gradient from a mini-batch which is a non-trivial task.

Next, we first overview the basic principles of SGLD (Sect. 4.1), then we derive an unbiased estimator of the true *similarity* gradient (Sect. 4.2), and finally present our privacy-preserving algorithm (Sect. 4.3).

4.1 Stochastic Gradient Langevin Dynamics

SGLD is an annealing of SGD and Langevin dynamics [23] which generates samples from a posterior distribution. Intuitively, it adds an amount of Gaussian noise calibrated by the step sizes (learning rate) used in the SGD process, and the step sizes are allowed to go to zero. When it is far away from the basin of convergence, the update is much larger than noise and it acts as a normal SGD process. The update decreases when the sampling approaches to the convergence basin such that the noise dominated, and it behaves like a Brownian motion. SGLD updates the candidate states according to the following rule.

$$\Delta \theta_t = \frac{\eta_t}{2} (\Delta \log p(\theta_t) + \frac{\mathcal{L}}{L} \sum_{i=1}^{L} \Delta \log p(x_{ti}|\theta_t)) + z_t; \qquad z_t \sim \mathcal{N}(0, \eta_t) \qquad (7)$$

where η_t is a sequence of step sizes. $p(x|\theta)$ denotes conditional probability distribution, and θ is a parameter vector with a prior distribution $p(\theta)$. L is the size of a mini-batch randomly sampled from dataset $\mathcal{X}^{\mathcal{L}}$. To ensure convergence to a local optimum, the following requirements of step size η_t have to be satisfied: $\sum_{t=1}^{\infty} \eta_t = \infty$; $\sum_{t=1}^{\infty} \eta_t^2 < \infty$. Decreasing step size η_t reduces the discretization error such that the rejection rate approaches zero, thus we do not need accept-reject test. Following the previous works, e.g. [13,32], we set step size $\eta_t = \eta_1 t^{-\xi}$, commonly, $\xi \in [0.3, 1]$. In order to speed up the burn-in phase of SGLD, we multiply the step size η_t by a temperature parameter ϱ $(0 < \varrho < 1)$ where $\sqrt{\varrho \cdot \eta_t} \gg \eta_t$ [6].

4.2 Unbiased Estimator of The Gradient

The log-posterior distribution of *similarity* S has been defined in Eq. (3). The true gradient of the *similarity* S over $R^{>0}$ can be computed as

$$\mathcal{G}(R^{>0}) = \sum_{(u,i) \in R^{>0}} g_{ui}(S; R^{>0}) + \lambda S \qquad (8)$$

where $g_{ui}(S; R^{>0}) = e_{ui}\frac{\partial \hat{r}_{ui}}{\partial S_i}$. To use SGLD and make it converge to true posterior distribution, we need an unbiased estimator of the true gradient which can be computed from a mini-batch $\Phi \subset R^{>0}$. Assume that the size of Φ and $R^{>0}$ are L and $\mathcal{L}$ respectively. The stochastic approximation of the gradient is

$$\mathcal{G}(\Phi) = \mathcal{L}\bar{g}(S, \Phi) + \lambda S \circ \mathbb{I}[i, j \in \Phi] \tag{9}$$

where $\bar{g}(S, \Phi) = \frac{1}{L}\sum_{(u,i)\in\Phi} g_{ui}(S, \Phi)$. $\mathbb{I} \subset \mathbb{B}^{M\times M}$ is symmetric binary matrix, and $\mathbb{I}[i, j \in \Phi] = 1$ if any item-pair (i, j) exists in Φ, otherwise 0. $\circ$ presents element-wise product. The expectation of $\mathcal{G}(\Phi)$ over all mini-batches is,

$$\mathbb{E}_\Phi[\mathcal{G}(\Phi)] = \sum_{(u,i)\in R^{>0}} g_{ui}(S; R^{>0}) + \lambda\mathbb{E}_\Phi[S \circ \mathbb{I}[i, j \in \Phi]] \tag{10}$$

$\mathbb{E}_\Phi[\mathcal{G}(\Phi)]$ is not an unbiased estimator of the true gradient $\mathcal{G}(R^{>0})$ due to the prior term $\mathbb{E}_\Phi[S \circ \mathbb{I}[i, j \in \Phi]]$. Let $\mathbb{H} = \mathbb{E}_\Phi[\mathbb{I}[i, j \in \Phi]]$, we can remove this bias by multiplying the prior term with $\mathbb{H}^{-1}$ thus to obtain an unbiased estimator. Follow previous approach [2], we assume the mini-batches are sampled with replacement, then $\mathbb{H}$ is $\mathbb{H}_{ij} = 1 - \frac{|I_i||I_j|}{\mathcal{L}^2}(1 - \frac{|I_j|}{\mathcal{L}})^{L-1}(1 - \frac{|I_i|}{\mathcal{L}})^{L-1}$, where $|I_i|$ (resp. $|I_j|$) denotes the number of ratings of item i (resp. j) in the complete dataset $R^{>0}$. Then the SGLD update rule is the following:

$$S^{(t+1)} \leftarrow S^{(t)} - \frac{\eta_t}{2}(\mathcal{L}\bar{g}(S^{(t)}, \Phi) + \lambda S^{(t)} \circ \mathbb{H}^{-1}) + z_t \tag{11}$$

4.3 Differential Privacy via Posterior Sampling

To construct a differentially private NBM, we exploit a recent observation that sampling from scaled posterior distribution of a Bayesian model with bounded log-likelihood can achieve ϵ-differential privacy [30]. We summarize the differentially private sampling process (via SGLD) in Algorithm 2.

Algorithm 2. Differentially Private Posterior Sampling (via SGLD)

Require: Temperature parameter ϱ, privacy parameter ϵ, regular parameter λ, initial learning rate η_1. Let K larger than burn-in phase.
1: **for** $t = 1 : K$ **do**
2:     • Randomly sample a mini-batch $\Phi \subset R^{>0}$.
3:     $\bar{g}(S^{(t)}, \Phi) = \frac{1}{L}\sum_{(u,i)\in\Phi} e_{ui}\frac{\partial \hat{r}_{ui}}{\partial S_i^{(t)}}$ ▷ gradient of S (mini-batch)
4:     $z_t \sim \mathcal{N}(0, \varrho \cdot \eta_t)$ ▷ $\sqrt{\varrho \cdot \eta_t} \gg \eta_t$
5:     $S^{(t+1)} \leftarrow S^{(t)} - \frac{\epsilon}{4B} \cdot \frac{\eta_t}{2}(\mathcal{L}\bar{g}(S^{(t)}, \Phi) + \lambda S^{(t)} \circ \mathbb{H}^{-1}) + z_t$
6:     $\eta_{t+1} = \frac{\eta_1}{t^\gamma}$
7: **end for**
8: **return** $S^{(t+1)}$

Now, a natural question is how to determine the log-likelihood bound B? ($\max_{u\in R^{>0}} \sum_{i\in R_u}(\hat{r}_{ui} - r_{ui})^2 \leq B$, and see Eq. (6)). Obviously, B depends on the max rating number per user. To those users who rated more than τ items, we randomly remove some ratings thus to ensure that each user at most has τ ratings. In our context, the rating scale is $[1,5]$, let $\tau = 200$, we have $B = (5-1)^2 \times 200$ (In reality, most users have less than 200 ratings [13]).

Theorem 2. *Algorithm 2 provides $(\epsilon, (1 + e^\epsilon)\delta)$-differential privacy guarantee to any user if the distribution $P'_{\mathcal{X}}$ where the approximate samples from is δ-far away from the true posterior distribution $P_{\mathcal{X}}$, formally $||P'_{\mathcal{X}} - P_{\mathcal{X}}||_1 \leq \delta$. And $\delta \to 0$ if the MCMC sampling asymptotically converges.*

Proof. Essentially, differential privacy via posterior sampling [30] is an exponential mechanism [15] which protects ϵ-differential privacy when releasing a sample θ with probability proportional to $exp(-\frac{\epsilon}{2\Delta\mathcal{F}}p(\mathcal{X}|\theta))$, where $p(\mathcal{X}|\theta)$ serves as the utility function. If $p(\mathcal{X}|\theta)$ is bounded to B, we have the sensitivity $\Delta\mathcal{F} \leq 2B$. Thus, release a sample by Algorithm 2 preserves ϵ-differential privacy. It compromises the privacy guarantee to $(\epsilon, (1 + e^\epsilon)\delta)$ if the distribution (where the sample from) is δ-far away from the true posterior distribution, proved by [30]. $\square$

Note that when $\epsilon = 4B$, the differentially private sampling process is identical to the non-private sampling. This is also the meaning of *some extent of free privacy*. It starts to lose accuracy when $\epsilon < 4B$. One concern of this sampling approach is the distance δ between the distribution where the samples from and the true posterior distribution, which compromises the differential privacy guarantee. Fortunately, [24,28] proved that SGLD can converge in finite iterations. As such we can have arbitrarily small δ with a (large) number of iterations.

5   Experiments and Evaluation

We test our solutions on two real world datasets, ML100K and ML1M [17], which are widely employed for evaluating recommender systems. ML100K dataset has 100 K ratings that 943 users assigned to 1682 movies. ML1M dataset contains 1 million ratings that 6040 users gave to 3952 movies. In the experiments, we adopt 5-fold cross validation for training and evaluation. We use root mean square error (RMSE) to measure accuracy performance: $RMSE = \sqrt{\frac{\sum_{(u,i)\in R^T}(r_{ui} - \hat{r}_{ui})^2}{|R^T|}}$, where $|R^T|$ is the total number of ratings in the test set R^T.

5.1   Experiments Setup

In the following, the differentially-private SGD based PNBM is referred to as DPSGD-PNBM, and the differentially-private posterior sampling PNBM is referred as DPPS-PNBM. The experiment source code is available at Github[1]. We compare their performances with the following baseline algorithms.

---

[1] https://github.com/lux-jwang/Experiments/tree/master/dpnbm.

- *non-private PCC and COS:* Differentially-private Pearson correlation (PCC) or Cosine similarity (COS) NBMs exist (e.g. [10,14,33]), with worse accuracy than the non-private algorithms. We directly use the non-private ones.
- *DPSGD-MF:* Differentially private matrix factorization from [4], which calibrates Laplacian noise into the SGD training process.
- *DPPS-MF:* Differentially private matrix factorization from [13], which exploits the posterior sampling technique.

We optimize model parameters using a heuristic grid search method, as follows.

- *DPSGD-PNBM:* The learning rate η is searched in $\{0.1, 0.4\}$, and the iteration number $K \in [1, 20]$, the regular parameter $\lambda \in \{0.05, 0.005\}$, the rescale parameter $\beta \in \{10, 20\}$. The neighbor size $N_k = 500$, the lower bound of $|S_i|I_u$: $C \in \{10, 15\}$. In the training process, we decrease K and increase $\{\eta, C\}$ when requiring a stronger privacy guarantee (a smaller ϵ).
- *DPPS-PNBM:* The initial learning rate $\eta_1 \in \{8 \cdot 10^{-8}, 4 \cdot 10^{-7}, 8 \cdot 10^{-6}\}$, $\lambda \in \{0.02, 0.002\}$, the temperature parameter $\varrho = \{0.001, 0.006, 0.09\}$, the decay parameter $\xi = 0.3$. $N_k = 500$.
- *DPSGD-MF:* $\eta \in \{6 \cdot 10^{-4}, 8 \cdot 10^{-4}\}$, $K \in [10, 50]$ (the smaller privacy loss ϵ the less iterations), $\lambda \in \{0.2, 0.02\}$, the latent feature dimension $d \in \{10, 15, 20\}$.
- *DPPS-MF:* $\eta \in \{2 \cdot 10^{-9}, 2 \cdot 10^{-8}, 8 \cdot 10^{-7}, 8 \cdot 10^{-6}\}$, $\lambda \in \{0.02, 0.05, 0.1, 0.2\}$, $\varrho = \{1 \cdot 10^{-4}, 6 \cdot 10^{-4}, 4 \cdot 10^{-3}, 3 \cdot 10^{-2}\}$, $d \in \{10, 15, 20\}$, $\xi = 0.3$.
- *non-private PCC and COS:* For ML100K, we set $N_K = 900$. For ML1M, we set $N_K = 1300$.

5.2   Comparison Results

We first compare the accuracy between DPSGD-PNBM, DPSGD-MF, non-private PCC and COS and show the results in Fig. 1 for the two datasets respectively. When $\epsilon \geq 20$, DPSGD-MF does not lose much accuracy, and it is better than non-private PCC and COS. However, the accuracy drops quickly (or, the

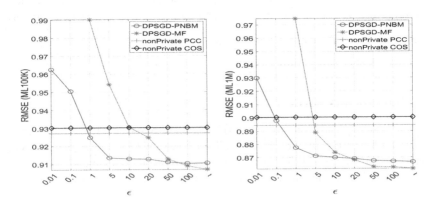

Fig. 1. Accuracy comparison: DPSGD-PNBM, DPSGD-MF, non-private PCC, COS.

RMSE increase quickly) when the privacy loss ϵ is reduced. This matches the observation in [4]. In the contrast, DPSGD-PNBM maintains a promising accuracy when $\epsilon \geq 1$, and is better than non-private PCC and COS.

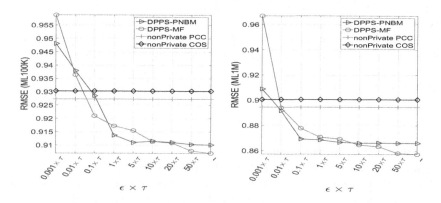

Fig. 2. Accuracy comparison: DPPS-PNBM, DPPS-MF, non-private PCC, COS.

DPPS-PNBM and DPPS-MF preserve differential privacy at user level. We denote the privacy loss ϵ in form of $x \times \tau$ where x is a float value which indicates the average privacy loss at a rating level, and τ is the max rate number per user. The comparison is shown in Fig. 2. In our context, for both datasets, $\tau = 200$. Both DPPS-PNBM and DPPS-MF allow accurate estimations when $\epsilon \geq 0.1 \times 200$. It may seem that $\epsilon = 20$ is a meaningless privacy guarantee. We remark that the average privacy of a rating level is 0.1. Besides the accuracy performance is better than the non-private PCC and COS, from the point of privacy loss ratio, our models match previous works [13,14], where it is showed that differentially private systems may not lose much accuracy when $\epsilon > 1$.

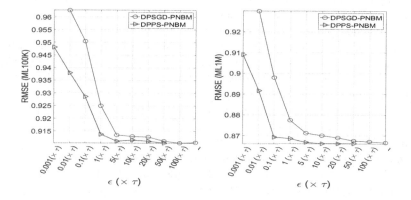

Fig. 3. Accuracy comparison between DPSGD-PNBM and DPPS-PNBM

DPSGD-PNBM and DPPS-PNBM achieve differential privacy at rating level (a single rating) and user level (a whole user profile) respectively. Below, we try to compare them at rating level, precisely at the average rating level for DPPS-PNBM. Figure 3 shows that both solutions can obtain quite accurate predictions with a privacy guarantee ($\epsilon \approx 1$). With the same privacy guarantee, DPPS-PNBM seems to be more accurate. However, DPPS-PNBM has its potential drawback. Recall from Sect. 4, the difference δ between the distribution where samples from and the true posterior distribution compromises differential privacy guarantee. In order to have an arbitrarily small δ, DPPS-PNBM requires a large number of iterations [24,28]. At this point, it is less efficient than DPSGD-PNBM. In our comparison, we assume $\delta \to 0$.

5.3   Summary

In summary, DPSGD-MF and DPPS-MF are more accurate when privacy loss is large. DPSGD-PNBM and DPPS-PNBM are better when we want to reduce the privacy loss to a meaningful range. Both our models consistently outperform non-private traditional NBMs, with a meaningful differential privacy guarantee. Note that *similarity* is independent of NBM itself, thus other neighborhood-based recommenders can use our models to differential-privately learn *Similarity*, and deploy it to their existing systems without requiring extra effort.

6   Related Work

A number of works have demonstrated that an attacker can infer the user sensitive information, such as gender and politic view, from public recommendation results without using much background knowledge, e.g. [5,31]. Randomized data perturbation is one of earliest approaches to prevent user data from inference attack in which people either add random noise to their profiles or substitute some randomly chosen ratings with real ones, e.g. [20,21]. While this approach is very simple, it does not offer rigorous privacy guarantee. Differential privacy [9] aims to precisely protect user privacy in statistical databases, and the concept has become very popular recently. [14] is the first work to apply differential privacy to recommender systems, and it has considered both neighborhood-based methods (using correlation as *similarity*) and latent factor model (e.g. SVD). [33] introduced a differentially private neighbor selection scheme by injecting Laplace noise to the *similarity* matrix. [10] presented a scheme to obfuscate user profiles that preserves differential privacy. [4,13] applied differential privacy to matrix factorization, and we have compared our solutions to theirs in Sect. 5. Secure multiparty computation recommender systems allow users to compute recommendation results without revealing their inputs to other parties. Many protocols have been proposed, e.g. [19,26]. Unfortunately, these protocols do not prevent information leakage from the recommendation results.

7   Conclusion

In this paper, we have proposed two different differentially private NBMs, under a probabilistic framework. We firstly introduced a way to differential-privately find the maximum a posteriori *similarity* by calibrating noise to the SGD training process. Then we built differentially private NBM by exploiting the fact that sampling from scaled posterior distribution can result in differentially private systems. While the experiment results have demonstrated that our models allow promising accuracy with a modest privacy budget in some well-known datasets, we consider it as an interesting future work to test the performances in other real world datasets.

Acknowledgments. Both authors are supported by a CORE (junior track) grant from the National Research Fund, Luxembourg.

References

1. Abadi, M., Chu, A., Goodfellow, I., McMahan, H.B., Mironov, I., Talwar, K., Zhang, L.: Deep learning with differential privacy. In: Proceedings of the 2016 ACM SIGSAC Conference on Computer and Communications Security. ACM (2016)
2. Ahn, S., Korattikara, A., Liu, N., Rajan, S., Welling, M.: Large-scale distributed bayesian matrix factorization using stochastic gradient MCMC. In: Proceedings of the 21th ACM SIGKDD International Conference on Knowledge Discovery and Data Mining, pp. 9–18. ACM (2015)
3. Beimel, A., Brenner, H., Kasiviswanathan, S.P., Nissim, K.: Bounds on the sample complexity for private learning and private data release. Mach. Learn. **94**(3), 401–437 (2014)
4. Berlioz, A., Friedman, A., Kaafar, M.A., Boreli, R., Berkovsky, S.: Applying differential privacy to matrix factorization. In: Proceedings of the 9th ACM Conference on Recommender Systems, pp. 107–114. ACM (2015)
5. Calandrino, J.A., Kilzer, A., Narayanan, A., Felten, E.W., Shmatikov, V.: "You might also like:" privacy risks of collaborative filtering. In: 2011 IEEE Symposium on Security and Privacy, pp. 231–246. IEEE (2011)
6. Chen, T., Fox, E.B., Guestrin, C.: Stochastic gradient Hamiltonian Monte Carlo. In: ICML, pp. 1683–1691 (2014)
7. Desrosiers, C., Karypis, G.: A comprehensive survey of neighborhood-based recommendation methods. In: Ricci, F., Rokach, L., Shapira, B., Kantor, P.B. (eds.) Recommender Systems Handbook, pp. 107–144. Springer, Heidelberg (2011)
8. Dwork, C., McSherry, F., Nissim, K., Smith, A.: Calibrating noise to sensitivity in private data analysis. In: Halevi, S., Rabin, T. (eds.) TCC 2006. LNCS, vol. 3876, pp. 265–284. Springer, Heidelberg (2006). doi:10.1007/11681878_14
9. Dwork, C., Roth, A., et al.: The algorithmic foundations of differential privacy. Found. Trends Theor. Comput. Sci. **9**(3–4), 211–407 (2014)
10. Guerraoui, R., Kermarrec, A.-M., Patra, R., Taziki, M.: D2P: distance-based differential privacy in recommenders. Proc. VLDB Endow. **8**(8), 862–873 (2015)
11. Kasiviswanathan, S.P., Lee, H.K., Nissim, K., Raskhodnikova, S., Smith, A.: What can we learn privately? SIAM J. Comput. **40**(3), 793–826 (2011)

12. Koren, Y., Bell, R., Volinsky, C., et al.: Matrix factorization techniques for recommender systems. Computer **42**(8), 30–37 (2009)
13. Liu, Z., Wang, Y.-X., Smola, A.: Fast differentially private matrix factorization. In: Proceedings of the 9th ACM Conference on Recommender Systems. ACM (2015)
14. McSherry, F., Mironov, I.: Differentially private recommender systems: building privacy into the netflix prize contenders. In: Proceedings of the 15th ACM SIGKDD International Conference on Knowledge Discovery and Data Mining. ACM (2009)
15. McSherry, F., Talwar, K.: Mechanism design via differential privacy. In: 48th Annual IEEE Symposium on Foundations of Computer Science (FOCS 2007), pp. 94–103. IEEE (2007)
16. Mobasher, B., Burke, R., Bhaumik, R., Williams, C.: Toward trustworthy recommender systems: an analysis of attack models and algorithm robustness. ACM Trans. Internet Technol. (TOIT) **7**(4), 23 (2007)
17. MovieLens. MovieLens Datasets. http://grouplens.org/datasets/movielens/
18. Narayanan, A., Shmatikov, V.: Robust de-anonymization of large sparse datasets. In: 2008 IEEE Symposium on Security and Privacy. IEEE (2008)
19. Nikolaenko, V., Ioannidis, S., Weinsberg, U., Joye, M., Taft, N., Boneh, D.: Privacy-preserving matrix factorization. In: Proceedings of the 2013 ACM SIGSAC Conference on Computer & Communications Security, pp. 801–812. ACM (2013)
20. Polat, H., Du, W.: Privacy-preserving collaborative filtering using randomized perturbation techniques. In: Third IEEE International Conference on Data Mining (ICDM 2003), pp. 625–628. IEEE (2003)
21. Polat, H., Du, W.: Achieving private recommendations using randomized response techniques. In: Ng, W.-K., Kitsuregawa, M., Li, J., Chang, K. (eds.) PAKDD 2006. LNCS (LNAI), vol. 3918, pp. 637–646. Springer, Heidelberg (2006). doi:10.1007/11731139_73
22. Rendle, S., Freudenthaler, C., Gantner, Z., Schmidt-Thieme, L.: BPR: bayesian personalized ranking from implicit feedback. In: Proceedings of the Twenty-Fifth Conference on Uncertainty in Artificial Intelligence. AUAI Press (2009)
23. Rossky, P., Doll, J., Friedman, H.: Brownian dynamics as smart monte carlo simulation. J. Chem. Phys. **69**(10), 4628–4633 (1978)
24. Sato, I., Nakagawa, H.: Approximation analysis of stochastic gradient langevin dynamics by using Fokker-Planck equation and Ito process. In: ICML (2014)
25. Su, X., Khoshgoftaar, T.M.: A survey of collaborative filtering techniques. Adv. Artif. Intell. **2009**, 4 (2009)
26. Tang, Q., Wang, J.: Privacy-preserving context-aware recommender systems: analysis and new solutions. In: Pernul, G., Ryan, P.Y.A., Weippl, E. (eds.) ESORICS 2015. LNCS, vol. 9327, pp. 101–119. Springer, Cham (2015). doi:10.1007/978-3-319-24177-7_6
27. Töscher, A., Jahrer, M., Legenstein, R.: Improved neighborhood-based algorithms for large-scale recommender systems. In: Proceedings of the 2nd KDD Workshop on Large-Scale Recommender Systems, p. 4. ACM (2008)
28. Vollmer, S.J., Zygalakis, K.C., et al.: (Non-) asymptotic properties of stochastic gradient langevin dynamics (2015). arXiv preprint arXiv:1501.00438
29. Wang, J., Tang, Q.: A probabilistic view of neighborhood-based recommendation methods (2016). https://arxiv.org/abs/1701.01250
30. Wang, Y.-X., Fienberg, S.E., Smola, A.: Privacy for free: posterior sampling and stochastic gradient monte carlo (2015)
31. Weinsberg, U., Bhagat, S., Ioannidis, S., Taft, N.: Blurme: inferring and obfuscating user gender based on ratings. In: Proceedings of the Sixth ACM Conference on Recommender Systems, pp. 195–202. ACM (2012)

32. Welling, M., Teh, Y.W.: Bayesian learning via stochastic gradient langevin dynamics. In: Proceedings of the 28th International Conference on Machine Learning (ICML 2011), pp. 681–688 (2011)
33. Zhu, T., Ren, Y., Zhou, W., Rong, J., Xiong, P.: An effective privacy preserving algorithm for neighborhood-based collaborative filtering. Future Gener. Comput. Syst. **36**, 142–155 (2014)

Privacy-Enhanced Profile-Based Authentication Using Sparse Random Projection

Somayeh Taheri$^{(\boxtimes)}$, Md Morshedul Islam$^{(\boxtimes)}$, and Reihaneh Safavi-Naini$^{(\boxtimes)}$

University of Calgary, Calgary, AB, Canada
{somayeh.taheri,mdmorshedul.islam,rei}@ucalgary.ca

Abstract. In a profile-based authentication system, a user profile is stored at the verifier and later used to verify their authentication claim. A profile includes user-specific information that is privacy sensitive. In this paper we propose a non-cryptographic approach to providing privacy for user profile data in profile-based authentication systems, using an efficient construction of *random projection*: a linear dimension reducing transform that projects the profile and the verification data to a lower dimension space, while preserving relative distances of the vectors and so correctness of authentication. We define privacy measures for two types of profiles: a single vector profile and a multivector profile, derive theoretical bounds on the privacy and correctness of privacy enhanced systems, and verify the results experimentally on two profile-based authentication systems: a face-biometric system and a behavioural based authentication system. We discuss our results and propose directions for future research.

Keywords: Profile privacy · Random projection · Profile · Biometrics

1 Introduction

Traditional entity authentication systems that rely on secrets (e.g. passwords, secret keys), or hardware tokens, are vulnerable to credential theft and credential sharing. This latter vulnerability not only allows users to share their credentials with others to bypass security of subscription services (e.g. online games), but also has been used for delegation (subcontracting) of work to others [1] resulting in the breach of the company security policy. In a *profile-based authentication system*, a user's *authentication claim* is compared with their stored *profile* that is constructed during a *trusted registration process*. A profile is one or more vectors of *feature values*, each sampling a feature that captures some user-specific property. The profile data is stored at the verifier and is used to accept or reject an authentication claim of a user that presents their *verification data*. The verifier uses a *matching algorithm* that compares the verification data with the stored profile and decides to accept, or reject, the claim. A traditional biometric system [2,3] is a profile-based authentication system where the profile data and

© IFIP International Federation for Information Processing 2017
Published by Springer International Publishing AG 2017. All Rights Reserved
S. De Capitani di Vimercati and F. Martinelli (Eds.): SEC 2017, IFIP AICT 502, pp. 474–490, 2017.
DOI: 10.1007/978-3-319-58469-0_32

verification data are each a single vector, and matching is by measuring the distance between the two. A more recent type of profile-based authentication system, sometimes referred to as *implicit authentication system (IA)* [4], uses a user profile that is a vector of *random variables* whose distribution is specific to the user. A feature is stored as a set of samples that represent the distribution of the feature, and the verification (matching) algorithm compares the distribution of the verification data (represented by a second sample set) with the profile data to determine if they are from the same distribution.

Privacy. Profile data carry sensitive personal information that must be protected from the verifier. Ideally the verifier should only be able to use the profile data for the verification decision. In practice however profiles can be used to learn about users' behaviour and interests for marketing and advertising, or track them across websites. Biometric profiles are uniquely identifying, and are of extreme sensitivity from privacy view point. Behavioural profiles also reveal user private information such as their health conditions, physical abilities or user skills and behaviour, as well as pattern of usage of applications and devices. Richer profiles (i.e. more behaviour data) lead to higher accuracy in authentication and this provides incentive to employ more user data, and "to keep it around for a longer period of time" [5].

An immediate solution to protecting privacy of profile data against the verifier is to store them in encrypted form and design the verification algorithm as a computation in encrypted domain, or use a secure two party computation protocol. These approaches in their general form [6] are computationally expensive and are primarily of theoretical interest. One can tailor more efficient secure computation systems for computationally simple verification algorithms, such as finding linear sums [7], but this cannot be easily extended to more general matching algorithms such as KS-test used in this paper (See Sect. 2). In [8] *random projection* of profile data was proposed to provide profile privacy for biometric data. Authors showed that, using a random transformation matrix whose elements are generated using a Gaussian distribution, one can project profile vectors to a lower dimension space, such that the correctness of the verification algorithm is maintained. Authors also showed that the approach allows *changeability* of the profile, which is a desirable security property. Our work builds on this result and strengthens and extends in a number of ways.

Our Work. *The setting.* We consider a *profile-based authentication system* with an honest-but-curious verifier who follows the protocol but would like to glean information about users from their stored data. We define correctness and security of the authentications system using *Success Rate (SR)*, *False Acceptance Rate (FAR)* and *False Rejection Rate (FRR)* (See Definition 1).

To provide profile privacy, a *trusted registration authority (RA)* performs user registration during which the following two things happen: (i) after checking the user's credentials, the RA generates a random matrix $R^{[u]}$ that will be stored on the user's device, and (ii) use the user's device (with the embedded transform) to generate their transformed profile $R^{[u]}\mathbf{X}^{[u]}$, where $\mathbf{X}^{[u]}$ is the original user profile. (Note that the user profile stays private to the RA also.) The user identifier and the transformed profile, $(u, R^{[u]}\mathbf{X}^{[u]})$, will be securely sent to the verifier. (The system can be designed such that the transform be generated by the device, and remain unknown to the RA.) In a user authentication session, verification data is generated by the device, transformed using the embedded transform, and sent to the verifier. For efficient computation we use *discrete random matrices* whose elements are generated according to Eq. (1) (Sect. 2).

Privacy model and theoretical results. We consider two cases: single-vector profiles, and multivector profiles. For *single-vector profiles* the adversary, denoted by $\mathcal{A}^{FV}$ *adversary*, wants to find the original *Feature Values*. Our notion of privacy in this case is in terms of the expected mean and variance of the adversary' error in finding these values (See Definition 3, item (1)). For *multivector profiles*, the *Feature Distribution* adversary denoted by $\mathcal{A}^{FD}$ *adversary*, wants to learn the distribution of the feature. Definition 3, item (2) introduces the notion of π-*Distribution-Privacy*, where π is the fraction of features (in the feature vector) that remain "close" to their original distributions, given the adversary's knowledge. We consider two types of *adversary knowledge*: (i) the adversary knows the distribution of random matrices, but does not know the random matrix $R^{[u]}$ that is assigned to the user, and (ii) the adversary knows $R^{[u]}$. This latter case corresponds to the extreme case that the user device has been compromised and $R^{[u]}$ has been leaked. These two types of knowledge are shown by subscripts D and R, respectively. Thus we have $\mathcal{A}_D^{FV}$, $\mathcal{A}_R^{FV}$, $\mathcal{A}_D^{FD}$, and $\mathcal{A}_R^{FD}$ adversaries, *where the superscripts show the goal, and the subscripts show the knowledge type.*

Single vector profiles. Proposition 1 gives the mean and variance of error for the best (least expected error) $\mathcal{A}^{FV}$ adversary strategy for finding the profile vector. Theorem 2 uses this result to quantify the privacy level of the system against this adversary. When the projection matrix $R^{[u]}$ is known to the adversary, Proposition 1, item (ii), gives the expected mean and variance of error, and Theorem 2, item (ii), shows the *privacy level against a* $\mathcal{A}_R^{FV}$ *adversary.*

Multivector profiles. Using the best estimation strategy on each profile vector we obtain an estimate of the multivector profile, that is compared with the original one, and closeness of each estimated feature with the original one is determined. To quantify closeness of an estimated feature distribution to its original distribution, we use KS-test [9] for two one-dimensional probability distributions. Proposition 1, items (i) and (ii), show that the variance of the estimated values is high and so the original feature distribution cannot be recovered. In our experiments we will experimentally find the π values of the adversaries $\mathcal{A}_D^{FD}$ and $\mathcal{A}_R^{FD}$.

We use the set of matrices that are generated using a discrete distribution. The correctness of authentication system in this case is shown in Sect. 3. Using a discrete distribution reduces the computation of profile transform to addition and subtraction only and so becomes very efficient (no multiplication).

Experimental results. To evaluate the above framework we considered the following profile-based authentication system.

Our profile-based authentication systems. For single-vector profiles we designed a simple face recognition algorithm with a matching algorithm that for verification uses *k-Nearest-Neighbors (kNN) algorithm* [10], with $k = 1$ (verification uses the closest profile in the profile database to the presented verification vector). This profile-based authentication was evaluated using the face-biometric data that was downloaded from AT&T Laboratories [11], and shown to have comparable performance to face-biometric system in [12].

For multivector system we used a profile-based behavioural biometric system called *Draw a Circle (DAC)* [13]. This is a challenge-response authentication system in which profile data and verification data consist of 30 and 20 profile vectors, respectively. The verification algorithm, for each feature, matches the distribution of the feature samples in the verification data against the corresponding distribution of feature samples in the profile data using *Kolmogorov Smirnov-test (KS-test)* [9], and then combines the results, using the meta-data analyzer *VoteP* [14], into a final *accept, reject* decision. More details about DAC is in Sect. 4. The success rate of the above systems, before using random projection, are 94.16% and 94.40%, respectively.

Profile projection. We assign a $m \times k$ random matrix $R^{[u]}$ that is generated using the distribution, described by Eq. (1), to each user. For *correctness*, our experimental results show that after projection, the *FRR and FAR* of both systems improve: in the case of face-biometric system, FRR and FAR both become close to 0.0, while for DAC, they are slightly lower than their original values. This is due to the combination of the distance preserving property of RP, and the fact that each user has an individual matrix. For *privacy evaluation* we use the same matrices and k values. For $\mathcal{A}_D^{FV}$ and $\mathcal{A}_R^{FV}$ adversaries in the face-biometric system, our results show that for higher k values, although the mean of estimated error becomes smaller, but as expected, because of large variance, the estimated value will be different from the original value. For DAC we used $\mathcal{A}_D^{FD}$ and $\mathcal{A}_R^{FD}$ adversaries that aim at feature distributions. We measured the similarity between the original and estimated profile and showed that feature distributions were not be preserved and this was even true for $\mathcal{A}_R^{FD}$ when the projection matrix is known. Details of experiments are given in Sect. 4.

Profile changeability. This property ensures that by changing user matrix, one can effectively refresh the stored (projected) profile. Although this is not the focus of this work, we report our experiment in Sect. 4.3. that shows perfect ability to refresh the profile.

The rest of the paper is organized as follows. Section 2 provides the background. Section 3 describes our setting, privacy attacks and measures for quantifying privacy, and provides privacy analysis for different attack scenarios, and Sect. 4 gives the experimental results. Section 5 summarizes related works, and Sect. 6 concludes the paper.

2   Preliminaries

A metric space $\mathcal{M}_m$ is a set of points equipped with a non-negative distance function $d : \mathcal{M}_m \times \mathcal{M}_m \rightarrow \mathbb{R}$ that satisfy, non-negativity, symmetry and triangular properties. We consider elements of $\mathcal{M}_m$ to be vectors of length m with components in $\mathbb{R}$, i.e. $\mathcal{M}_m \subset \mathbb{R}^m$. For two vectors $\mathbf{X}, \mathbf{Y} \in \mathcal{M}_m$, where $\mathbf{X} = \{\mathbf{X}_1, \mathbf{X}_2, ..., \mathbf{X}_m\}$ and $\mathbf{Y} = \{\mathbf{Y}_1, \mathbf{Y}_2, ..., \mathbf{Y}_m\}$, we consider the Euclidean distance $d(\mathbf{X}, \mathbf{Y}) = \sqrt{\sum_{i=1}^{m}(\mathbf{X}_i - \mathbf{Y}_i)^2}$.

For two subsets $\mathbf{A}$ and $\mathbf{B}$ of $\mathcal{M}_m$, we consider each set as samples of an underlying distribution, and use the distance between the two underlying distributions using *Kolmogorov-Smirnov (KS) test* in [9], as the distance $D(\mathbf{A}, \mathbf{B})$ between the two subsets.

Two-sample Kolmogorov-Smirnov (KS) test [9] is a non-parametric hypothesis testing method for equality of two distributions, each represented by a set of points. For two sample sets of size n and n', the test measures D, the maximum distance between two cumulative empirical distribution functions, and rejects the null hypothesis at level α if $D > c(\alpha)\sqrt{(n + n')/(nn')}$. The test outputs a *P-value* which is the confidence level of the test.

VoteP method [14] is a method of combining the results of multiple KS-tests, and obtain the combined P-value. We use this method to combine the result of feature similarity tests to obtain the verification decision. The method finds the number of P-values that are above a given threshold, and accepts the hypothesis if the fraction of these P-values (over all P-values) is above some specific threshold.

Performance Measures. Let *fa, tr, fr* and *ta* denote the number of false acceptance, true rejection, false rejection and true acceptance instances of an experiment (e.g. verification of claims). *False Acceptance Rate (FAR), False Rejection Rate (FRR)* and the *Success Rate (SR)* are defined as follows:

$$FAR = fa/(fa+tr), \quad FRR = fr/(fr+ta), \quad SR = (ta+tr)/(ta+fr+tr+fa).$$

Random projection(RP) is a *dimension reduction transformation* that uses random matrices to project a vector $\mathbf{X} \in \mathbb{R}^m$, to a vector $\mathbf{X}' = \frac{1}{\sqrt{k}\sigma_r}R\mathbf{X}$, $\mathbf{X}' \in \mathbb{R}^k$, using a random matrix $R^{k \times m}, k < m$, where σ_r is the standard deviation of entries of $R^{[u]}$. The important property of this transformation is that it preserves pair-wise Euclidean distances between the points in the metric space $\mathbb{R}^m$, up to an error that can be estimated for the dimension reduction parameter. Existence of distance-preserving dimension reduction transformations follows from the following Lemma.

Johnson-Lindenstrauss(JL) Lemma [15]. Let $\epsilon \in (0, 1)$ and $\mathcal{M}_m \subset \mathbb{R}^m$ be a set of n vectors and $k = \frac{4ln(n)}{\epsilon^2/2 - \epsilon^3/3}$. There exists a Lipshcitz mapping $f : \mathbb{R}^m \rightarrow \mathbb{R}^k$ such that for all $u, v \in \mathcal{M}_m$:

$$(1 - \epsilon)d^2(u, v) \leq d^2(f(u), f(v)) \leq (1 + \epsilon)d^2(u, v)$$

For a given projected dimension k, to satisfy the above inequality for a small ϵ (i.e. to preserve distances up to ϵ), one needs to have a sufficiently small n (sparse set). In profile-based authentication systems, sparseness of the profile vector space is a requirement for the correctness of the system (otherwise matching verification data against the profile will have high error) and so the required condition is satisfied.

The proof of JL Lemma constructs the RP transform using matrices whose entries are sampled from a Gaussian distribution [15]. It has been shown experimentally (e.g. in [16]) that the result also holds if R is generated by a zero mean and unit variance distribution. In [17], it is proved that the property will hold if the matrix entries are sampled individually and independently, from the following three-valued distribution,

$$\Pr(x = +1) = \frac{1}{2s}, \quad \Pr(x = 0) = 1 - \frac{1}{s}, \quad \Pr(x = -1) = \frac{1}{2s}, \tag{1}$$

Theorem 1 (*[17]*). *Suppose $\mathcal{M}_m \subset \mathbb{R}^m$ be a set of n vectors projected onto $\mathbb{R}^k$ using the transform $f : \mathbb{R}^m \rightarrow \mathbb{R}^k$ defined as $f(u) = \frac{1}{\sqrt{k}\sigma_r} Ru$ for $u \in \mathcal{M}_m$, where R is a $k \times m$ matrix generated using the distribution given in Eq. (1) and σ_r is the standard deviation of entries of R. Given $\epsilon, \beta > 0$ let $k_0 = \frac{4+2\beta}{\epsilon^2/2 - \epsilon^3/3} log(n)$. If $k \geq k_0$ then with probability at least $1 - n^{-\beta}$ for all $u, v \in \mathcal{M}_m$ we will have:*

$$(1 - \epsilon)d^2(u, v) \leq d^2(f(u), f(v)) \leq (1 + \epsilon)d^2(u, v)$$

We use $s = 3$ that results in many zeros in the matrix and speeds up the computation (only $\frac{1}{3}$ of the data are actually processed) and called it *sparse random projection*.

Minimum-norm solution. Let $\mathbf{X}' = R\mathbf{X}$, where $\mathbf{X}' \in \mathbb{R}^m$ and $R \in \mathbb{R}^{k \times m}$ and $k < m$. This system of linear equations has $m - k$ degrees of freedom. Among all solutions of the system, the solution $\hat{\mathbf{X}} = R^T(RR^T)^{-1}\mathbf{X}'$, known as the *minimum-norm solution*, minimizes the Euclidean norm of the solution $\|\hat{\mathbf{X}}\| = \sqrt{\sum_{t=1}^m \hat{\mathbf{X}}_i^2}$ [18]. In [19] the following result is proven about this solution.

For a fixed $\mathbf{X} \in \mathbb{R}^m$, let ℓ pairs $(\mathbf{X}'_j, R_j)$, $1 \leq j \leq \ell$ be given, where $R_j \in \mathbb{R}^{k \times m}$ entries are generated using a Gaussian distribution with zero mean and $\mathbf{X}'_j = R_j\mathbf{X}$. Let $\hat{\mathbf{X}}_j$ denote the minimum-norm solution of the linear system $\mathbf{X}'_j = R_j\mathbf{X}$. Then, the mean of the estimation error of $\mathbf{X}$ will be zero. This suggests that, given the projected value $\mathbf{X}'$ of a vector $\mathbf{X}$, the minimum-norm solution of the system of linear equation that can be written for the projected profile, provides a good estimation of $\mathbf{X}$.

3   Privacy-Preserving Profile-Based Authentication Systems

A *profile-based authentication system* consists of three types of entities: (i) a group of users $\mathcal{U}$ that must be authenticated; (ii) a trusted registration authority

(RA) that interacts with a user u and generates a profile $\mathbf{X}^{[u]}$ for them; and (iii) a verifier V that interacts with a user, and using the profile and the presented *verification data* decides if the user's claim is valid or not. The set of user profiles is stored in a profile database DB at the verifier. There are *two types of profile-based systems*, depending on the nature of profile data (and verification data).

(i) The profile of user u, $\mathbf{X}^{[u]}$, is a single vector $\mathbf{X}^{[u]} \in \mathcal{M}_m$, and can be represented as a $1 \times m$ vector with elements from $\mathbb{R}$. Biometric systems can generate such profiles (e.g. fingerprint data). In practice one may use multiple instances of the profile vector to achieve better accuracy in verification.

(ii) The profile of user u, $\mathbf{X}^{[u]}$, is *a set of n profile vectors* $\mathbf{X}_j^{[u]} \in \mathcal{M}_m$ (for $1 \leq j \leq n$) where each $\mathbf{X}_j^{[u]}$ consists of m *feature values*, i.e. $\mathbf{X}_j^{[u]} = \{\mathbf{X}_{j1}^{[u]}, \mathbf{X}_{j2}^{[u]}, ..., \mathbf{X}_{jm}^{[u]}\}$. We refer to these vectors as *feature vectors*. A profile thus can be represented as an $n \times m$ matrix with elements from $\mathbb{R}$. Behavioural authentication data (e.g. keystroke, mouse dynamics etc.) generate this kind of profile.

Note that in (i), the actual feature values provide information about the user, while in (ii), the *distribution of a feature* that is captured by a set of sample points, provide identifying information.

3.1   Correctness and Security

Correctness and security of profile-based authentication system is define by two parameters ϵ-*FRR*, and δ-*FAR*.

Definition 1. (ϵ, δ)-**security:** *A profile-based authentication system provides* (ϵ, δ)-*security if it satisfies the following:*
For the claimed identity u and the verification data $\mathbf{Y}^{[v]}$, the matching algorithm outputs $M(\mathbf{X}^{[u]}, \mathbf{Y}^{[v]}) = 0$ (reject) with probability at most ϵ, if $u = v$, and outputs $M(\mathbf{X}^{[u]}, \mathbf{Y}^{[v]}) = 1$ (accept) with probability at most δ, when $u \neq v$.

$$Pr[M(\mathbf{X}^{[u]}, \mathbf{Y}^{[v]}) = 0 \mid u = v] \leq \epsilon; \quad Pr[M(\mathbf{X}^{[u]}, \mathbf{Y}^{[v]}) = 1 \mid u \neq v] \leq \delta;$$

Changeability of a profile-based authentication captures the ability to refresh a user profile while maintaining correctness and security.

Definition 2. ζ-**changeability:** *A privacy-preserving profile-based authentication system provides ζ-changeability if it satisfies the following:*
For transformed profile $\mathbf{X}'^{[u]} = R^u\mathbf{X}^{[u]}$ and the verification data $\mathbf{Y}'^{[v]} = R^v\mathbf{X}^{[u]}$, the matching algorithm outputs $M(\mathbf{X}'^{[u]}, \mathbf{Y}'^{[v]}) = 1$(accept) with probability at most ζ, if $R^u \neq R^v$.

$$Pr[M(R^u\mathbf{X}^{[u]}, R^v\mathbf{X}^{[u]}) = 1 \mid R^u \neq R^v] \leq \zeta.$$

3.2 Privacy Model

Privacy transform must not be significantly adversely affect the correctness of authentication, and must protect the profile data.

Correctness after applying privacy transform. Let a profile $\mathbf{X}^{[u]}$ be mapped to $\mathbf{X}'^{[u]}$, and the verification date $\mathbf{Y}^{[v]}$ be mapped to $\mathbf{Y}'^{[u]}$. To preserve correctness of authentication, ideally we must have, $M'(\mathbf{X}'^{[u]}, \mathbf{Y}'^{[u]}) = 1$, if $M(\mathbf{X}^{[u]}, \mathbf{Y}^{[v]}) = 1$, and $M'(\mathbf{X}'^{[u]}, \mathbf{Y}'^{[u]}) = 0$, if $M(\mathbf{X}^{[u]}, \mathbf{Y}^{[v]}) = 0$ where $M()$ and $M'()$ are the matching algorithm used before applying the transform and the one used in the projected space.

Privacy Attacks. We define four types of adversaries $\mathcal{A}_{\mathcal{K}}^{\mathcal{G}}$ that are distinguished by their (i) attack goal ($\mathcal{G}$), and their (ii) prior knowledge ($\mathcal{K}$). The goal $\mathcal{G} \in \{\mathcal{FV}, \mathcal{FD}\}$ where FV denotes *Feature Value* and FD denotes *Feature Distribution*. These goals are for single and multivector profiles, respectively. The prior knowledge of the adversary is denoted by $\mathcal{K} \in \{\mathcal{D}, \mathcal{R}\}$, where D denote the distribution that is used for the generation of the random matrices, and R denotes the actual user matrix. Thus we have $\mathcal{A}_R^{FV}$, $\mathcal{A}_R^{FD}$, $\mathcal{A}_D^{FV}$ and $\mathcal{A}_D^{FD}$ adversaries. Assume the adversary has the transformed profile of a user $\mathbf{X}'^{[u]}$ (or transformed verification data).

Definition 3. *Let f be a random transformation. Our privacy notions are:*
*1. (μ, λ)-**Value-Privacy:** Let f applied to a profile vector $\mathbf{X}$ of length m, result in $\mathbf{X}'$. Then f provides (μ, λ)-Value-Privacy for the ith feature in $\mathbf{X}$ (i.e. $\mathbf{X}_i$), against an attacker $\mathcal{A}^{FV}$, if given $\mathbf{X}'$, the best strategy of $\mathcal{A}^{FV}$ for $\mathbf{X}_i$ satisfies, $E[\mathbf{X}_i - \hat{\mathbf{X}}_i] \le \mu$ and $Var[\mathbf{X}_i - \hat{\mathbf{X}}_i] \le \lambda$, where $E[\mathbf{X}_i - \hat{\mathbf{X}}_i]$ and $Var[\mathbf{X}_i - \hat{\mathbf{X}}_i]$ are the expected value and the variance of the attacker's normalized estimation error under the random transformation, respectively.*
*2. π-**Distribution-Privacy:** Let f be applied to a multivector profile $\mathbf{X}$, resulting in $\mathbf{X}'$. Then f provides π-Distribution-Privacy against an attacker $\mathcal{A}^{FD}$ if the best strategy of $\mathcal{A}^{FD}$ results in an estimated profile in which at most π-percent of features pass a statistical closeness test with the corresponding features in the original profile.*

3.3 Privacy Transform

We use the privacy transformation given in Eq. (1). A user u is associated with a $k \times m$ matrix $R^{[u]}$ that is generated using this distribution (in our experiments we use $s = 3$). Correctness of the privacy enhanced authentication follows from Theorem 1, using $M' = M$.

3.4 Privacy Analysis

We have the following results.

Privacy adversaries $\mathcal{A}^{FV}$. The system of linear equations $\mathbf{X}'^{[u]} = \frac{1}{\sqrt{k}\sigma_r} R^{[u]} \mathbf{X}^{[u]}$ is under-determined and has infinite number of solutions. For a fixed unknown $\mathbf{X}^{[u]}$ and the set of random $R^{[u]}$ matrices, the *minimum-norm solution* of the above system is known to be the best estimate in the sense that the estimation error of $\mathbf{X}^{[u]}$ will have a distribution with zero mean and small variance. We adopt this solution as the best estimate for $\mathcal{A}_R^{FV}$ attacker who knows $R^{[u]}$ and the projected profile.

In the case of $\mathcal{A}_D^{FV}$, they can generate an RP matrix $R'^{[u]}$ according to the distribution, and estimate $\mathbf{X}^{[u]}$ using minimum-norm solution, hoping that the estimated value is close to the real value. The following proposition gives the mean and variance of the best estimation for the cases, (i) attacker $\mathcal{A}_R^{FV}$ and (ii) attacker $\mathcal{A}_D^{FV}$. The proof is given in Appendix A.

Proposition 1. *Let $R^{[u]}$ be a $k \times m$ RP matrix with entries sampled from Eq. 1 with parameter s. For the projected profile $\mathbf{X}'^{[u]} = \frac{1}{\sqrt{k}\sigma_r}R^{[u]}\mathbf{X}^{[u]}$, we have, (i) If $\mathbf{X}'^{[u]}$ and distribution of $R^{[u]}$ entries are known and $\hat{\mathbf{X}}_i^{[u]}$ is the best estimation for the ith component of $\mathbf{X}^{[u]}$ obtained using minimum-norm solution, the mean and variance of the estimation error $\mathbf{X}_i^{[u]} - \hat{\mathbf{X}}_i^{[u]}$ will be $\mu_i = \mathbf{X}_i^{[u]}$, and $\sigma_i^2 = \frac{1}{k}\sum_{t=1}^m \mathbf{X}_t^{[u]^2}$.*
(ii) If $\mathbf{X}'^{[u]}$ and $R^{[u]}$ are known and $\hat{\mathbf{X}}_i^{[u]}$ is the estimation of the ith component of $\mathbf{X}^{[u]}$ obtained using minimum-norm solution, the mean and variance of the estimation error $\mathbf{X}_i^{[u]} - \hat{\mathbf{X}}_i^{[u]}$ will be, $\mu_i = 0$, and $\sigma_i^2 = \frac{1}{k}((s-1)\mathbf{X}_i^{[u]^2} + \sum_{t \neq i}\mathbf{X}_t^{[u]^2})$, respectively.

The above propositions lead to the following theorem.

Theorem 2. *(i) Random projection as defined in Proposition 1 provides (μ_i, λ_i)-Value-Privacy against $\mathcal{A}_D^{FV}$ for the ith component of $\mathbf{X}^{[u]}$, and we have $\mu_i = \mathbf{X}_i^{[u]}$, and $\lambda_i^2 = \frac{1}{k}\sum_{t=1}^m \mathbf{X}_t^{[u]^2}$.*
(ii) Random projection as defined in Proposition 1 provides (μ_i, λ_i)-Value-Privacy against $\mathcal{A}_R^{FV}$ for the ith component of $\mathbf{X}^{[u]}$, and we have $\mu_i = 0$, and $\lambda_i^2 = \frac{1}{k}((s-1)\mathbf{X}_i^{[u]^2} + \sum_{t \neq i}\mathbf{X}_t^{[u]^2})$.

Note that in both above cases, due to the large variance of the estimation error, the attacker's best estimation will be highly unreliable.

Privacy adversaries $\mathcal{A}^{FD}$. Proposition 1 shows that for $\mathcal{A}_D^{FD}$ the expected error and variance of the ith feature, when $s = 3$, will be $\mu_i = \mathbf{X}_i^{[u]}$, and $\lambda_i^2 = \frac{1}{k}\sum_{t=1}^m \mathbf{X}_t^{[u]^2}$, respectively. The high variance of error, results in the estimation values to vary significantly from the mean, and so the original feature distributions will not be recovered by the attacker. For $\mathcal{A}_R^{FD}$, using Proposition 1 and $s = 3$, we have $\mu_i = 0$ and $\lambda_i^2 = \frac{1}{k}(2\mathbf{X}_i^{[u]^2} + \sum_{t \neq i}\mathbf{X}_t^{[u]^2})$. Again due to the large variance of the error, the probability that an estimated value be close to the original feature values will be negligible.

Table 1. Comparison of correctness before and after projection. Random projection improve the system correctness a bit.

Matrices	Face-biometric				
	Before RP	After RP			
		k = 56	k = 66	k = 110	k = 355
FAR(%)	3.66	0.0	0.0	0.0	0.0
FRR(%)	16.66	0.0	0.0	0.0	0.0
SR(%)	94.16	100.0	100.0	100.0	100.0
Matrices	DAC				
	Before RP	After RP			
		k = 25	k = 35	k = 45	
FAR(%)	5.64	5.12	2.82	2.30	
FRR(%)	5.40	5.40	2.70	2.70	
SR(%)	94.40	95.09	97.42	97.89	

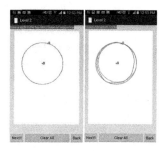

Fig. 1. A Challenge from server side and the user's response

4 Experiments

We will use our *privacy transform* on a single vector, and a multivector, profile-based authentication system, referred to as *face-biometric system* and *DAC*, respectively. We will measure the correctness and privacy of the transformed systems against $\mathcal{A}_D^{FV}$, $\mathcal{A}_R^{FV}$, $\mathcal{A}_D^{FD}$, and $\mathcal{A}_R^{FD}$ adversaries. First we give a brief overview of the face-biometric system and DAC and their corresponding matching algorithms.

A face-biometric user authentication system. We use the face database used in the paper [12] and published in [11]. A face image is represented by a vector of length 10304 (each value [0,255]). The database has 40 users, each represented by 10 face images. We designed and implemented a simple matching algorithm that uses kNN algorithm with $k = 1$. Using multiple sample face for each user we obtained success rate of 98.0%, FRR of 2.0% and FAR of 0.0%, which are comparable with the original results reported in [12].

DAC (Draw A Circle). DAC is a behavioural authentication for mobile devices. DAC is a challenge-response system that is implemented as a two level game: In *Level 1*, the challenge is a random circle that must be drawn from a given starting point. In *Level 2*, the challenge is a circle with a given starting point, that disappears after 3 s. There are 55 features in Level 1, and 56 in Level 2 (Table 1 in [13]). Figure 1 shows the system interface of DAC. Verification algorithm, for each feature, measures closeness of presented verification data with the corresponding profile feature data using KS-test, and combines the resulting *P-values* using VoteP method [14].

4.1 Correctness Experiments

Face-biometric. We measured the correctness of face-biometric system before and after RP, using FAR, FRR and SR metrics. We used, $k = \{56, 66, 110, 355\}$. From

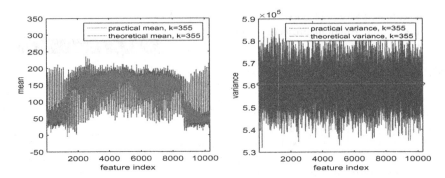

Fig. 2. Comparison of theoretical and experimental mean of error $\mathbf{X}_i^{[u]} - \hat{\mathbf{X}}_i^{[u]}$ for $k = 355$ where distribution of $R^{[u]}$ is known to the attacker. The experimental mean and variance of the estimation error is large for all k.

the 10 available feature vectors for a user, one vector models their single vector profile and the remaining 9 vectors are used as verification claims. For this dataset kNN with $K = 1$, the results are given in Table 1, showing that the privacy transform with individual user RP matrices, has improved the correctness, for all k values, making it close to 1.0. As discussed earlier this is because of the combination of distance preserving property, and the use of individual matrices that increases the distinguishability of the data of different users in the space.

DAC. For DAC we use a database of 39 users. Each profile consists of 30 feature vectors (collected during registration), and 20 other vectors for verification. We calculate FAR, FRR and SR of DAC, before and after projection, for $k = \{25, 35, 45\}$. By reducing k, we expect FAR and FRR of the system to increase because more information will be lost. Table 1 shows that FAR and FRR will remain below 6.0% for different values of k, even when $k = 25$. The success rate in all cases is higher than 94.0%, and again random projection improves the correctness results.

4.2   Privacy Evaluation

Privacy Evaluation for the two systems are below.

Face-biometric system. We transformed each profile in the face-biometric system using 10,000 random matrices of size $k \times m$, where m is the length of the feature vector. Matrices are generated using the distribution in (1).

For $\mathcal{A}_R^{FV}$ attacker, for each projected profile we found the minimum-norm solution, $\hat{\mathbf{X}}^{[u]}$, as the best estimate of the original profile assuming the matrix was known. For $\mathcal{A}_D^{FV}$ we repeated the same process, using a random matrix that was generated according to the known distribution. We calculated the mean and the standard deviation of the estimation error for each feature i, $\mathbf{X}_i^{[u]} - \hat{\mathbf{X}}_i^{[u]}$, for each profile, and compared the results with Theorem 2, for $k = \{56, 66, 110, 355\}$.

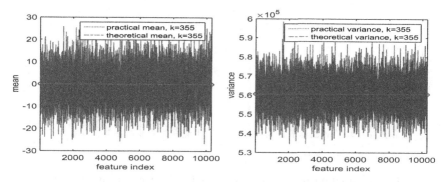

Fig. 3. Comparison of theoretical and practical mean of error $\mathbf{X}_i^{[u]} - \hat{\mathbf{X}}_i^{[u]}$ for $k = 355$ where $R^{[u]}$ is known. The experimental mean and variance of the estimation error is large for all k.

Using Theorem 2, these choices of k correspond to $\epsilon = \{1, 0.75, 0.50, 0.25\}$ (accuracy of distance preservation) and $\beta = \{2.66, 2.64, 2.58, 2.62\}$, where $1 - n^{-\beta} = 0.99$ is the probability of successful distance preservation for $n = 50$. The first sub-figure of Fig. 2 gives the mean of estimation error for $k = 355$ for each feature, assuming $\mathcal{A}_D^{FV}$. This conforms with our theoretical results showing that the mean of the estimated value is zero. The second sub-figure of Fig. 2 gives the results for the variance of the estimation error for $k = 355$ and shows that the error has a very large variance of the order of 10^6, hence very unreliable estimation for the attacker.

The first sub-figure of Fig. 3 shows the theoretical and experimental results for the mean of the error for $\mathcal{A}_R^{FV}$, and the last sub-figure of Fig. 3 show similar results for variances of the estimation error for every feature. It can be seen that the variance is large (of the order of 10^6), indicating that even $\mathcal{A}_R^{FV}$ will obtain negligible information about feature values. For both cases, the results for other k values are given in the full version of the paper.

In both attack scenarios, decreasing k results in higher error variance and so further reducing the dimension of data will improve privacy but this will be at the cost of correctness. Note that dimension reduction must maintain sparseness of the space and so the optimum value of k must be found experimentally.

DAC. We transformed each profile using 10,000 random matrices generated using the distribution given by Eq. (1). For $\mathcal{A}_R^{FD}$, we obtained the best estimate of the 30 transformed feature vectors by calculating the minimum-norm solutions, assuming the matrix is known. Then we used KS-test to measure the similarity between the distribution of features in the estimated set of vectors and the original ones, as the measure of the attacker's success. For $\mathcal{A}_D^{FD}$ we performed the same experiment, using random matrices that were generated from the known distribution.

The first sub-figure of Fig. 4 shows the portion of features that passed the KS-test in game level 2, for 15 users, assuming $\mathcal{A}_D^{FD}$. The experiments are done with

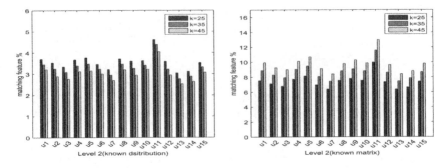

Fig. 4. The distribution of $R^{[u]}$ and $R^{[u]}$ itself is known: distribution of less than (4%) and (11%) of features estimated close to the original one in game Level 2, for 15 different users.

$k = \{25, 35, 45\}$ that according to Theorem 2 correspond to distance preserving parameters of $\epsilon = \{0.31, 0.26, 0.22\}$, and $\beta = 1.17$ which indicates $1 - n^{-\beta} = 0.99$ for $n = 10$. The second sub-figure of Fig. 4 shows similar results for same parameters, assuming $\mathcal{A}_R^{FD}$.

Our results show that for both attack scenarios only in a small fraction of features distributions could be correctly estimated. For $k = \{25, 35, 45\}$, in the case of $\mathcal{A}_D^{FD}$ this fraction is $\{3.78, 3.51, 3.24\}\%$. For $\mathcal{A}_R^{FD}$ the values increase to $\{7.80, 9.10, 10.19\}\%$. Thus, our approach achieves better than (4%)-Distribution-Privacy for $\mathcal{A}_D^{FD}$ and better than (11%)-Distribution-Privacy against the extreme attacker $\mathcal{A}_R^{FD}$. Similar results were obtained for game level 1 and are not presented due to limited space.

4.3   Changeability Evaluation

In [8] authors evaluated changeability property of RP for single vector profile. We extend this result to multivector profile. For a profile $\mathbf{X}^{[u]}$, for each k, we used 1,000 random matrices to transform $\mathbf{X}^{[u]}$ into $\{\mathbf{X'}_1^{[u]}, \mathbf{X'}_2^{[u]}, ..., \mathbf{X'}_{1000}^{[u]}\}$. We used our matching algorithm, to measure the similarity of every pair of profiles that are transformed using two different random matrices, to estimate the probability of $M(\mathbf{X'}_j^{[u]}, \mathbf{X'}_i^{[u]}), 1 \leq i, j \leq 1,000$ $(i \neq j)$ return accept. From $999 \times 1,000$ claims for each $k = \{25, 35, 45\}$, none of the $(\mathbf{X'}_j^{[u]}, \mathbf{X'}_i^{[u]})$ pairs was accepted. The average % of features that pass the KS-test $(\alpha = 0.05)$ for different k is as 15.26%, 14.70% and 14.46%, respectively.

5   Related Works

RP has been used for private data mining [19], and RP for profile privacy and achieving changeability of biometric data is considered in [8]. In this work the projection matrix uses continuous Gaussian distribution and a single matrix is used to transform all user's biometric data. Authors analyse correctness and privacy and provide experimental results for an attack scenario where the attacker knows, or tries to recover, the random matrix. The paper does not consider the case that only the distribution of the matrix entries are known to the adversary. The paper focusses on biometric profiles (not behavioural) and does not consider distribution privacy attacks where the attacker's goal is to recover the distribution of features. The accuracy results in [8] are worse than ours. This is because the same RP is used for all profiles. Using Gaussian distribution results in higher storage and computational overhead compared to discrete distribution that we use. Other non-cryptographic approaches to privacy includes data perturbation [20,21], or adding noise to the data [22]. These approaches cannot be directly used for profile privacy because they will affect the output of the matching algorithm.

Behavioural authentication systems [23] come in many forms such as keystroke, touch dynamics or game playing [24,25]. DAC is an active challenge-responses behavioural-based authentication system. Privacy protection of profiles can use cryptographic approaches [7], but this approach is limited to special matching algorithms.

6 Concluding Remarks

Profile-based authentication provides a powerful method of increasing confidence in authentication results, and protecting against a range of new attacks that defeat traditional authentication systems. Profile data is privacy sensitive and must be protected. We proposed a non-cryptographic approach, using RP, for privacy enhancement of profile-based authentication systems that rely on a single, or multivector, profiles. We provided a framework for analysing privacy enhancement of profile-based authentication systems, theoretically derived the privacy level that is offered by RP, and experimentally showed the effectiveness of RP as a privacy preserving transform. Our future work includes applying the transform to other profile-based authentication systems, and investigating optimal reduction of dimension such that the privacy is maximized while correctness results are maintained.

Acknowledgement. This research is in part supported by TELUS Communications and Alberta Innovates Technology Futures, Canada.

A   Proof of Proposition 1

Proof of Proposition 1(i)

Proof. Suppose σ_r be the variance of the distribution used to generate entries of $R^{[u]}$. Let ϵ_{ij} be the ijth entry of $R^{[u]T} R^{[u]}$. We have $\epsilon_{ij} = \sum_{t=1}^{k} r_{ti} r_{tj}$, and

$$E[\epsilon_{ij}] = E[\sum_{t=1}^{k} r_{ti} r_{tj}] = \sum_{t=1}^{k} E[r_{ti} r_{tj}] = \begin{cases} k\sigma_r^2 & i = j \\ 0 & i \neq j \end{cases}$$

that means $R^{[u]T}R^{[u]} \approx \frac{1}{k\sigma_r^2}I$. We know, the minimum-norm solution of the linear system of equations $\mathbf{X}'^{[u]} = \frac{1}{\sqrt{k}\sigma_r}R^{[u]}\mathbf{X}^{[u]}$ is given by $= R^{[u]T}(R^{[u]}R^{[u]T})^{-1}R^{[u]}\mathbf{X}^{[u]}$, which due to $R^{[u]T}R^{[u]} \approx \frac{1}{k\sigma_r^2}I$ can be written as $\approx \frac{1}{k\sigma_r^2}R^{[u]T}R^{[u]}\mathbf{X}^{[u]} = \frac{1}{\sqrt{k}\sigma_r}R^{[u]T}\mathbf{X}'^{[u]}$.

Knowing the matrix $R^{[u]}$, the attacker can estimate the variance of the entries of $R^{[u]}$, $\hat{\sigma}_r$ and use it to calculate the minimum-norm solution as $\approx \frac{1}{\sqrt{k}\hat{\sigma}_r}R^{[u]T}\mathbf{X}'^{[u]}$. Therefore we will have $E[\hat{\mathbf{X}}_i^{[u]}] = E[\frac{1}{k\sigma_r\hat{\sigma}_r}\sum_{t=1}^m \epsilon_{it}\mathbf{X}_t^{[u]}] = \frac{\sigma_r}{\hat{\sigma}_r}\mathbf{X}_i^{[u]}$, and

$$Var[\hat{\mathbf{X}}_i^{[u]}] = E[\hat{\mathbf{X}}_i^{[u]2}] - E^2[\hat{\mathbf{X}}_i^{[u]}] = \frac{1}{k^2\sigma_r^2\hat{\sigma}_r^2}E[(\sum_{t=1}^m \epsilon_{it}\mathbf{X}_t^{[u]})^2] - (\frac{\sigma_r}{\hat{\sigma}_r}\mathbf{X}_i^{[u]})^2$$

$$= \frac{1}{k^2\sigma_r^2\hat{\sigma}_r^2}E[\sum_{t=1}^m \epsilon_{it}^2\mathbf{X}_t^{[u]2} + \sum_{\substack{p,q=1\\p\neq q}}^m \epsilon_{ip}\mathbf{X}_p^{[u]}\epsilon_{iq}\mathbf{X}_q^{[u]}] - (\frac{\sigma_r}{\hat{\sigma}_r}\mathbf{X}_i^{[u]})^2$$

$$= \frac{1}{k^2\sigma_r^2\hat{\sigma}_r^2}\mathbf{X}_i^{[u]2}E[\epsilon_{ii}^2] + E[\sum_{\substack{t=1\\t\neq i}}^m \mathbf{X}_t^{[u]2}\epsilon_{it}^2] - (\frac{\sigma_r}{\hat{\sigma}_r}\hat{\mathbf{X}}_i^{[u]})^2$$

$$= \frac{1}{k^2\sigma_r^2\hat{\sigma}_r^2}\mathbf{X}_i^{[u]})^2E[(\sum_{t=1}^k r_{ti}^2)^2] + \sum_{\substack{t=1\\t\neq i}}^m \mathbf{X}_t^{[u]2}E[(\sum_{f=1}^k r_{fi}r_{ft})^2]) - (\frac{\sigma_r}{\hat{\sigma}_r}\mathbf{X}_i^{[u]})^2$$

$$= \frac{1}{k^2\sigma_r^2\hat{\sigma}_r^2}\mathbf{X}_i^{[u]})^2E[\sum_{t=1}^k r_{ti}^4 + \sum_{p\neq q}^k r_{pi}^2r_{qi}^2] +$$

$$\sum_{\substack{t=1\\t\neq i}}^m \mathbf{X}_t^{[u]}E[\sum_{f=1}^k r_{fi}^2r_{ft}^2 + \sum_{\substack{p,q=1\\p\neq q}}^k r_{pi}r_{pt}r_{qi}r_{qt}]) - (\frac{\sigma_r}{\hat{\sigma}_r}\mathbf{X}_i^{[u]})^2$$

$$= \frac{1}{k^2\sigma_r^2\hat{\sigma}_r^2}(\mathbf{X}_i^{[u]2}(ks\sigma_r^4 + k(k-1)\sigma_r^4) + k\sigma_r^4\sum_{\substack{t=1\\t\neq i}}^m \mathbf{X}_t^{[u]2}) - (\frac{\sigma_r}{\hat{\sigma}_r}\mathbf{X}_i^{[u]})^2$$

Assuming $\hat{\sigma}_r = \sigma_r$ we will have: $E[\hat{\mathbf{X}}_i^{[u]} - \mathbf{X}_i^{[u]}] \approx 0$ and $Var[\mathbf{X}_i^{[u]} - \hat{\mathbf{X}}_i^{[u]}] = \frac{s-1}{k}\mathbf{X}_i^{[u]2} + \frac{1}{k}\sum_{t\neq i}(\mathbf{X}_t^{[u]})^2$ where s is the parameter of the distribution of $R^{[u]}$.

Proof of Proposition 1(ii)

Proof. The attacker can generate a $k \times m$ matrix $\hat{R}^{[u]}$ using the known distribution (as an estimate for $R^{[u]}$) and use it to estimate $\mathbf{X}^{[u]}$ similar to the case of known $R^{[u]}$, as follows.

$$\hat{\mathbf{X}}^{[u]} = \frac{1}{\sqrt{k}\sigma_r^2}\hat{R}^{[u]T}\mathbf{X}'^{[u]} = \frac{1}{k\sigma_r^2}\hat{R}^{[u]T}R^{[u]}\mathbf{X}^{[u]}$$

Let $\hat{\epsilon}_{ij}$ be the ijth entry of $\hat{R}^{[u]T}R^{[u]}$. That is $\hat{\epsilon}_{ij} = \sum_{t=1}^k \hat{r}_{ti}r_{tj}$ and $\hat{\mathbf{X}}_i^{[u]} = \frac{1}{k\sigma_r^2}\sum_{t=1}^k \hat{\epsilon}_{it}\mathbf{X}_t^{[u]}$.

We have $E[\hat{\epsilon}_{ij}] = E[\sum_{t=1}^k \hat{r}_{ti}r_{tj}] = 0$ and $E[\hat{\epsilon}_{ij}^2] = E[(\sum_{t=1}^k \hat{r}_{ti}r_{tj})^2] = E[\sum_{t=1}^k \hat{r}_{ti}^2r_{tj}^2 + \sum_{\substack{p,q=1\\p\neq q}}^k \hat{r}_{pi}r_{pj}\hat{r}_{qi}r_{qj}] = k\sigma_r^4$

Therefore, we get $E[\hat{\mathbf{X}}_i^{[u]}] = \frac{1}{k\sigma_r^2}E[\sum_{t=1}^m \hat{\epsilon}_{it}\mathbf{X}_t^{[u]}] = 0$ and

$$Var[\hat{\mathbf{X}}_i^{[u]}] = E[\hat{\mathbf{X}}_i^{[u]2}] - E^2[\hat{\mathbf{X}}_i^{[u]}] = \frac{1}{k^2\sigma_r^4}E[\sum_{t=1}^m \hat{\epsilon}_{it}\mathbf{X}_t^{[u]2}] = \frac{1}{k^2\sigma_r^4}E[\sum_{t=1}^m \hat{\epsilon}_{it}^2\mathbf{X}_t^{[u]2} +$$

$$\sum_{\substack{p,q=1 \\ p \neq q}}^m \hat{\epsilon}_{ip}\mathbf{X}_p^{[u]}\hat{\epsilon}_{iq}\mathbf{X}_q^{[u]}] = \frac{1}{k}\sum_{t=1}^m \mathbf{X}_t^{[u]2}$$

Therefore we will have: $E[\mathbf{X}_i^{[u]} - \hat{\mathbf{X}}_i^{[u]}] = \mathbf{X}_i^{[u]}$ and $Var[\mathbf{X}_i^{[u]} - \hat{\mathbf{X}}_i^{[u]}] = \frac{1}{k}\sum_{t=1}^m \mathbf{X}_t^{[u]2}$.

References

1. BBC News: US employee 'outsourced job to china' (2013). http://www.bbc.com/news/technology-21043693
2. Maltoni, D., Maio, D., Jain, A., Prabhakar, S.: Handbook of Fingerprint Recognition. Springer Science & Business Media, London (2009)
3. Jain, A.K., Li, S.Z.: Handbook of Face Recognition. Springer, London (2011)
4. Shi, E., Niu, Y., Jakobsson, M., Chow, R.: Implicit authentication through learning user behavior. In: Burmester, M., Tsudik, G., Magliveras, S., Ilić, I. (eds.) ISC 2010. LNCS, vol. 6531, pp. 99–113. Springer, Heidelberg (2011). doi:10.1007/978-3-642-18178-8_9
5. Bonneau, J., Felten, E.W., Mittal, P., Narayanan, A.: Privacy concerns of implicit secondary factors for web authentication. In: SOUPS Workshop on "Who are you?!": Adventures in Authentication (2014)
6. Lindell, Y., Pinkas, B.: Secure multiparty computation for privacy-preserving data mining. J. Priv. Confidentiality 1(1), 5 (2009)
7. Safa, N.A., Safavi-Naini, R., Shahandashti, S.F.: Privacy-preserving implicit authentication. In: Cuppens-Boulahia, N., Cuppens, F., Jajodia, S., Abou El Kalam, A., Sans, T. (eds.) SEC 2014. IFIP AICT, vol. 428, pp. 471–484. Springer, Heidelberg (2014). doi:10.1007/978-3-642-55415-5_40
8. Wang, Y., Plataniotis, K.N.: An analysis of random projection for changeable and privacy-preserving biometric verification. IEEE Trans. Syst. Man Cybern. Part B (Cybern.) 40(5), 1280–1293 (2010)
9. Massey, F.J.: The kolmogorov-smirnov test for goodness of fit. J. Am. Stat. Assoc. 46(253), 68–78 (1951)
10. Altman, N.S.: An introduction to kernel and nearest-neighbor nonparametric regression. Am. Stat. 46(3), 175–185 (1992)
11. AT&T Laboratories Cambridge: An archive of AT&T laboratories cambridge. (2002). http://www.cl.cam.ac.uk/research/dtg/attarchive/facedatabase.html
12. Samaria, F.S., Harter, A.C.: Parameterisation of a stochastic model for human face identification. In: Applications of Computer Vision, pp. 138–142. IEEE (1994)
13. Islam, M.M., Safavi-Naini, R.: POSTER: a behavioural authentication system for mobile users. In: Proceedings of ACM CCS 2016, pp. 1742–1744. ACM (2016)
14. Cooper, H., Hedges, L.V., Valentine, J.C.: The Handbook of Research Synthesis and Meta-Analysis. Russell Sage Foundation, New York (2009)
15. Dasgupta, S., Gupta, A.: An elementary proof of a theorem of johnson and lindenstrauss. Random Struct. Algorithms 22(1), 60–65 (2003)

16. Bingham, E., Mannila, H.: Random projection in dimensionality reduction: applications to image and text data. In: Proceedings of SIGKDD 2001, pp. 245–250. ACM (2001)

17. Achlioptas, D.: Database-friendly random projections: Johnson-lindenstrauss with binary coins. J. Comput. Syst. Sci. **66**(4), 671–687 (2003)

18. Demmel, J.W., Higham, N.J.: Improved error bounds for underdetermined system solvers. SIAM J. Matrix Anal. Appl. **14**(1), 1–14 (1993)

19. Liu, K., Kargupta, H., Ryan, J.: Random projection-based multiplicative data perturbation for privacy preserving distributed data mining. IEEE Trans. Knowl. Data Eng. **18**(1), 92–106 (2006)

20. Liew, C.K., Choi, U.J., Liew, C.J.: A data distortion by probability distribution. ACM Trans. Database Syst. (TODS) **10**(3), 395–411 (1985)

21. Lefons, E., Silvestri, A., Tangorra, F.: An analytic approach to statistical databases. In: VLDB, pp. 260–274. Citeseer (1983)

22. Agrawal, R., Srikant, R.: Privacy-preserving data mining. ACM Sigmod Rec. **29**, 439–450 (2000). ACM

23. Revett, K.: Behavioral Biometrics: A Remote Access Approach. Wiley, West Sussex (2008)

24. Frank, M., Biedert, R., Ma, E., Martinovic, I., Song, D.: Touchalytics: On the applicability of touchscreen input as a behavioral biometric for continuous authentication. IEEE Trans. Inf. Forensics Secur. **8**(1), 136–148 (2013)

25. Alimomeni, M., Safavi-Naini, R.: How *to Prevent* to delegate authentication. In: Thuraisingham, B., Wang, X., Yegneswaran, V. (eds.) SecureComm 2015. LNICST, vol. 164, pp. 477–499. Springer, Cham (2015). doi:10.1007/978-3-319-28865-9_26

Supporting Privacy by Design Using Privacy Process Patterns

Vasiliki Diamantopoulou[1(✉)], Christos Kalloniatis[2,1], Stefanos Gritzalis[3], and Haralambos Mouratidis[1]

[1] School of Computing, Engineering and Mathematics,
University of Brighton, Brighton, UK
{v.diamantopoulou,h.mouratidis}@brighton.ac.uk
[2] Department of Cultural Technology and Communication,
University of the Aegean, Lesvos, Greece
chkallon@aegean.gr
[3] Department of Information and Communication Systems Engineering,
University of the Aegean, Samos, Greece
sgritz@aegean.gr

Abstract. Advances in Information and Communication Technology (ICT) have had significant impact on every-day life and have allowed us to share, store and manipulate information easily and at any time. On the other hand, such situation also raises important privacy concerns. To deal with such concerns, the literature has identified the need to introduce a Privacy by Design (PbD) approach to support the elicitation and analysis of privacy requirements and their implementation through appropriate Privacy Enhancing Technologies. However, and despite all the work presented in the literature, there is still a gap between privacy design and implementation. This paper presents a set of Privacy Process Patterns that can be used to bridge that gap. To demonstrate the practical application of such patterns, we instantiate them in JavaScript Object Notation (JSON), we use them in conjunction with the Privacy Safeguard (PriS) methodology and we apply them to a real case study.

Keywords: Privacy Process Patterns · Requirements engineering · Information security modelling

1 Introduction

Information Privacy is considered as an important challenge for Information and Communication Technology (ICT). With more and more sensitive and confidential information stored, shared and manipulated at digital level [1], both individuals and organisations expect appropriate measures to ensure privacy of such information. However, this is not easy, as privacy is a multifaceted concept with various impact and ways of achievement which depends, amongst other things, on the environments in which it is required to be achieved.

© IFIP International Federation for Information Processing 2017
Published by Springer International Publishing AG 2017. All Rights Reserved
S. De Capitani di Vimercati and F. Martinelli (Eds.): SEC 2017, IFIP AICT 502, pp. 491–505, 2017.
DOI: 10.1007/978-3-319-58469-0_33

Although the paradigm of Privacy by Design (PbD) has been proposed as a feasible solution to such situation, there are still major challenges that require further research and development. In particular, a challenging task in the context of PbD is moving from a design (where the privacy requirements of an information system have been elicited) to an implementation that fulfils those requirements. This is problematic for two main reasons. On one hand, there is little expertise on how best to align privacy requirements (from the design stage) to Privacy Enhancing Technologies (PETs) [2] at implementation stage. On the other hand, software engineers, who need to deal with both the design and the implementation stages, lack detailed knowledge of PETs to ensure correct implementation. This paper contributes towards these two challenges by proposing a set of Privacy Process Patterns to enhance detailed knowledge of PETs and a clear alignment between privacy properties (requirements) and PETs. Moreover, we are demonstrating how these patterns can be used as part of a privacy-aware methodology to bridge the gap between design and implementation. To improve the usability of such patterns, we instantiate them with JavaScript Object Notation (JSON), using a template that could be adapted by any programming language. Moreover, we present our patterns in the context of an existing privacy-aware methodology called PriS [3] and we apply our work to a real case study to illustrate practical applicability of the work.

The paper is structured as follows. Section 2 discusses the related work, while Sect. 3 presents the Privacy Process Patterns. Section 4 describes their implementation and Sect. 5 illustrates their application to a case study. Finally, Sect. 6 concludes the paper.

2   Related Work

Patterns have been adopted into software engineering as they encounter each problem in a systematic and structured way. Privacy patters, specifically, have been used as a way to model privacy issues. In [4] privacy patterns are used for web-based activity and especially for conveying privacy policies to end-users during online interactions. Traditional design patterns are described in [5], identifying 45 patterns for the design in ubiquitous computing environments, 15 of which focused on privacy. The authors in [6] propose a pattern language which contains 12 patterns for developing anonymity solutions for various domains, including anonymous messaging, anonymous voting and location anonymity. This work moves on the right direction regarding the modelling of privacy requirements but it fails to combine privacy elicitation concepts for capturing privacy requirements. In [7], six patterns that focus on how to establish boundaries for interaction are presented, focusing on the filtering of personal information in collaborative systems. Finally, the author in [8] presented two privacy patterns, applying this approach to security issues by proposing a set of security patterns to be applied during the software development process.

3   Privacy Process Patterns

Privacy Process Patterns are patterns being applied on privacy related processes in order to specify the way that the respective privacy issues will be realised through a specific number of steps, including activities and flows connecting them. They assist developers to understand, in a better and more specific way, how to implement the various privacy properties. The use of Privacy Process Patterns is considered as a more robust way for bringing the gap between the design and the implementation phase of a system or module of it.

The proposed pattern structure follows the so-called Alexandrian format [9] which is already accepted and used for the definition of security patterns [10]. This format is efficient enough for the description of the Privacy Process Patterns, matching the fields of each pattern when this is expressed with JSON. Through *definition* field, we give a comprehensive definition of the property. The fields *problems* and *forces* present the goals that need to be fulfilled and the forces that need to be considered when choosing to use this pattern, respectively. The fields *benefits* and *liabilities* present the advantages and the disadvantages that are identified in each privacy property. The field *implementation techniques* covers all the possible techniques that satisfy the respective property. From the range of the proposed implementation techniques, the developers can choose the most appropriate technology based on the privacy process patterns applied on every privacy-related process. Finally, the field of *related patterns* indicates which patterns have similar characteristics with the examined one, which patterns are closely related in terms of functionality and with which other patterns it can be utilised.

This work describes the five basic privacy properties [11–14] namely *anonymity, pscudonymity, unlinkability, undetectability* and *unobservability.* Our intention is to define a general template for privacy properties that can be used to describe other properties additionally to the five we enlisted above. This is a preliminary work aiming to identify all possible privacy concepts that need to be addressed when designing privacy-aware systems and provide a structured description in order for the developers to take advantage of and manage to handle privacy in a robust way, linking the gap between design and implementation phases. The impact of the selection of respective privacy concepts and the complexity of their applicability is a very interesting topic, but it is not the main focus of this paper. This template comprises a guide for the developers who can understand in a better and more structured way how to implement each privacy concept.

3.1   Anonymity

- *Definition:* Anonymity is a characteristic of information that does not permit a personally identifiable information principal to be identified directly or indirectly. During anonymization, identity information is either erased or substituted
- *Problem:* The user of a service cannot be identified

- *Forces:* Large number of users in the same network is required
- *Benefits:* (i) Supports users in accessing services without disclosing their identity, (ii) Users are more freely expressed, since freedom from user profiling is achieved (behaviour of users or other privacy-infringing practices), (iii) Freedom from location tracking, (iv) Minimal user involvement (they do not have to modify their normal activities for anonymity services)
- *Liabilities:* (i) Maintain users' accountability while anonymous, Performance (latency, loss of functionality, bandwidth, etc.), (ii) Usability of information (too much data obfuscation can undermine the usefulness of data), (iii) Abuse of privacy (malicious users), (iv) User count (large anonymity set), (v) User friendliness (if the users have to adapt a lot to achieve anonymity, they may start judging where they should have anonymity), (vi) Law enforcement (the anonymity might have to be liftable to investigate on crime suspects)
- *Implementation techniques*:
  - Anonymizer products, services and architectures: Browsing pseudonyms [15], Virtual Email Addresses, Trusted third parties, Crowds [16], Onion routing [17], DC-nets [18], Mix-nets (Mix Zone) [19], Hordes [20], GAP [21], Tor [22], Aggregation Gateway [23], Dynamic Location Granularity
  - Track and evident erasers: Spyware detection and removal, Hard disk data eraser, User data confinement pattern, Use of dummies
- *Related patterns:* Pseudonymity, unlinkability

3.2 Pseudonymity

- *Definition:* Pseudonymity is the utilisation of an alias instead of personally identifiable information
- *Problem:* Ensuring that an entity cannot be linked with a real identity during online interactions
- *Forces:* Use authenticated services without disclosing identifiable information
- *Benefits:* (i) Supports users in accessing services without disclosing their real identity, (ii) Permits the accumulation of reputational capital, (iii) The user is still accountable for its actions, (iv) A user may have a number of pseudonyms, (v) Fills the gap between accountability and anonymity, (vi) Hides the identity of the participants, (vii) Prevents unforeseen ramifications of the use of online services
- *Liabilities:* (i) Maintains users' accountability while pseudonymous, (ii) Abuse of privacy (malicious users) (iii) Forgery/impersonation, (iv) Law enforcement (the anonymity might have to be liftable to investigate on crime suspects), (v) Extensive usage of the same pseudonym can weaken it
- *Implementation techniques:*
  - Administrative tools: Identity management, Biometrics [24], Smart cards [25], Permission management
  - Pseudonymizer tools: CRM personalisation [26], Application data management, Obligation management, Mixmaster
- *Related patterns:* Anonymity, authentication

3.3   Unlinkability

- *Definition:* Unlinkability is the use of a resource or a service by a user without a third party being able to link the user with the service
- *Problem:* (i) Users' identifiable information is not protected, (ii) The strength of unlinkability is depended on the number of nodes belonging to the unlinkability set
- *Forces:* Enforce users' privacy regarding the linkability with the service used
- *Benefits:* (i) Protect users' privacy when using a resource or service by not allowing malicious third parties to monitor which services are used by the user, (ii) The intentional severing of the relationships (links) between two or more data events and their sources, ensures that a user may make multiple uses of resources or services without others being able to link the uses together, (iii) Requires that users and/or subjects are unable to determine whether the same user caused certain specific operations in the system, (iv) Minimise risks to the misuse of the privacy-relevant data and to prohibit or restrict profiling
- *Liabilities:* (i) Maintain a large unlinkability set, (ii) Equal distribution of traffic between the potential senders and the potential recipients, (iii) Unidirectional pseudonyms should be preferred because omnidirectional pseudonyms are susceptible to profiling
- *Implementation techniques:*
    - Anonymizer products, services and architectures: Trusted third parties, Surrogate keys, Onion routing, DC-nets, Mix-nets, Hordes, GAP, Tor, Aggregation Gateway
    - Pseudonymizer tools: CRM personalisation, Application data management
    - Track and evident erasers: Spyware detection and removal, Browser cleaning tools [27], Activity traces eraser, Hard disk data eraser, Use of dummies, Identity Federation Do Not Track Pattern
- *Related patterns:* Undetectability, anonymity

3.4   Undetectability

- *Definition:* Undetectability is the inability for a third party to distinguish who is the user (among a set of potential users) using a service
- *Problem:* The strength of undetectability depends on the number of nodes belonging to the undetectability set
- *Forces:* Enforce users' privacy by allowing them to use a service without being detected by a malicious third party
- *Benefits:* (i) Protect users' privacy when using a resource or service by not allowing malicious third parties to detect which services are used by the user, (ii) The attacker cannot sufficiently detect whether a particular Item of Interest (IOI) exists or not, e.g. steganography, (iii) The attacker cannot sufficiently distinguish whether it exists or not
- *Liabilities:* (i) Maintain a large undetectability set, (ii) Equal distribution of traffic between the potential senders and the potential recipients

- *Implementation techniques:*
  - Administrative tools: Smart cards, Permission management
  - Information tools: Monitoring and audit tools
  - Anonymizer products, services and architectures: Hordes, GAP, Tor
  - Track and evidence erasers: Spyware detection and removal, Browser cleaning tools, Activity traces eraser, Hard disk data eraser, Identity Federation Do Not Track Pattern
  - Encryption tools: Encrypting email [28], Encrypting transactions [29], Encrypting documents
- *Related patterns:* Unlinkability, unobservability

3.5 Unobservability

- *Definition:* Unobservability is the inability of a third party to observe if a user (among a set of potential users) is using a service
- *Problem:* The strength of unobservability set depends on the strength of: (i) The sender/recipient anonymity set, (ii) The sender/recipient undetectability set
- *Forces:* Users privacy is enforced since they can use a resource or service anonymously and without being detected regarding the service used when the state of IOIs should be indistinguishable from any IOI (of the same type) at all when we want to send messages that are not discernible from e.g. random noise
- *Benefits:* (i) Anonymity and Undetectability enforcement per service, (ii) Ensures that a user may use a resource or service without others, especially third parties, being able to observe that the resource or service is being used, (iii) Requires that users and/or subjects cannot determine whether an operation is being performed
- *Liabilities:* (i) Depends on the successful implementation of both anonymity and undetectability, (ii) Strong encryption required demanding many resources, (iii) Slower communication due to complex calculations
- *Implementation techniques:*
  - Administrative tools: Smart cards, Permission management
  - Anonymizer products, services and architectures: Hordes, GAP, Tor
  - Track and evidence erasers: Spyware detection and removal, Hard disk data eraser, Identity Federation Do Not Track Pattern
- *Related patterns:* Anonymity, undetectability

4   Privacy Process Patterns Implementation

4.1 PriS Methodology

The implementation of the aforementioned Privacy Process Patterns follows an abstract approach, enabling them to be applied to any requirements engineering methodology. In order to substantiate the applicability and usefulness of the Privacy Process Patterns that have been presented in Sect. 3, we opted to apply them on a privacy requirements engineering methodology, i.e. PriS (Privacy Safeguard). This methodology incorporates privacy requirements into the system design process and has been developed so as to assist designers on eliciting, modelling, designing privacy requirements of the system to be and also to provide guidance to the developers on selecting the appropriate implementation techniques that best fit the organisation's privacy requirements. PriS provides a set of concepts for modelling privacy requirements in the organisation domain and a systematic way-of-working for translating these requirements into system models, adopting the use of Privacy Process Patterns as a way to (i) describe the effect of privacy requirements on business processes and (ii) facilitate the identification of the system architecture that best supports the privacy-related business processes. PriS methodology comprises the following four activities that are presented below in an abstract way, as the implementation of them will be thoroughly described in Sect. 5, through a real case study:

1. *Elicit privacy-related goals.* This step concerns the elicitation of the privacy goals that are relevant to a specific organisation. It usually involves a number of stakeholders and decision makers (managers, policy makers, system developers, system users, etc.)
2. *Analyse the impact of privacy goals on organisational processes.* The second step is to analyse the impact of these privacy goals on processes and related support systems
3. *Model affected processes using privacy process patterns.* Having identified the privacy-related processes, the next step is to model them, based on the relevant privacy process patterns
4. *Identify the technique(s) that best support/implement the above process.* The final step is to define the system architecture that best supports the privacy-related process identified in the third step. Again, privacy process patterns are used to identify the proper implementation technique(s) that best support/implement corresponding processes

The proposed framework uses the concept of *goal* as the central and most important concept. Goals are desired state of affairs that need to be attained. Goals concern *stakeholders*, i.e. anyone that has an interest in the system design and usage. Also, goals are generated because of issues. An issue is a statement of a strength, weakness, opportunity or threat that leads to the formation of the goal. Privacy is a highly regulated area in Europe. The protection of users' privacy is stated in many European and national legislations through the form of laws, policies, directives, best practices, etc. [30]. Thus, *legal issues* need to be taken under consideration during the identification of functional and non-functional requirements. Goal identification needs to take under consideration all these elements before further analysis is conducted.

As shown in Fig. 1, there are two types of goals in the proposed framework, namely *organisational goals* and *privacy goals*. Organisational goals express the organisation's main objectives that need to be satisfied by the system into consideration. In parallel, privacy goals are introduced because of specific *privacy*

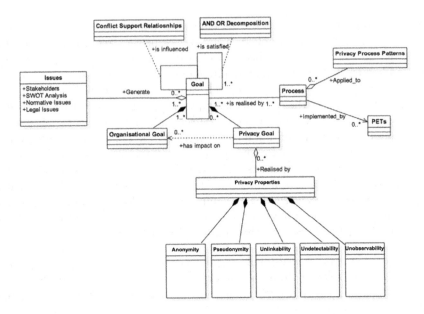

Fig. 1. Conceptual model

related properties. Through the privacy goals, the *realisation* of the identified privacy properties is achieved. Thus, all privacy related properties that need to be realised, should be addressed as specific privacy goals. Privacy goals may have an *impact* on organisational goals. In general, a privacy goal may cause the improvement/adaptation of organisational goals or the introduction of new ones. In this way, privacy issues are incorporated into the system's design. Every model has at least one organisational goal, but may have no privacy goals, thus the respective relationships (1..* and 0..*) among the organisational and privacy goal with the generic concept of goal. Goals are realised by *processes*. The relationship between goals and subgoals is many to many, in the sense that one goal can be realised from one or more processes and one process can support the realisation of one or more goals.

4.2   Expression of PriS with JSON Format

Another reason for choosing PriS in order to apply the proposed structure of the Privacy Process Patterns is their expression of its structure in JSON format [31] and the reasoning it facilitates through this format. Prior to PriS, the transmission from the design to the implementation phase was vague; developers did not have a methodology to automate this process, i.e. the selection of most suitable privacy enhancing technologies to apply in their context. PriS extended version is expressed in the JSON format, which is an Open Standard used to transmit data objects consisting of attribute-value pairs [32]. The *attribute* is immutable and corresponds to the concepts of the model. The suggested patterns are generic enough for being used in every Requirements Engineering method. The JSON format is an example to represent their ability to link the expressed knowledge in a more structured and closer to programmer format in order to bridge the gap between the design the and the implementation phase. One of the most common issues in the RE world is that developers find hard to implement the design outcomes, especially if these are related to system's non-functional requirements. JSON format assists the developers in the realisation of the identified privacy concerns (requirements) and a way that they can be implemented using a structured low level expression language and not generic/abstract software engineering diagrams. Of course, JSON can be replaced by other structured XML-like formats. However, its wide use and dynamic nature of the template inspired us to express our work using this format. The *value* is mutable and corresponds to the values assigned based on the analysis of the respective system. JSON template assist on the direction of simplifying the process for the developers of implementing what had been suggested from the design phase, by expressing the conceptual business process in this format. This format is preferable since it can raise developers' awareness in understanding the outcomes of the aforementioned reasoning. Based on the proposed framework, every identified privacy requirement is expressed in a structured textual format using the JSON format. Through this JSON template, a more formalised expression of the whole set of concepts is achieved, and developers can understand the privacy requirements that need to be satisfied and the processes that need to be altered for addressing the privacy properties.

The PriS JSON template, presented in Fig. 2a, is in accordance with the four activities of PriS presented previously. The object **Privacy requirement** consists of the *Title*, the *Privacy Goal* that it wishes to achieve, the specific *Organisational Goal* that it relates to, the *Process*, and the *Privacy Enhancing Technologies*. The organisational goal consists of its *Title*, its *Parent Goal*, its *Child Goal*, and its *Decomposition Type*. The attribute **Process** indicates which process is affected. It contains the *Title*, the *Parent Process*, the *Child Process* and finally, the *Process Pattern* that needs to be satisfied. From the field of process pattern, we realise which privacy pattern we will implement. Finally, the attribute **Privacy Enhancing Technologies** assists developers on the selection of the set of most appropriate existing privacy enhancing technologies related to the specific privacy properties.

Figure 2b depicts the Privacy Process Pattern template expressed with JSON format, enhancing PriS methodology. The template follows the same structure as it was described in Sect. 3, containing the fields *name, context, problems, forces, benefits, liabilities, implementation techniques,* and finally, *related patterns*. This final field contains all the available techniques that *can* satisfy the examined privacy requirement. The difference among this field and the one of *Privacy Enhancing Technologies*, which is included at the general template, is that the first one contains all the *potential solutions*, where the latter picks only the ones that satisfy the specific organisational goal. The template of the privacy process

{
  "privacy requirement":
  [
    {
      "Title": " ",
      "Privacy Goal": " ",
      "Organisational Goal":
      {
        "Title": " ",
        "Parent Goal": " ",
        "Child Goal": " ",
        "Decomposition type": " "
      },
      "Process":
      {
        "Title": " ",
        "Parent Process": " ",
        "Child Process": " ",
        "Process Pattern": " "
      },
      "Privacy Enhancing Technologies":
      {
        "Option 1": " ",
        "Option 2": " ",
        "Option ...": " ",
        "Option n": " "
      }
    }
  ]
}

{
  "Name": " ",
  "Context": " ",
  "Problems": " ",
  "Forces": " ",
  "Benefits": [" ", " ", " ", ..., " "],
  "Liabilities": [" ", " ", " ", " ", " ", " ", ..., " "],
  "Related patterns": [" ", ..., " "],
  "Implementation techniques":
  [
    {
      "Category Name": " ",
      "Option 1": " ",
      "Option 2": " ",
      "Option ...": " ",
      "Option n": " "
    },
    {
      "Category Name": "...",
      "Option 1": " ",
      "Option 2": " ",
      "Option ...": " ",
      "Option n": " "
    }
  ]
}

(a)   (b)

Fig. 2. PriS and Privacy Process Pattern JSON template

pattern will be included in the general template of the PriS JSON template to enhance the *Process Pattern* attribute.

5   Illustration of the Privacy Process Patterns

A real case study, in which PriS methodology has already been implemented to, and can be used to examine the applicability of the proposed Privacy Process Patterns' template, is the one of Aegean Career Unit. Specifically, University of the Aegean has built a software system for its Aegean Career Office. A detailed description of the Career Office System can be found in [33]. The scope of this case study was the identification of all respective concepts based on the PriS framework for conducting privacy-aware analysis based on the system's context and the stakeholders' requirements. The main objective of the Career Office system of the University of the Aegean is boundary management, i.e. helping students to manage the choices and transitions they need to make on exit from their studies in order to proceed effectively to the next step of their life. The Career Office system is described by three main principles that form the three primary organisational goals, namely: (a) Provide Career Information, (b) Offer Guidance through Events and (c) Maintain a lifelong communication with the graduates. In Fig. 3, the goal model of the examined case study is depicted. We analyse only the principle 'Maintain a lifelong communication with the graduates' for simplicity reasons.

In accordance with the first step of PriS, the main privacy requirement identified along with stakeholders, was the following: "Graduates' anonymity should

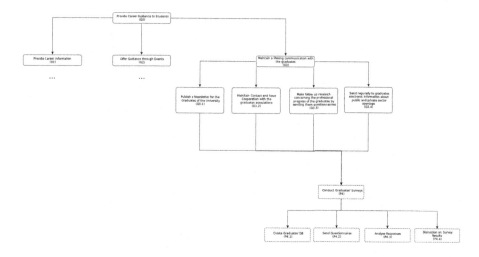

Fig. 3. Goal model

be enforced when collecting the completed questionnaires". For protecting graduates' privacy, it is of major importance to ensure that all types of analysis and produced results don't lead to any form of privacy violation directly or indirectly. Based on the organisation's context, graduates must be ensured that nobody, especially malicious third parties, will be able to reveal the name or other elements that may lead to the identification of the graduate that submits the answered questionnaire; when graduates send information through the career office portal, it must be ensured that others will not be able to reveal any personal identifiable information. Following the identified requirement, the privacy goal that needs to be addressed and fulfilled is the anonymity goal.

Proceeding to the second step of PriS methodology, we need to identify the impact of this goal in the Career Office system, and thus, the identification of the organisational goals and subgoals that deal with the specific requirement is vital. For satisfying the anonymity goal, the main goal, subgoal and process affected are the following:

- Main Goal: Maintain a lifelong communication with the graduates (G3)
- Subgoal: Make follow up research concerning the professional progress of the graduates by sending them questionnaires (G 3.3)
- Main Process: Conduct Graduates Surveys (P4)
- Subprocess: Collect Responses (P 4.3)

The third step of PriS indicates the modelling of the affected processes, using privacy process patterns. For realising the identified privacy goals, the respective processes that implement the privacy-related subgoals were identified. Thus, for the anonymity goal, the respective process that identifies the operationalised subgoal G3.3 is P4 and specifically, the 'P4.3 Collect Responses'. For assisting the realisation of privacy goals on processes, privacy process patterns are introduced.

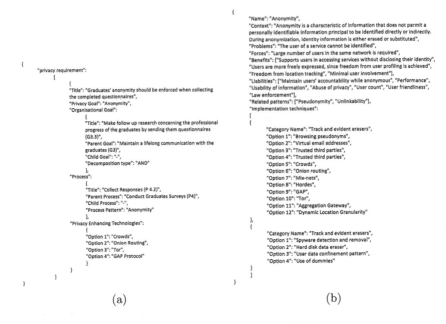

(a)   (b)

Fig. 4. Instantiation with JSON

Specifically, for every privacy goal, a respective privacy process pattern may be introduced on to the privacy-aware processes leading to the realisation of the privacy requirements by the respective PET in a more mature and concrete way.

By applying the relevant privacy process pattern on the respective privacy-related process, it is easier for the designer to identify the appropriate PETs, leading to the successful satisfaction of the respective goals. In the anonymity pattern, the user initiates a request for using a service to the system. The system checks the request and proceeds with the decision of preserving user's anonymity (in case the type of service requested should satisfy this privacy goal) or executes the identification task which leads the user to the process of providing their real credentials for granting access to use the requested service. Finally, according to PriS, the final step is the identification of the technique(s) that best support/implement the aforementioned procedures, the designer along with the stakeholders and the organisation's developer team decide the most appropriate PET for realising the identified privacy goals. The definition of selection criteria for the most adequate PET is out of the scope of this paper. In the given scenario, from the different options presented in Fig. 4b, our analysis has identified and suggested to the stakeholders the following PETs, presented in Fig. 4a: *Crowds*, *Onion Routing*, *Tor* and *GAP Protocol*.

6   Conclusions

This paper presents a set of privacy process patterns that can be used to bridge the gap between privacy design and implementation, and their instantiation in JSON. These patterns are illustrated using the Career Office system of the University of the Aegean. Although, due to lack of space we have focused on the definition of five patterns, more patterns can be defined using the same template.

Future work includes the development of a privacy pattern language that will further assist developers in building the gap between design and implementation phase. In addition, we are planning to extend our work to elicit and define privacy patterns in new domains, such as Internet of Things and Cloud Computing.

Acknowledgments. This research was partially supported by the Visual Privacy Management in User Centric Open Environments (VisiOn) project, supported by the EU Horizon 2020 programme, Grant agreement No. 653642.

References

1. Duncan, G.T., Pearson, R.W.: Enhancing access to microdata while protecting confidentiality: Prospects for the future. Stat. Sci. **6**(3), 219–232 (1991). Institute of Mathematical Statistic
2. Hes, R., Borking, J.: Privacy Enhancing Technologies: the path to anonymity. ISBN. vol. 90(74087), p. 12 (1998)
3. Kalloniatis, C., Kavakli, E., Gritzalis, S.: Addressing privacy requirements in system design: the PriS method. Requirements Eng. **13**(3), 241–255 (2008). Springer
4. Romanosky, S., Acquisti, A., Hong, J., Cranor, L.F., Friedman, B.: Privacy patterns for online interactions. In: Proceedings of the 2006 Conference on Pattern Languages of Programs, p. 12. ACM (2006)
5. Chung, E.S., Hong, J.I., Lin, J., Prabaker, M.K., Landay, J.A., Liu, A.L.: Development and evaluation of emerging design patterns for ubiquitous computing. In: Proceedings of the 5th Conference on Designing Interactive Systems: Processes, Practices, Methods, and Techniques, pp. 233–242. ACM (2004)
6. Hafiz, M.: A pattern language for developing privacy enhancing technologies. Softw. Pract. Experience **43**(7), 769–787 (2013). Wiley Online Library
7. Schümmer, T.: The public privacy-patterns for filtering personal information in collaborative systems. In: Proceedings of the Conference on Human Factors in Computing Systems (CHI) (2004)
8. Schumacher, M.: Security Patterns and Security Standards. In: EuroPLoP, pp. 289–300 (2002)
9. Alexander, C.: A Pattern Language: Towns, Buildings, Construction. Oxford University Press, New York (1977)
10. Mouratidis, H., Weiss, M., Giorgini, P.: Security patterns meet agent oriented software engineering: a complementary solution for developing secure information systems. In: Delcambre, L., Kop, C., Mayr, H.C., Mylopoulos, J., Pastor, O. (eds.) ER 2005. LNCS, vol. 3716, pp. 225–240. Springer, Heidelberg (2005). doi:10.1007/11568322_15
11. Fischer-Hübner, S.: IT-Security and Privacy: Design and Use of Privacy-Enhancing Security Mechanisms. Springer, Heidelberg (2001)

12. Cannon, J.C.: Privacy: What Developers and IT Professionals Should Know. Addison-Wesley Professional, Reading (2004)
13. Pfitzmann, A., Hansen, M.: A terminology for talking about privacy by data minimization: Anonymity, unlinkability, undetectability, unobservability, pseudonymity, and identity management (2010)
14. ISO/IEC 29100:2011(E): Information technology - Security techniques - Privacy framework (2011)
15. Gabber, E., Gibbons, P.B., Matias, Y., Mayer, A.: How to make personalized web browsing simple, secure, and anonymous. In: Hirschfeld, R. (ed.) FC 1997. LNCS, vol. 1318, pp. 17–31. Springer, Heidelberg (1997). doi:10.1007/3-540-63594-7_64
16. Reiter, M.K., Rubin, A.D.: Crowds: anonymity for web transactions. ACM Trans. Inform. Syst. Secur. (TISSEC) 1(1), 66–92 (1998). ACM
17. Goldschlag, D., Reed, M., Syverson, P.: Onion routing. Commun. ACM 42(2), 39–41 (1999). ACM, Chicago
18. Chaum, D.: The dining cryptographers problem: Unconditional sender and recipient untraceability. J. Cryptology 1(1), 65–75 (1988). Springer
19. Chaum, D.L.: Untraceable electronic mail, return addresses, and digital pseudonyms. Commun. ACM 24(2), 84–90 (1981). ACM
20. Shields, C., Levine, B.N.: A protocol for anonymous communication over the Internet. In: Proceedings of the 7th ACM Conference on Computer and Communications Security, pp. 33–42. ACM (2000)
21. Bennett, K., Grothoff, C.: GAP - practical anonymous networking. In: Dingledine, R. (ed.) PET 2003. LNCS, vol. 2760, pp. 141–160. Springer, Heidelberg (2003). doi:10.1007/978-3-540-40956-4_10
22. Dingledine, R., Mathewson, N., Syverson, P.: Tor: The second-generation onion router. DTIC Document (2004)
23. Akers, T., Ware, B., Zheng, W., Kostet, M., Clark, B.: Service Aggregation Gateway. U.S. Patent Application No. 11/551,066 (2006)
24. Jain, A., Flynn, P., Ross, A.A. (eds.): Handbook of Biometrics. Springer Science & Business Media, New York (2007)
25. Weis, S.A., Sarma, S.E., Rivest, R.L., Engels, D.W.: Security and privacy aspects of low-cost radio frequency identification systems. In: Hutter, D., Müller, G., Stephan, W., Ullmann, M. (eds.) Security in Pervasive Computing. LNCS, vol. 2802, pp. 201–212. Springer, Heidelberg (2004). doi:10.1007/978-3-540-39881-3_18
26. Mulvenna, M.D., Anand, S.S., Büchner, A.G.: Personalization on the Net using Web mining: introduction. Commun. ACM 43(8), 122–125 (2000). ACM
27. Himmel, M.A., Rodriguez, H.: Method and apparatus for selective caching and cleaning of history pages for web browsers. U.S. Patent No. 6,453,342 (2002)
28. Bacard, A.: Computer Privacy Handbook: A Practical Guide to E-Mail Encryption, Data Protection, and PGP Privacy Software. Peachpit Press, Berkeley (1995)
29. Wells, J.R., Felt, E.P.: System and method for message encryption and signing in a transaction processing system. US Patent No. 7,363,495 (2008)
30. European Parliament: Regulation (EU) 2016/679 of the European Parliament and of the Council of 27 on the protection of natural persons with regard to the processing of personal data and on the free movement of such data, and repealing Directive 95/46/EC (General Data Protection Regulation) (2016), April 2016
31. Crockford, D.: The application/json Media Type for JavaScript Object Notation (JSON) (2006). https://www.ietf.org/rfc/rfc4627.txt

32. Mavropoulos, O., Mouratidis, H., Fish, A., Panaousis, E., Kalloniatis, C.: Apparatus: reasoning about security requirements in the internet of things. In: Krogstie, J., Mouratidis, H., Su, J. (eds.) CAiSE 2016. LNBIP, vol. 249, pp. 219–230. Springer, Cham (2016). doi:10.1007/978-3-319-39564-7_21

33. ICTE-PAN: Methodologies and Tools for Building Intelligent Collaboration and Transaction Environments in Public Administration Networks. In: Project Deliverable D 3.1b. University of the Aegean (2005)

Evaluating the Privacy Implications
of Frequent Itemset Disclosure

Edoardo Serra[1], Jaideep Vaidya[2(✉)], Haritha Akella[1], and Ashish Sharma[1]

[1] CS Department, Boise State University, Boise, USA
[2] MSIS Department, Rutgers University, New Brunswick, USA
jsvaidya@rutgers.edu

Abstract. Frequent itemset mining is a fundamental data analytics task. In many cases, due to privacy concerns, only the frequent itemsets are released instead of the underlying data. However, it is not clear how to evaluate the privacy implications of the disclosure of the frequent itemsets. Towards this, in this paper, we define the k-distant-IFM-solutions problem, which aims to find k transaction datasets whose pair distance is maximized. The degree of difference between the reconstructed datasets provides a way to evaluate the privacy risk. Since the problem is NP-hard, we propose a 2-approximate solution as well as faster heuristics, and evaluate them on real data.

Keywords: Inverse Frequent itemset Mining · Column generation

1 Introduction and Related Work

Frequent itemset mining [1] is a crucial data mining task which has numerous applications in knowledge discovery such as recommendation, classification, etc. Many efficient implementations exist, [5], all of which assume that the underlying database is accessible to the data miner. However, often privacy concerns prohibit the direct release of data. Since frequent itemsets can serve as a good proxy for the underlying data and still enable different kinds of analysis, often they are released instead. Prior work has examined whether it is possible to find the original dataset from the frequent itemsets, defined as the Inverse frequent set mining (IFM) problem and studied from several different perspectives [4,6,7,9]. IFM aims to find a transaction dataset D that satisfies a given set of itemset support constraints (i.e., the support or frequency of an itemset should be contained within the specified numeric interval). Wang and Wu [13] also introduced the `ApproSUPP` problem, where they asked whether it is possible to satisfy the various support constraints

---

This work was supported by Idaho Global Entrepreneurial Mission (IGEM) program Grant 131G106011 (Precision Ag - Increasing Crop), the National Science Foundation Grant CNS-1422501 and the National Institutes of Health Award R01GM118574. The content is solely the responsibility of the authors and does not necessarily represent the official views of the agencies funding the research.

S. De Capitani di Vimercati and F. Martinelli (Eds.): SEC 2017, IFIP AICT 502, pp. 506–519, 2017.
DOI: 10.1007/978-3-319-58469-0_34

in an approximate fashion and presented an ILP formulation along with heuristic strategies. Several alternative heuristics have also been proposed [10, 14]. However, while IFM provides a measure of the degree of difficulty in inverting a set of support constraints into *a* dataset producing these, there is no notion of how different that dataset is from the original that needs to be protected.

In this paper, we precisely tackle this problem. We formulate a new problem called the k-distant-IFM-solutions which combines the IFM problem with elements of K-anonymity [11] and L-diversity [8]. Specifically, the problem consists in finding k IFM solutions (transaction datasets) whose pair distance is maximized. This ensures that we have at least k different solutions to the IFM problem that are all potentially quite different. Since any of these could be the source, and are as different as possible from each other, this gives a minimum bound on the degree of privacy afforded by the frequent itemsets. We show that the problem is NP-hard, and give a 2-approximation based on the greedy strategy. However, given the complexity of the underlying problem, we also develop a heuristic based on an ILP formulation (see [12]) that is quite efficient. Thus, our work is orthogonal to all of the prior work, since it considers the problem of finding multiple datasets meeting the given set of support constraints, and provides a better estimate of the risk of disclosure through the frequent itemsets.

2   Problem Statement

Let $\mathcal{I}$ be a set of items. An itemset I is a subset of $\mathcal{I}$. A transaction Dataset $\mathcal{D}$ is a pair $(T_{\mathcal{D}}, \#_{\mathcal{D}})$, where $T_{\mathcal{D}}$ is a set of transactions (i.e. itemsets) contained in $\mathcal{D}$ and $\#_{\mathcal{D}} : 2^{\mathcal{I}} \to N$ is a function assigning to each transaction a number of duplicates such that if $t \in T_{\mathcal{D}}$ then $\#_{\mathcal{D}}(t) > 0$, otherwise $\#_{\mathcal{D}}(t) = 0$.

Example 1. Let $\mathcal{I} = \{a, b, c\}$. Following is an example of a transaction database where $\#_{\mathcal{D}}(t) = 0$ for each transaction t that is not present in $T_{\mathcal{D}}$ and $\#_{\mathcal{D}}(t) > 0$ for transactions that are present in $T_{\mathcal{D}}$.

Given an itemset I, the support of I w.r.t. $\mathcal{D}$ is $support(I, \mathcal{D}) = \sum_{t \in T_{\mathcal{D}}, I \subseteq t} \#_{\mathcal{D}}(t)$ and its frequency is $frequency(I, \mathcal{D}) = \frac{support(I, \mathcal{D})}{|\mathcal{D}|}$. Given a dataset $\mathcal{D}$, the *frequent itemset mining* problem aims to find all of the itemsets whose frequency is greater than a given threshold.

D
{a,b}
{a}
{a,b}
{a,b}
{a,b,c}
{a,b,c}

$\Rightarrow$

$T_{\mathcal{D}}$	$\#_{\mathcal{D}}$
{a}	1
{a,b}	3
{a,b,c}	2

In our paper, we assume that instead of releasing the actual dataset, only a set of itemsets is released along with their frequencies due to privacy concerns. However, in this case, the problem that we study is the extent to which it is possible to retrieve the original dataset $\mathcal{D}$. This is related to the *Inverse Frequent itemset Mining (IFM)* problem, which aims to find a dataset such that the frequencies of a set of given itemsets for that dataset are in a specific range interval. IFM is formally defined as follows:

The IFM problem. Given a set of items $\mathcal{I}$, two integer numbers s_l, s_u, a set of support constraints S of the form (I, l, u) where I is an itemset on $\mathcal{I}$ and $l, u \in \mathcal{N}$ with $l \leq u$. The IFM problem, denoted as $IFM(\mathcal{I}, s_l, s_u, S)$, consists in finding a dataset $\mathcal{D}$ such that $s_l \leq |\mathcal{D}| \leq s_u$ and $\forall (I, l, u) \in S : l \leq support(l, \mathcal{D}) \leq u$.

Given a set of support constraints S, IFM provides information about degree of difficulty of generating a dataset that produces those frequent itemsets. However, note that while the solution to IFM enables malicious users to find a dataset that also meets the same support constraints, it does not say anything about whether this is the real dataset or how different it is from the real dataset. Indeed, given a set of support constraints S, more than one dataset solution can exist for the IFM problem. While this increases uncertainty in terms of the actual dataset, it may not significantly increase privacy since all of the datasets might be quite similar, thus actually reducing privacy.

Thus, to enable evaluation of the privacy risk associated with frequent itemset disclosure, we formalize a new problem called *k-distant-IFM-solutions*, i.e. find k IFM solutions whose pair distance is maximized. If we can find a sufficient number of solutions that are quite different from each other, then it significantly increases the degree of uncertainty and thus privacy. We can also take into consideration the problem of finding subset of support constraints or a perturbed version that can maximize the pair distance among all of the k IFM solutions.

2.1 K-distant-IFM-solutions Problem

We first define the distance between two datasets, and then formalize the actual problem. While Jaccard or Hamming distance is a good metric to measure the distance between two individual transactions, they cannot directly be used to measure the difference among the collection of transactions. In our problem, the number of duplicate transactions has a significant meaning and therefore we chose to define our own metric that extends the Hamming distance for collection of transactions. Furthermore, we use the edit distance constraint to ensure that the different datasets obtained are sufficiently apart from each other based on our distance metric. Consider a case where the dataset $\mathcal{D}_1 = \{\{a, b, c\}, \{a, b, c\}, \{a, b, f\}\}$ and $\mathcal{D}_2 = \{\{a, b, c, h\}, \{a, b, c, h\}, \{a, b, f, h\}\}$. Since there are no transactions in common, $(\mathcal{D}_1, \mathcal{D}_2) = 6$ is the maximum distance that can be obtained. However, these datasets are exactly the same except for the item h. The edit distance constraint addresses this issue.

Given two datasets $\mathcal{D}_1$ and $\mathcal{D}_2$ over $\mathcal{I}$, we define the function $dist(\mathcal{D}_1, \mathcal{D}_2)$ between $\mathcal{D}_1$ and $\mathcal{D}_2$ as

$$dist(\mathcal{D}_1, \mathcal{D}_2) = \sum_{t \in T_{\mathcal{D}_1} \cup T_{\mathcal{D}_2}} |\#_{\mathcal{D}_1}(t) - \#_{\mathcal{D}_2}(t)|$$

This distance is a metric, but we omit the proof due to lack of space.

2.2 k-distant-IFM-solutions

Given a set of items $\mathcal{I}$, a positive integer number k, two integer numbers s_l, s_u, a set of support constraints S of the following form (I, l, u) where I is an

---

Algorithm 1. Greedy Algorithm

1: **procedure** GREEDYALGORITHM($\mathcal{I}, S$)
2:     $SD = \emptyset$;
3:     Choose $\mathcal{D}^* \in SOL(\mathcal{I}, S)$
4:     **while** ($|SD| \leq k$) **do**
5:         $SD = SD \cup \{\mathcal{D}^*\}$;
6:         Choose $\mathcal{D}^* \in \arg\max_{\mathcal{D} \in SOL(\mathcal{I},S) \setminus SD} pairDist(SD \cup \mathcal{D})$;
7:     **end while**
8:     **return** SD;
9: **end procedure**

---

itemset on $\mathcal{I}$ and $l, u \in \mathcal{R}$. The k-distant-IFM-solutions problem consists of finding a set of k datasets $SD = \{\mathcal{D}_1, \ldots, \mathcal{D}_k\}$ such that for each $\mathcal{D} \in SD$, $\mathcal{D}$ is a solution of $IFM(\mathcal{I}, s_l, s_u, S)$, and the pair distance $pairDist(SD) = \sum_{\mathcal{D}_j, \mathcal{D}_i \in SD, i > j} dist(\mathcal{D}_i, \mathcal{D}_j)$ is maximized.

Theorem 1. *The k-distant-IFM-solutions problem is NP-hard.*

Since finding even one solution of $IFM(\mathcal{I}, s_l, s_u, S)$ is NP-hard (as shown in [4]), finding k solutions is also NP-hard.

3 Proposed Approach

We now discuss how this problem can be solved. Let us assume $SOL(\mathcal{I}, S)$ is the set of all datasets that are the solution of $IFM(\mathcal{I}, S)$.

Thus, the k-distant-IFM-solutions can be formalized as

$$SD^* \in \arg\max_{SD \subseteq SOL(\mathcal{I},S), |SD| = k} pairDist(SD)$$

For this problem, Borodin et al. [3] show that if the function $dist$ is a metric, then the Greedy Algorithm (Algorithm 1) gives a 2-approximate solution. However, we still need to specify how steps 3 and 6 of Algorithm 1 will be executed, i.e. how to choose $\mathcal{D}^* \in SOL(\mathcal{I}, S)$ (for step 3) and $\mathcal{D}^* \in \arg\max_{\mathcal{D} \in SOL(\mathcal{I},S) \setminus SD} pairDist(SD \cup \mathcal{D})$ (for step 6). Step 3 simply requires finding a solution for IFM, which is well understood. For the sake of simplicity and efficiency, we simply choose the first feasible solution instead of choosing a solution randomly. We denote the problem in Step 6 as the *Maximum Distant Dataset* and now show how to solve it.

3.1 Maximum Distant Dataset

The goal of maximization is to maximize the difference between the created dataset and existing datasets. Thus, we would like to find a dataset $\mathcal{D}$ that maximizes $\sum_{\mathcal{D}' \in SD} dist(\mathcal{D}', \mathcal{D})$, which is equivalent to maximizing $pairDist(SD \cup \mathcal{D})$. In order to solve the Maximum Distant Dataset we provide an ILP formulation. This formulation is based on three kinds of variables:

- a real variable x_t, for each possible transaction $t \subseteq \mathcal{I}$, modeling the number of duplicates $\#(t)$ for each transaction t in the dataset that we have to generate (we relax the assumption that number of duplicates is an integer number); Effectively, the variable x_t gives the support count of the transaction t in the newly created dataset.
- a real variable $y_t^{\mathcal{D}}$, for each $\mathcal{D} \in S\mathcal{D}$ and $t \in T_{\mathcal{D}}$, modeling the values $|\#_{\mathcal{D}}(t) - x_t|$; Note that for all transactions t present in the existing datasets, $|\#\mathcal{D}(t) - x_t|$ gives the absolute difference in support for such transactions in each dataset $\mathcal{D}$. For the transactions t that are not present in the existing datasets, x_t directly gives the support of such transactions in the new dataset.
- a binary variable $z_t^{\mathcal{D}}$, for each $\mathcal{D} \in S\mathcal{D}$ and $t \in T_{\mathcal{D}}$, that is used to emulate the absolute value $|\#_{\mathcal{D}}(t) - x_t|$.

Now, the formulation is as follows:

$$maximize \sum_{\mathcal{D} \in S\mathcal{D}} \left(\sum_{t \in T_{\mathcal{D}}} y_t^{\mathcal{D}} + \sum_{t \subseteq \mathcal{I}, t \notin T_{\mathcal{D}}} x_t \right) \quad (1)$$

$$\sum_{t \subseteq \mathcal{I}, I \subseteq t} x_t \geq l \qquad (I, l, \_) \in S \quad (2)$$

$$\sum_{t \subseteq \mathcal{I}, I \subseteq t} x_t \leq u \qquad (I, \_, u) \in S \quad (3)$$

$$\sum_{t \subseteq \mathcal{I}} x_t \geq s_l \qquad (4)$$

$$\sum_{t \subseteq \mathcal{I}} x_t \leq s_u \qquad (5)$$

$$\#_{\mathcal{D}}(t) - x_t \leq y_t^{\mathcal{D}} \qquad \mathcal{D} \in S\mathcal{D}, t \in T_{\mathcal{D}} \quad (6)$$

$$-\#_{\mathcal{D}}(t) + x_t \leq y_t^{\mathcal{D}} \qquad \mathcal{D} \in S\mathcal{D}, t \in T_{\mathcal{D}} \quad (7)$$

$$\#_{\mathcal{D}}(t) - x_t + 2 * k_t * (1 - z_t^{\mathcal{D}}) \geq y_t^{\mathcal{D}} \qquad \mathcal{D} \in S\mathcal{D}, t \in T_{\mathcal{D}} \quad (8)$$

$$-\#_{\mathcal{D}}(t) + x_t + 2 * k_t * z_t^{\mathcal{D}} \geq y_t^{\mathcal{D}} \qquad \mathcal{D} \in S\mathcal{D}, t \in T_{\mathcal{D}} \quad (9)$$

$$x_t \geq 0 \qquad t \subseteq \mathcal{I} \quad (10)$$

$$y_t^{\mathcal{D}} \geq 0 \qquad \mathcal{D} \in S\mathcal{D}, t \in T_{\mathcal{D}} \quad (11)$$

$$z_t^{\mathcal{D}} \in \{0, 1\} \qquad \mathcal{D} \in S\mathcal{D}, t \in T_{\mathcal{D}} \quad (12)$$

Where, $k_t = \min(s_u, \min_{(I, \_, u) \in S, I \subseteq t} u)$.

As can be seen, we have two groups of constraints. The first group of constraints from 2 to 5 defines the minimum support, the maximum support, the minimum size and the maximum size, respectively. The second group constraints from 6 to 9 contribute in modeling the absolute value $|\#_{\mathcal{D}}(t) - x_t|$ is equal to $y_t^{\mathcal{P}}$. More specifically, constraints 6 and 7 impose that $|\#_{\mathcal{D}}(t) - x_t| \leq y_t^{\mathcal{P}}$ ensuring that the variable $y_t^{\mathcal{P}}$ is an upper bound of the absolute difference between x_t and $\#_{\mathcal{D}}(t)$. Constraints 8 and 9 impose that only one condition between $\#_{\mathcal{D}}(t) - x_t$ and $x_t - \#_{\mathcal{D}}(t)$ has to be greater than or equal to $y_t^{\mathcal{P}}$. Latter two constraints ensure that $y_t^{\mathcal{P}}$ is also the lower bound of the absolute difference between x_t and $\#_{\mathcal{D}}(t)$. The constraints from 6 to 9, together, ensure that $y_t^{\mathcal{P}} = \#_{\mathcal{D}}(t) - x_t$. However, note that only one of the constraints between 8 and 9 can be met. $z_t^{\mathcal{D}}$ is the decision variable activating one of these two constraings, while $k_t^{\mathcal{D}}$ is the smallest constant that is large enough to ensure that these constraints are met. Finally, the maximization function (expression 1) maximizes the degree of difference in support for transactions present, which exactly models the maximization of distance metric defined in Sect. 2.1.

Usually, adding more constraints to an integer linear program reduces the search space by improving the bound obtained by the linear formulation and consequently reduces the computation time. Therefore, we define additional constraints and variables imposing that the value $y_t^{\mathcal{P}} = |\#_{\mathcal{D}}(t) - x_t|$ is $\max(\#_{\mathcal{D}}(t), x_t) - \min(\#_{\mathcal{D}}(t), x_t)$. The real variables $y_{t,max}^{\mathcal{P}}$ and $y_{t,min}^{\mathcal{P}}$ model $\max(\#_{\mathcal{D}}(t), x_t)$ and $\min(\#_{\mathcal{D}}(t), x_t)$, respectively. The revised ILP is given below. Note that in this case, the integer variables and the constraints are polynomial in the description of $S\mathcal{D}$ and S, respectively. The main issue is represented by the exponential number of real variables x_t due to all the possible transactions $t \subseteq \mathcal{I}$. Thus, these linear programs cannot really be directly solved. However, we can use an alternative technique called the branch and price algorithm (see [2]).

$$\#_{\mathcal{D}}(t) \geq y_{t,min}^{\mathcal{D}} \qquad \mathcal{D} \in S\mathcal{D}, t \in T_{\mathcal{D}} \qquad (13)$$

$$x_t \geq y_{t,min}^{\mathcal{D}} \qquad \mathcal{D} \in S\mathcal{D}, t \in T_{\mathcal{D}} \qquad (14)$$

$$\#_{\mathcal{D}}(t) \leq y_{t,max}^{\mathcal{D}} \qquad \mathcal{D} \in S\mathcal{D}, t \in T_{\mathcal{D}} \qquad (15)$$

$$x_t \leq y_{t,max}^{\mathcal{D}} \qquad \mathcal{D} \in S\mathcal{D}, t \in T_{\mathcal{D}} \qquad (16)$$

$$\#_{\mathcal{D}}(t)(1 - z_t^{\mathcal{P}}) \leq y_{t,min}^{\mathcal{D}} \qquad \mathcal{D} \in S\mathcal{D}, t \in T_{\mathcal{D}} \qquad (17)$$

$$x_t - k_t * (1 - z_t^{\mathcal{P}}) \leq y_{t,min}^{\mathcal{D}} \qquad \mathcal{D} \in S\mathcal{D}, t \in T_{\mathcal{D}} \qquad (18)$$

$$(\#_{\mathcal{D}}(t) - k_t) * z_t^{\mathcal{P}} + k_t \geq y_{t,max}^{\mathcal{D}} \qquad \mathcal{D} \in S\mathcal{D}, t \in T_{\mathcal{D}} \qquad (19)$$

$$x_t + k_t * z_t^{\mathcal{P}} \geq y_{t,max}^{\mathcal{D}} \qquad \mathcal{D} \in S\mathcal{D}, t \in T_{\mathcal{D}} \qquad (20)$$

$$y_{t,max}^{\mathcal{D}} - y_{t,min}^{\mathcal{D}} = y_t^{\mathcal{D}} \qquad \mathcal{D} \in S\mathcal{D}, t \in T_{\mathcal{D}} \qquad (21)$$

$$y_{t,max}^{\mathcal{D}} + y_{t,min}^{\mathcal{D}} = \#_{\mathcal{D}}(t) + x_t \qquad \mathcal{D} \in S\mathcal{D}, t \in T_{\mathcal{D}} \qquad (22)$$

$$y_{t,min}^{\mathcal{D}} \geq 0 \qquad \mathcal{D} \in S\mathcal{D}, t \in T_{\mathcal{D}} \qquad (23)$$

$$y_{t,max}^{\mathcal{D}} \geq 0 \qquad \mathcal{D} \in S\mathcal{D}, t \in T_{\mathcal{D}} \qquad (24)$$

Algorithm 2. HeuristicSolver

1: **procedure** HEURISTICSOLVER$((SD, S, s_l, s_u))$
2:     Generate integer linear program P according SD, S, s_l and s_u where the set of variables with prefix x is only equal to $\{x_t | \mathcal{D} \in SD, t \in T_{\mathcal{D}}\}$;
3:     Relax in P the binary constraints the variables with prefix z;
4:     Solve the program P;
5:     Find a new transaction t (if it exists) by solving the price problem;
6:     **while** (t exists) **do**
7:         Add the variable x_t in P;
8:         Solve the program P;
9:         Find a new transaction t (if it exists) by solving the price problem;
10:    **end while**
11:    Add in P the binary constraints on the variables with prefix z;
12:    Solve the program P;
13:    Obtain from the solution of P the dataset $\mathcal{D}$;
14:    **return** $\mathcal{D}$;
15: **end procedure**

3.2   Heuristic Solver

The branch and price algorithm is a branch and bound algorithm that at each branch solves the relaxed problem (i.e. the linear one) by using column generation techniques. Given that the number of variables is huge, column generation techniques make the problem tractable. Instead of working on the entire set of variables, the column generation technique starts with a prefixed number (in our case the variables related to all the transactions in SD) and at each iteration it generates a new variable or column (a new transaction) whose reduced cost is negative [4,7]. In order to generate a new variable a new problem called price problem has to be solved. The price problem consists of finding a new column with negative reduce cost, which is strictly related to the simplex algorithm [12] and how it works. Note that the specific price problem changes based on the underlying LP or ILP formulation. In prior work [7] the problem in Definition 2 has already been formalized as a linear program whose constraints are the constraints from 2 to 5. [7] also solves it with a column generation techniques and its price problem. In our problem we start by considering all the variables referring to all the transactions in SD. Then the new variables or columns that we have to generate are those not involved in the constraints from 6 to 22. The main idea is to use the column generation techniques to solve the relaxation formulation where all the binary variables are substituted with real variables restricted to $[0, 1]$. Then, use all the columns generated in the column generation algorithm to solve the ILP version. Algorithm 2 gives the details.

Price Problem. The pricing problem consists in finding a new transaction different from all the previous transactions whose reduced cost is negative. It is known that the reduced cost of a column can be expressed as a linear combination of the dual variable associated to each constraint of the linear program (see [6]).

Let dsl, dsu, dl_I and du_I (where $(I, \_, \_) \in S$) be the dual variables associated to the constraints of the kinds 2, 3, 4 and 5. The reduced cost of a transaction t is $rc(t) = 1 + dsl + dsu + \sum_{I \subseteq t, (I, \_, \_) \in S}(dl_I + du_I)$. Given the set of current datasets generated $S\mathcal{D}$, the set of all the different transactions present in $S\mathcal{D}$ is defined as $tr(S\mathcal{D}) = \bigcup_{\mathcal{D} \in S\mathcal{D}} T_{\mathcal{D}}$. Now, we show an integer linear program solving the price problem. A generic transaction is a set of items then we can represent this transaction by using $|\mathcal{I}|$ binary variable $\{q_i | i \in \mathcal{I}\}$ s.t. if the item i is contained in t then $q_i = 1$ or $q_i = 0$ otherwise. In order to model the reduced cost function, it is essential to know which of the itemset in S are contained in the new transaction. Therefore, we define a set of binary variables $\{h_I | (I, \_, \_) \in S\}$ s.t. if the itemset I (with $(I, \_, \_) \in S$) is contained in the new transaction then $h_I = 1$ or $h_I = 0$ otherwise.

The objective function represents the reduced cost of the new transaction. The first two constraints 26 and 27, impose that whether the transaction represented by the set of variables $\{q_i | i \in \mathcal{I}\}$ contains an itemset I, the variable h_I is equal to 1 or 0 otherwise. The third constraint 28 imposes that the edit distance between each transaction in $tr(S\mathcal{D})$ and the new one has to be greater than or equal to the constant $minED$. $minED$ can be one if we only want that the current transaction should be different by each other, but can be more than one to enforce that all the transactions in all the K datasets generated are very different. This parameter is very important in order to produce datasets different not only in terms of number of duplicates, but also in terms of transaction structure. The last constraint 29 imposes that the transaction is not an empty set. Thus, the following integer linear program finds a new transaction s.t. its reduced cost is minimized. Note that after solving this ILP program we have to check if the reduced cost is negative, and only continue to iterate if so. Otherwise, the heuristic solver stops because there does not exist any transaction with negative reduced cost.

$$minimize \ \ 1 + dsl + dsu + \sum_{(I, \_, \_) \in S} h_I \cdot (dl_I + du_I) \tag{25}$$

$$h_I \leq q_i \qquad\qquad (I, \_, \_) \in S, i \in I \tag{26}$$

$$\sum_{i \in I} q_i \leq |I| - 1 + h_I \qquad\qquad (I, \_, \_) \in S \tag{27}$$

$$\sum_{i \in t}(1 - q_i) + \sum_{i \in \mathcal{I} \setminus t} q_i \geq minED \qquad\qquad t \in tr(S\mathcal{D}) \tag{28}$$

$$\sum_{i \in \mathcal{I}} q_i \geq 1 \tag{29}$$

$$q_i \in \{0, 1\} \qquad\qquad i \in \mathcal{I} \tag{30}$$

$$h_I \in \{0, 1\} \qquad\qquad (I, \_, \_) \in S \tag{31}$$

4   Experimental Evaluation

We now discuss the experimental evaluation. Three datasets – 2 real datasets (BMS-Webview-1, BMS-Webview-2) and a synthetic one (T10I4D100K) – were used to conduct experiments. The dataset parameters are given in Table 1. Each instance of our problem is represented by several parameters: sizemax (s_u), sizemin (s_l), set of items ($\mathcal{I}$), set of support constraints S (at different levels of support), support values (ρ), k (number of different datasets to be generated), edit distance (minED). Sizemax and Sizemin were obtained for each dataset by adding and subtracting 10000 from the size of the original dataset, respectively

Table 1. Dataset description

Dataset name	Real dataset size	Distinct items	Avg. trans. Size	Max trans. Size	s_l	s_u
BMS WebView1	59602	497	2.5	267	49602	69602
BMS WebView2	77512	3340	4.6	161	67512	87512
T10I4D100K	100000	870	10	300	90000	110000

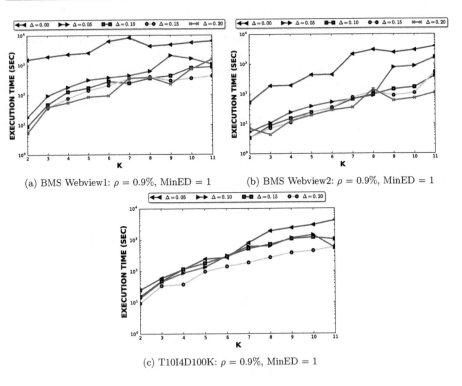

(a) BMS Webview1: $\rho = 0.9\%$, MinED $= 1$ (b) BMS Webview2: $\rho = 0.9\%$, MinED $= 1$

(c) T10I4D100K: $\rho = 0.9\%$, MinED $= 1$

Fig. 1. Varying k and interval threshold Δ

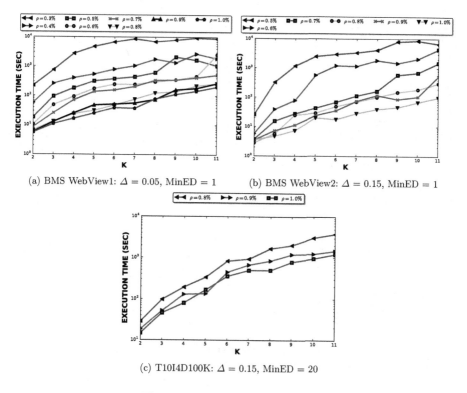

(a) BMS WebView1: $\Delta = 0.05$, MinED $= 1$ (b) BMS WebView2: $\Delta = 0.15$, MinED $= 1$

(c) T10I4D100K: $\Delta = 0.15$, MinED $= 20$

Fig. 2. Varying support threshold

(as noted in Table 1). $minED$ was set to 1, 10, 20, 30, and K was varied from 2 to 11 (inclusive).

In order to generate the support constraints, of the form (I, l, u), we compute the set of the frequent itemsets from each datasets where the minimum support value δ was varied in the range 0.2%, 0.3%, 0.4%..., 0.9%, 1%. The lower and the upper bound threshold for each frequent itemset I were obtained by using the following formulas $l = support(I, \mathcal{D}) * (1 - \Delta)$ and $u = support(I, \mathcal{D}) * (1 + \Delta)$ where the interval threshold (Δ) was set to values 0.0, 0.05, 0.1, 0.15, 0.2. Thus, when $\Delta = 0.0$, we have that $l = u = support(I, \mathcal{D})$.

All experiments were carried out on machines with CentOS7 (x86-64) Operating System, 2 Xeon Processors (E5-2620 v3 @ 2.40 GHz), and 256 GB RAM. We report the execution time as well as the $pairDist$ calculated for each dataset.

Varying Δ: We first observe the impact of varying itemset interval threshold Δ on execution time. k (the number of datasets to create) has been varied from 2–11. It was observed that the execution time was almost constant with varying interval threshold Δ values in the interval $\{0.0, 0.05, 0.1, 0.15, 0.2\}$ for all the three datasets except for $\Delta = 0.0$ for which execution time increased. Figures 1a–c represent the impact of k-anonymity values and interval threshold values on

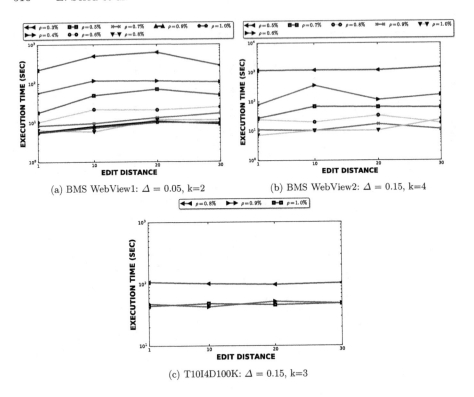

(a) BMS WebView1: $\Delta = 0.05$, k=2

(b) BMS WebView2: $\Delta = 0.15$, k=4

(c) T10I4D100K: $\Delta = 0.15$, k=3

Fig. 3. Varying edit-distance for different Δ and k

execution time for the three datasets. The results show that as we increase the value of delta, the flexibility allowed to the solver also increases and it quickly finds a feasible solution.

Varying support threshold values: We next observe the impact of varying k along with varying support threshold values on the execution time for solving a k-distant-IFM-solution. Figures 2a–c show the impact of varying k on execution time. It can be noted that while the time required is different for the three datasets for the different support threshold values, it does not change much with respect to k. For BMS Webview-2 and T10I4D100K datasets with varying $\rho\%$, similar trend is observed. In [7] (which models IFM with linear programs), increasing $\rho\%$ decreases the execution time. However, for integer linear formulations with more constraints, search space is decreased and it is easier to find a solution. Therefore, increase in $\rho\%$, increases the execution time.

Due to the significant computational resources required and the large number of experiments to be carried out, we were only able to carry out experiments for a few values of support for BMS Webview2 dataset. But we did check to make sure that the overall behavior is the same. For T10I4D100K dataset, lower values of support lead to a huge number of frequent itemsets. Therefore, we limited the

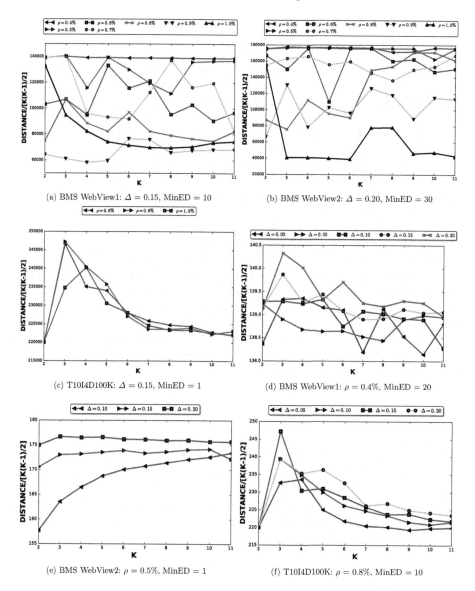

Fig. 4. Average Distance w.r.t varying ρ and Δ

experiments to higher values of support. Also, the behavior of execution time with respect to k is clear even when k is limited to 11, which was sufficient reason not to go beyond 11 for k as these operations are computationally expensive.

Varying edit-distance values: We next observe the impact of varying edit-distance values in the range $[1, 10, 20, 30]$. Figures 3a–c show the impact on execution time for the three datasets. We can generally observe that time does not significantly change by varying the edit distance.

Pairwise average distance varying k, ρ and Δ: Finally, we observe the effect of varying k, ρ and Δ on the pairwise distance. Firstly, for varying support constraints ρ and k, Figs. 4a–c show the impact of k w.r.t. $distance/((k*(k-1))/2)$ values for the three datasets. Here, no specific trend can be observed. However, if we consider that our approach is based on 2-approximation algorithm, these trends can be considered constant within an approximation range. Similarly, if we consider the case where we vary ρ, it can be observed that as the support increases, the average distance decreases and vice-versa (of course within the approximation range). This shows that as the amount of information about the distribution of the itemsets disclosed increases, the privacy risk increases (several transaction databases nearby each other).

Secondly, for varying interval threshold Δ, Figs. 4d–f show the impact of k values w.r.t. $distance/((k*(k-1))/2)$ for the three datasets. We can observe that as interval Δ decreases, the average distance also decreases. Essentially, increasing the support interval size for each itemset increases the uncertainty of the itemset distribution and thus decreases the privacy risk. Additionally, note that in Fig. 4c and f, there is a peak in the plots between $k = 2$ and $k = 3$. This is because Algorithm 1 in line 3 initialize the SD with an arbitrary transaction database which is not chosen in a way that would maximize the distance of the future transaction database candidates.

5   Conclusion

In this paper we define the K-distant-IFM-solutions problem, that enables evaluation of the frequent itemset disclosure risk and propose a solution for it. The experimental evaluation shows that the proposed approach is effective. In our future work, we plan to develop methodologies that are able to perturb the support of the itemsets disclosed in order to minimize the disclosure risk. In addition, we plan to extend these techniques to work with sequence mining as well – where we consider sequences rather than itemsets.

References

1. Agrawal, R., Imieliński, T., Swami, A.: Mining association rules between sets of items in large databases. ACM SIGMOD Rec. **22**(2), 207–216 (1993)
2. Barnhart, C., Johnson, E.L., Nemhauser, G.L., Savelsbergh, M.W.P., Vance, P.H.: Branch-and-price: column generation for solving huge integer programs. Oper. Res. **46**, 316–329 (1996)
3. Borodin, A., Lee, H.C., Ye, Y.: Max-sum diversification, monotone submodular functions and dynamic updates. In: Proceedings of the 31st Symposium on Principles of Database Systems, PODS 2012, pp. 155–166. ACM, New York (2012). http://doi.acm.org/10.1145/2213556.2213580

4. Calders, T.: Itemset frequency satisfiability: complexity and axiomatization. Theor. Comput. Sci. **394**(1–2), 84–111 (2008)
5. Goethals, B., Zaki, M.J.: Fimi03: workshop on frequent itemset mining implementations. In: Third IEEE International Conference on Data Mining Workshop on Frequent Itemset Mining Implementations, pp. 1–13 (2003)
6. Guzzo, A., Moccia, L., Saccà, D., Serra, E.: Solving inverse frequent itemset mining with infrequency constraints via large-scale linear programs. TKDD **7**(4), 18 (2013). http://doi.acm.org/10.1145/2541268.2541271
7. Guzzo, A., Saccà, D., Serra, E.: An effective approach to inverse frequent set mining. In: Ninth IEEE International Conference on Data Mining, ICDM 2009, pp. 806–811, December 2009
8. Machanavajjhala, A., Kifer, D., Gehrke, J., Venkitasubramaniam, M.: l-diversity: privacy beyond k-anonymity. ACM Trans. Knowl. Discov. Data (TKDD) **1**(1), 3 (2007)
9. Mielikainen, T.: On inverse frequent set mining. In: Society, I.C. (ed.) Proceedings of the 2nd Workshop on Privacy Preserving Data Mining (PPDM), pp. 18–23 (2003)
10. Ramesh, G., Maniatty, W., Zaki, M.: Feasible itemeset distributions in data mining: theory and application. In: Proceedings of the 28th International Conference on Very Large Data Bases, pp. 682–693 (2002)
11. Samarati, P.: Protecting respondents identities in microdata release. IEEE Trans. Knowl. Data Eng. **13**(6), 1010–1027 (2001)
12. Schrijver, A.: Theory of Linear and Integer Programming. John Wiley & Sons Inc., New York (1986)
13. Wang, Y., Wu, X.: Approximate inverse frequent itemset mining: Privacy, complexity, and approximation. In: ICDM, pp. 482–489 (2005)
14. Wu, X., Wu, Y., Wang, Y., Li, Y.: Privacy-aware market basket data set generation: an feasible approach for inverse frequent set mining. In: Proceedings of the 5th SIAM International Conference on Data Mining (2005)

Digital Signature, Risk Management, and Code Reuse Attacks

Forward-Secure Digital Signature Schemes with Optimal Computation and Storage of Signers

Jihye Kim[1] and Hyunok Oh[2]($\boxtimes$)

[1] Kookmin University, Seoul, Korea
jihyek@kookmin.ac.kr
[2] Hanyang University, Seoul, Korea
hoh@hanyang.ac.kr

Abstract. Forward-secure signatures minimize damage by preventing forgeries for past time periods when a secret key is compromised. Forward-secure signature schemes are useful for various devices such as logging systems, unattended sensors, CCTV, dash camera, etc. Considering sensors equipped with limited resources and embedded real-time systems with timing constraints, it is necessary to design a forward-secure signature scheme with minimal overhead on signer's side.

This paper proposes the first forward secure digital signature schemes with constant complexities in signature generation, key update, the size of keys, and the size of a signature. The proposed algorithms have $O(k^3)$-time complexity for each signing and key update algorithm and $O(k)$-size secret keys where k is an RSA security parameter. We prove the security of our proposed schemes under the factoring assumption in the random oracle model and present a concrete implementation of our schemes to demonstrate their practical feasibility.

Keywords: Forward secure · Digital signature · Fast signing/update · Factoring

1   Introduction

Forward-secure signature schemes mitigate the damage caused by a secret key exposure. The role of the digital logs and data as forensic values has boosted the need for strong authenticity of data. For example, audit logs record the "what happened when by whom" of the system. The forensic value of audit logs makes them an attractive target for attackers [1]. An active attacker compromising a logging machine can modify log entries related to the past, erasing records of the attacker's previous break-in attempts. Forward secure digital signature schemes, of which goal is to preserve the validity of past signatures even if the current secret key has been compromised, become an effective solution to prevent this active attack as well as to provide strong authenticity for the recorded video frames.

© IFIP International Federation for Information Processing 2017
Published by Springer International Publishing AG 2017. All Rights Reserved
S. De Capitani di Vimercati and F. Martinelli (Eds.): SEC 2017, IFIP AICT 502, pp. 523–537, 2017.
DOI: 10.1007/978-3-319-58469-0_35

Briefly, a forward-secure signature scheme divides the total time into T time periods and uses a different secret key in each time period (while the public key remains fixed). Each subsequent secret key is computed from the current secret key via a key update algorithm. Although it is ideal to have constant complexities regardless of the parameter T in computations and storage sizes overall, it is a challenging work. In the first forward-secure signature scheme proposed by Anderson [2], the size of secret key increases linearly with T. In the Bellare and Miner (BM) scheme [3] both public and secret key sizes are constant, but the signing and the verification time (of a single signature) grows linearly with T. Itkis and Reyzin [4] (IR) propose a scheme to have constant complexities in signing and verification, however, at the expense of key update time and the secret key size which grow logarithmically with T. Malkin et al. [5] (MMM) proposed a generic forward secure signature scheme based on a hash chain tree with a constant size public key. Although the secret key size, the signature size, signing and verifying time are $O(\log T)$, theoretically, the actual computation time and the storage requirement seem to be independent of T since the hash computation and size are relatively small compared with a public key signature scheme which it uses internally. However a signature in MMM contains two public keys and two signatures with an $O(\log T)$ size hash chain. The resulting signature size is 4 times larger than BM and IR.

One of main hurdles when forward-secure signature schemes are deployed in the real systems is located in their non-constant signing/update overhead. For example, in the video recording devices for streaming applications, a captured video frame is compressed periodically, e.g., every 33 ms. If a signature is generated for each frame, the signature computation with key update should be completed within 33 ms. When an incident occurs, the stored video frames and their signatures are used for forensic analysis. In this scenario, the signing and update time should be short enough to meet the time constraint. On the contrary, the verification of the signatures may be performed when a forensic is required.

The goal of this paper is to construct forward-secure signature schemes efficient enough to cover even resource- and/or time-constraint devices such as unattended sensors and surveillance real-time streaming systems. To achieve this goal, the computation and size complexities on signer's side should be short and constant at least. For the practical usage like other previous schemes, the public key size also needs to be constant. Setup and verification times not directly related with the signing device are comparatively less important.

Contributions. Our schemes extend the Bellare-Miner (BM) scheme [3] and the Abdalla-Reyzin (AR) scheme [6] to provide *a short and constant signature computation time*. The proposed schemes, denoted as Fast-BM and Fast-AR, require the same constant size memory for secret/public keys, and generate the same constant size signatures as BM and AR, respectively. The signature computation time complexity is $O(k^3)$ in our schemes, while the signature computation time complexity is $O(k^2 T)$ in the BM scheme, and $O(k^2 l T)$ in the AR scheme, where l is a security parameter representing the bit length of the hash output,

k is a security parameter denoting the bit length in RSA (modulo N is k-bit integer), and T represents the number of periods. Surprisingly, there is no significant performance degradation in other metrics, while we optimize the signing algorithms of BM and AR. In the experiment, our algorithms generate a signature and update their secret keys in 25 ms with security parameters $k = 2048$ and $l = 160$ regardless of the total number of periods T. The results show that our proposals are fast enough not only for normal applications but also for real-time streaming applications. The proposed Fast-BM and Fast-AR schemes are secure under the factoring assumption in the random oracle model.

We begin, in the next section, by describing background for forward secure digital signature schemes. Section 3 proposes our fast forward secure digital signature schemes with explaining the underlying schemes. Section 4 discusses the security of the proposed schemes. In Sect. 5, experimental results present quantitative measurements. We describe related work in Sect. 6 and summarize our conclusion in Sect. 7.

2   Background

This section reviews the syntax and security definitions of a forward secure digital signature scheme and defines its formal notion of security. All definitions provided here are based on those given in [3,6]. We also present the underlying cryptographic assumptions that our proposal relies on. We introduce some basic notations. If S is a set then $s \xleftarrow{\$} S$ denotes the operation of picking a random element s of S. We write $A(x, y, \cdots)$ to indicate that A is an algorithm with inputs $x, y, \cdots$ and by $z \leftarrow A(x, y, \cdots)$ we denote the operation of running A with inputs $(x, y, \cdots)$ and letting z be the output.

2.1   Forward Secure Signature Schemes

A forward secure signature scheme is a key-evolving signature scheme. We follow the definition of forward secure signature schemes in [3,6].

Definition 1 (Key-evolving signature scheme). *A key-evolving digital signature scheme is a set of four algorithms:* FSIG = (Setup, Sig, Upd, Ver), *where:*

- Setup: The key generation algorithm is a probability algorithm which takes as input a security parameter l and the total number of periods T and returns a pair (SK_0, PK), the initial secret key and the public key.
- Sig: The signing algorithm takes as input the secret key SK_i for the current time period i and the message M to be signed, and returns a pair $\langle i, s \rangle$, the signature of M for time period i.
- Upd: The key update algorithm takes as input the secret key SK_i for the current interval and returns a new secret key SK_{i+1} for the next interval.
- Ver: The verification algorithm takes as input the public key PK, message M and a candidate signature $\langle i, s \rangle$, and returns 1 if $\langle i, s \rangle$ is a *valid* signature of M, or 0, otherwise. It is required that $\mathsf{Ver}_{PK}(\mathsf{M}, \mathsf{Sig}_{SK_i}(\mathsf{M})) = 1$ for every message M and time period i.

We assume that the secret key SK_j for period $j \leq T$ always contains the value j itself and also contains the value T of the total number of periods. Finally, we adopt the convention that SK_{T+1} is the empty string and $\mathsf{Upd}(SK_T)$ returns SK_{T+1}.

Security: The adversary executes the usual adaptive chosen-message attack (cma) until it breaks in and learns the secret key for a given time period. The adversary is then considered successful if it can create a valid forgery on a new message for a *previous* time period. Formally, this adversary, denoted by F, is modeled via the following experiment. The adversary, denoted by F, runs in three phases. In the cma phase, F has access to a sign oracle. F is allowed to query multiple signatures in the same period. In the break-in phase, F is given the secret key SK_j for the specific interval j. Finally, in the forgery phase (forge), F outputs a pair of a signature and a message. The adversary is successful if it forges a signature of any new message (not previously queried to the signing oracle) for any time period prior to j. The formal experiment is described in the following:

F-Forge(FSIG, F) :

$(SK_0, PK) \xleftarrow{\$} \mathsf{Setup}(\mathsf{k}, \cdots, T);$

$j \leftarrow 0$

repeat

$\quad j \leftarrow j + 1;\ SK_j \leftarrow \mathsf{Upd}(SK_j);\ d \leftarrow F^{\mathsf{Sig}_{SK_j}(\cdot)}(\mathsf{cma}, PK)$

until $(d = \mathbf{breakin})$ or $(j = T)$

If $(d \neq \mathbf{breakin})$ and $(j = T)$ then $j \leftarrow T + 1$

$(M, \langle b, s \rangle) \leftarrow F(\mathbf{forge}, SK_j)$

If $\mathsf{Ver}(M, \langle \mathsf{b}, \mathsf{s} \rangle) = 1$ and $1 \leq \mathsf{b} < j$

$\quad$ and M was not queried of $\mathsf{Sig}_{SK_b}(\cdot)$ in period b

$\quad$ then return 1 else return 0

Definition 2 (Forward-security). *Let* $\mathsf{FSIG} = (\mathsf{Setup}, \mathsf{Sig}, \mathsf{Upd}, \mathsf{Ver})$ *be a key-evolving signature scheme and F an adversary as described above. Let* $\mathbf{Succ}^{\mathrm{fwsig}}$ $(\mathsf{FSIG}[\mathsf{k}, \cdots, T], F)$ *denote the probability that the experiment* **F-Forge**$(\mathsf{FSIG}[k,$ $\cdots, T], F)$ *returns 1. Then the insecurity of* FSIG *is the function*

$$\mathbf{InSec}^{\mathrm{fwsig}}(\mathsf{FSIG}[\mathsf{k}, \cdots, T]; \mathsf{t}, \mathsf{q}_{\mathsf{sig}}) = \max\{\mathbf{Succ}^{\mathrm{fwsig}}(\mathsf{FSIG}[\mathsf{k}, \cdots, T], F)\},$$

where the maximum is taken over all adversaries F making a total of at most q_{sig} queries to the signing oracles across all the stages and for which the running time of the above experiment is at most t.

3   Fast Forward Secure Digital Signature Schemes

Our proposed schemes extend the previous forward secure signature schemes proposed by Bellare and Miner (BM) [3] and by Abdalla and Reyzin (AR) [6].

Since the way of extension is the same for each, we describe our scheme focusing on the AR version (which has a simpler parameter setting). We first overview the scheme proposed by Abdalla-Reyzin (AR) in [6] and then describe our proposed schemes.

3.1   Overview of the AR Scheme

The AR scheme [6] defines T the maximum number of periods and extends the 2^l-th root signature scheme [7] to have the forward security property. The initial secret key S_0 is arranged as $2^{l(T+1)}$-th root of a public key U. For each period, the secret key is updated by raising it to the 2^l power and thus the secret key at the period j becomes $S_j = S_0^{2^{l(T+1-j)}}$. At period j, the signer proves the knowledge of the $2^{l(T+1-j)}$-th root of U, of which computational cost is proportional to T. Thus, as T increases, the signing time increases. The size of T depends on the application and is possibly large in general to avoid frequent setups. For instance, assume that a signature is generated and a secret key is updated every second. In order to provide a forward security in this device for a year, T should be no less than 31,536,000 (=$60 \times 60 \times 24 \times 365$). AR (of which signature computation depends on T) may be impractical to be used for applications with this large T setting.

3.2   Fast-AR

Algorithm 1 summarizes the key setup, the secret key update, the sign, and the verification of our proposed algorithm called Fast-AR. In the proposed algorithm, all numbers including secret keys (S_j), a public key (U), random numbers (R), and their exponentiations (Y) are chosen in $\langle g \rangle$ where g is a generator of a large subgroup in Z_N^*. In the following, we describe our approach and details of each algorithm.

Setup: We generate a safe RSA (or a safe-prime product RSA) modulus $N = pq$ where p, q, p', and q' are primes such that $p = 2p' + 1$, and $q = 2q' + 1$. Note that p and q are congruent 3 mod 4 and N becomes a Blum integer. Pick a random element g s.t. g generates a maximum subgroup in Z_N^*, i.e. $ord(g) = 2p'q'$ and s.t. $-1 \notin \langle g \rangle$. Note that this holds for about half of the elements in Z_N^*, and it is easily tested. In addition, the Jacobi symbol of g, $(g|N) = -1$.

Additionally, we compute $X = g^{2^{l(T+1)}} \bmod N$. Using g and X, we can efficiently compute $l(T + 1)$ squaring operations of any group element in $\langle g \rangle$, given the order of the element. Thus, to compute $U = S_0^{2^{l(T+1)}} \bmod N$ where $S_0 = g^s \bmod N$ for some known s, we compute $X^s \bmod N$ instead. (The same technique is used in the sign algorithm.)

Since the group size $\phi(N)(= (p-1)(q-1))$ is known at setup, computation of $X = g^{2^{l(T+1)}} \bmod N$ has $O(k^3)$-time complexity. A secret key S is chosen from $\langle g \rangle$ by selecting a random number s in $Z_{N/2}$ and computing $S = g^s \bmod N$. A public key U ($\equiv S^{2^{l(T+1)}} \equiv g^{s2^{l(T+1)}} \equiv X^s (\bmod N)$) is computed by raising X to the s as we describe above. After computing a secret key and a public key, the primes p, q and the chosen random number s are discarded. g and X are stored in a secret key.

Sign and Update: In AR, the signing overhead occurs mainly due the computation of $Y \leftarrow R^{2^{l(T+1-j)}} \bmod N$ for a chosen random R at period j. Since the computation requires $l(T + 1 - j)$ squaring operations of R, the computation complexity is proportional to T. Recall that we select a generator g (of a maximum subgroup of Z_N^*) and compute $g^{2^{l(T+1)}}$ denoted as X in advance. In the signing procedure of our scheme, we generate R by raising g to a random number e in $Z_{N/2}$. Then since Y is $R^{2^{l(T+1)}} \equiv g^{e2^{l(T+1)}} \equiv X^e (\bmod N)$, Y can be computed by raising X to the e. So the computation time of Y does not rely on T. After computing R and Y, e is erased. Note that the computation of Y in our scheme is different from AR: $Y = R^{2^{l(T+1)}}$ in our scheme, while $Y = R^{2^{l(T+1-j)}}$ in AR. I.e., the computation of Y in our scheme is independent of period j, unlike AR. Therefore, after we compute $X = g^{2^{l(T+1)}}$ once (in setup), it can be reused at every period. The verification in our scheme is modified accordingly, which is slightly different from AR and slower than AR, but has the same computation complexity as AR.

Algorithm 1. Fast-AR

---

function Setup(k, l, T)
    Pick random p' and q' such that $p(= 2p' + 1)$, $q(= 2q' + 1)$, p', q' are prime, and p and q are $k/2$ bit and set $N \leftarrow pq$
    Pick a random element g s.t. g generates a maximum subgroup in Z_N^*, i.e. $ord(g) = 2p'q'$, and such that $-1 \notin \langle g \rangle$
    $x \leftarrow 2^{l(T+1)} \bmod (p-1)(q-1)$; $X \leftarrow g^x \bmod N$
    $s \xleftarrow{\$} Z_{N/2}$; $S_0 \leftarrow g^s \bmod N$; $U \leftarrow X^s \bmod N$
    $SK \leftarrow (N, T, g, X, 0, S_0)$; $PK \leftarrow (N, U, T)$
    return (PK, SK)
end function

---

function Upd(SK) : parse SK as (N, T, g, X, j, S_j)
    if j=T then $SK \leftarrow \epsilon$
    else $SK \leftarrow (N, T, g, X, j+1, S_j^{2^l} \bmod N)$
    end if
    return SK
end function

---

function Sig(M, SK) : parse SK as (N, T, g, X, j, S_j)
    $e \xleftarrow{\$} Z_{N/2}$; $R \leftarrow g^e \bmod N$; $Y \leftarrow X^e \bmod N$; $\sigma \leftarrow H(j, Y, M)$; $Z \leftarrow RS_j^\sigma \bmod N$
    return $(j, (Z, \sigma))$
end function

---

function Ver$(M, PK, sign)$: parse PK as (N, U, T); parse $sign$ as $(j, (Z, \sigma))$
    if $Z \equiv 0 (\bmod N)$ then return 0
    else
        $Y' \leftarrow Z^{2^{l(T+1)}}/U^{\sigma 2^{lj}} \bmod N$
        if $\sigma = H(j, Y', M)$ then return 1
        else return 0
        end if
    end if
end function

The key update algorithm is the same as AR, which requires l times squaring operations only.

Verification: As mentioned early, our verification algorithm is slightly different from AR due to the different exponentiation number for Y. While the verification tests whether Y is equal to $Z^{2^{l(T+1-j)}} U^{\sigma}$ in AR, it checks whether Y is equal to $Z^{2^{l(T+1)}}/U^{\sigma 2^{lj}}$ in our scheme. On average, our verification requires twice computation than AR.

Correctness: For a given signature of $(j, (Z, \sigma))$ for message M, the verification is to check whether $\sigma = H(j, Y', M)$ where $Y' \leftarrow Z^{2^{l(T+1)}}/U^{\sigma 2^{lj}}$. Since $Z = RS_j^{\sigma} = g^e S_0^{2^{lj}\sigma}$ and $(g^e)^{2^{l(T+1)}} = X^e = Y$, $Z^{2^{l(T+1)}} = YS_0^{2^{lj}2^{l(T+1)}} = YU^{\sigma 2^{lj}}$. So the verification works correctly.

4   Security Analysis

Since the proposed Fast-AR scheme is similar to the existing AR scheme except that numbers are chosen in $\langle g \rangle$ rather than Z_N^* in a signature generation, the security proof is similar to the proof of AR.

Let k and l be two security parameters. Let $p = 2p' + 1$, $q = 2q' + 1$, p', and q' be primes and $N = pq$ be a k-bit integer (Since $p \equiv q \equiv 3 \pmod 4$, N is a Blum integer). Let Q denote the set of non-zero quadratic residues modulo N. Note that for $x \in Q$, exactly one of its four square roots is also in Q. In the following description, $x \xleftarrow{\$} \langle g \rangle$ denotes that $r \xleftarrow{\$} Z_N$ and $x \leftarrow g^r \bmod N$ for $ord(g) = 2p'q'$.

Lemma 1. *Given $\alpha \neq 0$, $\lambda > 0$, $v \in Q$ and $X \in \langle g \rangle$ such that $v^{\alpha} \equiv X^{2^{\lambda}} \pmod N$ and $\alpha < 2^{\lambda}$, one can easily compute y such that $v \equiv y^2 \pmod N$.*

Proof. Let $\alpha = 2^{\gamma}\beta$ where β is odd. Note that $\lambda > \gamma$. Let $\beta = 2\delta + 1$. Then $(v^{2\delta+1})^{2^{\gamma}} \equiv v^{\alpha} \equiv X^{2^{\lambda}} \pmod N$, so $v^{2\delta+1} \equiv X^{2^{\lambda-\gamma}} \pmod N$. Note that it is allowed to take roots of degree 2^{γ} since both sides are in Q. Let $y = X^{2^{\lambda-\gamma-1}}/v^{\delta} \bmod N$. Then $y^2 \equiv X^{2^{\lambda-\gamma}}/v^{2\delta} \equiv v \pmod N$. Note that since $\alpha < 2^{\lambda}$, $\lambda - \gamma - 1 \geq 0$.

Theorem 1. *If there exists a forger $\mathcal{F}$ for $\mathsf{FSIG}[k, l, T]$ that runs in time at most t, asking at most q_H hash queries and q_S signing queries, such that $\mathbf{Succ}^{\mathrm{fwsig}}(\mathsf{FSIG}[k, l, T], F) \geq \epsilon$, then there exists an algorithm $\mathcal{A}$ that factors Blum integers generated by $\mathsf{FSIG.key}(l, T)$ in expected time at most t' with probability at least ϵ', where $t' = 2t + O(k^2 lT + k^3)$, and $\epsilon' = \frac{(\epsilon - 2^{3-k}q_S(q_H+1))^2}{2T^2(q_H+1)} - \frac{\epsilon - 2^{3-k}q_S(q_H+1)}{2^{l+1}T}$.*

Proof. Suppose that there exists a forger $\mathcal{F}$ against $Fast - AR$ scheme that succeeds with ϵ in time t. We construct an algorithm $\mathcal{A}$ using $\mathcal{F}$ as a subroutine to factor a given Blum-Williams integer N with a probability of ϵ' within t' time. The goal is to find a pair (p, q) such that $N = pq$.

$\mathcal{A}$ is constructed as follows:

Setup

1. select $g \overset{\$}{\leftarrow} Z_N^*$ such that $-1 \notin \langle g \rangle$ [Given a safe RSA modulus N, with probability about $1/2$ we have $ord(g)=2p'q'$.]
2. $w \overset{\$}{\leftarrow} \langle g \rangle$; $v \leftarrow w^2 \bmod N$ [Will try to find a square root of v that is different from w.]
3. $b' \overset{\$}{\leftarrow} \{1, \cdots, T\}$ [Choose break-in period hoping that the break-in will occur after b' period, and the forgery will be at b' or earlier.]
4. $U \leftarrow v^{2^{l(T-b')}}$ [The intention is that $S_{b'}{}^{2^l} = v \bmod N$.]
5. $PK \leftarrow (N, T, U)$ [Build a public key.]

Now, we will explain how $\mathcal{A}$ simulates.

Simulation

1. **Hash query** simulation: If $H(j, Y, M)$ is undefined then $H(j, Y, M) \overset{\$}{\leftarrow} \{0, 1\}^l$. It returns $H(j, Y, M)$.
2. **Sign query** for M at the j-th period: If $j \leq b'$ then $Z \overset{\$}{\leftarrow} \langle g \rangle$; $\sigma \overset{\$}{\leftarrow} Z_{N/2}$; $Y \leftarrow \dfrac{Z^{2^{l(T+1)}}}{v^{2^{l(T-b'+j)}\sigma}} \bmod N$. Y satisfies that $Z^{2^{l(T+1)}} \equiv YU^{2^{lj}\sigma}(\bmod N)$ since $U^\sigma = v^{2^{l(T-b')}\sigma} \bmod N$. If $H(j, Y, M)$ is defined then $\mathcal{A}$ sets $fail_1 \leftarrow$ true and aborts the execution of $\mathcal{F}$; otherwise $H(j, Y, M) \leftarrow \sigma$. $\mathcal{A}$ returns $(j, (Z, \sigma))$. Since there are at most q_H entries defined in tables H, the probability that $fail_1$ happens is at most $q_H/2^l$ per sign query. Consider $j > b'$. Since secret $S_j = v^{2^{l(j-b'-1)}}$, $Sig(M, SK)$ can be performed and $(j, (Z, \sigma))$ is returned.
3. **Update simulation**: If $j \leq b'$ then nothing is performed. Otherwise $Upd(M, SK)$ is called.
4. **Break-in simulation** at the b-th period: If $b \leq b'$ then $\mathcal{A}$ sets $fail_3 \leftarrow$ true and aborts the execution of $\mathcal{F}$. Otherwise, $\mathcal{A}$ returns S_b such that $S_b = S_{b'}^{2^{l(b-b')}} = v^{2^{l(b-b'-1)}}$.

Factoring of N

Assume that $\mathcal{F}$ outputs a forged signature $(j, (Z, \sigma))$ for a message M where σ is a hash query for $H(j, Y, M)$. Assume that the forgery period j is no later than the break-in period b' or $j \leq b'$. If $\mathcal{F}$ forges the signature without querying on $H(j, Y, M)$ then A sets $fail_2 \leftarrow$ true and aborts the execution of F. $\mathcal{A}$ resets $\mathcal{F}$ with the same random tape as the first time, and runs it again, giving the exact same answers to all $\mathcal{F}$'s queries before the hash query of $H(j, Y, M)$. On the query of $H(j, Y, M)$, $\mathcal{A}$ comes up with a new answer $\sigma' \overset{\$}{\leftarrow} \{0, 1\}^l$, sets $H(j, Y, M) \leftarrow \sigma'$. Then $\mathcal{F}$ returns $(j, (Z', \sigma'))$. If the second forgery was not based on hash query on $H(j, Y, M)$ then $\mathcal{A}$ fails.

We know the following two equations must hold: $Z^{2^{l(T+1)}} \equiv YU^{2^{lj}\sigma} \pmod{N}$ and $Z'^{2^{l(T+1)}} \equiv YU^{2^{lj}\sigma'} \pmod{N}$. Dividing, we get $(\frac{Z}{Z'})^{2^{l(T+1)}} \equiv U^{2^{lj}(\sigma-\sigma')}$ $\pmod{N}$. From the setup, we know that $U \equiv v^{2^{l(T-b')}} \pmod{N}$. So we can write $(\frac{Z}{Z'})^{2^{l(T+1)}} \equiv v^{2^{l(T+j-b')}(\sigma-\sigma')} \pmod{N}$. Taking roots of degrees $2^{l(T+j-b')}$ of both sides, which we are allowed to do because both sides are in Q and remain in Q, because v is a square, $v^{\sigma-\sigma'} \equiv (\frac{Z}{Z'})^{2^{l(b'+1-j)}} \pmod{N}$. By applying Lemma 1, our algorithm can easily compute a square root of v, denoted as x, by setting $\alpha = \sigma - \sigma'$, $X = Z/Z'$, and $\lambda = l(b'+1-j)$. If $x \equiv \pm w \bmod N$ then abort. Otherwise, we compute $h \leftarrow \gcd(w - x, N)$ which is a non-trivial factor of N. Note that to argue the extracted square root of v differs from $\pm w$, subgroup $\langle g \rangle$ should contain at least another square root of v which is not $-w$. It cannot be $-w$ since -1 does not belong to $\langle g \rangle$ by construction. Such an element exists in $\langle g \rangle$ because, if the Jacobi symbol of g equals to -1 (or $(g|N) = -1$), $g^{p'q'}$ must be a non-trivial square root of unity in Z_N^*. As a consequence, $g^{p'q'} \cdot w$ is another square root of v that belongs to $\langle g \rangle$. Since the signing oracle and the break-in oracle never use w, the knowledge extractor allows to extract $g^{p'q'}$ with probability $1/2$. The computations of the probability and the running time are identical to [6].

5   Experiment

We implement the proposed Fast-BM and Fast-AR schemes using openssl library in C. For comparison, we implement BM [3], AR [6], IR, optimized IR (IROpt) [4], and MMM [5]. We use GQ [8] as public key signature scheme in MMM. All schemes except MMM generate a short size signature of which size is k while MMM generates a signature of which size is $4k$, where k is the bit-length of RSA modulus N. The experiment is performed on Intel i5 2.6 GHz laptop with 16 GB RAM under OS X. The hash length (l) is fixed to 160 bit.

Figure 1 illustrates the key setup time, the signing time per message, the key update time, and the verification time per message by varying the number of periods T from 10 to 100000 denoted as x axis when the security key parameter k is 2048. The y axis represents the execution time in second.

Figure 1(a) shows the setup time. As T increases, the setup time becomes significantly large in IR and IROpt. For instance, it is 1,000 s when $T = 100,000$, and it will be 10,000 s when $T = 1,000,000$ in IR and IROpt while in Fast-BM and Fast-AR it is a few ten seconds in which a safe RSA is generated.

Figure 1(b) represents the signing time per message. The signing time is proportional to T in BM and AR while it is independent of T in IR, IROpt, MMM, Fast-BM and Fast-AR. Note that the signing time complexity is $O(k^3)$ in Fast-BM and Fast-AR where k represents the bit length of modulus N.

Figure 1(c) indicates the key update time. In BM, AR, MMM, Fast-BM, and Fast-AR, the key update time is constant only depending on k and l while it is proportional to T and $\log T$ in IR and IROpt, respectively.

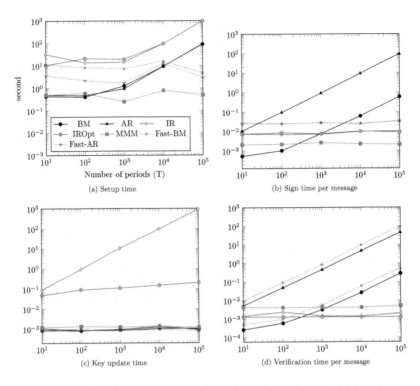

Fig. 1. Execution time variation as T varies when $l = 160$ and $k = 2048$

Figure 1(d) denotes the verification time. The verification time is proportional to T in BM, AR, Fast-BM and Fast-AR since T number of exponentiation operations are performed for verification in those algorithms, while it is irrelevant to T in IR, IROpt, and MMM.

Figure 2 illustrates the setup, signing, update, and verification times by varying k which is the bit-length of RSA modulus N when $l = 160$ and $T = 10000$. The setup time increases faster in IR, IROpt, Fast-BM, and Fast-AR since they use a safe RSA where $N = pq$, $p = 2p' + 1$, $q = 2q' + 1$, and p, q, p', q' are prime. When k is 2048, BM, AR, MMM, Fast-BM, and Fast-AR algorithms show a similar setup time.

Figure 2(b) shows the signing time per message. Since the signing time in all algorithms except Fast-BM and Fast-AR is proportional to k^2 if T and l are fixed, the signing time increases similarly in all algorithms as k increases. On the other hand, the time increases faster in Fast-BM and Fast-AR as k increases. Fast-AR is as fast as Fast-BM while AR is l time slower than BM since Fast-AR does not require $l(T + 1)$ squares.

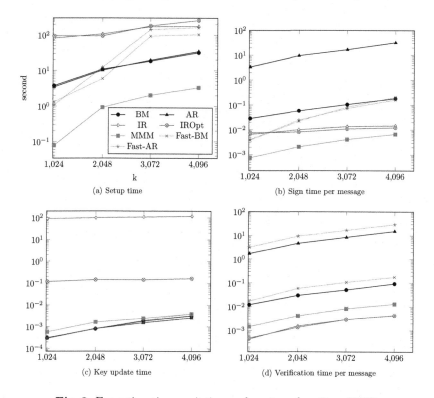

Fig. 2. Execution time variation as k varies when $T = 10000$

Figure 2(c) shows the key update time. As k increases, the key update time increases in all schemes. In IR and IROpt, the key update time increases slowly since the effect of T against k decreases where the update time complexities in IR and IROpt are $O(k^2 T)$ and $O(k^2 \log T)$ while they are $O(k^2)$ in the other algorithms.

Figure 2(d) represents the verification time. Regardless of k, IR and IROpt show the shortest verification time.

Table 1 summarizes the key sizes, setup time, signing time per message, key update time, and verification time in BM, AR, IR, IROpt, MMM, Fast-BM and Fast-AR. Fast-BM and Fast-AR reduce the signing time compared with BM and AR without sacrificing the other parameters.

Table 1. Comparison of BM, AR, IR, optimized IR, MMM, Fast-BM, and Fast-AR.

Criteria	BM	AR	IR	IROpt	MMM	Fast-BM	Fast-AR
Public key size	$k(l+1)$	$2k$	$2k$		l	$k(l+1)$	$2k$
Secret key size	kl	k	$3k+l$	$k(\log(T)+2)+l$	$(\log l + \log t + 2)l + 2k$	kl	k
Signature size	$2k$	$k+l$	$k+2l$		$(\log l + \log t + 2)l + 4k$	$k+l$	$k+l$
Setup	$O(k^3 + lTk^2)$	$O(k^3 + lTk^2)$	$O(l^3T + k^3)$	$O(l^3T + k^3)$	$O(k^3 + l^2\log l)$	$O(k^3 + lk^2\log(T))$	$O(k^3 + k^2\log(lT))$
Sign	$O(k^2(T+l))$	$O(k^2lT)$	$O(k^2l)$		$O(k^2l)$	$O(k^3)$	$O(k^3)$
Update	$O(k^2l)$	$O(k^2l)$	$O(k^2lT)$	$O(k^2l\log(T))$	$O(k^2l + l^2\log t)$	$O(k^2l)$	$O(k^2l)$
Verification	$O(k^2(T+l))$	$O(k^2lT)$	$O(k^2l)$		$O(k^2l)$	$O(k^2(T+l))$	$O(k^2lT)$
Security	Factoring		Strong RSA		One way hash	Factoring	

6 Related Work

The pioneering studies addressing the forward secure signatures were first proposed by Anderson [2] and subsequently formalized by Bellare and Miner in [3]. In a forward-secure signatures scheme, the forward- security property is attained by dividing time into T discrete intervals, and using a different secret key within each interval. The main challenge in designing forward-secure signature schemes is efficiency: an ideal scheme must have constant (public and secret) key sizes, constant signature size as well as constant signing, verification, and (public and secret) key update operations.

In the first category, the schemes use some generic method in which a master public key is used to certify the current public key for a particular time period (via a chain of certificates). Usually, these schemes increase storage space by noticeable factors in order to maintain the current (public) certificates and the (secret) keys for issuing future certificates. They also require longer verification times than ordinary signatures do, because the verifier needs to verify the entire certificate chain in addition to verifying the actual signature on the message. There is, in fact, a trade-off between storage space and verification time. These schemes include the tree-based scheme of Bellare and Miner [BM99] (requiring storage of about $O(\log T)$ secret keys and non-secret certificates, and verification of about $O(\log T)$ ordinary signatures), the scheme of Krawczyk [9] (requiring storage of T non-secret certificates, and verification of only 2 ordinary signatures), and the scheme of Malkin et al. [5] has constant-size public key while the secret key size, the signature size, signing and verifying time are $O(\log t)$ where t denotes the time interval index which is less than T. The scheme of Holt [10] has constant-size secret key and signatures but requires T non-secret certificates storage/communication to verify signatures. The generic construction proposed by Libert et al. [11] has a non-constant signature size and computational overhead and the exact complexities depend on the underlying schemes.

In the second category, the schemes are built upon standard signature schemes. The main advantage of these schemes is that they achieve better dependence on T. In particular, they typically have constant size parameters. The first such scheme is based on the Fiat-Shamir signature scheme [3]. Abdalla and Reyzin scheme [6] shortens secret and public keys of at the expense of signing and verifying time. Itkis and Reyzin scheme [4] has shorter signing and verifying time derived from the underlying Guillou-Quisquater signature scheme [8] at the expense of logarithmic key update time and the secret key size. Kozlov and Reyzin [12] propose another scheme based on a similar optimizing technique used in [4]. The scheme is an improved version of [4], and the key update time and the secret key size grow logarithmically in T. However, linear-time operations are needed at the beginning of each period in the scheme.

Boyen et al. [13] proposed a forward-secure signature scheme, where the secret key is encrypted with a second factor such as a user's password and can be updated in its encrypted form. The scheme in [13] based on [14] features a constant signing time at the expense of its key update time in $O(\log T)$, its secret key size in $O(\log^2 T)$, its public key size in $O(\log T)$, and comparatively stronger cryptographic assumption. It makes use of a very specific mathematical setting consisting of groups equipped with a bilinear mapping whose computation is expensive. Abdalla et al. [15] proposed a variant of [4] to have a much tighter security reduction, however, assuming stronger security assumptions.

7 Conclusion

In this paper, we propose fast forward secure digital signature schemes called Fast-BM and Fast-AR which provide fast signing and key update with constant size public and secret keys, and a short constant size signature. The proposed schemes are applicable to real-time surveillance streaming applications as well as the traditional forward secure signature systems. In the proposed schemes, the signing and the key update are performed in $O(k^3)$ meaning that they are independent of the maximum period T, where k denotes the bit length of module N in RSA. In real implementation, the signing and the update can be performed within 25 ms in the proposed schemes regardless of T when $k = 2048$ while they require 200 ms in the optimized IR. The signature size is only 2240 bit when $k = 2048$, and $l = 160$ in our schemes. Fast-BM and Fast-AR schemes are secure under the factoring assumption in the random oracle model which is a weaker assumption than a strong RSA which IR is based on.

Acknowledgments. This research was supported by IT R&D program MKE/KEIT (No. 10041608, Embedded system Software for New-memory based Smart Device), by Next-Generation Information Computing Development Program through NRF funded by the Ministry of Science, ICT & Future Planning (No. NRF-2016M3C4A7937117), and by Basic Science Research Program through NRF funded by the Ministry of Education (No. 2016R1D1A1B03934545).

References

1. Bellare, M., Yee, B.: Forward-security in private-key cryptography. In: Joye, M. (ed.) CT-RSA 2003. LNCS, vol. 2612, pp. 1–18. Springer, Heidelberg (2003). doi:10.1007/3-540-36563-X_1

2. Anderson, R.: Two remarks on public-key cryptology - invited lecture. In: The Fourth ACM Conference on Computer and Communications Security (CCS) (1997)

3. Bellare, M., Miner, S.K.: A forward-secure digital signature scheme. In: Wiener, M. (ed.) CRYPTO 1999. LNCS, vol. 1666, pp. 431–448. Springer, Heidelberg (1999). doi:10.1007/3-540-48405-1_28

4. Itkis, G., Reyzin, L.: Forward-secure signatures with optimal signing and verifying. In: Kilian, J. (ed.) CRYPTO 2001. LNCS, vol. 2139, pp. 332–354. Springer, Heidelberg (2001). doi:10.1007/3-540-44647-8_20

5. Malkin, T., Micciancio, D., Miner, S.: Efficient generic forward-secure signatures with an unbounded number of time periods. In: Knudsen, L.R. (ed.) EUROCRYPT 2002. LNCS, vol. 2332, pp. 400–417. Springer, Heidelberg (2002). doi:10.1007/3-540-46035-7_27

6. Abdalla, M., Reyzin, L.: A new forward-secure digital signature scheme. In: Okamoto, T. (ed.) ASIACRYPT 2000. LNCS, vol. 1976, pp. 116–129. Springer, Heidelberg (2000). doi:10.1007/3-540-44448-3_10
7. Ong, H., Schnorr, C.: Fast signature generation with a fiat shamir-like scheme. In: Advances in Cryptology - EUROCRYPT 1990, Workshop on the Theory and Application of of Cryptographic Techniques, Aarhus, Denmark, 21–24 May 1990, Proceedings, pp. 432–440 (1990)
8. Guillou, L.C., Quisquater, J.-J.: A practical zero-knowledge protocol fitted to security microprocessor minimizing both transmission and memory. In: Barstow, D., Brauer, W., Brinch Hansen, P., Gries, D., Luckham, D., Moler, C., Pnueli, A., Seegmüller, G., Stoer, J., Wirth, N., Günther, C.G. (eds.) EUROCRYPT 1988. LNCS, vol. 330, pp. 123–128. Springer, Heidelberg (1988). doi:10.1007/3-540-45961-8_11
9. Krawczyk, H.: Simple forward-secure signatures from any signature scheme. In: Proceedings of the 7th ACM Conference on Computer and Communications Security (CCS 2000), Athens, Greece, 1–4 November 2000, pp. 108–115 (2000)
10. Holt, J.E.: Logcrypt: forward security and public verification for secure audit logs. In: The proceedings of the Fourth Australasian Symposium on Grid Computing and e-Research (AusGrid 2006) and the Fourth Australasian Information Security Workshop (Network Security) (AISW 2006), Hobart, Tasmania, Australia, pp. 203–211, January 2006
11. Libert, B., Quisquater, J., Yung, M.: Forward-secure signatures in untrusted update environments: efficient and generic constructions. In: Proceedings of the 2007 ACM Conference on Computer and Communications Security (CCS 2007), Alexandria, Virginia, USA, 28–31 October 2007, pp. 266–275 (2007)
12. Kozlov, A., Reyzin, L.: Forward-secure signatures with fast key update. In: Cimato, S., Persiano, G., Galdi, C. (eds.) SCN 2002. LNCS, vol. 2576, pp. 241–256. Springer, Heidelberg (2003). doi:10.1007/3-540-36413-7_18
13. Boyen, X., Shacham, H., Shen, E., Waters, B.: Forward-secure signatures with untrusted update. In: Proceedings of the 13th ACM Conference on Computer and Communications Security (CCS 2006), Alexandria, VA, USA, 30 October–3 November 2006, pp. 191–200(2006)
14. Boneh, D., Boyen, X., Goh, E.-J.: Hierarchical identity based encryption with constant size ciphertext. In: Cramer, R. (ed.) EUROCRYPT 2005. LNCS, vol. 3494, pp. 440–456. Springer, Heidelberg (2005). doi:10.1007/11426639_26
15. Abdalla, M., Ben Hamouda, F., Pointcheval, D.: Tighter Reductions for Forward-Secure Signature Schemes. In: Kurosawa, K., Hanaoka, G. (eds.) PKC 2013. LNCS, vol. 7778, pp. 292–311. Springer, Heidelberg (2013). doi:10.1007/978-3-642-36362-7_19

RiskInDroid: Machine Learning-Based Risk Analysis on Android

Alessio Merlo[1(✉)] and Gabriel Claudiu Georgiu[2]

[1] DIBRIS, University of Genoa, Genoa, Italy
alessio@dibris.unige.it
[2] Talos Security, s.r.l.s., Savona, Italy
gabriel.georgiu@talos-sec.com

Abstract. Risk analysis on Android is aimed at providing metrics to users for evaluating the trustworthiness of the apps they are going to install. Most of current proposals calculate a risk value according to the permissions required by the app through probabilistic functions that often provide unreliable risk values. To overcome such limitations, this paper presents RiskInDroid, a tool for risk analysis of Android apps based on machine learning techniques. Extensive empirical assessments carried out on more than 112 K apps and 6 K malware samples indicate that RiskInDroid outperforms probabilistic methods in terms of precision and reliability.

Keywords: Risk analysis · Android security · Static analysis · Machine learning

1 Introduction

Android is still the most widespread mobile operating system in the world, as more than 300 millions Android-enabled smartphones have been sold only in the third trimester of 2016 [1]. Therefore, it remains a sensitive target for malware that aim at exploiting its diffusion to reach a high number of potential victims. Since users have access to a high number of apps through public markets and external web sites, they need reliable tools to rate the trustworthiness of apps they are going to install. App rating is empirically calculated according to different risk analysis techniques. Currently, most of them calculate a *risk index value* (hereafter, RIV) through probabilistic methods applied to the set of permissions required by the app. We argue that such approaches suffer from intrinsic limitations in terms of both methodology and setup. To prove this, we apply some optimizations to existing techniques at the state of the art, and we evaluate them through an extensive empirical assessment on a dataset made by 112.425 apps and 6.707 malware samples. Then, we propose a novel approach based on machine learning techniques that we implemented in an open source

S. De Capitani di Vimercati and F. Martinelli (Eds.): SEC 2017, IFIP AICT 502, pp. 538–552, 2017.
DOI: 10.1007/978-3-319-58469-0_36

tool, i.e., `RiskInDroid`[1] (Risk Index for Android). Finally, we evaluate the performance of RiskInDroid on the same dataset, thereby proving that the proposed methodology outperforms probabilistic approaches.

Structure of the Paper. The rest of the paper is organized as follows: Sect. 2 briefly introduces the Android architecture and the permission system, while Sect. 3 summarizes the related work and introduces probabilistic approaches. Section 4 discusses some optimization for probabilistic methods and proves their reliability through an extensive experimental assessment. Section 5 proposes our machine learning-based methodology while Sect. 6 summarizes its empirical evaluation. Finally, Sect. 7 concludes the paper and points out some future work.

2   Android in a Nutshell

Android is made by a layered architecture (see Fig. 1) where the top layer hosts both system and user apps. System apps come with the Android distribution itself and provide basic functionality (e.g., calendar, email, ...), while user apps are packed into compressed archives (i.e., the `APKs`) and made available to users on different external sources (e.g., app markets or web sites). Below the app layer lies the Application Framework that provides a set of modular components that apps can use to access system and device resources.

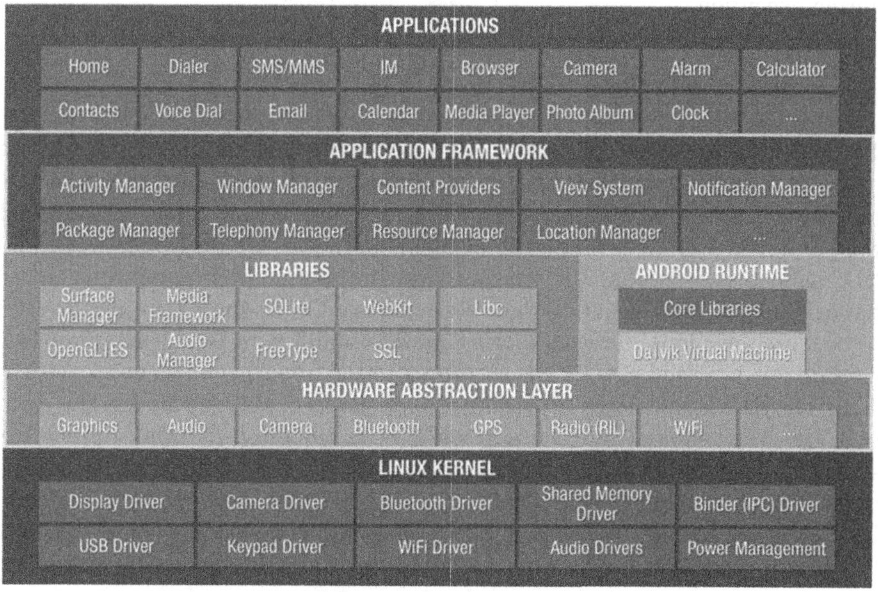

Fig. 1. The Android OS architecture.

---

[1] Freely available at: http://www.csec.it/riskindroid.

Android also contains a set of C/C++ native libraries granting optimized core services (e.g., DBMS, 2D/3D graphics, Codecs, ...). The Android Runtime provides virtual machines to execute the apps bytecode. The Hardware Abstraction Layer (HAL) is a set of libraries allowing the Application Framework to access the actual hardware. The Linux Kernel is at the bottom of the architecture and grants basic OS functionality as Interprocess Communication (IPC), memory and process management.

Security and Permissions. Android assigns a unique Linux user ID at Kernel layer to each app upon installation, thereby *sandboxing* the execution of apps in separate Linux users. Android authorizes apps to access core system resources through *Android Permissions* (hereafter, APs) that are required by the app and granted by the user upon installation or at runtime[2]. APs are declared in an XML file, i.e., the *Android Manifest*, contained in the APK. To get services from core Android APIs, the app should have the corresponding AP. There currently exist more than 130 APs[3], divided into four categories, namely, (1) *Normal*, i.e., basic authorizations that are automatically provided by the system upon installation, (2) *Dangerous*, required for accessing core APIs, they are granted by the user, (3) *Signature*, granted to apps signed by the same developer, and (4) *SignatureOrSystem*, automatically granted to system apps. We refer to the whole set of Android permissions as APSet. Apps are expected to require the least set of permissions sufficient to work properly, albeit they are often overprivileged [2]. Apps can also be underprivileged, but in this case they are expected to fail during execution.

3   Related Work

The scientific literature related to risk analysis of Android apps is rather limited and mostly focused on APs, so we also take into account works regarding malware classification because we expect to see some relationships between malware and high risk apps. Currently available proposals are probabilistic, i.e., the RIV indicates the probability that an app can be a malware, according to statistical analysis carried out on datasets containing both apps (that are expected to be mostly benign) and well-known malware samples. In [3], authors propose a method for detecting *risk signals* according to the frequency of security-sensitive APs. The RIV is calculated according to bayesian probabilistic models that compare the APs required by each app with those requested by other apps in the same category (that must be known a priori). Furthermore, authors define three properties that should be granted by any probabilistic function calculating a RIV for apps, namely, (i) *monotonicity* (i.e., removing an AP should lower the RIV), (ii) *coherence* (i.e., malware should have higher RIVs than apps), and

---

[2] It depends on the Android version. Older Android versions (<v. 6) require all permissions to be granted at install time, while newer versions allow the user to grant them dynamically at runtime.

[3] https://developer.android.com/guide/topics/manifest/permission-element.html.

(iii) *ease of understanding* (i.e., the RIV of an app should be clearly under-standable to the user, and it should allow straightforward comparison among values).

Also [4] proposes a methodology for calculating a RIV for apps according to their category. More specifically, for each category, the kind and number of required APs are empirically inferred, thereby identifying permission patterns belonging to apps in each category. Then, the RIV is calculated by measuring a *distance* between the set of APs required by the app and the permission patterns of its category. Notwithstanding the encouraging empirical results obtained on a dataset made by 7.737 apps and 1.260 malware samples, the main limitation of the approach is in the need to know in advance the category of the app. Such information can be often unreliable as categories are manually chosen by developers[4]. Maetroid [5] evaluates app risk according to both APs and metadata information related to the developer's reputation and the source app market. The risk is calculated according to declared APs only, and by assigning static weights to each AP. Maetroid does not provide a quantitative RIV, but assigns each app in one (out of three) risk category. A *framework* for app risk analysis is discussed in [6]. It is made by three layers carrying out static, dynamic and behavioral analysis, respectively. The framework combines the results from each layer and builds up the RIV. Unluckily, the framework is purely theoretical and lacks of any empirical evaluation, thereby making difficult to assess the viability of the approach. DroidRisk [7] is a quantitative method for calculating a RIV. DroidRisk is trained on a set of 27.274 apps and 1.260 malware samples, whereby it calculates the distribution of declared APs (i.e., those contained in the *Android Manifest* file). Then, DroidRisk applies a probabilistic function that calculates a RIV according to the kind and the potential impact of APs required by the app. More specifically, DroidRisk calculates a RIV for an app A according to two values for each AP p_i, namely the probability and the impact. Slightly extending the original notation, given a set of APs S, the probability $L(p_i, S)$ is the probability that $p_i \in S$ is required in the dataset, i.e., the number of apps requiring p_i on the total set of apps in the dataset; the impact $I(p_i, S)$ is a weight statically applied to each $p_i \in S$ according to its category (i.e., $I(p_i, N) = 1$, $I(p_i, D) = 1.5$, where N stands for the set of *Normal* APs and D for the set of *Dangerous* ones). Then, the RIV R_A for an app A is calculated as $\sum_{p_i \in \{N \uplus D\}} (L(p_i, \{N \uplus D\}) * I(p_i, \{N \uplus D\}))$, where $\uplus$ indicates the *disjoint union* between N and D.

Discussion. We argue that probabilistic methods suffer from some limitations.

1. They are unable to recognize as dangerous the malware that require a limited set of APs; conversely, they averagely provide high RIVs for apps requiring many APs.
2. Current proposals deal with declared APs only, without deepening, for instance, which APs are actually exploited by the app. Due to the

---

[4] https://support.google.com/googleplay/android-developer/answer/113475?hl=en.

monotonicity of probabilistic risk indexes, relying only on declared permissions can impact the reliability, as apps are often overprivileged by their developers [2] and can therefore obtain too high RIVs.

3. Probabilistic methods statically define the impact of APs, that is, all APs belonging to the same category (e.g., *Normal*, *Dangerous*, *Signature*, *SignatureOrSystem*) equally impact the estimation of the RIV. This choice does not allow to provide different impacts to APs, e.g., according to their distribution on the set of malware.

4. The validity of RIV is strictly dependent with the chosen dataset, as well as the ratio between apps and malware samples; therefore, the dataset should be large enough - w.r.t. the set of available apps and malware samples - to be statistically significant to calculate a reliable RIV.

We argue that more reliable RIVs can be obtained through a machine learning approach based on

- four sets of permissions for each app A, namely
  1. *Declared* Permissions (DAP_A), i.e., declared in the Android Manifest file;
  2. *Exploited* permissions (EAP_A), i.e., APs that are actually exploited in the app code;
  3. *Ghost* permissions (GAP_A), i.e., APs that the app tries to exploit in the code, but they are not declared in the Android Manifest file;
  4. *Useless* permissions (UAP_A), i.e., declared APs that are not exploited in the app code.
- a statistically significant dataset. Our dataset is made by 112.425 apps and 6.707 malware samples from different sources. In details, apps comes from the Google Play Store[5] (98.162 apps), Aptoide[6] (7.516 apps), and Uptodown[7] (6.747 apps). Malware samples have been mostly taken from the DREBIN dataset [8] (5.560 samples); the remaining samples come from publicly available repositories, namely the Contagio dataset [9], the Husted's dataset [10] and the Bhatia's dataset [11].
- *dynamic impact* for each AP, calculated on the basis of its distribution on the whole dataset. The aim is to weigh APs according to their statistical distribution over malware samples and apps.

4   Reliability of Probabilistic Risk Indexes

In this section, we empirically evaluate the reliability of RIVs calculated through probabilistic methods. To this aim, we extend the methodology proposed in [7] by introducing the notion of **dynamic impacts**. Dynamic impacts allow to take into account the characteristics of a statistically significant dataset in the calculation of a probabilistic RIV. It is worth noting that all current proposals adopt static impacts, i.e., defined according to some heuristics but independently from the characteristics of the dataset. In order to apply dynamic impacts, an extensive statistical analysis on the dataset must be carried out in advance.

---

[5] http://play.google.com/store/apps.

[6] http://www.aptoide.com/page/apps.

[7] http://en.uptodown.com/android.

4.1 Statistical Analysis on APs

We took into account the dataset described in the previous section, i.e., made by 112.425 apps and 6.707 malware samples. We systematically extracted information on the four sets of permissions from each app in the dataset. We built a Permission Checker tool that given an app A (i.e., an APK file) in input, it provides back statistics on each AP set. DAP_A is straightforwardly retrievable from the *Android Manifest* file, while EAP_A, GAP_A and UAP_A are inferred through static analysis. More in details, the Permission Checker carries out reverse engineering on the APK to retrieve the app bytecode. Then, for each method invocation in the bytecode, the Permission Checker analyzes the APs required to execute the method. In the end, the Permission Checker builds a set PS_A containing all APs exploited in the bytecode. Remaining sets are built as follows:

- $EAP_A = \{p_i | p_i \in DAP_A \wedge p_i \in PS_A\}$;
- $GAP_A = \{p_i | p_i \notin DAP_A \wedge p_i \in PS_A\}$;
- $UAP_A = \{p_i | p_i \in DAP_A \wedge p_i \notin PS_A\}$;

We indicate with DAP, EAP, GAP, and UAP, the disjoint union of single app permissions sets, for all apps in the dataset, namely: $DAP = \biguplus_A DAP_A$, $EAP = \biguplus_A EAP_A$, $GAP = \biguplus_A GAP_A$, and $UAP = \biguplus_A UAP_A$.

Table 1. Statistics on APs on the dataset

AP Set	MALWARE			APPS		
	MAX AP	AVG AP	Std. dev.	MAX AP	AVG AP	Std. dev.
DAP	87	10.67	5.76	96	5.84	4.39
EAP	15	4.25	3.19	24	3.81	2.40
GAP	9	1.15	1.26	23	2.9	2.11
UAP	84	6.42	4.58	91	2.03	2.78

Discussion. Table 1 summarizes global statistics on the four AP sets. Such values indicate that malware declare more APs than apps on average (i.e., 10.67 vs. 5.84) but they exploit very few of them (i.e., 4.25). Furthermore, malware seldom try to exploit undeclared APs ($AVG_{GAP} = 1.15$) in comparison to apps ($AVG_{GAP} = 2.9$). Figures 2 and 3 show the distribution of the top ten APs for malware and apps, respectively. For each AP, the y-axis shows the percentage of malware/apps having the AP.

Some APs related to networking are equally divided between malware and apps, e.g., INTERNET, ACCESS_NETWORK_STATE and ACCESS_WIFI_STATE; since apps often require to connect to Internet, it is difficult to evaluate the RIV according to these APs. Other APs are required more frequently by malware than apps; for instance, a comparison between DAP plots in

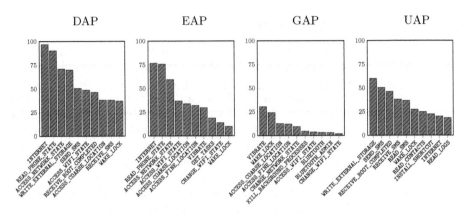

Fig. 2. Top 10 APs for malware

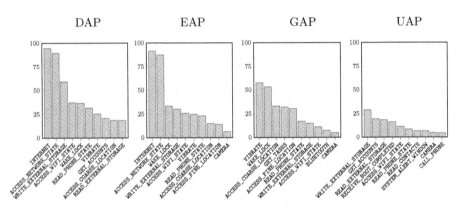

Fig. 3. Top 10 APs for apps

Figs. 2 and 3 suggests that an app requiring the READ_PHONE_STATE, the RECEIVE_BOOT_COMPLETED and the READ_CONTACTS could be potentially dangerous. The biggest gap between malware and apps is related to SMS APs; in fact, as shown in the DAP plot of Fig. 2, 2 out of 10 APs deal with SMS (i.e., SEND_SMS and RECEIVE_SMS), while no SMS-related APs appear in the DAP plot of Fig. 3. It is worth noticing that albeit almost 50% of malware require SEND_SMS, and more than 40% require RECEIVE_SMS, they seldom exploit them (as shown by the absence of such APs in the corresponding EAP set)[8].

4.2   Dynamic Impacts

We argue that calculating a RIV according to the distribution of APs on malware and apps in the dataset may improve the accuracy of current probabilistic risk

---
[8] Complete statistics are available at: http://www.csec.it/riskindroid.

indexes. To empirically assess this thesis, we apply the probabilistic method proposed in DroidRisk [7] on our dataset using both static and dynamic impacts. We consider static impacts as defined in the original DroidRisk paper, namely, $I(p_i, N) = 1$ for p_i being a *Normal* AP, and $I(p_i, D) = 1.5$ for p_i being a *Dangerous* one. We define a dynamic impact as follows:

$$I(p_i, S) = \frac{P(p_i|M, S)}{P(p_i|A, S)} \tag{1}$$

being $P(p_i|M, S)$ the probability that a malware requires p_i in the set S, and $P(p_i|A, S)$ the probability that an app requires p_i in the same set S. In this way, the impact value increases as APs are more often required by malware than apps, and vice versa. Note that also in this case, the probability for p_i is calculated as the number of malware/apps requiring p_i on the total number of malware/apps in the dataset. It is also worth noting that the value of dynamic impacts is independent from the AP category. Since DroidRisk takes into consideration only declared permissions, we calculated dynamic impacts only for declared APs, i.e., $I(p_i, DAP)$. Table 2 shows an excerpt of dynamic impacts w.r.t. the dataset.

Table 2. Dynamic impacts for DAP on the full dataset.

AP values in DAP	$P(p_i|M, DAP)$	$P(p_i|A, DAP)$	Dyn. Imp.	AP values in DAP	$P(p_i|M, DAP)$	$P(p_i|A, DAP)$	Dyn. Imp.
INTERNET	96.66	94.83	1.02	READ_PHONE_STATE	90.04	30.97	2.91
ACCESS_NETWORK_STATE	70.84	89.32	0.79	WRITE_EXTERNAL_STORAGE	69.79	58.49	1.19
SEND_SMS	50.45	1.83	27.51	ACCESS_WIFI_STATE	48.61	36.02	1.35
RECEIVE_BOOT_COMPLETED	46.31	14.55	3.18	ACCESS_COARSE_LOCATION	38.03	18.26	2.08
RECEIVE_SMS	37.93	1.80	21.02	READ_SMS	36.72	1.48	24.88
ACCESS_FINE_LOCATION	36.29	16.77	2.16	READ_EXTERNAL_STORAGE	6.38	17.38	0.37
READ_CONTACTS	24.66	5.73	4.31	READ_CALL_LOG	0.46	0.91	0.51
READ_SYNC_SETTINGS	0.60	0.73	0.82	WRITE_SYNC_SETTINGS	0.72	0.78	0.92
RECORD_AUDIO	12.26	5.40	2.27	READ_CALL_LOG	0.46	0.91	0.51
READ_CALENDAR	10.97	1.16	9.44	NFC	0.03	0.61	0.05

4.3 Evaluating Probabilistic Methods

We carry out an empirical assessment aimed at evaluating (i) if the usage of dynamic impacts could improve the quality of probabilistic RIV, (ii) to which extent probabilistic methods are reliable, and (iii) understand potential improvements towards more reliable RIVs.

Discussion. Our analysis indicates that the average RIV for apps is slightly lower with static impacts (i.e., 52.87 vs. 58.43); on malware, this gap is wider (i.e., 71.29 vs. 86.10). Figure 4 shows the RIV distribution for both malware and apps in the dataset based on static and dynamic impacts. We consider 20 classes of RIVs, each comprising all apps having a RIV between $5i$ and $5i + 5\%$, where $i \in \{0, \dots, 19\}$. The x-axis of each plot indicates the RIV, while the y-axis indicates the number of RIVs in each class. It is worth noting that in both cases malware have higher RIV on average, thereby suggesting that

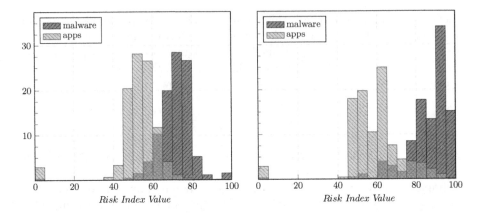

Fig. 4. Risk Index Values with static (left) and dynamic (right) impacts.

probabilistic methods are reliable in principle. However, our results also bring out their limitations. First, malware and apps histograms in Fig. 4 often overlap, thereby indicating that probabilistic methods may sometimes provide similar RIVs for malware and apps. In this case, the reliability of RIV depends on the gap between the overlapping histograms. For instance, let us consider the 60%–65% class for static impacts, where both histograms are almost equal; this indicates that each app having a RIV in this interval have rather the same chance to be a malware or not: this would be acceptable for RIVs around 50% only. Dynamic impacts allow to keep the gap in each class wider, at the cost of widening the overlap interval (i.e., histograms overlap from 50% and 80% with static impacts, and from 40% to 95% for dynamic impacts). Furthermore, RIV is averagely high for apps (>40%) and it does not span on the whole value interval (i.e., from 0% to 100%). Finally, as previously conjectured, probabilistic methods are unable to recognize as risky the malware that declare few or none APs (consider the overlap on class 0%–5% in both plots).

5   RiskInDroid: A Machine Learning-Based Risk Index

We argue that the intrinsic limitations of probabilistic methods applied to APs can be overcome by machine learning techniques able to build up more reliable RIVs. In this section we present the methodology at the basis of RiskIn-Droid, then we provide an extensive empirical assessment of the tool.

5.1   Methodology

Machine learning techniques are used for classifying elements, i.e., given a set of classes, they evaluate each element and assign a class to it. Therefore, they are particularly suitable for binary classification of malware. However, some techniques also provide a probability value related to the prediction. We leverage machine learning techniques to classify apps into two classes, i.e., *malware* and *non malware*, and we use the classification probability to build up a RIV. For our purpose, we adopt the *scikit-learn* library [12], that implements a set of machine learning techniques and provides a probability function for some of them.

Machine learning techniques require feature vectors to compare and classify elements. In our context, elements are apps, and features are APs. We define feature vectors as follows: given $APSet$ the set of APs, for each app A we define four feature vectors FV_S^A, with $S \in \{DAP_A, EAP_A, GAP_A, UAP_A\}$. Each FV is a binary vector of cardinality —APSet—, where $FV_S^A[i] = 1$ if $p_i \in S$, and $FV_S^A[i] = 0$ otherwise. We adopt a supervised learning approach. Supervised learning requires classifiers to be trained on a training set before being applied to classify new elements. We train a set of supervised classifiers on a subset of the dataset and then we use them to classify the remaining APKs.

5.2 Selection of Classifiers

The scikit-learn library implements 15 *supervised* classifiers with probability estimation, which means that they adopt proper techniques to provide a probability value for each classification result (also for algorithms that do not natively provide a probability on classification like, e.g., SVM and Decision Trees). In order to choose the more reliable ones, we empirically evaluated them on three sets randomly extracted from the dataset and containing the same number of apps and malware samples each (i.e., 6.707 malware samples and 6.707 apps), considering only DAP as permission set. We select classifiers according to three empirical rules:

1. **Accuracy > 90%**, in order to discard the less reliable classifiers.
2. **4% < AVG Score < 95%**, to avoid binary classifiers, i.e., that tend to provide scores around 100% for malware and 0% for apps.
3. **5% < Std. Dev.** to exclude classifiers that distribute in a little subset of the whole interval.

We evaluated the classifiers (using the default parameters provided by scikit-learn) by applying the `K-fold cross validation` [13] with $K = 10$. In a nutshell, the K-fold cross validation (see Fig. 5 for an example with $K = 4$) is an iterative statistical method where the dataset is divided into K independent sets (i.e., *folds*), each with approximately the same number of elements. At each iteration on K, the ith fold acts as the *testing set*, while the remaining $k - 1$ folds form the training set. The testing set is used to validate the model built through the training set. The accuracy value is calculated according to the number of samples in the testing set whose class have been predicted correctly. The advantage of K-fold cross validation is that all samples are used both to train and to test the model, thereby reducing the *overfitting* problem that occurs when a model classifies correctly in the training set but not in the testing one.

At each iteration, a classifier is trained on a training set of about 1342 elements (i.e., 671 apps and 671 malware samples) and tested with the remaining

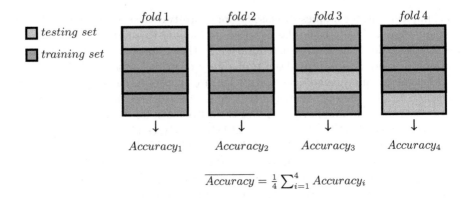

$$\overline{Accuracy} = \frac{1}{4} \sum_{i=1}^{4} Accuracy_i$$

Fig. 5. Example of 4-*fold cross validation*

Table 3. Empirical evaluation of classifiers in the *scikit-learn* library

Classifier	AVG accuracy	Malware		Apps	
		AVG Score	σ	AVG Score	σ
Support Vector Machines (SVM)	94.89	94.83	7.42	4.73	8.34
Gaussian Naive Bayes (GNB)	84.64	99.87	1.82	0.05	1.11
Multinomial Naive Bayes (MNB)	90.69	94.88	7.65	4.89	6.29
Bernoulli Naive Bayes (BNB)	89.97	99.07	4.87	0.69	4.19
Decision Tree (DT)	95.68	99.68	3.29	0.73	3.62
Random Forest (RF)	96.73	97.31	8.19	4.09	8.87
AdaBoost (AB)	94.19	52.83	1.45	47.48	1.44
Gradient Boosting (GB)	95.11	94.28	8.99	6.88	10.26
Stochastic Gradient Descent (SGD)	93.62	97.61	6.89	4.80	9.30
Logistic Regression (LR)	94.96	93.36	8.23	4.85	9.38
Logistic Regression CV (LR-CV)	94.93	96.41	8.21	4.71	9.21
K-Nearest Neighbors (K-NN)	94.29	98.69	6.22	4.82	11.34
Linear Discriminant Analysis (LDA)	93.88	98.11	6.42	1.93	6.18
Quadratic Discriminant Analysis (QDA)	78.18	100	0.31	0.06	1.32
Multilayer Perceptron Neural Network (MPNN)	97.06	99.12	4.31	1.68	5.51

9 sets, assuming that a score (i.e., the probability associated with the classification) $\geq 50\%$ implies recognizing the element as malware, while a score $<50\%$ implies that the element is not malware. By comparing the nature of the element with its classification, we are able to recognize the correctness of the evaluation. The accuracy value is calculated as the ratio between the number of correct classifications on the total number of classified elements. The average score and standard deviation (i.e., σ) statistics are calculated on the classification probabilities returned by classifiers in the testing phase. Results are reported in Table 3. Since all classifiers had a very similar behavior on all three sets, we report the average value for each metric.

Discussion. GNB, BNB and QDA grant low accuracy, while DT, RF, SGD, LR-CV, K-NN, LDA and MPNN have too high average score for apps. Finally,

Table 4. Average RIV calculated by probabilistic methods and RiskInDroid.

APK category	Static impacts	Dynamic impacts	RiskInDroid
Malware	71.29	86.10	84.34
Apps	52.87	58.43	16.89

AB has a low standard deviation and provides similar scores for malware and apps (i.e., from 47% to 53% in both cases). Only four classifiers meet all requirements, namely, SVM, MNB, GB and LR. Therefore, we chose to adopt them in RiskInDroid.

6 Experimental Results

RiskInDroid has been developed in Python and implements the selected four classifiers. For each app A, RiskInDroid calculates the RIV on all four APs sets (i.e., DAP_A, EAP_A, GAP_A, and UAP_A), by combining the corresponding feature vectors in a unique one, i.e., $FV_{all}^A = FV_{DAP_A}^A \| FV_{EAP_A}^A \| FV_{GAP_A}^A \| FV_{UAP_A}^A$. The RIV is calculated as the average score value of all four classifiers. To train each classifier in RiskInDroid, we applied the 10-fold cross validation on one of the three sets used to evaluate the classifiers. We also used the same set to empirically assess whether applying all four APs sets may improve the accuracy. To this aim, our tests returned the following average accuracy values: 92.93% for DAP, 88.36% for EAP, 79.12% for GAP, 91.09% for UAP, and 94.87% for all sets. Therefore, we chose to consider all sets.

Discussion. Table 4 shows the average RIV calculated by RiskInDroid, w.r.t. probabilistic methods in the previously discussed configurations. RiskIn-

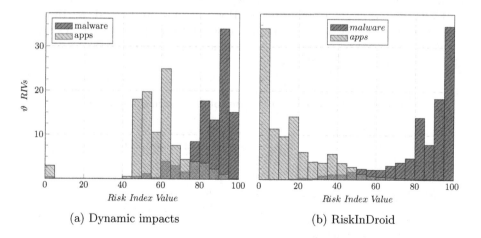

(a) Dynamic impacts   (b) RiskInDroid

Fig. 6. Distribution of RIV: probabilistic methods vs RiskInDroid.

Droid substantially lowers the average RIV for apps. Figure 6 compares the distribution of RIVs with probabilistic methods based on dynamic impacts and RiskInDroid. The latter distributes RIVs on the whole risk interval, and restricts the histogram overlapping in the center of the interval. This is reasonable as the median value implies the maximum uncertainty (i.e., $RIV = 50\%$ means that the APK has the same probability to be malware or not).

RiskInDroid and Malware Detection. We further evaluated the reliability of RIVs by assessing the relationship between apps with high RIVs and malware. More in detail, we selected all apps having RIV > 75%, and we analyzed them through VirusTotal[9], a free suite hosting more than 50 online antivirus. Such antivirus are *signature-based*, i.e., they compare the app with a set of known malware footprints. For each analysis, VirusTotal also provides the number of antivirus (i.e., *flags*) recognizing the submitted APK as malware.

Table 5 summarizes the results. They indicate that the methodology at the basis of RiskInDroid is promising and the corresponding RIVs are reliable, since some apps having high RIV are also recognized as malware by VirusTotal. However, it is worth pointing out that high RIV does not necessarily imply that an app is malware. For instance, social network apps require a lot of dangerous permissions and manage user data; such apps are risky for the security and privacy of the end user, but they are not malware. Finally, the experiments with VirusTotal indicate that apps from Google Play are less likely to be malware w.r.t. those provided by Aptoide and Uptodown: this is an expected result as Google Play carries out security assessments on its apps[10].

Performance of RiskInDroid. The performance of RiskInDroid has been evaluated on a general purpose desktop PC equipped with an Intel i7-3635QM @ 3.40 GHz, and 16 GB RAM. Table 6 summarizes the results. Performance of classifiers is evaluated in terms of average time and standard deviation, during the training and the testing phase. Using all sets decreases the average performance up to 240% during the training phase. However, it is worth noticing that this phase is executed once at the beginning. Instead, the testing phase is very quick and lasts in few millisecs both with one and all sets, thereby suggesting to adopt all four sets to obtain a higher accuracy.

Table 5. App analysis with VirusTotal: Experimental Results.

APK source	# apps with RIV >75%	% of apps with Flags > X				
		Flags > 1	Flags > 3	Flags > 5	Flags > 10	Flags > 15
Google Play	635	14.6%	9.4%	8.7%	7.8%	7.1%
Aptoide	125	26.5%	12.6%	123%	12%	8.5%
Uptodown	86	24.4%	15.6%	8.9%	4.4%	2.2%

---

[9] http://www.virustotal.com.
[10] http://googlemobile.blogspot.it/2012/02/android-and-security.html.

Table 6. Performance of RiskInDroid on a set of 13.414 APKs (6.707 apps and 6.707 malware samples)

Classifiers	Training phase				Testing phase			
	DAP only		All sets		DAP only		All sets	
	AVG T [ms]	σ [ms]	AVG T [ms]	σ	AVG T [ms]	σ [ms]	AVG T	σ [ms]
SVM	43460	60	97170	870	15	4	18	5
MNB	32	4	53	11	6	3	7	3
GB	5620	52	21806	403	9	3	11	5
LR	81	9	188	11	4	2	5	2
Total	**49193**	**67**	**119220**	**890**	**34**	**12**	**41**	**15**

7   Conclusion and Future Work

In this paper we empirically assessed the reliability of probabilistic risk index approaches for Android apps, and we proposed a novel methodology based on machine learning aimed at overcoming the shortcomings of the probabilistic solutions. We implemented the methodology in a tool, RiskInDroid, that we empirically evaluated. Future development of this research includes extending the feature set beyond APs, by taking into account suspicious API calls and URLs, both recognizable in the bytecode through the static analysis technique we adopted to build the permission sets.

References

1. Gartner. Gartner Says Five of Top. 10 Worldwide Mobile Phone Vendors Increased Sales in Second Quarter of 2016
2. Felt, A.P., Chin, E., Hanna, S., Song, D., Wagner, D.: Android permissions demystified. In: Proceedings of the 18th ACM Conference on Computer and Communications Security (CCS 2011), New York, NY, USA, pp. 627–638. ACM (2011)
3. Gates, C.S., Li, N., Peng, H., Sarma, B., Qi, Y., Potharaju, R., Nita-Rotaru, C., Molloy, I.: Generating summary risk scores for mobile applications. IEEE Trans. Dependable Sec. Comput. **11**(3), 238–251 (2014)
4. Hao, H., Li, Z., Yu, H.: An effective approach to measuring and assessing the risk of android application. In: 2015 International Symposium on Theoretical Aspects of Software Engineering (TASE), pp. 31–38. IEEE (2015)
5. Dini, G., Martinelli, F., Matteucci, I., Petrocchi, M., Saracino, A., Sgandurra, D.: Risk analysis of android applications: a user-centric solution. Future Gener. Comput. Syst. (2016). doi:10.1016/j.future.2016.05.035
6. Li, S., Tryfonas, T., Russell, G., Andriotis, P.: Risk assessment for mobile systems through a multilayered hierarchical bayesian network (2016)
7. Wang, Y., Zheng, J., Sun, C., Mukkamala, S.: Quantitative security risk assessment of android permissions and applications. In: Wang, L., Shafiq, B. (eds.) DBSec 2013. LNCS, vol. 7964, pp. 226–241. Springer, Heidelberg (2013). doi:10.1007/978-3-642-39256-6_15

8. Arp, D., Spreitzenbarth, M., Hubner, M., Gascon, H., Rieck, K.: DREBIN: effective and explainable detection of android malware in your pocket. In: NDSS (2014)
9. Contagio mobile malware mini dump. http://contagiominidump.blogspot.com/. Accessed 6 Apr 2017
10. Husted, N.: Android malware dataset (2011)
11. Bhatia, A.: Collection of android malware samples (2016)
12. Pedregosa, F., Varoquaux, G., Gramfort, A., Michel, V., Thirion, B., Grisel, O., Blondel, M., Prettenhofer, P., Weiss, R., Dubourg, V., Vanderplas, J., Passos, A., Cournapeau, D., Brucher, M., Perrot, M., Duchesnay, E.: Scikit-learn: machine learning in python. J. Mach. Learn. Res. **12**, 2825–2830 (2011)
13. James, G., Witten, D., Hastie, T., Tibshirani, R.: An Introduction to Statistical Learning: With Applications in R. Springer, New York (2014)

Using Fraud Patterns for Fraud Risk Assessment of E-services

Ahmed Seid Yesuf[(✉)], Jetzabel Serna-Olvera, and Kai Rannenberg

Deutsche Telekom Chair of Mobile Business & Multilateral Security,
Goethe University Frankfurt, Frankfurt am Main, Germany
{ahmed.yesuf,jetzabel.serna,kai.rannenberg}@m-chair.de
http://www.m-chair.de

Abstract. Every year, e-service providers report losses of billions of dollars due to fraud. Despite their huge efforts in implementing sophisticated fraud detection systems on top of their e-services, fraud effects seem to be rather increasing than decreasing. As a result, *fraud risk assessment* has been introduced as a fundamental part of e-service providers' prevention strategies. In particular, identifying potential fraud risks and estimating their impacts are two essential requirements to prevent fraud risks while developing and delivering e-services to customers. In this paper, we show that *fraud patterns* can be used to perform fraud risk assessment. We analysed real fraud incidents from an e-service domain – Telecom, and identified six fraud patterns, which are recurrently used to commit fraud. We then use those patterns in the same scenario in order to demonstrate their applicability to fraud risk assessment.

Keywords: Fraud pattern · Risk assessment · Security · Fraud · E-service

1 Introduction

Over the past years, security and risk assessment have become essential requirements in the successful development of information systems and electronic services of enterprises [1]. In particular, since e-services (e.g. Internet marketing, telecommunication services and banking services) are delivered using technological means, it is of utmost importance to perform risk assessment in order to minimise or even prevent risks. One of the most relevant forms of risks which prevail in a wide range of e-service domains is fraud risk [2]. Fraud risk is a complex combination of social, financial and technological risks including misuses resulting from the flaws and weaknesses of e-services themselves. Therefore, preventing fraud is extremely relevant, since fraud negatively affects the global e-service revenue; for instance, in 2015, fraud affected the global Telecom revenue by almost $38.1 billion (USD) [3]. Thus, risk assessment is essential not only to counter fraud but also to keep e-services profitable and secured [4,5].

© IFIP International Federation for Information Processing 2017
Published by Springer International Publishing AG 2017. All Rights Reserved
S. De Capitani di Vimercati and F. Martinelli (Eds.): SEC 2017, IFIP AICT 502, pp. 553–567, 2017.
DOI: 10.1007/978-3-319-58469-0_37

Typically, frauds are perpetrated by individuals, organised groups of individuals, employees or third parties with a set of goals targeting the weak parts of e-services [6]. For an individual who has a service contract with a service provider and uses it for individual purposes, the goal of perpetrating fraud is limited to individual benefit (e.g. using the service without/little payment). Beyond the individual benefit, organised fraudsters can potentially disrupt the business process of an enterprise (e.g. by colluding with third parties). In order to achieve their goals, they target customers, infrastructures of service providers (e.g. Private Branch Exchange – PBX systems), the service or product itself (e.g. service plan, credit card) and the entities involved in the process of delivering the e-services.

Until recently, a number of researches has focused on fraud detection methods such as [7–9]. In [2,6], authors present an extensive review and comparison of fraud detection approaches. Contrary to the many approaches which exist in fraud detection, fraud risk assessment has not been the target of many works. Authors in [10,11] have focused on fraud risk assessment. They proposed a value-based approach which can be used to identify and prioritise frauds, in particular, those occurring due to collusion with third parties. Although authors identified and focused on one of the most recurrent patterns that fraudsters use, they pointed out the need of performing fraud risk assessment with other types of fraud patterns in order to strengthen the security of e-services.

Considering that and given the wide range of methods and techniques to perpetrate fraud in e-services, fraudsters are able to use common but interchangeable patterns to achieve their goals. Thus, in this paper, we identify six fraud patterns from an e-service domain – the Telecom services. We therefore demonstrate how fraud patterns could be used to perform risk assessment of e-services and serve as a tool for preventing fraud risks.

The rest of the paper is organised as follows. Section 2 highlights concepts of fraud, e-services and fraud assessment in e-service. Section 3 presents the main methodology followed to produce the fraud patterns and use them towards fraud risk assessment. Section 4 describes the fraud domain model used to ease the interpretation of frauds. Section 5 presents an overview of the fraud incidents observed to identify the fraud patterns. Section 6 presents the identified fraud patterns followed by the application of the fraud patterns in a given scenario, namely Telecom services, which is then introduced in Sect. 7. Section 8 discusses the main advantages of this approach and highlights the open challenges and the limitations of the proposed approach; followed by the main conclusions of this paper in Sect. 9.

2   Background

2.1   Fraud Risk in E-services

Fraud has several meanings that depend on the contexts. According to the Fraud Advisory Panel (www.fraudadvisorypanel.org), an anti-fraud community based in England, "fraud is the deliberate use of deception or dishonesty to deprive, disadvantage or cause loss (usually financial) to another person or party". While this definition can be applied to a wide extent of auditing fraud, the Communication Fraud Control Association (CFCA) [3] has defined fraud as "the use of telecommunication services or products with no intention of payment". Therefore, fraud risks in e-services are understood as events that allow fraudsters to misuse the service either to gain personal benefit or to the benefit of organised fraudsters. In this paper, we focus and explore those fraud risks that have impact on the service providers from the perspective of fraudsters.

2.2 Fraud Risk Assessment

Based on ISO 31000 [12], the risk management process includes five processes: establish context, risk assessment, risk treatment, monitoring and review, and communication and consulting. Risk assessment is an integral part of the risk management process, which is the concept of managing risks against enterprise objectives. More specifically, fraud risk assessment (FRA) is defined as the process of identifying, analysing and estimating fraud risks in a service.

Considering the impact of fraud on service providers, it is essential to prevent, detect and prepare the appropriate counter-measures. There exist a number of different approaches for fraud detection [2,6]; however, preventing fraud through identifying and analysing business processes, transaction flows and other entities, still lacks the focus of the research community [4].

2.3 Fraud Patterns

The concept of patterns for security was initially introduced by Yoder and Barcalow [13]. The authors proposed seven security patterns that software developers should consider when developing their software applications. Since then, different types of security patterns were proposed (e.g. patterns for cryptography and access control [14]). "A security pattern describes a particular recurring security problem that arises in specific contexts, and presents a well-demonstrated generic solution for it" [15]. As such, the use of patterns has benefited security in several areas including software development. Inspired by this concept, we developed fraud patterns from the recurring fraud risks in the e-service domain. Fraud patterns not only help to describe recurring fraud risks in e-services but increase the potential of having in place preventive solutions. As a first step we have focused on the identification of the most relevant fraud risks.

3 Methodology

The whole process of a service provider from services delivery to the service payment process can be considered as a system. In such systems, one of the main challenges that directly or indirectly affect the revenue of service providers is fraud. Fraud risks are enabled when the weaknesses of the valuable assets (including their service) of service providers are exploited by fraudsters. Fraud risk assessment (FRA) is an approach to reduce the effects of fraud risks substantially – which is the goal of service providers. To develop a FRA approach, it is necessary to first develop a domain model or ontology of concepts related to fraud risks of such systems. Thus, we first adopted and extended the model introduced by [16]. By extending this model, we were able to develop a domain model specific for FRA. The domain modelling allowed us to better describe fraud risks in a particular domain. We considered the Telecom domain, and analysed five real fraud incidents in this domain. The analysed fraud incidents are business-related and are the result of different types of Telecom services (e.g., voice, PBX, roaming and Internet services). To develop the patterns, we applied the FRA domain modelling and interpreted the real fraud incidents. We identified six recurring and relevant patterns currently used by most fraudsters and actually present in more than one fraud incident. Finally, the applicability of the identified patterns is demonstrated by modelling the entities involved in the use case (Telecom domain scenario) and directly applying the fraud patterns to the model.

4   Fraud Risk Assessment Domain Model

In Information Systems Security Risk Management (ISSRM) [16] there exist different concepts that can easily be interpreted as concepts of FRA. The three groups of concepts mentioned in ISSRM – risk-based, asset-based and treatment-based concepts – could be adapted to the FRA domain model into concepts of fraud, assets and preventive measures. Based on this model, we defined a FRA domain model as shown in Fig. 1.

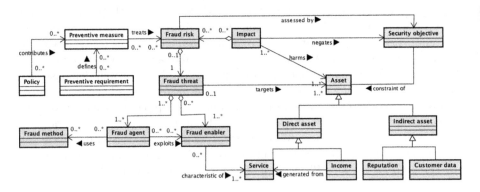

Fig. 1. Domain model for FRA (Fraud Risk Assessment): From left to right – *concepts of preventive measures, concepts of fraud and concepts of assets*

Concepts Related to Fraud

- *Fraud enabler* – is the potential weakness or possibility that enables a fraud to happen when exploited by a fraud agent.

- *Fraud agent* – is a fraudster or attacker who acts as an agent to perpetrate the fraud. A fraud agent uses fraud method and exploits fraud enablers.
- *Fraud method* – is an approach that a fraud agent follows to perpetrate the fraud.
- *Fraud threat* – is the combination of fraud agent and one or more fraud enablers. It targets one or more assets and its frequency/likelihood contribute for a fraud risk to happen.
- *Fraud risk* – is the combination of a fraud threat with one or more fraud enablers which negatively impacts one or more of the assets – direct or indirect assets.
- *Impact* – the negative effect of a fraud risk that harms one or more of the assets of the service provider. The impact on service provider can be interpreted in terms of money or reputation, by which both affect the revenue of the service provider.

Concepts Related to Assets

- An *asset* is any valuable entity of a service provider which could be targeted by one or more fraud agents (attackers/fraudsters); assets can be direct or indirect.

  Direct Assets can be directly estimated when affected by fraud; they include *income* of a service provider or revenue/income for a given *service* (e.g. call, messaging, data, Internet services) by a service provider.
  Indirect Assets cannot be directly estimated when affected by fraud; they include reputation and customer data.
- *Security objective* – is the protection measure that is applied to one or more assets. From the perspective of service providers, the security objectives include protection of direct and indirect assets including confidentiality, integrity and availability of services, prevention of service misuses and customer data protection (privacy).

Concepts Related to Preventive Measures

- *Preventive measure* – is a part of fraud risk management; it is not part of a FRA. We include it into the domain model as it contributes to show the importance of FRA (e.g. preventive requirement specification based on FRA). It describes the treatment approach to a given fraud risk. This can be achieved by:
  producing a *prevention requirement* – potential prevention requirements that need to be implemented in the system to protect the assets of the service provider, and/or
  producing a new or modified *policy* – which is designed based on the assessment results of FRA. It could be enforced at the service level, organisational level, or customer level.

5   Modelling the Telecom E-services Domain

The FRA domain model is applicable to different types of e-service domains (e.g. health insurance, Internet marketing, Telecom), where fraud is part of the risks of the respective services. In this paper, we considered the Telecom domain. In this domain customers subscribe to Telecom services. In the process of delivering the services, the Telecom providers are suffering from different types of frauds leading to important revenue loss [3,17,18].

5.1   Fraud Scenarios

Due to space limitation, we briefly describe the five scenarios spanning different types of real frauds. In the next subsection we further focus on two of the most relevant frauds, which are then interpreted using the domain model in Tables 1 and 2.

Fraud case 1

Name: Service plan misuse with the involvement of a third party
Target: Income of the targeted Telecom service provider
Goal: To gain financial benefit and use the service without payment.

Fraud case 2

Name: Identity theft to use the call-forwarding functionality of (a) post-paid contract(s)
Target: Income of the targeted Telecom service provider
Goal: Call selling, using service without payment

Fraud case 3

Name: Stealing credentials to make unauthorised calls from a PBX system
Target: Credentials of the PBX system and income of the Telecom service provider
Goal: Financial gain (e.g. by call selling) and using service without payment

Fraud case 4

Name: Abusing fixed line network credentials during service set-up process of an Internet access service
Target: Income of the Telecom service provider
Goal: Using service without payment

Fraud case 5

Name: Service plan misuse to perform roaming fraud
Target: Income of the Telecom service provider
Goal: To gain financial benefit

Table 1. Fraud case 3. Stealing credentials to make unauthorised calls from a PBX (Private Branch Exchange) system

Description	A fraudster is able to retrieve a victim's telephony credentials from a PBX and sets up a call divert to a destination number of his choice for the victim's phone number. The fraudster then activates call forwarding to other Telecom destinations – mostly located abroad. The fraudster then makes the highest number of possible parallel calls through the diverted phone number. Calls or forwards triggered by the attacker are billed on a per-minute-basis to the victim's postpaid account. The destination Telecom passes a share of the received call-termination fees to the fraudster, thereby providing a payout per minute for incoming calls as incentive to generate as much incoming traffic as possible to the Telecom network
Fraud enabler	– Vulnerabilities of the PBX – Weak configuration of policies at PBX (e.g. remote access to the PBX) – The availability of Telecom providers that could pay out the income share to the fraud agents who can manage to generate a lot of call traffic to customers of those Telecoms
Fraud agent	A fraudster who is an outsider
Fraud method	Call forwarding, social engineering, impersonation
Fraud threat	Revenue share
Asset	Credentials and income of the service provider
Security objective	Confidentiality of credentials and misuse protection
Fraud risk	– A bill with high cost to the customers – The customer might not pay the bill
Impact	Financial damage and service disruption (unavailability)
Preventive measure	– Implementation of strong PBX policies – Create awareness of social engineering to the customer – PBX maintenance

5.2 Fraud Pattern Development

In order to identify the fraud patterns, we modelled the Telecom domain using the five aforementioned scenarios. We have interpreted these frauds using the fraud domain model developed in Sect. 4. Tables 1 and 2 show the modeling of two of the five scenarios. Note that the goals of fraudsters are diverse, but we only focused on those which have an important effect to the Telecom service provider.

6 Fraud Risk Patterns (FRPs)

Fraud risk patterns (FRPs) are similar to security patterns described in [15,19], which describe a particular recurring *security* problem that arises in specific

Table 2. Fraud case 4. Abusing fixed line network credentials during service set-up process of an Internet access service (DSL connection)

Description	A fraudster orders a land-line Internet connection with a Telecom provider. In doing so, he uses fake customer data. An order confirmation will be sent to the fraudster's address, stating a service connection date. Sometime before a technician visits the place, fixed line network credentials will be sent via letter to the fraudster. The fraudster takes the credential letter as soon as it arrives and uses the respective credentials for SIP authentication, logging on to the TSP's telephony server from another location (securing its anonymity)
Fraud enabler	– Poor identity check – Service availability before the necessary devices are installed
Fraud agent	A fraudster who pretends to be a real customer
Fraud method	– Exploiting poor identity checks – Exploiting the time interval before the service charge is recorded
Fraud threat	Call selling, service distortion and social engineering of service provider
Asset	Income of the service provider
Security objective	Misuse protection
Fraud risk	Impersonation of customers and scamming the service provider
Impact	Financial damage
Preventive measure	– The message conversations between the customer and the service provider should be certified – Start the service once the apparatus is configured – The credentials must be sent only to legal user with certified identify

contexts, and present a well-proven generic solution for it. In our context, we are interested in recurring *fraud risks* against the valuable assets of service providers.

After defining each of the five fraud incidents using the FRA domain model (cf. Sect. 4), we have observed each of the fraud cases and found a list of recurring fraud enablers targeting the assets of the Telecom (e.g. the service itself and the income). Fraud agents (fraudsters) have different goals in perpetrating a fraud, most of them target the Telecom service to gain a lot of money – which indirectly affects the income of the Telecom for that specific service. Each of the fraud cases has security objectives and can mainly be categorised into three security objectives: misuse protection, CIA (confidentiality, integrity and availability) and privacy (data protection). In the process, we produced three groups of FRPs: patterns related to service-misusing, patterns due to system vulnerabilities and patterns related to privacy (data protection). In this paper, we are interested analysing the first two groups of patterns. The FRPs identified below are distributed across the five fraud cases.

Patterns Related to *service-misusing*

FRP 1 – Impersonation (of customers or service providers)
Context. This describes a situation where a fraudster pretends as a legal customer or a representative from a service provider to achieve his/her goal. In the *Fraud case 3*, for instance, the fraudster provides wrong information about his personal information including the address to impersonate a legal customer in order to get credentials necessary to commit the fraud. Beyond this, the fraudster can have a different approach to get the credentials by impersonating the technician of the service provider to get the credentials from a legal customer.
Target. This pattern targets customers and service providers. It is observed in the *Fraud cases 3, 4* and *2*.

FRP 2 – Time interval-based misuses
Context. In this pattern, the fraud is perpetrated following the availability of a service without the knowledge of the service provider or in a condition where the service provider could not recover the damage caused by the fraud. In *Fraud case 4* (see Table 2), for instance, the service provider sends the call credentials before the necessary infrastructure is configured at the customer place, while the service is activated and available to be used. In the case of VoiP telephony, the credentials are enough to set up a remote connection and perform the fraud. Obviously the main fraud enabler is the availability of the service before it is accountable to the customer. Note: This kind of fraud could also be exploited by a third party – stealing the credentials, in which case it follows FRP1.
Target. The target of this pattern is generally time-dependent activities. It is observed in the *Fraud cases 4* and *5*.

FRP 3 – Misusing the service by overdoing beyond the expected limit
Context. In this pattern, a fraudster uses the service beyond the expected usage limit of "normal" customers. For example, in a service plan misuse case, a fraudster tries to generate a lot of call traffic while keeping himself undetected by the fraud detection system installed at the service provider side. This is a very common fraud that a Telecom service provider is facing, which needs careful service planning.
Target. The target of this pattern is the service and its tariff plan. We observed this kind of fraud pattern in all of the *Fraud cases 1 to 5*.

FRP 4 – Fraud due to invisible collusions
Context. In this pattern, a fraudster perpetrated the fraud in an organised entity where other customers or service providers are involved directly or indirectly to gain financial benefit. A rational fraudster uses all possible ways of getting the benefit from the service either by installing a PBX system that helps to sell calls or randomly generating calls to expensive destination. In this case, the fraudster will make an agreement with a third party (mostly another Telecom service provider) to terminate calls to expensive destinations. In return, the fraudster gets his income share generated by committing the fraud with the third party.

Target. This pattern targets the service providers and the weaknesses on their services. It is observed in the *Fraud cases 1, 2* and *5.*

Patterns Due to *vulnerabilities of the system*

FRP 5: Unsecured (uncertified) communication
Context. This describes a fraud pattern due to lack of secure communication between different business entities in a given context. For instance, when a user has a possibility to register as a new customer via the Internet, the user might use a forged identity and delivery address unless the system implements a way of user certification. This allows fraudsters to trigger the process of creating a contract or an account to gain the advantages that a forged identity can get.
Target. This pattern targets the communication channel between entities in the e-service. It is observed in the *Fraud case 4.*

FRP 6: Exploiting infrastructure vulnerabilities
Context. This is a situation where technical weaknesses of the infrastructure at a service provider or at a customer point contribute to a fraud. In *Fraud case 3,* for instance, a weak configuration of the remote access policy of the PBX system is the main triggering factor for fraudsters to target the PBX.
Target. This fraud pattern targets the infrastructures used to deliver the e-services. It is observed in the *Fraud cases 3* and *4.*

7   Application of FRPs to Telecom Services

So far, we have presented fraud patterns identified from the real fraud incidents. In this section, we use an e-service from the Telecom domain, namely the *roaming service*, to apply the fraud patterns and show how they could be used for fraud risk assessment. To do the fraud risk assessment, first the necessary entities need to be described. Then, for each fraud pattern, the potential fraud risks would be identified. At last, the potential fraud risks should be estimated based on their impact on the service provider.

7.1   Case Study Description

Roaming is one of the Telecom services which allows customers to use calling and messaging services while they are abroad. It involves different independent actors: the customer, the visited and the home service provider. We focus on the calling service of roaming for the sake of simplicity.

The customer. A customer creates a contract (either flat-rate or pre-paid) with the home service provider to get call services – roaming. He is responsible to pay for the services he has used.

The home service provider (HSP). A HSP is responsible for providing calling services to their customers within the coverage of customers' contract. The HSP maintains the usage data of customers including access locations in a database –

home location register (HLR). To prepare the invoice for the roaming service of a customer, the HSP should receive call detail records (CDR) from the visited service provider. The CDR is the usage data of a customer stored in the visited service provider. The payment for the roaming service is based on the number of minutes that the customer calls while roaming.

The visited service provider (VSP). A VSP will have a roaming service *agreement* with the HSP to provide roaming service to the customers of the HSP when the customers use the service within the VSP network. The VSP is responsible for storing and sending the CDRs of the customer to the HSP. Based on technologies implemented at the VSP, the reporting time varies. According to the technology Near-Real-Time Roaming Data Exchange (NRTRDE), the time to report is limited only to four hours.

Entities in the Case Study

The e-service under assessment can be represented in a structural model, which represents the necessary entities for the assessment. Each of the fraud pattern targets a specific set of e-service entities such as actors, activities, services, communication channels and infrastructures. Finding a suitable modelling language to handle all types of e-service entities is a future work. An example model to represent the relations between actors in a semi-structured model is shown Fig. 2.

- **Actors.** *Customer* (type: human), *HSP* (type: service provider), and *VSP* (type: service provider). The actor *HSP* can be expressed with its employees such as customer services, technicians and commercial managers.
- **Activities.**

  Time-dependent activities. VSP sends CDR file of customer to *HSP* within certain time interval; A flat-rate roaming customer pays every month for the service he used;
  Non-time-dependent activities. Customer creates contract or subscribes to a service; The HSP has roaming service agreement with the VSP; the *customer* is able to *use* the roaming service while being in the *VSP*'s network, and maybe creates an agreement with VSP to commit fraud (i.e., invisible to the HSP).

- **Services.**

  Assets. The roaming service (type: service); the payment (type: income)
  Service usage limit. Contracts between *customer* and provider (for pre-paid contracts – the customer can use as long as the account balance is above zero, for flat-rate contracts – mostly the customer has yearly contracts payable monthly); between *HSP* and *VSP* (payment for the services that the customer of the *HSP* gets – paid per number-of-minutes of calls)

- **Communication channels.** At the time of the contract creation, the communication between the customer and the HSP is either through letters, emails, on-line registration or personally at the customer service. File transfer from VSP to HSP is through encrypted channel between the two

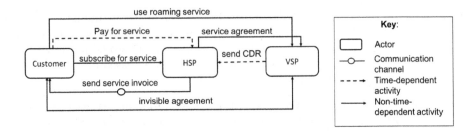

Fig. 2. A semi-structured model for the roaming service case

- **Infrastructures.** HSP database and VSP database systems (type: NRTRDE or other)

7.2   Risk Assessment

Fraud risk assessment is the process of describing the e-service under assessment, analysing fraud risks and estimating their impacts. The goal of risk analysis is to identify the potential fraud enabling factors using FRPs. To achieve this goal, we have to check all the fraud patterns against the service described above; due to space limitation, we only show this for FRP1 and FRP2. Each fraud pattern targets different entities in the e-service. A strategy of identifying the potential fraud enabling factors is by asking questions whether each FRP enables fraud targeting entities in the given e-service.

To estimate the potential impact to the HSP, we can use a qualitative measurement: *high*, *medium* and *low*. *High* is when the impact of the fraud is substantial to the HSP that they lose a lot of money beyond the expected expenses. *Low* is when the impact of fraud is within the customer's contract limit though has an effect on the income of the HSP. *Medium* is between the scale *high* and *low*. For each example fraud identified, we provide high level preventive measures in terms of security requirements.

FRP1 – impersonation. As the target of FRP1 is customers and service providers, and the goal of fraudsters in this fraud pattern is to gain financial benefit or use the service without payment, the question should be: *how could customer and HSP possibly be impersonated in the roaming case so that fraudsters gain financial benefit or use the service without payment?* Here are some examples:

1. A fraudster could impersonate the customer-service of the HSP to create a flat-rate roaming contract. The fraudster can then generate calls at least for a month until the service is interrupted.
    - *Impact. High* as the service provider is the main target by the fraudster.
    - *Preventive measures.* (1) Strong identity check (e.g. credit check with authorised third party) (2) train the personnel at customer-services about the threats of impersonation;

2. A customer who has a flat-rate roaming contract could be impersonated to clone his SIM-card or to lose his device as it allows a fraudster to commit fraud until the fraud detection system detects it or a customer informs the HSP to stop the service.
   - *Impact. Medium* because the customer is the main target affected by the fraudster, so enforced to pay. In the cases where the customers did not realise the fraud and did not report to the HSP or the fraud detection system didn't detect, the effect might go beyond the customer to affect the income of HSP.
   - *Preventive measures.* (1) Inform the customers who have contracts with the HSP about the common fraud patterns that they might be suspicious (2) advance the fraud detection mechanism to handle SIM cloning and similar impersonation techniques;
3. A fraudster creates a roaming service contract via the HSP's online registration portal with fake identity and credit information.
   - *Impact. High* because the fraudster could resell the service until identified and this directly affects the HSP.
   - *Preventive measure.* The registration portal should certify users and check their credit.

FRP2 – time interval-based misuse. The targets of FRP2 are time-dependent activities. So, the question should be: *How would time-dependent activities be used to misuse the service?* Here are some examples:

1. Because of the time-delay before the VSP sends the CDRs of a customer, fraudster could use the roaming service to call to an expensive destination without being detected or the service being interrupted. This is mainly dangerous if the fraud detection technology is weak at the VSP side.
   - *Impact. High* because (1) there is an unpaid bill by the fraudster and (2) the HSP has to pay the termination fee (for the calls terminated in the VSP network).
   - *Preventive measures.* (1) Limit the amount of time taken to send the CDRs of customers from VHP to HSP (2) Install standardised technologies with both HSP and VSP to prevent modification of CDRs – sometimes this is difficult to implement at VSPs due to lack of jurisdiction).
2. When a fraudster manages to get a flat-rate roaming service, the time-limit to pay the monthly service charge is in danger.
   - *Impact. High* because flat-rate services mostly have no usage limitation which leaves the HSP with the unpaid bill.
   - *Preventive measure.* The HSP should ensure that the customer has not been involved in a fraudulent behaviour (e.g. with the help of credit check organisations).

8   Discussion

Fraud patterns can successfully be applied not only in the process of FRA, but as well as for producing security requirements and policies. One of the main benefits relies on the fact the each of the fraud patterns targets a specific entity within the e-service model. The description of e-services (e.g. using appropriate modelling languages) thus plays an important role in using them for risk assessment. Since fraud patterns have been identified from five recurring fraud incidents in Telecom e-services, it would be valuable to perform the validation and improvement of those with real practices. Furthermore, the applicability of fraud patterns has only been shown in one domain; other e-services and domains would be interesting for demonstrating the applicability of fraud patterns in FRA of e-services in general. Note, that while performing FRA of e-services allowed us to identify fraud risks, it is also important to put fraud detection approaches in place to gain the full advantages of fraud management.

9   Conclusion and Future Work

Fraud pattern is a handy way of identifying fraud risks from the perspective of fraudsters. They are an essential part of fraud risk assessment to ease the task of fraud managers to put their preventive measures in place before the fraudsters damage the assets (directly or indirectly). This also increases the security and profitability of e-service providers.

Even though the fraud patterns identified in this paper are from a limited set of existing frauds, they are important to guide future development on fraud patterns. Therefore, to enhance the fraud patterns, we plan to develop a fraud risk assessment tool and apply the fraud patterns for different e-service domains beyond the Telecom domain.

References

1. Zuccato, A., Daniels, N., Jampathom, C.: Service security requirement profiles for telecom: how software engineers may tackle security. In: Sixth International Conference on Availability, Reliability and Security. IEEE (2011)
2. Rebahi, Y., Nassar, M., Magedanz, T., Festor, O.: A survey on fraud and service misuse in voice over IP (VoIP) networks. Inf. Secur. Tech. Rep. **16**(1), 12–19 (2011)
3. CFCA: Global telecom fraud report. Technical report, Communications Fraud Control Association (2000–2015)
4. Yesuf, A.S.: A review of risk identification approaches in the telecommunication domain. In: The 3rd International Conference on Information Systems Security and Privacy, ICISSP (2017)
5. Yesuf, A.S., Wolos, L., Rannenberg, K.: Fraud risk modelling: requirements elicitation in the case of telecom services. In: Za, S., Drăagoicea, M., Cavallari, M. (eds.) IESS 2017. LNBIP, vol. 279. Springer, Cham (2017)
6. Abdallah, A., Maarof, M.A., Zainal, A.: Fraud detection system: a survey. J. Netw. Comput. Appl. **68**, 90–113 (2016)

7. Hilas, C.S., Mastorocostas, P.A.: An application of supervised and unsupervised learning approaches to telecommunications fraud detection. Knowl. Based Syst. **21**(7), 721–726 (2008)

8. Ruiz-Agundez, I., Penya, Y.K., Garcia Bringas, P.: Fraud detection for voice over IP services on next-generation networks. In: Samarati, P., Tunstall, M., Posegga, J., Markantonakis, K., Sauveron, D. (eds.) WISTP 2010. LNCS, vol. 6033, pp. 199–212. Springer, Heidelberg (2010). doi:10.1007/978-3-642-12368-9_14

9. Farvaresh, H., Sepehri, M.M.: A data mining framework for detecting subscription fraud in telecommunication. Eng. Appl. Artif. Intell. **24**(1), 182–194 (2011)

10. Ionita, D., Wieringa, R.J., Wolos, L., Gordijn, J., Pieters, W.: Using value models for business risk analysis in e-Service networks. In: Ralyté, J., España, S., Pastor, Ó. (eds.) PoEM 2015. LNBIP, vol. 235, pp. 239–253. Springer, Cham (2015). doi:10.1007/978-3-319-25897-3_16

11. Ionita, D., Gordijn, J., Yesuf, A.S., Wieringa, R.: Value-driven risk analysis of coordination models. In: Horkoff, J., Jeusfeld, M.A., Persson, A. (eds.) PoEM 2016. LNBIP, vol. 267, pp. 102–116. Springer, Cham (2016). doi:10.1007/978-3-319-48393-1_8

12. ISO/TC 262 Risk management: ISO 31000:2009, ISO 31000:2009 Risk Management - Principles and Guidelines (2009)

13. Yoder, J., Barcalow, J.: Architectural patterns for enabling application security. Urbana **51**, 61801 (1998)

14. Braga, A., Rubira, C., Dahab, R.: Tropyc: a pattern language for cryptographic software (1999)

15. Schumacher, M., Fernandez-Buglioni, E., Hybertson, D., Buschmann, F., Sommerlad, P.: Security Patterns: Integrating Security and Systems Engineering. Wiley, West Sussex (2013)

16. Dubois, É., Heymans, P., Mayer, N., Matulevičius, R.: A systematic approach to define the domain of information system security risk management. In: Nurcan, S., Salinesi, C., Souveyet, C., Ralyté, J. (eds.) Intentional Perspectives on Information Systems Engineering, pp. 289–306. Springer, Heidelberg (2010)

17. Rosas, E., Analide, C.: Telecommunications fraud: problem analysis-an agent-based KDD perspective. Aveiro: EPIA 2009 (2009)

18. Ghosh, M.: Telecoms fraud. Comput. Fraud Secur. **2010**(7), 14–17 (2010)

19. Rrenja, A., Matulevičius, R.: Pattern-based security requirements derivation from secure tropos models. In: Ralyté, J., España, S., Pastor, Ó. (eds.) PoEM 2015. LNBIP, vol. 235, pp. 59–74. Springer, Cham (2015). doi:10.1007/978-3-319-25897-3_5

Gadget Weighted Tagging: A Flexible Framework to Protect Against Code Reuse Attacks

Liwei Chen[1,2(✉)], Mengyu Ma[1,2], Wenhao Zhang[1,2], Gang Shi[1,2], and Dan Meng[1,2]

[1] Institute of Information Engineering,
Chinese Academy of Sciences, Beijing, China
{chenliwei,mamengyu,zhangwenhao,shigang,mengdan}@iie.ac.cn
[2] University of Chinese Academy of Sciences, Beijing, China

Abstract. The code reuse attack (CRA) has become one of the most common attack methods. In this paper, we propose gadget weighted tagging (GWT), a flexible framework to protect against CRAs. In GWT, we firstly find all possible gadgets, which can be used in CRAs. Then, we attach weighted tags to these gadgets based on the lengths and types of the gadgets, and the weighted values are configurable. At last, GWT monitors the weighted tag information at runtime to detect and prevent CRAs. Furthermore, combining with the rule-based CFI, GWT+CFI can precisely confirm the gadget start and greatly reduce the number of possible gadgets, compared to the baseline GWT. We implement a hardware/software co-design framework to support GWT and GWT+CFI. The results show that the performance overheads of GWT and GWT+CFI are 2.31% and 3.55% respectively, and GWT can defeat variants of CRAs, especially those generated by automated tools.

1 Introduction

Code reuse attack (CRA) has become the primary attack vector nowadays. Attackers find special code snippets called gadgets, ending with an indirect branch instruction, and then manipulate program control flow to chain gadgets together to construct a malicious program. The CRA is proved to be Turing-complete and can be generated by automated tools [1]. Therefore, the CRA is an attack approach which is easy-to-use, hard-to-detect and can be applied to any purpose.

Many defense mechanisms have been proposed to protect against CRAs, and control flow integrity (CFI) [3,15] is thought to be one of the most promising ways. However, CFI has high complexity and low efficiency [4]. In order to design a practicable CFI, some researches [5,6,10,11] propose the coarse-grained CFI to realize a looser notion of control flow integrity without the static control-flow graph (CFG). Abandoning CFG to reduce complexity, the coarse-grained CFI

S. De Capitani di Vimercati and F. Martinelli (Eds.): SEC 2017, IFIP AICT 502, pp. 568–584, 2017.
DOI: 10.1007/978-3-319-58469-0_38

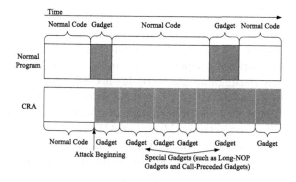

Fig. 1. The gadgets in normal program and CRA

is a tradeoff between security and efficiency. Hence, the security of the coarse-grained CFI is lower than the CFI based on CFG. Some recent papers [8,12–14] have proved that the coarse-grained CFI could be bypassed by CRAs with special gadgets.

We observe that all possible gadgets, which can be used in CRAs, only take a part of the whole code space. As shown in Fig. 1, gadgets in normal programs are discontinuous usually, whereas the CRA is composed of a **contiguous** sequence of gadgets. Additionally, with some special gadgets inserted, such as long-NOP gadgets and call-preceded gadgets [7,14], CRAs may pretend to be normal programs. Therefore, we can distinguish CRAs from normal programs by monitoring both normal gadgets and special gadgets at runtime.

In this paper, we propose gadget weighted tagging (GWT), a flexible framework to detect and prevent CRAs. In GWT, we classify all possible gadgets into three major types on the basis of their effects on CRAs: functional gadgets, NOP gadgets and normal codes. Then, we configure different weighted scores to these gadget types, and attach weighted tags to the gadgets in binary files. Finally, GWT computes the probability of CRA occurrence by dynamically monitoring the weighted tags at runtime.

Moreover, we propose GWT+CFI, since we discover that the control-flow rules in coarse-grained CFI are good supplements to the GWT. GWT+CFI can accurately identify the gadget start, and significantly reduce the number of potential gadgets. Hence, it is more precise to find possible gadgets in GWT+CFI, compared to the baseline GWT.

Several important parameters used in GWT, such as weighted scores for different gadget types, are configurable. Thus, users can modify the parameters as needed. Furthermore, if users discover some special gadgets, they can add the new gadget types into the GWT, and allocate different weighted scores for the gadget types. As a result, GWT can detect variants of CRAs with different gadgets, and the security of GWT can be further improved with adding more gadget types.

When a new CRA attack method or a new gadget type is proposed, the ways to construct the attack or to find the gadget should also be introduced. Hence, in GWT, we can reuse the ways to find the potential gadgets in programs, according to the descriptions in previous papers. Additionally, we can find and mark possible gadgets in GWT by reusing automated tools for CRA generation [1].

We apply GWT and GWT+CFI in a hardware/software co-design framework. The results show that the performance overheads of GWT and GWT+CFI are 2.31% and 3.55% respectively. Moreover, GWT can detect all CRAs generated by Q [1], and variants of CRAs with special gadgets.

The key contributions of this paper are summarized as follows:

(1) We propose gadget weighted tagging (GWT), a novel framework to prevent CRAs, which is of high-flexibility, high-security, low-overhead and easy to apply.
(2) We propose GWT+CFI, GWT combining with the rule-based CFI, which can find possible gadgets more precisely, compared to the baseline GWT.
(3) We implement a hardware/software co-design to support GWT and GWT+CFI, and evaluate its security effectiveness and performance overhead.

2   Background and Related Work

2.1   Code Reuse Attacks (CRAs)

The basic idea of CRAs is to reuse instructions from the existing code space to implement malicious operations. In order to achieve attack purposes, attackers should firstly find a set of instruction sequences (called gadgets) from the entire code space, and then link the selected gadgets into a gadget chain to construct a malicious program. In short, the CRA is composed of a contiguous sequence of gadgets.

A gadget usually has several normal instructions for computation and an indirect branch instruction to change control flow to link gadgets. For simplicity, we focus on three most common indirect branch instructions in this paper: call, return and indirect-jump. Furthermore, the gadgets used in CRAs have two important features as follows:

(1) **Sparse Distribution.** Every gadget should end with an indirect branch instruction, however, the indirect branch instructions only take a small part of the whole program. Moreover, attackers need gadgets containing special operations to construct a malicious program, or to bypass defense mechanisms, such as CFI. Thus, many existing gadgets may not meet for the special needs of attackers. As a result, the gadgets, which are useful for CRA construction, are quite rare in normal programs.
(2) **Small Size.** The gadgets with more instructions can perform more operations, however, they also inevitably lead to more side effects and some of them may conflict with each other. Hence, attackers usually prefer to discover the short and simple gadgets only with the intended operations [1],

instead of using long and complex gadgets. In fact, the gadgets in real CRAs usually have only 2 to 6 instructions [6].

According to the difference of the indirect branch instructions, CRAs can be classified into return-based ROP (return-oriented programming) and jump-based JOP (jump-oriented programming). In ROP, the stack pointer *esp* is used as the program counter in a return-oriented program. Instead, JOP uses a dispatch table to manage gadget addresses. The program counter of JOP is the register pointing into the dispatcher table [2], and an special **dispatcher gadget** is used to drive control flow. Thus, the dispatcher gadget is a key sign of JOP, which usually contains an self-modification operation and an indirect jump instruction. Generally, any gadget ending with an indirect jump instruction, that carries out the following algorithm, can be considered as a candidate of dispatcher gadget [2].

$pc \leftarrow f(pc)$;
$goto$ $*pc$;

2.2 Control Flow Integrity (CFI)

There are many CFI implementations that have been proposed [3–6, 10, 15]. We divide these CFI methods into two main kinds: CFG-based CFI and rule-based CFI.

CFG-based CFI, also is known as fine-grained CFI, enforces the control flow to adhere to control-flow graph (CFG) generated by static program analysis. CFG-based CFI is high security, and can detect any illegal control flow transfers. However, it is almost impossible to generate an ideal CFG containing all possible control-flow paths, and the performance overhead of CFG-based CFI is high [4]. Furthermore, some recent works [16,17] have proposed CRA attack methods to bypass the CFG-based CFI with unideal CFG. In addition, even the ideal CFG-based CFI could be also bypassed by control flow bending [18] combining with the non-control-data attack.

Rule-based CFI, that is also called coarse-grained CFI, uses several control-flow rules to defend against CRAs, instead of CFG. Therefore, the rule-based CFI is low-overhead and easy to implement. The control flow rules can be classified into two types as following.

(1) **Control-Flow Transfer Rules.** These rules stipulate the destinations of different indirect branch instructions [9, 11].

(1.1) **RETURN:** a return instruction should point to an instruction right after a call instruction.

(1.2) **CALL:** a call instruction should start execution at the entry point of a function.

(1.3) **Indirect-JUMP:** an indirect-jump instruction should point to either a position inside the same function, or an entry point of another function.

(2) **Code Length Rules.** These rules stipulate the code length of gadgets, and the chain length of CRA attacks [5, 6].

(2.1) **Gadget Length:** a short code snippet (e.g. 2–6 instructions) ending with an indirect branch instruction is a gadget, whereas a longer code snippet is not a gadget.

(2.2) **CRA Length:** a long gadget chain (e.g. 6 gadgets) is a CRA, whereas a shorter gadget chain is not a CRA.

2.3 Legal Gadgets

The rule-based CFI has several definite rules to recognize gadgets. However, attackers can find some special gadgets that obey these rules, called legal gadgets in this paper. As a result, legal gadgets are mistaken for normal codes by the rule-based CFI, so that CRAs consisting of legal gadgets can bypass the rule-based CFI. There are several kinds of legal gadgets to bypass different control-flow rules.

(1) **Call-Preceded (CP) Gadget.** A call-preceded instruction is any instruction in the address space of the application that immediately follows a call instruction [14]. A call-preceded gadget is a gadget that its first instruction is a call-preceded instruction. Thus, CP gadgets are legal destinations of any *return* instruction.

(2) **Entry-Point (EP) Gadget.** An entry-point gadget is a gadget starting at the entry point of a function. Hence, EP gadgets are legal destinations of any *call* or *indirect-jump* instruction.

(3) **Long-NOP Gadget.** A long-NOP gadget [7,14] is a gadget that contains enough instructions to obey the gadget length rule of rule-based CFI, and does not induce any side effects, i.e., the content of all registers and memory area used by the CRA is preserved. Therefore, attackers can use short and useful gadgets to perform malicious operations, and use long-NOP gadgets to bypass the rule-based CFI.

3   Threat Model

In this paper, we focus on defending against code reuse attacks. We assume that attackers have full control over data and stack/heap memory regions. In addition, we also assume that the attackers can modify all key registers of processors.

We assume that the DEP technology has already been realized, thus it forces the attackers to use CRA attacks. Moreover, we do not consider the gadgets consisting of a sequence of unintended instructions, such as in x86 platform with variable instruction sizes, since they can be detected by CFI [9].

Furthermore, we will introduce our approach, GWT, in two different systems.

(1) **Baseline System.** The baseline system does not have any special security mechanism, and is only protected by the DEP technology.

(2) **Protected System.** The protected system supports the DEP technology and the rule-based CFI with control-flow transfer rules as described in Sect. 2.2.

4 Gadget Weighted Tagging

4.1 Finding Gadgets

(1) **Finding Gadget End.**
The only strict limit of gadgets is ending with an indirect branch instruction (return, call and indirect-jump). Thus, all code snippets ending with an indirect branch instruction can be considered as gadgets in theory. Therefore, we should discover all indirect branch instructions in program codes, and take these instructions as the gadget end.

(2) **Defining Gadget Types.**
Q [1], the state-of-the-art automated tool for CRA generation, uses functional kinds to identify gadgets. Q defines nine kinds of gadgets, including NoOp, Jump, MoveReg, LoadConst, Arithmetic, LoadMem, StoreMem, ArithmeticLoad, and ArithmeticStore [1]. In Q, every gadget should have and only have one kind to define its function, and Q proposes a discovery algorithm to recognize the functional kind of each gadget.

In GWT, we define four types of gadgets as shown in Fig. 2. The functional gadget includes the eight kinds of gadgets defined in Q, except the NoOp gadget. The dispatcher gadget and the syscall gadget are two special types of functional gadgets. Because the two types of gadgets play critical roles in CRAs, we take them as separate types out from the normal functional gadgets.

(2.1) **Functional Gadget.** The functional gadget is a gadget that can perform a fixed and useful operation without any side effect, such as arithmetic calculation, branching, or loading data from memory. We use a method similar as Q [1] to identify functional gadgets. Details of the algorithm to identify the functional gadgets can be found in [1]. However, the original algorithm of Q can only be used to discover return-based gadgets and construct ROP chains. Hence, we have added new features, such as discovering indirect-jump instructions and syscall instructions, to find jump-based gadgets to construct JOP chains, and to discover syscall gadgets and legal gadgets in GWT.

(2.2) **Dispatcher Gadget.** The dispatcher gadget is an special functional gadget, which ends with an indirect jump instruction and contains an self-

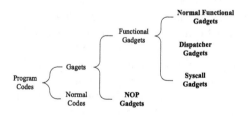

Fig. 2. The gadget types in GWT

modification operation to the jump destination. Furthermore, the dispatcher gadget plays a key role in the JOP [2]. It essentially maintains an virtual program counter and executes the JOP program by advancing it through one gadget after another.

(2.3) **Syscall Gadget.** The syscall gadget is an special functional gadget ending with an system call instruction. To make CRA attacks simpler, attackers can carefully construct attacks that consist of a small number of gadgets, and then inject code. For example, attackers can use the syscall gadget to invoke an system call to alter the execute bit on an attacker-controlled buffer (i.e. destroy the DEP protection), and then redirect control flow to it [12].

(2.4) **NOP Gadget.** The NOP gadget is a gadget which has neither useful operations nor side effects to CRAs. It includes the NoOp gadget in Q and long-NOP gadgets described in Sect. 2. To ensure that the NOP gadget does not break the semantics of the CRA chain, the NOP gadget should make use of only a small set of registers [14]. Generally, the NOP gadget can be used to confuse defense mechanisms, such as the rule-based CFI [5,6].

We define a parameter in GWT, MaxRegMod, which means the maximum number of registers modified by the NOP gadget. If a gadget is not a functional gadget and the registers modified by this gadget are not larger than MaxRegMod, then the gadget is a NOP gadget. Else, the gadget is not a NOP gadget (i.e. normal code).

(3) **Finding Gadget Start (Maximum Gadget Length).**
It is simple to find the gadget end (i.e. indirect branch instructions), whereas to identify the gadget start is difficult. In previous papers, the code length is always used to recognize gadgets, since longer gadgets lead to more side effects and may conflict with other gadgets. Usually, the maximum length of a meaningful gadget is 6 instructions [6]. However, attackers can still find some special gadgets (e.g. long-NOP gadgets), which are long enough and have few side effects to CRAs, to break the limits.

In GWT, the classified gadget type still depends on code length, however, we add a new gadget type (i.e. NOP gadget) to mitigate the above problem. A long enough gadget, which has few side effects, could be recognized as a NOP gadget in GWT, instead of normal code in previous papers. A gadget will be identified as normal code, only if the gadget contains too many instructions leading to significant side effects.

(3.1) **The Maximum Length of the Functional Gadget.** From the gadget end of a functional gadget, walks backwards one by one (instruction), until the gadget is not a functional gadget. Then, the instruction number is the maximum length of the functional gadget, and the first instruction is the start of the functional gadget. Because the dispatcher gadget and the syscall gadget both belong to the functional gadget, the maximum lengths of the two types of gadgets are the same as the functional gadget.

Table 1. Weighted scores of different gadget types

Gadget type value (3 bits)	Gadget type	Weighted score
000	Normal code	Zero clearing
001	Functional gadget	1
010	Dispatcher gadget	2
011	Syscall gadget	4
100	NOP gadget	0
Others	Undefined	–

(3.2) **The Maximum Length of the NOP Gadget.** It is similar as the functional gadget. Increases the code length of a NOP gadget, until the gadget is recognized as normal code. Then, the code length is the maximum length of this NOP gadget.

4.2 Weighted Tagging

In GWT, we attach the weighted tag to each gadget end (i.e. indirect branch instruction). The structure of weighted tag is shown in Fig. 3, and it has 32 bits and contains 3 parameters. The gadget type has 3 bits, and the meaning of this parameter is shown in Table 1. The maximum length of functional gadget has 14 bits, and the maximum length of NOP gadget has 15 bits.

We define five different gadget types, including normal code, functional gadget, dispatcher gadget, syscall gadget and NOP gadget. Normal code means the gadget can not be used in any CRA, and other four gadget types are introduced in Sect. 4.1. Different gadgets have different effects on CRAs, hence, we propose weighted scores to mark different gadget types. The foundation of weighted scores is the dangerousness and importance of each gadget type. With a higher score, the gadget type is more dangerous and important, and is also more possible to be used in CRAs.

The specific weighted score of each gadget type is shown in Table 1, and it is configurable. (i) The NOP gadget does not contain any useful operation for CRAs, and thus it has only 0 point. (ii) The functional gadget contains an useful and constant operation for CRAs, so it gets 1 point. (iii) The dispatcher gadget is a key sign of the JOP, and it is appeared every other gadget in the JOP, hence it has 2 points. (iv) System call is the start point of many important kernel functions of OS, and using the system call can significantly reduce the difficulty of CRA construction. Consequently, one common purpose of CRAs is to perform an special system call, and the syscall gadget is more important than other gadget types, which has 4 points. (v) Since the CRA is composed of a contiguous sequence of gadgets, if the current gadget is normal code, there is no CRA at present. As a result, the weighted score of the normal code is zero clearing.

We add the gadget tag information into the program executable file by annotation. The prior of every indirect branch instruction is a weighted tag annotation. Moreover, tag annotation starts with a prefetch instruction to retain binary compatibility, which is the similar as other methods [3,9]. The prefetch instruction is followed by the weighted tag information. Because we assume that the system supports the DEP technology, the weighted tag annotation can not be modified by attackers.

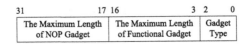

Fig. 3. Weighted tag information for gadget end

4.3   Monitoring Gadget Tags

At runtime, we assume that codes between two indirect branch instructions construct a potential gadget, and we identify the type of the potential gadget by its code length and the weighted tag information attached to the second indirect branch instruction. Furthermore, we define four simple intermediate variables to calculate the probability of CRA occurrence: current gadget type (CGT), current gadget length (CGL), real gadget type (RGT) and CRA occurrence index (COI).

CGL is used to record the code length of the current potential gadget, and CGT is used to record the gadget type of the current gadget tag. When an instruction is executed, the CGL adds one to itself. When an indirect branch instruction is executed, it is the boundary between two potential gadgets. Therefore, CGT records the gadget type of the corresponding tag, while CGL records the current gadget length for RGT computation, and then starts a new count of code length for the next gadget.

RGT, which is computed based on the CGT and CGL, records the real type of the current gadget at runtime. The detailed algorithm process of RGT is described in Fig. 4. The MaxFunc is the maximum length of the functional gadget, and the MaxNOP is the maximum length of the NOP gadget.

We use COI to denote the possibility of the CRA occurrence. If the COI is larger, then it is more likely CRA will occur. Furthermore, we define MaxCOI, the maximum value of COI. If the COI is larger than MaxCOI, then we assume that a CRA occurs. The COI is calculated based on RGT and weighted scores of gadget types, and the detailed algorithm process of COI is described in Fig. 4.

4.4   Hardware Implementation

Figure 5 shows the hardware implementation for GWT. It contains three important hardware modules: control-flow monitor (CFM), weighted tag configuration

```
if (CGT == Normal Code) {
    RGT = Normal Code;
}
else if (CGT == NOP Gadget) {
    if (CGL <= MaxNOP) {
        RGT = NOP Gadget;
    }
    else {
        RGT = Normal Code;
    }
}
else { // CGT == Functional/Dispatcher/Syscall Gadget
    if (CGL <= MaxFunc) {
        RGT = CGT;
    }
    else if (CGL <= MaxNOP) {
        RGT = NOP Gadget;
    }
    else {
        RGT = Normal Code;
    }
}
```

```
COI = 0; // initialization
while (each indirect branch instruction) {
    if (COI <= MaxCOI) {
        if (RGT == Normal Code) {
            COI = 0;
        }
        else {
            COI = COI + Weighted Score of RGT;
        }
    }
    else { // COI > MaxCOI
        exit(); // a CRA is detected
    }
}
```

Fig. 4. The algorithm process of RGT and COI

(WTC) and CRA detecting module (CDM). In addition, we assume that the rule-based CFI has already been implemented.

The CFM is the main module for weighted information monitoring. It records the number of instructions executed (CGL) and gadget type (CGT) of current gadget at runtime. When an indirect branch instruction is executed, the CFM computes real gadget type (RGT) based on CGL and CGT, and then sends the RGT to the CDM. The CDM computes COI, and compare it to the MaxCOI. If the COI is larger than MaxCOI, then a CRA occurs, and thus CDM should send an exception to report an attack. The detailed computation algorithms of these parameters are described in Fig. 4.

The WTC stores the parameters used by CFM and CDM, such as MaxCOI and weighted scores. Additionally, these parameters are configurable. Users can modify these parameters as needed. For example, if users want to improve system security, they can reduce the MaxCOI, or increase the weighted scores of gadgets. Furthermore, we assume that attackers can not directly change these parameters stored in WTC.

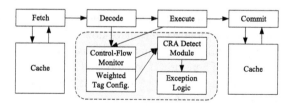

Fig. 5. Hardware implementation of GWT

5 GWT Combining with CFI

5.1 Motivation of GWT+CFI

One main shortage of GWT is that GWT can not precisely confirm the gadget start. Only using the gadget length to identify the gadget start is not clear enough. Therefore, we propose GWT+CFI, combining GWT and the rule-based CFI together. The rule-based CFI fits our approach very well, and introduces two benefits into the GWT.

(1) **Gadget Start.** In order to bypass the rule-based CFI, attackers can only use some special gadgets, such as call-preceded (CP) gadgets and entry-point (EP) gadgets. Fortunately, the two types of gadgets both have fixed start points: call-preceded instruction and the function entry. Consequently, we can precisely identify the gadget start in GWT+CFI.

(2) **Gadget Number.** Except legal gadgets, other illegal gadgets can be detected by the rule-based CFI. As a result, the number of gadgets that can be used in CRAs is reduced significantly in GWT+CFI. Therefore, we can locate useful gadgets in code space more accurately.

5.2 Finding Legal Gadgets

The major difference between GWT and GWT+CFI is the gadget discovery. In GWT+CFI, we only need to discover legal gadgets. On the other stages, such as gadget weighted tagging and monitoring, the GWT+CFI is almost the same as the GWT.

In GWT+CFI, we should find all indirect branch instructions firstly, and take them as the gadget end. Then, we should also find the gadget start. The start point of a CP gadget is a CP instruction, and the start point of an EP gadget is the function entry. Consequently, we can identify all legal gadgets based on the gadget start and end. At last, we should select useful gadgets from these legal gadgets. It is almost the same as the Sect. 4.1, to distinguish functional gadgets, dispatcher gadgets, syscall gadget, NOP gadgets and normal codes, as shown in Fig. 6.

Note that one indirect jump instruction can jump to any position inside the same function, that does not violate the control-flow transfer rules of CFI. Hence, attackers may find legal gadgets without CP instruction or function entry by indirect jump instructions. Therefore, if we find that a function contains indirect jump instructions, the gadget discovery inside this function should follow the baseline GWT, instead of GWT+CFI.

6 Security Analysis

Because the hardware architecture of GWT is very simple, it is only used to record gadget information and compute COI. As a result, for simplicity, we

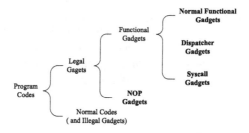

Fig. 6. The gadget types in GWT+CFI

implement a software method based on pintools [20] to simulate hardware functionality of GWT for security analysis. Pintools [20] are dynamic program analysis tools, which can manage the execution of every instruction. In addition, we select widely-used programs in Ubuntu */bin* and */usr/bin/*. In order to keep the balance between security and stability, we set the MaxRegMod is 6, MaxCOI is 6, and the weighted scores are the same as the Table 1.

Since the main difference between GWT and GWT+CFI is the gadget discovery, the CRA detection of GWT+CFI is almost the same as the GWT. Hence, we mainly focus on the security analysis of GWT in this section.

6.1   Gadget Discovery

In GWT, the average number of all possible gadgets is about 1072 in each program with average 40KB code size, and thus the gadgets take only a small part of the whole program codes. The average numbers of functional gadgets, dispatcher gadgets, syscall gadgets and NOP gadgets are 452, 7, 1.5 and 612 respectively. Furthermore, the average length of all possible gadgets is about 9.9 in each program. The average length of functional gadgets, including the dispatcher gadgets and syscall gadgets, is 5.3, and the average length of NOP gadgets is 13.3, as shown in Fig. 7.

In GWT+CFI, the average number of legal gadgets is about 471, which decreases significantly compared to the baseline GWT, especially the legal functional gadgets. The average numbers of functional gadgets, dispatcher gadgets, syscall gadgets and NOP gadgets are 45, 0.9, 0.15 and 425 respectively. Conversely, the average length of legal gadgets is about 13.5, which is longer than the GWT. The average lengths of functional gadgets and NOP gadgets are 7.7 and 14.1, as shown in Fig. 7.

MaxRegMod is the maximum number of registers modified, and defines the boundary between NOP gadgets and normal codes. Obviously, increasing the MaxRegMod will increase the maximum lengths of potential NOP gadgets, and include more normal codes into NOP gadgets. Thus, it may also increase the false positive rates of GWT. Figure 8 shows the changes of average lengths of NOP gadgets in GWT and GWT+CFI, with the MaxRegMod increasing. Although a processor has 32 registers, many registers have special purposes, and only 8 registers can be used for general-purpose computation usually. As a result, the average length of NOP gadgets has little change, after MaxRegMod is larger than 8. Additionally, because NOP gadgets have few effects on CRAs, and the weighted score of NOP gadget is zero, appropriately increasing MaxRegMod will not affect the CRA detection rate of GWT usually.

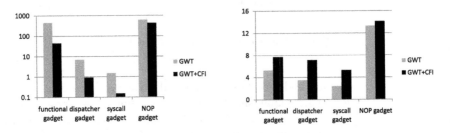

Fig. 7. The average numbers (left) and the average lengths (right) of different gadgets in GWT and GWT+CFI

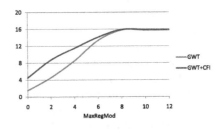

Fig. 8. The average lengths of NOP gadgets in GWT and GWT+CFI

6.2 Practical Attacks

We test GWT against CRAs generated by Q [1], which can automatically generate ROP payloads for given programs. Since we have already marked all possible gadgets in these programs, GWT can easily detect the attacks consisting of gadgets, and count the weighted scores of gadgets in the CRA chains. Moreover, since Q can only generate return-based gadgets, the gadgets are normal functional gadgets in GWT, thus their weighted scores are 1 point. As a result, if the gadget number is larger than the MaxCOI, a CRA is detected. At last, the GWT can successfully detect 100% all the payloads generated from more than 100 applications under the directory */bin* and */usr/bin/*.

Then, we try to build some CRAs manually to bypass GWT. A practical way is to structure a short and simple gadget chain to close DEP, and then to inject malicious codes [12]. At last, we build a few CRAs to close DEP in a well-designed targeted program, which contain only a syscall gadget, a functional gadget and several NOP gadgets. The COI of these CRAs is 5, which is smaller than MaxCOI (6). However, it is very difficult to construct practical attacks to bypass GWT, since we can not find such satisfactory gadgets in real-world programs.

The weighted score of gadget types and MaxCOI are two critical parameters for CRA detection. Larger weighted scores and smaller MaxCOI can offer higher security, but may also increase the false positive ratio. Thus, we should define proper values to balance the security and stability. Figure 9 demonstrates the CRA detection rate and false positive rate of GWT with different MaxCOI. With the MaxCOI increasing, GWT needs more gadgets to identify the CRAs. CRAs generated by Q usually consist of 20–40 gadgets, and thus to set MaxCOI less than 20 can detect most CRAs generated by Q. On the other hand, with the MaxCOI decreasing, GWT may mistake some normal programs for CRAs. For example, a normal program invokes a system call, and this system call may be recognize as a syscall gadget. If we set MaxCOI less than 4, GWT will mistake the system call invoked by this normal program for a CRA.

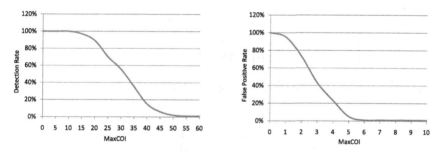

Fig. 9. The CRA detection rate (left) and the false positive rate (right) of GWT

7 Performance Analysis

In this section, we implement hardware architecture of GWT and GWT+CFI in RTL (Register Transfer Level) using Verilog on a Loongson processor. Moreover, we select workloads from the SPEC CPU2006 benchmark [19], and these benchmarks are compiled using the GNU version of GCC at O3 optimization level.

We compare the performance overheads of GWT, RBCFI (rule-based CFI) and GWT+CFI on the target applications and the system. Note that we only perform RBCFI with three control-flow rules as described in Sect. 3 (i.e. protected system). We perform assembly-level instrumentation of the binaries for both GWT and RBCFI to insert the additional information needed to perform the checks for both methods.

As shown in Fig. 10, the performance overhead of GWT is just about 2.31% on the average and it is less than 6% for all benchmarks. Furthermore, the performance overhead of GWT+CFI is about 3.55% on the average and it is less than 9% for all benchmarks, which includes the overhead of GWT as well as the overhead of rule-based CFI.

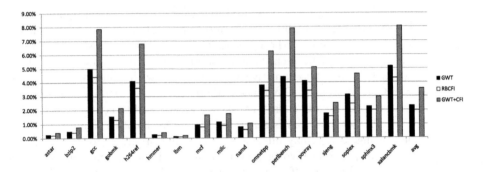

Fig. 10. Performance overheads of different methods (normalized to the baseline system)

8   Conclusions and Future Work

In order to defend against CRAs, we propose GWT, a flexible, low-overhead and high-security framework. GWT discovers and marks all potential gadgets with static program analysis, and then dynamically monitors the weighted gadget tags at runtime to calculate the probability of CRA occurrence. Furthermore, we propose GWT+CFI, GWT combining with the rule-based CFI, can more precisely find possible gadgets in code space, compared to the baseline GWT. We implement GWT and GWT+CFI in a hardware/software co-design system. The results show that the performance overheads of GWT and GWT+CFI are 2.31% and 3.55% respectively, and GWT can defeat variants of CRAs with different gadgets, especially those generated by automated tools. Moreover, GWT can be further optimized by adding more special gadget types and better gadget type classification.

The identification of the functional gadget, the NOP gadget and the normal code in GWT is not perfect. Attackers may manually find some useful gadgets which are identified as NOP gadgets in GWT, or find some NOP gadgets which are recognized as normal codes in GWT. Therefore, we plan to propose more precise methods to distinguish the gadget types. Additionally, it is our future work to insert discovery algorithms of special gadgets to improve the security of GWT, such as function-based gadgets.

Acknowledgement. This work is partially supported by the National Natural Science Foundation of China (No. 61602469).

References

1. Schwartz, E.J., Avgerinos, T., Brumley, D.: Q: exploit hardening made easy. In: Proceedings of the 20th USENIX Conference on Security (SEC), pp. 25–40 (2011)
2. Bletsch, T., Jiang, X., Freeh, V.W., Liang, Z.: Jump-oriented programming: a new class of code-reuse attack. In: Proceedings of the 6th ACM Symposium on Information, Computer and Communications Security (ASIACCS), pp. 30–40 (2011)
3. Abadi, M., Budiu, M., Erlingsson, Ú., Ligatti, J.: Control-flow integrity principles, implementations, and applications. ACM Trans. Inf. Syst. Secur. **13**, 4:1–4:40 (2009)
4. Burow, N., Carr, S.A., Brunthaler, S., Payer, M., Nash, J., Larsen, P., Franz, M.: Control-flow integrity: precision, security, and performance. CoRR. abs/1602.04056 (2016)
5. Pappas, V., Polychronakis, M., Keromytis, A.D.: Transparent ROP exploit mitigation using indirect branch tracing. In: Proceedings of the 22nd USENIX Conference on Security (SEC), pp. 447–462 (2013)
6. Cheng, Y., Zhou, Z., Miao, Y., Ding, X., Deng, R.H.: ROPecker: a generic and practical approach for defending against ROP attack. In: Proceedings of the 21st Annual Network and Distributed System Security Symposium (NDSS) (2014)
7. Kayaalp, M., Schmitt, T., Nomani, J., Ponomarev, D., Abu-Ghazaleh, N.: SCRAP: architecture for signature-based protection from code reuse attacks. In: Proceedings of the 2013 IEEE 19th International Symposium on High Performance Computer Architecture (HPCA), pp. 258–269 (2013)
8. Göktaş, E., Athanasopoulos, E., Polychronakis, M., Bos, H., Portokalidis, G.: Size does matter: why using gadget-chain length to prevent code-reuse attacks is hard. In: Proceedings of the 23rd USENIX Conference on Security Symposium (SEC), pp. 417–432 (2014)
9. Kayaalp, M., Ozsoy, M., Abu-Ghazaleh, N., Ponomarev, D.: Branch regulation: low-overhead protection from code reuse attacks. In: Proceedings of the 39th Annual International Symposium on Computer Architecture (ISCA), pp. 94–105 (2012)
10. Zhang, C., Wei, T., Chen, Z., Duan, L., Szekeres, L., McCamant, S., Song, D., Zou, W.: Practical control flow integrity and randomization for binary executables. In: Proceedings of the 34th IEEE Symposium on Security and Privacy (SP), pp. 559–573 (2013)
11. Zhang, M., Sekar, R.: Control flow integrity for COTS binaries. In: Proceedings of the 22nd USENIX Conference on Security (SEC), pp. 337–352 (2013)
12. Göktas, E., Athanasopoulos, E., Bos, H., Portokalidis, G.: Out of control: overcoming control-flow integrity. In: Proceedings of the 35th IEEE Symposium on Security and Privacy (SP), pp. 575–589 (2014)
13. Carlini, N., Wagner, D.: ROP is still dangerous: breaking modern defenses. In: Proceedings of the 23rd USENIX Conference on Security Symposium (SEC), pp. 385–399 (2014)
14. Davi, L., Sadeghi, A.-R., Lehmann, D., Monrose, F.: Stitching the gadgets: on the ineffectiveness of coarse-grained control-flow integrity protection. In: Proceedings of the 23rd USENIX Conference on Security Symposium (SEC), pp. 401–416 (2014)
15. Davi, L., Koeberl, P., Sadeghi, A.-R.: Hardware-assisted fine-grained control-flow integrity: towards efficient protection of embedded systems against software exploitation. In: Proceedings of the 51st Design Automation Conference (DAC), pp. 1–6 (2014)

16. Evans, I., Long, F., Otgonbaatar, U., Shrobe, H., Rinard, M., Okhravi, H., Sidiroglou-Douskos, S.: Control jujutsu: on the weaknesses of fine-grained control flow integrity. In: Proceedings of the 22nd ACM SIGSAC Conference on Computer and Communications Security (CCS), pp. 901–913 (2015)

17. Conti, M., Crane, S., Davi, L., Franz, M., Larsen, P., Negro, M., Liebchen, C., Qunaibit, M., Sadeghi, A.-R.: Losing control: on the effectiveness of control-flow integrity under stack attacks. In: Proceedings of the 22nd ACM SIGSAC Conference on Computer and Communications Security (CCS), pp. 952–963 (2015)

18. Carlini, N., Barresi, A., Payer, M., Wagner, D., Gross, T.R.: Control-flow bending: on the effectiveness of control-flow integrity. In: Proceedings of the 24th USENIX Conference on Security (SEC) (2015)

19. Henning, J.L.: SPEC CPU2006 benchmark descriptions. SIGARCH Comput. Archit. News. **34**, 1–17 (2006)

20. Luk, C.-K., Cohn, R., Muth, R., Patil, H., Klauser, A., Lowney, G., Wallace, S., Reddi, V.J., Hazelwood, K.: Pin: building customized program analysis tools with dynamic instrumentation. In: Proceedings of the ACM SIGPLAN Conference on Programming Language Design and Implementation (PLDI), pp. 190–200 (2005)

Author Index

Printed in the United States
By Bookmasters

Printed in the United States
By Bookmasters